Victimology and Human Security: New Horizons

SELECTION OF PAPERS PRESENTED AT THE 13TH INTERNATIONAL SYMPOSIUM ON VICTIMOLOGY, 2009, MITO, JAPAN

Hosted by the World Society of Victimology and Tokiwa University, Mito,Japan August 23-28, 2009

Morosawa, Hidemichi
Dussich, John J.P.
Kirchhoff, Gerd Ferdinand
(eds.)

Victimology and Human Security New Horizons

Selection of papers presented at the 13th International Symposium on Victimology, 2009, Mito, Japan

Morosawa, Hidemichi
Dussich, John J.P.
Kirchhoff, Gerd Ferdinand (eds.)

ISBN: 978-90-5850-819-5 (softcover)

Published by:

Wolf Legal Publishers (WLP)
P.O. Box 31051
6503 CB Nijmegen
The Netherlands
Tel: +31 24 355 19 04
Fax: +31 84 837 67 00
E-Mail: info@wolfpublishers.nl
www.wolfpublishers.com

Table of Contents

Victims and Restorative Justice

The Global Perspective on the UN Level

Introduction

by

Gerd Ferdinand Kirchhoff

Never before an International Symposium on Victimology of the World Society of Victimology has covered such a broad scope of victimology than the 13th held in August 2009 in Tokiwa University, Mito. The editors of the book had outstanding positions in this symposium: Hidemichi Morosawa was Chair of the Symposium Organizing Committee and Chairperson of the Incorporated Educational Institution Tokiwa University, the host of the symposium; John P.J. Dussich was President of the World Society of Victimology; and Gerd Ferdinand Kirchhoff was the Chair of the Scientific Program Committee, responsible for the selection of admitted papers. 532 participants from 51 countries registered, about 280 papers were presented.

The Executive Committee of the World Society of Victimology choose the Title of the Symposium: Victimology and Human Security. It determined the key note speakers. There were nine key note speakers. The key note addresses structure the content of the book widely. All key notes are included in this book except the excellent key note address by Nils Christie. It was separately published. This collection of selected papers in front of the reader contains only original not otherwise published contributions. The relevance of the contributions to the area demarked by the key note lectures served as the main criteria for conducting a content analysis on the book of abstracts of the 13rth conference. The reminder of the selection followed the tradition of the World Society of Victimology: This analysis yielded the initial database that was intensively discussed in the editorial team. Selected presenters were approached to deliver a full length article. Their submissions were subjected to a rigorous review process assisted by two independent peer reviewers. The review process led sometimes to substantial improvements of the papers included. We are grateful to reviewers and to the authors who usually followed review recommendations.

The first papers in this volume are taken **"From the Opening Session of the Symposium"**

In his Opening Statement, H. Morosawa (Japan) explained why this symposium was held in Japan, in this university which became a home of victimology studies. He summarized the development of victim related activities in Japan when the 1982 Second International Symposium held in this country 1982. In his Opening Statement as President of the World Society of Victimology, and as the Director of the Tokiwa International Victimology Institute, John P.J. Dussich (USA/Japan) praised the excellent cooperation within the organizing bodies and especially within his organizing team. Isao Okamura (Japan), Founder of the Japanese Victim Assistance Movement, Chair of Asunokai and famous lawyer in Tokyo, described how Asunokai emerged as leading Victim Assistance Organization in Japan and how it was able to influence Japanese victim related legislation in the next decade, starting the social movement for victims in Japan. The global stage was opened by Johan Cels, Representative of the UN High Commissioner on Human Refugees in Japan. He introduced the participants into the work of the UNHC for Refugees. This speech in the Opening Session was programmatic for the whole symposium: No longer exclusively the Crime Program of the United Nations was in the center of victimological considerations but the wider spectrum of the work of the UN on Human Rights Violations including crime, environmental change and disaster.

The Volume turns to "**Theoretical Victimology**". Here the reader finds three chapters. The first, written by A. Pemberton (NL) , is a theoretical discussion of "Just World Theory; revisiting Lerner in the study of victims of crime. It is a highly intelligent analysis of the current state of the debate. A. Davies (USA) considers "Claiming Victim Identity: A social Psychological Analysis." This is followed by an empirical study of Tai S.F. (Taiwan) who looks at the empirical side of "Blaming the Victims: Attributions of Convicted Offenders and Public Towards Victims of Various Crimes."

In the chapter **"Victimology and Human Security"** R. Letschert's (NL) key note speech analyses the main theme of the symposium. She deals with the topic "Towards a Victimology of International Crimes; incorporating nations from the Human Security Concept". She covers the basic relationships between the two constructs Victimology and Human Security. On a more practical side, L. Yamamoto (Japan) discusses "Past Violations of Indigenous Rights in the Inter-American Commission and Inter-American Court on Human Rights". Letschert's and Yamamoto's articles are augmented by an essay on "Human Security and Victimization in Venezuela" by L. Bastidas and Y. Parra (Venzuela).

The next chapter of the volume is devoted to "**Japan, Asia and Australia**" . It contains articles that give an overview on changes in victim policy in various countries. They demonstrate what is theoretically quite clear: That existing systems have their difficulties until they recognize and realize victim rights. Hidemichi Morosawa (Japan) demonstrates that in his article "Changing Victim Policy in Japan: The last Decade":, while Kim Jae Min (Korea) outlines a very similar development but apparently more applied, in his "Changing Victim Policy in Korea: The last Decade". Hong O.Y. (Korea) describes the "Juvenile Victimization Surveys in Korea" in the decade Kim Jae Min describes. M. O'Connell's excellent description of "Commissioner for Victims' Rights:Strengthening Victims' Rights shows the great experience of this author. Victims Rights are far too often desiderata, desired states of affairs, despite a language, that promises much more as the legal realities can hold. This chapter closes with a return to the brutal reality of victimization: Wang, S.-J. (Denmark) and her team describe "Individual and Collective Victimization in Bangladesh". They point out concrete measures of help.

The keynote for the section "**Refugees and Minorities as Victims**" is delivered by S. Takizawa (Japan): "Victims of Forced Displacement-Refugees and Internally Displaced Persons". Takizawa, a former UN diplomat and predecessor of Johan Cels als UNHCR Representative in Japan, describes the social career of a refugee and applies victimological concepts. The important topic of Minorities was worth a second separate key note: C. Noto (Japan) describes the collective victimization of the Japanese minority, the Ainu. Ainu herself, she vividly paints in her key note address "Ainu in Japan - Victimization of a Minority Group" a development of centuries of colonization and repression and a light of hope that under the rule of Human Rights the situation of her people in Japan will improve. G.F.Kirchhoff (Germany/Japan) and A. Tsuda (Japan) have conducted with Jun Kaneko (Japan) an empirical study "Victimization and Stress among Homeless in Japan" . They write about the homeless in Japan, the stress they endure by homelessness and by victimization, and they describe an innovative research design with cooperation of homeless and researchers.

The section "**Victimization in Family and Institutions**" contains several important highlights. Straus, M. in "Physical and Psychological Victimization of Students by Romantic Partners in Gender and World Perspective" analyzes his Dating and Parental Violence Victimization Study, using empirical data from some 16 000 students in twenty five countries. In the wake of this paper, A.Lysova (Russia) concentrates on "Corporal Punishment, Depressive

Symptoms and the Moderating Effect of Positive Partners and Parents in a Multi-National Perspective. D. Al-Badayneh in an excellent sober social science empirical study on "Wife Abuse in Jordan" informs clearly how underlying ideologies are reflected in the victimization of females by domestic violence. R. Peacock (South Africa) looks at "Institutional Victimization: Legislative Framework and Youth Marginalization in Post Apartheid in South Africa". He describes the conditions in prisons for juveniles. Institutionalization often means death penalty since the danger of infection with AIDS is so high.

In the chapter **"Sexual Victimization"** we find D.Kilpatrik (USA) and H.Resnick (USA) deal with "Rape in America. A Comparison after 15 years." The article is theoretically highly relevant and it argues stringently. A jewel in clear empirical work in a field full of political dangers: that is the study of Ben David a.o. (Israel) on "Sexual Harassment in Israel: in University and in Army". It is a typical example that victimologists do not want to silence and to beautify but to explain clearly the reality they find. Only then, change is possible. To this style, only Al_Badayneh comes close.

"**Victims of Human Trafficking**" is a very timely topic, importantly due to the political attention the field was awarded in recent years. J. Sigmon (USA) gives an overview on "Issues in Assisting Victims of Human Trafficking Worldwide". Her close involvement in the US Trafficking in Persons Report makes this contribution especially relevant. More local is the perspective of V. Ristanovic-Nikolic (Serbia): she contributes "Developing Needs-based, Gender Specific and Empowering Approach to Supporting Victims of Trafficking", a field in which she contrary to many activists maintains a clear victimological perspective.

The section "**Disaster Studies"** concentrates on a rather new development in victimology. K. Mundy (Japan) contributes a fundamental article on "Victims of Global Environmental Change". He opens the field of environmental change to victimological inspection. H. Susetyo (Indonesia), working in this field for a long time, writes on "Victimological Perspective on the Rights and Present Status of Disaster Victims: The Indonesian Situation." Disaster Studies in Victimology are a new and promising field that looks at victims of disasters and environmental change and on perceived inabilities and chances of amelioration.

The chapter "**Victims and Restorative Justice**" deals with an area that is better known to victimologists: The key note lecture of H. Strang (Australia) gives newest developments in "Restorative Justice and Victims of Crime: Evidence and Possibilities." Can short time interventions be of therapeutic value? P. Friday deals with "Principles of Restorative Justice" on a more fundamental base. Chockalingam (India) goes into the practice: he describes "Restorative Justice for Victims of Bullying in Colleges in India".

The last section "**Towards Global Perspectives**" looks into Europe and at the UN: Pemberton (NL) and Groenhuijzen (NL) describe "Developing Victims' Rights Within the European Union: Past, Present and Future". The European development is much less loud than the development in other parts of the world. It is less intensely discussed. However it might be that Victim Rights, a contentious concept, are developed there much more clearly than elsewhere. Dussich, J. P.J. (USA/Japan) reminds us that Justice and Support for Victims are global topics: His chapter "History of the Proposed UN Convention on Justice and Support for Victims of Crime and Abuse of Power" concludes this volume.

As Chair of the Scientific Program Committee, I was privileged to be able to work closely with so many participants and authors. Without the help of many already mentioned, this work would have not been possible. I am deeply indebted to my assistant Mari Doi. I am grateful for her reliable and efficient help and the encouragement during the years of preparation of the symposium and during most of our work on this volume.

From the Opening Session of the Symposium

Opening Address
The 13th International Symposium on Victimology
August 23, 2009

by

Hidemichi Morosawa

Ladies and gentlemen, it's my honor and privilege to have invited you to come here from all over the world to Mito to participate in the 13th International Symposium on Victimology.

It is especially to our great pleasure to announce that Her Royal Highness Princess Bajrakitiyabha of Thailand accepted our invitation and has graced our opening ceremony with her attendance tonight. A heartfelt welcome to Her Royal Highness and to all of my guests!

To say a few brief words in introduction of Her Royal Highness: She studied Law and Political Science in Thailand and continued her studies to receive a J.S. Doctoral Degree from Cornell Law School in New York in 2005.

It was last spring in the Vienna Congress of Crime Prevention and Criminal Justice when I first listened to a wonderful speech by Her Royal Highness. She is well known not only as a scholar in Criminology and Criminal Justice, but also as a person who puts theory into practice.

At this symposium, we are honored to have experts from both Japan and overseas in attendance. In particular, I would like to acknowledge Professor Hans Joachim Schneider, chairperson of the 3rd International Symposium in Muenster, Germany, and Prof. Sarah Ben-David, chairperson of the 6th International Symposium in Jerusalem, Israel.

In 1982, we held the 4th International Symposium on Victimology in Tokyo and Kyoto. At that time, the Professor Emeritus of Keio University Koichi Miyazawa was Chairperson of the Symposium Organizing Committee and I was the Secretary General. Now, we are here today celebrating the opening of the 13th Symposium, a full 27 years after the Tokyo-Kyoto Symposium. In this 13th Symposium, 532 participants have registered from 51 countries. I sincerely thank you all for coming from both near and far and taking the time to participate in this symposium.

This time we gather with the special purpose of contributing towards the development of victimological studies and educating young scholars in the Asian region. Unfortunately, Asia is comparatively behind the rest of the world in Victimology studies.

By the way, this year, the Incorporated Educational Institution Tokiwa University celebrates its centennial anniversary. One hundred years ago, when the now Incorporated Educational Institution Tokiwa University was established, the vision of the founders was to provide an educational setting that encouraged independence, creativity, and sincerity.

Now, we have further developed our educational philosophy to include the nurturing of individuals who have respect for human dignity and who think and behave from a global perspective. This new philosophical direction was identified because Tokiwa University strongly believed it was increasingly important for all of us to respect human dignity and to have a global perspective.
The theme of this year's symposium is "Victimology and Human Security." As you know, in 1985 the United Nations adopted the *Declaration of Basic Principles of Justice for Victims of Crime and Abuse of Power*. About a quarter of a century has passed since the adoption of this declaration, and many Western countries have provided for necessary domestic legislation based upon these Basic Principles. However, many countries in the world have still not taken any legislative action to implement these Basic Principles.

Japan also continued many years without changing its standpoint on victims. However, the Japanese government finally recognized victims' rights. The parliament nacted the Basic Act on Crime Victims in December, 2004. It was the first time the country recognized the rights and interests of victims by law.

In its preamble, the Basic Act says: "Now, everybody has a higher probability of becoming a crime victim, so it is required to make policies from the crime victims' viewpoints, and to make a step forward to realize a society where their rights and profits are well protected."

Additionally, Article 3 of the Basic Act says that the individual dignity of all crime victims shall be respected. Victims should be treated appropriately. In Japan too, the "Revival of Victims" is now coming.

I believe that Victimology is a science about how people protect human rights and human dignity. I've been involved with these issues for a long time. In my first paper on Victimology, in 1975, I insisted: Victimology is a science of victims' rights. But, at that time, this paper got an extremely bad evaluation by almost all professors of criminology and criminal law in Japan.
At that time, most scholars placed priority on protecting the interests of the accused, and opposed the protection of the rights of crime victims. Society had not much interest in victims, either, and I wondered if the rights of victims would never be addressed in this country. In 1982 when the Tokyo-Kyoto Symposium was held, the situation was still the same. But nowadays, everything has changed.

It was about a decade ago when I started to see some change. Experts increasingly began to fall into line with what I had to say, while the media began to express sympathy for victims. The overall climate began to change.

I believe that other nations, in particular in Asia, will be able to follow us. I truly hope that Japan's recent revision of the law on criminal procedures will influence movements in other nations in a positive manner.

I would like to take this opportunity to share with you recent developments in this country. Japan had tended to lag two or three decades behind Western countries in terms of victim support.

10 years or so ago, many experts took it upon themselves to establish voluntary community-based victim support centers, for example, the Mito Victim Assistance Center (now the Ibaraki Victim Support Center, Inc.) was established as the first private organization for victim support in 1995 by myself, and colleagues John Dussich, Nobuho Tomita, Susumu Nagai, Bunri Tatsuno, Satomi Nakajima and others.

Following this local initiative, today, other victim support centers have been established throughout the country and have formed a National Network for Victim Support. On their own initiative, victims in Japan have also raised questions about victim services and have started organizing victims' associations by themselves.

In terms of major historical developments in the victim support movement, in January 2000, the National Association of Crime Victims and Surviving Families (NAVS) was established and has actively worked to revise existing Japanese legislation.

The Japanese media generally refers to NAVS as "Asunokai," the *Association for Tomorrow*, meaning that victims do have both "a tomorrow," and "a future." Accordingly, ordinary Japanese people have started to take an interest in the suffering of victims, and the government has begun to redefine its policies in support of victims.

"Asunokai" carried out a lobby campaign for crime victims. It gathered 560,000 signatures from around the country to support a petition to the government to initiate changes for crime victims. "Asunokai" sponsored and carried out this spectacular action - and the Founder Chairperon of "Asunokai", Isao Okamura, will give the central key note speech of this Opening Ceremony.

In May 2000, the *Crime Victim Protection Law* was enacted. But, this legislation does not provide these rights as "victims' rights" as it is dependent on the discretion of judges or prosecutors. In November 2000, the *Anti-Stalking Act* and the *Child Abuse Protection Law* were enacted, followed in the April 2001 by the enactment of the *Domestic Violence Protection Law*.

In addition to these, several laws were revised with strong public support; for example, in December 2001, a provision was created to enable more severe penalties for cases of for traffic accidents caused by drivers under the influence of alcohol and drugs. Also, in July 2003, there was a revision of the law to raise the maximum penalty for the crime of rape. All the lobbying activities which brought these legal revisions had been initiated by victims themselves.

With these efforts as a backdrop, the *Basic Act for Crime Victims* was enacted in December 2004 (taking effect on April 1, 2005), and, for the first time in Japan, legally acknowledged victims' rights and benefits. Based upon this act, the Basic Plan for Crime Victims was formulated in December 2005. It provided a great impetus for further improvements of the legislation to protect victims in Japan.

To allow victims to participate in criminal court proceedings, major revisions of the Criminal Procedure Law were made in June 2007, and came into effect in November 2008.

In this way, the victim movement is gaining momentum in Japan; that is, it is working in favor of victim protection and is contributing to the revision of legislation for victim protection. Victims, themselves, are raising their voices and the mass media is supportive to report their activities.

Japanese society is also supporting such voices and moving the government in a positive direction. I sincerely wish that this kind of effective movement for victims will be seen in various parts of the world.

Finally, I hope that the 13th Symposium will be a great step in helping to enhance the development of Victimology throughout the world.

(Text of the Opening Address was edited for this publication.)

Opening Address of the 13th International Symposium on Victimology (Excerpts) by the President of the World Society of Victimology

By

John P. J. Dussich

Minasan, konichiwa. Good afternoon distinguished guests and participants of the World Society of Victimology's 13th International, I am greatly honored and pleased to be standing before you at this scholarly and meaningful event. I am happy to tell you that this symposium marks the 30th Anniversary of the WSV which was born in Munster, Germany in 1979. A very special welcome to our distinguished guest Her Highness Princess Bajrakitiyabha Mahidol of Thailand. I had the honor of meeting Her Highness in Vienna two years ago at the Crime Commission Meeting where she was promoting her special programs on behalf of the rehabilitation of women inmates and the wellbeing of their infants born in prison. Subsequently I was invited to visit and lecture in Bangkok and was able to see these programs in action. It was on that occasion that I realized that her deep dedication to these victims of the criminal justice system reflected a genuine concern for a class of victims that many countries do not protect. At that time the idea to invite Her Highness to be our special guest at this symposium came to my mind. I am very delighted that she accepted our invitation and honored that she is here with us today to open this important event. Your Highness, my deepest appreciation to you, and to the entire Thai delegation: *Khob-Khun-Mark. Krap Pom.*

I would like to share with you some words about the history of our symposia. The symposia of the World Society of Victimology started with a suggestion by the "Father of Victimology," Beniamin Mendelsohn in some of his seminal writings and speeches where he often suggested this new discipline needed: an international journal, victim clinics, university courses and an international society with periodic symposia. The First International Symposium on Victimology was organized by a well-known criminologist, Israel Drapkin, from Chile who subsequently moved to Israel where he became the Director of the Institute of Criminology at the Hebrew University in Jerusalem. He became aware of Mendelsohn work, collaborated with a number of victimologists and then decided to host the First International Symposium on Victimology in 1973. This was the first meeting of victimologists from across the globe. The success of this event prompted another pioneer in victimology to offer to host the next symposium; Stephen Schafer a Hungarian scholar teaching at Northeastern University in Boston, accepted the challenge and initiated the planning process for having the Second Symposium in 1976. Unfortunately the stress of preparations took his life about one month prior to the symposium; however, some of his colleagues and students finished the task and hosted the symposium in his honor. This American based event was also a success and it prompted the attendees to imagine a third symposium and the possibility of fulfilling another of Mendelsohn's expectations, an international society of victimology. In 1979 Hans Schneider hosted the Third International Symposium on Victimology in Muenster, Germany. It was at this event that the World Society of Victimology was formed and its Executive Committee met for the first time. Since then the WSV has been holding symposia every three years. Subsequently we met in: Japan, Croatia, Israel, Brazil, Australia, Netherlands, Canada, South Africa, USA, and in Japan. Our philosophy for these symposia has been to hold them in different continents and to make the unique victimological resources these symposia bring to as many different countries as possible.

The last time we held a WSV symposium in Japan was in 1982, 27 years ago hosted by Professor Koichi Miyazawa, the "Father of Japanese Victimology." It is a pity he cannot be with us, he very much enjoyed spending time with many of you whom he considered his long-time friends. He is in ill health and we extend to him and his family our very best wishes.

I am honored that I am wearing two hats at his event: President of the World Society of Victimology and Director of the Tokiwa International Victimology Institute. These two positions have given me the perspective and the insight to appreciate the collaboration of both organizations in the three yearlong planning process which has produced this symposium. I am most grateful to the Executive Committee of the WSV for placing their faith in me to lead our Society over these past three years, to be flexible with our internal Society decision-making and finally for showing great patience with the complex issues and problems that these events produce.

I am also very grateful to the Tokiwa University and my Institute staff for the hard work of many people who ate, drank, dreamed and talked almost nothing else but this 13th Symposium every day for the past 1,095 days since our last symposium in Orlando in 2006. I would be remiss if I didn't mention the very important leadership of the Chair of the Symposium Organizing Committee and the Chairperson of the Tokiwa Educational Corporation,

Professor Hidemichi Morosawa and his three vice-chairs, Professor Chockalingam, Professor Takenaka and Professor Itoga. We must also recognize the amazing and creative work of the Chair of the WSV Scientific Committee, the "king of the Program" Professor Gerd Ferdinand Kirchhoff of Tokiwa University.

Among the Tokiwa staff there were a small group of dedicated persons who "held it all together," they represented the core workers and who had an almost magical team spirit in spite of sometimes thinking they were losing their sanity, especially in these last six months with unbelievable dedication and endless "nemawashi meetings" sometimes lasting through the night: Mr. Otsuki, Ms. Sakaba, Ms. Maekoya, Ms. Tsuboi, and Mr. McManus. My personal gratitude to the five of you. I would like us all to give this "Tokiwa Dream Team" a special round of applause! Thank you.

I must also mention the many others who also gave their talents and energies: an army of Tokiwa students and faculty who contributed their time and energy and whom you will see helping in the rooms, sitting at the doors and standing in the hallways directing you to your destinations. Without all these dedicated people we would not have this symposium.

The theme of this symposium is "Victimology and Human Security" and there are nine sub-themes that cover the linked fields of victimology and victim assistance. Most of us have a fairly good idea what Victimology is; however, many of us are not so sure about what Human Security is. This term Human Security has emerged in the last decade as a response to the increase in fear from many sources: some recent major disasters and the awareness of wide-spread devastation that is threatening our planet due to climate changes, the pervasive and growing terrorist events that have invaded many of our countries, and the disturbing brutality of abuse of power victimizations that are on-going even now as I speak in Darfur. Of course crime still reaps a heavy toll in all nations, all of these victimizations have killed and injured thousands upon thousands of human beings, across the globe. And, like at no other time in history, these victimizations are reported on by an aggressive news media, that churns and dwells on all the gory details in living color with great regularity – not to mention the fictional blood baths that pass off as entertainment on our televisions which together can easily add up to the viewing of more than 100 persons injured or killed each day. Of course, in response, our fears have risen, and our concerns with protecting ourselves and our families have become a daily preoccupation. Aside from the real dangers and risks of being victimized are the man-made fictional dangers that add to our level of fear. And so, our job as victimologists, is to sort through the maze of digitized words and numbers in video and audio form, printed text, and real utterances that fill our lives and try to scientifically measure what is fact and what is fiction; identify what we can do to avoid these real dangers, find out how we can modify our vulnerabilities, learn how we should respond to the real needs of victims with evidence-based treatment, discover how we might create a new culture to restore those who become embroiled in conflict and, ultimately, teach new generations to anticipate and resolve minor arguments in gentle ways before they erupt into violence between humans. Reviewing the roughly 250 abstracts that make up the bulk of this symposium's Program, most of these issues will be discussed and debated; suggestions will be given; and, much will be learned about the links between Victimology and Human Security.

There are such a wide variety of topics being presented in our program, I am sure that each of you will find many sessions of direct relevance to your personal and professional interests and needs. One of the most important activities that the WSV has been engaged in and is still now working on is the promotion of victims' rights around the world. As a Society we are doing this by recommending that countries adopt our Proposed United Nations Convention for Victims of Crime and Abuse of Power. In partnership with INTERVICT and TIVI, the WSV has, for the past roughly six years, been working on a draft Proposal and has been actively lobbying, especially at the United Nations in Vienna every Spring to try to convince nations to sponsor the noble intents of this document. Last year TIVI hosted a two day symposium on this convention. Just last week TIVI published a book on the proceedings of that two-day symposium, which is filled with discussions and advice from world experts. Please take this publication, share it with others in your country, form a lobbying effort in your respective nation and join with the WSV in supporting this proposal at the United Nations. The WSV has a UN Liaison Committee which has the responsibility to coordinate this effort on behalf of our Society. Please contact this committee's chair and offer your help.

Most of you have come from immense distances, at great expense and at a significant sacrifice. The World Society, the Tokiwa University and the TIVI wish to extend to you our deepest gratitude for being here. Ultimately the symposium is about those who come to present and share their knowledge, wisdom and tell us about their discoveries. The symposium is also about those who come to listen, learn and react. Finally, it is also about renewing old friendships among victimologists who have known each other for many years; so, keeping the sense of family alive among our colleagues is also an important feature of these symposia. Use your time here to strengthen your ties and consider more transnational collaborations.

I sincerely hope that you will use this event to share what you know about victims, learn from others who have new information and, above all, make new professional contacts while you are here. This is your symposium, it is your turn to speak and be heard, it is your chance to make a difference for victims. I wish you all a good forum. Keep up the amazing work that you all do every day and every week, throughout the year, to help the plight of victims around the world. Finally, I want to wish you all a most pleasant time. Explore this wonderful Japanese culture and enjoy the warm, gentle and polite people who appreciate your being here and are eager to help you have a satisfying time in their country.

The Movement for Crime Victims' Rights and a Restoration System in Japan: Its History and Achievements

By

Isao Okamura

1. Why Did Crime Victims Take Action?

In Japan, criminal trials have a two-sided adversarial structure: the public prosecutor versus the defendant and his or her counsel. The victim used to be completely excluded from criminal proceedings. I myself pursued a legal career for 38 years without ever questioning this view, believing that the role of a lawyer lay in protecting the offender's human rights.

However, in 1997 my wife was murdered by a man who bore an unwarranted grudge against me in connection with my professional duties, and I became the survivor of a crime victim. Only then did I learn, through experience, just how much suffering this country's criminal justice system inflicts on the victims of crime, and I was stunned.

Victims had no rights. They were merely summoned unilaterally when needed for purposes of the investigation and trial. They were not even told the trial date, and they were not informed of the indictment, the main points of the prosecutor's closing arguments, or the verdict. They had no access to the trial records. Offenders could lie and defame the victims all they wanted in court, and the victims, unable to respond, could only suffer in silence in the public gallery. Japan's criminal justice system told victims to keep quiet. Members of the legal profession, myself included, had no idea of the amount of pain and suffering they caused the victims.

Consistent with the fact that, in the Japanese Constitution, ten articles provide for the human rights of offenders while those of victims are never mentioned, the emphasis has been entirely on the human rights of offenders, while those of victims have been ignored.

As a lawyer, once I became aware of this situation, I saw it as my duty to take back criminal justice for those victimized by crime; I saw this as the only way I could beg forgiveness of my wife, who had died in my place.

That was how I came, together with other crime victims, to found the National Association of Crime Victims and Surviving Families (NAVS) and to work on these issues. Nine years and eight months later, there is still a long way to go with regard to the system for aiding crime victims and restoring their losses, but we have seen many improvements, more rapidly than we expected, in the areas of victims' human rights and their rights within the criminal justice system.

Today, I would like to talk about how this movement grew and what it has achieved.

2. The Establishment of NAVS

In December 1998, I published an essay in a newspaper under the title "Open the Doors of Justice to the Victims." I proposed, among other things, the creation of systems to allow crime victims or their surviving families to participate in trials, to take parallel civil action against a defendant in a criminal case, and to have court-appointed representation. The legal profession paid no attention whatsoever. But the essay led to my meeting four fellow crime victims, and we agreed on the need to make society aware of the tragic situation in which victims found themselves. We planned a symposium titled "Crime Victims Make an Appeal" and put out a call through the media for people affected by crimes around the country to take part.

We were uncertain of the response, but in the event, on January 23, 2000, over 240 people—crime victims, members of the public, and journalists—crowded into a hall that seated 80, so that we could hardly breathe. As victims spoke of their frustration with the courts and their financial hardships, it was like looking into hell to hear their heartrending cries. It came as a great shock even to Professor Hidemichi Morosawa, who was present as an advisor; he said his mind went blank. This was the day that the victims of crime had been waiting for.

We realized that we could not leave this to other people, that we ourselves must act to obtain victims' rights and a system for aiding crime victims and restoring their losses. Thus, after the symposium, we established the Association of Crime Victims, which was later renamed the National Association of Crime Victims and Surviving Families.

The Association's prospectus read as follows:

> Because crimes originate in society and may victimize anyone, we believe that it is no more than the duty of the government and society to recognize the rights of crime victims and to create a system to aid them and restore their losses, including compensation for medical care and welfare, psychological support, and related services. Further, because the establishment of crime victims' rights and a restoration system is an issue that concerns them directly, crime victims must not leave their cause to supporters but must act on their own behalf.
>
> Accordingly, we, as victims of crime, have established the Association of Crime Victims in order to protest the unjust and tragic reality to which crime victims are subjected, to discuss crime victims' rights and a system to aid them and restore their losses, and to appeal to the government and society, thereby seeking on our own behalf the establishment of these rights and services.
>
> United in the Association of Crime Victims, we victims of crime throughout Japan will turn our individual pain and grief into the strength to live, and will dedicate our hearts and our efforts to making the society in which we live both just and secure.

News of the symposium and the Association was reported nationally on television and in the press. It drew a great response, and we were kept busy answering the enquiries that flooded in by telephone, fax, and post.

In Japanese NAVS is also called, for short, *Asu no Kai*, or the "Association for Tomorrow." We chose this name to signify that, although we are suffering today, we are determined to make tomorrow a better day.

3. Developments in Victim Assistance prior to the Founding of NAVS

In 1966, Mr. Asaichi Ichinose whose only son had been murdered, led the way in launching a movement to seek compensation from the government. He continued this work even after losing his eyesight, and in 1975 he appeared as a witness before the House of Representatives Committee on Judicial Affairs, together with Professor Minoru Oya of Doshisha University. Sadly, Mr. Ichinose passed away in January 1977; three months later, the government earmarked funds to study a compensation system, and in 1980 the Diet passed the Crime Victims' Benefit Payment Act. After that, no further measures for the relief of victims materialized until the mid-1990s.

In 1996, the Office for Crime Victims was finally created in the National Police Agency. It was charged with providing information, advice, counseling, and related services.

In 1999, the Ministry of Justice began notifying victims of the disposition of their cases, and also embarked on improving the legal provisions for victim protection and assistance. I submitted written opinions to the Ministry on matters including victims' trial participation, parallel civil actions, court-appointed representation, and access to trial records.

In 1999, the Judicial Reform Council was established under the Cabinet and began work on reforming the judicial system to serve the public in the 21st century.

Thus, NAVS came into being just as victims' issues were finally beginning to be addressed in Japan, 20 years behind Europe.

4. The Work of NAVS

After establishing NAVS, we began appealing to the public, the government, and the political parties, advocating the need for victims to participate in trials and to be able to take parallel civil action against a defendant in a criminal case, and the need for a restoration system and support services for crime victims.

In May 2000, two pieces of legislation proposed by the Justice Ministry were enacted. Referred to as the "two laws for protection of crime victims," these made sex crimes prosecutable without a complaint by the victim and instituted measures allowing crime victims to read and copy trial records, to have priority seating in courtroom galleries, and to be accompanied and/or shielded from view when appearing as witnesses. However, the wording of these laws (the court "may allow victims, etc., to ....") made these appear to be privileges rather than the rights we were advocating. There are some aspects of a right in just one area, the system that permits victims to state their own opinions, but this centers on victims stating their "feelings." As I noted at the time, it is like throwing a biscuit to the victim, who is still left out in the cold.

Also in May 2000, the Judicial Reform Council issued its interim report. This recommended steps to improve protection for offenders, for example, by providing a public defense system for suspects, but made no mention of victims' rights. They talked of justice serving the public, but the members of the public most closely involved with criminal justice are, on the one hand, suspects or defendants, that is, offenders, and, on the other hand, victims of crime. In a written opinion that I submitted to the Council, I argued that the administration of criminal justice does not serve the public unless it provides the justice that the victims are seeking, and I called for victims' rights, including the right to participate in trials and to take parallel civil action against a defendant.

5. The European Mission

After establishing NAVS, we formed the Research Group on Crime Victims and Criminal Justice consisting of scholars, lawyers, and former judges and prosecutors interested in victims' issues. This group met seven times to discuss trial participation and parallel civil actions, but it did not reach the conclusion we had anticipated. We wanted the existing system revised to create a three-sided adversarial structure with the victim as a party, and yet they concluded, "This cannot be done under the existing system." This was simply going round in circles.

In June 2001, the Judicial Reform Council delivered its final recommendations, but they were the same as those of the interim report. There was no sign they had even considered our views.

We therefore decided to send a fact-finding mission to Germany and France, where trial participation and parallel civil actions were already in effect, to see for ourselves whether it would be possible to introduce them in Japan. We organized a group of scholars and lawyers, and after a year of detailed preparations, our mission traveled to Germany and France in September 2002. We visited eleven institutions in Germany, including the Wiesbaden courthouse, the Federal Ministry of Justice, and the Berlin bar association, and eight institutions in France, including the Paris prosecutors' office, the Ministry of Justice, the Paris bar association, and the Paris Court of Assizes.

Jurists in both countries said unanimously, "Until 20 years ago, victims were mere exhibits in the courtroom. But we decided to have them participate in the proceedings since parties in the crime should also be parties in the trial." They also told us, "There was some opposition when we created the participatory system, but once it came into effect there were no problems, and today nobody opposes it." The word "exhibits" sounded very fresh to our ears. That's exactly what victims are in Japan: exhibits.

In both Germany and France, victims participate with almost the same rights as the defendant and prosecutor, in the capacity of trial participants and plaintiffs in parallel civil actions. Wherever we went, our hosts were in complete agreement with our view that criminal justice should exist not only for the public but also for the victims.

We also asked about possible reasons for opposition to introducing these systems, but we learned that there was no foundation to any of the foreseeable arguments.

There could indeed be three parties to a trial, including the victim of the crime, and the judge could be expected to arrive at a verdict based on their proofs of their arguments. Convinced that such a system, if designed appropriately, could be introduced in Japan, the mission returned home and prepared a detailed report.

6. The Conference Resolutions and the Petition Campaign

On December 8, 2002, at the fourth conference of NAVS, we held a symposium based on the European mission, under the title "Toward Victim Participation in Criminal Proceedings," and passed the following resolutions:

1. Victims are not exhibits but parties to criminal proceedings, and the criminal justice system should exist not only for the public but also for the victims of crime. (Criminal Justice for Victims)
2. Victims have an inherent right to participate in criminal proceedings and a system should be created for that purpose. (Trial Participation)
3. A system should be established to allow recovery of damages under civil law as part of the criminal process. (Parallel Civil Action)

We then decided to hold a nationwide petition campaign calling on the Prime Minister to make these resolutions a reality, and we began collecting signatures on the spot.

We would get nowhere dealing with conservative jurists, bar associations, and scholars. Instead, we adopted the strategy of appealing directly to the public and, backed by their support, moving politicians to reform the judicial system, over the heads of the legal profession, through political power.

The petition campaign was launched right there at the conference. In order to collect signatures in the streets, we needed to choose locations, obtain police permission, and prepare tables, chairs, microphones, petition forms, pens, and so on. Our officers and members made many trips to unfamiliar places.

For a year, from February 1, 2003, to February 1, 2004, we carried out a nationwide signature drive in the streets at 50 locations, from Hokkaido in the north to Okinawa in the south. NAVS members had no experience with this sort of thing and at first, when they picked up a microphone, they were too shy to speak. They went on rallying support for all they were worth, in the cold and in blazing heat.

We obtained cooperation from self-help and volunteer groups. We also had disabled people in wheelchairs helping us. Among the members of the public who signed, some arrived eager to do so, saying they had seen us on TV.

Since we could collect only about 1,000 to 1,500 signatures per day in the street, we had to turn to many contacts. But all-day media coverage of our petition campaigns made our work easier, and various companies, organizations, and others volunteered to collect signatures for us.

By June 15, 2004, we had gathered 557,215 signatures. As instructed by the Office of the Prime Minister, we presented the signed petitions to the Minister of Justice on two occasions.

The municipal assembly of Sakai City, Osaka Prefecture, passed a resolution in support of our movement and presented it to the Prime Minister, the Speakers of both Houses of the Diet, the Minister of Justice, and other officials. This movement spread to 107 local assemblies.

The petition campaign not only made the public aware of crime victims' real situation and where the problems lay; it also created a strong bond of solidarity among the victims themselves.

7. A Direct Appeal to the Prime Minister, and Political Action at Last

On July 8, 2003, backed by the signatures we had gathered at that point, the five officers of NAVS, including myself, met with Prime Minister Koizumi through the introduction of a member of the House of Representatives, Mr. Seiken Sugiura (a lawyer, later Deputy Chief Cabinet Secretary and Minister of Justice). We requested the Prime Minister to put the resolutions into effect. He was aghast when he heard the situation of crime victims. Also present was House of Representatives Member Okiharu Yasuoka, a lawyer and former judge who was chairman of the Research Commission on the Judiciary System within the Liberal Democratic Party (LDP). The Prime Minister asked him, "Is this true?" When Mr. Yasuoka replied that it was, Mr. Koizumi said, "That's serious. The government and the party should address this together." He then placed Mr. Yasuoka in charge of the party's response while taking on the government's himself. On September 25, in his key policy speech to the Diet, the Prime Minister expressed his strong commitment to realize investigations and trials that respect the human rights of crime victims. He made many similar statements in party leaders' debates and on other occasions.

Also, on his instructions, Justice Minister Mayumi Moriyama launched the Study Group on Measures for Crime Victims.

Political action was under way at last.

8. Passage of the Basic Act on Crime Victims

The LDP's Research Commission on the Judiciary System established a subcommittee chaired by Diet Member Yoko Kamikawa (later Minister of State for population issues) and began studying the question. In February 2004, Ms. Kamikawa held a hearing at the NAVS office with 15 of our members. I was told that on hearing the victims' heartrending accounts for the first time, she was very shocked, and she resolved, "We absolutely must see this work through."

The subcommittee met two or three times a month, and we attended every meeting and presented our opinions on all the issues that affect victims.

The draft interim report presented at an early morning session on June 8 spoke of enacting a basic act for assistance to crime victims. I urged strongly that the law be centered on victims' rights, not assistance. "Assistance" would only make crime victims objects of pity. The basic act, I insisted, must place victims' rights and dignity in the forefront. My opinion was incorporated into the subcommittee's *Recommendations on Comprehensive Measures for Crime Victims*, and on June 15, at the Prime Minister's Official Residence, these were personally submitted to Mr. Sugiura, who was now Deputy Chief Cabinet Secretary, by three Diet members, Mr. Yasuoka, Mr. Yasuhisa Shiozaki (later Chief Cabinet Secretary), and Ms. Kamikawa. The next day, June 16, Ms. Kamikawa explained the contents to the Prime Minister at his Official Residence. I was present on both occasions and requested Mr. Koizumi to put the recommendations into effect.

This was the process that led to the LDP's drafting the Basic Act on Crime Victims and approaching the other parties, so that the bill, submitted by members, came before the Diet with the support of all parties. On November 18, 2004, it passed the Lower House, and on December 1 it passed the Upper House and became law.

At that moment, we hugged one another with joy, completely forgetting our exhaustion.

In July 2004, NAVS published the *Draft Outline of a Victim Trial Participation System*. This would later serve as a basis for discussion in the Legislative Council of the Justice Ministry.

9. The Basic Act on Crime Victims and the Basic Plan for Crime Victims

I think the Basic Act on Crime Victims is the world's finest piece of legislation for victims. It is brief, consisting of only 30 articles. There is an English translation, which I hope you will read.

First, its Preamble recognizes that crime victims' rights have not been respected and that victims have been isolated in society, and declares that we should listen to crime victims and make a step forward to realize a society where their rights and interests are well protected. Article 3, paragraph 1 stipulates that "All Crime Victims shall have rights to be respected for their individual dignity and be assured of treatment appropriate for their individual dignity." Thus, for the first time, victims are endowed with their own rights. I call December 1, when the Basic Act became law, the "birthday" of victims.

The Basic Plan is required to contain 13 basic measures, including "developing a system to expand opportunities to participate in criminal procedures" (Article 18) and "organic linkage between the claims for damages and criminal procedures concerning the harm" (Article 12).
The Cabinet approved the Basic Plan (with the exception of matters requiring further study) on December 27, 2005. There is an English translation, which I encourage you to read.

In October 2005, NAVS had issued the *Draft Outline of a Parallel Civil Action System*. This, too, later served as a basis for discussion in the Justice Ministry's Legislative Council.

10. Enactment of Victim Participation and Orders for Compensation of Damages

On September 6, 2006, the Minister of Justice referred trial participation, parallel civil actions, and other matters to the Ministry's Legislative Council for deliberation. Over the course of eight sessions from October 3 to January 30, 2007, the Council deliberated on trial participation and parallel civil actions, and again I served as a committee member. As NAVS was the only entity to have made proposals, which we did by presenting the published draft outlines for the two systems, the deliberations began with my explaining their contents. Participation in criminal proceedings by the victims would be a revolutionary reform, and fierce debate ensued, with intense opposition from the JFBA and academic quarters.

The general public believes that victims should be treated with even more care than offenders, but many jurists see criminal trials as "the State versus the offender." In their view, even a heinous criminal is in a weak position before the State, and it is counsel's role to protect the rights of the weak. They spare no thought for the victim. The JFBA's stance is that it opposes victims' rights because they would weaken the relative position of the offender. One wants to ask whether it is not enough for them that a person has been robbed of their life—must the bereaved family also be robbed of their rights, their human rights?

Opponents argue mainly on the following grounds: (1) victim participation is possible under the inquisitorial system but not under the adversary system; (2) the victim's interests are adequately protected by the prosecutor; (3) victim participation would violate the defendant's right of defense; (4) it would cause disturbances in court; (5) the court would become a place for revenge; (6) the defendant would be too daunted to speak; (7) the victim would be hurt by the defendant's words and behavior; (8) victim participation would have a negative influence on lay judges.

These arguments are clearly groundless, as our studies in Germany and France have shown. I dealt with them one by one, pointing out that there is no need to limit the parties to two, prosecutor and defendant; that, especially in Japan, with its cause of action system, there is no risk of victim participation violating the defendant's right of defense; that the prosecutor represents the public good, not the victim; that participation would not cause disturbances in court, and that even if it did, to quote a German judge, it would be a question of how the judge conducted the proceedings. I asked how anyone could get revenge in a courtroom, and pointed out that it is only natural for the defendant to be daunted, having committed a crime, and that surely it is the role of counsel to encourage the defendant to speak. I noted that the victim has already been hurt, and that being hurt again as a participant is at least better than being hurt again as an observer in the public gallery. And I argued that the defendant is in a position to influence lay judges, and where is the logic in allowing that to the defendant but denying it to the victim?

Committee members who had been reluctant at the start gradually began to suggest compromises. It was proposed to adapt the two-party structure while maintaining it essentially intact by, for example, seating the victim or surviving relatives within the bar in order to facilitate communication with the prosecutor, and having the prosecutor act as intermediary in the victims' participation, their questioning of the defendant, and their statement of opinions. It was also proposed to limit victim participation to certain crimes and create a system that would provide counsel for participating victims at public expense (court-appointed attorney-at-law for victims).

With regard to parallel civil actions, renamed "orders for compensation of damages," one criticism was that it would prolong legal proceedings, and it was decided to limit this system to certain serious offenses committed with criminal intent.

When the bill to partially amend the Code of Criminal Procedure to protect the rights and interests of crime victims went before the Diet on March 13, 2007, after the Legislative Council had delivered its report, the JFBA voiced its opposition in the Diet and lobbied vigorously, stepping up its intense opposition campaign. They raise all sorts of theoretical objections, but it comes down to this: they don't want to recognize the human rights of victims.

I appeared as a witness before the Lower House, calling for rapid passage of the bill, and, with NAVS's membership, repeatedly petitioned members of the Diet in what became a fierce lobbying contest. On June 1 the bill was passed by the House of Representatives and sent to the House of Councillors, where deliberation in the Committee on Judicial Affairs began on June 12. But with the end of the Diet session near and party-political motives at stake, deliberations stalled and there was a risk that the bill would be abandoned. I therefore went with the other officers of NAVS on June 12 to appeal directly to Prime Minister Abe, urging him to ensure that the bill passed in the current session, and received his assent. And on June 20 the House of Councillors passed the bill into law. In view of subsequent political events, I get chills down my spine wondering whether the bill would ever have made it into law if it had been abandoned at the end of that session.

11. System for Aiding and Restoring Losses to Crime Victims

Needless to say, economic assistance or restitution by the government is important to victims, who usually cannot obtain satisfactory compensation from the offender. Benefits under the Crime Victims' Benefit Payment Act were a kind of solatium granted in a spirit of social solidarity and mutual aid, but they were one-time payments on a scale that depended on the victim's age, income, degree of disability, and other factors; payment was subject to strict conditions and the amounts were small. When NAVS was established, annual payments totaled 568 million yen, which was extremely inadequate as relief for victims. This was revised in 2000, but the total remains around 1.1 billion yen.

NAVS therefore sent missions to study the British and German compensation systems in October 2004. Britain makes a one-time compensation payment based on the spirit of social solidarity and mutual aid, while Germany pays an annuity and covers actual medical and other costs on the grounds that the State has failed in its duty to protect the citizen's security. In both cases, the amounts are far higher than in Japan. On returning home, the study missions produced detailed reports and made recommendations on the ideal type of compensation system.

The January 2005 NAVS conference adopted a resolution calling for a new compensation system based on these recommendations. It proposed a blend of the German and British systems, stipulating that payments were a form of state compensation, not a solatium, and providing for a one-time payment, an annuity, and coverage of the actual costs of medical care, long-term nursing care, and other needs. In 2006, a member of one of the missions served on the Cabinet Office's Panel on Economic Assistance and proposed the NAVS model of compensation system and, calculated on that basis, an annual disbursement of 9.5 billion yen by the State. In the end, however, only minor revisions were made to the existing framework, resulting in a total annual outlay of about 2.2 billion yen, or just twice the previous level.

This figure is extremely low compared to other major nations.

As of 2005, among the major nations, the burden on a per-capita basis was highest in France at 600 yen, followed by Britain at 483 yen, Germany at 271 yen, and the United States at 179 yen. In Japan, the figure was a mere 8.71 yen. Even when we factor in the doubling of payments, it still comes to 17.42 yen per capita.

On that basis, it is impossible to support victims "continuously from the time they receive harm until they return to leading a peaceful life again," as the Basic Act on Crime Victims says. We intend to redouble our efforts, noting that the Basic Plan is due for review after five years.

12. Other Results

Other results achieved by our movement include: passage of what is known as the Mental Illness Treatment and Observation Act; observation of trials in cases where protective measures are applied to juvenile offenders; victims being provided with information on the offender's release from prison; expanded access to and permission to copy trial records; provision of information to crime victims; concealment of personal information about crime victims; monetary rewards offered at public expense in criminal investigations; extension of the statute of limitations; improvement of shelters for crime victims; public coverage of the costs of transport and cosmetic restoration of a body after judicial autopsy; priority admission of crime victims to public housing; and non-inclusion of the victim's address in the complaint in cases where compensation for damages is sought.

With regard to observation of trials of juveniles, I made efforts to promote this as a member of the Legislative Council, but once again met with stubborn opposition from the JFBA and some scholars.

At one time there was a Crime Victim Support Day sponsored by the National Network of Victim Support, and we advocated the creation of a "Crime Victims Week" that would highlight the human rights and dignity of crime victims. This was realized in the Basic Plan, and events are now held annually around the country.

13. Conclusion

I have outlined the movement carried on by the National Association of Crime Victims and Surviving Families and the results achieved to date.

My involvement in this movement has made me feel that the legal profession, bound as it is by academic theory, precedents, and so on, is by nature too conservative to adapt to the needs of society. Issues can be tackled with a new mindset in fields where there were no existing legal provisions, such as the environment and pollution, but members of a field where a system is already firmly in place cannot think in terms of "scrap and build." I think this is a major defect in legal education.

By creating a movement of their own, crime victims have succeeded in obtaining many rights and new systems. However, it is future victims who will enjoy the rights and systems that we have won, not the victims who took part in the movement. They were moved to do so by an intense desire to spare future victims from having to go through what they themselves had suffered. I believe it is this spirit of self-sacrifice that won the public's support.

But success was not achieved by the victims alone. Our movement succeeded thanks to the cooperation of many people other than victims themselves.

It was made possible by cooperation of every kind, especially the judicious advice of Professor Hidemichi Morosawa, the energetic support of our legal advisory team, and the donations of funds, office space, and equipment and the loans of workers we received from many quarters, in particular, the Forum in Support of NAVS. Our Association does not collect membership fees; it is run solely on donations.

In closing, I have a request for the delegates gathered here from all over the world.

There are still countries without adequate legal provisions for victims, and I have heard that there are moves to learn from the example of our movement. It is true that, in Japan, we have the legal provisions that exist today because crime victims took the lead in campaigning for them. But it is a heavy burden on crime victims and bereaved relatives, who are already physically and mentally exhausted, to have to take the lead in such a movement. Japan was the first country where crime victims had to take on this demanding role, and I would like to ask you to ensure that it is also the last. Please create a system for victims before they are forced to take action themselves. Because one never knows who will become a victim tomorrow. I would particularly like to ask this of all of you, the delegates from around the world.

Looking at Refugees from the Victims Perspective

Address to the Opening Ceremony
of the Symposium

By

Johan Cels

It is a great privilege for me to be here and to represent the Office of the High Commissioner for Refugees at this symposium.

In this symposium, for the first time, victimology looks at refugees as victims. This is an important development from our perspective.

The second main reason why I am very pleased to be here is because I have worked for the Commission for Human Security a number of years ago in New York. I am very delighted to see that new disciplines - in this case victimology - are taking the concept of Human Security on board and are looking at it from different angles and see how it is relevant for its' research. It demonstrates that the concept of Human Security is relevant in analyzing today's challenges and also can come up with new policy prescriptions. I am also delighted because both Japan and Thailand have been the key proponents and supporters of Human Security. It was Japan with then Prime Minister Obuchi, who launched the concept of Human Security in response to the financial crisis in Asia a number of years ago. It was also Thailand through its former Foreign Minister, Dr. Surin Pitsuwan, currently the Secretary General of the ASEAN that can play a key role in promoting the concept of Human Security.

I am not a victimologist. I will not make any major academic contribution to your discussion.

I have worked primarily in refugee operations for the last 20 years. I look at it from an operational and practical point of view. When I was first approached to speak today it was at the U.N. Women's Day in Tokyo. I thought this was a very interesting invitation as it allows me to look at the work I have been doing from a different angle. It allows me to look at the refugee issue from the victims' perspective.

An advantage to listen to the previous speakers at this Opening Ceremony is that you learn a lot and pick up new ideas. So, I will put my prepared speech aside and I will try to make a number of comments, picking up on a number of issues that came up earlier today.

First, a look at victimology and the refugee question will reveal the link between the two. Some elements are drawn out where the discipline of victimology can contribute to the discussions in the UNHCR. Second, earlier comments on Human Security will be linked to the discussions on victimology and refugee issues.

At present there are worldwide approximately 45 million people who are forcibly displaced. I am talking about forcibly displaced people, I am not talking as such about migrants because then the figure would be much higher. Out of these 45 million people, 32 million people are of concern to the Office of the UN High Commissioner for Refugees: approximately 11 million are refugees, 13 million are internally displaced persons, and then there are another 5 to 6 million stateless persons.

Not only refugee issues have not been looked at sufficiently by the discipline of victimology, neither have stateless persons. Stateless people are persons without citizenship - without nationality. There are about 11 million stateless people in the world today. It is one of the forgotten issues. One of the reasons why this is so is because these people have no rights - no rights because they are no citizens. They have no voice. In your earlier discussions the problems of access to justice we discussed, problems of rights and about defending them. Stateless are a group of people who have clearly few rights in the international system and often none at the national system.

A few concrete examples: In Bangladesh, a group of people – the Biharis – were left in limbo for decades following the break-up of India and the subsequent independence of Bangladesh (formerly East Pakistan). In the case of Sri Lanka, many Indian Tamils worked in the tea plantations - for a very long time. Their rights as citizens were not recognized. Through working with host governments, UNHCR has been able to address these issues. Other examples include the former Yugoslavia and the former Soviet Union. When old states split and new states are created, gaps may occur due to a lack of updated nationality laws. Consequently, some groups of people are falling through the gaps and end up losing their nationality. This is clearly a group of people who also deserve our concern and attention.

Now back to refugee issues. I like to take you through the stages of a refugee's life. A refugee is a person - according to the Convention Relating to Refugees (UN 1951, Protocol 1967) - who has a well founded fear of persecution for reasons of race, religion, nationality, political opinion, or membership of a particular social group.

One of the key concepts is persecution. By persecution we mean "serious violation of human rights", which is of course one the concerns of victimologists. Victimologists are also focusing on human rights issues. But there is a difference between persecution and prosecution. Prosecution is another element of which you as victimologist are concerned about. However, we at the UN High Commissioner of Refugees are less concerned about prosecution. Except when there are situations where there is "cumulative prosecution" relating to one of the 5 reasons why a person is considered a refugee, i.e. race, religion, nationality, political opinion or membership of a particular social group. Under such circumstances, the person becomes of concern to us. And that is quite an important linkage between the two areas.

In addition to serious violations of human rights, the refugee definition has also been extended to include situations of war and conflict.

Since the end of the Cold War, we have noticed a trend: more and more internal conflicts are of concern to the UNHCR. The number of people who have been forcibly displaced internally, inside their country, is higher than the number of people who have been displaced externally, outside their country. At the international level - for those who have crossed the border - an international convention, namely the 1951 Convention relating to the Status of Refugees (UN 1951, UN 1967) – is applicable. However, for those who are still inside the country there is no such recognized international instrument. What we have there are the Guiding Principals on International Displacement. One thing I should highlight actually is that in Africa they are making the most progress in this area. The African Union will be adopting sometime in the near future an International Regional Convention on International Displacements protecting the rights of IDP.

A refugee - who is persecuted - has to flee, seeks protection, seeks asylum. The flight itself can be very traumatizing. There were references made to human trafficking earlier today. As more and more countries are closing borders and are becoming more restrictive in allowing people to enter, you will see more and more that people are forced to resort to trafficking, to traffickers to escape.

This is why it is so important in the discussion on human trafficking to highlight the need to protect the rights of those who have been trafficked because often they are victims. But they are not only victims of the traffickers themselves - extorting money, abusing them, raping women, or throwing them overboard at the high seas - as we see in the Gulf of Aden as Somalis are trafficked to Yemen. For many victims it is the only way they can escape the country.

So, when people are fleeing, they are being exploited: often their meager possessions are being taken away. They need to resort to false documentation among other issues.

Once a refugee arrives at the border and seeks asylum, then there are a number of other elements which may come into play: Many countries allow refugees or asylum seekers to enter and are very hospitable and very generous in receiving them. In other countries, including in Europe, it is becoming increasingly more difficult and much more restrictive. Refugees, the victims of persecution in their own country, are facing a number of new challenges when seeking asylum. Often because they have no documents, because they are trying to enter illegally, they are incarcerated or detained for often long periods of time. In other instances - and in the worst case scenarios - they are not allowed to enter, and are basically kept at the border. All of you are familiar with immigration at international airports. There is always somewhere a so-called "No - Man's Land" – a designated area at the airport where people who try to enter illegally are being held before they are allowed to "officially" enter the country. Some people are often held for quite a long period of time.

The most dramatic cases are those which relate to the violation of what we call the principle of "*non-refoulement*". It is a French word and refers to situations where people are sent back by force to the country where they most likely will face persecution. There have been some very dramatic instances in the past, resulting in people loosing their lives.

Another element of interest here is the process of determining refugee status. Once a person has arrived in a country of asylum they will go through a process determining whether they are refugees or not. That in itself - which is not a judicial process in many countries - can pose a number of issues regarding the protection of rights. Again it is an issue that can be examined by victimologists from different angles, for example access to social services, access to interpreters, to language, to information, to appeal, and so on.

The last phase relates to solutions. Basically, there are three solutions: voluntary repatriation home, integration in the country of asylum, and resettlement to a third country. We have had a number of very positive examples, where many of the refugees over the years have been able to integrate into a new community and have become a national of the new country.

But there are also the challenges that many of the refugees face when rebuilding their lives. Once in a country of asylum, many of them experience psycho-social trauma, depression, sometimes leading to violence in the community and in the family. They are facing alienation as they fail to successfully integrate into their new community. In addition, gaps between parents and children arise as the latter are able to integrate much easier than the parents.

Victimologists are interested in support networks that has been developed for victims. Many of those issues could be of relevance the UN work with refugees. This is another connection point where we could learn from what victimologists are doing.

The problem is also for those who voluntary return home. Returning home is considered the best solution for the majority of forcibly displaced people. In the last few years, we have witnessed large scale refugee return movements. What we often tend to forget: for example in the case of Afghanistan: over the last several years about 7 million Afghans returned from Pakistan and Iran. Many of them have taken part in the last elections and that is a major achievement. But there are still 3 million Afghans in Pakistan and 1 million in Iran. Many of the problems Afghans are facing once they return relate to how they can regain their property, their land, their houses. Most often, these were taken by others who are living there. How can they regain their property? Often when refugees go back to their community of origin, their neighbor may be the one who persecuted them and who forced them to flee. This is an issue that we have seen very intensely in the former Yugoslavia.

The question is how do two communities co-exist after a conflict? How can you make them live together? This is a big challenge and one of the reasons why we see in so many instances that after a peace agreement, after all the efforts of the international community in terms of peacekeeping and peacebuilding, still in 50% of the cases the peace process fails and there is a new outbreak of violence. So far, we have not been able to make a software - so to speak - of how you can bring people back together, how you can make them live together. This is one of the challenges and, again, hearing from the experiences by victim specialists, The UN can learn quite a lot in this area.

As I earlier said, I am not an expert in victimology, but what I have gathered is that you are very much concerned about human rights violations. This is what we share. We are also very much concerned about the impact, the consequences, upon people who need to flee because of human rights violations.

Equally, we are also very much interested in the process of becoming a victim. Having a better understanding of that from the victimology perspective would be very important to us. How victims are being perceived, how do they perceive themselves, how do others perceive them, as well as the whole response to victimizations. So these sets of issues are definitely of joint interest.

The victimological perspective includes three different dimensions, i.e., the emotional, the physical, and the material reactions to victimizations. In UNHCR, many of us are lawyers. Lawyers tend to focus a lot on the legal aspects and forget sometimes the emotional, the psychological, and the social aspects. These are areas where a closer relationship between the two groups can be of advantage.

A very important development is the work of WSV on the draft Convention on Victims. It might be useful to look at the implementation and the promotion mechanisms of, for example, legal instruments like the Convention on the Rights of the Child (UN 1989) and the Convention relating to the Status of Refugees (UN 1951). Not only in terms of rights, but also in terms of implementation and monitoring mechanisms. If you have a good convention with all the rights but you do not have the mechanisms on how to implement and how to monitor these rights - then key aspects are missing.

Regarding the earlier comments on Human Security, I like to mention that in the 2005 Millennium Declaration, adopted by nearly all Heads of States, a reference to Human Security was included (UN 2005). Remember that last year for the first time, the General Assembly had a discussion, an informal discussion, on Human Security. These developments imply that at the intergovernmental level there is increasing support for the concept of Human Security - and in that context the reference to the "Human Security Network" is an important one. The "Human Security Network" is a grouping of interested states who are promoting the concept of Human Security (see UN Human Security Unit 2009). Another grouping is the "Friends of Human Security" (Ministry of Foreign Affairs of Japan 2011) which is a group of like minded representations in New York, who are promoting issues relating to Human Security. If you can put the draft Convention on Victims within a similar framework or network, you can make quite a bit of progress in convincing states at the intergovernmental level to take the discussion forward.

These are some conversion points between Human Security, victimology and refugees:

First, we are all concerned about people and they are the focus of our attention. We are less concerned about institutions and processes.

Second, we are all concerned about rights. But then again, the issue of rights is a big field. There is a need to prioritize, to narrow it down, and see what type or what group of rights we are looking at. It is also important to adopt an approach which is situation sensitive. Certain rights, certain issues may be more prominent in some parts of the world but may be less important in other parts of the world. In Latin America very much attention is given to crime prevention, small arms, hand guns, and so on. In other parts of the world it is more freedom of speech. Detention is of concern to other areas. Adopting this situation sensitive approach will help identify the respective priorities for each region or country.

Third, and final, the concept of "Human Dignity" has been mentioned a couple of times. It is probably one of the most important elements, because in the end we are not only talking about people, but also about their dignity.

In this context a word of caution is in place. In the UNHCR we avoid portraying refugees as "victims" because a "victim" in public opinion is often seen as someone who is hopeless, who needs assistance. What we are arguing is what refugees need is respect. They do not need compassion per se. They do not need assistance. But what they need is respect. Respect for who they are, whom they represent, and that they themselves - if they have the tools - can make their own difference. They can be part of the solution rather than of the problem. This is what is meant by "Human Dignity".

The second dimension of Human Security, namely empowerment, is as relevant as protection. How do you empower people to make a difference? To contribute and to be part of the solution? When you succeed in empowerment, you create ownership and you create credibility. From my own personal experience and from colleagues who have worked with refugees, these are some of the key elements of the discussion.

References

Ministry of Foreign Affairs of Japan (2011): Friends of Human Security. http://www.mofa.go.jp/policy/human_secu/friends/index.html accessed August 15, 2011.

UN (1951). UN Convention Relating to the Status of Refugees. http://www.unhcr.org/3b66c2aa10.html accessed 15 May 2011.

UN(1967). UN Protocol Relating to the Status of Refugees. http://www.unhcr.org/3b66c2aa10.html accessed 15 May 2011

UN (1989)Convention on the Rights of the Child. General Assembly Resolution 44/25. http://www2.ohchr.org/english/law/crc.htm accessed May 15, 2011.

UN (1998). Special Rapporteur on the Human Rights of Internally Displaced Persons . International Standards. The Guiding Principles on Internal Displacement (E/CN.4/1998/53/Add.2) http://www2.ohchr.org/english/issues/idp/standards.htm accessed August 15, 2011.

UN (2005). Resolution 55/2: United Nations Millennium Declaration see under "Debates on the 2005 World Summit: at http://www.un.org/ga/59/hl60_plenarymeeting.html accessed on May 15, 2011.

UN Human Security Unit (2009). Human Security in Theory and Practice. Office for the Coordination of Humanitarian Affairs, UN, http://ochaonline.un.org/Reports/ tabid/2186/language/en-US/Default.aspx accessed August 15, 2011

Theoretical Victimology

Just-World Victimology: Revisiting Lerner in the Study of Victims of Crime

By

Antony Pemberton

Introduction

Good things happen to good people, bad things to bad people. You get what you deserve. From fairytales to religion, from Robin Hood to James Bond, this message is repetitively conveyed. The right side wins, even against all odds, and the wrongdoers do not get to profit from their ill-gotten gains. Crime does not pay, while hard work and cooperation do.

In a classic series of studies Melvin Lerner showed over three decades ago that this 'justice motive' is so engrained in people that they will adhere to it, even in the face of obviously conflicting evidence (e.g. Lerner and Simmons, 1966; Lerner and Miller, 1978; Lerner, 1980). In one of the most telling experiments, Lerner had two subjects work equally hard on a task, with their reward depending on a flip of the coin, one getting more, the other less. Observers who were aware of the manner of rewarding the workers, still overwhelmingly thought that the one who received the most, must have done the larger share. In Lerner's words, the justice motive is a fundamental delusion (Lerner, 1980). This fundamental delusion is of particular relevance in clear instances of injustice. Here the justice motive is threatened and much of Lerner's research and that of others concerning Just World theory has related to the strategies people employ to preserve their sense of a just world when faced with these situations.

Lerner's theory has played a role in the development of victimology (see Rock, 2007). It offered a particularly compelling theoretical explanation for the phenomenon of 'victim blaming'. Here the notion of good things happening to good people and bad things to bad people is reversed. The fact that something bad has happened to someone, implies that he or she must be a bad (or at least irresponsible) person. The tendency to blame victims for their own misfortune has henceforth been documented in a wide range of situations; from crime (even homicide and genocide) to sickness.

Lerner's notion of the importance of the belief in a just world was also an integral part of Janoff-Bulman's theory of 'shattered assumptions' (Janoff-Bulman, 1992). Janoff-Bulman theorized that psychological complaints following victimization could be explained by the fact that experiencing crime severely jeopardizes victims' previously held convictions about the world being a just place. This diminishes victims' sense of control over and predictability of their environment. This shattering of assumptions is associated with the onset of post-traumatic stress disorder. Although there has been some discussion of the 'shattering' mechanism that Janoff-Bulman assumed (e.g. Winkel, 2007), a diminished sense of control and the cognition that the world is an unjust, evil place both still are central elements of current theories of post-traumatic stress disorder (e.g. Ehlers and Clark, 2000).

It is important to note that the construct that Janoff-Bulman employed is slightly different from the justice motive that Lerner discerned (see Hafer and Begue, 2005). In the shattered assumptions theory, the belief in a just world is an individual difference measure which relates to the extent to which a subject actually believes the world is a just place (see Rubin and Peplau, 1975; for a review Furnham, 2003). However as Hafer and Begue (2005) note 'the essence of just-world theory is that most people have a "belief in a just world" in the sense that their underlying need to believe in a just world motivates them to behave as if they believed that the world is a just place and as if they wanted to preserve this belief, even if they do not explicitly endorse a belief in a just world on standard individual-difference scales'. This is also the reason why Lerner, Hafer & Begue and others prefer to speak of the justice motive (see also Ross and Miller, 2002), rather than the need to believe in a just world. As Lerner pointed out the latter construct was a metaphor rather than an actual description of the justice motive (Lerner, 1997). In particular the term "belief" is problematic, as this refers to conscious thought, while the justice motive is often implicit in the behaviour of people.

Except for reference to Lerner in studies into victim blaming or corollaries like rape myth acceptance and in studies into the mechanisms of the development of PTSD, the implications of just world theory and the ongoing research into this construct have been largely neglected in victimology. In a recent "Handbook on Victimology" there is just one reference to Lerner (Walklate 2007 p.59). This is unfortunate. Lerner (2003) himself provocatively stated: psychologists may have found the justice motive, they had also lost it. They were perhaps not likely to find it again. The title of this article by Lerner reflects this clearly (Lerner 2003). The body of research into just world theory is relevant in many ways to the development of victimological theory.

The current article is an attempt to make up some of the lost ground. First the current state of the just world theorizing will be discussed.

In this overview particular attention will be paid to the various strategies that people employ in the face of injustice. This discussion will be followed by the application of just world theory to a number of issues that are relevant to the development of victimology. First Nils Christie (1986)'s description of the ideal victim and criminological notions surrounding it will be compared to just world theory. Is the ideal victim really ideal? Secondly the justice motive will be used to unravel a number of notions included in restorative justice theory. Thirdly Van Dijk's recent work on the notion of victim labelling (see Van Dijk 2006; 2008) is discussed, as this proffers a different explanation for many of the victimological findings relating to just world theory. Finally the somewhat pessimistic implications of the justice motive for advancing the position of victims will be noted.

Throughout the article relevant victimological research will be used to demonstrate the use of just-world theory. In this process it will be shown that the research into the lived experience of victims is useful in the further development of just-world theory as well.

Just-world theory

Some fundamental notions

Hafer and Begue (2005) provide a comprehensive overview of the research into just-world theory. The current text is restricted to their discussion of the strategies people employ when faced with injustice. Added is the ongoing research into retributive justice, but three other features of their overview merit mentioning as well.

Hafer and Begue (2005) remind us that the need to believe in a just world is often implicit (see also Lerner, 1980, 1998; Lerner and Goldberg, 1999). This also calls into question whether it is in fact accurate to speak of the need to believe in a just world, as belief refers to a conscious deliberation (Hafer & Begue, 2005). People are mostly unaware that the justice motive underlies their behaviour (see also Dalbert, 2001), and therefore will not report it as a conscious motive (Lerner, 2003). This is an additional reason to discern research into the justice motive from research concerning individual differences in the belief in a just world. The latter reflects people's explicit or self-attributed motives. Although these may be correlated with the justice motive, this is not necessarily the case. There may only be a loose correspondence between explicitly endorsing just world beliefs and the role the justice motive plays in people's behaviour (Hafer and Begue, 2005). For example, experimental research into just-world theory has repeatedly shown the derogation of victims due to the justice motive. According to research by Callan et al (2007) this also involves negatively appraising a victims' physical appearance. But how likely is it that someone will state that the victim was unattractive, because she was a victim? Even if one was aware of this, social desirability bias would surely prevent one from revealing the motive to third parties? (e.g. Correia et al, 2001).

Secondly there is the function of the justice motive. According to Hafer (2000; see also Hafer et al, 2005) its primary function is that it allows one to invest in long-term goals and to do so according to society's rules for deservingness. Moreover 'given this function, people should have a greater need to believe in a just world if they have a strong focus on long-term investments and a strong desire to obtain goals through socially acceptable means'. The more people need to believe in a just world, the more they should be motivated to preserve a sense of justice in the face of contradictory evidence. (Hafer and Begue, 2005:44). In addition Dalbert (1999, 2001) suggested that the justice motive helps foster a sense of well-being, overall and in particular in the face of negative life events.

Finally the research into just-world theory shows that the necessity of employing the strategies for maintaining the justice motive increases with the degree of threat an event poses to the belief in a just world (Lerner, 1980). In other words: the higher the level of injustice, the more people need to take (cognitive, affective or behavioural) action to protect their just world beliefs. In particular both - the innocence of a victim and the persistence of his or her suffering - are threats to the belief in a just world (see Correia and Vala, 2003). As we will see these features can have perverse consequences. Where we may expect victims who are suffering indefinitely due to crime to be afforded the highest level of sympathy and support, just-world theory predicts negative responses to them to be more likely rather than less likely. As their suffering is difficult or hard to relieve, the social surroundings will employ strategies that involve a negative evaluation of or distancing from the victim to preserve the justice motive. These features may be further compounded by the so-called *severity* effect. This relates to the well-documented research finding that observers pay more attention to the victims' irresponsibility when the negative effect of an action is large rather than when it is minor (e.g., Feigenson et al., 1997). The victim's conduct therefore will be under closer scrutiny in the cases were his or her suffering is largest (see also Adams-Price et al, 2004).

Victim-focused strategies for dealing with injustice

Lerner's original work mainly addressed the strategies people employ with respect to the victims of injustice (Lerner, 1980). He divided the strategies into rational strategies, irrational strategies and so-called protective strategies.

Rational strategies involve the acceptance of the presence of injustice. These involve either acting to prevent injustice before it occurs and restoring justice to unjust situations, or in other words prevention and reparation. In one of Lerner's first experiments (Lerner and Simmons, 1966) observers watched a fellow student (actually a confederate) take part in a learning task and receive electric shocks for incorrect responses. In the first condition the observers were allowed to reassign the student involved in the task to a reward condition, in the second condition observers were not given this option. Most participants in the first condition decided to reassign the student, suggesting that if people are in the position to restitute victims they will do so. The crux of the experiment however, was that in both conditions the observers were asked to judge the student's character. This was judged to be positive in the first condition, but far less favourably in the second. The student's character was derogated due to his misfortune and the impossibility of undertaking restitutory activities (see also Haynes and Olson, 2006).

Victim derogation is an example of an irrational strategy. In this subset of strategies people preserve the justice motive by refusing to accept the presence of injustice. Lerner described four irrational strategies. Three of them involve reinterpretation of the event. In the first the *cause* is reinterpreted. Here victims are perceived to be (at least in part) to blame for the incident. The distress caused by injustice is diminished or even resolved by maintaining that the victim was also at fault. Victims who are perceived to have a degree of responsibility for their victimization are particularly prone to be blamed (Haynes and Olson, 2006). Victim blaming has been documented in a wide array of situations, such as unemployment, sexual abuse of women and children, battered women, cancer, elderly people, and HIV positive people (see for an overview Haynes and Olson, 2006).

In the second irrational strategy *personal characteristics* of the victim are reinterpreted. The tendency for negative appraisals of the victim's character (see Correia et al, 2001; 2003) and their attractiveness (Callan et al, 2007) is already noted earlier in this paper. Castano and Giner-Sorolla (2006) reveal a particular instance of victim derogation in the intergroup context. In their research they provided participants with evidence of mass-killing committed by their own 'in-group' (British and white Americans) against an 'out-group' (Australian Aborigines and Native Americans). Providing in-group members with this evidence led them to infra-humanize the out-group to a greater degree. Infra-humanization refers to the denial to an individual or group of some of the characteristics that make them human, and in particular of the uniquely human secondary emotions like love, guilt or hope (Leyens et al, 2000). Knowledge of 'our' inhumanities against 'them' therefore leads us to see 'them' as less human.

In the third irrational strategy the *outcome* of the event is revalued. The negative consequences of the event are downplayed. The possible positive consequences of undeserved suffering are stressed, for instance that the victimisation was a learning experience or that it builds character (Hafer and Begue, 2005). This is a topic that has not received much attention in the experiments into just world theory itself, but evidence of this is phenomenon is available from a variety of other sources. Bandura (1999) for instance notes the tendency to employ sanitizing euphemisms, like 'alternative career enhancement' for firing people or, in a far more extreme case, the 'Final Solution' for the Holocaust. The reactions of victims to their own suffering also show evidence of this strategy. Zoellner and Maercker's (2006) review of the concept of posttraumatic growth, shows that some victims find that their victimisation has positive consequences in the longer term. It strengthened their bonds with their close ones. It made them understand what is important in life. Nevertheless the same review shows post-traumatic growth to have an illusory aspect, in which the attempts of the victims to find something positive in their experience can be viewed as a cognitive effort to avoid the aversive consequences of victimisation.

Finally the observer may employ a fourth irrational strategy: one of denial/ withdrawal and the related construct of psychological distancing to the event. In denial/ withdrawal the observer attempts to avoid threats to the justice motive when they are encountered (Hafer and Begue, 2005). Psychological distancing involves creating a cognitive distance between oneself and the victim. The observer will attempt to discern cues that the victim is in some way different, so that the injustice that has befallen the victim will be unlikely to happen to the observer (Hafer, 2000).

Psychological distancing is related to the first of Lerner's so-called protective strategies, the 'two world theory' (Lerner, 1980), which may be summarized in the idea that where our world is just, theirs is not (Lerner and Goldberg, 1999; Hafer and Begue, 2005). Research that varies the group-status of victims shows that victims belonging to the same group as the observer pose a stronger threat to the justice motive than out-group members (see Correia et al, 2007; Aguiar et al, 2008). A more extreme form of this is moral exclusion (Opotow, 1990; Clayton and Opotow, 2003) in which the out-group is deemed to be outside the scope of justice. A good example of the consequences of two-world theory and moral exclusion is provided by the research into genocide. Where moral exclusion plays a role in the commission of genocide (see generally Waller, 2006), two-world theory is an explanation for the Western world's apparent indifference to intervene in genocide (see generally Power, 2003).

An additional protective strategy is what Lerner called 'ultimate justice' (Lerner, 1980). Here the justice motive is protected by the notion that although justice might not seem to be done in every instance, it will definitely be done in the long run (e.g. Maes, 1998). Lerner (1997) has connected this belief in ultimate justice with religion. As Hafer and Begue (2005) note the belief in ultimate justice reduces the threat posed by instances of injustice (what Maes calls 'immanent justice'). Consistent with this, Lerner (1997) found religious people to show less evidence of victim blaming than non-religious people.

Finally Lerner (1980) proposed a penultimate defence in which people maintain that they do not believe in a just world (and probably also have no need to hold such a belief).

Perpetrator-focused strategies for dealing with injustice

It is interesting to note that although Lerner was most interested in people's reactions to the victims of injustice, the threat to the justice motive also relates to people's reactions to *perpetrators* of injustice. There is a relative absence of studies that explicitly relate the justice motive to people's reactions to perpetrators of injustice (Hafer and Begue, 2005), but in the collection of essays in honour of Lerner '*The Justice motive in everyday life*' (Ross and Miller, 2002), both Vidmar and Darley connect their research into punishment and retributive justice to the need to believe in a just world (Vidmar, 2002; Darley, 2002). In the same volume Ellard and colleagues discuss the concept of demonizing of offenders within the framework of the justice motive (Ellard et al, 2002). Recent research by Wenzel and colleagues concerning retributive justice and other strategies for dealing with perpetrators of injustice shows a strong consistence with the victim-focused strategies discussed by Lerner (e.g. Wenzel et al, 2008, Okimoto et al 2009, Wenzel and Thielmann, 2006). A central question in the research Darley and his colleagues undertook is why we punish offenders (e.g. Darley et al, 2000; Darley, 2002, Carlsmith et al 2002). And the answer is as Darley himself says 'we punish others who have committed prototypic "crimes" –intentional infliction of wrongful, immoral harms on others- because we wish to give the actor his justly deserved punishment for the wrongful action he took' (Darley, 2002:331). Although this punishment may deter the offender or others from committing acts in the future, neither is the central purpose of punishment. Darley shows the punishment to be proportionate to the magnitude of the wrong committed, rather than its (perceived) effectiveness in the prevention of future offences. This notion of "just deserts" (e.g. Von Hirsch, 1993) or retribution is consistent with Lerner's theory. We punish in proportion to the threat posed by the offender's action to our need to believe in a just world.

The threat posed by the offender's action is more proportionate to the wrong committed rather than the harm caused. Alter, Kernochian and Darley (2007) showed transgression wrongfulness to outweigh harmfulness in determining sentence severity. Similarly the results of Gromet and Darley (2006; 2009a)'s research reveal the severity of crime to be related to the desire to meet out retributive punishment.

Research by Wenzel and colleagues outlines that an alternative reaction to the perpetrator's actions is what they call *value restoration* (see for an overview Wenzel et al, 2008). Here the injustice is undone through actions on the part of the offender to repair the harm caused and simultaneously reaffirm his or her commitment to the values breached by the transgression (or in other words through a restorative justice procedure, e.g. Braithwaite, 2002). In cases of lower severity Wenzel et al (2008; see also Gromet and Darley, 2006, 2009a, 2009b) show value restoration alone to be deemed a sufficient reaction by observers, while in high severity cases the value restoration may also be included in the reaction to crime, but only alongside a retributive response.

The importance of value restoration also depends on the question whether or not offender and victim are regarded as sharing membership in a relevant community or inclusive group (Wenzel et al, 2008). The strategy of value restoration applies to in-group perpetrators who are therefore expected to uphold community values, but not to out-group members. Support for value restoration is correlated with group cohesiveness, as this increases people's concern about group values (Wenzel et al., 2009). The ingroup-outgroup divide in reactions to perpetrators maps on to Lerner's protective strategy of the two-world theory. Our world is just, but "theirs" is not necessarily so.

The severity of the crime and the extent of shared identity interact (Gromet and Darley, 2009a). Severe crimes will lead to an attempt to distance oneself from the offenders and to exclude them from the in-group (see also Eidelman, Silvia, & Biernat, 2006). As Pemberton (2010) notes, crimes of a sufficient severity automatically convey a sense of 'otherness' to the perpetrator. This sense of otherness relates to an earlier notion of Darley that demonizing the offender serves to protect the justice motive (Darley, 1992).

As Ellard et al (2002) note, this may, at first glance, seem somewhat paradoxical. 'After all if evil behaviour is threatening, is not demonizing just the opposite of what people should do to protect their belief in a just world? Why would people want to populate their just world with evil people? (Ellard et al, 2002: 352). As Ellard et al (2002) point out, however, the alternative, the unfortunately empirically well supported fact that ordinary people commit extremely evil acts, is more disturbing. Waller, (2006) shows convincingly that it is ordinary people who commit genocide and mass killing.

If anyone can be the author of evilness, it is much harder to maintain a belief in a just world - believing that evil acts are undertaken by equally evil people makes it more recognizable and controllable. The threat that evil poses to the justice motive is located in individuals, who can be contained or even eradicated. The evildoers become the rare exceptions to the rule that the world is basically a just place. Moreover their humanness is called into question. Perpetrators of evil are dehumanized (Haslam, 2006), by using categories of subhuman creatures (for example, the word predator, relating to animals) or by using categories of negatively evaluated unhuman creatures (as is implied by demonizing) and are thereby morally excluded from the scope of justice (Opotow, 1990).

The research into (the motives behind the) punishment of perpetrators of crime reveals the existence of – in Lerner's terms, see above - both rational strategies (retribution, value restoration) and protective strategies (two-world theory, demonizing). Irrational victim-related strategies, in addition, may implicate offenders as well as victims. The reinterpretation of the cause of the event may reapportion blame between the victim and the offender, although victim blaming may coincide with a severe retributive response toward the offender (see below). Reinterpretation of the outcome, in more positive terms, can also reduce the perception of wrongdoing by the offender.

The relative importance of strategies

Hafer and Begue (2005) note that different just-world strategies may co-occur. People may at once attempt to compensate victims, while they psychologically distance themselves from them. Similarly the urge for retribution may coincide with either the protective strategy of demonizing or attempts to achieve value restoration. In the latter case, the compensatory strategy focused on the victim is an integral part of the strategy focused on the offender.

As noted throughout this article a variety of factors play a role in the choice of strategy. In the case of the offender, the severity of the crime stresses the need for retribution, while shared identity with the offender makes a value restoration strategy more likely. In the case of the victim, the possibility of offering compensation is important, with victim derogation and even blaming being more likely in the absence of such possibilities. Similarly failed attempts at compensation or enduring suffering of the victim heighten the need for non-rational strategies in coping with the injustice the victim suffered.

A particularly important issue for victimology is the relative importance of the rational strategies people may employ in the face of injustice. Do they prioritize punishment of offenders over compensation to victims or the other way around? The former rather than the latter appears to be true. The aversion at injustice, the anger or 'moral outrage' this causes (e.g. Miller, 2001; Darley & Pittman, 2003) are easily aligned with a punitive response towards the offender. In dealing with the victim however an observer is faced with two conflicting emotions, with the aversion at the situation sitting uneasily with the sympathy and empathy needed to address the plight of the victim (e.g. Folger & Pugh, 2002). Similarly where increasing severity of crime simply leads to a stronger desire to punish the offender, a similar increase heightens the tension of dealing with victims. As noted earlier, the more a victim suffers, the more likely it is that a non-rational strategy, like victim blaming, derogation or distancing, will be employed. Finally employing the strategy of psychological distancing to victims, will lead people to be relatively indifferent to the victims' needs (Loewenstein and Small, 2007), while people are rarely indifferent to offenders (e.g. Miller, 2001; Hogan and Embler, 1981; Van Prooijen, 2009).

The predominance of punishment over compensation is borne out by recent research by Van Prooijen, 2009 and Gromet and Darley, 2009. Van Prooijen (2009) showed the impulse to punish the offender to outweigh compensation of the victim in crimes ranging from relatively mild (pick-pocketing) to severe (kidnapping or rape). Gromet and Darley (2009) revealed punishing the offender to be the default reaction to crime, although instructing participants to think about the victims' fate did increase the importance of 'restorative' options.

Victimological concepts and just-world theory

The ideal victim?

In a seminal and much-quoted publication Nils Christie (1986) coined the term 'ideal victim'. Briefly, he described the ideal victim along the following lines (see also Dignan, 2005):

- The victim is weak in relation to the offender – the 'ideal victim' is likely to be either female, sick, very old or very young (or a combination of these).
- The victim is, if not acting virtuously, then at least going about their legitimate, ordinary everyday business.
- The victim is blameless for what happened.
- The victim is unrelated to and does not know the 'stranger' who has committed the offence.
- The offender is unambiguously big and bad.

According to Christie these 'ideal victims' are those who -when hit by crime – are most readily given the complete and legitimate status of being a victim, with the little old lady being his favourite example (Christie, 1986). They are the deserving victims, the ones that are most likely to receive our sympathy and in whose names victim services are justified (Spalek, 2006). Christie criticised the ideal victim for not adequately reflecting the reality of many instances of crime, as many victims of crime do not share the characteristics of the 'ideal victim'.

Except for its lack of a factual base, the notion of the ideal victim is also supposed to have subsequent negative consequences for the way offenders are viewed and treated. Many authors have noted that the ideal victim figures heavily in the media (e.g. Reiner, 2002) and in populist campaigns for more severe sentences (e.g. Scheingold et al, 1994; Miers, 2007). The concern is that offenders are increasingly seen as 'unambiguously big and bad' - although most of them are not – *because of* the emphasis on ideal victims. The subsequent punitive turn in punishment and pressure on suspects' and offenders' rights is, at least in part, caused by this stereotype (see also Christie, 2010).

However the research into the justice motive suggests two problematic features of this line of reasoning. First and foremost, viewed through the lens of the justice motive, ideal victims are in fact anything but ideal. They represent a clear challenge to the notion that bad things do not happen to good people. The research into the justice motive suggests that when faced with the injustice suffered by victims, the first inclination of observers is often to review the conduct and the character of the victim to see whether they are to blame for their misfortune. Moreover, the victim's enduring suffering, will not lead to an ongoing outpouring of support. This is instead likely to run out long before victims have had time to adequately cope with their ordeal.

Evidence is abundant of these phenomena. Miers (2007) for instance notes the importance of blamelessness in the compensation of victims in the United Kingdom. Where the victim's behaviour contributes to his or her victimization, compensation may be reduced or victims may be ineligible for criminal injuries compensation. Moreover, victims with a history of criminal behaviour of their own are also excluded, by the mere fact that they are 'criminals' themselves conveying a permanent sense of blameworthiness on them.

The phenomenon of secondary victimisation of victims and victim blaming by justice authorities is another case in point. Contrary to what one would expect when viewing the notion of the ideal victim, these phenomena are also well-documented in the case of 'ideal victims'. The experience of co-victims of homicide, even when they are clearly 'ideal victims', is often marred by instances of secondary victimisation (e.g. Spungen, 1998; Armour, 2007). In addition, as predicted by the research into the justice motive, the reaction of victims' social surroundings is often not one of enduring sympathy and empathy. Instead victims continuing suffering will lead to strategies of avoidance and distancing (e.g. Doka, 1988).

The mere existence of Victim Support can serve as a final illustration. A large part of Victim Support's work involves measures to reduce secondary victimization and deliver emotional support to victims (see Pemberton, 2009), efforts to fill in the void in the societal reaction to victimization. The necessity of these types of services stems from the fact that people's default reaction to victimization includes blaming victims, and that the victim's suffering often does not elicit (sufficient) sympathy and support from their immediate environment. That we needed an organization to provide 'tea and sympathy' (Fattah, 1999) to victims should serve as a lasting reminder of this fact.

A second problematic feature of the ideal victim is its proposed effect on the way the offender is viewed. In Christie's reasoning the deservingness of the ideal victim and the sympathy he or she elicits, affects negatively people's perception of the offender. This however sits uneasily with the evidence that the reaction to the offender is predominant in dealing with threats to the justice motive and that in cases of ideal victims, a severe retributive response co-occurs with victim-blaming and derogation.

This point is maybe best illustrated by the description of a different stereotype. In an equally seminal publication as Christie's, which is nevertheless largely ignored in victimological circles, social-psychologist Roy Baumeister described the so-called 'Myth of Pure Evil':

- The offender intentionally inflicted severe harm on the victim.
- This harm was primarily motivated by the wish to harm the victim, merely for the pleasure of doing so. The harm was not inflicted for instrumental reasons, nor was it used reluctantly.
- Evil and evil offenders are so by nature and this nature has a permanent quality.
- The harm is committed by the other, the stranger or even the enemy.
- The victim is innocent and good.

Although Christie's stereotype is obviously similar to Baumeister's, the latter situates the portrayal of ideal victims squarely as an element of a protective, offender-focused strategy to deal with threats to the justice motive, namely demonizing the offender. The populist campaigns that invoke the ideal victim, therefore are not so much focused on delivering higher levels of support and compensation to the victim, which should be expected if sympathy for the victim was the main driver for action, but instead on more severe sentences to the author of evil, the offender. The 'idealization' of the victim is then a *consequence* rather than a *cause* of the way the offender is viewed and the cases where the blameworthiness of victims is not called into question, are those where the offender is perceived as pure evil. A good example of this is the treatment of victims of mass terrorism, particular the acts committed by Al Qaeda (see Pemberton, 2011).

The justice motive in restorative justice theory

Christie contrasted the stereotype of the ideal victim with what he saw as the reality of victims' experience, but his own perception of reality proved to be a social construction in itself. Van Dijk (2006) described this 'ideal victim of restorative justice' as being 'free of vengefulness and mentally ready to accept apologies from the offender and to offer forgiveness.' Pemberton, Winkel and Groenhuijsen (2007:11) similarly consider this ideal victim to be 'forgiving, not punitive, more interested in restoration than punishment, and symbolic reparation at that, part of the same community as the offender, not afraid of the offender, wanting and capable of full participation in the case.'

The point to be made here, is not that this stereotype does not adequately capture the experience of many victims of crime, in particular those suffering the most severe forms of victimization (see already Pemberton et al 2007; Pemberton 2009, 2010). Instead it is relevant to emphasize that the 'ideal victim of restorative justice' concurs with the justice motive, in the sense that observers would much prefer victims to act in accordance with Christie's stereotype. The ideal victim of restorative justice does not suffer indefinitely, is capable in a large extent of dealing with the consequences of their victimization him or herself and his or her needs may be met by the offering of (often symbolic) reparation. These features all reduce the threat posed by injustice. Instead victims suffering indeterminately, for whom the damage has permanent qualities and who are vindictive and vengeful pose an enduring threat to the justice motive. Van Dijk (2006) provides an extensive discussion of the evidence of the negative societal reaction to angry, vengeful victims. Viewed through the lens of the justice motive, the unease caused by these victims is due to the fact that they serve as enduring reminders of injustice and our inability to resolve the tensions resulting from this. In sum: the justice motive predicts an observer bias for the 'ideal victim of restorative justice' and against the retributive, vengeful victim.

Similar evidence of the justice motive's role in restorative justice theory is provided by another seminal publication of Christie. His

1977 article 'Conflicts as property' is one of the most widely cited in criminology. Central in this paper is the notion that crime can be redefined as conflict and that conflict represents a most interesting property. This property is taken away, - and that is more relevant than the goods originally taken away from the victim, or given back to him (Christie 1977; 7). Again this can be viewed in conjuncture with the justice motive. Both notions may be seen as non-rational strategies for dealing with injustice. The event is reinterpreted, from being an unjust crime to a valuable conflict. That becomes also clear from Christie's catchphrase "Crime does not exist". The positive aspects of the outcome of the event are stressed, in the sense that the conflict has provided possibilities for 'norm-clarification'. It is not so much that I find the first notion to be erroneous (Pemberton 2010; see also Duff, 2003), and that the second only applies under certain circumstances (Pemberton 2010; see Wenzel et al, 2008): both the re-evaluation of the cause of suffering and the emphasis of positive outcomes can serve to reduce justice-related threat experienced by observers. The unease caused by the fact that bad things happen to good people is decreased by calling into question whether they are in fact bad things.

Taken together: the charge that just world theory offers against Christie's point of view, which resounds in the work of all too many other authors in the field of restorative justice, is that it attempts to resolve the problems in the reaction to crime by denying, in part or in whole, the injustice that is inherent to it (see also Pemberton, 2010). This may contribute to easing justice-related threat, but these non-rational strategies are not very conducive to developing a coherent theory of justice.

Victim labelling

Recently van Dijk discussed similar problematic features to the reaction to victimization (see Van Dijk, 2006, 2008). The author of the current article referred to and agreed with a number of his findings throughout this essay. His general notion of victims being disempowered, blamed and derogated in the societal reaction to them and the bias against their expression of anger concur with the gist of this article. He may not fully agree with van Dijk's description of 'treatment-oriented victimology', but he can quite follow the possibility that the ubiquitous overuse of the word trauma in the description of victims may not be in their interest (see also Pemberton, 2008). Van Dijk finds treatment-oriented victimology (i. e. the psychological services provided to victims of crime) to portray the image of victims as passive sufferers (van Dijk, 2006; 18). However a core feature of the most promising cognitive-behavioral techniques for reducing or recovering from post-traumatic stress disorder is in fact combating passivity (e.g. Ehlers and Clark, 2000).

Van Dijk's analysis reveals a rather intriguing phenomenon, that a desire for retribution and punishment of crime in the public (see also Carlsmith et al, 2002) may coexist with denunciation of retributive feelings on the part of the victim. In the light of the justice motive this may be explained through the fact that retributive justice may be a strategy for reducing the threat to justice, while the victims desire for retribution or even revenge may serve as a reminder of the enduring nature of this threat. An interesting avenue for experimental research into the justice motive would therefore be to explore whether anger displayed by victims leads to similar results as their enduring suffering. This is particularly relevant seeing that the anger rather than anxiety may be the more prevalent reaction to criminal victimization (Winkel, 2007).

However as to the cause of the phenomena, this author finds himself at odds with the cause of the phenomena van Dijk describes, and subsequently with the solution of his analysis. According to Van Dijk the core of the problem lies in the word victim itself. Van Dijk's version of victim labelling theory (see also Miers, 1989; Rock, 2004) traces the origin of the word victim to its religious roots (Van Dijk, 2006: 2008). Van Dijk (2006:4) shows that 'the word victim in European and Arab languages originates from an ubiquitous religious ritual, the offering of a sacrifice as part of the worship of a god.' And in the Christian tradition this refers to the figure of Jesus Christ. According to Van Dijk (2008;20) Jesus Christ does not just stand for innocent suffering. His image also stands for meekness and mandatory forgiveness. And subsequently (Van Dijk, 2008:21) ' In the context of Christian culture, victims are challenged to follow in the steps of Christ at the Cross. They are expected to play a healing role in the aftermath of the crime. The label of victim invites them to render a service to the community by relinquishing their natural right to seek vengeance. By labelling them as victims, those affected by crime are forced into a passive role.' He therefore concludes that relinquishing the term victim and/ or uncovering its hidden connotations will serve as a part of the solution to the problems faced by crime victims.

This author does not share the implicit optimism: the research into the justice motive also predicts the type of reaction to victims that Van Dijk observes. The question then becomes whether, the reactions to victimisation are due to Christian connotations with the term victim. Or are the latter better understood as a religious enshrinement of the justice motive?

My reading of the literature leads me to believe that the latter is the case. Just-world effects have also been documented in cases where the word victim is absent (see generally Hafer and Begue,

2005) or even where no words at all are used to describe the victims suffering (Pancer, 1988). Providing a description of the suffering of a person or the event that caused their suffering is sufficient. Similar effects are found in instances of non-criminal injustice (Hafer & Begue, 2005). Blaming or derogating people for their misfortune and attempting to psychologically distance oneself from them is not restricted to victimisation by crime or to those situations for which in the English the term victim is commonly used. Similar findings are also observed in job lay-offs or sickness, for whom the terms unemployed and sick are far more common than 'victim' (see e.g. Haynes and Olson, 2006).

There is cross-cultural evidence for the need to believe in a just world (e.g. Furnham, 1993, Pepitone and L'Armand, 1996; see also Lee et al, 1997). Research has negative reactions to victims in non-Western, non-Christian subjects as well, and there is also evidence that these effects are stronger rather than weaker (f.e. Mori et al, 1995, Yamawaki & Tschanz, 2005). Religious subjects are more inclined to employ the protective *ultimate justice* strategy. i.e. that although justice might not seem to be done in every instance, it will definitely be done in the long run, see above. The threat posed by these individual instances of injustice, (what Maes (1998) calls "immanent justice is therefore as a rule less than it is for non-religious subjects. There is evidence that they therefore are less rather than more likely to display many of the negative reactions to victims that Van Dijk perceives (see Spilka, Hood, Honsburger and Gorusch, 2003 and Saroglou, Pichon, Trompette, Verschueren and Dernelle, 2005; for the role of the justice motive in this phenomenon, see Pichon and Saroglou, 2009). Both the cross-cultural evidence and the research findings concerning religious subjects contradict the emphasis on the Christian connotations of the word victim.

This is also true for the evidence of differences within the Christian population. The findings mentioned in the previous section do not apply equally to more closed-minded religious subjects, i.e. those adhering to fundamentalism or orthodoxy, They are less likely to display helping behaviour (see Jackson and Esses, 1997, 2000), in particular if the suffering person does not belong to the same faith (Batson, Anderson and Collins, 2005). While it is hard to see how victim labelling theory would explain these findings, Saroglou (2003) shows both they can be helpfully understood through just-world theory, with fundamentalist religious subjects displaying higher levels of immanent justice, while more open-minded subjects display higher levels uiltimate justice (see also Pichon and Saroglou, 2009).

These research findings form a stark contrast to the importance Van Dijk places on the word used to describe victims and their ordeal. This leads to suspect that replacing the term 'victim' will not be effective in reducing the negative societal reactions to victims of crime. Using 'survivor' or 'aggrieved party' to describe a person who has suffered injustice will not obscure the threat to the need to believe in a just world that that person poses to observers.

The justice motive and improving the plight of victims of crime

Throughout the article we have seen evidence of victim-blaming being caused by the need to believe in a just world. Lerner's contention that the justice motive is a fundamental human characteristic implies that reducing the extent of victim-blaming in society will be a never-ending uphill battle. Moreover, the revelation that victims who are in greatest need of sympathy and support due to their enduring suffering may be withheld it for that same reason is quite unsettling. Those most deserving of our support are only 'ideal' victims if their victimization is invoked in strategies of demonizing the offender.

The justice motive provides equally pessimistic predictions of increasing the relative priority of victim reparation. In dealing with injustice, observers first and foremost include strategies in reaction to the perpetrator's behaviour. Punishing the offender is people's default reaction to crime. It outweighs the wish for victims' reparation. However, although retributive responses may be preferred, the victim's own vengefulness will be met with negative reactions, as this serves as a reminder to the injustice the victim suffered. Instead the 'ideal victim of restorative justice' may in fact be the most preferred victim-stereotype.
Replacing the word 'victim' will not be effective in reducing these negative societal reactions to victims. The Mark of Abel is conveyed by the mere fact that the victims suffered injustice, and that this injustice subsequently threatens the need to believe in a just world. The latter delusion is apparently fundamental to the human condition and in my opinion fundamental to the development of victimology as well.

This article was written with the support of the Dutch Victim Support Fund.

References

Adams-Price, C. E., Dalton, W.T. & Sumrall, R. (2004). Victim Blaming in Young, Middle-Aged, and Older Adults: Variations on the Severity Effect, Journal of Adult Development, 11(4), 289-295.

Aguiar, P., Vala, J., Correia, I., & Pereira, C. (2008). Justice in our world and in that of others: Belief in a just world and reactions to victims. Social Justice Research, 21, (1), 50-68.

Alter, A. L., Kernochan, J., & Darley, J. M. (2007). Transgression wrongfulness outweighs its harmfulness as a determinant of sentence severity. Law and Human Behavior, 31, 319–335.

Armour, M. (2007). Violent death. Journal of Human Behavior in the social environment. 14(4), 53-90.

Bandura, A. (1999). Moral disengagement in the perpetration of inhumanities. Personality and Social Psychology Review, 3(3), 193-209.

Batson, C.D., Anderson, S.L. & Collins, E. (2005). Personal religion and prosocial motivation. In Maher, M.L. et al (eds.) Advances in motivation and achievement, 14, 151-185.

Baumeister, R. F. (1997). Evil. Inside human violence and cruelty. New York: Henry Holt and Company.

Braithwaite, J. (2002). Restorative justice and responsive regulation. New York, Oxford University Press.

Carlsmith, K. M., Darley, J. M., & Robinson, P. H. (2002). Why do we punish?: Deterrence and just deserts as motives for punishment. Journal of Personality and Social Psychology, 83, 284–299.

Castano, E., & Giner-Sorolla, R. (2006). Not quite human: Infra-humanization as a response to collective responsibility for intergroup killing. Journal of Personality and Social Psychology, 90, 804–818.

Christie, N. (1977). Conflicts as property. British Journal of Criminology, 17(1), 1-17.

Christie, N. (1986). The ideal victim. In E.Fattah (ed.): From crime policy to victim policy. Basingstoke: Macmillan.

Christie, N. (2010). Victim movement at a crossroad. Punishment and Society, 12, 125-133.

Clayton, S., and Opotow, S (2003). Justice and identity: Changing perspectives on what is fair. Personality and Social Psychological Review, 7(4): 298–310.

Correia, I., & Vala, J. (2003). When will a victim be secondarily victimized? The effect of observer's belief in a just world, victim's innocence and persistence of suffering. Social Justice Research, 16, 379–400.

Correia, I., Vala, J., & Aguiar, P. (2001). The effects of belief in a just world and victim's innocence on secondary victimization, judgements of justice and deservingness. Social Justice Research, 14, 327–342.

Dalbert, C. (1999). The world is more just for me than generally: About the personal belief in a just world scale's validity. Social Justice Research, 12, 79–98.

Dalbert, C. (2001). The justice motive as a personal resource: Dealing with challenges and critical life events. New York: Kluwer Academic/Plenum.

Dalbert, C. (2002). Beliefs in a just world as a buffer against anger. Social Justice Research, 15, 123–145.

Darley, J. M. (1992). Social organization for the production of evil. Psychological Inquiry, 3, 199–218.
Darley, J. M. (2002). Just punishments: Research on retributional justice. In M. Ross & D. T. Miller (Eds.), The justice motive in everyday life (pp. 314–333). New York: Cambridge University Press.
Darley, J. M., Carlsmith, K. M., & Robinson, P. H. (2000). Incapacitation and just deserts as motives for punishment. Law and Human Behavior, 24, 659–683.
Darley, J. M., & Pittman, T. S. (2003). The psychology of compensatory and retributive justice. Personality and Social Psychology Review, 7, 324–336.
Dignan, J. (2005). Understanding victims and restorative justice. Maidenhead: Open University Press.
Doka, K. (Ed.). (1988). Disenfranchised grief: Recognizing hidden sorrow. Lexington, MA: Lexington Books.
Duff, R.A. (2003). Restoration and retribution. In: von Hirsch, A., Roberts, J.V., Bottoms, A., Roach, K. & Schiff, M. (ed.) Restorative and criminal justice: competing or reconcilable paradigms. Oxford, UK: Hart Publishing.
Ehlers, A. & Clark, D.M. (2000). A cognitive model of posttraumatic stress disorder. Behavior research and therapy, 38, 319-345.
Eidelman, S., Silvia, P. J., & Biernat, M. (2006). Responding to deviance: Target exclusion and differential devaluation. Personality and Social Psychology Bulletin, 32, 1153–1164.
Ellard, J. H., Miller, C. D., Baumle, T., & Olson, J. M. (2002). Just world processes in demonizing. In M. Ross & D. T. Miller (Eds.), The justice motive in everyday life (pp. 350–362). New York: Cambridge University Press.
Fattah, E. (1999). From a handful of dollars to tea and sympathy. The sad history of victim assistance. In J.J.M. van Dijk, R.G.M. van Kaam & J.A. Wemmers (eds.). Caring for crime victims: selected proceedings of the 9th International Symposium on Victimology. Monsey NY: Criminal Justice Press.
Feigenson, N., Park, J., & Salovey, P. (1997). Effect of blameworthiness and outcome severity on attributions of responsibility and damage awards in comparative negligence cases. Law and Human Behavior, 21, 597-617.
Folger, R., & Pugh, S. D. (2002). The just world and Winston Churchill: An approach/avoidance conflict about psychological distance when harming victims. In M. Ross, & D. T. Miller (Eds.), The justice motive in everyday life (pp. 168–186). Cambridge, UK: University Press.
Furnham, A. (1993). Just world beliefs in twelve societies. Journal of Social Psychology, 133, 317–329.
Furnham, A. (2003). Belief in a just world: Research progress over the past decade. Personality and Individual Differences, 34, 795–817.
Green, S. (2007). Crime, victimisation and vulnerability. In Walklate, S. (2007). Handbook of Victims and Victimology. Cullumpton, Devon, UK: Willan Publishing.
Gromet, D. M., & Darley, J. M. (2006). Restoration and retribution: How including retributive components affects the acceptability of restorative justice procedures. Social Justice Research, 19, 395–432.
Gromet, D. M., & Darley, J. M. (2009a). Retributive and restorative justice:

The importance of crime severity and shared identity on people's justice responses. Australian Journal of Psychology , 61, 50-57.
Gromet, D. M., & Darley, J. M. (2009b). Punishment and beyond. Achieving justice through the satisfaction of multiple goals. Law and Society Review, 43(1), 1-37.
Hafer, C. L. (2000). Do innocent victims threaten the belief in a just world?: Evidence from a modified Stroop task. Journal of Personality and Social Psychology, 79, 165–173.
Hafer, C. L. (2002). Why we reject innocent victims. In M. Ross & D. T. Miller (Eds.), The justice motive in everyday life (pp. 109–126). New York: Cambridge University Press.
Hafer, C.L. & L. Begue (2005) Experimental research on just-world theory. Problems, developments and future challenges. Psychological Bulletin, 131(1), p. 128-167.
Haslam, N. (2006). Dehumanization: An integrative review. Personality and Social Psychology Review, 10, 252-264.
Haynes, G. A., & Olson, J. M. (2006). Coping with threats to just-world beliefs: Derogate, blame, or help? Journal of Applied Social Psychology, 36, 664–682.
Hogan, R. & Emler, N. (1981). Retributive justice. In M. Lerner (Ed.), The justice motive in social behavior. New York, Plenum Press.
Jackson, L.M. & Esses, V.M. (1997). Of scripture and ascription: the relation between religious fundamentalism and intergroup helping. Personality and Social Psychology Bulletin, 23(8). 893-906.
Jackson, L.M. & Esses, V.M. (2000). Effects of perceived economic competition on people's willingness to help empower immigrants. Group processes and intergroup relations, 3, 419-435.
Janoff-Bulman, R. (1992). Shattered assumptions: Towards a new psychology of trauma. New York: Free Press.
Lee, Y.-T., Pepitone, A., & Albright, L. (1997). Descriptive and prescriptive beliefs about justice: A Sino-U.S. comparison. Cross-Cultural Research, 31, 101-120.
Lerner, M. J. (1978). "Belief in a just world" versus the "authoritarianism" syndrome. . . but nobody liked the Indians. Ethnicity, 5, 229–237.Lerner, M. J. (1980). The belief in a just world: A fundamental delusion. New York: Plenum Press.
Lerner, M. J. (1997). What does the belief in a just world protect us from: The dread of death or the fear of undeserved suffering? Psychological Inquiry, 8, 29–32.
Lerner, M. J. (1998). The two forms of belief in a just world. In: Montada, L. & Lerner, M.J. (Eds.). Responses to victimizations and belief in a just world (pp. 247–269). New York: Plenum Press.
Lerner, M. J. (2003). The justice motive: Where psychologists found it, how they lost it, and why they may not find it again. Personality and Social Psychology Review, 7, 388–399.
Lerner, M. J., and Goldberg, J. H. (1999). When do decent people blame victims? The differing effects of the explicit-rational and implicit-experiential cognitive systems. In Chaiken, S., and Trope, T. (eds.), Dual Process Theories in Social Psychology, Guilford, New York.

Lerner, M. J., & Simmons, C. H. (1966). The observer's reaction to the "innocent victim": Compassion or rejection? Journal of Personality and Social Psychology, 4, 203-210.
Lerner, M. J., & Miller, D. T. (1978). Just world research and the attribution process: Looking back and ahead. Psychological Bulletin, 85, 1030–1051.
Leyens, J. P., Paladino, P. M., Rodriguez-Torres, R., Vaes, J., Demoulin, S., Rodriguez-Perez, A., et al. (2000). The emotional side of prejudice: The attribution of secondary emotions to ingroups and outgroups. Personality & Social Psychology Review, 4, 186–197.
Maes, J. (1998). Immanent justice and ultimate justice: Two ways of believing in justice. In: Montada, L. & Lerner, M.J. (Eds.). Responses to victimizations and belief in a just world (pp. 9–40). New York: Plenum Press.
Maes, J. and Schmitt, M., 1999. More on ultimate and immanent justice: results from the research project "Justice as a problem within reunified Germany". Social Justice Research 12 2, pp. 65–78
Miers, D. (1989), Positivist Victimology; A Critique, International Review of Victimology, 1, pp. 3-22.
Miers, D. (2007). Looking beyond Great Britain: the development of criminal injuries compensation. In Walklate, S. (2007). Handbook of Victims and Victimology. Cullumpton, Devon, UK: Willan Publishing.
Miller, D.T. (2001). Disrespect and the experience of injustice. Annual review of psychology, 52, 527-553.
Mori, L., Bernat, J. A., Glenn, P. A., Selle, L. L., Zarate, M. G. (1995). Attitudes toward rape: Gender and ethnic differences across Asian and Caucasian college students. Sex Roles, 32, 457–467.
Okimoto, T. G., Wenzel, M., & Feather, N. T. (2009). Beyond retribution: Conceptualizing restorative justice and exploring its determinants. Social Justice Research. 22(1), 156-180.
Opotow, S. (1990). Moral exclusion and injustice: An introduction. Journal of Social Issues, 46, 1–20.
Pancer, S. M. (1988). Salience of appeal and avoidance of helping situations. Canadian Journal of Behavioural Science, 20, 133–139.
Pemberton, A. (2008). Over egels, vliegen vangen en herstelrecht. Een reactie op Daems, Kaptein en Walgrave. Tijdschrift voor Herstelrecht, 8(4), 53-65. (In Dutch: with an English summary).
Pemberton, A. (2009a). Victim Movements: from diversified needs to varying criminal justice agenda's. Acta Criminologica, 22(3), 1-23.
Pemberton, A. (2010). A victimological hedgehog examines restorative justice: a rebuttal to Daems, Kaptein and Walgrave. In: Pemberton, A. (2010). The cross-over: an interdisciplinary approach to the study of victims of crime. Antwerp, Belgium, Maklu Publishers.
Pemberton, A. (2011). Al Qaeda and vicarious victims. Victimological insights into terrorist strategy. In Van Dijk, J.J.M. & Letschert, R.M. (eds.). The new faces of victimhood. Globalisation, transnational crimes and victim rights. Dordrecht, the Netherlands. Springer.
Pemberton, A., Winkel, F.W. & Groenhuijsen, M.S. (2007). Taking victims seriously in restorative justice. International Perspectives in Victimology, 3, 1, 4 – 14.

Pepitone, A., & L'Armand, K. (1996). The justice and injustice of life events. European Journal of Social Psychology, 26, 581-597.
Pichon, I. & Saroglou, V. (2009). Religion and helping: Impact of Target Thinking Styles and Just-World beliefs, Archives for the Psychology of Religion, 31, 215-236.
Power, S. (2003). A problem from hell. America and the age of genocide. London. Harper/ Collins.
Reiner, R. (2002). Media made criminality. In Maguire. M., Morgan, R. & Reiner, R. (eds.): The Oxford Handbook of Criminology. Oxford: Oxford University Press.
Roberts, J. V., et al. (2003). Penal Populism and Public Opinion: Lessons from Five Countries. New York: Oxford Univ. Press.
Rock, P (2004). Constructing Victim's Rights; The Home Office, New Labour and Victims, Oxford: Oxford Universty Press.
Rock, P. (2007). Theoretical perspectives on victimisation. In Walklate, S. (2007). Handbook of Victims and Victimology. Cullumpton, Devon, UK: Willan Publishing.
Ross, M & Miller, D.T. (Eds.) (2002). The justice motive in everyday life. New York: Cambridge University Press.
Rubin, Z., & Peplau, L. A. (1975). Who believes in a just world? Journal of Social Issues, 31, 65–89.
Saroglou, V. (2003). Trans-cultural/ religious constants vs. cross-cultural/ religious differences in psychological aspects of religion. Archives for the psychology of religion. 25, 71-87.
Saroglou, V., Pichon, I. Trompette, L., Verschueren, M., & Dernelle, R. (2005): Prosocial behaviour and religion: New evidence based on projective measures and peer ratings. Journal for the Scientific Study of Religion, 44, 323-348.
Scheingold, S., Olson, T. & Pershing, J. (1994). Sexual violence, victim advocacy and republican criminology: Washington's Community Protection Act. Law and Society Review, 28(4), 729-763.
Spalek, B. (2006), Crime Victims; Theory, policy and practice, New York: Palgrave.
Spilka, B., Hood, R.W., Hunsberger, B., & Gorsuch, R. (2003): The psychology of religion: An empirical approach (3d ed.). New York: Guilford Press.
Spungen, D. (1998). Homicide: The hidden victims. Thousand Oaks, CA: Sage.
Van Dijk, J.J.M. (2006). The mark of Abel. Reflecting on the social labelling of victims of crime. Inaugural lecture, Tilburg University. Tilburg: INTERVICT.
Van Dijk, J.J.M. (2008). In the shadow of Christ? On the use of the word victim to describe those affected by crime. Journal of Criminal Justice Ethics, 2008, Winter/ Spring, 13-24.
Van Prooijen, J.W. (2009). Retributive versus compensatory justice. Observer's preference for punishing in response to criminal offences. European Journal of Social Psychology, DOI: 10.1002/ejsp.611.
Vidmar, N. (2002). Retributive justice: Its social context. In M. Ross, & D. T. Miller (Eds.), The justice motive in everyday life (pp. 291–313). Cambridge, UK: University Press.
Von Hirsch, A. (1993). Censure and sanctions, Oxford, Clarendon Press.
Walklate, S. (2007). Handbook of Victims and Victimology. Cullumpton,

Devon, UK: Willan Publishing.
Waller, J. (2007). Becoming Evil. How Ordinary People commit Genocide and Mass Killing. (2nd edition). Oxford. Oxford University Press.
Wenzel, M., Okimoto, T. G., Feather, N. T., & Platow, M. J. (2008). Retributive and restorative justice. Law and Human Behavior, 32, 375–389.
Wenzel, M., Okimoto, T. G., Feather, N. T., & Platow, M. J. (2009). Justice through consensus: Shared identity and the preference for a restorative notion of justice. European Journal of Social Psychology.
Wenzel, M., & Thielmann, I. (2006). Why we punish in the name of justice: Just desert versus value restoration and the role of social identity. Social Justice Research, 19, 450–470.
Winkel, F.W. (2007). Post-traumatic anger. Missing link in the wheel of misfortune. Inaugural lecture, Tilburg University. Tilburg: INTERVICT.
Yamawaki, N., & Tschanz, B. T. (2005). Rape perception differences between Japanese and American college students: On the mediating influence of gender-role tradionality. Sex Roles, 52, 379-392.
Zoellner, T., & Maercker, A. (2006). Posttraumatic growth in clinical psychology: A critical review and introduction of a two-component model. Clinical Psychology Review , 26, 626-653.

Claiming Victim Identity: A Social-Psychological Analysis

By

Andrew L. B. Davies[1]

When do people see themselves as victims? Most theory suggests victim perceptions of what happened will be key, though there is disagreement over which perceptual issues will be most important. This study examines the importance of three subjective dimensions of victimizations – the degree of harm perceived by the victim, the perceived cause of the victimization (internal or external to the victim themselves) and its perceived unfairness. The relationships of these perceptions to three responses - indignant anger, self-labeling as a victim, and the self-ascription of novel rights or entitlements - are assessed in a sample of undergraduates. The results suggest the pre-eminent role of harm and justice concerns in explaining victim responses.

Claiming Victim Identity: A Social-Psychological Analysis

Sometimes, all it takes to become a victim is to be in the right place at the right time. In an event like a car crash the victims include those who were in the car that were injured or killed, any passers-by who were also hurt, and – more tenuously – any others traumatized by witnessing the crash, hearing about it, or even made ever-so-slightly more anxious by the incremental effect of the addition of yet one more such event to the annual tally of car crashes in their region that they later hear on a news broadcast. Provided they come into contact with the event in some way, almost any person near the site of an unpleasant event can claim to be a victim.

The point of this exercise is not to reduce to absurdity the question of who qualifies as a 'victim'. Rather it is to illustrate the fact that in official statistics and most academic work the only thing truly necessary to obtain "victim" status is proximity to a victimization event itself. Most debates over the scope of victimology concern themselves entirely with the question of what a victimization

---

1 State University of New York at Albany

event is. Historically, proximity to crimes have almost always been sufficient to be considered for 'victim' status, though in recent years diseases, natural disasters or abuses by authorities have also become widely accepted (Best, 1997; Burt, 1983; Garkawe, 2004; Kirchhoff, 2010; Mendelsohn, 1976; Šeparović, 1985). It is even increasingly unfashionable to except instances in which the victim clearly brought their fate upon themselves (Davies, 1998; Felson, 1991; Schafer, 1977). Whether that individual identifies themselves as a victim is another question – but not one that concerns scholars very often. In fact, more than anything, the process of becoming a victim noted in official dispatches is very like contracting a disease. Victimizations are sites of infection. Victims are the infected. Victimhood is the affliction. Little wonder that literature on the psychological impact of victimization does not concern "identity", but rather "trauma", "coping" and "recovery".

Yet the recognition of such events as victimizations, and of one's own identity as victim, is not only a more complicated business than official statistics make it look. It is also one that may have implications for victim behavior. Victim identity is associated with many stereotypes – from the helpless waif to the defiant campaigner (Peterson and Seligman, 1983; Polletta, 2007). How victims see themselves – and whether they identify themselves as a 'victim' at all – might play a distinctive role in motivating and explaining how they respond to what happened to them. This study deals with the self-ascription of victim identity. When do victims identify themselves as victims and what are the consequences of such identifications? .

First, this study deals with the importance of examining victim identity claims by asserting their relevance for victim behaviors that are of policy concern. Next, it more clearly defines 'victim identity'. A theoretical framework is laid out to account for when victims are likely to make such identity claims. Then the measures for such claims themselves are described. The resulting model the is tested using survey data from a sample of undergraduate students. Victim identity claims arise when victimizations are perceived by individuals to be not only seriously harmful but also inherently unjust.

The Importance of Claiming Victim Identity

Victims – however they are defined – behave in a number of ways that are of unique and specific interest to policy-makers. They may invoke their right to call for assistance from police (Greenberg and Ruback, 1992). They may talk about what happened to their friends (Kahn, Mathie, and Torgler, 1994). They may take protective measures: building high walls, installing alarms or buying aggressive dogs for their houses (Maguire, 1980). They may change their daily routines (Silva and Wright, 2009). They may be active in a movement to seek redress for others similarly afflicted (Loseke, 1999). They may do all this and more besides.

Moreover, existing work suggests strongly that victim self-concept – that is, the ways victims think about themselves – matters tremendously to their decision-making and to their behavioral responses in the aftermath of victimizations. Self-identification as a victim and of events as victimizations may increase the likelihood an individual will take evasive action during a crime (LeJeune and Alex, 1973). It may improve victim engagement with the criminal justice system (Dunn, 2001), increase the likelihood of accessing victim services (Leisenring, 2006), increase the likelihood of the disclosure of victim experiences to others (Littleton, Axsom, Brietkopf, and Brenson, 2006), provoke the organization of social movements (Loseke, 1999), and, more pejoratively, result in more complaining (Sykes, 1992). Understanding when individuals will self-identify as such is likely to improve our understanding of victim responses generally.

Theorizing Victim Identity Claims

When will people claim "victim identity"? Individuals may be expected to be most likely to identify themselves as victims when they perceive an event to have been seriously harmful, caused by factors external to themselves, and unjust.

Symbolic interactionists such as Holstein and Miller (1990), Leisenring (2006) and Dunn (2001) have examined the nature of victim identity. Beginning with Holstein and Miller's pioneering piece, which specified for the first time "the *social processes* through which persons become 'victims'" as a research topic, these scholars have improved substantially our understanding of the ways that the word "victim" is used in public and private discourse, and have explored some of the complexities and ambivalences involved in individual and social decisions to apply the identity (Holstein and Miller, 1990, p. 103, emphasis in original)
Leisenring argues individuals identify as victims in situations where they emphasize the degree of harm they have suffered, their lack of personal responsibility for that harm, and the injustice inherent in their experience of it (Leisenring, 2006). This tri-partite definition is adopted in the present chapter.

Harm

The subjective seriousness of harm is not only central to most definitions of victimhood, it is also commonly assumed to predict victim behavior (Bayley, 1991; Montada, 1994). Building on an implicit rational-choice model of victim responses, studies in areas such as police reporting have often shown that when the harm or loss experienced by a victim is greater, the likelihood of their reporting the crime is larger too (e.g., Greenberg and Ruback, 1992; Skogan, 1976). Equally, the calculation not to report by some rape victims has often been assumed to be a rational response to the likely arduousness of the subsequent process (Estrich, 1987; Taylor, Wood, and Lichtman, 1983). In both cases, victim self-identification is characterized as a direct, rational response to the degree of harm suffered and the likely benefits or drawbacks of reporting the event itself (Loseke 1999, p. 77. Davies (1998).

Thus, the perception that an event was harmful may be expected to be a key predictor of claiming victim identity.

External Attribution

Victims have at least three choices for understanding the causes of unpleasant events. Firstly, they may have been caused by some other person or agent. Secondly, they might have been caused by some random and unpredictable factor in the environment – usually meaning that the event was an accident. Thirdly, they might have been caused by themselves – that is, the victim might 'self blame' (Hall, French, and Marteau, 2003). Montada (1994) argues that, from a legal and psychological point of view alike, victim status may only be attributed in the first two of these cases. That is, an individual may be considered a victim when the unpleasant event was perpetrated on them by a third party, or where the event was essentially unpredictable or accidental. But where an event was the result of 'their own risky actions, their own wrong decisions, or their own careless behavior....we hesitate to use the term victimization' (Montada, 1994, p. 6). Dunn's (2001) work on the treatment of stalking victims by prosecutors appears to substantiate this point empirically: when victims were interpreted to be able to control the behavior of the stalker, responsibility for any alleged victimization was judged to fall on the shoulders of the victim herself. The perception that the event was caused by some agent or environmental force external to the victim themselves is therefore expected to be the second key predictor of victim identity claims.

Injustice

Judgments of the overall unfairness of a situation, separate from questions regarding causation, are very common in discussions of victim status. In social psychology, "justice motive" literature suggests that perceived personal deservingness will be significant for responses to personal misfortunes and victimizations (Callan, Ellard, Shead, and Hodgins, 2008; Hafer and Bègue, 2005; Hafer and Olson, 1998; Lerner, 1980). Similarly, in the policy arena, victim compensation schemes almost always provide reduced awards where the victim is either judged to have caused their own victimization or where a criminal record renders them of dubious moral character (Miers, 2007). More generally, Loseke observes that sympathy is reserved only for individuals who are 'evaluated as moral', while Christie argues that the 'ideal victim' is one who at the time of victimization is engaged in a 'respectable project' in a place 'where she could not possibly be blamed for being' (Christie, 1986, p. 19; Loseke, 1999, p. 77). The 'victim' who is beaten up during a drug deal which went wrong, it seems, deserves everything he or she gets. An additional predictor of victim identity claims is therefore expected to be the understanding that the event itself was, for some reason, unjust.

Summary

To clarify this theoretical account of victim identity claims, a narrative might help. Firstly, we might agree that a person who loses $10,000 is more seriously harmed and – plausibly at least – more likely to see themselves as a victim than one who loses $10. But not all who lose $10,000 are victims. A gambler losing this much does not seem to be a victim, whereas someone who had it stolen by a thief does. In addition to serious harm, therefore, the event must have been caused by some agent or force external to the victim: hence the second criterion. Yet even when these two criteria are met – of serious harm and external attribution – one might not be a victim. Some externally inflicted harms are considered justified, as in the case of the punishment of wrongdoers. The third criterion, then, is that the individual must have endured serious, externally attributable harm that they consider unjust. When all three criteria are met, individuals are expected to identify themselves as victims.

Measuring Victim Identity Claims

How can we know when individuals are claiming victim identity? Certainly, we should ask victims directly 'do you consider yourself a victim?' As well as the imposition of a 'victim' label, however, victim identity might also have other affective and behavioral dimensions. In this study, victim identity claims were assessed in three ways: self-reported feelings of indignant anger related to the event, willingness to apply the label 'victim' to oneself, and the self-ascription of "secondary rights" or entitlements.

Anger

First, experiences identified as victimizations should result in feelings of anger (Winkel, 2007). Though anger is only one possible emotional reaction to unpleasant experiences, it is both the most common reported in associated with victimizations, and one which existing literature suggests should be related to harm, attribution and injustice assessments. Lazarus, for example, has suggested that the strength of angry responses to stress is associated with external attributions of the cause of the stress – suggesting that victimizations, as externally attributed events, should result in feelings of anger (Lazarus, 1998, p. 359). Regarding injustice, Weiner (2006) has pointed to evidence that anger is stronger in cases where a perpetrator is seen as having acted deliberately and culpably, suggesting that the perception of injustice increases these feelings (Weiner, 2006, p. 35. See also the more philosophical work by such authors as Murphy and Hampton (1988) that suggests the special importance of indignant anger in cases of victimization.

Where measures of perceived victimization are high, anger at the event in question is likely to result. One caveat is important, however: scholarship on guilt tends to suggest that when individuals feel personally responsible for a negative event they are equally capable of feeling anger directed at themselves as when another party is responsible (Lerner, 1998). It is also therefore possible that attributions are not important predictors of angry feelings.

Victim self-ascription

Second, the perception by an individual that an event meets the criteria specified above should also make them more willing and likely to label themselves as a 'victim'. Leisenring's (2006) study of victim discourses among a sample of domestic violence victims suggested self-description as a victim was an approach adopted by individuals when they wanted to stress that they had suffered serious harm, that they were not responsible for the suffering, and that it had been unjust. Leisenring suggests a formulation of victim identity which precisely reflects the descriptive model proposed here. Where individuals perceive events to be harmful, externally attributable and unjust they will be more likely to apply the term 'victim' to themselves.

Secondary Rights

Lastly, experiences identified as victimizations should result in the self-ascription of secondary rights. The term 'secondary rights' is chosen here to address the rights victims obtain a result of their victimization. It is derived from the notion of 'secondary victimization', already familiar to victimologists. Practically speaking, secondary victimization is used to refer to negative reactions towards victims from others in the social environment including friends, relatives, and agents of the criminal justice system such as police, prosecutors and court personnel (Kirchhoff, 2010). Montada proposes a rights-based definition of secondary victimizations, labeling them 'violations of rights and entitlements which victims claim after having been victimized' including the rights to be treated with respect and sensitivity by others (Montada, 1994, p. 7, emphasis omitted). The notion of secondary victimization is thus predicated on the notion of special 'secondary rights' implicitly or explicitly granted to victims. Events which appear to an individual to be victimizing will result in greater self-ascriptions of secondary rights.

Interactions

The three elements of the structure of victimizing events specified above are expected to interact in the production of victimhood. The experience of victimization can only be said to occur when all three elements are present (Bayley, 1991; Davies, 1998; Leisenring, 2006; Loseke, 1999; Montada, 1994). Thus, in statistical models we would expect a three-way interaction among perceptions of harm, external attribution and injustice to predict anger, secondary rights and victim self-ascription above the impact of each variable in isolation.

Method

Questionnaires were administered to a sample of 291 undergraduate students in order to gather quantitative data to explore the hypotheses specified in this paper. The survey instrument was divided into two sections referred to here as the 'personality' and 'victimization' sections, though not distinguished in the instrument subjects received. The 'personality' section included several personality measures the results of which are not reported here. The 'victimization' section included a screener questionnaire which asked whether respondents had experienced any of a total of fifteen unpleasant events, and if so which they had experienced most recently.

The screener questionnaire was developed through the combination and consolidation of items from three existing trauma screener questionnaires. These were the Traumatic Life Events Questionnaire (Kubany et al., 2000), the Life Events Checklist (Gray, Litz, Hsu, and Lombardo, 2004) and the Stressful Life Events Screening Questionnaire (Goodman, Corcoran, Turner, Yuan, and Green, 1998). The questionnaire used here covered all the substantive areas included in these other instruments while consolidating some items (e.g. items on car crashes and other types of accidents were combined into a single item on 'accidents'). Where respondents indicated they had experienced more than one of the category of events on the screener, they were instructed to think of the most recent event.

Respondents reporting having experienced such an event were instructed to fill out instruments which assessed perceptions of harm, external attributions and injustice in relation to the event. Situation specific measures of anger, self-ascribed secondary rights and self-description as a victim were developed for the purposes of this study from prior focus group research and were also included.

Perceived harm was measured using eleven items (six positive, e.g. 'I suffered a lot when this happened' and five negative, e.g. 'It was not really a big deal). Perceived external attribution was measured using fourteen items (seven positive, e.g. 'I did nothing to cause what happened' and seven negative, e.g. 'I can see how people might think I was responsible). Perceived injustice was measured using twelve items (seven positive, e.g. 'What happened was wrong' and five negative, e.g. 'On balance, what happened wasn't that unfair'). In addition, a nine-item measure of situation-specific anger (six positive, e.g. 'I feel outraged about the situation' and three negative, e.g. 'It doesn't really bother me') and a five item measure of secondary rights (e.g. 'In a fair world, I would be compensated somehow for this') were developed. Responses were scored on six-point Likert-type scales ranging from 'Strongly disagree' to 'Strongly agree'.

The order of administration of the 'personality' and 'victimization' sections was randomized, and controlled for in subsequent analysis.

Results

Of the 290 surveys distributed in criminal justice classes, 271 (93%) were received with usable data. Of these, 170 reported at least one victimization experience on the victimization portion of the questionnaire, or 63% of responses received.

Construction of Measures

Factor analysis using half the sample of responses of the 37 situation-specific victimization perception measures led to their reduction to an inventory of just 21 items in a model that explained over 67% of the variance in the items. Reliability analyses conducted on each scale using the whole dataset revealed coefficients of 0.898, 0.934 and 0.838 respectively. A similar procedure was adopted for the measure of feelings of anger. All nine original items were included in the final anger measure (Cronbach's alpha coefficient 0.923).

Scale scores for each of the measures of injustice, harm and external attribution were summed for each subject, transformed into z-scores and mean-centered to minimize collinearity problems. Interaction terms between each were then computed. Secondary rights were measured as a simple count of the number of rights subjects considered they acquired as a result of their victimization from a possible five, with the average subject self-ascribing 3.86. Victim self-ascription was measured with a single item in the survey which asked whether subjects agreed with the statement 'I consider myself a victim'. Answers were on a six-point scale and the average score was 3.48 – a position at the mid-point of the scale, between 'slightly agree' and 'slightly disagree'.

Regression analyses

The measures of perceived victimization were entered into regression equations to predict, respectively, individual anger, self-ascriptions of secondary rights, and self-ascriptions of victim identity. Victimization type was controlled using a series of fifteen dummy variables. In each case, models were run with and without interaction terms present to test for their importance. Two-way interactions and a single three-way interaction between perceived harm, external attribution and injustice were included in the full model.

The results of the regression analyses showed that perceptions of harm predicted all three outcomes, resulting in increased feelings of anger, increased self-ascription of secondary rights and increased willingness to use the term 'victim' to describe oneself. The importance of the perceived harm was not uniform, however. In the case of self-labeling as a victim, the introduction of the interaction terms caused statistical significance to drop below conventional levels. Contrary to expectations, the belief that causal responsibility for the event lay outside the victim was unrelated to any outcome in any model. Perceived injustice, however, was a significant predictor of feelings of anger, the self-ascription of secondary rights and victim self-ascription in all models.

Regarding the interaction terms, the three-way interaction between perceived harm, external attribution and injustice did not predict the victim identity outcomes in the way that existing theoretical accounts suggested it would. The combination of high levels of perceived harm in conjunction with external attribution and injustice did not prove to be the alchemical formula that was expected. Moreover, although other two-way interaction terms provided some additional findings of empirical significance, the addition of the interaction terms did little to change the overall fit of the models. Only in the case of secondary rights was the increase in the R^2 (from 0.388 to 0.452) significant, $F(4,99) = 3.02$, $p<0.025$.

Discussion

The results of the regression analyses show that the perceptual variables of interest in this study are highly relevant to the victim responses, though not in ways consistent with the hypotheses made earlier. Bearing in mind the inherent limitations of a student sample, three findings are of particular note. First, perceived harm and injustice appear, respectively, to be the predictors of principle importance in explaining victim responses such as anger, self-labeling as a victim and the self-ascription of secondary rights. Second, the perception that the victimization was caused by some agent or force external to the victim was unrelated to any of the responses of interest. And third, the three-way interaction between perceptions of harm, external attribution and injustice did not predict any of the responses.

In sum, these findings suggest that the descriptive theory advanced above of the correlates of victim identity claims requires revision. Specifically, they suggest a simpler picture than was first suggested. Rather than a complex combination of harm, attribution and justice perceptions, victim responses appear instead to be driven by two factors. Firstly, individuals appear to respond to victimization events in terms that are recognizably rational. Victim identity claims were more likely where the deprivation or suffering endured was worse or more serious. In keeping with the economic assumptions that have underpinned studies of police reporting since Skogan (1976), individuals appear to be more likely to call themselves 'victims' when there is more at stake – and, potentially, more for them to gain. Where harm is severe, the services or redress that available services offer may be more valuable to victims. Their inclination to avail themselves of those services (and in doing so assume a victim identity) may thus be understandable as a simple, rational response to their experiences.

Secondly, and somewhat in contrast, individuals also appear to respond to victimizations in ways that speak to one particular motive in particular – the preservation of justice. Victim identity claims are significantly more common where individuals claim an injustice. The indignation that a 'victim' of an attempted murder might feel, for example, at the injustice of such an attempt might yet move them to anger, self-labeling as a victim and the self-ascription of secondary rights. Victim identity claims, in short, may not require one to experience any harm at all.

Conclusion

Individual perceptions of victimizations remain an unexplored area within victimology, yet these are likely to be critical for understanding and explaining victim responses. The present study suggests that although victims may respond rationally to victimization – as is often implicitly assumed in literature on the subject – other profound motivations may also attend their reactions. In particular, the importance of justice in victim perceptions should not be ignored, and future research should investigate further the role of individual perceptions of personal deservingness – that is, whether one is a good person who deserves better – in determining individual responses to victimizations.

References

Bayley, J. E. (1991). The Concept of victimhood. In D. Sank and D. I. Caplan (Eds.), *To be a victim: Encounters with crime and justice* (pp. 53-62). London: Plenum.

Best, J. (1997). Victimization and the victim industry. *Society, 34*, 9-17.

Burt, M. R. (1983). A Conceptual Framework for Victimological Research. *Victimology: An International Journal, 8*, 261-269.

Callan, M. J., Ellard, J. H., Shead, N. W., and Hodgins, D. C. (2008). Gambling as a search for justice: examining the role of personal relative deprivation in gambling urges and gambling behavior. *Personality and Social Psychology Bulletin, 34*(11), 1514-1529.

Christie. (1986). The ideal victim. In E. Fattah (Ed.), *From crime policy to victim policy: Reorienting the Justice System* (pp. 1-17). London: Macmillan.

Davies, J. (1998). *Safety planning with battered women: complex lives/ difficult choices*. Thousand Oaks, CA: Sage.

Dunn, J. L. (2001). Innocence lost: Accomplishing victimization in intimate stalking cases. *Symbolic Interaction, 24*(3), 285-313.

Estrich, S. (1987). *Real rape*. Cambridge, MA: Harvard University Press.

Felson, R. B. (1991). Blame analysis: Accounting for the behavior of protected groups. *The American Sociologist, 22*(1), 5-23.

Garkawe, S. (2004). Revisiting the Scope of Victimology - How Broad a Discipline Should it Be? *International Review of Victimology, 11*, 275-294.

Goodman, L. A., Corcoran, C., Turner, K., Yuan, N., and Green, B. L. (1998). Assessing traumatic event exposure: general issues and preliminary findings for the Stressful Life Events Screening Questionnaire. *Journal of Traumatic Stress, 11*(3), 521-542.

Gray, M. J., Litz, B. T., Hsu, J. L., and Lombardo, T. W. (2004). Psychometric properties of the Life Events Checklist. *assessment, 11*(4), 330-341.

Greenberg, M. S., and Ruback, R. B. (1992). *After the crime: Victim decision making* (Vol. 9). New York: Plenum Press.

Hafer, C. L., and Bègue, L. (2005). Experimental research on Just-World Theory: problems, developments, and future challenges. *Psychological Bulletin, 131*(1), 128-167.

Hafer, C. L., and Olson,

J. M. (1998). Individual differences in the belief in a Just World and responses to personal misfortune. In L. Montada and M. J. Lerner (Eds.), *Responses to victimizations and belief in a Just World* (pp. 65-86). New York, NY: Plenum Press.

Hall, S., French, D. P., and Marteau, T. M. (2003). Causal attributions following serious unexpected negative events: a systematic review. *Journal of Social and Clinical Psychology, 22*(5), 515-536.

Holstein, J. A., and Miller, G. (1990). Rethinking victimization: an interactional approach to victimology. *Symbolic Interaction, 13*(1), 103-122.

Kahn, A. S., Mathie, V. A., and Torgler, C. (1994). Rape scripts and rape Acknolwedgment. *Psychology of Women Quarterly, 18*, 53-66.

Kirchhoff, G. F. (2010). History and a theoretical structure of victimology. In S. Shoham, P. Knepper and M. Kett (Eds.), *International handbook on victimology* (pp. 95-126). Boca Raton, FL: Taylor and Francis.96-123

Kubany, E. S., Leisen, M. B., Kaplan, A. S., Watson, S. B., Haynes, S. N., Owens, J. A., et al. (2000). Development and preliminary validation of a brief broad-spectrum measure of trauma exposure: The Traumatic Life Events Questionnaire. *Psychological Assessment, 12*(2), 210-224.

Lazarus, R. S. (1998). The stress and coping paradigm. In R. S. Lazarus (Ed.), *Fifty years of the research and theory of R. S. Lazarus: An analyses of historical and perennial issues* (pp. 182-221). Mahwah, NJ: Lawrence Erlbaum.

Leisenring, A. (2006). Confronting "victim" discourses: The identity work of battered women. *Symbolic Interaction, 29*(3), 307-330.

LeJeune, R., and Alex, N. (1973). On being mugged: The event and its aftermath *Urban Life and Culture, 2*(3), 258-287.

Lerner, M. J. (1980). *The Belief in a Just World: A fundamental delusion*. New York: Plenum Press.

Lerner, M. J. (1998). The two forms of belief in a just world: some thoughts on why and how people care about justice. In L. Montada and M. J. Lerner (Eds.), *Responses to victimizations and belief in a just world* (pp. 247-269). New York, NY: Plenum Press.

Littleton, H. L., Axsom, D., Brietkopf, C. R., and Brenson, A. (2006). Rape acknowledgment and postassault experiences: How acknowledgment status relates to disclosure, Coping, worldview, and reactions received from others. *Violence and Victims, 21*(6), 761-778.

Loseke, D. R. (1999). *Thinking about social problems: An Introduction to Constructionist Perspectives*. New York: Aldine de Gruyter.

Maguire, M. (1980). The Impact of burglary upon victims. *British Journal of Criminology, 20*(3), 261-275.

Mendelsohn, B. (1976). Victimology and contemporary society's trends. *Victimology: An International Journal, 1*(1), 8-28.

Montada, L. (1994). Injustice in Harm and Loss. *Social Justice Research, 7*(1), 5-28.

Murphy, J., and Hampton, J. (1988). *Forgiveness and mercy*. New York: Cambridge University Press.

Peterson, C., and Seligman, M. E. P. (1983). Learned Helplessness and Victimization. *Journal of Social Issues, 2*, 103-116.

Polletta, F. (2007). *Victim Stories*. Paper presented at the American Sociological Association. from http://www.allacademic.com/meta/p_mla_apa_research_citation/1/8/3/4/3/p183439_index.html

Schafer, S. (1977). *Victimology: The Victim and His Criminal* (2nd ed.). Reston, VA: Reston Publishing Company, Inc.

Šeparović, Z.-P. (1985). *Victimology: Studies of victims*. Zagreb: Samobor-Novaki.

Silva, L. C., and Wright, D. W. (2009). Safety rituals: How women cope with the fear of sexual violence. *The Qualitative Report, 14*(4), 747-773.

Skogan, W. G. (1976). Citizen reporting of crime. *Criminology, 13*(4), 535-549.

Sykes, C. (1992). *A nation of victims* (1st ed.). New York: St. Martin's Press.

Taylor, S. E., Wood, J. V., and Lichtman, R. R. (1983). It could be worse: selective evaluation as a response to victimization. *Journal of Social Issues, 39*(2), 19-40.

Weiner, B. (2006). *Social motivation, justice and the moral emotions: An attributional approach*. Mahwah, NJ: Lawrence Erhbaum Associates.

Winkel, F. W. (2007). *Post traumatic anger: Missing link in the wheel of misfortune*. Nijmegen, NL: Wolf.

Questionnaire and detailed statistical tables are available on request from the author.

Blaming the Victim: Attributions of Convicted Offenders and the Public Towards Victims of Various Crimes

By[1]

Tai Shen-feng and Lin Chung-Tin

Abstract:
The present study examines different attributions of guilt toward victims of different crimes. Attitudes towards victims of different crimes are analyzed: victims of physical violence – especially of sexual violence -, of robbery, and of fraud. Just World Theory is applied to predict and interpret the different attributions that are done by convicted inmates on one side and non-convicted people on the other side. Non convicts will attribute less guilt to the victims, more to offenders. Offender will generally blame victims, regardless of the kind of victimization. The sample consists of inmates (n=404, 214 female and 190 male) and of not convicted members of the general public (n=93, 49 female and 44 male). Main Results: Attitudes of convicted inmates differed from those of the general public. As predicted, the general public showed more sympathy toward victims than inmates did. On the other hand, inmates attributed generally more responsibility toward victims. While they blamed all victims more than the general public did, they blamed especially the victims of sexual crimes.

Introduction

According to the data published by the National Police Agency, Ministry of the Interior of Taiwan (2007), the numbers of victims of atrocious violence offendings such as murder have decreased, however, victims of fraud, of sexual violence, and of theft have increased. Why do people become victims of criminal offending? Do criminal victims have resposibilities of their own harm? Numerous investigations have used theories to explain the responsibility of crime victims, such as the lifestyle/exposure model of personal victimization, the routine activity theory of victimization. However, research about the public opinion and convicted offenders' attributions towards victims of crime were rare, especially in Taiwan. The purpose of the

---

1 Assistant professor of Department and Graduate Institute of Criminology; Master graduated from Graduate Institute of Criminology, National Chung Cheng University, Chia-Yi, Taiwan

present study is to examine the public opinion and the attributions of convicted offenders towards victims of murder, fraud, sexual violence and of theft.

The belief in a just world

Lerner (1965) developed the Just- World -Theory, suggesting that people tend to believe that the world they live in is basically a just world. People who behave „correctly", get rewarded. On the other hand, if someone gets victimized, it indicates that he/she must have done something wrong.

Numerous studies suggested that people do believe in a just world (BJW) when they attribute why people become victims of crime (Dalbert, 1997, 1999, 2001, 2002, 2004; Otto, 2005). People tend to believe that criminal victims 'must' have done something wrong. They wear e.g. sexually attractive fashion. Or they show off their fortune. According to the belief in a just world, people tend to blame criminal victims. They attribute: victims have responsibilty for their own damage. However, the belief in a just world is admitted to be a kind of attribution error when people attribute peoples' behaviors and the results (Furnham & Procter, 1989).

Therefore, the first purpose of the present study is to examine the „Belief in a Just World" by a sample of the (Taiwanese) public and to find out how they attribute behavior of victims in cases of physical violence – especially of sexual violence –, of robbery, and of fraud. These people seldom have real chance to get into contact with criminal victims. They therefore may have erroneusly attributed that victims are resposible. That is different with convicted inmates. Actually, convicted inmates may have enough information about the victim's behavior and about the surrounding environment. However, studies about convicted inmates' attributions toward victims are rare in Taiwan.

The second purpose of the present study is to examine how convicted inmates attribute behavior of victims in cases of physical violence – especially of sexual violence - ,of robbery, and victims of fraud.

The difference between both attributions then will be analyzed.

Method

Participants

According to the purpose of the present study, participants come from two parts: convicted inmates and from the non-convict population. Both samples are non-representative purposily selected. Convicted inmates participants were from 3 prisons: Changhua prison, Taichung women's prison, and Kaohsiung women's prison. Researchers went to the prison and distributed 500 questionaires to participants directly and collected 404 useful answers (male:190, female:214) from Febuary, 20, 2008 to March, 20, 2008. The age of convicted inmates participants ranged from 23 to 68 years (*M* = 47.8; *SD* = 12.44).

A sample of 93 purposly selected non-convict participants were gathered by interview directly. We trained 4 undergraduated students to be the interviewers. The interviewing period were from March,15, 2008 to May, 1, 2008. There were 93 useful answers with 44 males and 49 females. The age of this sample ranged from 19 to 69 years (*M* = 39.96; *SD* = 13.32) and was clearly lower than the age of the convicts.

Questionare

In order to exam particiants' attitudes and attributions toward criminal victims, the present study developed a questionare including 3 parts. The first part contains questions for demographic variables (gender, age, education level). Besides, we asked participants to answer that if their relatives or friends have real experiences of criminal offending.

The second part of the questionaire contains questions about attitudes towards victims of crime. We translated the Attitudes Toward Rape Victins Scale (ARVS) (Ward, 1988), Rape Myth Acceptance Scale (Burt, 1980), and Attitudes Toward Rape Incidents Scale (Field, 1987) into traditional Chinese and reorganized questions into 4 sub-questionaures to exam participants' attitudes toward victims of sexual violence, victims of physical violence, victims of robbery, and victims of fraud. We asked each participant to rate each of the four different kind of victimizations (10 to 12 items) on a 5-point Likert scale (1: not at all ; 5: definitely).

The third part of the questionnaire examined participants' believe in a just world. We created a 20 items questionnaire based on The Just World Scale (JWS) (Rubin and Peplau, 1975) and General Believe in a Just World Scale (, 1987). Again, the 5-point Likert scale described earlier was used.

Results

Non-convict and inmates' attitudes toward victims of sexual violence, of physical violence, of robbery, and of fraud and theft

First, we combined responses from the non-convicts and the convicted inmates and factor-analyzed responses to attitudes toward criminal victims of sexual violence, victims of physical violence, victims of robbery, and victims of fraud.

Victims of sexual violence

We did a factor analysis aof the answers that pertained to victims of sexual violence only. The results of the factor analyses of answers pertaining of other victims (victims of physical violence) ......

The factor analysis used the responses to 15 items by a principal component analysis with direct oblimin rotation. Three factors were obtained with a total contribution of 45.96%.

Factor 1 comprised these items: "Sexually experienced people will not get victimized" " Victims are inconsiderate"; "Victims feel kind of pleasure during the assault "Victims are victimized due to their own weakness"; "Only people who wear sexy clothes will get victimized"; "A good girl (boy) will never be sexually victimized". These items had the highest factor loadings. We called this factor as "Blaming the Personal Character".

Factor 2 comprised these items: "Victims should not be blamed"; " Victims deserve our empathy"; " Victims are innocent"; and " Victims had no means to prevent the assault". We called this factor "Sympathy toward the Victims".

Factor 3 comprised these items: "Victims are responsible themselves for what happened"; "The most important contributing factor is the lack of resistance of the victim"; and "Victims should be punished, too". These items presented that people tend to emphasize the responsibility of sexual assaults victims, we interpreted this factor as "Holding Victims Responsible for the Sexual Assault".

High internal consistency of these factor scores (alpha = 0.75, 0.88, and 0.77, respectively) established reliability of these scores. The factor scores correlated significantly with each other, $r = 0.55$, 0.49, and 0.39, ($p < .01$ for each coefficient).

Victims of physical violence

We factor-analyzed the responses to 12 items by a principal component analysis with direct oblimin rotation. Three factors were obtained with a total contribution 46.24%. The "Victims" in the following items are all "victims of physical violence".

The first factor included these items: "Victims provoke their victimization"; "Victims of are physically weak" "Victims contributed through inappropriate behavior"; "Victims contributed by going into an unsafe area."; "People become victims due to their own weakness"; and "The most important contributing factor the lack of resistance of the victim". We called this factor "Blaming the Victim's Character" .

The second factor included these items: "Victims should not be blamed"; " Victims deserve our empathy"; " Victims are innocent"; " Victims had no means to prevent the assault". We called this factor

"Sympathy toward Victims" ".
The third factor includes these items: "Victims are responsible themselves for their damage"." and "Victims should be punished,too". We called this "Responsibility of the Victims".
High internal consistency of these factor scores (alpha = 0.77, 0.78, and 0.76, respectively) established reliability of these scores. The factor scores correlated significantly with each other, $r = 0.35$, 0.46, and 0.49, ($p < .01$ for each coefficient) .

Victims of Robbery

Here too, we analyzed the the responses to 12 items by a principal component analysis with direct oblimin rotation. Three factors were obtained with a total contribution 47.01%.
Factor 1 included these items: "Victims contributed by being in an unsafe area". "Victims are responsible for their own damages"; "Victims show off their fortune"; " Victims of robbery should be punished, too"; and "Only people who display their money get victimized." We called this factor "Responsibility of Victims for Their Own Victimization".
Factor 2 included "Victims should not be blamed"; " We should sympathize with victims"; " Victims are innocent"; and " Victims had no means to prevent the attack" We called this factor: "Sympathy Toward Robbery Victims".
Factor 3 consisted of these items: "Victims were damaged due to their inappropriate behaviors";; "Victims were careless"; and "Victims did not protect themselves". This factor was called : Blaming the Personal Characters of Robbery Victims".
High internal consistency of these factor scores (alpha = 0.64, 0.72, and 0.79, respectively) established reliability of these scores. The factor scores correlated significantly with each other, $r = 0.53$, 0.46, and 0.45, $p < .01$ for each coefficient.

Fraud Victims and theft Victims
We factor-analyzed the responses to 12 items by a principal component analysis with direct oblimin rotation. Three factors were obtained with a total contribution 46.30%.
Factor 1 consisted of "Victims were careless"; "Victims were damaged due to their own inconsiderateness"; " Victims should be punished, too"; and "Victims did not pay enoug attention". This factor is "Blaming the Personal Weak Character"
Factor 2 included these items: "Victims should not be blamed"; "We should sympathize with victims"; "Victims are innocent"; " Victims had no means to prevent the attack" . This factor we called "Sympathy Toward Victims".

Factor 3 was made up of these statements: "Victims should be held responsible for their own damages"; "Victims did not protect themselves" and " Victims are only the rich people". This was the factor "Holding Victims Responsible".
High internal consistency of these factor scores (alpha = 0.65, 0.64, and 0.93, respectively) established reliability of these scores. The factor scores correlated significantly with each other, *r* = 0.54, 0.43, and 0.36, p <.01 for each coefficient.

Summarizing, we conclude that participants had three main dimensions of attitudes toward victims of crime: blaming the personal characters of victims (blaming factor), asking for behavioral responsibility of victims (responsibility seeking factor), and sympathy toward victims (sympathy factor). According to these results, people had multidimensional attitudes toward victims of crime. People on the one side tend to sympathize with victims of crime, on the other hand, people also criticize weaknesses or inappropriate behaviors of victims.

The belief in a just world
In order to exam participants' attitudes of the belief in a just world, we combined responses from the non-convict group with the answers of the convicted inmates. We factor-analyzed 20 item-responses to attitudes toward the belief in a just world, using principal component analysis with direct oblimin rotation, and deleted 3 items of low fator loadings. Five factors were obtained by 17 items with a total contribution 50.60%. Factor 1 reflected: "Unfairness of Society" and included "I feel that there are lies in the world"; "Many criminal offenders had not be punished enough"; and "Many athletes violated rules without having been exposed".
Factor 2 was called "Fair World". It is made of these items: "The world is a fair world"; "Innocent people will not be sent to the jail"; "People will not get ill if they take care of themselves".
Factor 3 we called the "Own Efforts" ". It included "Even the bad one has power, finally the good one will win"; " People will be promoted if they worked hard", and "People will get the benefit of their own efforts".
Factor 4, the "Punitive Punishment" , included "Rich people should pay more tax"; " I agree that strict laws can help to improve the security of the society", and "Most people have no ideas to cheat others" .

Attitudes differences between public people and convicted inmates: Attitudes toward victims and the belief in a just world
In order to compare attitude differences between convicted inmates

and the non-convicted group, we conducted ANOVA for the factor scores of attitudes toward victims of physical violence, sexual violence, robbery, and fraud, by groups as independent variables. A main group effect was significant for sympathy toward victims of sexual violence, of robbery, and of fraud and theft (F (1, 462) = 7.248, 8.359, 6.626, p<.01), with the convict group having lower sympathy values toward victims of sexual violence, of roberry, and of fraud and theft.

Besides, we conducted ANOVA for the factor scores of the belief in a just world by groups as independent variables. A main effect of group was significant by "punitive factors" and "punitive sense of value" (F(1, 495) = 5.599, 16.583, p<.05). Convicted inmates showed higher punitive attitude scores than public people.

Finally, in order to examine how belief in a just world influences attitudes toward victims of crimes, we conducted a path analysis, and used the stepwise multiple regression analysis. All the variables of attitudes toward victims and the demographic variables were used as independent variables. Belief in a just world factors were the dependent variable by every attitude domain respectively. The results showed that people who have strong the belief in a just world attitude tend to blame and assign responsibility of victims of crime directly. Convicted inmates have more belief in a just world than the non-convicts. Convicts exhibit more punitive attitudes and blame the victims more.

Discussion

The present study examined peoples' attitudes toward victims of physical violence, of sexual violence, of robbery, and of fraud and theft, and compared the belief in a just world attitudes differences between the non-convicts and convicted inmates. Results showed that the first group has higher sympathy toward victims compared to convicted inmates. Convicted inmates showed higher punitive attitudes than the public people toward victims of crime. Finally, we found that convicted inmates believed more in a just world. They tend to blame and to attribute more responsibility to victims than the other group.

Why do convicted inmates tend to have stricter punitive attitudes toward victims of crime? Taylor and Joudo (2005) suggested that male, low education level, and low income subjects tend to have punitive attitudes toward victims of crime. On the other hand, people with high educational level and high income tend to sympathize victims of crime. According to the official data of Taiwan government, the average education level and income of convicted inmates are lower than the average of all state. Besides, convicted inmates are under punishment of their criminal behaviors. They may have much more grudges or negative attitudes toward victims of crime. That might lead to convicted inmates having much more punitive attitudes and less sympathy toward victims of crime.

Reference

Dalbert, C. (1997). Coping with an unjust fate: The case of structural unemployment. *Social Justice Research,* **10,** 175-189.

Dalbert, C. (1999). The world is more just for me than generally: About the personal belief in a just world scale's validity. *Social Justice Research,* **12,** 79-98.

Dalbert, C. (2001). The justice motive as a personal resource: Dealing with challenges and critical life events. New York: Plenum Press.

Dalbert, C. (2002). Beliefs in a just world as a buffer against anger. *Social Justice research,* **15,** 123-145.

Dalbert, C., and Dzuka, J. (2004). Belief in a just world, personality and well-being of adolescents. In C. Dalbert & H. Sallay (Eds). *The justice motive in adolescence and young adulthood: Origins and consequences*(pp. 101-116). London: Routledge.

Furnham, A., and Procter, E. (1989). Belief in a just world: Review and critique of the individual differences literature. *British Journal of Social Psychology,* **28,** 365-384.

Lerner, M.J. (1965). The effect of responsibility and choice on a partner's attractiveness following failure. *Journal of personality,* **141(4),** 341-357.

Otto, K. and Dalbert, C. (2005). Belief in a just world and its functions for young prisoners. *Journal of Research in Personality,* **39,** 559-573.

Taylor, N. and Joudo, J. (2005). The impact of prerecorded video and closed circuit television testimony by adult sexual assault complainants on jury decision-making: and experimental study. Canberra: Office of Director of Public Prosecutions.

Ward, C. (1988). The attitudes toward rape victims scale. *Psychology of women quarterly,* **12,** 127-146.

Victimology and Human Security

Towards a Victimology of International Crimes; Incorporating notions from the human security concept

By

Rianne Letschert

1.1 Introduction

Victimology as an academic discipline has achieved a lot by bridging concepts stemming from different academic disciplines such as law, psychology, traumatology and criminology, and by studying how to develop adequate victim-centred legislation and policy as well as effective evidence-based psycho-social intervention programmes. What is often referred to as "mainstream" victimology has until recently mainly focused on victimization through so-called ordinary or conventional criminal acts. Important issues relating to what can be referred to as mass or collective victimization have received less focused attention. Neuman (1984) and Elias (1985) argued that Victimology should not define its subject matter in terms of criminal law but in terms of human rights. Also Separovic (1985) argued that Victimology should extend its definitions to include victims of human rights abuses. Kirchhoff (2005) points into the same direction. Dussich (2000) contents that while abuses of power have killed and injured far more people than has crime or war, there is very little empirical research on the subject. This has, however, changed in the last ten years.

Although human rights abuses are increasingly becoming a topic of study in Victimology (Kirchhoff 2005) questions relating to victims of war crimes, crimes against humanity and genocide (the international crimes covered by the International Criminal Court) have for a long time remained to a large extent blind spots on the victimology map. Albrecht (2002) notes that large scale victimizations, in modern societies unprecedented waves of organized and collective violence, have long been neglected by traditional Victimology and Criminology. Although there have been attempts to develop concepts of collective victimization, mainstream Victimology is still focused on the individual victim, the individual perpetrator and mediation or victim-offender reconciliation as the leading models of analysis, explanation and policy. Research on victims of crimes in and around war zones and areas of civil unrest have largely been left to other disciplines such as political studies, peace studies, international law and human rights law, history, international traumatology and journalism. And only recently have critical criminologists begun a systematic exploration of state crimes like genocide, war crimes and crimes against humanity.

This contribution will explore whether existing theories and concepts developed within mainstream victimology are adequate to address issues pertaining to mass victimization resulting from international crimes or gross atrocities crimes, a generic term that covers the three categories of crimes just mentioned. This kind of victimization comes with its own problems. These stem from the very nature of these particular crimes, relating mainly to the magnitude which is often inherent to them. Enormous challenges lie in developing victimological approaches relating to the complexities of victimization by international crimes. In particular, it will explore whether victimological theories and concepts – some already in existence, but mostly in need of development to apply to international atrocity crimes – can be construed or enriched through insights offered by the concept of *human security*. This concept has been launched 15 years ago as an answer to a wide range of current threats to human life.

Section 1.2 will provide a brief introduction on the kind of crimes we are dealing with. Section 1.3 will give arguments why victimologists should more intensively address victimization caused by international crimes. Thirdly, section 1.4 will elaborate on the concept of human security, in particular in relation to international crimes. Lastly, in section 1.5 an analysis is made how human security can contribute to the development of a victimology of international crimes. Given the multiple dimensions they encompass, space limitations do not allow for an in-depth discussion of all related aspects of both victimology and human security. Nonetheless, this paper tries to present the relevance of both in reflecting on issues pertaining to international crimes.

1.2 International crimes

Over the past century, millions of civilians have fallen victim to acts of violence during war on a vastly larger scale than in the preceding centuries. This has not only led to a dramatic increase in the numbers of civilian casualties of war during the 20th century, but also to a likewise dramatic increase in the proportion of civilian casualties as opposed to military casualties: From about 14 % in World War I over

67% in World War II, to 90% by the end of the last century (Levy et al. 2007). Civilians, notably women and children, are increasingly targeted. Conflicts involving child soldiers, widespread attacks on civilian populations, destruction and looting of civilian residences and institutions, abductions and the use of rape as an instrument of warfare, and massive deportations and ethnic cleansing have become common practices.
According to the UNHCR's annual "Global Trends" report of June 2009, at the end of last year, the number of people forcibly uprooted by conflict and persecution worldwide stood at 42 million. The total includes 16 million refugees and asylum seekers and 26 million internally displaced people uprooted within their own countries.

On the other hand, the first Human Security Report of 2005, the Human Security Brief of 2007 and the Human Security Report (Levi et al. 2007) of 2009 document a dramatic, but largely unknown, decline in the number of wars, genocides and human rights abuses over the past decade.

To demonstrate the complexity and magnitude of the issues we are talking about, some figures and facts from Rwanda are briefly presented: In 1994, the beautiful country of Rwanda – also known as the country of one thousand hills – was engulfed by one of the most effective and most public genocides of all time. Within 100 days, from April 7 to July 18, about one million Tutsi and moderate Hutu were brutally murdered by Hutu militia, including their Hutu neighbours, friends and acquaintances. In those 100 days, an estimated 250,000 to 500,000 women and girls were raped and experienced other forms of sexual violence (UN report of 1996). As a 1996 United Nations report observed, "rape was the rule and its absence the exception". For many survivors, rape, the resulting HIV infection and stigmatisation by their community constitute the ultimate violation of their human rights. But the fallout does not stop here. The genocide left hundreds of thousand children as orphans and a similar large number of survivors as widows or widowers. The country's economy, its judicial institutions and social services were completely destroyed. Slowly but with strong determination, the country is trying to recover from its horrific past. Programmes of reparation and reconciliation, national and local, have been developed, and tradition-based justice mechanisms put in place. It is still hard to imagine how reconciliation can work in a society like Rwanda, where the crimes were so brutal, and victims and perpetrators live close to each other in the same communities again.

The final decade of the twentieth century saw the revival of global efforts aimed at tackling some of these most atrocious crimes. At the global, regional and national levels, several initiatives were undertaken to criminalize the commission of genocide, war crimes and crimes against humanity and to prosecute and punish those most responsible for them. The establishment of the *ad hoc* international criminal tribunals for the crimes committed in the former Yugoslavia and for Rwanda, and of the permanent International Criminal Court, is the most publicized outcome of these initiatives. Alternatives to traditional criminal litigation, such as commissions of inquiry, exemplified by the South African Truth and Reconciliation Commission, or the tradition-based justice system used in Rwanda (the Gacaca), have been tried and tested. The field of transitional justice explores the complexities of doing justice in societies ravaged by war. Social scientists have initiated studies on the psychological consequences for victims of international crimes, the possibilities and difficulties of meeting their needs in the aftermath of conflicts and the mechanisms that play a role in overcoming the damage to society at large caused by gross atrocities crimes (see, for instance, scholars such as Danieli (2009), Wemmers and De Brouwer (2011), Staub (1992), Horn (2009), Stover (2005, 2007), Letschert, Haveman, De Brouwer, Pemberton (2011).

1.3. Why should Victimology become more involved?

The founding fathers of victimology, Hans von Hentig and Benjamin Mendelsohn, started their academic work on victims' issues adhering to a broad scope. Von Hentig got 'inspired' by the horrific crimes committed in the Second World War and began seeking to analyse the causes and effects of this victimization. Benjamin Mendelsohn also believed that the subjects of study should include not only victims of crime and abuse of power, but also victims of accidents, natural disasters and other acts of God (van Dijk 1999:5, for a detailed overview on the history of victimology Kirchhoff 2010).

Notwithstanding these early efforts, in subsequent years, victimologists focused primarily on victims of ordinary crime. Also Goodey (2005) underlines the relative absence of victimological perspectives to these crimes and urges to become more involved (p.231). This is also reflected in developments in the legal sphere where the emphasis was for a long time put on victims of conventional crime. The UN 1985 Declaration of Basic Principles of Justice for Victims of Crime and Abuse of Power clearly focuses on victims of ordinary crime, covered in 17 Articles, while victims of abuse of power are covered only in 4, rather vaguely formulated articles see Lamborn (1987), Elias (1994), Friday et al. (2005). The UN Basic

Principles and Guidelines on the Right to a Remedy and Reparation for Victims of Gross Violations of International Human Rights Law and Serious Violations of International Humanitarian Law and the Statute of the International Criminal Court have partially filled this gap by respectively establishing reparation principles for victims of serious and gross human rights violations and granting far-reaching victims' rights before the ICC. They were adopted and proclaimed by the United Nations General Assembly on 16 December 2005, after a 15-year period of negotiation. The principles are often referred to as the Van Boven/Bassiouni Principles, referring to the drafters. Other Declarations worth mentioning are the Principles on Housing and Property Restitution for Refugees and Displaced Persons adopted by the Sub-Commission on the Promotion and Protection of Human Rights in 2005, also referred to as the Pinheiro Principles, and the Nairobi Declaration on Women's and Girls' Right to a Remedy and Reparation (UN 2007, Nairobi 2007).

The recent initiative of the Draft UN Convention on Justice and Support for Victims of Crime and Abuse of Power (2005) includes victims of the latter category under its entire scope of protection but fails to clearly recognize the peculiarities and complexities that massive and collective victimization bring about. Further revisions have been discussed and agreed upon during a Symposium held at the Tokiwa International Victimology Institute on February 15&16, 2008. The whole language of the Draft Convention seems inspired by the many achievements Victimology has reached with regard to ordinary crimes.

From a psycho-social perspective, an important question that merits further research is whether the consequences of mass victimization are similar to or different from those of conventional victimization, thus justifying also a new victimological research agenda. Without going into details, a few insights into some specific features of victimization through these crimes are offered here, thereby not claiming to be exhaustive (Letschert et al. 2011 and Wemmers 2011).

According to various studies, in the case of mass victimization (based for instance on studies relating to terrorism), victims have essentially the same needs as victims of other violent crimes (Albrecht et al. 2007, Letschert et al. 2009). Victimization, be it conventional crime or gross atrocities crimes, affects, first of all, the individual. To this extent, they can evoke similar reactions in victims, such as shock, anger, depression, guilt, fear, etc. But crimes leading to mass victimization may also have a different impact on victims than ordinary crimes have. The impact can be longer lasting and more encompassing.

Most international crimes target specific groups that not only affect individual victims but also other group or community members. Victims are concerned about the safety of family, friends and other community members or share their experience of crime and victimhood with them. Victimization of a whole community or group also deeply impacts the circumstances within which victims attempt to rebuild their lives and come to terms with what happened. In some cases, the perpetrators of the crimes will themselves be a part of that context; possibly as perpetrators and victims at one and the same time. This also shows that the conceptualization of victimhood in societies in transition poses several additional complexities. Many conflicts are characterized by, as Roth-Arrizia calls it, shades of gray, whereby in the aftermath society (often through trials) tries to divide the population into a small group of guilty parties and an innocent majority, which was thereby cleansed of wrongdoing (Roth-Arriaza 2006). Rama Mani (2004, 69) argued that 'by ignoring [...] vast categories of society but creating deep and often fallacious and misleading distinctions between people defined solely in terms of victims and perpetrators, transitional justice as currently practiced divides and alienates. What is needed in the aftermath of conflict and political crisis for a peaceful and just transition is a more inclusive notion that encompasses all parts of society whatever their past role/s during the conflict or crisis. It is a notion based on all individuals within society defined collectively as 'survivors' rather than victims, perpetrators or beneficiaries and bystanders.'

Also, the trauma of extreme group victimization, such as the Holocaust or the Rwandan Genocide, is *more* likely to be transmitted from one generation to the next (Danieli 2009, Barankowski et al. 1998).) Research has shown that not only survivors of the Holocaust live on average 5 years less than others, and have more illnesses, but the same results have been found also with children of Holocaust survivors.

With regard to mass victimization, it has furthermore become evident that for many people victimization will not be a single event. Instead they will have *multiple victimizations, both direct and indirect.* A victim may experience multiple group rapes, but may also witness the death or torture of family members and experience loss of property or other possessions. The impact of multiple victimization is cumulative and the trauma may therefore be different.

Mass victimization may furthermore often lead to additional tragedy through, for instance, the spreading of contagious diseases suffered not only by survivors but also by their newborn children. In Rwanda,

70% of women who survived multiple rapes during the genocide turned out to be HIV-positive. The spreading of HIV through rape was used as a weapon of war and an additional means to accomplish the genocide (Shaw 2001, De Brouwer 2005).

Lastly, the degree of physical and social power individuals possess, and how they and others perceive their own vulnerability, are key to understanding their experience of crime (Goodey 2005 p.123) Physical power affects the impact of crime on victims and the extent to which they can be expected to make a full and speedy recovery. As Goodey (2005 p.231) observes, especially in conflict situations because of the brutality of the violence, the often complete absence of proper medical care in the immediate aftermath of the conflict and the consequent collapse of formal and social structures (compare Ewald 2002). The effect of victimization is therefore not only on the individual losing control and power balance (see Fattah 1986: 4), but it is supplemented by the fact that victimization occurs in a situation where structural conditions to stop threats and injuries and to cope with them are absent.

To conclude this part, for many victims the road to recovery and reconciliation is a long and bumpy one. They do not only suffer from the terrible crimes they had to endure and witness, but also face serious socio-economic and health problems. On top of that, achieving some form of justice is often incredibly difficult. As human beings entitled to enjoy the basic human rights and freedoms enshrined in the 1948 Universal Declaration of Human Rights and other international human rights and victims' rights instruments, these victims are, more often than not, experiencing yawning gaps between entitlements and realities.

The gaps are found in different layers of society, making the call for a comprehensive approach all the more urgent. As eloquently described by Tomuschat, first, inadequate laws, restrictions in legal scope and content relating to the committed crimes, impediments in getting access to justice and restrictive attitudes of courts are some of the *legal obstacles*. Second, often societies face *political obstacles* mainly from authorities and certain groups in society unwilling to recognise that wrongs were committed. Third, *severe economic consequences* as a result of a shortage or unjust distribution of resources further preclude easy recovery. Especially in those countries that already belonged to the developing countries, ensuring economic recovery is extra difficult. In addition, most conflicts lead to an enormous number of victims, putting stress on any proposed reparation regime. Prioritizing the allocation of resources thus poses vexing questions (Duthie 2009). Fourth, *under-empowerment* of victims themselves should be mentioned, mainly because of a lack of knowledge and capacity to present and pursue their claims. All these factors are compounded by the vulnerability of groups of victimized persons, notably women, children, and members of specific racial, ethnic or religious groups. In addition, most contemporary conflicts are intra-state in nature, posing additional pressure and difficulties for reparation processes. Fletcher & Weinstein (2002) refer in particular to the human suffering on a communal level which is a shared feature in many contemporary conflicts, where neighbour-on-neighbour violence is characteristic of this form of aggression

1.4. Notions from the Human Security Concept

Human security, as argued by one of its apostles, former Canadian Minister of Foreign Affairs Lloyd Axworthy, is in essence, an effort to construct a global society. The safety of the individual is at the centre of international priorities. Axworthy believes it to be a motivating force for international action (Axworthy 2008). Three main reports form the basis for the human security concept as it stands today: the *Human Development Report* issued by the UN Development Programme (1994), *Human Security Now* (2003) drafted by the Independent Commission on Human Security (initiated by Japan), and *Human Security Report, War and Peace in the 21st Century* by the Human Security Centre of the University of British Columbia in Canada (2005). As the forword of the report makes it clear (pages iv-v), the said commission was inspired by the 2000 UN Millennium Summit; funded by Japan under UN facilitation (UN 2003, UNDP 1994, Human Security Report 2005).

Whereas its predecessor, the concept of human development, exclusively focused on the right to a long and healthy life, education and access to health care, human security adds the right to live free of violations of human rights, criminal acts and political violence. It highlights the interrelationships between the threats of global crimes and other security risks such as those of extreme poverty or health.

The human security concept thus tries to complement other related notions. For example, many of the existing human rights, such as the right to food and the right to education, are part of the holistic approach of the human security notion. The often proclaimed specific characteristics of human rights, being universal, interdependent and interrelated, are also reflected upon in the human security debate. The 1994 Human Development Report, for instance, notes that human security is a universal concern, of which the components are interdependent (UN 1994 p.28). Other notions which the human security concept aims to combine are those of national security, the previous mentioned concept of human development and humanitarian intervention such as the concept of 'responsibility to protect.' (details at Tadjbakhsh et al.2007). Human security aims to overcome the compartmentalization of these other notions. In that sense it is more and more developing into an approach with its own theories.

There is still discussion how wide the scope of human security should be. The narrow approach limits it to violent threats to individuals from internal violence (an approach promoted by Canada), while the broad approach also includes threats such as hunger, disease and natural disaster (as promoted in the UNDP Human Development Report of 1994 or by the Government of Japan).

The wide approach of the human security concept aims to include under its scope each and every individual living in each and every country; everyone means the women who survived the multiple rapes in Rwanda, but also the single mother living in a dangerous neighborhood in New York, or the business man residing in Tokyo. The concept evolved from the notion that in a global society the safety of one person is strongly interdependent with the safety of another. As a prominent human security scholar, Mary Kaldor, explains, 'insecurity can no longer be contained. Violence tends to cross borders. This does not happen through military attacks by foreign regimes. It happens through terrorism, organized crime or extreme ideologies (Kaldor 2007 p.196).

The concept of human security can therefore only be understood in the context of a globalized world. Human beings in different parts of the world are more and more interconnected. Through technological development and media coverage we are more and better informed about what happens on another side of the world. This results in an increasing awareness of the pain and suffering of people in different parts of the world. Globalization, consequently, may lead to a conviction that such pain and suffering, wherever it takes place, is of universal concern and should invoke joint action to end it, which can be referred to as a process of moral globalization (Bodelier 2011).

But globalization has also affected the nature of crime itself. The effects of globalization processes in the economic, political and cultural spheres have profound implications for the world of crime and justice. The playing field for offenders, and sometimes also for victims (think of their role in international tribunals), has expanded from the local or national to the global, leading to new – international and transnational – forms and manifestations of crimes. States with their traditional systems of criminal prosecution and security policies have often found themselves powerless to deal with these new forms of crimes. Finding solutions for 'problems without passports' has proved to be extremely difficult.

Main characteristics; holistic and bottom-up approach

The main characteristics of the human security concept can be described as follows: It entails a holistic or comprehensive approach which means that it aims to systematically and coherently address the various threats. The word "threat" includes helping countries to recover from conflicts. Ceasefires agreements and peace settlements may mark the end of armed conflict but they do not ensure human security (Human Security Now p.57). Human security comprehensively addresses both "freedom from fear" and "freedom from want". It aims to deal with the capacity to identify threats and the underlying interdependencies, prevent them when possible and mitigate their effects when they do occur. In order to do so, a wide range of actors as potential providers of security and protection need to be involved, multiplying the opportunities for coordinated, international responses within a normative framework as well as for new institutional arrangements (Tadjbakhsh, Chenoy.2007 : 236).

Its direct relevance to the field of Victimology is that human security claims to be individual-oriented, thereby moving away from the State-centred approach that we see in traditional security debates (Tadjbakhsh,Chenoy 2007:40). Elements of both protection and empowerment play an important role (see also the Barcelona Report of the Study Group on Europe's Security Capabilities,' A Human Security Doctrine for Europe, Barcelona, 15 September 2004, Executive Summary). Emphasis is therefore placed on a bottom-up approach: on communication, consultation, dialogue and partnership with the local population in order to improve early warning, intelligence gathering, the mobilization of local support, implementation and sustainability. The individual should always be involved in the promotion of his or her security. Individual empowerment is both a means as well as an objective of human security (Tadjbakhsh and Chenoy,2007. 238).

The emphasis is thus on agency or strength of individuals, particularly relevant to the human security debate in the sense that it prioritizes people above institutions. This actor-oriented approach forms a sharp contrast to established approaches in the national security domain. These approaches often present people as passive victims of violence or merely recipients of emergency relief. They overlook the possibility of empowerment and emancipation and denying them their agency (Frerks and Godewijn p.39).

Some critique

Considering the range of different perspectives, 'human security' is either criticized for being an additional conceptual idea lacking any substantial meaning and practicability, *or* seen as part of an evolving, genuine paradigm shift, offering an alternative and attractive language to rethinking and furthering the protection of human beings beyond currently dominant paradigms. Concepts, so says Upadhyara (2005:1; compare Paris 2001) come and go. They do not stay forever.

First some of the critique. The concept lacks a clear-cut definition and a clear listing of priorities. For various reasons, it has still not been possible to develop a so-called Human Security Index (compare the Human Development Index) that would monitor the security of persons worldwide. The Human Security Report that came out in 2005 and 2009, and the Human Security Brief and the Human Security Atlas try to analyse the state of affairs, but these reports adhere to the narrow approach, thereby neglecting the human development part (see Human Security Report Project 2010, Letschert and van Dijk, 2010).

Its comprehensive, or holistic, approach also meets with criticism. The fact that human security overarches different threats in very diverse societal domains, including a variety of state and non-state actors, and has far-reaching ambitions in terms of peace, development and human rights, makes it difficult to operationalize in practice.

In addition, critics hold that all the issues the human security concept aims to address are becoming more and more problematic under the present circumstances. Meaning an ever more fragmented world, divisive discourses, and a multilateral system that is hold back by lack of political will and consensus, under-funded (especially now with the worldwide economic crisis), and undermined by attacks and the selfish behaviour of States.

We cannot neglect these observations. While the language and the objectives of human security are increasingly establishing themselves within the discourse of the UN and the European Union, and individual countries such as Japan, Canada and the United States forming the Human Security Network, institutional changes to promote human security remain negligible. With one exception: in March 1999, with a view to make the human security approach more operational, the Government of Japan and the United Nations Secretariat launched the United Nations Trust Fund for Human Security (there are three types of pooled funds: Emergency Response Funds, Common Humanitarian Funds and the Central Emergency Response Fund, compare UN 2011). On the other hand, more and more scholars, of which Sen (1979) and Nussbaum (2000) are most prominent, embark upon studies that further conceptualize and operationalize human security. Also, international research institutes on human security were set up, in Canada, France, India, and South-Africa.

1.5. How can Human Security contribute to a victimology of international crimes?

Does the human security concept contribute to the further development of a victimology of international crimes? The discussion here is limited to the context of international crimes. It is within this context that I see most relevance to the benefits of the underlying notions of human security for victimology. It is also within this context that freedom from want and freedom from fear are most seriously threatened and interrelated. Before attempting to address this question, first the main differences and similarities between the two will be discussed.

Differences
First, in the field of Victimology, victims are often defined in terms of national criminal law whereas human security uses international and moral-political criteria. The concept of 'human security' thus goes far beyond the prevailing practice in victimology which, while filling the gaps in early human rights instruments by providing for victims' rights, mainly focuses on a limited category of victims. *Second*, mainstream Victimology mostly concerns people who have been victimized, whereas human security also aims to prevent persons from falling victim. *Third,* mainstream Victimology is more realistic, whereas human security is more utopian but therefore maybe also more performative. In that sense they pertain to different ideologies or sensitivities.

Similarities
First, both are increasingly influenced by processes of globalization which also influence the perception of fear or risk of becoming victimized. The concepts of fear of crime or fear of insecurity are apparent and at the same time problematic for both. Goodey (2005: 16-19) states that people experience risk and insecurity at the local level but that reflects global shifts to the established social order. Ewald,

referring to Giddens, lists four global risk areas which determine the manufactured insecurity in contemporary world society: ecology (global warning), the expansion of absolute poverty, uncontrolled distribution of weapons of mass destructions, and the suppression of democratic rights. The new quality of these risks is their general and ubiquitous nature which does not differentiate between rich and poor (Ewald 2002: 92).

Second, many human security notions, just as Victimology, also include criminal justice elements.

Third, both put the individual victim first. Whereas victimologists criticize criminologists for putting the interest of the state or society first, human security proponents criticize human development scholars who often think in terms of state support.

Fourth, both are inherently critical towards the status quo; they challenge institutional foundations; for victimology this would be criminal law and criminology, and for human security the focus on state security.

How can human security contribute to a victimology of international crimes? Victimologists should not embrace each and every idea promoted by the human security concept, but should critically assess whether some of them can be useful *and* further developed by using or incorporating a victimological lens. In general, three crucial pillars are discerned under the human security concept that could be foundational for a victimology of international crimes.

1. Protection and empowerment of individuals worldwide
2. Importance of a bottom-up approach
3. Holistic or comprehensive approach

1. *Protection and empowerment of individuals worldwide*

With regard to the protection and empowerment of individuals *worldwide*, it is already discussed in this paper why victimologists should set up more specific studies relating to victims of gross atrocity crimes (section 1.3.). Therefore I will focus on the bottom-up and holistic approach.

2. *Bottom-up approach*

The human security concept claims that through a bottom-up approach, individuals will be empowered by encouraging their ability to act on their own behalf. In Rwanda, a clear example can be found of a bottom-up approach. After the Genocide, the new government struggled with developing just means for the humane detention and prosecution of the more than 120,000 people accused of genocide and related crimes against humanity. By 2000, most of these people were still held in Rwanda's prisons without a trial being held. The ordinary courts would never have managed to try all these perpetrators in due time. Therefore, the government, urged also by local leaders, decided to re-implement the Gacaca court system, which has evolved from traditional cultural communal law enforcement procedures. Local people were trained to become judges, and communities would literally sit down in the grass to hear the stories of both perpetrators and victims. The Gacaca courts therefore became a method of transitional justice, designed to obtain three objectives: The speeding up of the legal proceedings by using as many courts as possible, the reconciliation of all Rwandans and building their unity, promote healing and moving on from the crisis (Kaitese and Haveman 2011). The Gacaca court system has received a lot of criticism, mainly from Western scholars, who argue that important principles relating to, for instance, a fair trial are violated. Whereas on the other hand, anecdotal evidence from survivors claims that they are reasonably satisfied. Two of the main reasons for this are (1) that survivors got to know what happened with their loved-ones and (2) had a chance to speak out about what happened to them. The fact that local leadership and public discussion about the genocide was encouraged by the Gacaca, are important elements of empowerment.

Too often, the international community treats conflicts and victimization in different contexts alike. Too often, international experts are flown into crisis areas to bring in their expertise to help individuals and societies recover. Too often, they fail to take the local, cultural and historical context into account when developing policies for reconstruction or reconciliation. The question should however not be: What can we do? It should be: How does this activity build on the efforts and capabilities of those directly affected? Orentlichter (2007:18) noted that no one could expect to find a universally valid formula for transitional justice given the great range of national experiences and cultures. Increasingly, scholars argue that transitional justice initiatives should be established 'bottom down', 'from the grass root level', 'including local ownership'; an understanding also encouraged by the human security concept. The idea of local ownership reflects also the increasing tendency to give due regard to tradition-based conceptions of providing justice (See Schotsmans in Letschert et al. 2011).

For victimologists, a task is to assess how victims' needs are respected in these tradition-based mechanisms, thereby not losing sight from the specific cultural and historical contexts, of the country and its victims trying to overcome their past (Rohne 2006). In particular it should be underlined to including the historical context in any analysis, since often in conflict-torn societies, gross victimizations are linked to historical victimizations and how they are perceived in the collective memory (Danieli 2009).

3. Holistic approach

Recent international legal developments in relation to the prosecution of international crimes still show serious shortcomings in dealing with victims of genocide, war crimes and crimes against humanity. The focus has been too one-sidedly on the punishment of offenders and on retribution, with the often main purpose of involving surviving victims being to serve these goals. International criminal justice mechanisms seem to overlook the fact that, while the damage caused to society and humanity at large is real, the suffering incurred by the direct victims is, at least, as great and is deserving of much more attention than has been the case so far. The International Criminal Court tries to implement a more comprehensive approach in its mandate. The option of combining the granting of individual rights and collective reparations comes close to the integrative approach the human security concept aims to achieve and was actually also inspired by the human security lobby. Nevertheless, the enormous number of victims wishing to participate in the Court's procedures poses for the Court a still unresolved challenge.

The notion that the needs and views of victims and survivors of international crimes are insufficiently represented in the formal criminal justice response is the main drive behind the development of various commissions of inquiry, such as for instance truth commissions and of reparations programs. With regard to the truth commissions, the emphasis is not on the punishment of offenders, but on unraveling the narrative of the international crimes committed, simultaneously offering victims an opportunity to voice their experiences and receive acknowledgement of the wrongs committed against them. Truth commissions, just like reparation programs, can offer monetary and symbolic reparations, educational programs, memorials and projects to strengthen democratic institutions. However, where the formal criminal justice response may lay too much emphasis on punishing the offenders of crimes, the experience with truth commissions or reparations suggests that here, from the victims' point of view, there is too little emphasis on retribution. This implies that from a human security and victimological point of view, one of the most intriguing questions confronting the development of transitional justice is how to balance and more importantly combine the strengths of truth commissions or other forms of reparation programs with an (international) criminal justice response.

Some final words on a holistic approach

Already in 1968, Maslow developed his pyramid of needs. Taking a closer look at these needs, we can argue that he was not far away from promoting a human security concept. Maslows's needs theory was also applied to victims of international crimes by Wemmers and De Brouwer (in Letschert and van Dijk, 2010). According to Maslow, people first have to satisfy their basic needs like food and shelter as well as medical care. A survivor of genocide, who lost her house, her family and is unable to work due to injuries suffered as a result of her victimization will, in the first place, need urgent medical care for her injuries as well as food and a place to stay. In addition, immediate trauma counselling is of utmost importance. However, Becker et al argue that "victims know that individual therapeutic intervention is not enough. They need to know that their society as a whole acknowledges what has happened to them" (Becker et al. 1990:174).

The second level of needs identified by Maslow is safety. People need to feel safe and secure. The third and fourth levels of needs are a feeling of belonging or affection and self-esteem. Informal support can provide victims with a sense of feeling loved and accepted which in conflict setting is often difficult to realise because of all the casualties within families and communities. The fifth need of self-actualization is the last stage, and according to Maslow only achievable if all the other needs are satisfied. While Maslow's hierarchy of needs was developed independent of both human security and victimology, it is important to note the convergence between the needs identified by Maslow and those of victims of international crimes. Interesting to note furthermore is that both Sen (1979) and Nussbaum (2000), two prominent human security scholars, touch close upon Maslow's ideas with their capabilities theory.

Thinking this through to the field of Victimology, it implies that victimological studies relating to international crimes should encourage a similar comprehensive approach as promoted by the human security concept. It thus means encompassing all the different consequences of victimization, seeking to include different actors by, for instance, combining private and public partnerships (Goodey 2005: 21), and acknowledging that a legal response alone is not enough and will often even be impossible due to the collective nature of the victimization.

This being said, does this mean that victimology should further expand its scope and, for instance, include victims of poverty or natural disasters to its field of study? That would not be my plea. However, I would argue that victimologists should include all factors that influence the often continuing victimized status of survivors of international crimes. That means more than they do now, to study and develop theories that analyze the interplay and interdependencies of continuing personal security threats *and* socio-economic threats. In other words, victimologists should not study the causes of poverty or social exclusion, but should analyze their effects on victims on possibilities to recover from their trauma. In addition, while victims' rights form an integral part of the normative framework of many Western domestic legal systems, it has been more difficult to enact, let alone implement, these rights in several countries in the developing world. Perhaps Victimology could achieve more in countries that struggle on a daily basis with potential political, financial and administrative collapses, not to mention AIDS pandemics, when it adheres to a more encompassing human security *and* victim-oriented approach.

1.6. Conclusions

Human security as a concept can make a significant contribution to the protection and empowerment of victims of international crimes. But as yet, it is still too much of an abstract framework and needs to be translated into a pragmatic agenda for concerted action, in which different actors work according to their capabilities to achieve different, but ultimately compatible, human security goals. A key consideration in that regard must be how, if, and, where possible, should the individual be involved in the promotion of his/her own human security. For indeed, individual empowerment is both a means as well as an end of human security (Tadjbakhs et al. 2007: 238).

This is where victimologists should come in: on the one hand, by learning from and further elaborating a comprehensive individual-oriented human security approach to victim protection; and, on the other hand, enriching the human security concept by incorporating results achieved in the victimological empowerment studies.

This paper has argued that the complex situation of victims of international crimes calls for a holistic approach that links various relevant fields such as development studies, traumatic stress studies, the social psychology of group conflict and resolution, and the psychology and sociology of national and international legal processes. The latter is important in its own right, but also for the ongoing efforts in transitional and international criminal justice, as it can provide the empirical foundation for the choices and developments in this field. It is exactly this holistic approach that is the cornerstone of the human security concept. The analysis of collective victimization and post-conflict coping in conflict regions by a combined human security and victimological approach can significantly contribute to understanding the unique situation of human exposure to threats, risks, suffering and fear, and hence, how to react appropriately to (re)gain security (see Ewald 2002). By doing so, the scientific study of victimization becomes more and more diverse, justifying the development of a differential victimology that takes the specific features of different crimes, victims, and contexts into account.

References

Albrecht, H.J. (2002). Preliminary Remarks, *European Journal of Crime, Criminal Law and Criminal Justice.*, 2002, 2-3, pp. 87-89.

Albrecht, H.J. and Kilchling, M. (2007). Victims of Terrorism Policies: Should victims of terrorism be treated differently? *European Journal on Criminal Policy and Research,* volume 13, numbers 1-2, 13-31 (2007)

Axworthy, L. (2001). Human Security and Global Governance: Putting People First, Global Governance 7, 2001, pp. 19-23.

Axworthy L. (2008). talks to Canada World View. http://www.dfait-maeci.gc.ca/canada-magazine/special/se1t3-en.asp (accessed on 14 august 2008)

Barankowsky, A., M. Young, M., Johnson-Douglas,S., Williams-Keeler,L. & McCarrey, M. (1998). PTSD Transmission: A Review of Secondary Traumatization in Holocaust Survivor Families. *Canadian Psychology*, 39, 4, pp. 247-256.

Becker, D., Lira E., Castillo, M.I., Gomez, E., & Kovalskys, J. (1990). "Therapy with Victims of Political Repression in Chile: The Challenge of Social Reparation". *Journal of Social Issues,* Vol. 40, No. 3.

v, R. (2010). Human Security and the Emergence of a Global Conscience, in Letschert, R.M. and van Dijk, J.J.M., *The New Faces of Victimhood,* Springer Publishers.

Brouwer, A.L.M. de (2005). *Supranational Criminal Prosecution of Sexual Violence: The ICC and the Practice of the ICTY and the ICTR. Antwerp -* Oxford: Intersentia. (School of Human Rights Research, 20).

Brouwer, de, A.L.M. and S. Ka Hon Chu, The Men Who Killed Me: Rwandan Survivors of Sexual Violence, Vancouver: Douglas & McIntyre, 2009.

Danieli, Y. (2009). in Ferstman,c.; Goetz, M. & Stephens, A. (Eds), (2009). Reparations for Victims of Genocide, War Crimes and Crimes against Humanity, Nijhoff Publishers.

Danieli, Y. (2009). Massive Trauma and the Healing Role of Reparative Justice, *Journal of Traumatic Stress*, Volume 22, Issue 5, pages 351–357.

Danieli, Y. (1998). *International Handbook of Multigenerational Legacies of Trauma*. New York: Plenum Press.

Dussich, J.P.J. (2000). The Past Millenium's Abuse of Power: An Analysis of Offenders and Victims. In: Gaudreault, A.&Waller, I. (eds.) X International Symposium on Victimology. Selected Symposium Proceedings. Montreal (Associacion Quebecoise Plaidoyer-Victimes) pp. 255-275.

Dussich, J. & Mundy, K. (eds.) (2009). Raising the Global Standards for Victims: The Proposed Convention on Justice for Victims of Crime and Abuse of Power, Mito, Seibundo Publishing Co., Ltd.

Elias, R. (1985). Transcending our Social Reality of Victimization: Toward a New Victimology of Human Rights, *Victimology*, 1985, 10 (1/4), pp. 6-25.

Elias, R. (1994). 'Paradigms and Paradoxes of Victimology',in: Sumner, C., Israel,M.,O'Connell, M.& Sarre, R. International Victimology.

Ewald, U. (2002). Victimization in the Context of War. *European Journal of Crime, Criminal Law and Criminal Justice*, Vol. 2-3.

Fattah, E.A. (1986). *From Crime Policy to Victim Policy,* London.

Fletcher, L.E. and Weinstein, H.M. (2002). Violence and Social Repair: Rethinking the Contribution of Justice to Reconciliation, *Human Rights*

Quarterly 24, 573–639.
Frerks, G.E, Klein Goldewijk, B. (2007). Human Security and International Insecurity: The quest for humane global governance. In: Human security and international insecurity. Frerks, G.E., Klein Goldewijk, B (eds) Wageningen : Wageningen Academic Publishers, pp. 21 – 44.
Friday, P. and De la Luz Lima, M. (2005). Abuse of Power, Issues of theory and policy, in *Victims of Crime and Abuse of Power, Festschrift in Honour of Irene Mellup*, Bangkok (11th UN Congress on Crime Prevention and Criminal Justice) pp. 567-582.
Goodey, J. (2005). *Victims and Victimology, Research, Policy and Practice*, Longman Criminology Practice.
Henry, N. (2009). Witness to Rape: The Limits and Potential of International War Crimes Trials for Victims of Wartime Sexual Violence, *International Journal of Transitional Justice*, March 2009.
Horn, R. (2009). Testifying in an International War Crimes Tribunal: The Experience of Witnesses in the Special Court for Sierra Leone, *International Journal for Transitional Justice*, March 2009.
Human Security Now. Protecting and Empowering People. Commission on Human Security. Washington 2003.
Human Security Report 2005: War and Peace in the 21st Century, University of British Columbia, Canada, New York/Oxford, Oxford University Press, 2005.
Kaldor. M. (2007). *Human Security, Reflections on Globalization and Intervention*, Polity Press.
Kaitese, U. and Haveman, R. (2011). Prosecution of Genocidal Rape and Sexual Torture before the Gacaca tribunals in Rwanda, in Letschert et al, *Developing Victimological Approaches to International Crimes, Focus on Africa*, Intersentia, Antwerp.
Kirchhoff, G.F. (2005). What is Victimology? Monograph Series nr.1., Tokiwa International Victimology Institute. Mito (Seibundo Publishing, Tokyo).
Kirchhoff, G.F. (2010). History and a Theoretical Structure of Victimology. In: Shoham, S.G., Knepper, P. & M. Kett (eds.) International Handbook of Victimology. Boca Raton, Taylor and Francis CRC Press), pp. 95-123.
Kramer, R.C. and Michalowski, R. (2005). War, Aggression and State Crime, A Criminological Analysis of the Invasion and Occupation of Iraq, *Br J Criminol* (July 2005) 45 (4): 446-469.
Lamborn, L.L. (1987). The United Nations Declaration on Victims, 19 *Rutgers L.J.* 59, pp. 59-95.
Letschert, R., Staiger, I. & Pemberton, A. (eds.) (2009). *Assisting Victims of Terrorism, Towards a European Standard of Justice*, New York, Springer.
Letschert, R.M. and van Dijk (eds). (2010). *The New Faces of Victimhood*, Springer Publishers.
Letschert, R., Haveman, R., de Brouwer, MA.-M., Pemberton, A. (eds.) (2010). *Developing Victimological Approaches to International Crimes. Focus on Africa*. Intersentia, Antwerp.
Levi, B. & Sidel,V. (1997). *War and Public Health*, New York, Oxford University Press.
Mani, R. (2005). Reparation as a Component of Transitional Justice: Pursuing 'Reparative Justice' in the Aftermath of Violent Conflict. in

K. de Feyter, S. Parmentier et al (eds.) *Out of the Ashes: Reparation for Victims of Gross and Systematic Human Rights Violations* (Antwerp/ Oxford: Intersentia.

Maslow, A.H. (1968). *Toward a Psychology of Being* (2nd Edition). New York: Van Nostrand Reinhold.

Mullins, C.W. and Rothe D.I. (2008). *Blood, Power, and Bedlam: Violations of International Criminal Law in Post-colonial Africa*, New York (Lang).

Mullins, C.W (2009). He Would Kill Me With His Penis, Genocidal Rape in Rwanda as a State Crime, *Critical Criminology*, Vol. 17, No. 1.

Neuman, E. (1984). Victimologia. El rol de la victim en los delitos convencionales y non concencionales. Buenos Aires (Editorial Universidad).

Nussbaum, M. (2000). Women and Human Development: The capabilities approach. New York: Cambridge University Press.

Orentlichter, D. (2007). Settling Accounts Revisited: Reconciling Global Norms with Local Agency, *International Journal of Transitional Justice*, Vol. 1, No. 1, pp. 10-22.

Paris, R. (2001). Human Security, Paradigm Shift or Hot Air, *International Security*, Vol. 26, No. 2 (Fall 2001), pp. 87–102.

Rohne, H.C. (2006). Opferperspektiven im interkulturellen Vergleich.Eine viktimologische Untyersuchung im Kontext der Al-Aqsa-Intifada. Max Planck Institut fuer Auslaendisches und Internationales Strafrecht.

Ph. Pham, Vinck, P., Balthazard, M., Hean, S., Stover, E. (2009). So We Will Never Forget: A Population-Based Survey On Attitudes About Social Reconstruction and the Extraordinary Chambers in the Courts of Cambodia, Human Rights Center, University of Berkeley, California, Berkeley.

Roth-Arriaza, N. (2003-2004). Reparations Decisions and Dilemmas, *Hastings International & Comparative Law Review*, Vol. 157,

Roth-Arriaza, N (2006). *Transitional Justice in the Twenty–First Century: Beyond Truth Versus Justice* (Cambridge University Press 2006) (with Javier Mariezcurrena).

Sen, A. (1979). Equality of What? The Tanner Lecture on Human Values. Stanford University 22.

Separovic, Z.P. (1985). Victimology: Studies of Victims, Croatia, Samobor.

Shaw, M. (2001). Time Heals All Wounds? In: G. Farrell and K. Pease (eds.) Repeat Victimization. Crime Prevention Studies, volume 12, (pp. 218-233). Monsey NY, Criminal Justice Press.

Smeulers, A. and Havemann, R.H. (eds.) (2008). *Supranational Criminology: Towards a criminology of international crimes*, Antwerp: Intersentia

Staub, E. (1992). *The Roots of Evil: The origins of genocide and other group violence*, Cambridge University Press.

Stover, E. (2005). *The Witnesses: War Crimes and the Promise of Justice in The Hague*, Philadelphia, PA: University of Pennsylvania Press,

Stover, E. and Weinstein, H. (2004). *My Neighbor, My Enemy: Justice in the aftermath of Mass Atrocity*. Cambridge University Press.

Tadjbakhsh, S. and Chenoy, A.M. (2007). *Human Security, Concepts and Implications,* Routledge, London, New York, 2007.

Upadhyaya,P.(2005). Human Security, Humanitarian Intervention, and the Third World Concerns', 33 Denver *Journal of International Law and*

Policy nr. 1, 71-91.

Van Boven, T. (2009). Victims' Rights to a Remedy and Reparation: The New United Nations Principles and Guidelines, in Ferstman,C., Goetz, M., and Stephens, A. *Reparations for Victims of Genocide, War Crimes and Crimes against Humanity, Systems in Place and Systems in the Making*, Martinus Nijhoff Publishers.

van Dijk, J.J.M. (1999). Introducing Victimology. In: Van Dijk, J.J.M., van Kaam, R.G.H. & Wemmers, J. (eds) 1999. *Caring for Crime Victims. Selected Proceedings of the 9th International Symposium on Victimology*. Monsey NY, USA (Criminal Justice Press), pp. 1-9.

Wemmers, J.M. & De Brouwer, A.M. (2010). Globalization and Victims Rights at the International Criminal Court. in: Letschert and van Dijk (Eds.), The New Faces of Victimhood, Springer.

Wemmers, J. (2011). The Needs of Victims of International Crimes, in: Letschert, Haveman, De Brouwer, Pemberton, *Developing Victimological Approaches to International Crimes, Focus on Africa,* Intersentia.

Past Violations of Indigenous Rights in the Inter- American Commission and Inter-American Court on Human Rights

By

Lilian Yamamoto[1]

Indigenous societies of the Americas, like those in Africa and Asia, have suffered the destruction of their culture and traditions due to colonialism (Lâm, 2007, p.424). Indigenous peoples had their culture and way of life systematically assaulted by colonial powers which tried to force assimilation and expand the concept of private property at the expense of the communal holdings of indigenous peoples. European colonists in Latin America, used indigenous labor first as slaves and subsequently as forced wage laborers (Hannum, 2004, p.323) In the American continent, approximately 400 indigenous groups of varying sizes remain, numbering more than 30 million people (Hannum, 2004, p.323).

The Inter-American Commission (IACHR Inter-American Commission on Human Rights) and the Inter-American Court on Human Rights(IACtHR Inter-American Court on Human Rights) have provided interpretation of the system's American Declaration on Human Rights and American Convention on Human Rights which follows the international instruments which protect indigenous rights. In addition, it has been overcoming the lack of *ratione temporis* issues, by examining cases which took place before the ratification of the American Convention(ACHR American Convention on Human Rights) by the states. In these cases, the lack of investigation, prosecution, punishment and the ancestral lands are discussed.

1. Inter-American Commission on Human Rights and Inter-American Court on Human Rights

The Inter-American Commission on Human Rights was established in 1959 by Resolution VIII of the Fifth Meeting of Consultation of Ministers of Foreign Affairs (Cerna, 2004, p.65). It entered into force

[1] United Nations University-Institute of Advanced Studies

in 1960 when its first members were chosen.

The Commission initially was doing on-site visits to analyze the human rights situation of each country. From 1965 the Commission also started examining individual petitions. The functions of the Commission are (1) to develop an awareness of human rights, (2) to make recommendations to the governments of member states regarding measures that favor human rights, (3) to prepare studies and reports, (4) to take action on petitions and (5) to submit an annual report to the General Assembly of the Organizations of American States, American Convention on Human Rights (ACHR, Art.41). Regarding the indigenous rights, in 1990 the Inter-American Commission on Human Rights established the Office of the Special Rapporteur on the Rights of Indigenous people, so it could give special attention to the indigenous peoples of the Americas.

The Inter-American Court on Human Rights (ICtHR) was established many years after the creation of the Inter-American Commission on Human Rights (IACHR) in 1979. The Court could not be organized until the Convention entered into force on 18 July 1978 (Information and History, n.d.). The ICtHR has adjudicatory and advisory functions. In the first one it can examine cases submitted by the IACHR or by a State Party as long as the state has accepted the jurisdiction of the Court (ACHR, Art.62 [3]). The latter function consists of the interpretation of the Convention or of other treaties concerning the protection of human rights in OAS member states (ACHR Art.64).

The main difference between the IACHR and the IACtHR is that the former does make decisions that are not binding to the state parties. They are recommendations which accepted the jurisdiction of the Cou Twenty-one States Parties have acknowledged the Court's contentious jurisdiction: Costa Rica, Peru, Venezuela, Honduras, Ecuador, Argentina, Uruguay, Colombia, Guatemala, Suriname, Panama, Chile, Nicaragua, Paraguay, Bolivia, El Salvador, Haiti, Brazil, Mexico, Dominican Republic, and Barbados.
rt. Conversely, the IACtHR produces decisions which are legally binding to the state parties.

Regarding the right to petition before the IACHR, the "injured party" (Art. 63.1 of the ACHR) and Arts. 46, 1.b and 2.b refers to "party alleging violation of his rights". In the rules of the procedure, Art.23, the Court referred to victims, as persons "whose rights have been violated, according to a judgement pronounced by the Court", or their "next-of-kin", referring to the successors.

The right of petition is not limited to the alleged victims and their relatives. Any 'person or group of persons, or any nongovernmental entity legally recognized in one or more member states' of the OAS has the right to petition in the Inter- American system (ACHR Art.44).

In the context of indigenous victimization, the non- governmental organizations had played an important role, representing the indigenous peoples in many petitions. In the Case of Yakye Axa Indigenous Community v. Paraguay (IACHR, Case of Yakye Axa Indigenous Community v.Paraguay, case No.12,420) "Tierraviva a los Pueblos Indigenas del Chaco paraguayo" and the Center for Justice and International Law (CEJIL) submitted to the Inter- American Commission the complaint. In the case of Moiwana Community v. Suriname (IACHR, Case No.11.821), the human rights organization Moiwana 86 filed a petition before the IACHR. Individuals cannot bring a petition before the IACtHR. Most of the complaints are filed by human rights organizations. That is explained by the fact that the victims and their relatives, but also their lawyers, are susceptible to intimidation, having the possibility of becoming the next victims (Pasqualucci, 2003, p.101)

2. Protection of indigenous rights in the Inter-American system

Although the Inter-American system does not provide a treaty specialized in the protection of indigenous rights it has been interpreting the American Declaration of the Rights and Duties of Man (American Declaration) and the American Convention of Human Rights (ACHR) as best interpretation for such rights. In both instruments, the articles which are related to property rights (article XXIII of the Declaration and article 21 of the American Convention) are present in various cases (Yakye Axa Indigenous Community v.Paraguay; *Sawhoyamaxa Indigenous community v. Paraguay*; Mayagna (Sumo) community of *Awas Tingni v. Nicaragua*). Other instruments that have been applied for interpretation of the articles in the Declaration and in the Convention are the Convention No.169, the United Nations Declaration of the Rights of Indigenous Peoples, the Draft American Declaration of the Rights of Indigenous Peoples and other relevant sources.

Other legal documents such as United Nations Charter (Art.55), the International Covenant on Civil and Political Rights (Art.1[1]), the International Covenant on Economic, Social and Cultural Rights (Article 1[1]) or the Vienna Convention on the Law of Treaties (Preamble regarding self-determination) are also source of reference to the Inter-American organs.(Raisz, 2008)

In addition to the protection of the property rights, the lack of proper investigation causing a situation of impunity by the government authorities regarding violations against members of the indigenous communities (Plan de Sanchez v.Guatemala), is also brought to the Inter-American Commission and Inter-American Court on Human Rights.

The Organization of American States (OAS) adopted only one instrument on the rights of indigenous peoples prior to the adoption of the Draft International American Declaration on the Rights of Indigenous Peoples by the Inter- American Commission on Human Rights in 1995.

3 Past violations in the context of indigenous rights –lack of investigation and remedies

Many of the injustices that indigenous communities have suffered cannot be repaired by any legal means now. There is a discussion centering around the extent to which past injustices committed against indigenous people can be redressed after many years have passed since the occurrence of the original injustice. This question is discussed in Sawhoyamaxa Indigenous Community v. Paraguay since the lands that are in question were purchased by British businessmen in the London stock market in the end of the nineteenth century, without the acknowledgement of the native populations. The indigenous populations were losing their territory to ranches that started using them as slaves (IACtHR, Sawhoyamaxa Indigenous community v. Paraguay, Merits, Reparations and Costs, para. 73).
Is it fair to ask the current landowners to return these lands to the original indigenous populations?

The question of time is also addressed when the British government broke the Waitangi treaty in which Maori chiefs agreed to cede the governance of New Zealand in return for protection against invaders (Thompson, 2002, p.73).The treaty was broken by the British Crown. Would it be reasonable to consider that non-Maori New Zealanders who live now can be hold responsible for the redress of a wrong committed long time ago? Thompson explains that there is the common sense assumption that reparative entitlements and obligations fade away as time passes. The evidence tends to disappear and memory becomes less reliable as an injustice recedes into the past. However, the same thinking cannot be applied to the case of historical injustice, as in the case of criminal procedures, it is necessary to determine guilt or innocence. (2002, p.78)

In the injustices committed against the indigenous people there is no doubt who the perpetrators are. In this case, the passage of time seems irrelevant. This idea might be applied by the international human rights bodies in order to consider the claims made by indigenous peoples. The Inter-American system of human rights made efforts to overcome procedural barriers relating to the jurisdiction *ratione temporis* of events which took place before the Court had jurisdiction on the state in question. However, the Court would not examine the crime *per se*. It would examine the lack of action by the state to provide necessary remedies to the victims of the violations. It is the question whether the procedural remedies can be disconnected from the causal facts or incidents. Can the killings which occurred in Moiwana village (IACtHR, Moiwana village v. Suriname), be disconnected from investigations that were supposed to be done by the Suriname authorities?

This effort was done by applying the "Concept of Continuing Violations" which consists of the application of the Convention to facts which occurred before the ratification of the Convention by the State party or facts that took place before the state recognized the jurisdiction of the Court.

A continuing violation according to Joost Pauwelyn is *the breach of an international obligation by an act of a subject of international law extending in time and causing a duration or continuance in time of that breach* (1996, p.415)

It would be an exception to the principle of non- retroactivity of the treaties provided in art. 28 of the Vienna Convention on the Law of Treaties which sets out that "unless a different mention appears from the treaty or is otherwise established, its provisions do not bind a party in relation to any act or fact which took place or any situation which ceased to exist before the date of entry into force of the treaty with respect to that party".

The exception to the principle was recognized by the Inter-American system of human rights in order to remedy victims of human rights violations. One case that could be an example is the Moiwana Village case.

This case examined the massacre of an ethnic group descended from "Bush Negroes" or "Maroons", former slaves who fled enslavement and lived in independent communities. The American Convention on Human Rights entered into force for Suriname on November 12, 1987. From this date on, the jurisdiction of the Court was recognized. On 29 November 1986 the village belonging to the N'djuka community was surrounded, its property burned, and many members of the community were killed, causing the displacement of the survivors to other regions.

The Moiwana massacre occurred before the State of Suriname ratified the American Convention on Human Rights and accepted the Court's jurisdiction, a fact which led the State of Suriname to question the competence *ratione temporis* of the Court.

Suriname claimed that the IACtHR lacked jurisdiction *ratione temporis* once the Commission treated it as a Convention State for the entire case, applying the Convention to the State *ex post facto* (IACtHR, Case of Moiwana village v. Suriname para 34b). Regarding the violations which occurred before the Convention entered into force for Suriname, the IACHR recognized the violation of Articles I, VII, IX, XXIII of the American Declaration of the Rights and Duties of Man and violations of a continuing nature, occurring after the Convention entered into force for the State (Moiwana village v. Suriname par. 34 a ii). Suriname claimed that the only continuing violations the Court had had recognized were forced disappearances, which were not at issue in the case (Moiwana village v. Suriname para 34e).

The Commission replied to the State's claims, contending that Suriname had been treated as a state party to the Convention with respect to the entirety of the claims once the claims directly connected to the attack and related violations were argued to be violations to the Declaration (Moiwana village v. Suriname para 35d). The representatives argued that the denial of justice in the case and omission had a continuing nature (Moiwana village v.Suriname para.36 b).

The Court stated that in the case of a continuing or permanent violation, the Tribunal was competent to examine the actions and omissions occurring after the recognition of jurisdiction (Moiwana village v. Suriname para. 39). A continued or permanent violation begins before the acceptance and lasts after the acceptance of the Court's jurisdiction.

The Court admitted that the failure to investigate, prosecute and punish the people responsible for the massacre constituted ongoing violations to the Arts.8 and 25 of the ACHR, right to humane treatment (Art. 5), freedom of movement (Art. 22), and property (Art.21) (Moiwana viollage para. 43. In relation to the murder of the victims, the jurisdiction of the IACtHR was not applied. Furthermore, the IACtHR ruled that the failure to investigate the crime in due time constitutes a violation to the right to judicial protection.

The IACtHR's judge Antonio Cançado Trindade emitted in his separate opinion of the *Moiwana village v. Suriname* case (Trindade, A.C. Separate Opinion) among other issues, the projection of human suffering in time. He quoted the U.N. World Conference against Racism, Racial Discrimination, Xenophobia and Related Intolerance (Durban, 2001) in his judgment. He also pointed out the salience of par. 98 of the instrument which stresses the *"importance and necessity of teaching about the facts and truth of their history of humankind".*

The document emphasizes that *"remembering the crimes or wrongs of the past, wherever and whenever they occurred...are essential elements for international reconciliation and the creation of societies based on justice, equality and solidarity"* (par.72). In addition, Judge Trindade points out that: "forgetfulness can simply not be imposed on anyone. Legal or institutionalized means of imposing oblivion, -such as amnesty or prescription, - utilitarian as they may seem to be appear rather as obstruction to justice. The search for, and investigation of, past violations of human rights render the past an eternal present". (para.89).

His statement makes us think of the historical dimension of events, a past event is one that has happened and is now lost, a situation that was at hand now and no longer exists. It is an event which continues to have significance for our present time, as a piece of past with contemporary effects, such as a historical artifact in a museum remains present-at-hand.

In this sense it can be assumed that the IACHR extends the competence *ratione temporis* in order to make governments remember and not repeat the past wrongs in issues that- if left exclusively to the involved governments to decide - would have a high probability of being forgotten. IACHR and the IACtHR played a historical role in causing state governments to acknowledge their mistakes where, in addition to addressing the victims of the violations, the memory could be preserved even if the whole claim of the petitioners were not accepted.

In Ovelário Tames v. Brazil (IACHR, Ovelário Tames v. Brazil), civil police officers had arrested Mr. Ovelário Tames on October 1988. He was found dead in his cell next morning. The petitioners alleged a violation of rights guaranteed in Article I (right to life, liberty and personal security) of the American Declaration of the Rights and Duties of Man, and in Arts.8 (right to a fair trial) and 25 (right to judicial protection) of the American Convention on Human Rights.

Brazil ratified the Convention on September 25, 1992, but at the time the petition was presented, had not accepted the IACtHR's jurisdiction. The IACHR decided that it would not exempt the State for violations of human rights which occurred prior to the ratification of the Convention, because the rights safeguarded in the Declaration have a binding character according to the Commission's decision (IACHR, Ovelário Tames v. Brazil para.15).

In this case, the IACHR also decided that it would have competence to decide on facts that took place before the ratification of the ACHR. That made it possible to examine the violations committed in a relatively recent past. The Moiwana case has historical significance, as it is connected to an intentional government policy which tried to destroy a community. Ovelário case is significant because it denounces the negligence of the Brazilian judiciary towards a member of an indigenous group. However, not only members of minority groups face a state of impunity as a result of the Brazilian judiciary's delays. That can be seen in other cases, such as in João Canuto Oliveira v. Brazil (IACHR, João Canuto Oliveira v. Brazil), a case examined by the Inter-American Commission as Brazil had not accepted the Court's jurisdiction by the time the Commission analyzed it.

In Ovelário's case, what was put into question was not only the assassination of the victim, but also the ongoing denial of justice by the Brazilian government. The IACHR decided that Brazil was responsible for the violation of the rights to life, liberty and personal security (Art. 1), to a fair trial (Article 18), and to protection from arbitrary arrest (Art. XXV) American Declaration on the Rights and Duties of Man, and to a fair trial and judicial protection (Arts. 8 and 25), and of the obligation of the State to respect the rights (namely, Art. 1[1] ACHR). The violations occurred in connection with the death of Ovelário Tames as a result of injuries inflicted by members of the civil police force, in addition to the failure to actively investigate, try and punish those responsible, and also for the failure to make reparations to his family and other legitimate claimants.
In this case, what was challenged was not the retroactivity of the

Commission's competence over the assassination of the victim, but the lack of judicial response to the case. This approach was the same as that of the Commission in the João Canuto de Oliveira v. Brazil, where the victim, who was a labor union leader of rural workers in Brazil had been killed under the plan of local landlords. The Commission based its recommendation on violations of the American Declaration of the Rights and Duties of Man in relation to the events which occurred before September 25, 1992, the date Brazil ratified the American Convention on Human Rights.
Furthermore, the Commission recognized its own competence regarding the facts which took place after Brazil ratified the Convention, as they constituted the "continued denial" of the right to judicial guarantees (Arts. 8 and 25 of the ACHR) (IACHR, João Canuto Oliveira v. Brazil para.13). The victim was assassinated on December 18, 1985 by gunmen over a land dispute. João Canuto had reported to the local police that he was threatened by landlords and politicians. But the authorities failed to take measures to protect him. Nine years after the crime occurred, no suspects for the murder of João Canuto had been arrested or tried. The investigation also took eight years to be completed. After its conclusion, the case was still being held up at the time the petition was brought to the IACHR. The IACHR referring to Article XVIII of the American Declaration, recognized its competence *ratione temporis* to examine the facts occurred before the ratification of the Convention.

It found a violation of Art. XVIII of the American Declaration of Human Rights. This is related to the right of access to justice. The IACHR ruled: the unjustified delay in the investigation and procedures conducted by the Office of the Public Prosecutor exonerated the petitioner from his obligation to exhaust domestic legal remedies (IACHR, João Canuto Oliveira v. Brazil para.63)..

As we can see in the aforementioned case, the delay of procedures would not be targeted exclusively at members of indigenous groups, but in the broader context of the Brazilian judiciary's activities.

Parmak (2003, p.49) discusses whether the duty to investigate, prosecute and punish can be applied to the "concept of continuing violations". He states that the duty to investigate, prosecute and punish can be separated from the main event that occurred before the critical date. The mentioned author follows the same view of the Inter-American court which considered as under its jurisdiction the part in that it ocurred a denial of justice in Moiwana village case.
Following the Moiwana case, other decisions were handed down

which related to the continuing denial of justice which would enter the classification of Madrigal- Borloz (2003, p.242) as a lack of executive action. In the following cases the critical date was not discussed, only the lack of action by the state authorities.

In *Yakye Axa case* (IACtHR Yakye Axa Indigenous Community v. Paraguay) the Court analyzed Paraguay's failure to process in due time an indigenous community's claim to regain access to its traditional lands, as it is established in the Constitution. The community had submitted its claim before the national courts in 1993. However, by the time the IACtHR had examined their decision in 2005 the case was still being processed. The IACtHR came to the conclusion that Paraguay's delay of more than 12 years was not acceptable. In the meantime, members of the tribe had to live on the side of the road adjacent to its ancestral territory, an area that lacked the most basic amenities such as access to clean water. The IACtHR recognized the close relationship between the indigenous people and the land, and found a violation of right to property (article 21) of the ACHR. In addition, the IACtHR also found a violation of articles 1(1), 2, 4, 8, and 25 of the ACHR. The IACtHR also ordered reparations to the community either by ensuring its access to its ancestral lands or identifying alternative land that the state could acquire for that objective.

4. Past-violations- property rights

Other aspects of indigenous culture were dealt with by the Inter-American Human rights system, such as the right to communal property in the Case of the Mayagna (Sumo) community of Awas Tingni v. Nicaragua . Through these decisions, which respect the cultural aspects of indigenous peoples, the Inter-American human rights system is seeking to ensure that the tradition and memory of these groups survive the states' attempts to impose foreign values to their communities.

The IACHR presented the case and asked the IACtHR to decide whether the state violated articles 1(obligation to respect rights), 2(Domestic legal effects), 21(Right to property), and 25(Right to Judicial protection) of the ACHR, as Nicaragua has not demarcated the communal lands. The Commission asked the Court to decide (1) that the State had to establish a rapid demarcation and official recognition of the property rights of the Mayagna community, (2) the payment of compensation for material and moral damages suffered by the community, (3) the payment of costs and expenses incurred in prosecuting the case under the jurisdiction of the inter-

American system. In the petition presented to the IACHR it was requested precautionary measures as the State was about to grant Sol de Caribe, S.A. (SOLCARSA) a concession to start the logging in communal lands.

The community of Awas Tingni is comprised of more than six hundred persons. It is an indigenous community of the Mayagna or Sumo ethnic group, located in the Northern Atlantic Autonomous Region (RAAN) of the Atlantic Coast of Nicaragua. They subsist on family farming and communal agriculture, fruit gathering and medicinal plants, hunting and fishing. These activities, as well as the use and enjoyment of the land they inhabit, are carried out in a determined area (Mayagna (Sumo) Awas Tingni Community *v.* Nicaragua para. 2 d). The Court ruled that "...among indigenous peoples there is a communitarian tradition regarding a **communal form of collective property of the land** in the sense that ownership is not centered on an individual but rather on the group and its community...".(emphasis added)(Mayagna (Sumo) Awas Tingni Community *v.* Nicaragua para. 149). The IACtHR decided that the state should create an effective mechanism to delimit the territory of the community, abstain from allowing third parties to affect the existence, value, enjoyment of the property where the community lives and allow them to carry out their own activities. In addition, the IACtHR established that reparations should be paid to the community.

If there is a clash between indigenous communal property and individual private property, the IACtHR established that the restrictions of the former have to follow 4 criteria: (1) they must be established by law; (2) they must be necessary; (3) they must be proportional, and (4) their purpose must be to attain a legitimate goal in a democratic society (Yakye Axa Indigenous Community v. Paraguay para24)

The Yakye Axa and the Sawhoyamaxa cases against the Paraguayan government dealt with the internal displacement of the indigenous communities and with their right to return to their lands. The IACtHR stated that when there is no way of returning the tribes to their ancestor's lands, these peoples shall be provided in all possible cases with lands of quality and legal status at least equal to that of the lands previously occupied by them, suitable to provide for their present needs and future development. Where the peoples concerned express a preference for compensation in money or in kind, they shall be so compensated.

In Sawhoyamaxa case (Sawhoyamaxa Indigenous community v. Paraguay), the Court examined the time- restriction on the right to restitution. The Court decided: as the indigenous people still identify with the lands which were taken away from them, their right to restitution was not lapsed (Sawhoyamaxa Indigenous community v. Paraguay para.131).However, regarding the dispute over the lands, the Court stated that it did not have authority to decide the dispute regarding the private parties. However, it dealt with the arguments of the state.

The State claimed (1) lands have been conveyed from one owner to another "for a long time" and this process has been duly registered; (2) lands are being adequately exploited, and (3) that the owner's rights "is protected under a bilateral agreement between Paraguay and Germany, which has become part of the law of the land (Sawhoyamaxa Indigenous community v. Paraguay para. 137).

The IACtHR decided claim (1) that in case of a conflict of interests, it must assess in each case the legality, necessity, proportionality and fulfillment of a lawful purpose in a democratic society. Regarding claim (2), the Court stated that productivity is not recognized by indigenous people. As to the claim (3), the Court stated that enforcement should always be compatible with the American Convention that is a multilateral treaty of human rights. In this way, The IACtHR dismissed all the state's claims (Sawhoyamaxa Indigenous community v. Paraguay para.138).

Conclusions

The Inter-American Commission and Inter-American Court on Human Rights ruled: past violations against indigenous populations - violations that started even before the existence of the inter-American human rights system - are not past but current issues for their decisions. This was possible because the IACtHR has accepted that the duty to investigate, prosecute and punish the violations can be separated from the crimes itself, which allowed the examination by them of these cases.

The application of the continuing violations concept (made to protect victims of human rights violations) was also applied in the Inter-American Human Rights system to preserve the memories and history of indigenous peoples. The outstanding decision of Moiwana village by the IACtHR considered that the denial of justice by the Suriname authorities was a continuing violation.

The interpretation of the IACtHR and IACHR made it possible to bring up once more questions that could have been left without legal remedy. The evidence vanishes with time. Memory becomes less reliable as an injustice recedes into the past. However, the Court interpreted that these memories cannot be forgotten.

The IACtHR also criticized the state's paradigm of the private property. It ruled that productivity is not a value recognized by indigenous people. In addition, the communal characteristic of the indigenous lands were to be taken in consideration in decisions.

References

Alt Parmak, K.(2003) The application of the concept of continuing violation to the duty to investigate, prosecute and punish under international human rights law'(1994-2004) Turkish Yearbook of human rights. http://papers.ssrn.com/sol3/papers.cfm?abstract_id=926281. Accessed on August 15, 2011.

Borloz, V.M. (2003) Damage and Redress in the Jurisprudence of the Inter-American Court of Human Rights. In UlrichD. & Krabbe Boserup, L. (eds.) Human Rights in Development- Reparations: redressing past wrongs (pp.212-274) Kluwer Law International, Nordic Human Rights Publications

Cerna, C (2004) The Inter-American Commission on Human Rights: its Organization and Examination of petitions and communications. In Harris, DJ.& Livingstone, S. (eds.), The inter-American system of human rights (pp 65-114) Oxford University Press

Hannum, H. (2004) The Protection of Indigenous Rights in the Inter-American System. In Harris, D. J. & Livingstone, S.(eds.), The inter-American system of human rights (pp. 323-344).. Oxford University Press

Lâm, M. C.(2007) Remembering the country of their birth - Indigenous people and territoriality.'. In., Falk R., Hilal E. & Hajjar, L.(eds), Human rights-critical concepts in political science. vol.II, pp.424

Pasqualucci, J. M. (2003) The practice and procedure of the Inter-American Court of Human Rights .Cambridge University Press.

Pauwelyn, J. (1996) The Concept of a 'Continuing Violation of an International Obligation: Selected Problems 66 British Yearbook of International Law, pp.415-450

Risz, A. (2008) Indigenous communities before the Inter-American Court of Human Rights-new century, new era? Miskolc Journal of International Law, Vol5, No.2 (pp.35-51), http://www.uni-miskolc.hu/~wwwdrint/20082raisz1.htm accessed on August 15, 2011.

Thompson, J. (2002) Taking responsibility for the past- reparation and historical justice, Polity.

History of the Inter-American Court on Human Rights, available at http://www.corteidh.or.cr/historia.cfm, accessed on August 15, 2011.

Cases

Inter-American Commission on Human Rights

João Canuto de Oliveira, Case 11.287, Report No.24/98, available on the Internet at <www.cidh.org>

Ovelário Tames v. Brazil, Case No.11.516, Report No.19/98, available on the Internet at <www.cidh.org>

Inter-American Court on Human Rights

Case of Yakye Axa Indigenous Community v. Paraguay (Merits, Reparations and Costs) Decision from 17 June 2005, available on the Internet at <www.cidh.org> *and at* <www.corteidh.or.cr>.

Case of Moiwana village v. Suriname, (Preliminary Objections, Merits, Reparations and Costs), Decision from 15 June 2005, available on the Internet at <www.cidh.org> *and at* <www.corteidh.or.cr>.

Case of the Mayagna (Sumo) community of Awas Tingni v. Nicaragua, Decision from 31 August 2001, available on the Internet at <www.cidh.org> *and at* <www.corteidh.or.cr>.

Case of Plan de Sanchez v.Guatemala, Decision from 29 April 2004, available on the Internet at <www.cidh.org> *and at* <www.corteidh.or.cr>.

Case of Sawhoyamaxa Indigenous community v. Paraguay (Merits, Reparations and Costs) Decision from 29 March, 2006. available on the Internet at <www.cidh.org> *and at* <www.corteidh.or.cr>

Separate Opinion of Judge Antonio Augusto Cancado Trindade for Moiwana village v.Suriname, (Preliminary Objections, Merits, Reparations and Costs) Decision from 15 June 2005, available on the Internet at <www.corteidh.or.cr>

Correspondence concerning this article should be addressed to yamamoto@ias.unu.edu

Perspectives on Human Security and the on the National Victimisation Survey in Venezuela

By

Laura M. Bastidas and Yasmely Parra

I. Introduction

Two basic freedoms are the pillars on which Human Security rests: The "freedom from want " and the "freedom from fear". Human Security is related to the Prevention of the Crime closely, inasmuch as both topics are of public interest in all territorial and social political ambits.

In the case of Venezuela, there are special problems due to tensions at the border between Colombia and Venezuela. Venezuela has many disadvantaged living areas like slums. This is connected with the fact that there are many refugees from Colombia, who lack the minimum guarantees of human security. There no recognition of the existing rights for the refugees. That creates groups that are marginalized, devoid of security, and with the feeling of neglect. They do not feel that they are respected as human beings.

In the center of the following text stands the concept of Human Security. We first look at the historical development of the concept. Then we describe some general and special aspects of the concept. We will then discuss the relationship of Human Security to the United Nations Development Program. Finally we will summarize the results of the Venezuela National Victimization Survey 2009 who sheds a specific light on Human Security in Venezuela.

II. Human Security - the Evolution of the Concept

Traditionally the concept of security has been related to the absence of crimes, wars and physical violence. Since the seventeenth century the concept of security has been linked to the state. In the twentieth century, after the consolidation of the modern Western states, that did not change. The commonly used approach is focused on the state, not on the person. This has built the welfare state with its main emphasis on social security. It entails the concept of national security as well.

Social security often awakes political worries: the notion of social security in the modern State is seen to have sought to substitute the traditional common family networks of the capitalist economic system. Family networks protected the people in case of problems in the area of health, work, or aging which in turn leads to the welfare state. The social weaving changes by processes of urbanization, by the effects of the industrial revolutions, the changes of modes of production, the labor market. Many countries adopt this model with different variations in politics and programs. Generally speaking, the welfare state – characterized by formally equal rights for all and full employment – is held responsible for providing security in face of certain risks and contingencies that can be presented in the cycle of labor life: unemployment, illness, joblessness and old age. Nevertheless, from the seventies begins a crisis of the welfare state by the economical insecurity – the goal of a universal cover by of the social security system is less attainable.

The International Labor Organization (ILO 1991) defines social security as protection, provided by society to its members. The means applied are a series of public measures against economical and social deprivation. It means protection against a rapid decrease of income in cases of sickness, maternity, work accident or occupational disease, unemployment, invalidity, old age and death. It means as well protection in the form of medical assistance and aid to families with children.

In Venezuela, like in many other countries with similar Human Development Indicators, the major source of income for large parts of the population is informal work. People in this situation face a multitude of risks: They are not protected by a formal contract of employment. They do not have access to most social security benefits. Their fundamental labor rights such as equity in pay, holidays or bonuses, are not respected. Yet, though to a lesser extent, those with formalized working relationships face such risks as well. There are contracts that grant less protection - day work or casual or temporary work. In many cases these contracts are set up so that the employer can avoid to fully respect workers' rights.
The inability of the informal economy to cover all the needs, has led to difficulties in social security in its original form. It has led to to challenges to meet economic and social needs in situations of risk. To resolve these problems, it has been proposed that in addition to the creation of new jobs in a global area, we need to create policies for labor markets and alternative forms of social protection. Hence, the human security approach provides a useful vision not only to incorporate the concept of social security, but also provide strategies

for prevention and attention to new risks that the world-wide population faces.

A new chapter in the history of public security began in the Nineties, with the dismantling of the communist block and the end of the Cold War. In a less polarized world, other threats surface, no longer the adverse ideological and military powers. Now the risks of drug trafficking and the organized crime are emphasized. They are seen now as threats for the social stability. What begun as problem to public security as manifestations of the concept of national security, that now becomes a problem to the inner security of states. The governments start to employ strategies similar to those used to protect national security, but now focused on the criminal policy at national level to prevent and to combat crime.

Similarly, new aspects of the concept of Human Security appear: Our contemporary world has to cope with genocide, civil wars, natural disasters, disasters caused by climate change, epidemics and pandemics such as HIV / AIDS. They all have a severe impact on employment stability and social benefits. Discrimination to minority groups continues. There is a general lack of social security policies. There is the poverty of millions of people throughout the world. This all leads to a more comprehensive reflection of the various risks shared by the countries of the world, regardless of their economic or ideological positions. To accommodate these new global challenges, the concept of Human Security emerged.

It was common to refer to security problems in terms of the North - South conflict, i.e., between developed and underdeveloped, or in terms of an East - West conflict. These notions already indicate a design based on different stages of development. The Brandt Report 1980 approach was on regions rather than on nation states. From this perspective originated the concept of economic security.

The Brandt Report 1980 deals with the concept of economic security. It observes that the South were most threatened by underdevelopment and by armed conflicts. The report demanded that the concept of security must be expanded beyond the purely military aspect. According to this report, peace cannot prevail under conditions of hunger. It is morally no difference if a human dies because of the war or because of starvation. The Brandt Report seeks development policies with a comprehensive approach that includes trade, financial and monetary policies, as well as the areas of energy, ecology, population growth and the problem of refugees, among others.

Subsequently, the Brundtland Commission (1987) introduced the concept of environmental security. This report also elaborated on the concept of sustainable development. This concept of "Sustainable Development" emerged in the "Conference on the Human Environment" (UN 1972). Like the concept of Human Security, it was growing and expanding its scope. Thus, in 1980 with the rise of the International Union for the Conservation of Nature (IUCN), it acquired international recognition. The concept of environmental security and economic development are closely related. This is why the Brundtland Report in its comprehensive and multidisciplinary vision not only influences, but even determines a new concept of Human Security, thus establishing the close relationship between development and security.
The broad nature of the security was taken up by the Organization of the North Atlantic Treaty (NATO). The NATO was originally a purely military security treaty. But consequently it included in its concept of security an emphasis on political, economic and environmental security.
We turn now to the relationship of Human Security and the quality of life.

III. Human Security and Quality of Life

The concept of Human Security is introduced to the world in the mid-nineties, as the leading paradigm to explain the international security system after the Cold War. Intense theoretical and practical discussions about the traditional concepts of military security and national security inspired the actions of countries throughout much of the nineteenth and twentieth centuries. From academia, international organizations and even some States such as Canada and Japan, the concept of human security was used to better capture the new security challenges. There was a change of emphasis to the perspective of individuals or citizens, with less emphasis on state security.

The main purpose is clearly protection of individuals. In this regard, the term "Broad" Human Security, first outlined in the Human Development Report 1994 of the United Nations Program for Development argues that human security rests on two pillars: the freedom from need and freedom from fear (UNDP 1994).

The concept "Broad Human Security" advocates a comprehensive concept of Human Security. It includes food security, adequate shelter, security from poverty, and sometimes security from "threats to human dignity." Its supporters argue: hunger, disease and natural disasters kill more people than war, genocide and terrorism together. Often, these threats are interrelated. Therefore they advocate a comprehensive approach.

In contrast to this, the concept "Limited Human Security focuses on freedom from violence. This includes both, criminal violence as well as political violence, since it is not always easy to distinguish between them. Is there any practical difference between a gang of criminals cultivating drugs and use weapons to protect their crop, and a group of insurgents who grow drugs to finance their rebellion? Where is the difference between an off-duty soldier who sexually assaulted someone and a campaign of military mass rape as a strategy employed in war? There is no difference between criminal violence and political violence.

Both approaches to Human Security - limited or broad - are people-centered. They are complementary rather than contradictory. Nevertheless, since "comprehensive" includes everything from poverty to genocide, it is held to be too general, to be not concrete enough to be useful for policy development.

III.1. Human Security and Quality of Life : Water, Housing and Utilities

When discussing the quality of life, the right to an adequate standard of living serves as general right containing other specific and concrete rights. Thus, the right to an adequate standard of living includes the right to water and housing. The Report studies them each as autonomous in its own relevance and its regulation. It also discussed the provision of public services as means for the realization of human rights. Moreover, adequate provision of public services has a clear link to the right of everyone to an adequate standard of living, which includes the right "to sustained improvement in living conditions", recognized by the International Covenant on Economic, Social and Cultural Rights - inadequate housing means a constant state of helplessness.
In the sector on housing, the report looks at housing shortage, lack of access to housing or limitations on access for people with lower income, the perception of housing as a means of speculation and not as a human right. It deals with limitations on legal loopholes, the irregularities in the possession or ownership of housing, poor quality residency, the lack of basic services related to housing, the location of the homes of people in informal settlements and with settlements in high-risk areas.

III. 2. Human Security and Quality of Life : Irregular settlements

It is difficult to maintain a balance between the right to housing and the right to a healthy environment. An issue of importance is the situation of families who are forced to resort to non-formal mechanisms for access to housing and forming the so-called "settlements" in different areas, including those considered as ecological conservation areas.

III.3. Human Security and Quality of Life: Utilities: the Path to the Realization of Rights:

The provision of public services is a prerequisite for full realization of rights, particularly economic, social, cultural and environmental human rights. The main deficit was found in inadequate service delivery and in a lack of proper planning that meets the differing needs of different social groups as women, youth, older persons and persons with disabilities, among others.

The provision of public services has to do directly with adequate budgetary allocation to address the magnitude of the needs of the people. Another deficit is often the lack of awareness among the authorities. They are not aware of their obligation to observe the principles of progressivity, not of reduction, in budgeting. They are not aware that they must design policies that have a direct positive impact on the human security of people living in and transiting through the city.

III.4. Human Security and Quality of Life : Using Public and Trade on the Road: Between Law and Chaos

There are not enough public spaces. The misuse of existing social fragmentation increases the already existing inequality in economic living conditions. The resulting conflict generates poverty and exclusion. For decades, informal trade in public places has grown rapidly, a consequence of the economic crisis and of unemployment. This has become an option to deal with labor needs of thousands of people who opt for this kind of activity as a means of survival.
We will now look at the consequences of the concept for the United Nations Development Program (UNDP)

IV. The UNDP and Human Security

The team that prepared this report used a holistic view in the research (UNDP 1994). It also paved the way for the Human Rights

Commission (Mexico City) that serves to defend Human Rights as well as the development of outreach programs and measures of public education in the fields of economic, social, cultural and environmental rights (CDHDF 2011).

UNDP (1994) provided a new basis for understanding and security, realizing that for most people the feeling of insecurity is a main concern in everyday life. The feeling of insecurity in relation towards armed conflicts is not so pervasive.

Since the publication of the Human Development Report of UNDP 1994 considerable efforts have been made to refine the concept. Through research and meetings of experts, the UN and interested parties sought to make human security a priority of the policy agenda, both nationally and regionally. A special concern were innovative activities in this field to meet the needs and concerns of the most vulnerable populations. This report first attempted to generate a comprehensive analysis on the topic and defines the concept of security on a new footing. For UNDP, two conditions guarantee human security: a) a population free of fear, and b) a population free of shortcomings. In this report, UNDP refers to human security as a change in the concept of security, stressing the emphasis on people and not the nation-state. Security implies "Freedom from Fear" and "Freedom from Want (see: Anan 2005). These concepts are not new to the United Nations. Since the San Francisco Conference where the UN Charter was decided, ideas of freedom from fear and freedom from unfulfilled basic needs are discussed. Anan's Report "In Larger Freedom" Towards Development, Security and Human Rights For All" was written after a process of deliberations with independent experts from academia, civil society activists and representatives of states about the course the UN and its member states should take. The report states:

> "78. The threats to peace and security in the twenty-first century include not just international war and conflict but civil violence, organized crime, terrorism and weapons of mass destruction. They also include poverty, deadly infectious disease and environmental degradation since these can have equally catastrophic consequences. All of these threats can cause death or lessen life chances on a large scale. All of them can undermine States as the basic unit of the international system " (Koofi Anan 2005 nr. 78).

Today, collective security depends on accepting this fact: In our globalized world, the threats we face are interconnected. A threat for one region is a threat for all. The rich are vulnerable to the same threats that affect the poor. The strong are vulnerable to the weak, and vice verse. A terrorist nuclear attack against the United States or Europe would have devastating effects for the whole world. The same is true of the emergence of a new virulent pandemic in a poor country without an effective health care system - left alone, it soon would endanger the whole world.

Given this interconnectedness of threats, we must reach a new security consensus. Basic principle must be that we are all entitled to live free from fear. Threats are not isolated - threats for one are threats for all. Once this is general understanding, we have no choice but to confront the whole range of threats.

In analyzing these ideas from the human rights approach, it can be argued that conditions exist to allow for greater exercise of freedom, equal opportunity and processes. There are greater possibilities for people to enjoy their fundamental rights in everyday life . As seen above, the definitions of human security have been based mainly on two aspects: a life free from fear and a life free from misery ("freedom from fear" and "freedom from want"). The concept of Human Security covers threat and risk caused by both: by violence and by poverty.

It is the national situation in Venezuela we will now turn to.

V. The Venezuela National Victimization Survey 2009

A unique aspect on human security of the people in Venezuela is made visible by the most recent victimization survey, the first in the state. It describes - through the answers of people to a survey how people perceive that the state provide for their security. As it turned out, Venezuelan's do not trust the state's ability to secure their safety.

The Encuesta Nacional de Victimización y Seguridad Ciudadana 2009 was begun in August 2009. A joint effort between the Consejo Nacional de Prevención y Seguridad Ciudadana and the Instituto Nacional de Estadística (INE), which was created out of the police reform in 2006. INE assumed responsibility for carrying out this survey to obtain information for the creation and tracking on security policies.(OAS 2011).

This survey is one of the most complete surveys made in the country, even if the present results cannot immediately be taken as a reference for making policy decisions in crime prevention. A random sample of 5 500 households participated in the survey.

The results can be summarized in ten points:

1 - Criminal victimization by conventional crimes against property, including theft and robbery constitute 67.8% of the occurrences of victimhood. These rates are well above official statistics.
2 - The murder victimization rate is higher than the rate derived from official records.
3 - The corruption of officials turned out to be high while in official statistics corruption ranks as minimal and insignificant.
4 - The Personal Injuries occurred at a rate of 5.2 per 100,000 inhabitants, three times the official rate.
5 - In the average, 30% of all crimes are reported to police.
6 - The main reasons for not reporting these victimizations are: distrust that police does not handle the report at all or incorrectly.
7 - Victims want to see the perpetrators punished so that the offender does not reoffend.
8 – Most victims of interpersonal violence are injured by juvenile offenders they know. This is the same in cases of fraud but not in other property victimizations.
9 - Almost one eighth of the offenders are members of the police or the National Guard, often in cases of corruption, illegal arrests and extortion..
10 - The victimization tends to occur mainly in the residential sites of victims. Afternoon and the first part of the night are the most dangerous times.

The victimization survey indicates a robbery victimization rate of 578 per 100,000 inhabitants, while the rate for theft is 1 735 per 100,000 inhabitants. Fraud rate is 387 per 100 000.

The victimization survey results in a homicide rate of 75 per 100 000 inhabitants. Personal injuries yields a rate of 272 per 100 000. Kidnapping shows a rate of 95 per 100 000, while sexual victimization result in a rate of 32 per 100 000 inhabitants.

2.7% of the all homicide victimization (614 out of 19 113 homicides) are attributed to members of the police force or the National Guard.

It is no surprise that most Venezuelan citizen do not believe in the power of the state to protect them from victimization.

As these victim survey shows, the conviction in the efficiency of the state is quite low. In states that bordered to other countries, 15% of the respondents believed that the state presence was strong or very strong. 75% believed that the state presence was weak or very weak. In states with no borders to neighboring countries the figures were very similar. About 80% believe that the state cannot guarantee the security of its citizen.

The lack of trust in the efficiency of state poses a special problem for the government of Venezuela and its criminal justice system. Victims do not feel protected by the state.

References:

ACNUR Agency of the United Nations for the Refugees in Venezuela, (2007), "Profile of the Colombian population, with necessity of protection ".

BIRKBECK, Christopher. (2004) Experticia and prevención of the crime: A comparative study of Canada and Venezuela. CC. vol.32, no, p.147-189. ISSN 0798-9598.

Bolivariana Republic of Venezuela (2000) National Constitution. Official newspaper N° 5,453, Presses National, Caracas, Venezuela.

Bolivariana Republic of Venezuela (2006) Law of the Communal Councils. Official newspaper N° 5,806, Editorial NJR, Caracas, Venezuela.

Bolivariana Republic of Venezuela (2008) Statutory law of the service of police and the body of National Police. Official newspaper N° 5.880

Electronic sources

Brandt Report (1980): The Brandt Report. In: http://www.stwr.org/special-features/the-brandt-report.html accessed June 15, 2011.

Brundtland Commission (1987), Our common future. Available in: HTTP www.oarsoaldea.net the Report Brandt (1980). Accessed June 15, 2011

CDHDF Comision de Derechos Humanos del Distrito Federal. In: http:// www.cdhdf.org mx/ accessed on June 15, 2011.

Commission of Aid for the Development of the OECD. Available in: http://www.nuso.org/upload/articulos/884_1.pdf accessed June 10, 2011.

Human Development Report 1994. Published for the United Nations Development Programme (UNDP) New York, Oxford (Oxford University Press) 1994. *hdr.undp.org/en/media/hdr_1994_en_contents.pdf accessed June 15, 2011.*

Human Security Report (2005), Oxford University Press and Human Security Brief (2006). Summary on Human Security. Available in: http:www.hdr.undp.org/es/indh/.../oxford/2006/lecturas accessed June 10, 2011. .

ILO (2001) "Social security: A new consensus. 2001. International Labour Office Geneva " available in http://www.ilo.org/public/english/protection/secsoc/downloads/353sp1.pdf accessed on June 15, 2011.

Instituto Nacional de Eestatistica Republica Bioliviarana de Venezuela. 2009. Encuesta Nacional de Victimizacion y Percepcion de Seguridad Ciudana 2009 (ENVPSC-2009) Documento Technico. Caracas. 2010. In : http://www.oas.org/dsp/PDFs/encuestavictimizacion2009.pdf accessed August 30, 2011.

Koofi Anan. In Larger Freedom 2005. Report of the Secretary-General In larger freedom: towards development, security and human rights for all -: Towards Development, Security And Human Rights. The Secretary General Statement to the General Assembly, New York, 21 March 2005. http://www.un.org/largerfreedom/sg-statement.html. accessed June 15, 2011.

Organization the International of Trabajo (OIT) (1991), "Administration of the social security". Available in: HTTP www.ilo.org.

OAS 2011. Alertamerica.org. The OAS observatory of citizen. Victimization Surveys in the Americas. http://www.oas.org/dsp/english/cpo_observatorio_enlaces_victimizacion.asp#VZ. Accessed on August 30, 2011.

Symposium on Human Rights and Human Security (2001). San Jose, Costa Rica. Available in: HTTP catarina.udlap.mx/u_dl_a/tales/documentos/.../bibliografia.pdf

UN 1972. Report of the United Nations Conference on the human environment. Stockholm1972. http://www.unep.org/Documents.Multilingual/Default.asp?documentid=97 accesssed January 3, 2012.

UNDP 1994. Report on the human development (1994), New dimensions of the human security. program of the United Nations United for the development. Human Development Reports 1990 - 2011. http://hdr.undp.org/en/reports/global/hdr1994/ accessed June 15, 2011.

Japan, Asia, Australia

The Road to Victim Rights Establishment in Japan

By

Hidemichi Morosawa

1. Introduction

In modern nations, human dignity is respected and people are ensured their rights. Victims are people whose rights have been abused. Victim recovery should be facilitated with the compliance of the victimizers and the state (Right to Recovery). In particular, to help victims to economically recover, the state should enhance its compensation (Right to Compensation) and its use of restitution orders (Right to Restitution). In addition, victims should be informed of their rights regarding recovery. They also have the right to know why, how and by whom they were victimized as well as the victimizers profile, how they were tried, treated, and rehabilitated (Right to Notification). Also, victims have the right to be involved and offer their opinion in court. The victim can attend the criminal trial, give testimony, and allege the defendant's guilt or innocence (the Right to Trial Attendance).

In Japan, the recognition of victim rights has been late compared to other industrialized modern nations because there has not been sufficient awareness of victim rights during the early years of victimology. It was only recently that the Japanese government developed a compensation system. Although Japan launched the Victim Benefit Law in 1981, this system was limited. It was a benefit system which did not give victims the right to compensation but paid ex gratia. The actual number of payments was about 230 cases a year. As a result of these circumstances, the matter was brought up at the State Victim Benefit System's 10th Memorial Symposium in 1991. The following year, victimologists organized a large victimization survey.

In response to this survey, the National Police Agency began to discuss victim procedures, which have subsequently have been agreed upon. In 1997, the Ministry of Justice and the Japan Bar Association considered further measures. From 2000 to 2001, four new victim assistance laws were instituted and five existing laws were amended.

The process has not always been stable and critics often attack these reforms. Japan continues to experience obstacles in its search for reform. Victimologists continue to strive for the improvement of conditions for victims.

As early as 1976, Morosawa presented the thesis entitled, 'Victims' Rights and Victimology', making the point to introduce the concept of 'victims' rights' for the first time in Japan (Morosawa 1976). As expected, this paper was met with strong resistance in the scientific society concerning criminal law and criminal policy. In the late 1970s, the necessity of having a compensation system for crime victims had begun to attract public attention in Japan. The argument over 'victims' rights' should have been made under such circumstances. However, even the specialists who contributed to the establishment of the Crime Victim Benefits Act were skeptical of the concept of 'victims' rights'. While the phrase 'victims' rights' began to gain attraction in the late 1990s, the government had not officially used it yet.

2. Establishment of National Association of Crime Victims and Surviving Families (NAVS)

On January 23, 2000 "NAVS - National Association of Crime Victims and Surviving Families" - Japanese name Asunokai - was founded in Japan. The chairperson of this association is Mr. Isao Okamura, a lawyer, and a one-time vice-chairman of the Japan Federation of the Bar Association. Until the time of his wife's murder at the entrance of their house, he did not know that the position of victims in the criminal justice system was inadequate. Japanese criminal justice had, until that point, left victims out in the cold. That is to say, victims were outsiders of criminal justice system.

The movement of victim assistance in Japan began by presenting the problem to scholars in the 1990s, initiating victim assistance with the police, and then starting an amendment of laws with the Ministry of Justice and the Japan Federation of the Bar Association. However, in these movements victims and surviving families have continuously been placed in a position outside of the main issue with few exceptions.

One incident that demonstrates how much disregard there is for victims happened in 2008. The Tokyo Metropolitan Police Department held a symposium for victim assistance and invited the Governor of Tokyo. The co-sponsors were the victim support groups in Tokyo, specialists, and concerned police. Although this plan got wide coverage by the media, the victims and the surviving families who wanted to join the symposium that day were rejected. The reason given was that they were not invited. Only a few surviving families who had already been selected to speak at the symposium were allowed to join the symposium.

Indeed, there have been meeting within the Criminal Justice community about the development of victim support, and indeed, victim support measures were developed. This movement has a kind of paternalistic approach. It justifies a separation of victims and criminal procedure. The motto seems to be:"I support you and you are supported" - and that is it. Such attitude positions the victims as poor objects only to be supported but not as a group that has rights. It does not emphasize that these rights must be recognized by government and society, let alone that recovered victims would support other victims after they have gotten over their own hardships. Victims were constructed as people only to be sympathized, not as people with an own agency. Victims with own agency might become aware of their own rights and might demand changes from the government! This approach may result in an attempt to control victim activities (compare Kirchhoff and Morosawa 2008). This author has cautioned against this tendency but no one in the country agreed with his approach. Even some victim specialists supported the "government oriented" paternalistic approach.

A number of victims had concerns against the police symposium held in Tokyo. Consequently, they decided to establish the 'Organization of victims, by victims, for victims". They organized their preparatory committee in November 1999. Although they were sure that there must be many victims who held the same opinion, they chose a room fit for 150 people as the place for the inaugural general meeting because they thought that only a few people would actually come. To their great surprise and pleasure; however, many more people than expected came in from all over the nation and filled the symposium with an excited atmosphere starting in the early morning. More than 50 TV cameras and journalists of many newspapers and magazines came with great interest. The preparatory committee allowed the media in on the condition that only one TV camera would be used from each TV station. Also, the media was not allowed to film in the building where the meeting was held because they were strongly concerned about the victim's privacy.

The symposium began at 10:00 am and was broadcasted on the main national network "NHK's news" at noon. In the afternoon, many victims who watched the news came to the symposium. The room and the passageways were packed with participants and this sometimes caused a lack of oxygen. Even though some people were in uncomfortable conditions, the participants discussed their plight eagerly, caring for each other especially for the old and for the sick. At the symposium, opinions were voiced such as 'The current Japanese victim support program is not appropriate', and 'Let the government realize that the law needs to be amended'. Taking this opportunity, the media simultaneously carried out a campaign bringing to the public the idea of victim support. These special programs were often on aired on TV and there were sequential special features in magazines about victim support.

Prejudice towards victims exists in all societies, but it seems that such prejudice is notably stronger in Japan (see Morosawa 2001 p.372-378). For 20 years this author explained such prejudice, resulting in reactions such as 'It is because they have done something bad ...' or 'It could not have happened unless they did something wrong'. The participants at the symposium reconfirmed this hypothesis. Although the media documented the victims' miserable state, there were few people who could complain their hardships to friends and families. A meeting of victims was a rare event - and the participants seemed to use this rare opportunity to blow off steam after years of suffering.

3. Victim Benefits and Out-of-Court Settlements in Japan

The victim support programs in Japan are approximately 20 years behind most Western countries. While many Western countries have formed 'compensation systems for victims' in the Sixties and Seventies of last century, Japan enacted the "Crime Victim Benefit Act" in 1980, starting from January 1st, 1981 on. However, it was not an actual "victim compensation program". It was more a "money gift program" - it was repeatedly explained in parliament that this money gift was meant as a token of sympathy for victims. In the past 18 years, the government annually had supplied benefits to 216 surviving families in the average. Annually 3.6 victims of serious injury received this benefit. That corresponds to an average sum of 2,990,000 yen for each surviving family. It means too that in cases of serious injury, victims received in the average 5,340,000 yen (Morosawa 2001 p. 515).

Restitution, rarely ordered and if, then only in serious cases, have scarcely been paid in Japan. According to the investigation on surviving families - conducted by the Japanese Association of Victimology - in all of Japan, only about 16% of the surviving families have been able to reach an out-of-court settlement about restitution.

Most offenders did not - and could not - pay at all. The Ministry of Justice, influenced by these investigations, made an analysis of the use of out - of - court settlements in cases of victimizers sentenced to life imprisonment with labor in 1996. Such settlements were achieved in 27% of the murder cases and in 18% of the of the cases of manslaughter in connection with burglary. The Research and Training Institute of the Ministry of Justice (Houmu Sougou Kenkyujo) in 1999 focused on the offenders convicted at the district courts in all over Japan from 1997 to 1998. 18% of the surviving families achieved out-of-court settlements. The study of Morosawa (2001) on out-of-court settlements and their fulfillment in cases of murder revealed: in these cases, only one surviving family out of seven received any money. Six families received no money at all. The full amount was paid only in one case out of 20, that is in 5% of all cases. In most cases, nothing was paid. If surviving families received money from the offenders through out-of-court settlements in addition to state benefits, they had to pay back the money received from the state.

In the last thirty years, Morosawa interviewed more than 500 bereaved families. Never the settlement payment was paid in a lump sum. If money was paid at all, then in installments.

Till now the paper dealt with state benefits and with out of court- settlements. The situations of both legal institutions are not satisfactory. The paper turns to further systems in the next paragraph.

4. The Influence of the National Association of Crime Victims and Surviving Families (Asunokai) on the Coming Legislation

Before the activities of the National Association of Crime Victims and Surviving Families (Asunokai) are described, two concepts have to be separated which are often discussed synchronously without observing the proper difference between the two. The first concept is the concept of "Victim Participation". The other concept is the concept of "Lay Judge Participation in Criminal Justice", or less precise the short name "Lay Judge System". Victim Participation means that crime victims actually have an active role in the criminal proceedings, they "participate". The Lay Judge System means that the court in criminal trials is a mix between professional judges and lay people. Both systems do not have a common victimological background - the "Victim Participation" is an old standing demand of victimologists. The Lay Judge System has no special victimological background.

In Japan, the Victim Participation System in the criminal proceedings was put into effect in December 2008 and the Lay Judge System in May 2009. It has been about two and half years since the enforcement of the victim participation system and about two years since the lay judge system. Because Japanese are a very conservative nation and dislike change, both systems are considered completely progressive, signifying a transformation in the standards of the Japanese criminal justice system. Many Japanese believe that criminal law must not be changed so easily. However, my point of view is to consider what was realized and what it brought.

Although the number of serious and lethal violent crimes went up by the end of the twentieth century, the Japanese government did not want to change the justice response. To advocate changes in the justice system, seems to imply that various opinions stated against the previous justice systems were justified.

The government was eventually pushed to organize a Council for Reform of the Justice System in July 1999. Discussions within this gremium dragged on for two years. The main issues were the duration of court processes (they seemed to take too long time), the participation of the public in criminal cases (there was no lay judge participation in trials) and the reform of the law education (too old traditional) The reform of criminal justice for victims was not one of their discussion points.

In response, the National Association of Crime Victims and Surviving Families (NAVS), established in January 2000, began appealing to the public, the government, and the political parties. They advocated the need for victims to participate in criminal proceedings. They also advocated a restitution system and demanded support services for crime victims.

In May 2000, two pieces of legislation proposed by the Justice Ministry, referred to as so called "Two Laws for the Protection of Crime Victims" were enacted. These laws instituted measures allowing in a limited way crime victims to have access to copies of trial records and to have priority access to the courtroom galleries in addition to the option of being accompanied by a person of their trust and/or being shielded from view when appearing as a witness.

However, these new positions were "limited": the wording of these laws was like 'the court may allow victims, etc". These laws established privileges depending on the decision of the judges - rather than granting rights. This was not what NAVS had been advocating. It was the first step into the right direction. This system permitted victims to state their opinions but in just one area: they were allowed to state the emotional impact of the victimization.

In December 2002, the NAVS held its 4rth conference titled "Toward Victim Participation in Criminal Proceedings.". The association had sent a major fact finding mission to Europe. The symposium was based on the results of this commission. At the closing session, the members of ASUNOKAI decided to begin a nationwide petition campaign calling on the Prime Minister to improve the existing laws by instituting the privileges as rights.
They began collecting signatures on the spot.
By June 2004, they had gathered about 560,000 signatures. The petition campaign not only made the Japanese public aware of crime victims' reality and where the problems lay, it also created a strong bond of solidarity among the victims and their supporters themselves.

This public activity resulted finally in the "Basic Act for Crime Victims".

5. Contents of the Basic Act on Crime Victims

The Basic Act on Crime Victims is one of the world's finest pieces of legislation for victims. It is brief. It consists of only 30 articles. But these articles are very important.

First, its Preamble recognizes that crime victims' rights have not been respected and that victims have been isolated in society. It declares that we should listen to crime victims and make a step forward to realize a society where victims' rights and interests are well protected. Article 3, paragraph 1 stipulates that "All crime victims shall have their rights and individual dignity respected as well as be assured of appropriate treatment of their individual dignity." Thus, for the first time, victims are endowed with their own rights.

The Basic Act goes on to say, in Article 3, paragraph 3, "The measures for crime victims shall be taken so that crime victims may receive necessary support continuously from the time they receive harm until they return to leading a peaceful life again." Article 8 requires the government to establish a "Basic Plan for Crime Victims", to promote measures for crime victims and to seek a Cabinet decision thereon. The Basic Plan is to be drafted by a panel, the "Council for the Promotion of Policies for Crime Victims" established in the Cabinet Office (Article 24) and chaired by the Chief Cabinet Secretary. This shows the political importance the government attributed to this problem.

6. Formulation of the Basic Plan for Crime Victims

In 2005, the Cabinet Office formed a panel to draft this Basic Plan. The panel met 11 times between April 28 and November 21. This author was member of the panel. We faced a massive task, as 1,066 requests from victims and support groups had been compiled into 258 items for consideration. The Basic Plan was to contain 13 basic measures, including "developing a system to expand opportunities for victims to participate in criminal procedures" (Article 18) and "organic linkage between the claims for damages and criminal procedures concerning the harm" (Article 12). At last, trial participation and parallel civil actions were within striking distance.

The fact that trial participation and parallel civil actions were being discussed, caused the Japan Federation of Bar Associations (JFBA) to go into crisis mode. Not only did their executive body pass a resolution opposing these systems, but they launched a full-scale opposition campaign; for example, each local bar association was made to vote against the measures. JFBA was represented on the Council for the Promotion of Policies for Crime Victims, but, far from promoting the policies, their members firmly opposed them.

In the end, the panel failed to reach a consensus. The Ministry of Justice called for further study aiming to reach conclusions and implement them within two years regarding parallel civil actions and trial participation. Nevertheless, our primary aim was achieved, because the draft of the Basic Plan included the statements "Criminal justice exists not only for the public but also for the victims," and "This holds equally true in cases where protective measures are applied to juvenile offenders." The Cabinet approved the Basic Plan (with the exception of matters requiring further study) on December 27, 2005.

In October 2005, NAVS had issued the Draft Outline of a Parallel Civil Action System. This later served as a basis for discussion in the Justice Ministry's Legislative Council.
In December 2007, a new law went into effect allowing victims of crimes and their families to participate in criminal proceedings. Previously, victims were virtually shut out of criminal courts unless they were called on to provide testimony. It is this system of victim participation in criminal procedures we turn to next.

7. Victim Participation in Criminal Procedures

In Japan, criminal trials have a two-sided adversarial structure: the public prosecutor versus the defendant and his or her counsel. The victim used to be completely excluded from criminal proceedings. The Supreme Court concurred in this casting aside of the victim when it ruled on February 20, 1999, that "Criminal investigation and the institution of prosecution exist to serve the maintenance of public order, not to serve the victims of crime"

Victims had no rights. They were merely summoned unilaterally when needed for the purposes of the investigation and trial. They were not told the trial date, not informed of the indictment, not of the main points of the prosecutor's closing arguments, not of the verdict. They had no access to the trial records. Offenders could lie and defame the victims in court but the victims were unable to respond. They had to suffer in silence in the public gallery. The victims' cooperation was all taken for granted in the investigation and trial. Victims were used and discarded. There was no consideration for their feelings, of their desire to know the truth about what happened, to know what sort of person the offender was, to protect the honor of the deceased, or to refute the defendant's statements. They also could not ask questions, nor could the survivors' speak on behalf of a deceased victim who had been deprived of stating its own position. In addition they were not given the chance to urge the court to impose an certain punishment. In short, Japan's criminal justice system told victims to keep quiet.

Consistent with this is: In the Japanese Constitution, ten articles provide for the human rights of offenders while those of victims are never mentioned. The emphasis has been entirely on the human rights of offenders, while those of victims have been ignored. The new legislation gave victims of certain crimes the right to participate in criminal trials, be present in court, question the defendant, question witnesses to challenge the credibility of statements relating to mitigating circumstances, and state opinions about matters of fact or law following the prosecutor's summation and sentencing recommendation. The new legislation introduced the "Victim Participation in Criminal Proceedings". § 316.33 to § 316.39 of the Code of Criminal Procedure proscribe: When victims demand permission to appear in court as Victim Participants and when the court permits it, the victims can have a seat next to the public prosecutor and attend the trial as Victim Participant. This is possible in cases of homicide, rape, kidnapping and negligent homicide,

And the new law introduced the system of parallel civil claims: A victim of a serious offense committed with criminal intent may, before the conclusion of oral proceedings in the criminal case, file with the court a claim for damages against the accused as part of the criminal process (restitution order). If the court finds the accused guilty it will immediately begin hearings with the aim to issue a restitution order, an order that is able to be swiftly executed. The revenue stamp to be affixed to the claim costs only 2,000 yen; thus, there is a much smaller financial burden on the victim.

These systems both came into effect on December 1, 2008. They are very well regarded and widely utilized. In addition, the participation of victims in the oral proceedings has completely changed the atmosphere in courtrooms. Now that judges, prosecutors, and counsel are all aware of the victim's existence. Their attitude has become attentive. Under the Victim Participation Law, victims may sit next to prosecutor during trials, talk to the judge and even question the defendants themselves. People can use the victim participation system in criminal cases resulting in death such as homicide, burglary, rape, forcible indecency, dangerous driving, abandonment, illegal detention, injury and so on.

Even at the Council of Legislation, the law is a controversial topic for discussion. The critics claim that allowing victims to make statements during proceedings will prejudice judges and undermine the fundamental principle of criminal trial, which assumes the defendant is innocent until proven guilty. Its proponents say that victims and their families should be given the right to face suspects in court and confront them with the results of their alleged crimes.

Under the Victim Participation System, victims are able to, with regard to the facts and application of the law, examine witnesses to test the probative value of their testimony, question the defendant when necessary and state their opinions. According to the Criminal Statistic of Japan for 2009, 560 victims participated in the criminal district courts that year, 344 victims questioned the defendant, and 288 victims demanded a desired length of the imprisonment and explained the reason.

8. The Lay Judge System in Japan

Although the Lay Judge System Law was enacted by the Diet on May 2004, the launch was delayed until May 2009. Soon after the Council for Reform of Justice System began discussions, the Justice Ministry held that the Victim Participation System should be established first and then the Lay Judge System. Therefore the Lay Judge System had to wait for about five years before it was launched. Under the new system, six randomly selected citizens will work as lay judges alongside three professional judges to deliver joint verdicts in trials involving serious crimes (homicide, acts of arson at houses where people are staying, counterfeiting money, narcotic related crimes, illegal holding of guns and swords in addition to cases of burglary, rape, forcible indecency, dangerous driving, abandonment, illegal detention, injuries resulting in death).

Based on the 2002 figures, the government estimates that around 25,000 people per year will be appointed as lay judges, including those who will be appointed as reserves. This means that one out of every 67 people will take part in trial proceedings as a lay judge once in their lifetime. People who refuse to serve without a valid reason may be fined of up to 100,000 yen. It should be self understood that victims do not qualify to be lay judges in their own cases since this would be irreconcilable with the idea of justice.

The system of Lay Judge Participation in Criminal Proceedings does not specially serve the interest of the victims. If at all, it is a system that serves the interest of all Japanese to improve the criminal justice system in the country - there are no special direct victim interest served. There might be an indirect "service" to victims: One might speculate that in the long run, since so many lay judges will be involved, many more Japanese citizens will be confronted with the suffering of victims, and that might change the societal climate in favor of victims.

9. Victim Protection Provisions in Japan

About ten years ago, Japanese Government shifted away from anti-victim policies toward pro-victim policies. But in the early stage, it was not enough for victims. Although the Government enacted finally the Victim Protection Law (see above), which demands from judges to consider witnesses and especially victims in the criminal procedure, it does not give rights to victims.
The following special provisions for victims have been installed since 2001.

1) Victim Impact Statement
   §292 - subsection 2 Code of Criminal Procedure: "The court shall give the opportunity to state their feelings or other opinions on the date of the trial if they have applied to express their feeling about damages and opinions on the case."
2) Victim Impact Statement by Documents
   §292 sub-section 7 Code of Criminal Procedure: "If an oral statement is not appropriate, the opinion can be given in writing.
3) Screen for Victims in the Court
   This allows the placement of a screen between defendant and witness - § 157 sub-section 4 Code of Criminal Procedure)

4) Video-links for Witnesses
   This enables victims/witnesses to testify in a room separate from the courtroom by establishing a TV link to the courtroom (see Morosawa 2004 p.72, § 157 sub-section 4 Code of Criminal Procedure).
5) Escort System for Witnesses
   Trusted persons (victim attendants: relatives, victim supporters) can escort the victim in the court room . In praxi, family members and victim supporters are admitted at police level as well.
6) Reconciliation Records for Victims
   If there is a reconciliary settlement agreement between victim and defendant, such agreement can be recorded in the official court records of the trial. (Victim Protection Law 2000 Art.13 till Art.16.) Such record permits immediate compulsory execution of the settlement (Kensatsu 2012).
7) Copying of Public Trial Records
   Once the request for allowing inspection and photocopying of records of the trial has been granted, e.g. for preparing a claim of restitution or an insurance claim), the victim or their bereaved family is allowed to inspect and/or photocopy trial records (Victim Protection Law 2000 Art.3, Kansetsu 2012 p.26).
8) System to Protect Victims' Privacy (2008)
   § 299 sub - section 3 Code of Criminal Procedure: particular care to be taken so that the address, work place and ordinary whereabouts of victims are not disclosed to those concerned (including the accused).
9) Restitution Order (2009)
   Victim Protection Act Art. 17 till 22. Restitution orders are explained in the previous text of the article.

According to 2011's White Paper, the applications of these systems are listed in Table1.

Table 1: Number of Victims using 9 types Victim Protection Systems (2006-2010)

Year	2006	2007	2008	2009	2010
1) Victim impact statement(VIS)	917	1,010	1,068	1,119	1,198
2) VIS with documents	253	270	339	490	557
3) Screen against defendant	1,233	1,222	1,007	1,094	1,295
4) Video-links for witnesses	234	224	202	235	261
5) Escort for witnesses	77	70	86	79	102
6) Reconciliation Records	73	38	35	46	34
7) Copying of Public Trial Records	903	846	1,012	1,348	1,175
8) Protection of victim's privacy	-	-	2,490	3,849	3,854
9) Restitution Order	-	-	-	162	238

Over 10 years has passed since the establishment of these systems. In particular, systems number 1, 3 and 7 have become widely put into practical use. In three years, the protection system of victim's privacy such as the use of their name, address and information which can be identified or concealed in court was used by more than ten thousand victims.

Table 2: The Numbers of Victims Using Victim Participation Methods (2009 & 2010)

Year	2009	2010
Number of victims participating in criminal court	560(22*)	839(232*)
Number of victims examining the witness in criminal court	130	217
Number of victims questioning the defendant	344	484
Number of victims demanding the length of punishment	288	115
Number of victims using a screen	50	40
Number of victims escorted to the court	24	557
Number of victims hiring lawyers	367	272

**The number victims participating under the lay judge court system.*

Crimes with the largest rate of victim participation are:
1) Negligent driving resulting in injury or death
2) Rape and forcible indecency,
3) Murder,
4) Injury,
5) Burglary

The number of cases with potential victim participation in the trial is about 15,000 cases. Hence, about 5.6% of victims participated in criminal court during 2010.

10. The Evaluation of Victim and Lay Judge Systems

Various kinds of problems in the systems are worth pointing out. First, the objects of many crimes in the two systems are overlapping one another because the government thought both systems should pass judgment on serious crimes. A central concern about the victim-participation system is that it will unduly influence these new lay judges, who may pass out harsher sentence because they are perceived as being more emotional than tested.

Evidence shows that this may not be the case. About 50 mock tribunals have been conducted throughout Japan to test both the lay judge courts and victim-participation systems. The example case is usually vehicular manslaughter and the victim always asks for the maximum 20-year sentence. In every case, however, the mock tribunals - simulating the lay judge courts - have handed down sentences which were clearly below the demand of the victims - four to eight year sentences.

Presently, there are no research studies concerning the victim participation system, especially no research of the victims who actually have participated in this system. Although two years have passed since its enactment, we sometimes hear the voices of participating victims. Currently, this author is conducting a large scale research to evaluate the situation from a victimological point of view.

References:

The author has quoted in the text only references in English language except his contribution of 1976. That decision was made not to burden the text with Japanese quotations which for most readers are not understandable. Where references to Japanese resources are missing, the reader is asked to turn to the author for further information.

Basic Act on Crime Victims (Act No.161 of 2004). English translation of the original Japanese texts as published in the Official Gazette.

Kensatsu 2012= Public Prosecutors Office: For the Victims of Crime. About Protection and Support Systems for Victims. http://www.kensatsu.go.jp accessed January 24, 2012.

Kirchhoff, G.F. and Morosawa, H.: The Study of Victimology. Basic considerations for the study of theoretical victimology. In: Winkel, F.W., Friday, P.C. , Kirchhoff, G.F. and Letschert, R. (eds.): Victimization in a multi-disciplinary key: Recent advances in victimology. Nijmegen (Wolf Legal Publishers) 2009 p.271 - 312.

Morosawa, H. (1976) The Rights of Victims and Victimology—The New Trial of Victimology. (In Japanese language) Study of Law, Vol.49, No. 1, 1976, pp.205-225.

Morosawa, H. (2001) Victimology - An Interdisciplinary Study of Victims and Victimization (in Japanese language). Tokyo (Seibundo) 2001, Third Edition), p.515.

2011 White Paper (Hanzai Hakusho) of Japan, Department of Justice (Homusho), Dec. 2011, p.183.

The Changes of Korean Victim Policy in the Last Decade

By

Kim,Jae Min

1. Introduction

The victim issues had not been handled seriously until the middle of 1980's in Korea. Even in these days, some arguments have been made whether crime victim is the real subject on the criminal process or not. Victims have often been treated as the forgotten party in the criminal justice system, a party outside the criminal justice proceedings (Wallace & Roberson, 2011, p. 216). Today there is widespread consensus: victims should be considered as 'the significant subjects' who are to be assured of their legal rights. This indicates a substantial change: The traditional criminal justice system has mainly focused on securing the defendants' rights.

This change means: criminal justice authorities have been unavoidably confronted with a new environment of criminal justice system. This has been affected the Korean criminal justice system for the last decade as well. All the criminal justice authorities try to consider victim as the meaningful subject of the criminal process. It seems to be a good opportunity to solve the chronic victim alienation issue. Korean victim policy has been greatly improved for several years. This paper is to touch upon this changing facet of Korean victim policy for the recent 10 years and tries a first look at the results.

2. Overview about Korean criminal procedure

The Republic of Korea (afterwards, we call it as 'Korea'), an important Asian country with close relationship with United States and Japan, is a constitutional Republic. It covers all the southern area of latitude 38 of Korean peninsula. Korea was emancipated from Japanese colonialism in 1945, and put under the military administration of U.S.A by the time of establishing the independent government in 1948. After that, the Korean peninsula was divided in two parts due to Korean War in 1950. It is an area that has been politically separated from the communist Northern part of the country since the armistice agreement in 1953 (Chulsu Kim, 2004. p. 118). Korea is governing all the southern area of the demilitarized zone located latitude 38. According to the constitution, however, Korean sovereignty reaches to the North Korea (Article 3 Korean Constitution; Chulsu Kim, 2004. p. 118).

Korean old criminal procedure law of 1912 ("Choseon Hyungsalyung", the Code of the Choseon Dynasty) was influenced by Japan which itself was affected by continental legal system such as Germany (Jongdae Bae & Lee, Sangdon , 2004, p. 6). During the US military administration the anglo-american exercised its influence. But mainly it was the German law that had a great effect on Korean modern criminal procedure law through the Japanese legal literature (Choi Jonggo 2001. p. 261) Establishing a new criminal procedure law in 1954, Korea adopted the European continental system in that a public prosecutor had initiative in the criminal investigation. This institution led the investigation phase. Police worked as assistant of the prosecutor. They worked under his supervision. Only the prosecutor can decide on "accusation or dismissal", not the police. A court judge may sentence the defendant to a fine, to imprisonment and other punishment.

As in other countries, so in Korea, the traditional justice system has mainly focused on offenders, on their crime, on their rights. The victim was treated as a piece of evidence in the functional system of vertical justice (regarding offender orientation in criminal justice, see Kirchhoff 2005. p. 45). In the last decade, however, many innovations have taken place or been on the way that is to promote the position of the victim. In Korean Criminal Justice, the victim is no longer "the forgotten person". The new legislation and rules use the term "victim" rather often. The term "victim care" is used to denominate all efforts that are made to change the role of the victim "from a forgotten person" to "a respected significant subject" in the criminal proceedings.

3. The changes of Korean victim policy in the last decades

Most victim related innovations find their origin in the 1985 UN Declaration on Basic Principles of Justice for Victims of Crime and Abuse of Power (Dussich & Mundy 2008. pp. 184-187). The Korean case is a good example. The UN instrument serves basically a "shopping list" from which the member states can take what they find most adequate for their countries. The UN Declaration deals with access to justice and fair treatment, restitution, compensation and assistance. We shall look into the Korean victim policies with corresponding to the UN Declaration lists, just focusing on "Victims of Crime."

3.1 Treatment of the victim with respect of his dignity

Korean Constitution has prescribed the respect for human dignity from 1962 such as "All citizens shall be assured of their human worth and dignity and shall have the right to pursue happiness. It shall be the duty of the State to confirm and guarantee the fundamental and inviolable human rights of individuals (Article 10, Constitution of the Republic of Korea)." Needless to say, victim belongs to the citizens addressed in article 10. Consequently, according to "Beomjoe Piheja Bohobeop" (BPB 2005 article 2), victims have the right to be respected in their human dignity. The Korean government follows obviously the UN 1985 Declaration.

3.2 Judicial and administrative mechanisms

Judicial and administrative mechanisms are closely related to the field of victim assistance. This field is to be taken care of not only by the official sector, i.e. by government agency such as police, public prosecutor and court, but also by the civil organization or private sector. In this part of the paper, the judicial and administrative mechanisms are described as official type of the victim assistance, setting the private type aside to be dealt with in the second part.

3.2.1 Police

The Korean Police Agency (KPA) - a national police organization under the Ministry of Public Administration and Security - plays a very important role in the reform of victims' position in the criminal justice system. Its police force has a manpower of about 131 thousand people with about 99,500 police officers and other police personnel (mainly obligatory combat police) of about 32,000 (Korean National Police University 2010. p. 170). The KPA launched a small organization called "Pihaeja Daechekgye" under the Criminal Investigation Bureau. That is an office that specializes on protecting the victims of crime in KPA. Such a special office has an advantage: By creating this unit, the victim policy could be implemented more intensively and consistently then before. However, it had a disadvantage as well: Human rights issues have already been handled by the various departments, e.g. in the Office of Inspection, in the Criminal Investigation Bureau and in the Crime Prevention Bureau of KPA. Consequently, it has resulted in discordance and inconsistency in the course of vindicating the victim's rights. That led to the foundation of the Human Rights Center which belongs to the Criminal Investigation Bureau. It was to supplement the confused and weakened police activity for victim's human rights. This can be seen as a great step forward for victim protection (KPA 2005. p. 13-14).

A special feature of the KPA victim assistance mechanisms is the management of the "Victim Supporter" in charge of protecting crime victims at the first response to the crime. This system enables easier contact between police and victims. By this, assistance is given more effectively, such as offering information, giving notice to the relatives and securing personal safety of the victim. It has been run by each police station of all over the country since 2004. It is very crucial for the victim to get the initial support as soon as possible when crime occurs, because it could effect on victim's recovery to the great extent (Moriarty, 2002. pp. 20-21; Bree Cook, 1999. p. 46).

There is another unique victim assistance system in Korean police: In 2006, KPA employed 11 special agents that were in charge of psychological intervention and in charge of crisis intervention. They were stationed at each of the eight metropolitan provincial police agencies. For their effective crisis intervention, they were specially trained for the task in a 6 months course in 2007(Korean Police Agency 2009. p. 175). This kind of a special recruitment project has been interrupted for several years, but since 2011, this project has been resumed again. The professionals who want to be the special agents must have at least a bachelor degree in psychology and having professional experiences as practicing or researching in psychological area more than 3 years.

There is a lot of activities on the police level. These are matched by reforms on the level of the Office of the Prosecutor. They will be described next.

3.2.2 Public Prosecutor and Ministry of Justice

Korean Public Prosecutor's Office and Ministry of Justice have taken various measures to improve the organizational obstacles of victim protection since 2001. Since 2004, there is a special prosecutor in charge of monitoring how the rights of the victim are taken care of. This special prosecutor is appointed by the Superintendent Public Prosecutor with the exclusive responsibility to assist victims (Ministry of Justice 2006. p. 45). The officer has a duty to consult with his/her utmost sincerity and offer various support to victims. In the same year, a comprehensive strategy for victim protection was published by Ministry of Justice (Kim Youngse 2010. pp. 146-147).

Following the plan outlined in the Comprehensive Strategy for Victim Protection by the Ministry of Justice, the Crime Victim Protection Law was legislated in 2005. This law - revised in 2010- regulates victim-offender mediation, the victim compensation system and the obligatory establishment of a Plan of Action by the each chief of the central agencies of government (Article 12, Crime Victim Protection Law 2010). Before this, victim-offender mediation had been carried out by a non official committee supported by the prosecutors' office until it was regulated by the mentioned law of 2010. This law as well incorporated the former Criminal Victim

Compensation Law. The following section will deal with the various consequences of this comprehensive law. We will start with the consequences on courts.

3.2.3 Criminal court

Amendments of the Criminal Procedure Law in 2007 have brought many changes to the criminal court in Korea. Firstly, the victim-witness has the right to be accompanied and supported by person of his personal trust (Article 244-5, Criminal Procedure Law). Secondly, the court is able to use the video-link system, if necessary, while interrogating victim-witnesses (Article 165-2, Criminal Procedure Law). Thirdly, the court should give victims an opportunity to present his/her opinion about their damage and the expected punishment of the offender. This kind of victim impact statement widens clearly the scope of the victims input (Article 294-2, Criminal Procedure Law). These norms create an obligation for the court. Already in 2003, a Special Law to Protect Victims of Sexual Assault (SLPVSA) introduced compulsory video-recording when a child under 13 years of age or when a disabled persons is interviewed. It has been now expanded to the children under 16 years old through the second amendment of the Law (Article 21-3, SLPVSA).

4. Protection of victims in the criminal proceedings

4.1 Personal safety

Whenever the physical safety of a victim is endangered, police officers have to respond appropriately. That is especially important in cases of domestic violence. Police has to assess reasonably the degree of danger. "Reasonably" means that police has to take into account the type of offence, previous criminal records of the suspect, the level of danger emanating from the suspect and from the surrounding situation, taking into account the ongoing investigation and the expected punishment. Within this framework, police has the duty to protect the physical safety of the victim from present or expected dangers (Korean Supreme Court 1998. 5. 26. 98da 11635). In the wake of this decision, the legislator issued the Special Laws to protect (1) crime victims and victims that reported to police (Special Law 2006 art.7-8; Kim 2006 p.478), (2) victims of sexual assault, (Special Law 2006a, art. 20; Kim, 2006. p.468), and (3) victims of domestic violence (Special Law 2006b, art. 5; Kim, 2006. p. 450)". Victims of the crime have the right to demand from the chief of the local police station of their residence that measures are taken to protect their safety. The same applies to other persons who have reported the crime to police. Such protective measures can be implemented after a specific request of the applicants. Independent from such application, the chief of police has the duty to provide security for these persons ex officio (Special Law 2006 art. 13; Kim, 2006. p.478).

4.2 Victim interviewing

Recently, criminal investigation authorities have tried to improve the way of interrogation of victims by police. Aim of these measures was to avoid secondary victimization resulting from blaming the victim for its conduct or from otherwise disregarding victim's dignity and needs.

Since 2003, the Supreme Prosecutor's Office began to put in force the rules of interviewing a child victim under 13 years of age and have set the guideline on the process of victim interviewing (Kim, 2010, 146). The Investigation Rules prescribe the use of video-recording facilities. It permits that the trustworthy persons of victims can be present during police interrogations (Investigation Rules art. 47-48). Similar provisions were introduced into the Criminal Procedure Law in 2007 as well.

This started a series of training programs and guidelines for child victim interviewing since 2004. The program covers proper attitude to victims, the suitable place for interviewing and the necessary aids for solving psychological problems.

The Manual for Criminal Victim Protection made by Korean Police Agency provides several possibilities to prevent secondary victimization through improved interviewing methods; investigators should prepare thoroughly lest they should call for the victim's attendance repeatedly. They should avoid the direct confrontation between the victim and offender especially in cases of murder, robbery and rape. If a line-up has to be carried out to identify the criminal, then the investigator should not permit such direct confrontation. In these cases, a special room protecting the victim with a one-way mirror should be used. The victim has the right to have a trustworthy person taking part in the interviewing process, considering the age and mental situation of the victim (KPA Manuel for Criminal Victim Protection, 2007, p. 60)

Korean Police Agency enacted the Official Regulations (2005). According to these rules, female victims should be handled by female police officers. To avoid repeated appearance of the victim in the police station, video-recording facilities are to be used. Such measures may provide less burden for the victim. It too serves the transparency of the investigation (Article 70).

While these measures are directed to improve police performance, they indirectly favor the victim if they achieve the goal: avoidance of secondary victimization. A similar purpose has the rules for information of victims.

5. Information for victims

All over the world, victims are said to complain that they do not have enough information (Dussich & Mundy, 2008. p. 60). Victims find themselves in a system that is unfamiliar to them. Therefore, there is a need for information and orientation from the criminal justice authorities (Moriarity, 2002. p. 21). Criminal justice system should react to these needs. They must try to furnish information to victims. Fortunately, all of the Korean criminal justice authorities have consistently emphasized the importance of information offering for victims. We shall review the present situation of information offering system in Korea briefly.

5.1 Contents of Information Offering

Before the 'Beomjoe Piheja Bohobeop' was enacted, the issue of information to victims was regulated in diverse special laws including service guidelines of the related national authorities. These special regulations were summarized in a unified basic principle about information offering by the Crime Victim Protection Law (2007).

According to the Criminal Procedure Law, public prosecutors should inform victims within 7 days from the time of final decision whether to prosecute the suspect or not if the victim requested such information from the prosecutor (Article 258 Criminal Procedure Law). The prosecutor, on demand of the victims and their family, has to inform about date and place of the trial, the result of judicial decision, the arrest or release of the defendant. This information is to be given as soon as possible (Article 259-2 Criminal Procedure Law).

As far as this author knows, there are no cases that victims got reparation because of the violation of information norms such as article 258, 259-2 and 262. The court decided that it was illegal not to inform the suspect of his/her rights according to the Criminal Procedure Law (Korean Supreme Court 2000. 7. 4. 99do4341, gong 2000, 18510). It would make sense if a failure of notifying on victim's rights would be included in the illegal actions that lead to reparation by the state. However, such cases are not known. .

While it is principally the competency of the prosecutor to decide whether to prosecute or not, such decision is no longer free from judicial review: Like in the German system, in Korea too victims can appeal the decision of the prosecutor to dismiss the case. If they are without success on this level, they can appeal to the High Court. The High Court should decide as soon as possible (Article 262 (3) Criminal Procedure Law).

The Supreme Prosecutors' Office began to enhance the information system from 2004 on. It now includes the notification about ongoing process of the criminal cases and their results.

Korean Police Agency established also the essential grounds of the information offering system for the victim in the Criminal Investigation Rules (CIR) in 2004. Police officers should inform victims of their case within 3 days after they have given the case to the public prosecutors officer, or to other authorities (Article 204 CIR). According to the CIR, the police investigators should inform the victim on the outline of the criminal procedure, on the return process of their seized property, the management of state compensation and restitution system, the victim statement in the court, the rights to get help from the lawyer or service provider and the medical support mechanism for the sexually abused persons (Article 203 CIR). But what happens when these rules are not obeyed?

Most of the notification norms are inner service rules of police organization such as the Criminal Investigation Rules. As far as this author knows, the court has not award any reparation on the grounds that police did not inform the victim in accordance to the CIR. CIR are administrative rules binding police internally - but they do not create any rights of victims to demand reparation. They don't directly empower victims to sue for damage. That is different in case of a violation to return seized property (Art. 133,135 Criminal Procedure Law). It is also different in the case which police were responsible for not providing enough security for the victim (see III. 3-1. Personal safety). In this context it is mentioned that a victim impact statement in Korean criminal procedure can be hardly considered a "right" of the victim since the victims' position as witnesses are rather passive - victims as witnesses react to questions of the judge.

5.2 Form of the information

Each Korean police station must provide guide books or leaflets containing the information about the criminal procedure, compensation and restitution system for the victims according to the criminal patterns. These guidebooks are available in several non Korean languages. Additionally, Korean Police Agency has run the Criminal Intelligence Management System (CIMS). That is a nationwide computerized data bank. The useful information for victims could be printed out and be offered to them. Police investigation offices can provide the information for the victims with the type of printout leaflet whenever they need it. This again serves effective police work directly. Only indirectly it serves victims.

Above all, on May of 2010, the Bureau of Investigation in Korean National Police Agency, decided to conduct the notification system of victim's rights orally, so called "Reverse Miranda Warning (Moriarity, 2002, p. 19)", so that in early time of criminal incident, victims is able to get verbally informed of their legal rights. When the victims are interviewed by investigators, police agency must make it a rule for the victims to sign on the paper including the message that they are properly noticed about their rights by criminal investigation authorities. All these rules do not constitute a right of victims since there are no consequences if these norms are violated - and that is very different in the case of Miranda Warning violations. That renders Moriarity's dictum doubtful.

6. Restitution

6.1 Definition

Restitution means the offender's payment to the victims for the harm or loss suffered, reimbursement of expenses incurred as a result of the victimization, the provision of services, the restoration of rights and the return of victim's property. Important is the source of the payment: restitution comes from the offenders (UN 1985, art.8, Declaration of Basic Principles of Justice for Victims of Crime and Abuse of Power). Restitution is ordered by the criminal court to be paid by the offender to the victim.

6.2 Restitution orders

Korea adopted the restitution order system first in 1981. Even though the scope of awards to the victims was enlarged through the revision of the Special Law for Facilitating Legal Procedure in 2005, the types of the crime that victim can get restitution are still limited to injury, assault, injury or death from negligence, larceny; burglary, fraud, blackmail, embezzlement, misappropriation and damage to the property. The court can order the offender to pay the victims the restitution of the material damage, the cost of medical treatment and consolation money.

6.3 Criminal mediation program

6.3.1 Definition

Mediation is a voluntary process whereby parties in dispute meet with a trained and impartial mediator in order to facilitate a prompt and effective resolution. The Mediator listens to each party's version of the dispute without making any determination of right or wrong. The mediator uses these positions as a starting point from which compromise and creative problem-solving strategies are employed toward achieving amicable resolution for all affected parties. Criminal mediation program has adopted this general mediation method in the various criminal cases.

6.3.2 Criminal Mediation Committee

The criminal mediation program of Korea had been started voluntarily by a few district public prosecutors' office since 2005. After Ministry of Justice established the inner rule for the criminal mediation, 33 public prosecutors' offices put that program into practice in connection with the Crime Victim Support Center (CVSC) from 2007. The Crime Victim Support Centers are part of the private sector, not part of the criminal justice system - even if they cooperate with the local prosecutor closely. The first CVSC was launched first at Gimcheon city in 2003. It provides the victims with financial, medical, legal, psychological supports and the other various services including criminal mediation program. In the meantime, the program was officially and clearly induced into the Criminal Victim Protection Law in 2010. According to the law, the Criminal Mediation Committee has been organized under the each district public prosecutors offices to run the program. The cases are able to be delivered to the committee for mediation by not only the request of the victims but also the authority of public prosecutors (Song, Gilyong, 2007. p. 57).

7. Compensation

7.1 Definition

Victim compensation is a direct payment to, or on behalf of, a crime victim for crime-related expenses such as unpaid medical bills, mental health counseling, funeral costs, and lost wages. Crime victim compensation programs exist to provide financial assistance to crime victims and reduce some of these stressors (Harvey Wallace & Cliff Roberson, 2011, pp. 274-275). The government has a duty to compensate the victims for their loss resulted from crime in this program, while the offenders should pay the victims in the restitution programs.

7.2 Development of Compensation Program

After legislating the victims' rights for compensation in Korean Constitutional Law in 1987, Korean government established the special law, so called "the Crime Victim Aid Law." The law was to facilitate putting the constitutional victims' rights into practice. According to that law, the criminal victims who get the life-threatening impact and injury from criminal act can receive the aid from the government for their damage if the essential factors are met to the criteria. But this system had been usually criticized because the amount of the compensation and the number of beneficiary was smaller than various other countries (Kyunsuk Cho, 2006. p. 339).

In the meantime, this Crime Victim Aid Law was absorbed in

the Criminal Victims Protection Law which was greatly revised in May 2010. As a result of that, the Crime Victim Aid Law was finally abolished. The new compensation system was loosened at its specific criteria for bestowing the aid, enlarged the scope of the beneficiary and heighted the amount of the money for the victims to receive. For example, the scope of the victim who could get compensation was restricted to the death or to serious disability resulting from crime. The new law, however, covers serious injury as well. Additionally, funding for compensation has been started from January 2011 according to the law and the fund has been raised mainly through the fine which the offender should pay (Ministry of Justice 2010).

8. Victim assistance

As it was mentioned previously, there are two major types in the victim assistance. The government initiative type is one, and the private initiative type is the other. As a matter of course, there is an intermediate sector also which connects these two parts intimately. We shall look into the private and intermediate sector for victim assistance first.

The Korean Counseling Center for Sexual Assaulted Woman was founded already in 1991. It can be considered as the first emergence of civil organization for victim assistance. These services of the center include: counseling victims, supporting their rehabilitation, and carrying out research about the cause of sexual crime and victim policy since it began.

After this Korean pioneer organization, others followed. They appear under various names: "the Call for Woman", "the Refuge for Woman" and "the Call for Love" and so on. They relied on volunteer work and did not have many professional positions. That was regarded as a disadvantage – such difficult work was seen as work for professionals (social workers, counselors, psychologists, nurses) that can be effectively supported by volunteers, but not substituted by volunteers.

Meanwhile, the specific civil counseling centers and shelters for victims opened all over the country after the legislation of the Special Law for Protecting Victims against Sexual Assault in 1994 and Special Law for Family Violence in 1997 (Special Law 2006a, 2006b). This law provided public finances for these centers. Moreover, the Ministry of Woman which was newly organized in 2001, began to improve the victim assistance system more rapidly because it has enabled to put the greater concern on the women victim than ever before (Kim, Youngse, 2010. p. 427).

Among these organizations, as we said before, there is a mixed shape constituted both of official and private sector. Those are called by the name of One-Stop Support Center and Crime Victim Support Center. The first are connected closely with police and the latter cooperate with the public prosecutor. We shall briefly look at the two kinds of organizations.

8.1 One-Stop Support Center

Experiencing a traumatic event as a crime, people might fall into psychological and physiological suffering. These traumatic events could be called as 'individual crisis' (Handbook on Justice for Victims, 2011. p. 17). These individual crises have to be taken care of in a way that is convenient and not burdening for victims.

In Korea, on August of 2005, the One-Stop Support Center which had set a goal for clearing up the victims' crisis resulted from the crime, was established in Seoul at first. Today there are 16 of these centers nationwide (KPA 2009, p. 78). They are the prototype of victim assistance provided by the police in Korea. They run as 24-hour crisis intervention facilities. The victims, especially the vulnerable people such as women, children and the disabled, can get their medical, psychological and legal services simultaneously with the concept of on-site crisis intervention. This kind of an emergent supporting system has been proliferating to 16 service centers all over the country since that time on.

The One-Stop Support Center is typically equipped with the emergency medical facility, with a comfortable room for interview with video recording facilities for investigation. The staff is lead usually by a police woman for investigation. Other staff members include counselors for emergency psychological treatment and trained nurse for medical service. All these services are offered free of charge to the extent of 300 million won in Korean currency for victims on 24 hours base.

The establishment of these centers is very helpful for victims, not only because they could prevent the victims from being secondary-victimized but also offer the victims a proper medical or emotional assistance which could not be provided if the police investigation would be carried out in a police station. While they are theoretically a low-step offer for citizen, however, many victims served in these institutions, has been brought in by the investigating police officer from the police center next door. Drop-in clients are relatively rare. Consequently, these centers have possibility to be managed by criminal justice oriented attitude. That does not take away from the fact that they are very helpful institutions for victims. The low barrier open access victim assistance service available for "drop in" will be described next.

8.2 Crime Victim Support Center

The Crime Victim Support Centers (so called "Beomjoe Pihaeja Jiwon Center" in Korean. here addressed it as CVSCs), are the second local kind of victim assistance centers. The first was established in 2003. They operate in 57 local areas. Each center is closely connected with district public prosecutor's offices. This mix of private service and connection to prosecutorial work is reflected in the persons who founded this successful model: One was the public prosecutor, named Kyunseok Cho who played a great role to launch the Crime Victim Support Center firstly in Korea. He cooperated closely and kept the strong partnership with other professionals. The other is Dr. Kenjae Jung, who runs a hospital as a psychiatrist and medical expert in Gimcheon city in Korea. Dr. Jung became aware of the needs of victims and he was able to convince the leading prosecutor to engage in this kind of victim assistance.

The CVSCs carry out a variety of works: Firstly, they offer victims the information which is useful for their recovery from criminal damage (that is a kind of legal advice for victims). Secondly, they provide victims with the financial aids for their survival and medical treatment. Thirdly, they assist victims by securing their personal safety on the crime scene and accompany them to the investigation authorities or to the court. Additionally, the CVSCs had performed the criminal mediation program before the revision of the Criminal Protection Law. According to the results of the quantitative and empirical research, it showed that the program highly satisfied victims and offenders (An, Heejun 2009. p. 79).

In addition, the centers provide individual counseling for victims in emotional difficulties, a very much needed and used service. The Gimcheon Center among others features self help groups of victims of sexual assaults who meet once a month. In these privately organized but publicly funded organizations the main bulk of victim assistance is Korea is delivered.

9. Conclusion

With regard to the improvement of victim policy, this author has developed the mutual corresponding aspects (Kim, Jae Min, 2006 p.256 – 258). The first aspect pertains to the level of the police officer and deals with his sensitivity and attitude and behavior towards victims. This more individual microscopic aspect has direct implications for victims.

There is another "macroscopic" aspect in victim policy. It is concerned with the improvement of the institutional and legal environment dealing with victims. It is more system oriented, while the first is more personnel oriented. In victim assistance organizations, both aspects may not be always discriminated clearly. That is obviously the case due to their mutual intimate relationship.

This paper cannot deepen the discussion of these concepts. It will end with an outlook which might even serve cross cultural comparisons. A police oriented way of looking at victim assistance definitely will include both aspects of institutional social control. A more decidedly clearly victimological way of looking at victim assistance will put the victim and its needs and wishes in the center. It is less concerned with the microscopic or macroscopic dimensions of police interests. There might be a conflict between the two ways of looking at the relevant features. This conflict must – and can - be solved under the umbrella of social control. One way of social control is serving directly the victim while another is to improve the personal and institutional aspects of formal social control via the criminal.

References

An, Heejun. (2009). Trend and Development Directions of Crime Victim Support Policy. In Korea. Korean Journal of Victimology, Vol. 17. No. 2.
Anonymous. (2011). Handbook on Justice for Victims, Reprints from the collection of the University of Michigan Library.
BPB = Beomjoe Piheja Bohobeop. engl. Transl. Criminal Victim Protection Law (2005). In http://likms.assembly.go.kr/ law/jsp/ Law.jsp? WORK_TYPE =LAW_BON&LAW_ID= A1972&PROM_NO = 10283 & PROM_DT=20100514&). Accessed April 30, 1010
Bae, Jongdae & Lee, Sangdon. (2004). Criminal Procedure Law, Hongmunsa.
Cho, Kyunsuk. (2005). Overview about Victim Assistance, victim support center.
Choi,Youngseong. (2006). The Strategy for Revitalization of Crime Victim Support Center, Symposium of Korean Journal of Victimology.
Cook, Bree. (1999). Victims' Needs, Victims' Rights, Australian Institute of Criminology Research and Public Series, No. 19.
Chulsu Kim. (2004). Overview about Korean Constitution. Parkyungsa.
Dussich, P. J. John & Mundy, G. Kieran (Eds.), (2008). Raising the Global Standards for Victims, TIVI.
CIR = Criminal Investigation Rules, Korean Police Agency(2011). In http://www.law.go.kr/ /admRulSc.do?menuId=1&p1= &subMenu=1&query= #AJAX. Accessed April 30, 2011. Jonggo Choi. (2001). The History of Korean Legal Thought. National Seoul University.
Kim, Chulsu. (2004), Overview about Korean Constitution, Parkyungsa.
Kim, Jaemin. (2006). Criminal Victim Policy. Seoul, Jinlitamgu.
Kirchhoff, F. Gerd., & Morosawa, Hidemichi. (2009). The Study of Victimology, Victimization in a Multi-disciplinary Key : Recent Advances in Victimology, WLP.
Kirchhoff, G. F. (2005). What is Victimology? TIVI.
Kim, Youngse. (2010). Victimology. Hyungsul.
Korean National Police University. (2010). Police Administration.
Korean Police Agency. (2005). "We are the Korean Police for Human Rights"
KPA (2007) = Korean Police Agency PA Manuel for Crime Victim Protection, 2007. Seoul)
KPA (2009) Korean Police Agency. White Paper. Seoul 2009.
Korean National Police University (2010). Department of Police Administration.
Korean Society of Victimology & Human Rights Bureau in Ministry of Justice. (2006). Proceedings of Academic Symposium.
Maguire, M. (1982). Burglary in a dwelling. London : Heinemann
Ministry of Justice, The Resource for reporting, 2010.
Moriarty, L. J. (Eds.), (2002). Policing and victims, Prentice Hall.
Official Regulations 2005 = Official Regulations for Police to Protect Human Rights(2005). In : http://www.law.go.kr/admRulSc.do? menuId =1&p1=&submenu =1&query = #AJAX, accessed April 5. 2011.
Shapland, J. (1984). Victims, the criminal justice system, and compensation. British Journal of Criminology, 24.
Song, Gilyong. (2007). Overview about the Criminal Mediation Program and its Manual, Victim Support Center, Gimjeon.

Special Law 2006 = Special Law to Protect Crime Victims and Victims Reporting to the Police (2006). In: http://likms.assembly.go.kr/law/jsp/Law.jsp? WORK _TYPE= LAW_BON &LAW_ID=A1670&PROM_NO=09139&PROM_ DT= 20081219&. Accessed April 30, 2011.

Special Law 2006a = Special Law to Protect Victims of Sexual Assaults(2006). In: http://likms.assembly.go.kr/law/jsp/Law.jsp? WORK_TYPE= LAW_BON &LAW_ID=A3346&PROM_NO=10521&PROM_DT=20110330&. Accessed April 30, 2011.

Special Law 2006b = Special Law to Protect Victims of Domestic Violence(2006). In: http://likms.assembly.go.kr/law/jsp/Law.jsp? WORK_TYPE =LAW _BON&LAW_ID=A1028&PROM_NO=10573&PROM_DT =20110412&. Accessed April 30, 2011.

UN 1985: Declaration on Basic Principles of Justice for Victims of Crime and Abuse of Power. Wallace, Harvey. & Roberson, Cliff. (2011). Victimology, Prentice Hall.

The Victimization of the Juveniles in Korea: Findings from the Korean Juvenile Victimization Survey 2008

By

Hong, Young Oh[1]

This paper describes juvenile victimization in Korea. It looks at the current situation on juvenile victim support for young people. While this is mainly based on official statistics, it relies too on the results of the Korean Juvenile Victimization Survey (Hong 2008). Finally, this paper suggests several possibilities to support juvenile victims.

1. Introduction

When people read or hear about 'adolescents' or 'juveniles', they usually associate images of 'delinquency,' 'problematic behavior,' 'violence', and 'perpetration of violence'. Few people think of juveniles as of 'victims'. However, many adolescents become victims of crime. That has been documented in the "Analytic Report on Crimes" (Supreme Prosecutor's Office, 2010). For example, the percentage of crime against juveniles (13 – 20 years old) in 2009 is reaching 5.5% of the total number of crimes. 26% of these events are sexual assault victimizations, with robbery making up18.7%. Physical assaults account for 9.2% while murder victimization are 3.3%.

That shows: the rate of victimizations of juveniles is fairly high. There is no way of knowing all cases of victimization through the official statistics collected by the Supreme Prosecutors' Office. Many crimes not reported to police and prosecutor. This is the problem of hidden crimes. The proportion of juvenile victimization reported to police is much lower than the proportion of adult victimization. Therefore it is expected that the actual victimization rate will be much higher than the rate represented by the official statistics. But although many juveniles had been victimized, there had been comparatively little interest in juvenile victims in general and especially in support of juvenile victims.

1 Korean Institute of Criminology

It is quite necessary to look at the needs of juvenile victims, at measures for their protection and at means of their support. This is so because the impact of crime on a physically and mentally not fully matured adolescent can be much more severe compared to the adults. Also, if protection and support are insufficient, it may be harder for the juveniles to recover from the criminal victimization, which may subject them to suffer for the rest of their lives. In addition, as a result of many studies including the one by Shaffer and Ruback (2002), the consequence of juvenile victimization is that they are more likely to become victims of such crimes again. There also might be a higher possibility that in future they may become the offenders of such crimes. According to the studies of Woodward and Fergusson (2000), the strongest single predictor for criminal behavior during teenage years was previous victimization.

Also, juveniles with experiences in such victimizations were more likely to experience psychological problems as depressions, personality disorders, and Posttraumatic Stress Disorders (PTSD) compared to young people who do not have such experiences (Boney-McCoy and Finkelhor, 1996; Kilpatrick, Ruggiero, Acierno, Saunders, Resnick and Best, 2003). They also had higher rates of running away from home, of drug abuse, and of other delinquent acts. In the wake of victimization, they experienced other serious problems that might even lead to suicide. Especially, when juveniles are victimized by violence or sexual assault, not only are there severe after-effects, but there is also the vicious cycle of having a higher chance that they will use violence on their children when they become adults (Finkelhor, Cross, and Cantor, 2005).

The Korean government has long been supporting the juvenile victims through various measures. Recently there is a growing interest in juvenile victims. New provisions have been added to the Criminal Procedure Law in 2007 Also many laws (their titles are given here in English, not in the original Korean version) are issued to protect juveniles from harm, e.g. the Act for Protection of Juveniles, the Act to Protect Juveniles from Sexual Abuse, the Child Welfare Act, the Crime Victim Protection Act, the Crime Victims Aid Act, the Act for the Prevention of Sexual Assault and Protection of the Victims, Act for Prevention of Domestic Violence and Protection of the Victims, Act on the Prevention of and Countermeasures against Violence in Schools.

2. Prevalence of Juvenile Victimization in Official Statistics

This paper analyzes the prevalence and trend of juvenile victimization.

It covers the years 2000 to 2009. It is based on the "Analytic Report on Crimes" of the Supreme Prosecutors' Office 2000 to 200 (Supreme Prosecutors' Office, 2010; KOSIS, 2010.)
The incidence of reported juvenile victimizations in 2000 was 39,993. That corresponds to a victimization rate of 6.8 cases per 1,000 juveniles. The victimization rate is defined as number of victims per 1,000 juveniles. From 2000 to 2003 the number of victimization declined, reaching 28,750 in 2003. The number started to rise in 2004 with 42,038 and it continuously increased till 2009 when it arrived at 69,692. There is a downward trend till 2003 and a constant rise till 2009.

Not only the numbers of victimization show this trend. The victimization rates do so as well. In 2003, this victimization rate came down from the previous year to 5.5 cases per 1,000. Like the numbers of victimizations, the rate of victimizations started to increase in 2004 with 8.1 cases per 1,000 juveniles. It continuously increased to 13.1 cases in 2009.

When classified by sex, the number of victimization for male juveniles was 27,087 in 2000 and the victimization rate was 8.8 per 1,000 male juveniles. Later, the number decreased to 17,892 in 2003 and then sharply increased in 2004 compared to the year before, reaching 25,000 cases. The increase continued year for year up to 44,797 in 2009. The victimization rate was 6.5 cases in 2003. It started to increase in 2004 to 9.2 cases. It continued its increase to 15.8 in 2009. In the case of male juveniles, the numbers increased sharply in the years 2004, 2006, and 2009.

For females, the victimization rate was generally lower than the rate for males. The number of victimization for female juveniles was 12,906 in 2000 and the victimization rate was 4.5 cases per 1,000 female juveniles. Unlike the decrease for male juveniles, the number of victimization for females increased from 2000 to 2001 reaching 13,769. It decreased until 2004 to 10,858 cases. In 2004, the number increased sharply compared to the preceding year (reaching 17,038) and continued to increase up to 24,895 cases in 2009. The victimization rate also increased to 5.0 per 1,000 female juveniles in 2001 and then went down to 4.3 cases in 2003 to be followed by an increase to 6.9 cases in 2004. From this year, it climbed continually, reaching 10.0 cases per 1,000 in 2009. In the case of female juveniles, the number increased sharply compared to the preceding years in 2004 and 2007.

In summary, it showed that the number of juvenile victimization is recently on the rise. The development of male and female victimization is astonishingly parallel. The figures and rates for male victimizations regularly are higher than the figures for female victimization. From 2003 on, the numbers and the victimization rates increase annually, reaching a height in 2009.

The following paragraph describes juvenile victimization rate by the type of crime. Again, the data are from the Korean Supreme Prosecutor's Office 2010. The description covers rates of victimization by larceny, robbery and of sexual assault.
For most of the victimizations, the figures decrease till 2004. Then the figures increase: For larceny from 4,150 (2004) to 9,390 (2009). Corresponding rates (victimizations per 1,000 juveniles in the age from 13 to 20 years) change from 0.8 to 1.8. The figures for robbery have a similar tendency: numbers increase from 579 (2006) to 1,153 (2009). Numbers of sexual assault victimizations - including victimizations by rape, attempted rape, and by indecent forceful acts - grow from 1,448 (2003) to 4,090 (2009). In the same time the rates increase from 0.3 to 0.8. From 2003 to 2009 the numbers of violent victimizations - including assault, injury, and other violent acts - increase from 9,995 to 21,699, while the rates increase from 1.9 to 4.1 (Supreme Prosecutor's Office, 2010).
Larceny Victimization: The juvenile victimization rate of larceny showed a downward trend from 0.66 cases in 2000 to 0.54 cases in 2003. From this time, it sharply increased to 0.8 cases. Afterwards, except for the 0.94 cases in 2006, there the number oscillated around 1 cases but continued to be on the rise.
Robbery Victimization: The victimization rate of robbery, unlike the victimization rate of larceny, showed an upward trend from 0.07 cases in 2000 to 0.13 cases in 2004. It decreased to 0.12 in 2005 and 0.11 in 2006 and since then has been showing an increasing trend from 0.14 cases in 2007 to 0.22 cases in 2009.
Sexual Assault Victimization: The victimization rate of sexual assault continuously decreased from 0.34 cases in 2000 to 0.27 cases in 2002 and 2003 but started to increase with 0.45 cases in 2004 and continued to increase in 2009 (0.77). The victimization rate showed a decreasing trend from 0.25 cases in 2000 to 0.19 cases in 2003 and then sharply increased to 0.23 cases in 2004. Afterwards, except for the 0.27 cases in 2006, there has been a continuously increasing trend with 0.41 cases in 2009.
Year after year the victimization rates per 100.000 juveniles for sexual assaults show the lowest level, followed by the victimization by larceny and then by robbery. Consistently and considerably higher than these three - among themselves relatively close - is the rate for the victimizations by violence. That pattern characterizes the rates from 2000 to 2009.

3. Prevalence of Juvenile Victimization in the Juvenile Victimization Survey

The purpose of the Korean Juvenile Victimization Survey was to examine the extent and nature of juvenile victimization, to discover specific characteristics of juvenile victims and offenders, and to analyze those factors affecting juvenile victimization in Korea (Hong, 2008).

The survey population covered the juvenile population residing in Korea. A representative sample of 2,500 respondents was randomly selected across the country. Data were collected from respondents through face-to-face interview. The data collection was done from June 2007 to June 2008. The respondents were asked about various forms of victimization experiences.

The method used to identify victims was by asking a screening question whether they have experienced certain types of crimes during the past year. If they responded positively to the screening question, then they were asked to describe the situation in more details. The events asked for specifically, covered six different victimizations.

The Mental Health status of the respondents was measured by the scales for anxiety, depression, hostility and life satisfaction. Anxiety was measured by the related 20 items of the Korean version of STAI (Spielberger, 1983; modified by Hahn, Lee, and Chon, 1996), depression by the related 10 items of the Korean version of SCL-90 (Derogatis, 1977; modified by Kim, Kim, and Won, 1984)), hostility by the related 6 items the Korean version of SCL-90(Derogatis, 1977; modified by Kim, Kim, and Won, 1984). Life satisfaction was measured by a single question, "How satisfied with your life are you overall?"

The victimization rate of all six crimes, including violent and property offenses was 136 per 1,000 people in the past year (July 2007 to July 2008). This results in a victimization rate for violent events of 72 per 1,000. For property violations, the victimization rate was 82 of 1,000. Clearly there were more property victimizations than violent victimizations.

The overall victimization rate was 374 per 1,000 juveniles in the age group of 13 to 18 in the reference period. Comparing violent and property victimizations: The rate was higher for violent victimizations: 215 as compared to 158 for property victimizations.

The victimization rate of sexual assault for only female juveniles was 49 over 1,000 . Sorted by crime types, among the victimization of violent offense, damages from extortion of valuables happened most frequently and among property offense, robbery was most frequent .

As expected, juvenile victimization is not a one time event but a repeat event. Looking at cases where the same type of victimization happened more than once, the total number was 2.76 per victim. Comparing violent victimization and property victimization: violence made up 2.99, property offense 1.94. Classified by crime types, the victims of extortion of valuables reported in the average 2.74 victimizations. Corresponding averages are for fraud (2.18 cases) and assault (2.03 cases). The chances of repeated victimization were found to be comparatively lower in the cases of pocket-picking (1.63) and theft (1.65). In the case of sexual offenses, attempted rape was 2 cases in average and sexual harassment was 1.2 cases in average.
According to results on the analysis based on only middle school and high school students in the Seoul area, the overall victimization rate decreased dramatically from 1990 to 1999. Both violent crime and property crime seemed to have decreased drastically.

4. Reporting to Police

We cautioned already against the expectation to get a "true" picture of juvenile victimization by looking at official police data or prosecutor's statistics. Do juveniles report their victimization to the police? To start with the result: Rarely. The police reports are very low.
The report rate to the police was a mere 2.3% - that means that only about 2 out of 100 cases of victimization were reported to the police. The report rate of violent events was only 1.6%, for property victimizations it was 2.8%. The rate that juveniles report crime to the police was very low regardless of whether it was a violent offense or a property offense.
The results in detail: Violent victimization, including robbery, assault and threat, in total 185 incidents surprised with an average reporting rate of 1.6%. Property victimization faired slightly "better": included were theft, fraud, and pick- pocketing, a total of 251 events. In the average, 2.8% were reported to police. Of 436 total incidents, police was informed about 10, that is an overall reporting percentage of 2.3%.
There are several possible reasons for these low reporting rates: Obviously, police authorities are not the receivers of information of juveniles. Juveniles seem to prefer other networks. The current study asked exclusively for reports to police. It did not ask for sharing the information with other people. Juveniles may tell in many cases tell their experiences of victimization to parents or teachers. But this study did not ask for such reports. Another reason might be that the events in general have been rather trivial and not so serious – victimizations with minor damage are less often reported to police.

5. The Impact of Criminal Victimization on Mental Health

There is a relationship between victimization and mental health problems and with life satisfaction. Victimized juveniles had a higher degree of anxiety, depression, and hostility and a lower degree of life satisfaction compared to those without victimization experiences. That is documented in the results for violent victimization but not for property victimization. The mean anxiety score for the 1873 juveniles with no violence experience was 5.9, while this score for victims of violence was 6.24 ($t=2.74$, $p<.01$). The differences for both groups on the depression scale (violence victims 8.05, non-victims 7.12, $t=4.51$, $p<.001$), on the hostility scale (non-violence 4.71, violence victims 5.54, $t=3.60$, $p<.001$) and on the measure for Life Satisfaction (No violence 2,09, violence victims 1.85, $t=1.32$, $p<.001$) show all into the same direction.
The differences between juveniles who have been victims of property offences, and those who did not experience property victimizations, were non-significant for each subscale. Violent victimization has a more negative effect on the mental health status of the victims compared to property offences where such negative effect cannot be secured.

6. Suggestions for Supporting Juvenile Victims

In the final paragraphs, the paper will deal with Support Centers for Young Victims (1).. Then it turns to counseling and support for the parents of these victims (2). It calls for efforts to increase the reporting rate of juvenile victimization (3) and to reduce the fear of crime among young people (4). In general there must be an increased awareness of the seriousness of the problem of juvenile victimization (5). The paper ends with an outlook on Parallel Justice (6).

Until recently the Korean juvenile justice system and policy on juveniles related to crimes were focused more on the arranging legislations and systems of reactions to juvenile delinquents (for example, suspension of indictment with the condition of proper guidance, diversion, counseling protective juveniles, juvenile education and juror system) rather than on the victim. There were not many protective or supportive policies for juvenile victims. Of course, as mentioned above, in Korea there were enacted various new laws. Also, newly installed support centers attempt to support the juvenile victims, but it is still not enough, which brings us to suggest several measures for juvenile victim support.

6.1 Support Centers for Young Victims

Studies on juvenile victimizations have shown that the juveniles with experiences in criminal victimization, especially with violent offenses, were found to have a more mental health (Boney-McCoy and Finkelhor, 1995; Hong, 2008; Kilpatrick, et al., 2003) compared to those with no such experience. Juveniles with experiences in criminal victimizations had higher degrees of anxiety, depression, and hostility and lower degree of life satisfaction compared to the juveniles without such experiences of victimization. Generally, victimizations are perceived by the victims as traumas. Such traumatic experiences induce symptoms other than the effects mentioned in this research, such as behavioral traumas like social phobia, avoidance of public places, and helplessness from emotional symptoms (i.e. sense of guilty, anger, and sense of alienation (Hong and Lee, 2006). As mentioned earlier, as a result of many studies, the problem of juvenile victimization is not only that they are more likely to become victims again compared to non-victims. But they are also more likely to become later offenders of such crimes (Shaffer and Ruback,2002). Therefore, there is a dire need for an early intervention for the juvenile victims. Currently in Korea, the institutions that support victimized juveniles are mainly the Center for Victims of Crime, Sunflower Center for Children, One-stop Support Center for Women Victims of Violence, Sunflower Center for Women and Children, and the National Child Protection Agency.

The Center for Victims of Crime (http://www.bcvc.or.kr/main/main.html) is a private organization established in regional areas. It supports victims through counseling, providing medical treatment. It helps with medical expenses. It supports by assisting in covering living and school expenses, and assists in the contact with police and courts.

The Sunflower Center for Children(http://www.child1375.or.kr/index.asp) is an institution that professionally supports sexually assaulted children under 13 years of age and provides counseling, psychological treatment, medical support, legal support, and investigative support. The merit of this center is that there are professional psychological therapist residents in the institution to provide an in-depth psychological treatment.One-stop Support Center for Women Victims of Violence(http://www.smone stop .or.kr/ html/main.asp) provides counseling, support in psychological treatment, investigative and legal support, and etc. The merit of this center is that it provides a 24-hour free counseling service. A police woman is working there 24 hours so that the crime reports can be filed in the center and not at the police station.

The Crisis Intervention Center for Women and Children(http://www.helpo 365.or.kr/index.php#) provides a one-stop service of counseling,

medical, legal, investigative support 24 hours a day, 365 days a year for victims of sexual assault, domestic violence, and trafficking. Its aim is to support victims in handling the emergency situation and to prevent repeated victimizations.
Lastly, the National Child Protection Agency(http://korea1391.org/index_new.php) works to prevent child abuse. It is an institution to support abused young people under 18 years of age.
There are also other places like the Sexual Violence Relief Center, Domestic Violence Relief Center, and the Counseling Center for the Juveniles. However, the number of support centers for juveniles is still insufficient at the moment. There is a crucial need for an increase in the number of institutions and for more aggressive support measures on counseling and psychological treatment.

6.2 Counseling and Education for Parents of Victimized Juveniles

With the recently established Support Center for Women and Children Victims of Violence, support services started to be extended to the parents of victims by developing programs and manuals for women, victimized youth, and family. However, the change in the perception of parents of victimized juveniles and supportive measures must be more strengthened. It is very important to take on the mental trauma of juvenile victims, and that starts often in the way parents treat the victims. Also, along with the fact that parents need to play the role of providing help in treating the psychological wounds of their children, there needs to be a change in perception: parents must be considered as the subject of counseling and treatment. When juveniles are victimized in their teenage years, the psychological pains of the parents are comparable in severity to the problems of the juvenile victims. Parents need also support. In order to do so, a change in perception of parents of victimized juveniles is needed. It is urgently recommended to develop and to produce a guidebook to support them, to develop counseling programs for parents and to specialize and counseling education.

6.3 Efforts to Improve the Victimization Reporting Rate

Korean juveniles report only about 2% of their victimizations to police. Especially, the report rate of violent offense was only 1.6%. These low reporting rates are causes for concern. We need to intervene in the early stages of juvenile victimization to minimize the after-effects of the crime. We need to support juveniles to recover from such harms before anything else. It is therefore of utmost interest to boost the report rate of juvenile victimization. Although the report rate was very low in studies on the harm done, generally the report rate of juvenile victimization is even lower than that of adults. Concerned related institutions need to find a solution to increase the number of crime reports through increased cooperation and promotion. They have to give victims a feeling of comfort. They must foster the belief that the offenders will not be able to retaliate. For example, the police will need to emphasize the fact that they are interested in the reports of juveniles and that they take these victims seriously. Police must put their efforts in trying to give the impression that a juvenile victimization is a crime. Most of all; the police should build trust by demonstrating that they can safely protect the victims from being retaliated. Schools should also emphasize that reporting crimes does not mean betrayal or a sign of weakness. Schools should also convince the juveniles that reporting helps to prevent not to become harmed again. Relating to public order, efforts to properly dispatch police in places with high chances of juvenile victimization should be made.

6.4 Measures Against Fear of Crime

According to the studies on victimization, juveniles with experiences of victimizations had a greater fear of crime than the juveniles without such experiences. Especially, the juveniles with experiences in property offenses only had a considerably higher degree of fear in property crimes compared to juveniles without such experiences. However, in the case where the juveniles had experiences in a violent offense, not only did they have a higher degree of fear in violent offenses, but they also had a higher degree of fear in property offenses. Also, it has been observed that girls in middle school show the highest rate of avoidance, accompanying other people, delay of work, avoiding carrying even small amounts of money due to fear of crime. Thus, to decrease the degree of fear on crimes, we need to stop violent offenses above anything else.

6.5 Promotion of Awareness of the Importance of Support for Juvenile Victims

Protection and support for victims are also an important issue in Korea. Various laws and systems are under way. However, they are not focused on juveniles. Thus, in order to expand the support for the juvenile victims, first of all, the criminal justice authorities and the institutions of education have to change their perception: the seriousness of the juvenile victimization needs to be recognized as well as the importance of support. Since the Criminal Justice System concentrates so much on adults, staff has to learn how to interact better with juveniles. There is a need to educate the employees of in the criminal justice system, to train them in various ways how to treat juvenile victims.

Because the victims usually try to hide the crime or feel guilty about it, the need for an aggressive promotion on the victims' rights is crucial. In order to do so, there is a need to actively educate the policy makers, public servants, and others to change the general perception, laws, and systems in place. Promotional activities using mass media or nationwide campaigns, such as the Public Awareness Campaign should be extensively utilized.

6.6 Introduction of Parallel Justice

Recently in Korea, Restorative Justice, an alternative to the traditional legislative system, has been introduced and much interest has been placed on the recovery of victims and offenders of the criminal victimization. However, restorative justice is also criticized to focus on the offenders rather than the victims of the crime. The recovery of a crime victimization is more complicated than a simple apology, restitution, and reparation of relationships. It may require a long-term psychological counseling and support to regain a sense of security.

As long as - like in Korea - the restorative justice system is in the beginning of its develop,ent, only a few are given the chance to profit from it. There is an inbuilt limitation: the offender basically has to concede to his wrongdoings and he has to want to be a part of the process. Accordingly, Parallel Justice, which combines the legislative system of the offender and the victim, came to the fore (Herman, 2000, 2010). In a legislative system of the victim, offenders acknowledge the evil brought on by the crimes and contribute to victims recovery. Likewise, there is a need for a justice system for juvenile victims that puts recovery of the victim at the top of the list aside from the treatment of the offender.

7. Conclusion

According to the official statistics and studies on victimization, many juveniles are experiencing victimizations.

Within the criminal justice system, there were a lot of efforts to establish laws and systems for guidance and protection than the criminal penalties against juvenile delinquents through various methods, such as suspension of prosecution with supervision, diversion, counseling for juvenile at risk, increased training and qualification of police, and court hearing participation. Nevertheless, for the victimized juvenile, there was not only little interest but also an insufficient number of supportive systems and policies.

Juveniles belong to the Korean people. Since the Korean state is obliged to protect its people, it should put its efforts more on the establishment of protective and supportive measures for victimized juveniles along with the guidance and protection of juvenile delinquents.

Reference

Boney-McCoy, S., and Finkelhor, D.(1995). Psychosocial sequelae of violent victimization in a national youth sample. *Journal of Consulting and Clinical Psychology, 63(5),* 726-736.

Boney-McCoy, S., and Finkelhor, D.(1996). Is youth victimization related to trauma symptoms and depression after controlling for prior symptoms and family relationships? A longitudinal prospective study, *Journal of Consulting and Clinical Psychology, 64(6),* 1406-1416.

Derogatis, L.R.(1977). SCL-90: Administration, scoring, and procedure manual - I. Baltimore, MD: Johns Hopkins.

Finkelhor, D. Cross, T. P., and Cantor. E. N.(2005). The justice system for juvenile victims. *Trauma, Violence, and Abuse 6(2),* 83-102.

Hahn, D-W., Lee, C-H., and Chon, K-K.(1996). Korean adaptation of Spielberger's STAI(K-STAI). *Korean Journal of Health Psychology, 1(1),* 1-14.

Herman, S.(2000). *Seeking Parallel Justice - A New Agenda for the victims movement,* National Press Club Luncheon(December 15, 2000). The National Center for Victims of Crime.

Herman, S. (2010). *Parallel justice for victims of crime.* Washington, DC : The National Center for Victims of Crime.

Hong, Y. O., and Lee, S. J.(2006). *Protection and assistance aystem for juvenile victims of crime.* Seoul : Korean Institute of Criminology.

Hong, Y. O. (2008*). Juvenile victimization in Korea, 2008.* Seoul : Korean Institute of Criminology.

Kilpatrick, D. G., Ruggiero, K. J., Acierno, R., Saunders, B.E., Resnick, H. S., and Best, C. L.(2003). Violence and risk of PTSD, major depression, substance abuse/dependence, and comorbidity: Results from the National Survey of Adolescents. *Journal of Consulting and Clinical Psychology, 71(4),* 692-700.

Kim, K-I., Kim, J-H., and Won, H-T.(1984). SCL-90. Seoul : Central Aptitude Publishing.

KOSIS (2010). Korean Statistical Information Service. Available at http://www.kosis.kr.

Ministry of Government Legislation. (2011). Korean laws in English. Available at http://www.moleg.go.kr/english/

Shaffer, J. N., and Ruback, R. B.(2002). *Violent victimization as a risk factor for violent offending among juveniles.* U.S. Department of Justice. Office of Justice Programs, Office of Juvenile Justice and Delinquency Prevention.

Spielberger, C. D. (1996). Manual for the State-Trait Anxiety Inventory: STAI(Form Y). Palo Alto, CA: Consulting Psychologists Press.

Supreme Prosecutors' Office.(2010). *Analytical report on crimes.* Seoul: Supreme Prosecutors' Office, Republic of Korea.

Woodward, L. J. and Fergusson, D.(2000). Childhood and adolescent predictors of physical assault: A prospective longitudinal study. *Criminology, 38,* 233-261.

Commissioner for Victims' Rights: Strengthening Victims' Rights?

By

Michael O'Connell[1]

Crime impacts on victims, their families and witnesses; and, as well affects the social, economic and health of communities (Bard, & Sangrey 1983 & Markesteyn1992). Those victims who choose to report crime expect to be treated with respect for their dignity, amongst other things. Yet, the criminal justice system does not necessarily address their needs or their losses. Rather, it can compound the trauma victims may have suffered causing 'secondary victimisation'. Many factors have been identified as contributing to this 'secondary victimisation', which is also known as 'second injury'.

With the rise of state-centred criminal justice systems, crime victims lost fundamental rights and their personal satisfaction was substituted by an intangible satisfaction of knowing that justice would be done for the state (Young 2001). Elevating victims' rights is one way to improve outcomes for victims; however, victims' rights should not compromise the right of the accused to a fair trial.

Australia's political system consists of an Australian Parliament; six State Parliaments and two Territory Parliaments. In addition to the two self-governing territories, Australia has six territories that come under the jurisdiction of the Australian Parliament. All States, except one, and both self-governing Territories have promulgated principles on how public officials should treat crime victims. These principles, amongst other entitlements, focus on respect for victims, informing them about the investigation, prosecution and court outcomes and informing them about health and welfare services to help them deal with the effects of crime. It also examines the role of the Commissioner for Victims' Rights in South Australia. The Commissioner reviews the effect of the law on victims, monitors officials and agencies' compliance with the Declaration Governing Treatment of Victims of Crime and reports annually to Parliament.

---

[1] Commissioner for Victims' Rights South Australia.

The Commissioner can also recommend that an agency or public official make a written apology to a victim where there has been a breach of victims' rights. Notably, the Commissioner has procedural rights in certain criminal proceedings, which is peculiar in common law jurisdictions.

Evolution of Victims' Rights in Australia

In 1985, the United Nations General Assembly adopted the *Declaration of Basic Principles of Justice for Victims of Crime and Abuse of Power*. This Declaration is based on the philosophy that victims should be adequately recognised and accorded access to justice and prompt redress for the harm they have suffered. It is a non-binding international declaration; however, it is complimented by other international instruments, such as the Commonwealth of Nations *Statement of Basic Principles of Justice for Victims of Crime* (2005). The Commonwealth of Australia has endorsed both instruments. It is also a signatory to other international instruments that acknowledge crime victims' rights, for example, the *Declaration on the Elimination of Violence against Women; United Nations Convention against Transnational and Organised Crime* and the *Convention on the Rights of the Child. Contrary to Declarations or Statements, conventions bind those member states that have signed (ratified) the Convention.*

Australia's *Constitution* distributes political power between the founding States (such as South Australia) and the Commonwealth Parliament, which is sometimes called the Australian Parliament. The States surrendered many powers to the Commonwealth but responsibility for criminal justice and related areas of policy and programs, including victim assistance remained with the States and Territory Governments. Since the 1990s, however, a number of significant Federal criminal laws have been enacted that involve natural persons as crime victims. Currently, on Australian soil there are nine different criminal codes: six State criminal codes, two Territory criminal codes and a Federal criminal code.

The push for the recognition of victims as an integral component of the criminal justice system in Australia began in the 1980's in South Australia, which set the trend. Nowadays, each State (except Tasmania) and both self-governing Territories have a declaration of victims' rights. All, except Northern Territory have enshrined their declaration in law. Northern Territory has a legal provision that authorises the incorporation of a declaration on victims' rights in law but its declaration is an administrative statement. Tasmania's

Government is consulting on a declaration on victims' rights. All states and territories have provision for victim impact statements in criminal sentence hearings and financial assistance or compensation schemes for crime victims. These schemes vary considerably from jurisdiction to jurisdiction. Each jurisdiction also has service networks some of which are located within the government sector and some within the non-government sector. There is no Federal declaration on victims' rights, yet there has been an encouraging trend in favour of the Commonwealth Parliament enacting one.

A National Charter on Crime Victims' Rights

Under the auspices of co-operative federalism many bodies have been established such as the Australian Police Ministers Council (APMC) and the Standing Committee of Attorneys-General (SCAG). In 1990 the APMC received a discussion paper on victims' rights sponsored by the Commissioner of Police for South Australia (Woodberry 1989). The Commissioner argued for a national approach to victims' rights. A similar debate happened in the SCAG. A discussion paper sponsored by the Attorney-General for South Australia was debated by the Attorneys-General (SCAG 1992). By the mid-90s the SCAG promulgated a National Charter for Victims' Rights, which was consistent with the United Nations' Declaration (1985) and modelled on the Declaration on Victims' Rights in South Australia.

The Charter set minimum standards for the treatment of victims in the criminal justice system. It recognises that crime victims should:

- be treated with compassion and respect for their dignity
- have access to services
- be informed of their rights
- be informed of the progress of proceedings
- be allowed to present their views at appropriate stages of the proceedings
- be afforded measures to protect their privacy, ensure their safety and minimise inconvenience.

The SCAG Secretariat was tasked with monitoring the implementation of the Charter. *It issued* a report in 1996 that revealed all States and Territories had taken steps towards the implementation of the Charter. Although the Australian Government (that is Commonwealth) had taken no action, some federal agencies – in particular the Commonwealth Office of the Director of Public Prosecutions (Bugg 2004; Commonwealth DPP no date) – had begun to adopt victim-oriented policies and practices. A decade later the Australia Government joined Commonwealth Nations in developing a *Statement of Basic Principles of Justice for Victims of Crime*, which was approved in 2005 (South Australian Attorney General's Media Release 2005). The communiqué on the Statement reflects the good practice guidelines developed by an expert group for the Commonwealth Secretariat (Commonwealth Secretariat 2002). Then in 2008 the Federal Attorney-General's Department hosted a Summit on Criminal Justice that listed victims and criminal justice as a key theme (See: <http:// www.ag.gov.au/www/agd/agd.nsf/Page/Consultations_reforms_and_reviews2008_Federal_Criminal_Justice_Reform_Forum?open&query=Justice Summit>). The workgroup on victims of crime at that summit recommended the draft convention developed by the World Society of Victimology and partners as a framework to guide the development of a federal declaration on victims' rights. Also that year, the SCAG established a workgroup to report on a federal declaration on crime victims' rights and 'good practice guidelines' for a national approach to victim assistance (O'Connell 2008; Garkawe & O'Connell 2007).

The SCAG workgroup identified many federal offences that involve natural persons as crime victims. The *Criminal Code and Crimes Act*, for example, outlaws human trafficking; child sex tourism; slavery and sexual servitude, and terrorism (see also Kelly 2008). It also noted that there are international instruments and issues that concern victims; and benefits and support for crime victims have increased. Emerging issues of national and local significance for law enforcement agencies and crime victim services include the trafficking in human beings into Australia and the exploitation of children, for instance, child pornography facilitated by the Internet. The workgroup also noted that special efforts are required to address the needs of victims of terrorism. Despite the absence of a federal charter on crime victims' rights, Commonwealth social and justice policy, for example, in education and social security, has impacted positively on crime reduction and prevention victimisation. Furthermore, important federal questions are raised where crimes are committed overseas against Australians or where residents of one Australian jurisdiction are victimised in another jurisdiction. The recommendations of the workgroup are yet to be made known but clearly the proliferation of these issues and others now requires a concerted and coordinated federal response of which a Federal Declaration on Victims' Rights should be a core element of that response. Notably, the former Labor Government (under Prime Minister Rudd) announced that it would implement a declaration (ABC News 2008; Pearlman 2008 & ALP 2009); whether that happens depends on political will. That Government also revamped the assistance scheme for victims of human *trafficking. It* funded a Victim-Witness Assistance Officer for the Office of the Commonwealth Director of Public Prosecutions. Recently, the Federal Attorney-General for the current Labor Government (under Prime Minister Gillard) announced that a federally funded compensation scheme for victims of terrorism will likely be established.

Crime victims' rights in States and Territories

Charters and declarations enacted by the States and Territories mirror the ten fundamental rights in both the United Nations Declaration and Australia's National Charter to a significant extent. However, the declaration in New South Wales, South Australian and Queensland respectively has been amended since the former declaration and charter were approved. In New South Wales and South Australia, for instance, there has been greater emphasis on procedural rights such as the right to be consulted before charge decisions are varied. Victoria's Justice Department reviewed all Australian charters and declarations before enacting its *own* charter (Victim Support Agency 2004). Queensland and the Australian Territory Governments reviewed their declarations and redrafted them before enacting new legislation. Western Australia is reviewing its charter on victims' rights that is a schedule under the *Victims of Crime Act* (Porter 2011; Cordingley 2010). Tasmania adopted the United Nations Declaration, however, its Attorney-General announced in 2010 that State would introduce a local charter on victims' rights (see http://www.justice.tas.gov.au/victims).

All declarations or charters are intended to ensure a recognised position for victims within the criminal justice system and to minimise any secondary victimisation. They comprise a set of principles (often called rights) that oblige public officials to treat victims accordingly.

There are many commonalities in the declarations and charters that exist in Australia, for example,

- Treating victims with respect, compassion and dignity, as well as cultural sensitivity
- Providing protection from the accused person (and his or her family and associates)
- Avoiding unnecessary intrusion into victims' privacy, including protecting the identity of the victim
- Providing medical, psychological and practical assistance that is easily accessible for the victim
- Providing information of the criminal justice process and victims' role and responsibilities as witnesses

- Providing accurate and timely information about: the investigation, the charges laid, about the outcome of a bail application (including information on conditions imposed to protect the victim), the prosecution, the court outcome and the impending released, escape or recapture of the offender
- Giving victims opportunities to participate in decisions that affect them, such as taking into account victims on their perceived safety concerns when deciding whether to bail the accused; consulting victims before any decision to modify or not to proceed with charges laid against the accused; and the opportunity to make submissions at parole hearings.
- Giving victims the opportunity to make statements on how the crime affected them and giving those who choose to make statements accurate information and appropriate assistance
- Providing for offender paid restitution and, when the offender cannot afford to pay restitution, state-funded compensation for victims of violent crime
- Reducing inconvenience by, for instance, returning victims' property held by the State for the purpose of investigation or evidence

It is increasingly common that jurisdictions acknowledge that victims can complain if their rights are not honoured. For example, in South Australia public officials are obliged to give victims information about making a complaint about a breach of their rights. No Australian jurisdiction has provided penalties for non-compliance with victim rights legislation by a public officer, except in South Australia the Correctional Services Act sets a maximum penalty of $10,000 for officials who breach confidentiality with respect to certain information, including information about victims that is kept on the Victims Register (see Section 84D *Correctional Services Act* 1988). The New South Wales, Queensland and South Australia legislation prohibit criminal or civil liability being attached for breaches. However, no Act excludes disciplinary action against a public official for a breach. Indeed, crime victims may, in all jurisdictions, access existing *bodies* (such as the Ombudsman) and *they can make use of procedures of the relevant agency to pursue* a complaint. None of these authorities, however, is known to monitor and/or report on the complaint's relevance to victims' rights.

Compliance mechanisms are needed. They are an important tool to strengthen victims' rights. They also enable governments to determine whether victims' rights are being implemented properly in agencies. It is important to ensure that public officials and public agencies have appropriate procedures and practices in place to meet their obligations to victims.

Enforcement of victims' rights in Australia's States and Territories

Although victims' rights declarations aim to ensure that, wherever possible, victims' rights are received consistently and reliably, there are still gaps in the way the criminal justice agencies and other public officials *are seen to* respond to victims (Wilkie et al 1993; Cook et al 1999; Curtis & Pankhurst 2003; Gardner 1989; Erez et al 1994; JSU 1999 & 2000).

For example, in 2009 the New South Wales Sentencing Council (2009) reported that 62% of residents in that State thought that the criminal justice system did not meet the need of victims. Victim surveys reveal that many victims are not aware of their rights and many victims, despite victims' rights, still feel they are treated with ambivalence (Wilkie et al 1993; Social Systems & Evaluation 1997; Cook et al 1999; Curtis & Panhurst 2003; Gardner 1990; Erez et al 1994; JSU 1999 & 2000; NSW Victim Services 2010).

These short-comings might be because victims continue to be seen as only witnesses. It might also be because the language of 'rights' suggests the declarations or charters carry more weight than in reality (Groenhuijsen, 1999). In other words, victims' rights are arguably symbolic and will likely remain so until they are enforceable. Other reasons for the patchy implementation of victims' rights are the attitude of public officials and inadequate resources that limit the ability and capacity of public officials and public agencies to respond effectively to victims

In order to raise the profile of victims' rights not only for victims but also for public officials several jurisdictions have enshrined victims' rights in statute law. Arguably a statutory obligation on officials and agencies is a better way to ensure that victims are treated with the respect and dignity afforded to them under a declaration or charter. This, however, has not proven to be as effective as some anticipated. Research indicates that the existence of a set of rights for victims does not in itself ensure that victims are able to exercise the entitlements they provide. Whether victims' rights come through a statutory scheme or administrative direction, there is a need for the principles to be clearly articulated and compliance mechanisms to be established for them to operate effectively. Thus, in addition to affording rights to crime rights States and Territories have introduced ways to resolve victims' grievances when those rights are violated. A brief overview on each follows before an elaboration on South Australia's approach that incorporates the appointment of a Commissioner for Victims' Rights.

The Australian Capital Territory enacted the *Victims of Crime*

Act in 1994, which sets out principles that, as far as practical and appropriate, govern the treatment of victims of crime. A public official who breaches a guideline can face disciplinary proceedings within his or her own agency. A Commissioner for Victims of Crime (yet to be appointed) will promote efficient and effective services to victims of crime and in*vestigate alleged breaches of these principles by criminal justice agencies.*

In New South Wales the "Victims Services NSW" (within the Attorney-General's Department) has the authority to receive a complaint, attempt to resolve it and, where this is not possible, to advise the Attorney-General who may table the report in Parliament. This State's charter applies to public agencies and public officials, as well as non-government organizations and their employees that receive public funds to deliver victim assistance. This is unique to New South Wales.

The *Victims of Crime Rights and Services Act* in the Northern Territory consolidated a range of victim related legislation. The Act established the new Crimes Victims Services Unit (CVSU) and the Victims Register. The CVSU is charged with promoting and overseeing victims' rights, including raising public awareness on these rights. Victims with grievances, however, should first utilise existing complaint authorities.

Queensland has appointed a 'Victims of Crime *Co-ordinator'. The Co-ordinator* manages "VictimAssist", which is a government agency. If a victim complains about a violation of his or her rights, there should be an investigation by the respective public agency and the result of the investigation must be reported to VictimAssist. Furthermore, public agencies ought to co-operate with VictimAssist in resolving victims' complaints.

A Victims Assistance section in the Department of Justice in Tasmania administers the victims register, liaises with other justice agencies, provides information and court support to victims and manages a counselling service for victims of crime. The section monitors compliance with victims' rights laws but it does not investigate complaints from victims of crimeIn Victoria, the Secretary for the Ministry for Justice is tasked with establishing a victim-complaint process. The Secretary has delegated that responsibility to the Victim Support Agency, which operates the Victims Help-line and runs the victim assistance counselling programme.

The Attorney-General for Western Australia currently should report annually on the operation of the Victims of Crime Act, including the Schedule of Guidelines on the Treatment of Crime Victims.

The incumbent Liberal Attorney-General has announced that Government intends to establish a crime victims advocate or similar position. The statutory officer's functions would be based on South Australia's Commissioner for Victims' Rights (see below).

Most Australian jurisdictions have a designated entity to receive, inquire into and attempt to resolve victims' complaints. The limited information publicly available suggests that the majority of victims' complaints are resolved by providing information or referrals, or reminding public officials of their obligations. At first glance, none of Australia's declarations or charters creates legally enforceable rights. Rather, all victims' rights declarations or charters state that violation of a right does not create a civil or criminal cause of action against a public official or agency.

Establishment of a Commissioner for Victims' Rights in South Australia

The *Victims of Crime Act* 2001 in South Australia incorporates the Declaration of Principles Governing Treatment of Victims of Crime and provides for the Governor to appoint a Commissioner for Victims' Rights. A Commissioner for Victims' Rights was conceived as a response to the fact, that - despite victims' rights legislation - many victims still are not receiving the rights to which they are entitled under that law. The Premier and Attorney-General for South Australia asserted that victims should no longer be by-standers in the criminal justice system.

The Commissioner is independent of direction or control by the Crown or a Government Minister. The Act makes it clear that any directions or guidelines given to the Commissioner about the carrying out of his or her functions must, as soon as practicable after they have given, be published in the Gazette and laid before each House of Parliament. Then Attorney-General, Hon. Michael Atkinson MP (2007) said, "This will help to ensure that the Commissioner is free to make independent recommendations for change that arise from any review of laws and practices", amongst other things. This level of separation from government ensures objectivity (Uhrig Review 2003). According to Holder (2008), a statutory advocate for victims must be free to act within the criminal justice system, with enabling legislation, to ensure individual's interests and rights are upheld and to allow victims effective engagement with the system. Furthermore, she stated that independence from government is one means by which a Commissioner for Victims' Rights can undertake the statutory duties with "due diligence, objectivity, efficiency, competence, specialisation and equity".

The Commissioner for Victims' Rights is an *ex officio* member of the Victims of Crime Ministerial Advisory Committee. That Committee is appointed by the Attorney-General under section 15 of the *Victims of Crime Act* 2001. It is required to advise on:

- practical initiatives that the Government might take to ensure that victims of crime are treated with proper consideration and respect in the criminal justice system;
- to help victims of crime to recover from harm suffered by them;
- to advance the interests of victims of crime in other ways; and
- any other matter referred to the Advisory Committee by the Attorney-General for advice.

The Committee is made up of public officials, representatives for non-government organisations and a community member. The Attorney General ensured that any public official on the Committee is at the appropriate level to make decisions on behalf of his or her agency. The Attorney-General also appoints the chair, after consultation with the Commissioner for Victims' Rights. The Committee facilitates liaison between public agencies and non-government organisations. It has developed initiatives to assist agencies in complying with the Declaration Governing Treatment of Victims of Crime. A statement of commitment (known as an Administrative Agreement) endorsed by most chief executives of public agencies and the Commissioner of Police to collaborate in light of their obligations to victims of crime is a prime example (O'Connell 2009). The Committee has also conducted a review on training and education on victim assistance and criminal justice. It has overseen the preparation of an inventory of crime prevention and victimisation prevention programmes funded by government. It has in addition produced a list of victim-oriented priorities such as funding victim assistance for specific 'at risk' groups.

The Commissioner in addition:

- advises the Attorney-General on how to use available government resources to effectively and efficiently help victims of crime.
- assists victims in their dealings with the criminal justice system
- consults with the Director of Public Prosecutions in the interests of victims and in particular cases about matters including victim impact statements and charge bargains
- consults with the judiciary about court practices and procedures and their effects on victims
- monitors the effect of laws on victims and victims' families.
- makes recommendations to the Attorney-General on matters arising from the performance of these functions.

Several of these functions, which the leader of the Opposition in the South Australia Parliament described as "interesting developments" (Redmond 2007), have afforded the Commissioner avenues to intervene in criminal proceedings in ways traditionally associated with civil (inquisitorial) criminal justice systems than common law systems.

Since his appointment, the Commissioner has sought to change the legal culture with respect to observance of victims' rights. For this purpose, amongst other strategies, he has provided direct legal representation for individual victims in consultation with prosecution, in criminal and civil proceedings and coronial inquests as well as initiated legal matters that affect victims in general. (The Commissioner has about $A250,000 per year to engage legal representation for his or her office and for victims.) The presence of victims' lawyers has increased attention to victims' rights by police officers, prosecutors, magistrates and judges – and defence counsel.

In spite of these victims' rights advances, the tradition of excluding victims from criminal proceedings in Australia prevails. Although a court room is a public place, unless the court is closed, victims are not even afforded the same entitlement as members of the public in most States and Territories.

Victim presence in court is traditionally discouraged when the victim is likely a prosecution witness. The tradition is justified primarily as essential to ensure the integrity and quality of the 'fact-finding' process. The Commissioner's interventions have sought to strike a balance between the defendant's right to due process and the victim's legitimate interest.

The Commissioner monitors compliance with the Declaration of Principles Governing Treatment of Victims in the Criminal Justice System. It was evident to the Commissioner that, despite the police giving an *Information for Victims of Crime* booklet to victims who report offences, too many victims were unaware of their rights and how to exercise them.

Therefore, in September 2008 the Commissioner implemented a victim-letter notification programme. The South Australia Police provide data for the letter whenever a first court date is registered in its computer. Since the programme began, the Commissioner has posted approximately 1,000 letters per month. A "Common Questions Fact Sheet" enclosed with each letter, informs victims on how to exercise their rights to information about, for instance, the progress of the prosecution and the court outcome. In 2009-10 (financial year), about 1300 victims followed up the letter seeking further information from the Commissioner.

In order to inform victims on their right to complain and to whom they should complain, a chapter was inserted into the *Information for Victims of Crime* booklet that the police and other agencies distribute. A pamphlet summarizing the role of complaint authorities, including the Commissioner for Victims' Rights, has been produced. Each year several hundred victims raise their grievances with the Commissioner. In 2010-11, for instance, the Commissioner received 143 complaints; 583 inquires about compensation, including grievances; and, 201 inquires and/or requests for advocacy (often as a result of a public official not responding to a victim's request for information, assistance and so on). Many grievances focus on the attitude or behaviour of public officials that are contrary to the governing principles, as opposed to negligent behaviour on the part of the agency. The most common grievances raised with Commissioner are about the failure to keep the victim informed and that the victim has been left out of the criminal justice process (for example, not asked to provide information about their perceived safety concerns to a bail authority; not consulted by the prosecutor; or not given an opportunity to make a victim impact statement). Some victims complain that they are only provided with *ad hoc* measures that are predominantly aimed at facilitating the criminal investigation. They felt that police priorities dominate victims' needs.

In appropriate cases, the Commissioner may recommend that the official or agency make a written apology to the victim. The Commissioner can report on compliance with a recommendation in his or her annual report to Parliament.

Encouraging compliance or urging a genuine apology when a grievance is substantiated is seen as more effective than the threat of punishment. The aim of the actions of the Commissioner is to bring about attitudinal change or behaviour modifications. These changes are seen necessary to improve respect for victims' rights and improve practical outcomes for victims. The Commissioner has not had to recommend an apology since he acquired the authority to do so in July 2008. Several public officials, however, have volunteered apologies.

The *Victims of Crime Act* 2001 does not prevent disciplinary action being taken against an official under the agency's, or the Government's, code of conduct, or via another statutory authority such as the Police Complaints Authority or the Ombudsman. This, coupled with the Commissioner's authority, may be sufficient to ensure victims' grievances are in most cases satisfactorily resolved.

The appointment of the Commissioner happened at a time when the main political parties in South Australia embarked on a 'law and order' campaign. The Commissioner from this perspective could be seen as having much to do with the war on crime (see Harding 1994).

The Commissioner in particular and victims' rights in general however should be disentangled from that war. Instead the focus should be on victims as people and victims' rights as human rights. Victims are people who, in many cases, have endured the traumatic crisis of crime. Crime is a violation of a person's human rights. Human rights require that people are treated with respect. Victims' rights also require the people as victims be treated with respect and not treated as an after-thought. In this context, the role of the Commissioner for Victims' Rights is better understood as being about transforming the brute power of the state. The Commissioner's primary challenge is to urge others take victim seriously and to respect the rights of victims of crime. If there is systemic change then, as Dubber (2002, p342) concluded, respect for victims' rights will become more important than protecting their rights.

Conclusion

Crime victims' rights have increased exponentially in the years since 1985 when the first declaration was promulgated in South Australia. In reality, however, all the declarations and charters in Australia have been drafted to give victims information and participatory rights in our criminal justice systems but – perhaps deliberately - not control of them. Thus, another way of looking at the victim status in general is to say that the victim has been re-introduced into the criminal justice process that they once dominated

Enshrining victims' rights into legislation may not necessarily achieve the outcomes sought. It is the complaints and compliance mechanisms in place which give effect to the 'rights'. Important as well is appropriate training for public officials in relation to their obligations in accordance with the declarations and charters on victims' rights.

Reference List

ABC News 2008, Debus flags Federal charter of victims' rights, <http://www.abc.net.au/news/stories/2008/03/06/2182303.htm>

Atkinson, Hon. M. 2007, Victims of Crime (Commissioner for Victims' Rights) Amendment Bill, Second Reading Speech, House of Assembly, *Hansard*, 24 July.

Attorney-General's Department 2008, Federal Criminal Justice Forum <http://www.ag.gov.au/www/agd/agd.nsf/Page/Consultations_reforms_and_reviews2008_Federal_Criminal_Justice_Reform_Forum?open&query=Justice Summit>

Bard, M. & Sangrey, D. 1986, *The Crime Victim's Book*, Brunner/Mazel, New York, US.

Bugg, D. 2004, Accountability, independence and ethics in the prosecution practice < http://www.cdpp.gov.au/Director/Speeches/20040808db.aspx >

Bugg, D. No Date, The role of the prosecutor in the 20th century, <www.jca.asn.au/attachments/BuggPaper.pdf >

Commonwealth Director of Public Prosecutions No Date, Victims of Crime Policy, < http://www.cdpp.gov.au/Publications/Victims-of-Crime-Policy/CDPP-Victims-of-Crime-Policy.pdf >

Commonwealth Secretariat 2002, *Guidelines for Treatment of Victims of Crime: Best Practice*, Human Rights Unit, Commonwealth Secretariat. <http://www.childtrafficking.com/Docs/commonwealth_secretariat_20.pdf >

Commonwealth Senior Law Officers 2005, *Statement of Basic Principles of Justice for Victims of Crime*, Annex Three, pp 26–27, of the Commonwealth Law Ministers' communique see: <www.thecommonwealth.org/shared_asp_files/uploadedfiles/2A07BB49-003F-4916-8B21-C368B0DE486C_FINAL-LMM-COMMUNIQUE.pdf>.

Cook, B., David, F. & Grant, A. 1999, *Victims' Needs, Victims' Rights: Policies and Programs for Victims of Crime in Australia*, Australian Institute of Criminology, Canberra.

Cordingley, G. 2010, 'Victims could be given sentencing power – Attorney-General', *Perth Now*, 9 October. <http://www.perthnow.com.au/news/western-australia/victims-could-be-given-sentencing-power-attorney-general/story-e6frg13u-1225936403339>

Coroner's Court 2008, Inquest into death of Christopher Stuart Wilson, <www.courts.sa.gov.au/courts/coroner/findings/findings_2008/Wilson_Christopher_Stuart.pdf>

Coroner's Court 2011, Inquest into death of Daniel Buddy Raphael, <www.courts.sa.gov.au/courts/coroner/findings/findings_2011/Raphael_Daniel_Buddy.pdf>

Curtis, M. & Pankhurst, G. 2003, 'New South Wales: Phone-in Survey of Victims of Crime', *Journal of the Australasian Society of Victimology*, vol. 2, pp. 10-20

Department of Justice & Community Safety 2008, *Issues Paper: Review of the ACT Victims of Crime Act 1994*, June.

<www.justice.act.gov.au/resources/attachments/Issue_Paper_VOC2008.pdf>

Draft Convention on Justice and Support for Victims of Crime, Abuse of Power and Terrorism, (2005), found at <http://www.tilburguniversity.nl/intervict/convention.pdf>.

Dubber, M.D. 2002, *Victims in the war on crime: The use and abuse of victims' rights*, New York University Press, NY, USA.

Erez, E., Morgan, F. & Roeger, L. 1994, *Victim Impact Statements in South Australia: An Evaluation*, Attorney General's Department, Adelaide.

Gardner, J. 1989 'Victims' Satisfaction with the Criminal Justice System', paper presented at the *5th Annual Conference of the Australian and New Zealand Society of Criminology*, July.

Gardner, J. 1990, *Victims and Criminal Justice*, Attorney-General's Department, Research Report, Series C, South Australia.

Garkawe, S. & O'Connell, M. 2007 'The Need for a Federal, Australia-Wide Approach to Issues Concerning Crime Victims', *Current Issues in Criminal Justice*, 18(3), March, pp488-493.

Groenhuijsen, M. 1999, 'Victims rights in the criminal justice system: A call for more comprehensive implementation theory', in van Dijk, J.J.M., van Kaam, R.G.H. & Wemmers, J. (eds) *Caring for victims: Selected proceedings of the 9th International Symposium on Victimology*, Criminal Justice Press, Monsey, USA, pp85-114.

Harding R, 1994, 'Victimisation, Moral Panics and the Distortion of Criminal Justice Policy: A review essay of Ezzat Fattah's "Towards a Critical Victimology"' 6(1) *Current Issues in Criminal Justice* pp27-42.

JSU 1999, *Review on Victims of Crime - Report One*, Attorney-General's Department, Justice Strategy Unit, South Australia, Adelaide, <www.voc.sa.gov.au>.

JSU 2000, *Review on Victims of Crime - Report Two (Victims Survey)*, Attorney-General's Department, Justice Strategy Unit, South Australia, Adelaide, <www.voc.sa.gov.au>.

Kelly, E. 2008, Federal Victims Policy, unpublished paper presented at the National Victims of Crime Conference, Adelaide, South Australia, 23 September.

Markesteyn, T. 1992, *The Psychological Impact of Nonsexual Criminal Offenses on Victims*, Ministry of the Solicitor General of Canada, Ottawa.

National Charter for Victims' Rights in Australia (1993) Standing Committee of Attorneys-General (Australia), Meeting in Darwin 24 June 1993, Agenda Item 18 - Victims of Crime.

New South Wales Sentencing Council 2009, *Public Confidence in the NSW Criminal Justice System,* NSW Sentencing Council Government of New South Wales.

O'Connell, M. 2008, Crime Victims' Rights – Taking a closer look, presentation to the Standing Committee of Attorneys-General, Barossa Valley, South Australia, March.

O'Connell, M. 2009, 'Implementing victims' rights: A case study on the South Australia Police', in F.W. Winkel, P.C. Friday, G.F. Kirchhoff & R.M. Letschert, (eds.). *Victimization in a multi-disciplinary key: recent advances in victimology,* Wolf Legal Publishers, Nijmegen, the Netherlands.

O'Connell, M. 2010, To do the victim justice, requires more than kindness: The case for greater victim participation in criminal justice, plenary paper given at the National Victims of Crime Conference - Victims Needs, Victims Rights "Let's get real" – Hobart, Tasmania, 22-23 November. < http://www.cdesign.com.au/voc2010/program.html>

Pearlman, J. 2008, "Rights Charter to Vindicate Victims", *Sydney Morning Herald*, 7 February.

Redmond, Hon. I. 2007, Victims of Crime (Commissioner for Victims' Rights) Amendment Bill, Second Reading Speech, House of Assembly, *Hansard*, 12 September.

Porter, Hon C. 2011, Community members sought to represent victims of crime, Media Release. <http://www.mediastatements.wa.gov.au/Pages/default.aspx?ItemId=139226>

Sanders, A., 1999, *Taking account of victims in the criminal justice system: A review of the literature*, Central Research Unit Report, Edinburgh, Scotland.

Social Systems & Evaluation 1997, *A Review of the Operations and Effectiveness of the Victims of Crime Act (WA)*, Ministry of Justice, Perth, WA.

South Australian Attorney General's Media Release 2005, dated 28 July 2005, found at: <www.voc.sa.gov.au/Publications/News/Victims%20of%20Crime%20Communique%2028-7-05.doc>.

Standing Committee of Attorneys-General, National Charter on Victims' Rights, Item 19, Documents and Summary Matters, Taupo, New Zealand, 14 October, 1992, Volume 2.

United Nations *Convention against Transnational and Organised Crime* (UN *Treaty Series*, vol. 2555, No. 39574).

United Nations *Convention of the Rights of the Child* (UN *Treaty Series*, vol. 1577, no. 27531).

United Nations 1985, *Declaration of Basic Principles of Justice for Victims of Crime and Abuse of Power*, <www.victimology.nl/onlpub/declar/declar.htm>

United Nations Declaration on the Elimination of Violence against Women, 1993, UN Resolution 48/104 (444).

Uhrig, J. 2003, *Review of the corporate governance of statutory authorities and office holders*, June. < http://www.finance.gov.au/financial-framework/docs/The_Uhrig_Report_July_2003.pdf>

Victims of Crime Coordinator (ACT) 2008, *The Quality of Justice: Operation of the Victims of Crime Act 1994 in the Australian Capital Territory 1996–2007*, Victims of Crime Coordinator, Victim Support ACT. <http://www.victimsupport.act.gov.au/res/File/Quality%20of%20Justice%20June%202008.pdf>

Waller, I. 2007 *Less Law, More Order: The truth about reducing crime*, Praeger, Westport, Connecticut.

Wilkie, M., Ferrante, A. & Susilo, N. 1992, *The Experiences and Needs of Victims of Crime in Western Australia*, Crime Research Centre, UWA, Perth.

Woodberry, J. 1989, *A national charter of victims' rights: Minimising the risk of victimisation and recognition of victims' rights as fundamental tenets of crime prevention*, Australian Police Ministers' Council.

Young, R. 2001, 'Just Cops Doing "Shameful Business?", in A. Morris and G.

Maxwell (eds) *Restorative Justice for Juveniles: Conferencing, Mediation and Circles*, Hart, Oxford, pp. 195–222.

Prevalence, Correlates and Health Consequence of Household Exposure to Violence and Human Rights Violations in Western Bangladesh: A Population-Based Approach Assessing Individual and *Collective Victimization*

By*

Shr-Jie Wang[1], Mohammad Akramul Haque[2], Saber–ud-Daula Masum[2], Shuvodwip Biswas[3], Jens Modvig[1], Edith Montgomery[1]

Abstract

The study assesses the victimization by organized crime, political violence (OPV) and human rights violations in a troubled area in Western Bangladesh. A cross-sectional, population-based cluster survey of 1,101 households using structured questionnaires was conducted 2008. From the surveyed households, 236 victims of massive violence were recruited for a detailed study at a mobile clinic. Most often, they were victims of police action. These victims suffered mainly from police. More than three quarters of the victims reported having had at least two injuries and suffered from pain.

In the district under study, victimization by organized crime and political violence (OPV) and human rights violations are frequent. The population suffers from violence-related injuries and traumas. Victimization is not random; OPV is often driven by economic interests and political goals.

Background

Bangladesh has been exposed to a power struggle between its two major parties since the independence war in 1971. The dominant parties have used armed groups and militias to fight for power and resources(Human Rights Watch 2006; AHRC 2006). Political polarization, lawlessness and institutionalized corruption have hampered the development of democracy in Bangladesh. It appears that there is a serious lack of understanding regarding prevalence and risk factors of organized crime, political violence (OPV) and human rights violations in Bangladesh. The consequences for the victims, the impact of OPV and of human rights violations with regard to population health and financial burden was never explored before.

Objectives

The general objective of this study is to promote understanding of violence epidemiology and of the extent of individual and collective victimization. The study consists of two components: a household survey and a report on health screening at a mobile clinic. The study aims at: 1) describing the magnitude and patterns of OPV and human rights violations, 2) estimating the prevalence of injury, OPV-related injury and pain in the conflict-affected area, 3) identifying the risk determinants of victimization and 4) investigating the association between OPV exposure and general health conditions. This article deal with selected aspects.

Methods

Site

The study was done in Meherpur, the smallest district on Bangladesh, 680000 inhabitants as of 2008. Its wider surroundings were especially hit by in the Bangladesh Independence War of 1971 and later experienced two governmental security operations in 2002 and 2004. It borders to the Indian state West Bengal in the north. Data were collected in February-March 2008.

Determination of Sample Size Sample

A generic protocol was developed based on the guidance provided by WHO document "Guideline for conducting community surveys on injury and violence"(Sethi et al. 2004). The protocol was modified to focus on OPV-related injury and mortality. In order to determine the optimal sample size, a standard statistical formula was used that is developed by United Nations Children's Fund (this formula is given in UNICEF 2000). The number of households to be surveyed in order to estimate the prevalence of a lifetime experience of violence-related injury within the whole population was determined to be 500-1000.

Study sites and sample selection

The sampling frame was based on the 2001 Bangladesh Census, adjusted with an annual population growth rate in the urban and in the rural area (Statistics Bangladesh 2006). A multistage cluster sampling was used. The district was stratified into urban and rural areas. A cluster consists of 50 households. This results in 3,117 clusters. To reflect the ration of rural to urban population, 20 rural clusters and 2 urban clusters were randomly selected for the household survey. A total of 1,101 households in 22 clusters were visited.

The Household Survey

A focus group discussion was carried out with the objective of building trust within the local community and to collect public opinions about the causes and consequences of violence. Questionnaires for the household survey were then created in English and translated into Bengali. A household was defined as a group of people eating from the same pot and sleeping under the same roof. The definition of "torture and other cruel, inhuman or degrading treatment or punishment" is provided by The UN Convention against Torture (UN 1984). The legal definition of "forced or compulsory labour" is provided by the International Covenant on Civil and Political Rights, article 8 (UN 1966). The Geneva Convention additional protocol II (UN 1949) , which addressed the protection of objects indispensable to the survival of the civilian population (article 14) and the prohibition of forced movement of civilians (article 17), were also referenced. The definition of violence was adapted from the WHO report(6). Violence-related injury included interpersonal violence, self-directed violence, legal intervention, war, civil insurrection and disturbance (demonstration or riot). Violence-related deaths therefore included homicide and suicide. Reports on deaths and injuries were classified according to the WHO guideline (Sethi et al. 2004) and the International Statistical Classification of Diseases and Related Health Problems (ICD-10; WHO 1994).

The interviewers began their work in the village centre. The household sampling interval (n) depended on the approximate estimate of the village size. The interviewer visited the *n*-th house on the street in the selected direction and subsequently walked along the street from the centre to the periphery. In the selected households, the head of the household or his/her spouse was interviewed upon providing his/her informed consent. All the answers were reviewed for completeness by the interviewer, the deputy team leader and the principal investigator.

Health screening at mobile clinic

After the household interview, the screening in the mobile medical clinics was an option. For subsequent screening, families were invited who reported one or more of the following experiences: 1) torture or other cruel, inhuman or degrading treatment or punishment; 2) sexual harassment or forced sexual contact by members of a law enforcement agency; 3) arrest and detention without warrant or order; or 4) extrajudicial execution of family members.

Victims were invited to be examined and treated at the mobile clinics. Four mobile clinics were deployed after the household survey. 356 people from the selected households followed the invitation. During the screening process at the entrance to the clinic, we excluded 120 people who were either mentally ill or who reported having no experience with OPV or human rights violations. Altogether,

236 people satisfied the criteria and were recruited. A physical examination was performed that included a routine medical check-up and pain and injury examination (adapting the body mapping from the Istanbul Protocol 1999). Height, weight and standing balance were measured. Participants were asked to stand barefoot on the flat floor on one foot with their eyes open. The physiotherapist/interviewer measured the time that each participant could maintain the balance without assistance; participants were asked to stop after 90 seconds. If balance on one leg was held for more than 30 seconds, it was considered a successful outcome (Hermodson et al. 1994). The "WHO-5 Well-Being" scale was used to assess the subjective emotional well-being of the study participants. A raw score beneath 13 is considered poor emotional well-being. After the physical examination, a consultation was provided to the participants.

Quality assurance

Only four households refused or did not complete the interview. During the household survey, every tenth to twentieth of the participants were interviewed twice by different interviewers or supervised by the deputy team leader. The data set was checked three times for discrepancies.

Ethics evaluation

The study abides by the Declaration of Helsinki and the Danish law. Permission to conduct the study was obtained from the Bangladesh NGOs Bureau. Informed consent was provided and confidentiality was guaranteed. A basic treatment in the mobile trauma clinic was offered to victims of torture or ill-treatment identified during the subsequent screening. Severe cases were referred to the Bangladesh Rehabilitation Centre for Trauma Victims. The sponsor had no role in the study design, data collection and analysis, interpretation of the data, or writing of the report.

Results

Household and participant profile

4,870 persons in 1,101 households were surveyed. The average size of a household was 4.4 people (range 1-15). The mean age of the sample was 28 years old. 8% were younger than 5 years.

The prevalence of injury within 12 months was 36%. The lifetime experience of violence-related injury amounted to 50% while pain complaints within 2 weeks preceding the survey were at 57%. Half of the sample population (n=2,426) have been injured due to violence at some point in their lifetime, and 19% (n=456) of violence-related injury was due to OPV. Among the 87 household members who died within the previous 12 months of the survey, five (6%) were reported to be killed due to violent attacks, which is 1.02 per 1,000 people. Thus, in 2007, we estimate that there were approximately 679 deaths in the district due to violent attacks.

The pain complaints increased with age reaching a plateau after the age of 35. Gender effect on the frequency of pain complaints was small. The prevalence of pain complaints was more than 80% among those over 35 years old and those who reported to have been injured due to violence at some point in their lifetime.

Prevalence and risk factors

Six different forms of household victimizations were measured.

Forced evacuation or displacement , victimized in the liberation war with Pakistan and illegal demolition of household property or food supply essential for survival made up relatively rare occurrence (under 15%). Occupation of the house or searches of the house by legal authority or law enforcement agency happened relatively often (up to 30%) while most often in about 66%, the household was victimized by gunshot, shelling or bombing in the neighbourhood.

From these household victimizations, the study distinguished individual victimizations of household members.

Relatively rare were: Experience of sexual harassment, molestation, rape or insering blunt object into genital or rectum by law enforcement agency members; forced separation from family members; Kidnapping, trafficking or disappearances; participation in combat and "cross fire"; extrajudicial execution by law enforcement agency members; and forced labor for law enforcement agency.

Relatively often were experienced arrest and detention without warrant or order and Torture or cruel inhuman degrading treatment and punishment.

Most often, household members saw relatives being arrested, assaulted, tortured, humiliated, injured or killed (about 70%) and about 80% saw friends or neighbours being mistreated in the same way.

Household-level reporting of OPV and human rights violations was high: 83% reported having been exposed to at least two categories of OPV or human rights violations. Two thirds of the households have experienced gunshots, shelling or bombing in the neighbourhood; and in 75% of the households the members have witnessed a violent action against their friends, neighbours or relatives.

A multivariate model was built up and tested in a stepwise manner,

taking parameters of univariate associations into account. Household served as the unit of analysis and weighting of family size was adjusted. We identified the following predictors: Most probably a family member was arrested or detained if someone from this family: 1) is involved in party politics; 2) has ever participated in a demonstration, a strike or a human rights rally; or 3) has a personal or financial conflict with other families. The likelihood increases as well with the income level of the household. Adjusted for the cluster effect of village, monthly household income level, and size of the household, a significantly increased risk is observed for families involved in the Awami League (the oldest opposition party in Bangladesh) and for families whose members have ever participated in a demonstration, a strike or a human rights rally.
Families whose members are involved in politics or have a conflict with other families in the community are also more likely to report that a family member experienced combat or cross-fire incidents or was extra-judicially executed by members of a law enforcement agency. If relatives or friends of the family work with a law enforcement agency, the likelihood that a family member reported the above experience was significantly lower.

Consequences for family health and financial burden
A generalized linear model was adjusted for the cluster effects of village, location of residence, household income level, and level of political involvement and social activity of family members. The family exposed to at least four categories of OPV and human rights violations yielded higher regression coefficients for the proportion of household members reporting injury, lifetime experience of violence-related injury and pain complaints within two weeks preceding the survey: 14.10, (95% CI: 4.23-23.97, P<0.005), 22.36, (95% CI: 12.48-32.24, P<0.001) and 6.65, (95% CI:0.51-12.80, P<0.05), respectively, compared to families exposed to less than four categories of OPV or human rights violations. Adjusted for income level of household, education and occupation of the head of household, village, and number of family members who had a lifetime experience of violence-related injury, families exposed to at least two categories of OPV and human rights violations were likely to have declining household income level due to the presence of an injured person (OR=2.29, 95% CI: 1.22-4.31, P<0.01), or because family members had stopped working to take care of the injured person (OR=2.89, 95% CI: 1.37-6.11, P<0.005). (An OR > 1 implies that the event is moiré likely in the first group).

Screening at mobile clinic
The mean age of 236 victims of massive violence admitted to the mobile clinic was 42 years. The patterns of victimization shows that

most of the 270 incidents reported by the 236 participants, occurred at their home (46%), 21% at police stations, in military camps, custody or prison facilities. Perpetration. Most often, police were the perpetrators (75%) responsible for 1
The participants endured a total of 719 torture victimizations. 14 types of torture methods were applied to them (Figure 3c). 78% reported having had one or two injuries on the body map. The five most frequently injured areas were the lower back and the abdomen (n=128), the legs (n=100), the chest (n=58), the shoulders (n=40) and the ankles (n=26). The participants were at an increasing risk of having leg and knee injuries if they were subjected to falanga (beating on the soles of the feet) (OR=2.10, 95% CI=1.28-3.67, P<0.01) and being kicked (OR=2.7, 95% CI=1.32-5.53, P<0.01), respectively. An association is established between falanga and sole injury (OR=4.26, 95% CI=1.45-12.49, P<0.01). The results showed that 25% and 50.0% of 236 participants experience consistent and periodic pain within two weeks, 75% and 13% of 236 participants reported moderate and high level of pain intensity, respectively.

In total, 225 participants have completed the WHO-5 Well-Being questionnaire: 86% scored less than 13, which implied that the majority had poor emotional well-being. Out of 229 participants who were able to take the standing balance test, 102 (45%) were able to stand on either foot for 30 seconds. Ability to maintain standing balance is significantly poorer for older participants (above 55 years (OR=0.37, 95% CI: 0.21-0.65, P<0.001).

Discussion

Case reports of violence and human rights violations by human rights NGOs have mainly focused on individual experiences. A few studies showed that family members live with pervasive feeling of pain and perceived or real threat of violence(Montgomery and Foldspang 2001; Baro 2006). However, the risk and adverse health impact on family members who have experienced direct and indirect violence were poorly documented. We used the household as a unit to study the prevalence, correlates and the impact of collective violence. This unique approach allowed us to study collective victimization. We reported that elevated annual injury rates, lifetime experience of violence-related injury, and pain complaints within 2 weeks were related to the levels of collective exposure to OPV or human rights violations. We showed that violence-related mortality rate in the Meherpur district is similar to the rate reported in Iraq(Alkhuzai et al. 2008) and a majority of the study population is suffering from pain.

This study identified several individual, family, relational and community factors that are associated with the risk of victimization among the study population. We confirmed that OPV and human rights violations are often instigated with a political goal or an economic interest. Understanding these factors can help identify various opportunities for prevention at individual and population levels(Adler et al. 2004).

Since Bangladesh gained its independence, the leadership of the two major parties has promoted hatred of rival groups for political and economic gain, which led to a cycle of violence(Andersen 2006, Sreeradha 2005). A similar situation has been reported in the neighbour country Pakistan: political activity is a risk factor for attack and homicide(Chotani et al. 2002; Jamali 2000, Mian et al. 2002) .

It is also known that vengeance, family disputes, dowry disagreements, land disputes and political conflicts have been the sources of violent clashes between families in Bangladeshi society (Monsoor 2007, Begum 2004). Family members share the sense of collective victimhood and their collective fear and hatred spark revenge-driven violence. During the focus group discussion, the victim families mentioned that they could bribe the police and the army to attack the members of rival families. We also found that members from the richest families have higher risk of being arrested or detained than members from the poorest families, but there is no evidence showing that they are more likely to be tortured or executed. This findings support the public opinion collected from the focus group discussion and recent ethnographic research that Bangladeshi police extort money from the population (Sreeradha 2005; Monzoor 2006; Redress Trust2004). The police offer to drop the charges in exchange for a bribe. Richer families are more likely to arrange bribes to save victims from detention, and this may explain why the risk of being tortured or executed is lower for victims from the richest families(Cowdhury 2007). To break the cycle of violence, the authority in Bangladesh needs to launch an anti-corruption reform in the public sectors and establish independent and credible judicial and penal system and.

We also provided a detailed clinical and functional assessment of a sample of 236 victims of massive violence. A combination of physical examination and simple physical tests, a questionnaire and interviews were used to record the history of individual victimization and to assess their physical functioning and well-being. Many victims showed poor subjective emotional well-being. We provided evidence that the effects of exposure to OPV and human rights violations are not temporary. This is also the first study assessing the standing balance performance of victims of massive violence. The standing balance test is a simple and rapid tool for initial assessment. The victims showed poor standing balance, which was associated with their leg and knee injury. Literature showed that impaired lower extremity performance is associated with reduced physical activity levels, which may contribute to subsequent disability in elderly persons(McDermott et al. 2002; Guralnik et al. 1995). To avoid further physical deterioration, we recommend carrying out a comprehensive balance and mobility assessment when a victim of massive violence showed poor standing balance performance outcome.

Limitations

The major limitations of this study are the cross-sectional and retrospective nature of the survey. Memory bias could affect the responses, although a 10 year-recall is considered reliable (Buurt et al. 2001; Schroots et al. 2004) . There is a selection bias in the fact that only one person from each household was interviewed and most of the respondents were women. It is also possible that people in the village misunderstood the definition of each category of OPV and human rights violations. There was inevitably some risk of bias in the recruitment of the study group for the subsequent screening at the mobile clinic. The health-seeking behaviour of the individuals concerned is one possible source of bias. We had expected to use the results as a baseline for a large-scale intervention in this community and to repeat the study afterwards to monitor the quality and outcome of rehabilitation. Unfortunately, these could not be realised for various reasons.

Conclusions

The baseline was established for collective exposure to OPV and human rights violations among the general population in the Meherpur district. The prevalence of the household experience of different OPV manifestations and human rights violations is high. We have developed a simple and rapid tool to assess whether the oppressed population has fair physical and functional capacity in maintaining daily life after being attacked or abused. Both qualitative and quantitative methods should be employed to study individual and collective victimization in order to address the complexity of the situation.

Acknowledgements

The work was supported by the Novo Nordisk Research Foundation. We wish to acknowledge Bangladesh Rehabilitation Centre for Traumatized Victims and Manab Unnayan Kendra (MUK) for their coordination and logistic support, Salma Chowdury and Nuzhat-e-rahman for their contribution in the field. Special thanks go to Per-Erik Isberg, Department of Statistics, Lund University, Sweden for the advice on data analysis. We also thank Andrei Chirokolava and Janni Hansen for editing this manuscript.

References

Asian Legal Resource Center and Asian Human Rights Commission (AHRC): Lawless law-enforcement and the parody of judiciary in Bangladesh. In *Article 2 of the International Covenant on Civil and Political Rights. Volume 5.* Hong Kong: Asian Human Rights Commission (AHRC); 2006.

Adler RN, Smith J, Fishman P, Larson EB: To prevent, react, and rebuild: health research and the prevention of genocide. *Health Serv Res* 2004, 39(6 Pt 2):2027-2051.

Alkhuzai AH, Ahmad IJ, Hweel MJ, Ismail TW, Hasan HH, Younis AR, Shawani O, Al-Jaf VM, Al-Alak MM, Rasheed LH *et al*: Violence-related mortality in Iraq from 2002 to 2006. *N Engl J Med* 2008, 358(5):484-493.

Andersen MK: The borderlands of violence: the making of capable victims. *Master thesis.* Roskilde University, International Development Studies and Geography; 2006.

Baro D: Children witnessing atrocities against parents or caregivers, a human rights perspective. *Torture* 2006, 16(3):190-219.

Begum AA: Acid violence: a burning issue of Bangladesh--its medicolegal aspects. *Am J Forensic Med Pathol* 2004, 25(4):321-323.

Burt CD, Kemp S, Conway M: What happens if you retest autobiographical memory 10 years on? *Mem Cognit* 2001, 29(1):127-136.

Chotani HA, Razzak JA, Luby SP: Patterns of violence in Karachi, Pakistan. *Inj Prev* 2002, 8(1):57-59.

Chowdhury AH: Prisons Centers of Bangladesh: an Overview. Dhaka; 200.

Guralnik JM, Ferrucci L, Simonsick EM, Salive ME, Wallace RB: Lower-extremity function in persons over the age of 70 years as a predictor of subsequent disability. *N Engl J Med* 1995, 332(9):556-561.

Hermodsson Y, Ekdahl C, Persson BM, Roxendal G: Standing balance in trans-tibial amputees following vascular disease or trauma: a comparative study with healthy subjects. *Prosthet Orthot Int* 1994, 18(3):150-158.

Human Rights Watch: Judge, jury, and executioner: torture and extrajudicial killings by Bangladesh's elite security force. 2006, 18(16 c):79.

ICRC 1949: International Committee of the Red Cross: The Geneva Conventions of 1949 and their Additional Protocols. In: http://www.icrc.org/eng/war-and-law/treaties-customary-law/geneva-conventions/index.jsp accessed July 20, 2011

Istanbul Protocol (1999) The Manual on the Effective Investigation and Documentation of Torture and Other Cruel, Inhuman or Degrading Treatment or Punishment. http://www.irct.org/investigation---documentation/the-istanbul-protocol.aspx . accessed July 20, 2011.

Jamali AR, Ghulamullah S, Qureshi I, Mehboob G: Human cost of political violence. *J Pak Med Assoc* 2000, 50(1):25-29.

McDermott MM, Greenland P, Ferrucci L, Criqui MH, Liu K, Sharma L, Chan C, Celic L, Priyanath A, Guralnik JM: Lower extremity performance is associated with daily life physical activity in individuals with and without peripheral arterial disease. *J Am Geriatr Soc* 2002, 50(2):247-255.

Mian A, Mahmood SF, Chotani H, Luby S: Vulnerability to homicide in Karachi: political activity as a risk factor. *Int J Epidemiol* 2002, 31(3):581-585.

Misra A: Revisions of cut-offs of body mass index to define overweight and obesity are needed for the Asian-ethnic groups. *Int J Obes Relat Metab Disord* 2003, 27(11):1294-1296.

Montgomery E, Foldspang A: Traumatic experience and sleep disturbance in refugee children from the Middle East. *Eur J Public Health* 2001, 11(1):18-22.

Monsoor T: Violence against women in Bangladesh. An unpublished report of multi-sectotoral programme on violence against women (MSPVAW) a project of Ministry of Women and Children Affairs and DANIDA. Dakar; 2007.

Monzoor H: Corruption in Bangladesh: a household survey. Dhaka: Transparency International Bangladesh; 2006:2.

Sethi D, Habibula S, McGee K, Peden M, Bennett S, Hyder AA, Klevens J, Odero W, Suriyawongpaisal P: Guideline for conducting community surveys on injury and violence. Geneva: World Health Organization; 2004:151.

Singapore Ministry of Health and Health Promotion Board: Revision of body mass index (BMI) cut-offs in Singapore. Singapore; 2005.

Sreeradha D: Political violence in Bangladesh: trends and causes. *Strategic Analysis* 2005, 29(3):427-447.

Schroots JJ, van Dijkum C, Assink MH: Autobiographical memory from a life span perspective. *Int J Aging Hum Dev* 2004, 58(1):69-85.

Statistics Bangladesh 2006 (http://www.bbs.gov.bd/dataindex/stat_bangladesh.pdf)

UNICEF 2000 United Nations Children's Fund: Monitoring progress toward the goals of the world summit for children: End-decade multiple-indicator survey manual. New York, NY. 2000.

UN 1966: International Covenant on Civil and Political Rights. 1966. In: http://www2.ohchr.org/english/law accessed on 20 August 2011.

UN 1984: United Nations :Convention against Torture and Other Cruel, Inhuman and Degrading Treatment or Punishment. GA 39/46 of December 10, 1984. In: http://www2.ohchr.org/english/law/cat.htm accessed on 20 August 2011.

The Redress Trust: Torture in Bangladesh 1971-2004 In *Making international commitments a reality and providing justice and reparations to victims.* London: The European Initiative for Democracy and Human Rights; 2004.

UN 1984: United Nations :Convention against Torture and Other Cruel, Inhuman and Degrading Treatment or Punishment. GA 39/46 of December 10, 1984. In: http://www2.ohchr.org/english/law/cat.htm accessed on 20 August 2011.

UN 1966: International Covenant on Civil and Political Rights. 1966. In: http://www2.ohchr.org/english/law accessed on 20 August 2011.

WHO1990: International Classification of Diseases (ICD) in: http://www.who.int/classifications/icd/en/ accessed
Accessed July 20, 2011.

WHO 2002 : World Health Organization: WHO report on violence and health. Geneva: WHO Violence Prevention Alliance; 2002:372.

Refugees and Minorities as Victims

Victims of Forced Displacement – Refugees and Internally Displaced Persons

By

Saburo Takizawa[1]

Refugees and Internally Displaced Persons are the "clients" of the UN High Commissioner of Refugees . A very suitable introduction into the work of this part of the UN Administration is a video "Working with Refugees" (UN.DVD).

Refugees are defined as persons who are outside one's own countries of origins owing to persecution, for reason such as race, religion, and political opinion. Internally displaced persons are those who have been uprooted from home to elsewhere within their country. The office of the United Nations High Commissioner for Refugees, or UNHCR, was established in 1950 as the UN agency mandated to protect the human rights of refugees and to resolve their problems. In 1951, the Refugee Convention was adopted. UNHCR's Headquarters is in Geneva, Switzerland. The Agency maintains offices in 117 countries throughout the world, including Japan, and it has staffs over 6300. UNHCR's activities are wide-ranging. The number of people in need of UNHCR support is currently estimated to be 33 million world-wide, or nearly one quarter of population in Japan. UNHCR activities at large are financially supported by voluntary contributions from governments as well as donations from private sector.

People on the run

As we have seen in the video, throughout history, there have always been refugees. Wars, political upheavals, ethnic discrimination, religious strife and other human rights abuses have forced people to flee their homes and countries. Those "people in the run", particularly women, girls, boys and the elderly, are very vulnerable people. And there are many of them in today's world. At the end of 2008, there were as many as 46 million displaced persons including 15 million refugees and 26 million Internally Displaced Persons or IDPs. 46 million people mean that one in every 140 people worldwide is either a refugee or an IDP. In Asia alone, there were 3.4 million refugees and 3.5 million IDPs in 2008.

---

[1] Toyo Eiwa University

Some people cross international borders and seek asylum in other countries in an attempt to receive refugee status. A refugee is any person who is outside their country of origin and because of a well-founded fear of persecution due to their race, religion, nationality or political opinion, is unwilling or unable to receive the protection of his or her home country. On the other hand, IDPs also flee their homes and communities, but do not cross international borders because they either wish to stay in their home country, or they are unable to reach the border. The main difference between refugees and IDPs is whether they have crossed international borders or not.

But why do so many people have to flee their homes and countries, often risking their lives and not even knowing what await them? People flee because the victimization inflicted upon them is so severe. They have experienced, or they are afraid of, for example: intimidation, physical assaults, arbitrary detention and forced labor, abduction, torture, murder of family members or friends. Extreme cases of victimization include mass rape, mass killing and "ethnic cleansing". These acts are difficult to imagine in a peaceful county like here in Japan, but they are taking place in the world today. The numbers of IDP assisted by the UNHCR in the last decade has increased from 4 to 14 million while in the same period the numbers of assisted refugees have been slightly decreased. Why is this so?

The first reason is that the nature of armed conflicts has changed. In the past, wars were fought among States. All major wars were inter-State, like the Korean War and the Vietnam War where more than two countries fought against each other. This type of inter-State war has diminished since the end of the Cold War in 1989. Indeed, the last large-scale international war was almost 20 years ago when Iraq invaded Kuwait in 1990. Today, wars are mostly fought inside a country among armed groups belonging to different ethnic or religious groups, like civil wars in the Balkans, Great Lakes region in Africa, Northern Iraq, West Africa, Caucasus, Afghanistan and Darfur, Sudan. Those intra-State conflicts within a country tend to produce more displaced people than Inter State wars.

The second reason is that, after the Cold War, the legitimacy of certain Nation-States was seriously challenged by various ethnic, religious, political groups whose interests and aspirations were suppressed or completely ignored during the Cold War period. Previously, the USA and former-USSR tended to support repressive, dictatorial, undemocratic and corrupt States, so long as they remained loyal to the two Superpowers. With the loss of the Superpowers' support in the post-Cold War period, various ethnic, religious or political minorities revolted against those State authorities and sought to assert their rights and justifiable aspirations. These States in turn activated their security and judicial systems to maintain their political and social control via repression of those whom the State considered to be offenders or criminal dissidents.

Graph 1 State as Protector

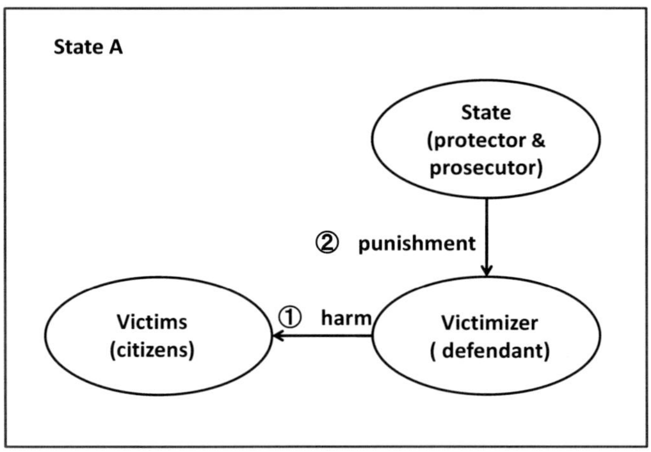

Graph 2 State as Victimizer

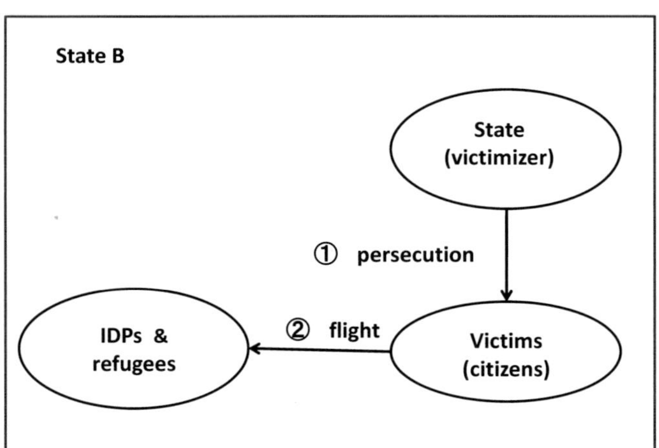

The two graphs are based on an idea of Kirchhoff (2005). The first (Graph 1) shows, let's say, a "democratic" State A which acts as a protector of its citizens, and when necessary acts as a prosecutor of offenders who have harmed other citizens. Graph 2 shows, on the other hand, an "undemocratic" State B whose power is dominated by certain groups and who acts as a victimizer and persecutor to suppress minority groups who are demanding that their rights and aspirations be recognized. Alternatively, a State may be simply unable to control serious internal conflicts, like the failed State of Somalia or a fragile State like Afghanistan. The two diagrams are exactly the same, but the consequences are opposite. State A does not produce displacement, but State B produced IDPs and refugees. Forced displacement is related to failed or weak governance. It is related to abuse and misuse of political power by States at the expense of neighboring States.

The third reason for the increase in the number of IDPs is that the strategy of war has changed. Today, warring factions and armed groups often target unarmed civilians and deliberately kill them, torture them, maim them and rape them, with the intention to terrify and terrorize people so that affected populations flee the disputed territories in large numbers. An example are presentations on mass victimizations in Cambodia and Bangladesh. The combination of intra-State conflicts and the deliberate targeting of unarmed civilians, cause millions of people to flee their homes and countries. And this is a new post-Cold War phenomenon.

In addition, it has to be kept in mind that not everybody who wishes to flee their county can actually do so. For example, in North Korea, where severe human rights violations and starvation are reported, there are a large number of people wishing to flee their country, but cannot do so as it is illegal and in violation of the Constitution to leave the country without permission. If anyone is caught at the border trying to flee, he or she will face severe punishment, imprisonment in labor camps, or even the death penalty. People do not even have the freedom to flee.

In other countries, some people refuse to flee despite experiencing state persecution and continue fighting for what they believe is right for their country, like democratization. And we must remember that there are millions of people who can never flee – as they have already been killed during armed conflicts, or died of disease or hunger when the country's social infrastructure collapsed. For instance, in southern Sudan alone, it is estimated that up to two million people have died during internal armed conflicts that have lasted 30 years. They did not survive conflicts and starvation.

Cycle of Forced Displacement

The victimization of refugees and IDPs during their flight and displacement is the topic of Graph 3. First, when an armed conflict occurs in a country, or persecution by a government starts, people flee to a safer place in their own country, such as in the mountains or rural areas, hoping that the conflict will cease shortly. Some people may wish to flee to a foreign county as a refugee, but many people cannot flee their country, because of the long distance to the border, lack of transportation means, lack of money, or because they do not want to leave behind family members and friends. Today there are 26 million IDPs across 52 countries in the world.

Graph 3 People on the Move

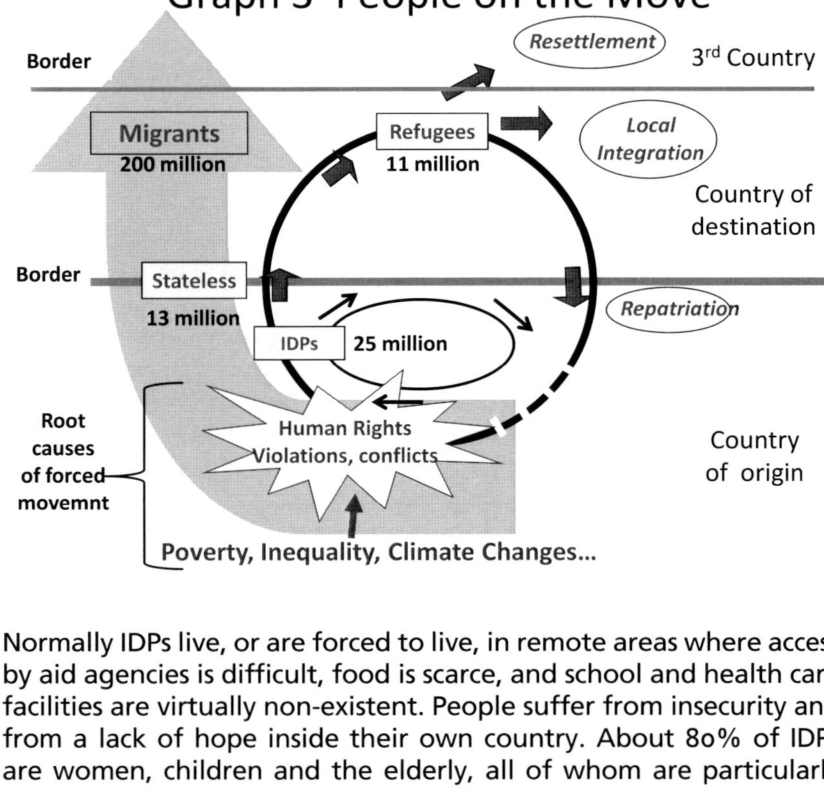

Normally IDPs live, or are forced to live, in remote areas where access by aid agencies is difficult, food is scarce, and school and health care facilities are virtually non-existent. People suffer from insecurity and from a lack of hope inside their own country. About 80% of IDPs are women, children and the elderly, all of whom are particularly vulnerable. Men are either fighting with government or other armed forces, are detained or are simply dead. Many IDPs remain in this refugee-like situation, without protection and assistance by their own country, for years and even decades. They are in a protracted IDP situation.
Why is this so? The main reason for the absence of international

protection of IDPs is the issue of State Sovereignty and the still common principle of non-interference in the internal affairs of other countries. While States are responsible to protect their own citizens, failed states like Somalia or fragile states like Afghanistan cannot do so. Other States are capable of helping their own citizens, but lack the intention to do so and yet refuse international humanitarian assistance. International society's reluctance to forcibly intervene in the conflict in Darfur where massive victimization has been taking place is one example in this respect.

Even if we know that there are serious human rights violations which cause a large number of IDPs in a country, the international society cannot simply intervene to help these victims. If UNHCR and others help IDPs, they need to obtain permission from the very political authorities who are responsible for the victims of forced displacement! The case in point is Myanmar/Burma, where international community has failed to obtain the consent of the government to help IDPs in the border regions.

Asylum seekers and Refugees

Every year hundreds/thousands of people cross international borders to seek asylum. Once recognized as a refugee, he or she is protected by the country of asylum and shielded from possible harm by his or her own country. But not all asylum seekers are recognized as refugees. Roughly 80 % of asylum seekers are rejected. Consequently, they and are either deported or have to find asylum in another country. The 1951 Refugee Convention provides that States should not forcibly send asylum seekers back to their country of origin where they face the risk of persecution. This is called the principle of "*non-refoulement. It* is at the core of the international protection of refugees.
However, the situation surrounding asylum seekers and refugees is not encouraginging. First, since the 9/11 terrorist attacks in NY, States have become more concerned about national security and more countries have introduced restrictive refugee policies. As a result, the number of asylum seekers in industrialized countries has been reduced from 600,000 in 2000 to 300,000 in 2007. This does not mean that there are fewer asylum seekers, but simply means that reaching the shores of asylum countries is more difficult than before. This perhaps means that there are more people who continue to be victimized due to persecution and armed conflicts in their home countries.

Second, another development that narrows the asylum space in

developed countries is the issue of migration. As globalization continues, more and more people move towards industrialized countries to seek better economic opportunities. And developed countries have become more concerned about the entry or influx of migrants, particularly during times of economic recession like today. Realizing that getting a working visa is more difficult than before, some migrants do in fact abuse the asylum system. Modern migratory patterns can be extremely complex and contain a mix of economic migrants, refugees and others. Separating refugees from the various groups of migrants through fair asylum procedure can be a daunting task for governments.
Third, there is the problem of the long-term detention of asylum seekers. An increasing number of asylum seekers are detained pending determination of their status. They are confined in jail-like facilities for long and unknown periods. Many asylum seekers develop physical, mental and psychological problems.

This type of victimization is inflicted on asylum seekers in particular. Many asylum seekers already suffer from post-traumatic stress disorder (PTSD) because of their experience of persecution or armed conflict. Long term detention can aggravate the situation and cause additional detention-related PTSD. For asylum seekers arriving in a developing country, the situation is worse, as mental health care is usually totally inadequate. There are only 30 psychologists in Cambodia, a country that experienced one of the most serious genocides. In emergency situations when trauma care is needed, assistance providers are preoccupied trying to provide basic materials for survival, like food, water, and shelter. Trauma care is not given high priority and this is the case within UNHCR as well.

Fourth, refugees suffer many losses. They have lost homes, land, loved ones and personal property. Some of their family members and close friends may have been killed or detained. Most refugees consistently worry about their family members who have been left behind, as maintaining communication with them is usually difficult. They have lost occupational and social roles and this could lead to loss of their identity as an individual. In refugee camps where there is no gainful employment, adult males are forced to be idle. This often leads to domestic violence against spouses and children. All these losses are demoralizing and traumatic and these in turn, may lead to loss of a sense of dignity and meaning in life.

Fifth, many of the world's refugees are in a protracted refugee situation, that is, they have spent years or more than a decade of their life in exile. Out of 15 million refugees in the world, more than six million have been staying in a refugee camp or a camp-like situation for more than five years. The average duration of life in a camp is 17 years. Fear and insecurity are everywhere: fear for one's own life, fear for family members and relatives and anxiety over the children's future. A refugee's life is full of worry and helplessness. Such a protracted situation creates further problems, as desperate refugees may be attracted by armed groups which may cause security concerns in the host country. Protracted refugee situations can also cause regional security concerns.

Finally, in the host countries, refugees face victimization by xenophobia. They are repeatedly discriminated when they are perceived as a security threat to the host country and a burden to the host community. In victimology, there is the concept of "secondary" or of "multiple" victimization. This is a sad reality in many countries, including in Japan. There is xenophobia One presentation in the parallel session deals with refugee victims of xenophobia in South Africa. Xenophobia against refugees is everywhere. There exists "structural victimization" of asylum seekers and refugees around the world._

Solutions (voluntary repatriation, local integration, resettlement)

There are three basic solutions to refugee problems, as defined by UNHCR: voluntary return, repatriation to the home county, local integration in the country of asylum and resettlement to a third country. These three solutions also apply to IDPs.

Voluntary return

The best solution for displaced persons is to return to their homes once conflicts or human rights violations have ended. In Africa, hundreds of thousands of refugees went home after peace negotiations ended internal conflicts in Angola, Burundi, Liberia and South Sudan. When refugees arrive to their home after years of exile, meet separated family members and find old friends among those waiting for their arrival, the scene is truly emotional. It is the best moment for UNHCR staff as well.

Very important is the positive role of refugees in post-conflict peace building. Many returned/repatriated refugees have been trained, educated and empowered by assistance providers like UNHCR, and have new ideas and skills that they acquired during their time spent abroad. They are willing to join in the efforts to build peace. Many of them have courageously fought for freedom and democracy. Many have survived persecution. Therefore they know very well the importance of democratic values. Their experience during their life in exile has made them stronger and some of them will be able to assume leadership roles in the State and society where peace has been re-established. Returned refugees can be "agents for change" and "agents for democracy".

Local integration and resettlement

When returning to one's home country is not possible because of continued conflict or ongoing fear of human rights violations, alternatives may exist in form of local integration and resettlement in third countries. This means that refugees live permanently in a host country and may eventually become citizens of that country. In fact, many refugees have integrated permanently in their country of asylum. Einstein was a refugee from Nazi-controlled Germany and Former US Secretary of State, Madeleine Albright was a refugee from Czechoslovakia.. Such people have made valuable contributions to their host country in economic, political, social and scientific fields. Refugees can, without doubt, be excellent assets to a host society.

However, refugees may continue suffering disadvantage, discrimination and xenophobia for many years in the host country. This is particularly so when initial integration support is not sufficient. For instance, some 11,000 Indochinese refugees have been accepted by Japan over the last 30 years, but many of them have faced difficulties because their Japanese language training was totally inadequate – the training was only three to four months. Imagine how difficult it would be if those of you who came from abroad have to live and work in Japan with only three months language training!

From a victimological point of view, there are five aspects to be taken into account:

First, displacement entails massive victimization. There are over 40 million victims of persecution, people who are on the run.

Second, refugees and IDPs may face secondary, or even multiple, victimization during their flight and time in exile. Refugees are routinely victimized by power holders like immigration officials, security officials and human traffickers.

Third, when commonly refugees are perceived as a threat to the host country and as a burden to the host community, and when they face systematic discrimination and xenophobia in many parts of the world, we say that refugees face "structural victimization".

Fourth, their victimization can become protracted - over 6 million refugees have spent more than 5 years in refugee camps in 30 countries, without freedom of movement amidst other human rights violations.

Finally, and this is perhaps the most important attribute that make refugees and IDPs a unique category of victims: Many refugees and IDPs are victims of abuse or misuse of political power by the State. Certain States are unable to protect their own citizens. Some abusive States become victimizers and persecutors, forcing refugees to seek asylum in other countries.

International protection regime

Despite the longstanding historical significance of refugees, it was only in the twentieth century that a formal institutional structure was created to address refugee issues. Following the atrocities and victimization of hundreds of millions of people during Second World War, the United Nations General Assembly adopted the Refugee Convention (UN 1951) to provide international protection to refugees. The Convention defines the rights of refugees who no longer enjoy the legal protection of his home country, such as access to national courts, the right to employment and education, and other social, economic and civil rights on par with a national of the host country. The most significant right granted to refugees is *non-refoulement*; the right of refugees not to be forcibly returned to a country where they risk persecution. This remains the cornerstone of international refugee protection.

As for IDPs, in 1998, the United Nations adopted the *Guiding Principles on Internal Displacemen(UN 1998)*. Based on standards enumerated by human rights law, refugee law and international humanitarian law, the Guiding Principles provide a framework to prevent internal displacement and to protect and find solutions for those who have been displaced. While the Guiding Principles are not binding, some countries have already incorporated them in their national laws, thus binding themselves to their implementation.

Although there is no formal international legal framework yet, there is an emerging consensus that the international community has a collective responsibility to protect the most vulnerable victims when a State is unwilling or unable to protect its own citizens. This principle is called "the Responsibility to Protect" (or "R2P") and has gained increasing acceptance since the late 1990s. The 2005 United Nations strongly and unanimously endorsed the principle. In response to these developments, UNHCR and other UN agencies have been strengthening their support to States in protecting and assisting IDPs.

UNHCR

At the same time as the adoption of the 1951 Refugee Convention, the General Assembly established UNHCR, the UN Refugee Agency, so as to provide protection to refugees and find durable solutions to refugee problems. UNHCR, as the guardian of the 1951 Refugee Convention, has been providing relief and care to refugees and, when requested by the United Nations, some of the IDPs who are in need. It has facilitated consultation and negotiations among States. It monitored their compliance with the 1951 Convention. UNHCR is a part of the international social response to massive, multiple, protracted and structural victimization of displaced populations. However, it should be pointed out that it does not directly deal with the root causes of forced displacement in the countries of origin. The focus is on refugees outside the home country.

It is fair to label UNHCR as a kind of victim service organization. It has served and saved tens of millions of lives of victims of armed conflicts and human rights violations. UNHCR has resettled a large number of refugees from the East to West during the Cold War and addressed the massive outflow of millions of refugees from the South to surrounding countries in the post Cold War period throughout the world. On a separate but related issue, UNHCR is also mandated to look after stateless persons, whose number is estimated as high as 12 million, Stateless persons fall between the cracks of national borders, having no State to protect them.

From a small office of some 30 staff based mostly in Europe in the early 1950s, UNHCR is now a global organization with more than 6500 staff in many conflict-affected Countries. UNHCR is a front-line humanitarian agency of the United Nations system, protecting and empowering tens of millions of victims of forced displacement. It was awarded the Nobel Peace prise twice in the past.

Limitation

Now, the established international refugee regime has come under pressure due to the following issues, all of which are outside the scope of the 1951 Refugee Convention: (A) restrictive refugee policies of developed countries; (B) the emerging norm of "the responsibility to protect" with respect to IDPs; (C) the asylum/migration nexus in which refugees and migrants move together, albeit for different reasons; and (D) the emergence of so-called "environmental refugees". UNHCR spends almost half of its resources on IDPs, voluntary returnees, and stateless persons. With an increase in the number of persons displaced by natural disasters, and a dramatic rise in the number of economic migrants in the world, coupled with predictions that these numbers will rise further with the consequences of climate change and globalization, the challenge facing UNHCR is likely to increase in scale and complexity in the future.

Situation in Japan

Japan has long been criticized by the international community for closing its doors to refugees and asylum seekers. Indeed, other than the 11,000 Indochinese refugees who have been accepted over the last 30 years, Japan has recognised a little over 500 refugees in the last 27 years under the Refugee Convention. This is very low compared to the number of refugees accepted by other industrialized countries. On the other hand, Japan has been generous in providing financial resources to UNHCR. Last year Japan's financial contribution to UNHCR of over US$100 million was second only to the United States despite decreasing Japanese foreign aid (ODA). Some commentators criticize Japan's approach as using "check book diplomacy" – we will give you money, so please take care of refugees outside Japan (Knight 2009).

Fortunately the situation is changing and beginning to move in the right direction. In December 2008, the Japanese government announced that it would start a pilot refugee resettlement program from 2010 for a period of three years. Each year, it is planned that 30 Burmese/Myanmar refugees who have been living in refugee camps in Thailand will be resettled to Japan. While this is a pilot program and the number is extremely small, it is significant because Japan will be the first Asian country to become an official resettlement country, and because Japan is starting this programme without any foreign pressure (known as *Gaiatsu* in Japanese), as was not the case when resettling Indochinese refugees during the 1970s and 1980s.

Furthermore, the number of asylum seekers in Japan reached 1600 last year, of whom 57 were recognized as refugees. In 2008, an additional 350 asylum seekers were granted special permits to stay in Japan temporarily, although their refugee claims were rejected. All in all, some 400 asylum seekers were granted some form of protection in Japan last year. If one recalls that a decade ago, only a handful of asylum seekers were recognized as refugees in this country each year, this is a remarkable development. Japan seems to be opening its doors to refugees at long last in the spirit of humanitarian principles and international solidarity. The humanitarian space in Japan is indeed expanding (UNHCR 2010).

Summary: Refugee Studies and Victimology

Refugees and internally displaced persons have been described as victims of serious human rights violations, and as victims of abuse and misuse of political power. The article gives some explanations why there is an increasing number of IDPs in today's world. It traced the physical movement of displaced people along the cycle of forced displacement, and it described what sort of specific victimization they may face. IDPs and refugees face massive, multiple, protracted and even systematic victimization. Three solutions (voluntary repatriation, local integration and resettlement) are described within the framework the international society's response to refugee problems, that is, the international refugee protection regime, including UNHCR. Finally, some recent developments in Japan in terms of protection of refugee victims are described.
For the author, it is abundantly clear that all refugees and IDPs are victims. However, although there is a vast amount of literature on refugee studies from the legal and political perspectives, as well as studies on the mental health of displaced persons, there appears to be a very limited literature on refugees from the perspective of victimology. In April this year, he visited the Refugee Studies Center at Oxford University and found that there was no literature dealing specifically with both refugees and victimology, although there were quite a few books on the mental health of refugees, particularly those dealing with PTSD.

This author hopes that a new field of inquiry for victimology is opened. In this field, the focus on refugees and internally displaced persons as victims. Conversely, refugee studies can gain a lot from research and practice on the mental health of refugees, from the accumulated understanding of the victimizer-victim dynamics. New collaboration between Victimology and refugee studies will help to enhance the human rights and human security of victims of forced displacement, tens of millions people on the move.

References:

Guiding Principles on Internal Displacement (E/CN.4/1998/53/Add.2) http://www2.ohcr.org/english/issues/idp/
standards.htm accessed on May 5, 2011

Kirchhoff, G.F. (2005). What is Victimology? Tokiwa International Institute Monograph Series No.1. Tokyo (Seibundo Publishing).

Knights, Sophie: Closed Gates. Metropolis. 28. August 2009. http://archive.metropolis.co.jp/tokyo/800/feature.asp. Accessed on May 5, 2011

UN 1951 = Refugee Convention of 1951, http://www.unhcr.org/pages/49da0e466.html, accessed May 5, 2011

UN 1998=Guiding Principles on Internal Displacement (E/CN.4/1998/53/Add.2) http://www2.ohcr.org/english/issues/idp/ accessed May 5, 2011.
standards.htm accessed on May 5, 2011

U.N. DVD reveals plight of refugees. Yomiuri Shimbun/Daily Yomiuri. August 20, 2008 |
http://www.accessmylibrary.com/article-1G1-188313950/u-n-dvd-reveals.html accessed August 31, 2011.

UNHCR 2010= Welcome to Japan: First Asian country joins UNHCR's resettlement programme
News Stories, 28 September 2010. http://www.unhcr.org/cgiin/texis/vtx/search?page=search&docid=4ca1dbe66&query =japan, accessed on August 28,2011.

Ainu People in Japan – Victimization of a Marginal Group in Society

By

Chiori Noto

As a result of the modernization policy directed by the Japanese Government, the Ainu who were officially recognized as indigenous people of Japan in 2008, had been denied the ability to practice their native language, belief system and traditional customs, resulting in the subsequent loss of their sense of identity. This policy was created and implemented under the perception that Ainu needed to be protected because they were "inferior, illiterate and a non-agricultural race", an attitude that resulted from the prejudice and aversion towards the Ainu. The Ainu therefore, have been deprived of the freedom of choosing their own future.

This policy aimed to "protect inferior people". It served as an assimilation policy for the Ainu and created a vicious cycle that destroyed the Ainu people's basis for livelihood, subsequently talking away from them the opportunity to get education and leading them into poverty. The symbol of assimilation policy, the "Hokkaido Former Aborigines Protection Act" (1899), was finally abolished in 1997, and the "Law for the Promotion of Ainu Culture and for the Dissemination of Advocacy for the Traditions of the Ainu and the Ainu Culture" was enacted instead. This new law, however, emphasized only the need to protect, maintain and raise awareness about Ainu culture. But it has not provided a scheme strong enough to break the vicious cycle that Ainu have suffered since long before.

1. Introduction

In 2007, the UN General Assembly adopted the "Declaration on the Rights of Indigenous People" (UN 2007). Even if the declaration is not binding all UN members, it is recognised as an international standard which establishes the rights of about three hundred seven million of indigenous peoples - their identity, culture, education, economic rights, their land rights and their rights on the resources they have traditionally owned (Art.26). 144 nations in the General Assembly voted for the Declaration, 4 nations voted against it (America, Canada, Australia and New Zealand), and 11 abstained (Azerbaijan,

Bangladesh, Bhutan, Burundi, Colombia, Georgia, Kenya, Nigeria, Russia, Samoa and Ukraine, see BBC News 2007). Japan's government voted in favour and gave this reason: "We are requested by UN human rights monitoring bodies to make concrete steps to realize the purpose of the Declaration" (Diet 2008).

In June 6, 2008 both houses of the Japanese Parliament unanimously passed the "Resolution Calling for the Recognition of the Ainu People as Indigenous People in Japan" (Lewallen 2008). The Diet resolution states (in English translation) "Our historical awareness about *Ainu* has changed in the process of modernization. Our laws repeatedly said that Ainu are equal. However, many *Ainu* people unavoidably suffered from poverty." The Diet also expressed the wish to establish general guidelines for the *Ainu* policy. The Japanese government legally and politically regarded Ainu people as indigenous people. That meant a new step in direction of a multi- cultural society in Japan. However, in the past Ainu had experienced cultural, social, and economical damages - and they were about to loose their pride as *Ainu* while under the control of the Japanese. That constitutes a vicious circle even now. The survey "*Hokkaido Ainu* People – the Present Life and Attitudes of *Ainu* People" conducted by *Hokkaido* University *Ainu* Indigenous People Research Centre clearly shows the problems. This article looks at the history of *Ainu* people. It provides some ideas how Japan should proceed in future with its indigenous people.

2. The History of *Ainu*

Ainu settled in Hokkaido, Sakhalin and Kuril Islands. They lived from the natural resources and had trade relationships with the main island of Japan (Honshu), China and Russia. They preserved their own culture and trading areas. Meanwhile, the culture of rice cultivation was extended into their land, and that changed gradually the traditional way of life, economically and politically.

Eventually in about the middle of the 14th *century, Wajin* (Japanese living in Honshu, the main island of Japan) invaded the Ainu's territory in the southern part of *Hokkaido* and founded trade posts. The *Wajin* exploited the Ainu by unfair trade conditions. An example for such unfair trade policies was that the Wajin paid for hundred salmons not more than 30kg of rice. This exploitation caused conflict between Ainu and Wajin.

In the following time, Ainu uprisings occurred quite often. The resistance against the Wajin led to the Battle of *Kosyamain* (1457).

Other battles have been fought in 1669 (*Shakushain)* or in 1789 *(Battle of Kunashiri and Menashi*). The Ainu lost each time. After losing the Battle of Kunasiri-Menasi in particular, the Ainu fell completely under the control of the Japanese (Ainu Museum 2011).

Since 1855, territorial issues had been settled between Japan and Russia with the result that the Ainu inhabitants of the islands *Karafuto, Chishima, Etorofu and Wruppu* were deported. For the first time all territories where *Ainu* people lived, were controlled by the power of the Japanese government. In the Meiji Restoration, the original name of the area that were inhabited by Ainu, "*Ainumishiri*" (that is in Ainu language the "domain of humans" as opposed to "kamuymosir, the domain of the Gods) was changed into the Japanese name *Hokkaido.* In 1871, *Ainu* people were forced to be enrolled into the Japanese family register system according to the Japanese Family Register Law. But in contrast to other Japanese citizen, they were registered as "former natives" and actually treated as a second class of citizen. The next step in the "assimilation" came in 1872. Under the pretext of "civilizing *Ainu* people", their cultures and customs came under pressure. New regulations prohibited typical signs of cultural ethnic identification like the tattoos of females and the earrings of the male Ainu. Most of their land rights were taken away. Also, the Meiji government prohibited Ainu to exercise their rights to hunting and fishing - the traditional livelihood of the Ainu. If *Ainu* violated the law they were punished for poaching (Nomura1992). For those reasons, many *Ainu* people became impoverished. Diseases such as tuberculosis or syphilis undermined their health. The discrimination, based on the Japanese laws, has been continuing till today. Since then, discrimination replaced the old fashioned oppression and exploitation (Ainu 1994).

In 1875, Japan and Russia concluded the *Karafuto* and *Chishima* Exchange Treaty. In this Japan agreed to give up its claims on Sakhalin in exchange for undisputed ownership of the Kuril Islands. Ainu lived in both islands.
In its wake, *Ainu* people had to choose whether they would belong to Japan or Russia. Often they were forced to migrate..

In 1898, the Hokkaido Indigenous Protection Act passed the Diet. This law mainly prohibits *Ainu's* traditional livelihood, hunting and fishing, the foundation of their life. Instead, it tries to assimilate them to Japanese agriculture and school system. The Japanese government was to rule over the underprivileged people who lost the fight for their existence. Not only there was no viewpoint of the rights of the race but, also no recognition that the impoverishment. The written motives of the law say (English translation): "The time has not been long enough during which the *Ainu* received the blessings by our Emperor. Their intellectual enlightenment is very low. Therefore the blessings of nature which they have been relying on were occupied by the people from *Honshu. Ainu* people gradually lost their lifestyle. It looked as if the only thing they did was waiting for scarcity of food and clothing. This survival of the fittest is the course of nature which we cannot do anything for it" (Ainu 2000).

The Protection Act shows clearly disregard for the Ainu. The Ainu were characterized as in need of national protection. In the written reasons for the law, Ainu are called "children of the Emperor" - they are "Japanese", but they are regarded as immature and in need of special education until their cultural level reaches to the level of ordinary Japanese people - only then they are real citizen. The Protection Law provided that Ainu could own up to up to 49500 m2 - but only those *Ainu* who already were involved in farming or who started to become involved. But the land allotted to them was of poor quality, not suited for farming. There was a provision in the law that deprived Ainu of this property: If this land had not been cultivated within 15 years, the land would be confiscated. As the results of that, about 20% of Ainu's lands were taken away.

In 1922, *Hokkaido* government conducted "A Survey on the Natives". It revealed that 60% of the Ainu were engaged in farming-independent or dependent. The only way of making a living for Ainu was in agriculture. To make things worse, there was no agricultural education, no instruction how to farm. After the prescribed period of 15 years had run out, *Ainu* saw their lands being confiscated due to the inability of cultivation. In addition, many Ainu were swindled by Japanese out of their property and were led to give up their land at a cheep price. That is to say *Ainu* people were actually deprived their lands twice.

In the field of school education, in 1901, *Hokkaido* government started to regulate the education of "indigenous children". An important feature of the regulation was the principle of separate education from Japanese children. Following this law, the government provided 25 of "Schools for Indigenes" in areas where Ainu people were settling. If *Ainu* children had to attend other public schools than these "Special School for Indigenes", those children were to be separated from Japanese children as much as possible. Another feature of this assimilation policy, the policy to convert Ainu into "good Japanese citizen", was this: A*inu* children were forced to learn the Japanese language and to adopt Japanese lifestyle. The use of Ainu language was prohibited. With this prohibition of Ainu language, young people very early - even inside their home - were separated from their traditional lifestyle. In addition, *Ainu* children were provided a shorter obligatory education compared to Japanese children: their schooling period was only for 4 years while Japanese children went 6 years to school. On top of that, the enrolment for Ainu children started a year later than for Japanese children. Furthermore, for Ainu children a special subject called "*Shyushin*" was introduced. The goal of the special subject was to produce citizens of the Empire of Japan, devoted to the Emperor and to Japanese language and culture. *Ainu* had no chance to learn geography, history or science. This gap in education between Japanese and Ainu caused much dissatisfaction among Ainu. *In* 1937, the Protection Act was drastically amended and coeducation between Japanese and Ainu was introduced - however, it caused contempt and hate against *Ainu* in the classrooms. The policy was officially designed for protection of *Ainu* but it did not protect but it did discriminate - *it* positioned Ainu as minority in society. It was hardly possible for an Ainu to pursue a higher-level school career after they finished the minimum compulsory education. That in turn made it difficult to find a decent job. Such life circumstances caused a vicious circle.

3. Human Rights of Ainu: The Cultural Revival Movement

In 1946, *Hokkaido Utari* Incorporated Association (Utari means "fellow citizen") had been established. With this the movement for a renaissance of the Ainu, claiming independent status for *Ainu,* started. In 1972, *Hokkaido* government conducted a survey on the actual living conditions of *Ainu, to* improve their standard of living and to raise the percentage of students who go on to higher-level education "The first *Hokkaido Utari W*elfare Measure Plans" was settled. The plan was to differentiate between *Ainu* people and Japanese in the matter of welfare measures. In 1978, the Hokk*aido Ainu* Association drafted a "New *Ainu* Law". But the Governor of *Hokkaido* convocated an own Committee to deal with the problem. Later, the competence for this matter was shifted to the Cabinet Domestic Administration Policy Unit. These manoeuvres made it clear: There was no official political interest in improving the situation of the Ainu - the discussion disappeared in an administrative political jungle.

In 1986, the Prime Minister stated officially that Japan is a "homogeneous" nation. This statement stirred up controversies. The minority issue drew peoples' attention all over the nation. In

1991, the government incidentally acknowledged the existence of *Ainu* as minority people. This happened in a report which is based on the International Covenant on Civil and Political Rights. In 1992, the chairperson of the *Hokkaido Ainu* Association gave the Inauguration Address to the UN General Assembly for the "Year of the Wold's Indigenous People". Following the changing trend of the time, the Japanese government installed in the Cabinet Secretary a "Panel Discussion by Experts For the Measures of Utari". This group issued a report in 1996.

This report demands

- Promoting comprehensive and practical researches
- Promoting *Ainu* cultures including *Ainu* language
- Reconstruction of the traditional living space
- Promoting general understanding of *Ainu.*

It postulates to create a society that respects the identity of *Ainu*. It postulates to promote their original culture. However, deleted from the report were items that emphasized indigenous rights like the political right to self-determination - while the "New *Ainu* Act" drafted by *Hokkaido Ainu* Association contained these items. The report merely announced legislating promotion of traditional culture of the Ainu. In 1997 a "New *Ainu* Cultural Law", an act to promote *Ainu* culture and the awareness of *Ainu* tradition, passed the Diet. It created an incorporation entity that was financed from tax money. It was to promote Ainu culture and to conduct further research. It promoted the proliferation of Ainu traditional culture to coming generations and fostered international exchange.

In the same year there was the decision to plan the Nibutani Dam, a dam for hydro electricity. At the site of the dam, many *Ainu* people lived. Sacred grounds of the Ainu and other cultural resources were flooded. Ainu land owners were expropriated. *Ainu* brought this issue before *Sapporo* District Court. The dam was already built. In the decision, the judges acknowledged rights of the Ainu to "enjoy rights of an own culture". They based their decision on the Japanese constitution and on Art. 27 of the International Covenant on Civil and Political Rights. This article says: "States shall establish and implement, in conjunction with indigenous peoples concerned, a fair, independent, impartial, open and transparent process, giving due recognition to indigenous peoples' laws, traditions, customs and land tenure systems, to recognize and adjudicate the rights of indigenous peoples pertaining to their lands, territories and resources, including those which were traditionally owned or otherwise occupied or used. Indigenous peoples shall have the right to participate in this process" (UN International Convenant 2007). That was the first time in the history that a Japanese court acknowledged the *Ainu* race as minority, as indigenous people (Levin 1999) with its own rights. .

Law and jurisprudence stated that *Ainu* exist and that they contribute to the diversity of Japanese culture. On one side, equality before the law was a constitutional right in Japan. On the other side, even though there was no definition of *Ainu* given, Ainu people obviously had been treated differently from general Japanese citizens. It those social circumstances, in 2007, the UN Declaration on the Rights of Indigenous People was adopted after twenty two years of protracted discussions. This declaration was considered very meaningful since indigenous people participated in its draft.

The H*okkaido Ainu A*ssociation already had strongly demanded reforms in a written request to the Prime Minister. As a result, on June 6th in 2008, both the chambers of the Diet unanimously adopted a resolution that demanded the acknowledgement of Ainu as the original inhabitants. During the G8-Summit 2008 in Sapporo, the Japanese government faced questions for the Japanese Ainu policy. The government was driven into a corner when it had to answer for the definition of indigenous people in Japan. The answer was most shameful: "We do not have a definition for indigenes". That event is believed to be a major reason for the 2008 Diet resolution.

In its wake, on August 11th, 2008, the Japanese government held the first panel meeting to discuss a change of policy. The panel stated that the government's assimilation policy indeed had damaged *Ainu*'s life and culture. It stated that there is a gap in quality of life between *Ainu* and Japanese. Furthermore the panel stated: "Indigenous people had lived in certain places before these came under the rule of the government. They settled in the place as a race with different culture and identity from majority. These people constituted a nation. Even though they were controlled and influenced by the majority people, they still preserved their own culture and identity. Those people should be called indigenous people". (Cabinet Office 2009). This was a very similar language than the language used in the Nibutani Dam - decision in 1997.

Several concrete steps to improve the situation of Ainu followed.

Firstly, Ainu culture is to be recognized in school curricula. Elementary school teachers are to be trained to teach about *Ainu.*

Secondly, research institutes are to educate talented persons who can succeed to traditional art crafts. A Memorial Park is to be established, to respectfully preserve the human bones which have till now had been preserved in the university. They are to be kept and honoured as a symbol of the race. Furthermore, an improved livelihood support policy provides a scholarship. Originally provided only for further education of *Ainu* people it later will be applied nationwide.

A Membership Register to the Ainu Minority is implemented, following objective and transparent identification procedures.

Thirdly, a special governmental department at the level of the Secretary of Cabinet has the task to take care that the humiliating poverty of most Ainu will be systematically eliminated.

However the prevailing policy of the government is still one of assimilation to Japanese. This causes uneasiness and deep concerns for the *Ainu.* Some people say "Don't rock the boat". On the surface, direct discrimination can be hardly seen. But silencing the problems is a danger - and damage is generated by indifference to the issue of Ainu.

4. Prospect for the Future

In 2008, *Hokkaido* University's *Ainu* and Indigenous People Research Centre conducted a survey on actual living conditions of *Ainu (Hokkaido University 2010)*. The subjects of the survey were households of "*Hokkaido Ainu* Incorporated Association" aged 18 to 85. According to this survey, the average annual income of *Ainu* households was considerably lower than the average income in *Hokkaido*. On top of that, the percentage of welfare recipients among Ainu is 5.2% while the comparable number for total Hokkaido is 3.5%, for the whole nation 2.1%. Moreover it shows that the percentage of Ainu students (below age 30) in universities is 20.2% while the national average is 42.2%. Up to date, the measures to improve the living conditions of *Ainu*" were not effective enough. The "Protectionism" by the Japanese government let to the collapse the foundations of *Ainu* livelihood. It caused the Ainu to lose their pride. It brought them into vicious circles of poverty and health deterioration.
In order to avoid repeating the tragic history it is important to look back the footsteps *Ainu* have walked. "Why do young *Ainu* always have the word discrimination on their lips? They do not want us to do something for them. They just want to break away the trauma they always suffer from" (Okada 2008).

In order to create a better future the victimized Ainu themselves have begun to face their fear of discrimination and prejudice. Inner qualities are the true wealth of Ainu people. Self awareness of these inner qualities, is important for a future life in security. Now is the time for us living together to have open dialogue with each other so that Ainu will be able to recover the pride of who we are born as, acquire stable and secure lives, and choose our own path into the future.

References

Ainu (1994) = Ainu no rekisi to bunka [The history and cultures of Ainu], Ainu Museum, Shiraoi-cho, Hoddaito, April 30, 1994. http://www.ainu-museum.or.jp/

Ainu Museum (2011) Ainu History and Culture:History . http://www.ainu-museum.or.jp/en/study/eng01.html. accessed 11. May 2011.

Ainu (2000) *Ainu minzoku ni kansuru sidou shiryou* [The Education Text About Ainu Race]. The Foundation for Research and Promotion of Ainu Culture (ed.) Sapporo (The Foundation for Research and Promotion of Ainu Culture). March 2000.

Cabinet Office (2009) *Ainu seisaku no arikatani kansuru yushikisya kondanjai houkokusyo* [The report of the advisory panel by experts on the policies toward Ainu people], (Ed.) Advisory panel by experts on the policies toward Ainu people. July, 2009, Tokyo: Cabinet Office, Retrieved from: http://www.kantei.go.jp/jp/singi/ainu/dai10/siryou1.pdf

BBC News (2007)c News of 13th of September 2007. Indigenous Rights Outlined by UN. http://news.bbc.co.uk/2/hi/in_depth/6993776.stm. Accessed on May 5, 2011.

Diet (2008) Ainuminzoku wo senjyumin to surukotowo motomeru ketsugi [The resolution which demands for approval that Ainu are the original inhabitants], adopted on June 6, 2008 at the plenary sessions of both the House of Representatives and the House of Councillors, The National Diet of Japan, http://www.shugiin.go.jp/itdb_gian.nsf/html/gian/honbun/ketsugian/g16913001.htm and http://www.sangiin.go.jp/japanese/gianjoho/ketsugi/169/080606-2.html accessed 11August 1, 2011

Hokkaido University (2010) *Gendai Ainu no seikatsu to isiki – 2008 Hokkaido Ainu minzoku seikatsu jittai cyousa houkokusyo* [Living Conditions and Consciousness of Present-day Ainu: Report on the 2008 Hokkaido Ainu Living Conditions Survey, Hokkaido University Center for Ainu & Indigenous Studies, March 21, 2010. Sapporo: Hokkaido University. Retrieved from: http://www.cais.hokudai.ac.jp/en/archive.html

Levin, M. (1999). Kayano et al. v. Hokkaido Expropriation Committee: 'The Nibutani Dam Decision' (1999). International Legal Materials, Vol. 38, p. 394, 1999. Available at SSRN: http://ssrn.com/abstract=1635447 accessed May 15, 2011.

Lewallen, A.-E. (2008). Indigenous at last! Ainu Grassroots Organizing and Indigenous Peoples Summit in Ainu Mosir. The Asia Pacific Journal, Viol. 48-6-08, November 30, 2008. http://old.japanfocus.org/_ann_elise_lewallen-indigenous_at_last___ainu_grassroots_organizing_and_the_indigenous_peoples_summit_in_ainu_mosir_. Accessed on May 5, 2011.

Nomura, G (1992): Inauguration Speech to the UN General Assembly on December 10, 1992. http://www.ainu-assn.or.jp/english/eabout08.html., accessed May 6, 2011.

UN (2007) United Nations Declaration on the Rights of Indigenous Peoples, Adopted by General Assembly Resolution 61/295 on 13 September 2007. http://www.un.org/esa/socdev/unpfii/en/drip.html accessed August 1, 2011

Stress and Victimization - An Empirical Study on Homeless in a Japanese Metropolis

By

Gerd Ferdinand Kirchhoff and Aoi Tsuda in cooperation with Minoru Yamada and Sugao Shinohara

This TIVI Research Project could not have been completed without Sugao Shinohara who was widely responsible for the data analysis, and without Jun Kaneko MA who was responsible for the data collection in Osaka. Minoru Yamada was main consultant for the project in Osaka.

This study describes the connection between the stress level of homeless, their victimization and other demographic variables in Osaka, a Japanese metropolis in 2009. The paper describes the homeless in Osaka, their social environment in Nishinari Ward and the work program of an NGO that provided the participants for this study. The Japanese version of the TSQ was used to measure stress. An adaption of the CTS was used to measure victimization. While stress level is related to victimization, it is not related to length of homelessness.

Homelessness - Global and Local Issues

The Homeless Victimization Research looks at the relationship of stress and victimization. This research question is *global* as well as local. It is global since the relationship between stress and homelessness is a problem everywhere in this world. It is not limited to Japan. To become and to be homeless, we believe, is stress, whether this happens in Germany or in Japan. This stress is intensified by victimization.

At the same time, our research is *local.* It depicts characteristics of a group of about 1000 homeless that are part of a work program of a NGO in Osaka. It is this local group of homeless in Osaka's Nishinari Ward around the Sankaku Park we are interested in and for which our results are valid.

For sure, there are homeless in all countries of the world. The international "Dictionary of Homelessness" (Levinson 2004 p.240) lists words and English translations for "Cross-Cultural *Conceptions* of Homelessness". Most of these concepts transport certain unique usually "derogating" connotations. In Japanese, the most neutral term seems to be "hoomulesu". The term "hoomulesu" (pronounced with voiceless u) is of course "derived" from the English "homeless". You will not find the word "hoomulesu" in the well introduced Japanese dictionary (Nishio et al. 2000) - there is no explanation of "hoomulesu". Most Japanese people intuitively "know" that "hoomulesu" denotes something that is not really Japanese but "foreign", "alien" and "Anglo-American" - in any case, not part of the Japanese culture, something not Japanese.

Worldwide there might be over 100 million homeless (UN Commission on Human Rights 2005), - 79 million alone said to live in India- . But there are only about 15 800 officially counted homeless in Japan (Japan Times 2011). That is a very small group, compared to 147 million Japanese it means 1 homeless per 1000 Japanese people. That indeed is a small number. This official figure is based on headcount reports of local police. Such a headcount is most probably conservative (see Kirchhoff 2007). In Japan, there are several head count surveys of homeless people. For the time from 2007 to 2011, the total number of officially counted homeless decreased from 17.444 to 10,524. Most homeless counted are males (97%; Ministry of Health, Labor and Welfare 2011).

A society's ability to integrate people can be measured by the magnitude of its homeless population. Japanese homeless became a favorite topic for many social scientists, activists, and journalists to want to point their fingers to the inability of the Japanese social security system to handle a problem that lingers in the public discourse since the nineties of last century. This inability brought Japan into the international limelight when the UN Committee on Economic, Social and Cultural Rights gave a number of recommendations to the Japanese Government to improve the official "blindness" to a visible social problem (UN ECOSOC 2001).

Who are the "Homeless"?

Homeless here are defined here as people without a roof over their head, without a stable habitat that they can secure in advance for more than one night. These are people who sleep outside. They sleep in shelters which they have to leave during the day. They live in so called cardboard houses. They live in simple places that offer very cheap lodging with minimal services (the Japanese doya). Who has no money at all, sleeps outside. Who does not sleep outside, uses shelters with bunk beds and shared showers. Who can afford to pay for the night, can take advantage of the relatively cheap minimum standard facilities (doya). This shows that we do not follow the wide definition of homeless.

The wide definition maintains: those should be included who live in very fragile temporary facilities, with friends, in internet café's, in simple hotels. It should include young unmarried mothers, people who live in instable conditions, by the tolerance of friends or relatives in their apartments, in cars, etc. (wide definition of homeless). We have decided to use the narrow definition. The wide definition does not lend itself easily to such a survey as we have here.

Homeless lack a fixed, regular and adequate night-time residence. They have a primary night-time residence in any facility that is not designed for permanent living, or a place not ordinarily used for sleeping" (Wiedle 2005 for Alaska). The Japanese Special Measures Law Concerning Support etc. for Self Sustaining Living of the Homeless (2002) includes in the definition people who stay in certain locations (riverbeds, parks, public buildings) *without a right to stay there.* This definition excludes and places the status of homeless near to illegality.

Homeless in Osaka

Construction work was mainly done by day workers, by people who got contract and payment for one day only. The economic decline of the nineties of last century hit these people hard (for a good understanding description see Gill 1999, Hasegawa 2005). From about 190000 positions for day workers , about 20 000 remained. Most of the former day workers were somehow absorbed into society. But some became jobless permanently. They could not pay the rent even for the most modest permanent habitats. At the time we did our study (2009), the great majority of homeless were male - there are almost no homeless females. This coincides with the figures reported in the survey 2007. There were no young homeless.
These male homeless mostly were aging former day workers. Okamoto (2007) describes the population - a fifth of the Japanese homeless had some kind of job but did not make enough money to afford accommodations. A third got money from scavenging.

Public Assistance and Private Local Programs

3% in Japan (but 63% of the English homeless) received public assistance (unemployment benefits, income support, other state benefits). It is fair to say that Japanese homeless are left without any public support. There is a legal constitutional right to public assistance [Art.25 of the Constitution of Japan" All people shall have the right to maintain the minimum standards of wholesome and cultured living. In all spheres of live the state shall use its endeavors for the promotion and extension of social welfare and security and of public health" (Constitution 1946)]. Real life rules invented by public administrators however, demand that the recipient of welfare money has to be "registered". That presupposes a permanent place to stay - homeless by definition do not have such a place. Without registration people literally do not exist for the welfare administration, and it is astonishing - to put it mildly - how a civilized orderly administration could so liberally interpret clear constitutional rules. Famous became the Osaka citizen Yuji Yamauchi . He started a legal battle against the administration. The administration did not register his sleeping place under a bush in a public park and hence deprived him of getting any social security money, pension payments or health insurance. In 2007, the case is still undecided: The Supreme Court refused to take on the (appeal) case (Nagashima 2011). In the same line, in March 2007, the Osaka City government cancelled bogus resident registrations of about 2 100 homeless people and day laborers in one of Japan's largest slums (Kyodo News April 2007). Without registration - you do not exist. No welfare money. This practice is held by many unconstitutional, "completely illegal" and "totally unacceptable" (for all Kakita 2004 p.16, serious warning in Okamoto 2007, 539/540).) -

These conditions render the homeless without any income, without any health insurance. Many are dependent on the daily free soup that is provided by (mainly Christian) volunteer groups that give food to homeless for free. Other mainly Christian groups maintain free social services, a house to get rest and peace and medical counseling ("Tabiji no Sato" Jesuit Social Welfare Center, "Furusato no Ie" : open house for elderly homeless day workers) , General Social Service Center including a No-Kotsu-Do - this facility has a room to store individual urns (showing the foto of the homeless) and containing the ashes of the deceased cremated homeless so that a place of memory for their souls is maintained - very important in the Japanese society. That all happens in an area of a square- kilometer around in Sankaku Park in Kamagasaki.
Almost no literature published and available to us, mentions the enormous stress homelessness produces. To exist at the lowest level of society, to be without a permanent residence, not to know where to sleep next night, living completely unprotected, living in fear of

outsiders who victimize them or of insiders whom they do not trust, living alone, living exposed to health risks including death - especially in the cold winters or in rainy season - these stressors have to be mastered. They cause very intense stress - it is an emotional burden that most of the readers would not be able to shoulder without getting seriously ill or mentally disturbed.

Before we go into the details of our study, we want to emphasize that the homeless in Kamagasaki treated us foreigners with perfect respect and courtesy. There was no begging, there was no hostile behavior towards us "intruders". There were no visible signs of mental diseases. There were no women (see general figures above) - obviously women get absorbed into non-homeless society much easier than men. There was no young person, let alone children. Younger persons maybe maintain another pattern of survival. It was obvious that a lot of alcohol was consumed. This life, some homeless explained to us, is bearable only if you have had "enough" alcohol. The insecure form of existence (and its permanency] creates a lot of unsolvable problems for the homeless.

Homeless in Osaka are - contrary to public prejudice (Kirchhoff 2007) - by no means lazy, stinky and dirty. The homeless we met in Osaka impressed by their cleanliness. They are poor, for sure, but they maintain a clean appearance. In all surveys of homeless, most Japanese homeless tell that they have two main wishes: They want to have work and they want to have a habitat (instead of detailed references Kakita op.cit. p.17, Okamoto 2007 p.534). Exactly that is not provided by the social system, neither by the private nor by the administrative sector.

Local Typical Conditions

Participants in this study are about 1000 homeless men living in Kamagasaki' Nishinari Ward, a quarter of Osaka City. It was selected for several reasons: Osaka has a sizeable homeless population, concentrated in the Nishinari Ward, a place where traditionally many day workers used the "yoseba". Here in the "Yoseba", in the early morning, employers pick up the needed number of workers for this day and usually bring them back in the evening. Such day work is very much demanded by employable homeless (we already pointed out that most homeless want work), and the observer can see homeless waiting, sleeping, eating on the yoseba place. The existence of a yoseba means a concentration of homeless (if no day work is available), and exactly this happened in Nishinari Ward. All in all, there are about 1000 homeless in the area around Sankaku Park, a triangle square with not solid ground. The grass has disappeared under the many footprints of hundreds of pedestrians, customers of simple selling booths. Here simple food and alcohol are sold. Here groups of homeless sleep under the open sky, covered with paper boxes and maybe blankets. Others disappear in the dark neighborhood of Sankaku Park. The park is a "social center" - Christian NGOP's cook and distribute here the daily free soup is cooked and dispensed. Here, Christian NGOs run kindergartens, a "House for the Children", the Furusato no Ie (see above) where homeless can rest and recreate in silence or in talking to each other (free tea provided). Here is a minimal medical counseling service. Here is the center of the activities of the NGO Kamagasaki.

The history of this NGO is in a way typical for the approach to homelessness in Japan. In the end of the nineties of last century, with the homeless problem getting more and more ardent, a group of homeless started to organize themselves and rallied city administration and provincial administration for help. Public administration did not show any interest in changing the destitute situation of the homeless. But the city administration unofficially promoted the group of homeless under the leadership of a very skilled former homeless activist who lived with his family (a definite exception!) in the area. The interest of city administration was kept alive by the very fact that in Kamagasaki there lived non-homeless residents as well. They send their children to the school that was located in the center of homelessness. There was the city hospital that catered to both, residents and homeless. There were the many simple (substandard) overnight renting houses (doyas) which had to go out of business for the homeless could not even pay the 500 Yen (about 2 Euro) per night to stay there. Of course the resident citizen urged the city to remove the homeless. Forceful eviction actions followed. That caused - in rare instances even international - uproar and media protests. This is not the place to describe the successful work of the NPO "Kamagasaki Shien Kikou" (Support Organization Kamagasaki) guided by an "inspirational man with 38 years of experience in work for the homeless" (i.e. Minoru Yamada, Social Firms UK 2011). It was able to build shelter for (in 2009) about thousand homeless. The director of this NGO became member of our research team.

Access to the Homeless in Osaka

The research team had a problem to access the population under study. Between homeless and non-homeless, there are high walls of mutual rejection and a mutual strong awareness of the prejudices on both sides. Homeless and non-homeless live in different worlds, and these worlds never or rarely intersect (See Okamoto 2007, Kirchhoff 2007).

Getting access started three years before the actual survey was done. Together with students, the German researcher stayed several days in the area of Sankaku Park. The group - and later the research team did the same - helped cooking meals for the homeless from 4.00 in the morning till 11.00 noon when the soup was delivered. The "intruders" were asked what they wanted to do here in this environment that was certainly not their home. The homeless realized that group had travelled 5 hours by train and Shinkansen to learn about life and problems of homeless. In the following years, these visits were repeated. The research team developed very good working relationships with the NGO. We visited public festivals that the NGO organized for the homeless. We interviewed several homeless who were asked by the NGO to assist us - the interviews took place in the cafeteria that the NGO run (outsourced to homeless). We helped again cooking and distributing the food to the homeless. By and by, the homeless got to know that we were there to learn about their life. They accepted our presence. We never were treated in an impolite way. We never were bothered by drunk homeless or by begging men. And men we met almost exclusively - the Japanese researcher and the translator for the German researcher, were the only females around.

Special Conditions of Homeless in Osaka compared to the US

The Method of Sampling

The NGO featured a work program which the research team took advantage of: Under the guidance of a foreman, usually a former homeless himself who had the trust of the other homeless as employee of the NGO and as a former "brother in fate", four or five homeless constituted a work group. These work groups cleaned the streets around Sankaku Park. Each individual homeless had the opportunity to work in such a work group three times a month for a day. They were paid by the City of Osaka. These positions were very much in demand: almost no able man wanted to miss this rare opportunity to make some money. As a result, not only the environment of Sankaku Park was pretty clean. Since no one was allowed to work more than the fixed maximum, the NGO had developed a registration system that was accepted by the homeless. That enabled us to avoid that a homeless participated more than once in the survey. One work group consisted of 5 homeless. There were about twenty teams daily.

Therefore we could reach in ten days about 1000 homeless. That is almost the whole population of homeless in this part of the city.

The Administration

The administration of the test was done in this way: In a work brake, the foreman distributed the questionnaires to his team and provided pencils. He then explained the purpose of the study in simple words. He made sure that all understood that the questionnaire did not ask for their names nor allowed any identification. He made sure his group understood that cooperation was voluntarily. He then read the first question a loud, paused for the men having time to tick the box of the question (there was no writing necessary except ticking boxes), and went to the next question. He then collected the questionnaires in an extra file and cleaning work was presumed. The foremen reported that the questions were easy to understand and that very few clarifying questions were asked. The participant homeless received incentives - a bag with a towel, soap, tooth - brush and toothpaste. By this method, foremen were able to bring in total about 1000 questionnaires.

Homelessness and Stress

In the pretest, it became clear that the CTS was understood by the homeless. The scale includes victimizations by violent invasions into the self of the homeless as well as property invasions. Homelessness means stress. Jobless day laborers notoriously cannot find accommodation and they become rough sleepers ((Okamoto et al. 2004)" "No job leads to no money and no accommodation" (p.7). That alone is a traumatic event. That is especially so in Japan. Loosing the job is already shameful and degrading . People will not share this loss at home (if there is a home). They will try to use saved money to keep up the façade of being employed. Of course, that does not last long. Homelessness is forced upon the people, is not a chosen change (Tsumaki p.23). This downfall goes hand in hand with repeated failures to get a job. The decline into homelessness is traumatic as such.

The arrival in the homeless society is a scary event. Usually the novice is frightened, distrustful, desperately depressed about social location which - he knows very well - is the bottom of Japanese society. Deeper he cannot sink (information from interviews with newly arrived homeless in Sankaku Park). These newcomers liked to talk to us outsiders since they could express how alienated and how frightened they were in this social environment they were not

accustomed to. Being homeless is stress. It is generally accepted that victimization means additional stress.
From literature and from our own research, is was known that there is a deep gap between the world of homeless and the general population, let alone the world of universities. This gap might be the reason that till now, homeless were never asked for their emotional burden nor for their victimization.

The Development of the Research Questions

To get access to the homeless, we turned to the Director of the NGO "Kamagasaki Homeless Support", Minoru Yamada. The Bylaws of his NGO clearly stated "research" as the task of the group.
Repeated visits of members of the team and telephone contacts brought about a trustful working relationship. We soon discussed our research questions with the (often part time) employees of the NPO. These foremen were usually former homeless. In these discussions a mutual learning process happened. The foremen taught us that homeless will immediate block cooperation (1) when they fear to be identified and (2) when they fear that disappointing depressing memories will come up. Therefore the originally planned questions for supportive ties to families (which according to the local experts never exist!) were eliminated. The same was true for school education. Questions for stress caused by previous injustices (victimizations by "normal citizen" and by "other homeless") should be simple and clear. While the academics learned to respect the special situation of the homeless men, the foremen learned to overcome their mistrust against academic research. They learned that the academics listened to them and asked for their advice as to address problems and as to phrase the questions. That in turn sparked the willingness of the hitherto distrustful foremen to take on this research as their task - it was good for their self esteem to experience that without their support and help, the whole research would be impossible. Possible disadvantages were treated as acceptable costs.

This NPO not only collected the data (see below), it made considerable input into the realization of the research project. Such influence is new in victimological research projects in Japan. Our basically constructivist approach opens the sensitivity for different perspectives from different positions. Victimologists often look at power differentials. It is the conviction of many researchers that victims have experienced powerlessness and that they should be empowered as much as possible. It is then a contradiction when victims - as usual - are treated merely as the research objects. Most researchers maintain a hierarchical position to "their" victims, giving the researcher the sole almost dictatorial position over research topics. Maybe that helps to explain why victimologists over and over have to a ascertain themselves that they do have a "victim perspective" (Ben David 2000).

Since science follows normative rules, it is not possible to let non-scientists decide what can be researched and what not. But their expert voices must be heard. There is a shared responsibility between scientists and the experts on the ground.

The staff of the NPO Kamagasaki, often former homeless themselves, had longtime experience in interacting with their clientele. It convinced the researchers that it would be irresponsible to ask for critical life events without having any possibility to offer relief if emotional reactions like depression, sadness, despair that most probably would result from our research confronting homeless with these stressing events in their past. Homeless would simply refuse to cooperate to shield themselves from too intense memories.

The usual Anglo-American homeless research literature often reflects the dominant research interests: the main interest of authors from psychological side is often experiences with childhood violence experiences in the family of origin of the homeless. The feminist interest is often to connect domestic violence in the parental family with subsequent domestic violence in the partnership and its direct contribution to homelessness (see Crook in Johnston 2007:363f.). Many contributions from the psychiatric side establish a link between homelessness and the abolishment of ambulant care for released mental patients from institutions (see Alpert in Jackson 2007:355f.) When we started, we wanted to look at several independent variables like prior experience of violence in parental families, in school success, in critical life events like breaking up family, becoming homeless, relationships to supportive family members of lack thereof. All these events may contribute to greater emotional damages, to stress of homeless people. Therefore we restricted our research interest basically on the connections between stress and victimization.

We agree with Jasinski et al (2005): It is difficult to imagine a lifestyle that is more conducive to victimization than homelessness. Homeless spend their night and their days in run-down areas, in a relatively dirty environment that invites to dump garbage and stuff on the place. It is impressive nevertheless, how clean the homeless men appear.

Lifestyle Theory and Victimization of Homeless

From Anglo-American applications of lifestyle theory, we know that homeless live in dangerous regions where they get into easy contact with motivated offenders. As Jasinski et al (2005) observe: homeless do not possess much. But the low risk, the ease in which they are victimized, is said to compensate offenders for small gain. The victimological content of the situation might be: It is logical that property loss is the more painful, the less you have at your disposition. As regularly, the emotional harm characterizes the victimization, not the money value.

In Kamagasaki around Sangaku Park, cleaning teams of the NPO are visible in the streets. The environment - in spite of great difficulties to keep Osaka financing these work programs - does not make an abandoned uncared-for impression. The cleaning teams act as a kind of guardian. The belongings of homeless are packed in blue plastic bundles and stored on the side of the streets. The homeless themselves cannot guard their own deposits. Guardianship would be impossible without a kind of informal social control which prevents foreigners to mess with the bundles of homeless.

The places where homeless live are usually described as places where violence is commonplace. In our visits in Nishinari Ward, we did not observe a single incident of violence. Alcohol use and consumption of other drugs may generally increase vulnerability and decrease guardianship. Interview results suggest: when homeless do not use shelters but sleep outside, they flock at night in small units to guard themselves better against attacks from outside. Visual impressions do not reconfirm a lack of guardianship of property:

Anglo-American researchers stress that various survival strategies of homeless - trading sex, panhandling, drug dealing - increase exposure to risk. In Osaka, neither are these survival strategies visible in this population of elderly men nor are they reported by the NPO experts.

In the US homeless population, there are many women, many juveniles, many mentally deranged people, many drug users, characterized by excessive violence and excessive victimization. Lifestyle theory belongs into a society that is characterized by partially absent trusted institution of social control. From interview information we know that homeless do not like police. Especially they were appalled by the surveillance cameras which were used to observe the homeless in the streets round Sankaku Square. In 2009, these obvious signs of repressive observation were dismantled by police. In interviews homeless told us that they never would involve the police. On the bottom of society, there is no protection expected from the formal institutions of social control. Even a dead body of a homeless was not reported to police.

The Research Instrument

The questionnaire dealt (with victimizations and (2) with the stress level of the homeless.

The victimization questions were taken from the Conflict Tactic Scale (CTS) (Straus et al.,1979 Tjaden and Thoennes (1998,1999). Their usefulness for research with homeless was proven by Jasinski et (2005) et al. in their research on homeless women (and men). In this research, we used a Japanese translation of these questions:

The 12 victimization questions were: whether respondent was (1) insulted or whether someone showed openly contempt to respondent, (2) having an object thrown that could hurt, (3) having been pushed, grabbed or shoved, (4) having been pulled the hair, (5) having been slapped with hand or fist, (6) having been kicked or bitten, (7) having been choked or having been subjected to an attempt to drown (attempt),(8) having been hit with an object, (9) having been being beaten up, (10) having been threatened with a weapon (11) having been stolen from(12) having been stolen from with force. For each victimization, we asked whether it was done by a homeless or by another person.

A Japanese version of the Trauma Screening Questionnaire (Brewin et al 2002) was used to measure the Stress level of the participants. The questions were phrased in an easily understandable way. The Japanese questionnaire is available from the TIVI (tivi@tokiwa.ac.jp). For each positively answered question, the respondent earned one point on this scale. The answers were summed for each respondent and the total score was used to indicate the stress level.

The Japanese verbalization of the English scales were simple and geared to the language level of homeless people. It is well known that Japanese has a very stratified language and sentences understandable for one part of the population will not be of practical value in another part. We checked the acceptability of the Japanese version by retranslation into English. The result was satisfactory. The Japanese version used very simple language. The wording of the Japanese questionnaire was very simple. No complicated scaling was demanded from the respondents nor reading of Chinese signs for

the different words of the questions. In this simple language, the content of the English question was transported to the respondents. No writing was necessary. All questions could be answered by ticking the corresponding answer box.
The instrument consisted of a demographic part, a victimization part and the Trauma Screening questions.

The Sample

The questionnaire was distributed to 1000 homeless, 993 questionnaires returned. The high return rate is dependent on the design of the study. This does not mean that 993 questionnaires entered the data analysis of each question. Often, not all questions were answered.

Most respondents were male. That corresponds to results of other nationwide surveys (Japan Minister for Health, Labor and Welfare 2007 p. 6).

Of the 976 respondents, most (61%) were between 60 and 69 years old. The second biggest group were the men in their fifties (50-59 years old, 32%.) while 40 (4%) were in their seventies. Less than 1% was younger than 50 years old. That corresponds to the quoted nationwide survey of 2007.

For most of them, homelessness is an experience that lasts for longer than a year (51%, National Survey 20-0-7: 76%). For one quarter of them, it is a relatively new experience (less than three months, 9% in the National Survey 2007). 17% (National Survey 14%) are homeless between three months to one year. This question is not answered by 111 (11%), obviously these people feared that this details could assist to identify them. 92% of the respondents live in Kamagasaki one year and longer, only 2% live here les than three months. From this we infer: homeless are not moving (they do not have the money to do so!), they are stuck in one place. Most of them - 60% - are former construction day workers (61%).

As expected, these men do not have a stable habitat. In the following text, the figure in parentheses gives the percentage where they stay "usually overnight", while the first figures tells where they stayed "last night". 15% (17%) staid outside, without any roof over their head. That is remarkable since the survey was done in February, a time when it is very cold outside. The majority of them used a shelter (46% equal percentages for "last night" and "usually"). About a quarter of them - 26% (25%) could afford to stay even in the most simple overnight facility.

The Method of Data Collection

Each foreman had a work team of four to five respondents per day. Daily there were about 20 workgroups at work. At a work break, the men received the questionnaire and a pencil, then the questions were read to them and the marked their answer with a cross. No handwriting was demanded. At the end of the action, the foremen collected all questionnaires. That was successful (returning rate about 99%) since every homeless man wanted to get the incentives. Within two weeks, about thousand homeless in the workgroups answered the questions in the questionnaire. They were rewarded with a gift of toilet articles, tooth brush and toothpaste and the like. This resulted in a very high rate of cooperation. In total, 980 questionnaires returned. The quality of the data was – understandable – not of a high standard. Often question were not answered, presumably for homeless feared to be identified. 431 completed questionnaires contained all needed answers for victimization.

The resulting treatment of the Victimization scale and the TQS was certainly rough. The foremen read the text aloud to their group but we cannot control what they additionally explained. Therefore it was so important that the questions themselves were phrased in simple Japanese. Certainly the basic ideas of the original (English language) questions were successfully transported to the respondents. This is the main reason why the data do not lend themselves to a higher statistical analysis.

Results

431 respondents answered all victimization questions with "yes, it happened" or "no, it did not happen". These were included in the analysis.

The frequencies of victimizations that were done by other homeless, and the frequencies of victimization done by "outsiders" show a clear parallel pattern: Outsider Victimizations are leading in almost every victimization. There is a correlation coefficient of= .808 (p.01), indicating that both victimizations show the same pattern. In the following text, the letter O signifies the percentage of victimizations attributed to outsiders while H signifies the attribution of the victimization to other homeless. Theft is leading, (61% O, 39% H), followed by the open expression of disrespect or contempt (46% O, 29 % H.). From outsiders, homeless were pushed, grabbed or shoved - (46% O, 11% H) As it was expected, the most severe victimizations happened with less frequency: (threatened with a gun or knife (13%

O, 9% H) ; kicked or bitten (8% O, 15% H); being chocked (14% O, 9% H).

Of the 309 people who identify themselves as victims (77% of all who answered all questions for victimizations) only 7% report to be victimized once, 93% give us multiple victimizations.

Property victimizations are reported most often, violent victimization follow on the second place. 7% of the respondents did not experience any property victimization, for violent victimizations the corresponding figure is 32%. That corresponds to the usual picture that is known from police statistics for the general populations: property victimizations lead by far, violent victimizations are less frequent.

Homeless attribute these victimizations more to outsiders than to other homeless. The 95% - confidence interval around the arithmetic mean 4.35 for insiders is 3.00 – 3.90 while the same interval for victimization by outsiders, 4.52, extends from 3.99 to 5.05. The confidence intervals within the outsider group or within the insider group overlap.

Victimization is related to the length of homelessness. Those who are homeless less than three months report in the average 2.18 cases. For the group who are homeless between three months to one year, this figure is 3.95. Homeless longer than a year show an average of 4.87 ($p<.01$).
Victimizations by other people are in the average more frequent (7.60, 95% confidence Interval 6.9 - 8.3) than victimization by homeless (5.50, 95% Confidence Interval 4.87 - 6.10). Homeless believe that outside people are more dangerous compared to other homeless.

As expected, victimizations are related to positively related to stress level. While homeless who report no victimization show an average level of TSQ of 2.92 (99% confidence interval 2.32 – 3.52,), the homeless who report victimization, impress with a TSQ average of 4.59 (99% confidence interval = 4.23 - 4.95). The same is true for violent victimization: Homeless who report no violence victimization, have a TSQ mean of 2.92 (99% confidence interval 2.32 to 3.52) while victims of violence give us a TSQ mean of 4.38 (99% confidence interval 4.09 to 4.67). The same information we can draw from $r=.469$ ($p<.01$) between victimization and TSQ. Homeless who report victimizations are generally more stressed than homeless who do not report any victimization.

Only the stress levels for property victimization are different depending on who the homeless attributed the victimization to. With an arithmetic mean of 3,24 (95% confidence interval at 2.86 to 3.62), TSQ values related to property victimization from non-homeless show a clearly lower degree than the other groups. Stress by violent victimization by both, homeless and non-homeless, and property victimization by other homeless only appear to be clearly higher (values between 4.99 and 5.34 but overlapping confidence intervals permit no statement of differences).

Stress level is not related to the place where the respondents stay overnight, usually or in the last night. That result surprises. We expected that sleeping outside, is connected with higher stress levels.

Finally we are interested whether length of homelessness is related to stress and how. Whether we correlate duration of homelessness with TSQ or whether we compare means with confidence interval, there is no relationship between duration of homelessness and stress. Whether homelessness lasts for a long time or whether the respondents are homeless for a relative short time, the stress does not decrease with length of time. Such a decrease we would expect if homeless would get somehow used to their situation. That means that homelessness in itself is a factor for stress. Victimization may contributes to this stress, as we have shown before.

Discussion

In this study, stress is related to victimization, especially to victimization by violence.

Most of the victims report more than one victimization. Homeless victimization is not a one time and one type event, it is multiple victimization. That confirms the thesis that homeless live in a very dangerous world, if frequency is a measure for the dangerousness of victimization. We will come back to a related question when we discuss the TSQ.

In this analysis we do not distinguish how often any kind of victimization occurred. Nevertheless – and plausibly – the homeless report that they have been victimized by many types of events. The actual number might be misleading. It is possible that people who did not experience the victimization, overlooked to mark "none" and forgot that they had to give a (negative) answer. If this is so, they skipped the "no" and. Then this would have been recorded as a missing case. Except our suspicion, we do not have any reconfirmation.

The rank order between victimization by outsiders and victimization by homeless is almost identical (only in theft, the homeless are leading). The victimization follow the same pattern. But in each kind of victimization, the homeless attribute more to non-homeless than to homeless. Outsiders – that is our impression - are seen as more dangerous than homeless. Even if there is no solidarity of the homeless that leads to joint social actions to change their situation, there is a clear perception of "we" and "them". To whom the victimization is attributed, does not show a clear picture. As the TSQ values show, property victimization by other homeless is especially disappointing, resulting in higher stress values. That is plausible- from other homeless is expected that they do not damage the property but respect the (needy) situation of a fellow homeless. This difference between "insiders" and "outsiders" does not show for violent victimizations . That indicates that there is no intense "we-feeling", no active group solidarity.

For the first time this study measures the emotional damage of homeless by the TSQ. This scale is designed to measure the risk of developing PTSD. But it is justified through the logic of the scale to interpret it as measure for stress level, for emotional damage. We have shown that emotional damage is related to victimization. We have also shown that emotional damage is related to the frequency of victimization: the more victimization experienced, the higher is TSQ. That is an argument for measuring the severity of damage by the frequency of victimization – of course it is preferable to use a special measure like the TSQ – scale.

This study has serious limitations. It uses scales that correspond to CTS and to TSQ, however that treatment of the scales is rough. The translation of a scale from English to Japanese is always very difficult due to different language structures. In this case simplifications in the Japanese language might have obscured differences that would have shown up if a more precise correspondence between the original versions of the scales and the Japanese versions could have been granted. Therefore the data analysis gives only rough information. More complicated analyses like path analysis or regression analyses were conducted but resulted in rather low explanatory values (18%). That means that 82% of the variance was unexplained, a fact that has to do with the roughness of the scale treatment and with the quality of the data.

References

Ben David, S. 2000. Needed. Victim's Victimology. In: Friday P.C. & Kirchhoff, G.F. (eds.). Festschrift for Hans Joachim Schneider. Victimology at the Transition from the 20th to the 21st Century. Essays in Honor of Hans Joachim Schneider. Moenchengladbach. Aachen. (WSV Publishing and Shaker Verlag). 55 - 72.

Brewin 2002 = Brewin, C.R., Rose, S., Andrews, B., Green, J., Tata, P.,McEvedy, C.,Turner, S. and Foa, E.B. 2002 Brief screening instrument for post traumatic stress disorder. British Journal of Psychiatry. .158 - 162.

Constitution 1946 = The Constitution of Japan from Nov.3, 1946 in http://www.solon.org/Constitutions/Japan/English/english-Constitution.html accessed on July 7, 2011.

Gill,T. (1999) Wage Hunting at the Margins of Urban Japan. Lilies in the Field. Marginal People who Live for the Moment. Day, Papataxiarchis and Stewart (eds.) Boulder, Colorado and Oxfort (Westview Press). 119-136.

Hasegawa, M. 2005. Economic Globalization and Homelessness in Japan. American Behavioral Scientist Vol.48 (April) .989-1012.

Japan Times . 2011. Homeless Population totals 15 759. March 10, 2009. http://search.japantimes.co.jp/cgi-bin/nn20090310b2.html accessed on June 30, 2011.

Jasinski,Jana L., Wesley, J., Mustaine, E. and Wright, J.D. (2005). The Experience of Violence in the Lives of Homeless Women. Final report submitted to the National Institute of Justice. Washington D.C. (National Institute of Justice)

Kakita, Y. (2004) Homeless People in Japan. Characteristics, Processes and Policy Responses. Shidai Shakaigaku . The Annals of Sociological Association, Osaka City University No.5 p.7 - 20.

Kirchhoff, G.F. (2007). Prejudice Against Homeless as a Victimological Problem. Results from the Mito Prejudice Surveys. Tokiwa Journal of Human Sciences. No.15 March 2007. 117-129.

Levinson, D. (ed.) 2004. Encyclopedia of Homelessness. A Berkshire Reference Work. Thousand Oaks . London. New Delhi. (Sage Publications). 886 p.

Japan Ministry of Health, Labor and Welfare (2011) : The Results of Nationwide Surveys about Homeless and Their Actual Condition.(Japanese Text) In: http://www.mhlw.go.jp/stf/houdou/2r98520000019qr.html accessed on 2011/07/04

Nagashima (2011) . Oral communication of the advocate of Yamauchi with the authors from 26 July 2011. (Yasuhisa Nagashima, info@hirakata-lawoffice.com). Compare further references on http://blogs.yahoo.co.jp/stellar_mimiru/56638793.html accessed on July 27, 2011.

Nishio et al (2000) = Nishio, M., Iwanbuchi, E. & Mizutani, S. (eds.) *Iwanami Kokugo Jiten*. (Japanese Dictionary) Tokyo (Iwanami) 2000

Okamoto, Y. (2007) . A Comparative Study of Homelessness in the United Kingdom and in Japan. Journal of Social Issues. Vol.63. No 3. . 525- 542.

Okamoto et al. (2004). Okamoto, Y., Hayakawa, K., Noguch ,S. Shinya, M. . 2004. Homelessness and housing in Japan. . Paper presented at the International Conference "Adequate and Affordable Housing for All Research, Policy, Practice" : June 24-27, 2004. Nihon Fukushi University COE Program, 2004. 1 - 9.

Social Firms UK 2011. Tales from Japan Part 1. Posted on January 28, 2011. http://socialfirmsuk.wordpress.com p.1 accessed on July 7, 2011.

Special Measures Law 2002 (Kirchhoff 2007 p.129).

Steward B. McKinney Homeless Assistance Act. US PL 100.77, 42 U.S.C. 119. Summary in Levinson 2004 p.747.

UN ECOSOC, 24 September 2001. Concluding Observations of the Committee on Economic, Social and Cultural Rights: Japan. 09/24/2001 E/C12.1/ Add.67 (Concluding Observations/Comments) accessed June 15, 2011.. http://www.unhchr.ch/tbs/doc.nsf/%28Symbol%29/E.C.12.1.Add.67. En?Opendocument accessed July 23, 2011.

United States Department of Housing and Urban Development, in: http:// portal.hud.gov/hudportal/HUD?src=/topics/homelessness/definition accessed 26 June 2011.

Wiedle, J. (2005). Statewide Homeless Survey. Summer 2005. Anchorage (Alaska Housing Finance Corporation).

Victimization in Family and Institutions

Physical and Psychological Victimization of University Students by Romantic Partners and Parents in Gender and World Perspective

By

Murray A. Straus[1]

This article describes victimizations experienced by a sample of 17,404 university students who participated in the International Dating Violence conducted in 32 nations in all major world regions. The percent of students in each nation who were *physically* attacked by a dating partner ranged from 13% to 41% (median = 25%). These rates are about three times higher than has been found for married persons. About the same percent of male and female students were victims of a physical assault by their partner. For 69% of the couples, both partners were violent. The percent injured ranged from 2% to 65% (median = 7%). In most nations more women than men were injured. Almost all the students experienced at least one instance of a *psychological* attack by their partner. The average number of times in the previous 12 months ranged from a mean of 6 to 17 times (mean for all nations = 9 times). Victimization by *violence by parents* in the form of being spanked "a lot" ranged from 19% to 74% (median = 52%). Harmful effects were found for each of these forms of victimization. Each the three types of violence victimization were associated with an increased probability of the victim physically assaulting a partner, and an increased probability of depression. The equally high percent of men and women who were victims of violence by a partner and the evidence that most of the violence by women is initiated by women rather than an act of self-defense, contradicts the predominant theory of partner violence (PV) - that it is almost always perpetrated by men as a means of maintaining male dominance. This theory needs to be replaced by a family systems theory approach that recognizes the mutuality of most partner victimization and the multiple causes PV. Consequently, prevention and treatment of PV needs to be directed to women as well as men. The relationship between having been a victim of violence by parents in the form of corporal punishment

1 Family Research Laboratory, University of New Hampshire Durham

and physically assaulting a dating partner suggest that a substantial reduction in victimization of dating partners requires a substantial reduction in the victimization of children by parents.

This paper addresses the following questions about the victimization experiences of 17,404 university students in 32 nations:

1A. What percent of the students were victims of ***physical assaults*** by a romantic partner?

1B. Is being a victim of physical assault by a partner associated with an increased probability that the victim will injured, depressed, and physically assault the partner?

2A. What percent were victims of ***psychological aggression*** by a romantic partner

2B. Is being a victim of psychological aggression by a partner associated with an increased probability that the victim will be depressed?

3A. What percent of students were victims of physical assault ***by parents*** in the form of ***corporal punishment?***

3B. Is being a victim of physical assault by parents associated with an increased probability that the victim will be depressed and physically assault a partner?

4. What can be done to ***prevent or reduce*** these three types of victimization?

To answer these questions, all analyses were replicated to provide separate but comparable result s for men and women, for individual students, and for differences between the 32 nations in the study.

METHOD

Sample

The International Dating Violence Study. The research uses data from the International Dating Violence Study. The data were gathered by a consortium of researchers in all major world regions. Each consortium member used the same core questionnaire, except for the final section, which was reserved for each member to add questions about issues of specific local or theoretical interest. A detailed description of the study, including the questionnaire and all other key documents, is available on the website http://pubpages.unh.edu/~mas2, and in previous articles reporting results from this study (Douglas & Straus, 2006; Hines, 2007; Straus, 2004, 2008).

Questionnaire Administration. The data were gathered using procedures reviewed by and approved by the boards for protection of human subjects at each of the universities in the study, or where such a board was not in place, by a Dean or other administrator with responsibility for reviewing research ethics. The purpose of the study and the right to refuse to participate were explained to all students. They were assured of anonymity and confidentiality, and given a debriefing form that explained the study in more detail. The students were also provided contact information for area social service agencies should they need assistance.

Study Participants. The participants are a convenience sample of students at 68 universities in 32 nations. The regional coverage includes two countries in sub-Saharan Africa, seven in Asia, 13 in Europe, four in Latin America, two in the Middle East, two in North America, and two in Oceania. The data were obtained by administering a questionnaire during regularly scheduled classes. Most of the classes were in psychology, sociology, criminology, and family studies. The median sample size is 285 (range = 99 to 4,533). Seventy percent of the students were female because the questionnaires were administered in social science courses that tend to have a large percentage of female students. Because this study is focused on issues in which gender differences are crucial, the analyses either controlled for gender or were replicated for male and female students, or an interaction with gender was included in the models tested.

About 20,000 questionnaires were administered. Of these, about four percent could not be used because of a large number of unanswered questions. The questionnaires with sufficient data were examined for aberrant response patterns such as an implausibly high frequency of rare events, for example, 10 instances of being attacked by a partner with a knife or gun in the past year; or inconsistent answers, for example, reporting an injury but no assault. Based on this screening method, 6.2% of the approximately 19,200 completed questionnaires were dropped from the sample. This resulted in a sample of 17,404. Of these, 3,252 or 18% were not in a relationship that lasted at least one month or more. Therefore, when the analysis involves students in a relationship, the sample N is 14,252. Table 1 gives data on the characteristics of the students in each of the 32 nations.

Table 1. International Dating Violence Study Sample

Region	Nation		N	% Female	Mean Age	% In A Relationship ≥Month
All Nations			**17,404**	**70.1**	**22.9**	**81.9**
Africa	ZAF	South Africa	150	90.0	24.2	72.7
	TZA	Tanzania	247	43.7	26.3	70.9
Asia	CHN	China	1730	65.8	21.3	43.7
	HKG	China-Hong K	874	70.9	23.8	63.0
	IND	India	193	69.4	21.6	49.2
	JPN	Japan	207	52.2	20.3	64.3
	SGP	Singapore	260	68.1	24.7	83.1
	KOR	Korea	256	63.7	24.3	74.2
	TWN	Taiwan	258	71.7	20.1	62.8
Europe	BEL	Belgium	803	76.8	27.3	87.9
	DEU	Germany	522	68.8	24.2	92.9
	GBR	Great Britain	456	84.4	20.9	91.7
	GRC	Greece	288	74.3	21.1	80.2
	HUN	Hungary	179	67.0	22.2	90.0
	LTU	Lithuania	453	66.0	20.3	85.9
	MLT	Malta	124	78.2	22.2	83.1
	NLD	Netherlands	465	86.5	22.9	82.8
	PRT	Portugal	437	65.5	21.6	82.4
	ROU	Romania	274	90.2	21.0	89.1
	RUS	Russia	457	60.0	19.9	93.9
	SWE	Sweden	675	75.9	28.7	99.9
	CHE	Switzerland	369	72.4	34.2	86.0
Latin America	BRA	Brazil	289	68.2	21.0	84.8
	GTM	Guatemala	252	46.8	19.6	69.8
	MEX	Mexico	242	81.4	20.5	84.7
	VEN	Venezuela	285	61.1	24.1	91.6
Middle East	IRN	Iran	99	75.8	22.4	99.0
	ISR	Israel	349	80.1	30.7	91.1
North America	CAN	Canada	1275	71.3	21.6	89.0
	USA	United States	4533	67.8	21.7	91.8
Oceania	AUS	Australia	254	81.9	23.4	91.7
	NZL	New Zealand	149	77.9	21.5	87.3

Validity Of Data

The use of a convenience sample means that results describe what was found for the students in those classes in each country and cannot be taken as representative of the nation, or even of students in general. However, there is evidence that the behavior and beliefs of these students reflects the national context in which the students lived. Analyses of the degree of correspondence between seven concepts as measured by the International Dating Violence Study and as measured by studies using representative samples found correlations that ranged from .43 to a high of -.69 (Straus, 2009b). The -.69 correlation was between scores on a scale to measure male dominance in dating relationships. This correlation shows that the more male dominance reported by the students in this study, the lower the score on the Gender Empowerment Measure published by the United Nations Development Program (2005).

Control Variables

The analyses of the effects of victimization controlled for a number of variables.

Relationship length. Because the nature of a relationship changes over time, it was important to control for the length of time the couple had been together. The length of the relationships varied greatly.

Socioeconomic Status. It is important to control for the socioeconomic status (SES) of a student's family because SES can be correlated with the key variables of the study. We use a scale that combines father's education, mother's education, and family income. Because income has such different values in different nations, and because years of education may have different meanings in different nations, it was not appropriate to use raw scores for these variables. Instead, the SES of each student was measured relative to others at the student's university. This was done by first transforming the three SES variables into z-scores for the site, summing the three of them, and then calculating the z-score of that sum. The result is a scale that as a mean of zero and a standard deviation of 1 for each of the nations in the study. This scale cannot be used to compare nations. It measures SES as the number of standard deviations each student was above or below the mean of his or her respective site.

Gross Domestic Project Index. The GDP index for each nation was obtained from a United Nations Publication (United Nations Development Programme, 2006). It was calculated using the adjusted GDP per capita (PPP US$). GDP per capita is the total value of goods and services produced by a country in a year. It is measured in Purchasing Power Parity (PPP) in order to account for price differences between countries. Therefore, it better reflects people's living standards than using a traditional exchange rate. In theory 1 PPP dollar has the same purchasing power in the domestic economy of a country as 1 U.S. dollar has in the U.S. economy. The GDP Index is computed using an income of $40,000 (PPP US$) per capita as a maximum goalpost and $100.00 (PPP US$) is the minimum goalpost.

Limited Disclosure Scale. Differences in self-reported criminal behavior between groups could reflect differences in willingness to report socially undesirable behaviors as much or more than real differences in crime. To deal with this threat to validity, we controlled for scores on a scale which measures the tendency to avoid reporting socially undesirable behavior -- the Limited Disclosure scale of the Personal and Relationships Profile (Straus, Hamby, Boney-McCoy, & Sugarman, 2010; Straus & Mouradian, 1999). This is a13-item scale asking about behaviors and emotions that are slightly undesirable but true of most people, such as "I sometimes try to get even rather than forgive and forget." The more items a participant denies, the more likely a participant will avoid reporting PV. The response categories range from 1 (Strongly Disagree) to 4 (Strongly Agree).

Data Analyses

ANCOVA. Analysis of covariance was used to examine the relationship of the demographic characteristics to partner violence at the individual level. All analyses included the control variables listed above as covariates.

Scatter plots with regression lines were used to examine nation-to-nation differences in percent victimized and the relationship of the percent victimized to the dependent variables.

RESULTS ON QUESTION 1A: WHAT PERCENT OF STUDENTS WERE VICTIMS OF *PHYSICAL ASSAULTS* BY A ROMANTIC PARTNER?

The Conflict Tactics Scales

The data on physical assaults perpetrated by the partners of the students in this study was obtained using the Physical Assault Scale of the Revised Conflict Tactics Scales or CTS2 (Straus, Hamby, Boney-McCoy, & Sugarman, 1996). The CTS2 asks research participants to indicate whether they had engaged in a list of physically assaultive behaviors in the past year, and also if their partner had done so. Thus, it provides data on both partners. This is possible because the questions are about events in which the participant was either the perpetrator or the victim, or both. Consequently, participants in the study have full knowledge of the behavior of the partner.

However, that does not necessarily mean that they will accurately report either their own behavior of that of their partner.

In the past 30 years, the CTS have been used in over 400 studies, mostly in North America, but also in many other countries. It has demonstrated cross-cultural reliability and validity (Archer, 1999; Straus, 1990, 2004). The scale items and psychometric data are available in Straus et al (1996).

The Physical Assault scale of the CTS2 consists of 12 items, ranging in severity from less severe assaults (such as slapping or throwing something at the partner) to more severe attacks such as choking, punching, or attacks with objects or weapons. The alpha coefficient of reliability is .78 for the male students and .77 for the female students in this study.

The "past-year prevalence" scoring method was used for this paper, which means that if the participant reported any one or more acts of physical violence in the previous 12 months, he or she was classified as having perpetrated violence. The same procedure was used to classify the participant's partner as physically violent or non-violent.

Table 2. Percent assaulted by partner, by gender and nation
(In rank order of national context)

Median: Total = 25.0%, ***Males = 24.8%,*** ***Females = 26.2%***

High Half Of Nations				**Low Half Of Nations**			
	Total	Male	Feml		**Total**	Male	Feml
Iran	**41.0**	43.0	40.0	South Korea	**24.7**	19.5	28.3
Mexico	**39.5**	21.2	39.0	Lithuania	**24.4**	18.5	27.4
India	**35.8**	40.9	34.2	Germany	**24.3**	26.4	23.4
Great Britain	**33.3**	33.9	33.1	Venezuela	**24.1**	23.5	24.5
Tanzania	**33.1**	29.2	37.2	Canada	**23.1**	21.8	23.6
South Africa	**33.0**	28.6	33.3	Australia	**22.7**	28.6	21.5
New Zealand	**30.8**	35.7	29.4	Guatemala	**22.7**	20.9	24.7
Greece	**30.3**	34.5	29.0	Hungary	**21.7**	27.5	19.1
China -Taiwan	**29.0**	17.9	32.5	Brazil	**20.4**	16.7	22.2
Belgium	**28.2**	25.0	29.1	Singapore	**18.5**	13.4	20.8
Russia	**28.0**	29.2	27.1	Switzerland	**17.7**	23.3	16.0
Romania	**27.9**	41.7	26.4	Japan	**17.3**	19.4	15.5
United States	**27.9**	29.1	27.3	Sweden	**16.9**	22.7	15.1
China	**27.0**	24.7	28.4	Malta	**16.5**	31.8	12.3
China-Hong K	**25.4**	24.1	26.0	Portugal	**13.6**	11.9	14.5
Netherlands	**25.2**	31.3	24.3	Israel	**12.6**	15.8	11.9

Table 3. **Percent *severely* assaulted by partner, by gender and nation** (In Rank Order Of National Context)

Median: Total = 9.1%, Males = 9.1%, Females = 8.5%

High Half Of Nations				Low Half Of Nations			
	Total	Male	Feml		**Total**	Male	Feml
Tanzania	**17.1**	12.4	12.9	Russia	***9.1***	8.2	2.5
Greece	**15.6**	16.4	11.4	Canada	***8.0***	7.8	15.0
Iran	**15.3**	17.4	8.5	Belgium	***7.8***	5.3	8.1
Mexico	**15.1**	9.1	2.7	Germany	***7.6***	8.1	15.3
India	**14.7**	9.1	5.7	Japan	***6.8***	4.8	6.2
China	**13.6**	11.5	13.4	Brazil	***6.5***	7.7	3.7
China -Taiwan	**13.6**	15.4	10.3	Hungary	***6.2***	9.8	14.7
Great Britain	**13.4**	13.6	9.4	New Zealand	***6.2***	7.1	9.1
Venezuela	**13.4**	14.3	12.9	Portugal	***5.8***	5.1	9.7
South Korea	**12.6**	9.1	16.3	Israel	***5.7***	5.3	15.0
South Africa	**11.9**	18.0	10.8	Lithuania	***4.9***	2.3	4.9
China-Hong K	**11.1**	10.2	16.4	Malta	***4.9***	4.5	5.9
United States	**10.5**	10.9	10.8	Switzerland	***4.7***	8.2	7.4
Australia	**9.4**	11.9	6.0	Singapore	***4.2***	3.0	13.0
Romania	**9.4**	12.5	4.7	Netherlands	***3.9***	12.5	6.2
Guatemala	**9.1**	8.8	4.5	Sweden	***2.7***	3.1	1.7

Table 4. Ten other examples of the approximately 200 studies showing gender symmetry in perpetration of physical. assault

Study	**Severity Of Assault**	**Victim**	
		Female	**Male**
Canadian National Survey (Lupri, 1990)	Minor Severe	17.8% 10.1%	23.3% 12.9%
Canadian General Social Survey (1999)	Overall rate	7.0%	8.0%\
British Crime Survey (1996)	Overall rate	4.2%	4.1%
National Co-morbidity Study (Kessler, 2001)	Minor Severe	17.4% 6.5%	17.7% 6.2%
National Alcohol and Family Violence Survey (Straus, 1995)	Overall Severe	9.1% 1.9%	9.5% 4.5%
Dunedin Health and Development Study (US Dept of justice 1999)	Overall	27.0 %	34.0%
National Violence Against Women Survey (Tjaden & Thoennes, 2000)	Overall	1.3%	0.9%
Youth Risk Behavior Survey CCenters For Disease Control, 2006)	Overall	8.8%	8.9%
National Youth Survey (Wofford-Mihalic, Elliott, & Menard, 1994)	Overall Severe	20.2% 5.7%	34.1% 3.8%
% of Emergency room visits for PV (Ernst, et al.,2004)		19.0%	20.0%

Extent Of Victimization

The medians for all nations at the top of Table 2 shows that about one out of four of the students in this study (26% of male participants and 28% of female participants) were the victim of one or more of the violent acts in the CTS in the past year. Most of this partner violence (PV) was "minor" assaults as defined above. One out of four is more than double the rate of PV typically found in U.S. national surveys such as Kessler, (Kessler, Molnar, Feurer, & Appelbaum) and Straus (1980 (2006)). This is because PV, like other violent crime, peaks at about age 20 and then declines rapidly (Stets & Straus, 1989; Straus & Ramirez, 2007). The sample for this study is much younger (average age of 23) than the samples for national samples for which the average age is about 40, and the higher rate of PV is therefore to be expected. The high percentage who were victims of PV is also consistent with the rates from many dating partner studies (Archer, 2000; Sugarman & Hotaling, 1989). Another indication of the extremely high rates of PV among student couples is the difference between the way these data are reported and the way police statistics on assault are reported. Police statistics are usually expressed as a rate per 100,000, whereas the percentages in the article are the rate per 100.

The main part of Table 1, gives the percent of female and male students who were assaulted by a partner in each of the 32 nations in the International Dating Violence Study. The nations are listed in Table 2 in rank order in order to make clear that, although all are high relative to police statistics on assault, there are also large differences between nations. The highest rate of partner assault is in Iran. It is important to note that nations which are high in the percent of women who were assaulted by a partner also tend to nations where a high percent of men were assaulted by their partner. The similar rates of victimization for men and women is consistent with what has been found by over 200 studies (Fiebert, 2010). Table 4 summarizes the results for ten of those studies.

Table 3 is like Table 2 except that it gives the percentage in each nation who were *severely* assaulted as defined above. The percent who were victims of severe assault are much lower than the percentage in Table 2, which is to be expected. An important result in Table 3 is that, as was the case with overall assault rate, a similar percent of men and women were victims. The similar percentage of male and female victims of PV is consistent with what has been found by more than 200 general population studies (Archer, 2000; Fiebert, 2004; Straus, 1999; Sugarman & Hotaling, 1989). Ten of the leading studies are summarized in Table 4, which shows similar rates of victimization in all ten studies.

Victimization And Degree Of Injury Experienced. An important aspect of the similar rates of PV victimization of men and women in the current study and in the ten studies in Table 4, is that being the victim of an attack is only one aspect of victimization. Female victims, on average sustain more injury, both physical injury and psychological injury. Moreover, because women tend to have fewer economic resources, than men, it is more difficult for a woman to escape a violent relationship, and therefore there is a greater need for services for women victims.

Female Partner Violence In Male Dominant Societies

Both Table 2, which gives the percentages for any assault, and Table 3 which gives the percentages for severe assault may be a surprise to some readers of this article because they show that the nations with the highest rates of victimization tend to be low economic development and/or male dominant, although there are some important exceptions. Although studies of female victims of PV has attracted world-wide attention, as it should, the many studies showing high rates of male victims have been almost ignored. The International Dating Violence Study is one of the many studies which have found that, even in male-dominant societies, about the same percent of women as men physically assault partners. A forthcoming paper on this issue presents such data for women in 27 male-dominant nations and offers an explanation for the high rate of PV victimization by men in such societies(Straus, 2011). The high rate of male victimization in male-dominant societies is also illustrated by the following three studies. The Global School-based Health Survey conducted by the World Health Organization obtained data on students age13 to 15 in four presumably male-dominant societies (downloaded November 15, 2006 from www.who.int/school_youth_health/gshs). The students were asked if they had been hit, slapped or hurt on purpose by a boyfriend or girlfriend in the past 12 months. For Jordan the study found a 15% victimization rate for girls and a 29% rate for boys; for Namibia, 9% girl victims and 16% boy victims; for Swaziland, 6% girl victims, and 8% boy victims, and for Zambia, 18% girl victims and 23% boy victims

Although the above results are for adolescents, results for adults are given in 25 of the 27 studies reviewed in (Straus, 2011). For example, Kerley(2010) studied a sample of married women in Thailand. According to the women in this study, 40% of the men had been assaulted by the women interviewed. Kim(2003) studied a nationally representative sample of households in Korea and found 16% male victims and 28% female victims of assault by a partner.

Mutual Victimization

Table 5 summarizes the results on "mutuality" of victimization for ten major U.S. studies, shows that most physical assaults in romantic relationships are mutual, in the sense that both the male and female partners are victims. The percent of couples in which both are victims ranged from 17 to 78% (median = 42%). Tables 6 and 7 give this data in slightly different form for the 32 nations in the International Dating Violence study. Those two tables show the percent of mutual victimization as reported by the male students in each nation of the 32 nations, and by the female students in each of those nations. The medians in the top row of Table 6 indicates that, according the male students in this study, when there was violence, in 74% of the cases it was mutual; and according to the female students, it was mutual in 67% of the cases. Thus, according to both men and women, mutual victimization is the predominant pattern, and this applies to both the overall victimization rate and being the victim of a severe assault.

It is important to realize that these percentages are not for the total sample in each nation. They are the percentage of mutual violence among the part of the sample where one or more assaults occurred in the previous 12 months. This can be a high percentage of a small number of cases, as for example in Sweden, which has one of the lowest rates of victimization in Table 2, but among that relatively small group, Table 6 shows that it was mutual in 58% of the cases. In addition, it is important to keep in mind that, as noted previously, women victims sustain more injuries. But the fact that about a third of the injuries from PV are sustained by men (Archer, 2000), including a third of the lethal injuries (Catalano, 2006), must also be kept in mind.

Table 5. Mutuality of severe assaults In ten general population studies					
Study and Sample		**% Both**	**% Male Only**	**% Feml Only**	**N***
Natl. Survey Families And Households (Anderson, 2002)	Female Rept	**67%**	22%	22%	674
	Male report	**70%**	10%	20%	
University Survey (Jamilia Bookwala, et al., 1992)		**NR***	≥6%	≥20%	305
Cross-section of Manitoba couples, 1981 (Merlin B. Brinkerhoff, Grandin, & Lupri, 1992)		**28%**	22%	50%	121
New Zealand Birth Cohort (Magdol, et al., 1997)		**NR**	24%	76%	104
National Comorbidity Survey (Kessler, et al., 2001	Female Report	**57%**	24%	20%	146
	Male Report	**44%**	2%	54%	97
Korean national survey (Kim & Emery, 2003)		**17**	70	13	
Stonybrook NY Representative Sample (Slep & O'Leary, 2005)		**42%**	21%	37%	107
National Family Violence Survey (Straus, 2005)		**35%**	35%	30%	211
National Longitudinal Study of Adolescent Health (at age 18-28). (Whitaker, et al., 2007)		**78%**	10%	12%	760
Representative community sample (Kar & O'Leary, 2010)	Overall	**59**	19	21	264
	Severe	**27**	23	50	90

NR % "Both" Not reported. Presumably it is: 100- (% male-only + % female only)
** N refers to the subset of cases in which severe physical assault occurred, which is frequently a small percent of the study N*

Table 6. Percent b*oth* violent according to male and female students (among violent relationships. In rank order of national context)

Median: Total = 68.7%, Males = 74.3%, Females = 67.3%

High Half Of Nations	Total	Male	Feml	Low Half Of Nations	Total	Male	Feml
Iran	92.6	100.0	89.8	Canada	68.6	73.6	67.2
Tanzania	90.5	89.7	91.2	Venezuela	68.4	56.7	76.1
South Africa	89.5	100.0	88.9	China-Taiwan	66.7	87.5	63.6
India	81.1	88.9	78.6	Guatemala	66.0	80.0	56.7
Japan	79.3	85.7	73.3	Portugal	65.2	87.5	58.0
Great Britain	77.7	80.0	77.4	New Zealand	63.8	40.0	70.3
Mexico	77.3	77.8	77.3	Australia	63.5	53.8	66.0
Lithuania	71.9	88.9	67.3	Germany	63.2	64.4	62.6

South Korea	71.4	70.0	72.1	China	61.9	71.3	58.4
Russia	71.2	75.5	69.0	Switzerland	61.7	63.6	61.0
Netherlands	71.1	100.0	67.3	Greece	59.8	70.8	55.6
Brazil	71.0	76.5	68.9	Israel	58.7	81.8	53.8
Hungary	69.8	75.0	66.7	Sweden	58.0	71.8	53.2
United States	69.5	72.7	68.2	Singapore	57.9	41.7	62.2
Romania	69.0	54.5	71.1	China-Hong K	54.3	59.2	52.9
Belgium	68.8	67.3	69.1	Malta	50.0	55.6	46.7

Table 7. Percent both *severely* assaulted partner (among violent relationships. in rank order of national context)

Median: Total = 57.1%, AS REPORTED BY: Males = 61.7%, Females = 56.0%

High Half Of Nations				Low Half Of Nations			
	Total	Male	Feml		Total	Male	Feml
Japan	74.0	75.0	85.7	United States	57.0	60.4	55.7
Tanzania	73.0	73.3	72.7	Guatemala	55.6	44.4	66.7
Brazil	72.2	57.1	81.8	Germany	55.3	50.0	57.6
India	70.6	33.3	78.6	Russia	55.2	81.3	45.2
Portugal	69.6	100.0	58.8	Australia	53.6	80.0	47.8
South Korea	67.7	75.0	65.2	Lithuania	48.5	33.3	51.9
Iran	66.7	100.0	57.1	Belgium	48.3	46.2	48.6
Venezuela	64.3	64.7	64.0	Netherlands	47.8	66.7	41.2
Israel	64.0	75.0	61.9	China-Hong K	47.5	70.6	42.7
Canada	61.5	63.0	61.1	New Zealand	46.7	50.0	46.2
South Africa	61.1	100.0	56.3	Singapore	46.2	0.0	54.5
Mexico	60.5	50.0	61.8	Romania	44.1	66.7	41.9
Great Britain	59.7	33.3	63.5	Hungary	42.1	57.1	33.3
Greece	59.1	58.3	59.4	China	39.8	38.1	40.3
China -Taiwan	58.3	100.0	50.0	Sweden	25.0	40.0	21.1
Switzerland	57.1	83.3	46.7	Malta	24.0	0.0	14.3

RESULTS ON QUESTION 1B IS BEING A VICTIM OF PHYSICAL ASSAULT BY A PARTNER ASSOCIATED WITH AN INCREASED PROBABILITY THAT THE VICTIM WILL BE INJURED, DEPRESSED AND PHYSICALLY ASSAULT THE PARTNER?

Injury

Injury resulting from physical assault by a partner of the students in this study was measured by the injury scale of the revised Conflict Tactics Scales (Straus, et al., 1996). This is a six item scale consisting of two indicators of relatively minor injury which had occurred in the previous 12 months, such as "I had a sprain, bruise, or small cut because of a fight" and four relatively more serious injuries such as "I had a broken bone from a fight." The alpha coefficient of reliability for the men in this study was .65, and for the women .65.

Table 8.
Percent injured by partner (in rank order of national context)

Median: Total = 6.9%, *Males = 6.2%, Females = 7.2% , F% Of M = 116%*

High Half Of Nations				Low Half Of Nations			
	Total	Male	Fem.		Total	Male	Female
Iran	65.3	87.0	58.7	South Korea	6.8	6.5	7.1
Tanzania	17.7	14.6	20.9	Hungary	6.2	7.8	5.5
South Africa	13.8	28.6	12.7	Greece	5.6	7.3	5.1
India	12.6	4.5	15.1	Australia	5.2	0.0	6.3
China Taiwan	12.3	10.3	13.0	Germany	5.2	6.1	4.7
Venezuela	10.3	10.2	10.4	China Hong K	4.7	4.2	4.9
Mexico	9.8	9.1	9.9	Singapore	4.6	4.5	4.7
United States	8.7	9.2	8.5	Guatemala	4.5	6.6	2.4
Great Britain	8.6	6.8	8.9	Romania	4.5	4.2	4.5
New Zealand	8.5	3.6	9.8	Netherlands	4.2	6.3	3.9
Canada	8.1	6.8	8.6	Brazil	4.1	2.6	4.8
China	7.8	6.9	8.3	Sweden	3.9	4.9	3.5
Malta	7.8	9.1	7.4	Israel	3.8	5.3	3.4
Lithuania	7.5	6.2	8.1	Japan	3.8	0.0	7.0
Belgium	7.1	5.9	7.4	Portugal	2.2	1.7	2.5
Russia	7.0	4.1	8.9	Switzerland	1.9	0.0	2.5

Figure 1.
The more assaults by a partner, the higher the percent Injured

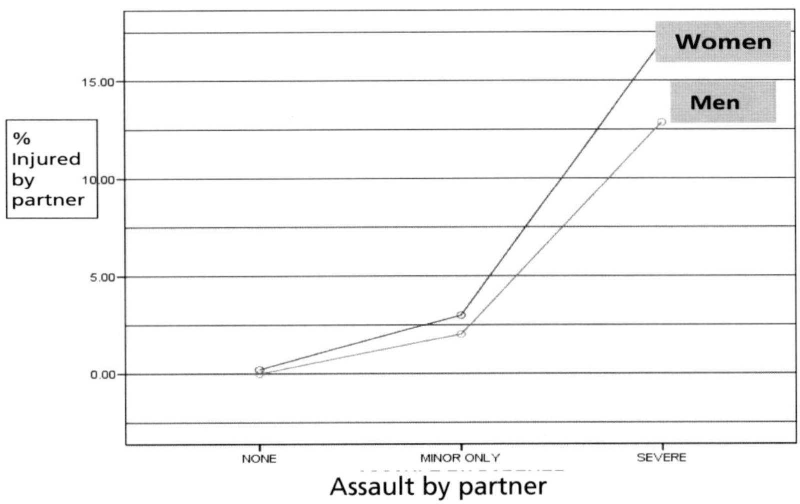

In the next figures 2,4,6,8 and 10 the abbreviations are:
AUS Australia; BEL Belgium; BRA Brazil; CAN Canada; CHE Switzerland; CHN China; DEU Ger-many; GBR Great Britain; GRC Greece; GTM Guatemala; HK Cong Kong; HUN Hungary; IND India; IRN Iran; ISR Israel; JPN Japan; KOR South Korea; LTU Lithuania; MEX Mexico; MLT Malta; NLD Netherlands; NZL New Zealand; PRT Portugal; ROU Romania; RUS Russia; SGP Singapore; SWE Sweden; TWN Taiwan; TZA Tanzania; USA United States; VEN Venezuela; ZAF S Africa

Figure 2 (A and B)
The higher the percent of students in a national setting who were physically assaulted by a partner, the higher the percent injured, especially women

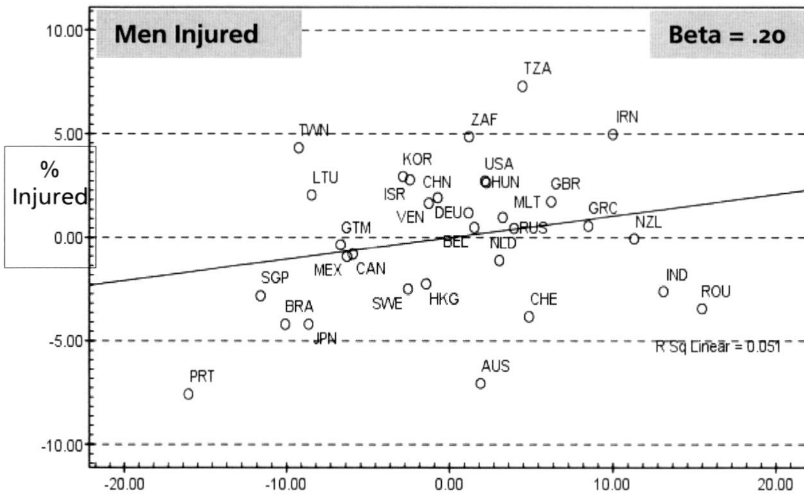

Fig. 2A: Percent assaulted by a female

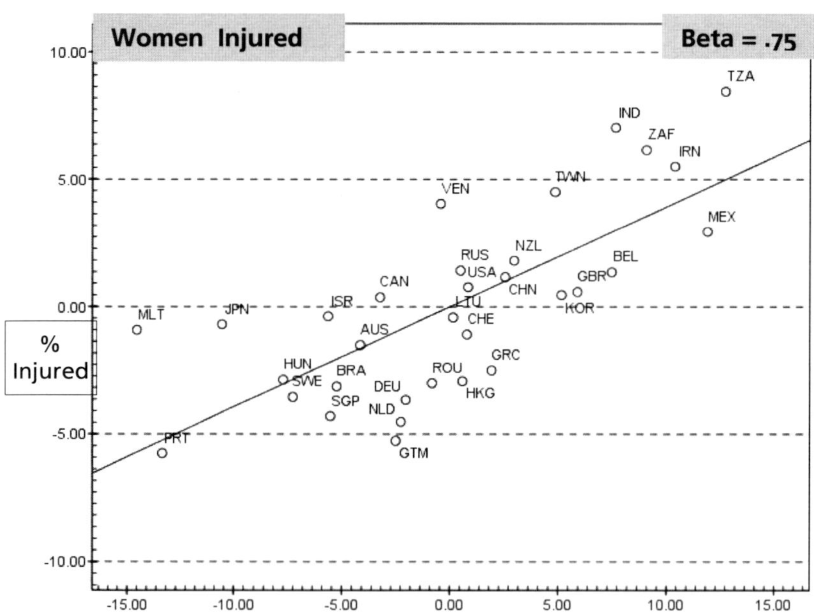

Fig. 2B: Percent assaulted by a male

Percent Injured In The 32 Nations. The medians at the top of Table 8 show that about seven percent of the students were physically injured by a dating partner during the previous 12 months. The percent of women injured was 16% higher than the percent of men injured by a partner. The somewhat greater injury rate sustained by women victims of PV is also shown in Figure 1. This is a much smaller gender difference than has been found by most other studies, but consistent the finding that the *difference* between men and women in injuries is lower when the sample consists of young couples or dating couples (Archer, 2000, 2002).

National Context And The Relation of Assault Victimization To Injury. In Figure 2, the cases are not the seventeen thousand students in the International Dating Violence study. The cases are the 32 national contexts in which those students resided. Figure 2 shows that the larger the percent of students in a nation who were victims of physical assault by a partner, the larger the percent that were physically injured. This suggests that in national contexts where there is more assault, it also tends to be more severe and injury producing. The left side of Figure 2 shows this for men and the right side for women. Comparing them shows that the link between the percent of students in a national context who are victims of assault and the percent that are injured by being assaulted is much stronger for women. The much stronger link between assault and injury among women probably occurs because women are more vulnerable to injury.

Depression

• Being a victim of physical assault by a partner can have many adverse psychological effects. For this article, we examine one of them – depression. Depression was measured by the Depressive Symptoms Scale of the *Personal And Relationships Profile* (Straus, et al., 2010). This is an eight item scale based on questions from previously validated depression measures such as "I am so sad, sometimes I wonder why I bother to go on living" and "My life is generally going well" (reverse scored.). The alpha coefficients of reliability for this sample are Males = .82, Females = .83, Total = .83

Table 9. Depressive symptoms by gender and nation (mean score in rank order of national context)							
Median: Total = 30.6, Males = 29.8, Females = 30.8, F% Of M = 103%							
High Half Of Nations				Low Half Of Nations			
	Total	Male	Feml		*Total*	Male	Feml
Japan	*45.3*	47.2	43.6	Singapore	*30.6*	30.1	30.8
China -Taiwan	*42.8*	38.5	44.5	Belgium	*30.5*	29.5	30.8
China	*40.4*	41.5	39.8	New Zealand	*29.9*	30.1	29.9
South Korea	*39.4*	34.0	42.6	Brazil	*29.2*	29.9	28.8
China-Hong K	*37.9*	38.8	37.6	Tanzania	*29.1*	28.0	30.6
Russia	*34.4*	33.9	34.7	Switzerland	*27.4*	28.8	26.9
Iran	*33.8*	32.3	34.2	Australia	*27.0*	25.4	27.4
Greece	*33.6*	31.7	34.3	Canada	*27.0*	25.8	27.5
Germany	*33.4*	33.2	33.5	Romania	*27.0*	22.2	27.6
Lithuania	*32.3*	31.0	33.0	United States	*25.8*	26.7	25.3
South Africa	*31.7*	28.1	32.1	Guatemala	*25.5*	25.0	26.0
India	*31.5*	27.4	33.3	Israel	*25.3*	27.7	24.7
Portugal	*31.5*	29.7	32.4	Netherlands	*24.2*	22.2	24.6
Great Britain	*31.3*	35.4	30.5	Mexico	*21.5*	20.2	21.8
Hungary	*31.3*	30.3	31.8	Venezuela	*20.2*	20.8	19.8
Malta	*30.7*	30.4	30.8	Sweden	*18.4*	19.1	18.2

Figure 3.
Both men and women victims of partner assault have elevated depressive symptoms, but especially women

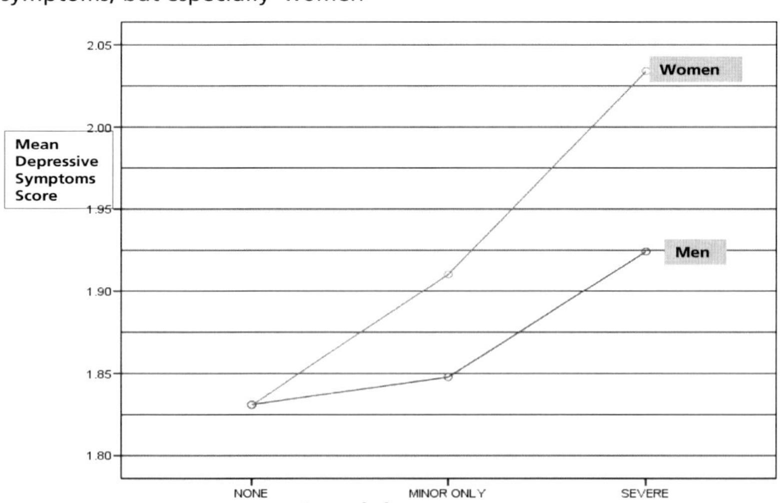

Figure 4. (A and B)
The higher the percent of students in a national who were *severely* assaulted by a partner, the higher the level of depressive symptoms among students in the nation

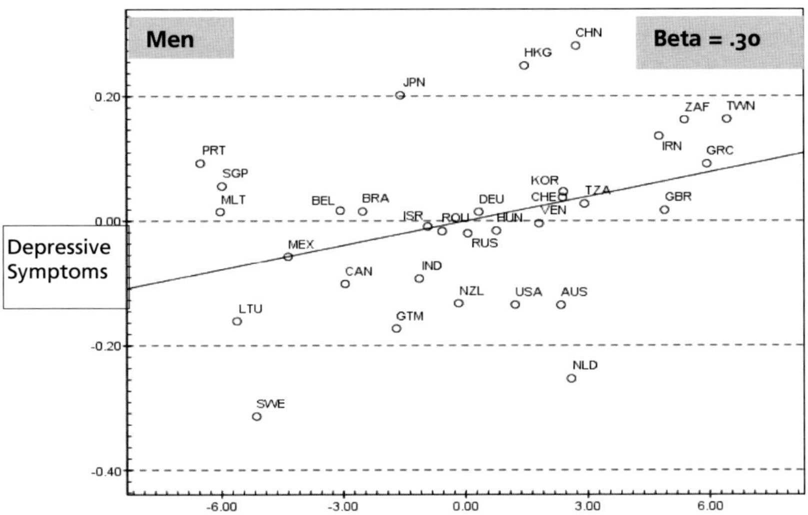

Fig 4 A: Severe assault by female partner

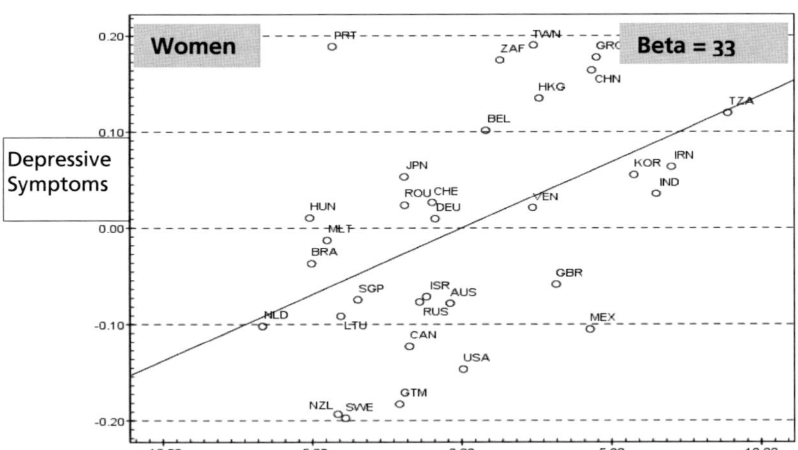

Fig 4 B: Severe assault by male partner

Table 10. Psychological aggression by partner, by gender and nation (mean number of times in rank order of national context)							
Median: Total = 9.1 times, *Males = 9.2, Females = 9.5, F% of M = 103%*							
High Half Of Nations				Low Half Of Nations			
	Total	Male	Feml		Total	Male	Feml
Great Britain	16.8	13.4	17.4	Iran	8.8	9.3	8.7
United States	14.4	12.8	15.1	Mexico	8.8	5.5	9.5
Canada	12.0	9.6	12.9	Singapore	8.6	6.8	9.4
Australia	11.6	8.5	12.3	Russia	8.5	9.5	7.9
Greece	11.6	11.5	11.7	Lithuania	8.3	5.8	9.5
New Zealand	11.6	7.3	12.7	Romania	8.0	11.6	7.6
Israel	11.2	12.4	10.9	Brazil	7.9	6.8	8.3
India	11.1	13.2	10.4	Tanzania	7.9	5.9	10.0
South Africa	11.1	12.6	11.0	China-Hong K	7.6	9.4	6.9
Germany	11.0	10.0	11.4	Japan	7.5	7.5	7.5
Malta	10.9	13.6	10.1	Netherlands	7.2	9.1	6.9
Belgium	10.5	9.4	10.8	China -Taiwan	6.5	6.2	6.6
Venezuela	10.5	8.0	12.0	South Korea	6.3	3.8	8.0
Sweden	9.9	11.6	9.3	China	6.0	7.7	4.9
Hungary	9.8	6.7	11.3	Portugal	5.6	5.3	5.8
Guatemala	9.4	10.6	8.1	Switzerland	5.5	6.2	5.3

Extent Of Depressive Symptoms In 32 Nations. Many studies have found that a larger percent of women than men suffer from depression or depressive symptoms. However, the gender difference is minimal or absent among adolescents or young adult students (Grant, et al., 2002). The medians at the top of Table 9 show that results for the students in the International Dating Violence Study are consistent with the minimal difference found by other student studies. The median for men is 29.8 and 30.8 for women, which is not a statistically significant difference. Moreover, the small difference in depressive symptoms between men and women students tends apply to all 32 nations. There are, however, large differences in depression between students in different national contexts, with the scores ranging from a low of .18.4 in Sweden to a high of 48.3 in Japan.

Relation Of Physical Victimization To Depressive Symptoms. Figure 3 shows that the more severe the assault experienced by the students in this study, the higher the average depressive symptoms score. This applies to male victims of assault by a partner as well as female victims. Figure 3 also suggests why, taking the sample as a whole, there is almost no difference between men and women in depressive symptoms. It is because there is no gender difference among the non-victimized students, and they are three quarters of the sample. However, among assault victims, the depressive symptoms score of women in much higher than that of men, especially those who were severely assaulted. Thus, being a victim of physical attacks by a partner results in more psychological injury to female victims than to male victims, just as being a victim of physical assaults by a partner results in more physical injury to women than to men.

In Figure 4, the cases are the 32 national contexts in which the students resided. It shows that the higher the percentage of students in a national context who were victims of assault by a partner, the higher the average depressive symptoms of students in the national context. This suggests that nation-to-nation differences in victimization by a partner is one of the reasons for the large nation-to-nation difference in depressive symptoms shown in Table 9.

Asymmetry in Effects: The Basis for Denial of Symmetry in Perpetration

Most Studies Find Gender Differences In Effects. The distinction between perpetration and the effects of the assault is extremely important. If the criterion for symmetry is whether an individual was physically attacked by a partner the data presented and the studies cited indicate symmetry *in perpetration*. However, if the criterion for symmetry is the extent to which the person attacked suffers physical, psychological, or economic injury, the results indicate gender differences. Thus, there can be symmetry in perpetration and asymmetry in effects. That is the case with PV. Attacks by male partners cause more fear, more physical and psychological injury (as illustrated by the results on depressive symptoms in Figure 3), and more deaths (Catalano, 2006; Rennison & Welchans, 2000; Straus, 2005). The greater adverse effect on women is an extremely important difference for theories of victimization. It is equally important for policy and practice because it indicates the need to continue to provide more services for female victims of PV than for male victims. Nevertheless, the greater harm suffered by female victims should not obscure the fact that many men are also harmed, including the previously cited research indicating that men sustain about a third of the injuries from PV, including a fifth of the homicide deaths (Catalano, 2006; Rennison & Welchans, 2000; Straus, 2005). In addition, from a legal perspective, in most jurisdictions in the U.S., a physical attack is a crime regardless of whether there is injury, or even contact. If a man or woman attacks their partner with a base ball bat and the partner dodges and gets out the door without being touched, it is an "aggravated assault" in the U.S. legal system. Psychologically, the partner is a victim of what in many cases is a traumatic experience, even though it is not as serious as when injury occurs.

RESULTS ON QUESTION 2A WHAT PERCENT WERE VICTIMS OF *PSYCHOLOGICAL* AGGRESSION AGAINST ROMANTIC PARTNER?

Table 10. Psychological aggression by partner, by gender and nation (mean number of times in rank order of national context)

Median: Total = 9.1 times, *Males = 9.2, Females = 9.5, F% of M = 103%*

High Half Of Nations				Low Half Of Nations			
	Total	Male	Feml		Total	Male	Feml
Great Britain	16.8	13.4	17.4	Iran	8.8	9.3	8.7
United States	14.4	12.8	15.1	Mexico	8.8	5.5	9.5
Canada	12.0	9.6	12.9	Singapore	8.6	6.8	9.4
Australia	11.6	8.5	12.3	Russia	8.5	9.5	7.9
Greece	11.6	11.5	11.7	Lithuania	8.3	5.8	9.5
New Zealand	11.6	7.3	12.7	Romania	8.0	11.6	7.6
Israel	11.2	12.4	10.9	Brazil	7.9	6.8	8.3
India	11.1	13.2	10.4	Tanzania	7.9	5.9	10.0
South Africa	11.1	12.6	11.0	China-Hong K	7.6	9.4	6.9
Germany	11.0	10.0	11.4	Japan	7.5	7.5	7.5
Malta	10.9	13.6	10.1	Netherlands	7.2	9.1	6.9
Belgium	10.5	9.4	10.8	China -Taiwan	6.5	6.2	6.6
Venezuela	10.5	8.0	12.0	South Korea	6.3	3.8	8.0
Sweden	9.9	11.6	9.3	China	6.0	7.7	4.9
Hungary	9.8	6.7	11.3	Portugal	5.6	5.3	5.8
Guatemala	9.4	10.6	8.1	Switzerland	5.5	6.2	5.3

Figure 5.
Overall psychological aggression is related to depressive symptoms only for victims of the most frequently aggressive fifth of partners

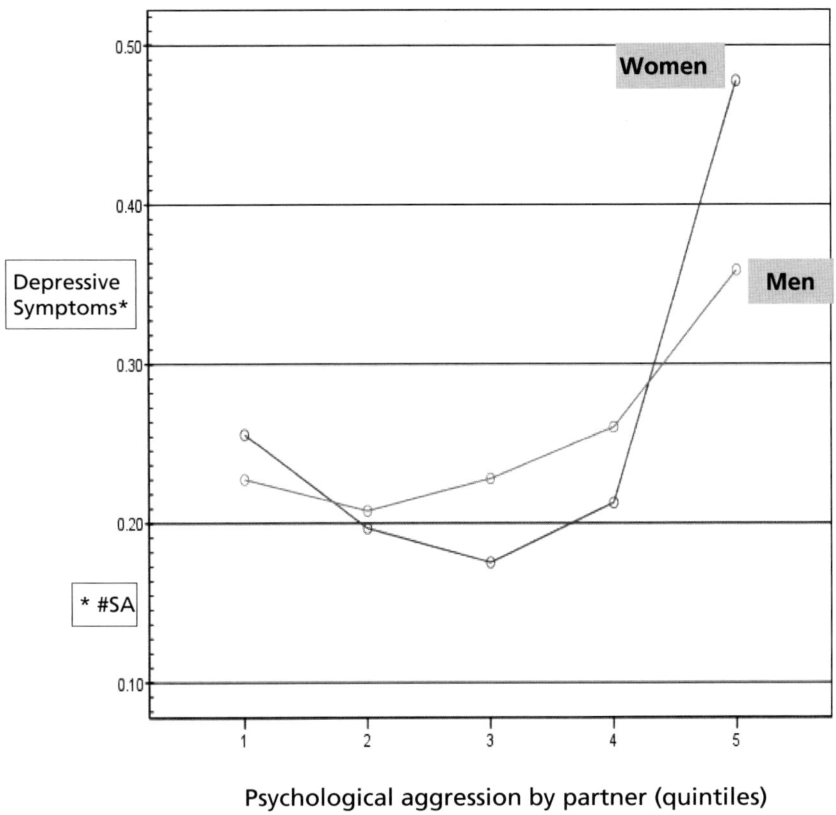

Figure 6. (A and B)
National settings in which students are *severely psychologically* aggressive to partners tend to have higher rates of depressive symptoms

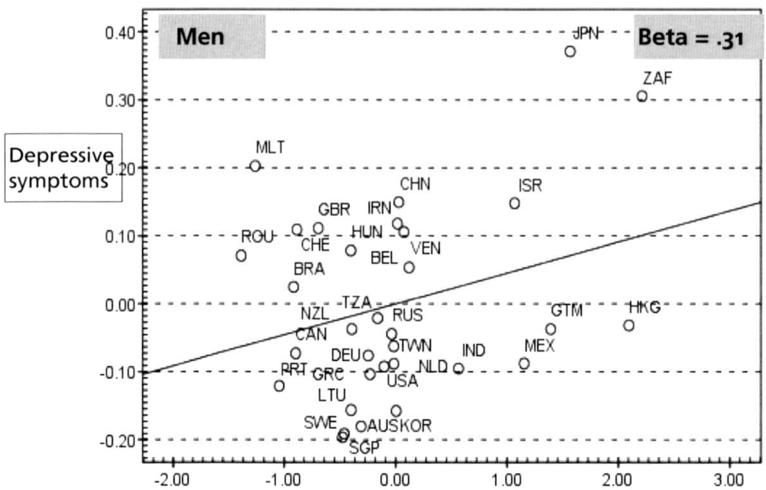

Fig 6A: Severe psychological aggression by male partner

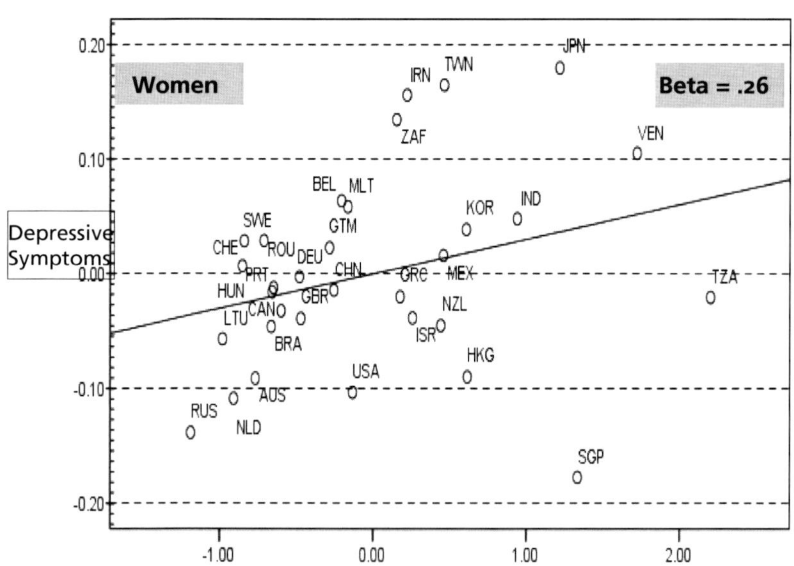

Fig 6B: Severe psychological aggression by male partner

Psychological attacks on a partner (also called verbal aggression) was measured by the psychological aggression scale of the Revised Conflict Tactics Scales (Straus, et al., 1996). This scale includes acts of minor aggression such as shouting or yelling at the partner and four acts judged to be more serious in the sense of being more hurtful, such as calling the partner a name such as fat or ugly. The students were asked if and how often these things happened in the previous 12 months. The alpha coefficient of reliability is .65 for the male participants in this study, and .71 for the female participants. The *percentage* who verbally attacked did not provide a meaningful basis for identifying differences between nations in psychological aggression or a basis for studying the effects of being a victim of psychological aggression by a partner because the percentages were almost all close to 100%. However, the nations did differ in *how often* the students were victims of verbal attacks. Therefore, the data in Tables 10 and 11 are the average number of times the partner verbally attacked, not the percentage who verbally attackThe medians at the top of Table 10 show that both the male female students reported having been victims of psychological aggression about nine times during the preceding 12 months. This may seem high, but it is probably lower than the actual frequency because this is such a common event that few keep track of the number of times. Also important is the nearly equal rates of victimization of men and women. The high frequency of psychological aggression against the men and the women in this study, and the preceding data on the high rate of physical assaults victimization of both men and women, contradict the stereotype that men attack physically and women psychologically. This is consistent with the results from a U.S. national survey (Straus & Sweet, 1992). What this and other studies show is that a similar percent of men and women are victims of both psychological attacks and physical attacks.

RESULTS ON QUESTION 2B
IS BEING A VICTIM OF PSYCHOLOGICAL AGGRESSION BY A PARTNER ASSOCIATED WITH AN INCREASED PROBABILITY THAT THE VICTIM WILL BE DEPRESSED?

Figure 5 shows that being a victim of psychological aggression by a partner does not seem to be associated with depression until the frequency of the verbal attacks is very high (top fifth of the sample. At that level, however, it is associated with a large increase in depressive symptoms. The students whose partners were in the fifth of the sample in how often they verbally attacked have a much higher number of depressive symptoms than the other four fifths of the sample

If the overall measure of psychological aggression is used as the independent variable, the national setting differences, no relationship was found between the percent of students in a nation who were victims of psychological aggression and the percent who are depressed. However, if *severe* psychological aggression is used as the independent variable, Figure 6 shows that there is a slight tendency for nations in which more students were victims of psychological aggression by a partner to have a higher average depressive symptoms score. This is consistent with the results in Figure 5 which show that psychological aggression is associated with elevated depressive symptoms scores only when the victimization is very frequent.

RESULTS ON QUESTION 3A
WHAT PERCENT OF STUDENTS WERE VICTIMS OF PHYSICAL ATTACKS *BY PARENTS* IN THE FORM OF *CORPORAL PUNISHMENT*

Table 11. Percent who did not strongly disagree that they were spanked or hit a lot before age 12, by gender and nation
All Nations Median: Total = 52%, Males = 55%, Females = 50%

High Half Of Nations				Low Half Of Nations			
	Total	Male	Female		*Total*	Male	Female
China-Taiwan	74.0	78.1	72.4	Canada	51.0	54.4	49.6
Tanzania	71.7	74.8	67.6	Hungary	50.8	45.8	53.3
South Africa	67.3	66.7	67.4	Lithuania	48.3	57.1	43.8
Mexico	65.7	71.1	64.5	Greece	47.6	63.5	42.1
Singapore	65.4	67.5	64.4	Switzerland	44.2	50.0	41.9
China-Hong K	60.2	65.7	57.9	Romania	41.6	51.9	40.5
United States	*60.0*	*68.3*	*56.1*	Japan	35.7	46.5	25.9
South Korea	59.8	65.6	56.4	Guatemala	33.7	41.8	24.6
Germany	59.4	62.6	57.9	Malta	32.3	40.7	29.9
China	57.6	64.4	54.0	Venezuela	28.1	40.5	20.1
Russia	56.0	61.2	52.6	Israel	22.6	22.4	22.7
Great Britain	55.0	62.0	53.8	Belgium	22.0	27.4	20.4
New Zealand	55.0	48.5	56.9	Portugal	21.5	29.1	17.5
India	54.4	50.8	56.0	Brazil	19.4	27.2	15.7
Australia	52.8	58.7	51.4	Sweden	17.0	19.0	16.4
Iran	52.5	54.2	52.0	Netherlands	14.6	33.3	11.7

Figure 7.
The more spanking experienced, the higher the probability of both women and men assaulting a dating partner

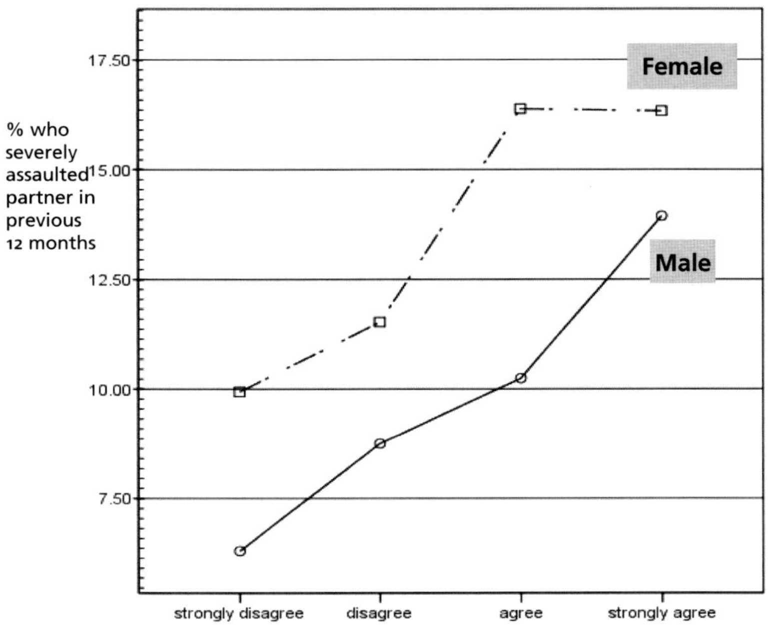

'When I was less than 12 years old, I was spanked or hit a lot by my mother or father'

Figure 8 (A and B).
Nations where more parents use corporal punishment tend to be nations where more students hit dating partners

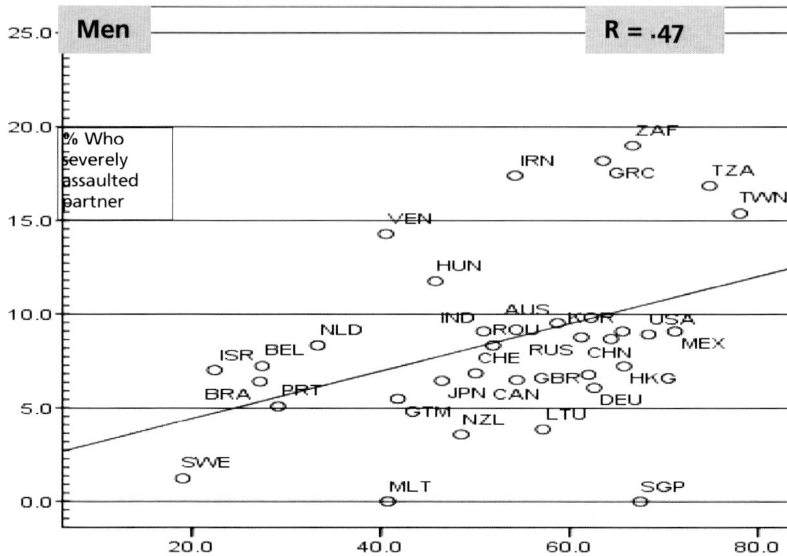

Fig: 8A: % Spanked or hit a lot before age 12

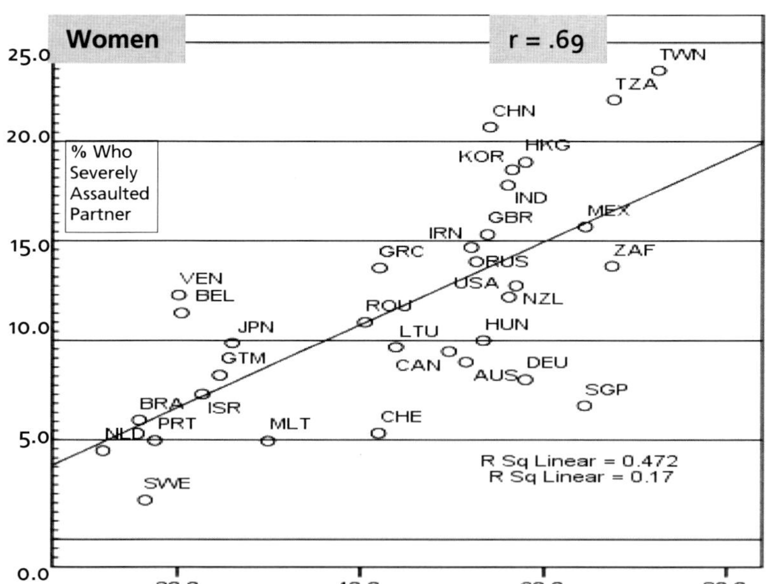

Fig 8B: % Spanked or hit a lot before age 12

Most research on physical attacks by parents has examined the causes and consequences of severe assaults such as kicking, punching, chocking, or burning a child, i.e. on perpetrators and victims of "physical abuse." However, the focus of this article is on what, in most nations, is legal and also morally approved corporal punishment (CP) by parents. In the U.S. this called "spanking" and in the U.K. it is called "smacking" a child. One reason for focusing on ordinary CP of children rather than "physical abuse" is that there is already a large body of research which shows the many adverse physical and psychological effects of "physical abuse" and further research on this linkage is not a high priority. Another reason for focusing on being a victim of legal parental assaults in the form of spanking and slapping a child is that it is far more prevalent than physically abusing a child -- perhaps a hundred times more prevalent. Consequently, if CP has adverse effects, many times more children will be at risk of those adverse effects than are at risk from physical abuse.

The definition of CP which guided this research is the use of physical force with the intention of causing a child to experience pain, but not injury, for the purpose of correction or control of the child's behavior (Straus, 2001, page 4). CP was measured by asking the students who participated in the study whether they agreed or disagreed that, "When I was less than 12 years old, I was spanked or hit a lot by my mother or father." The response categories in the questionnaire were Strongly Disagree, Disagree, Agree, and Strongly Agree. If the student chose any response category except Strongly Disagree, he or she was classified as having experienced CP. The logic behind using this cutting point was that students who did not strongly disagree had probably experienced at least some CP. This was supported by 16 exploratory correlations which compared the size of correlations of CP with hypothesized causes or consequences of CP. In all 16 comparison, the correlation using "did not Strongly Disagree" as the measure of CP was larger than the correlation using Agree or Strongly agree as the measure of CP.

Prevalence Of Corporal Punishment

Measuring CP in the way just explained, Table 11 gives the percent who experienced CP before age 12 for the entire sample and for each of the 32 nations in the study. The top row shows that, in the median nation, 52% of the students indicated that they had been "spanked or hit a lot" as a child. The column headed Total in Table 11 lists the rates for the 32 national settings in rank order, starting with the nation with the highest rate. This was in Taiwan, where three out of four students reported that they were spanked or hit a lot before age 12. At the bottom of the list is the Netherlands, where 15% reported being hit a lot before age 12. Thus, CP varied tremendously among the nations in this study. The next two columns show the percent of male and female students who reported being hit a lot, and the final column shows the ratio of females to males who reported being hit a lot. In 30 of the 32 nations in the study, somewhat more male than female students were hit as a child. This is consistent with the results from other studies, including two U.S. national samples(Giles-Sims, Straus, & Sugarman, 1995; Straus & Stewart, 1999) which also found that more boys than girls are hit by parents.

The percentages who experienced CP in Table 11 are almost certain to be much lower than the actual percent of children who experienced CP. This is because the question asked about being spanked "a lot" thus excluding those who were spanked only occasionally. That is like a study of partner violence which omits those women were only occasionally slapped by their partner. In addition, many or most adults remember little of what happened when they were aged 2, 3, or 4, which are the ages at which CP is most likely to occur. But even with these constraints, in six nations two thirds or more the students were spanked or hit *a lot*.

RESULTS ON QUESTION 3B
IS BEING A VICTIM OF PHYSICAL ASSAULT BY PARENTS ASSOCIATED WITH AN INCREASED PROBABILITY THAT THE VICTIM WILL PHYSICALLY ASSAULT PARTNER AND BE DEPRESSED?

Figure 9.
The more spanking experienced as a child, the more depressive symptoms as a university student

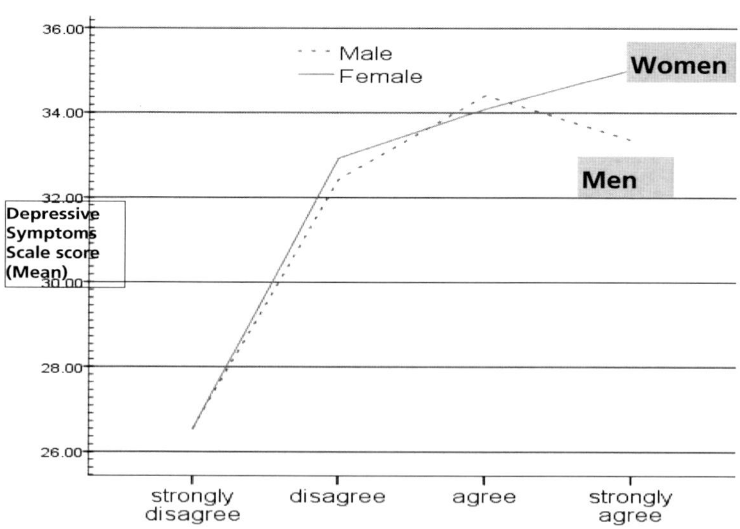

'I was spanked or hit a lot by my parents before age 12'

Figure 10 (A and B).
The higher the percent of students in a nation who were spanked a lot, the higher the higher the more depressive symptoms

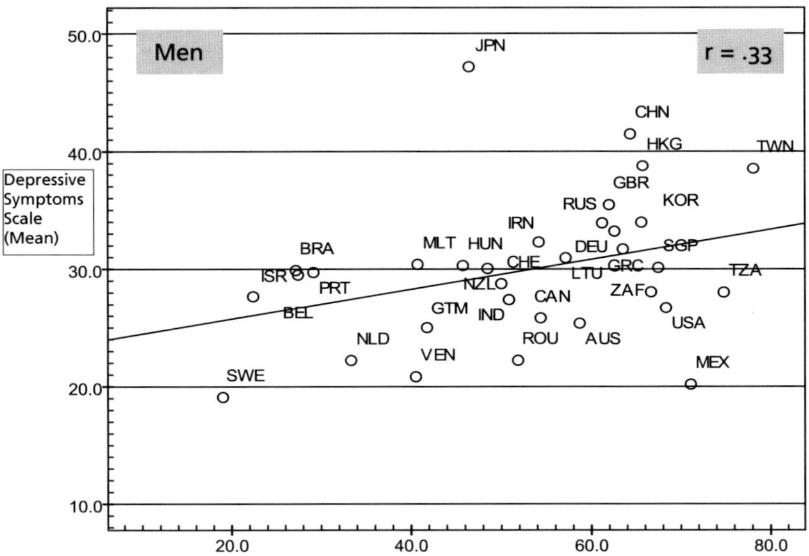

Fig. 10 A: Percent spanked or hit a lot before age 12

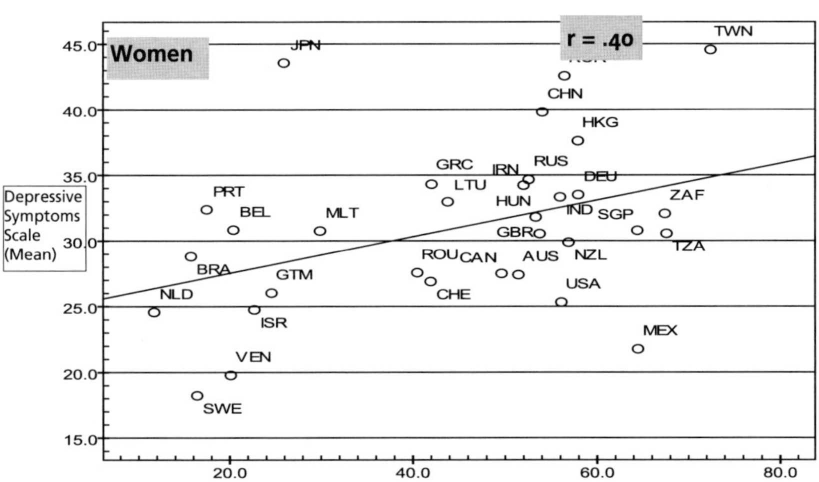

Fig. 10B: Percent spanked or hit a lot before age 12

More than a hundred studies have found many harmful side effects of being physically assaulted by parents in the name of "discipline." Moreover, there is an unusually high agreement between the studies of the different adverse outcomes – 93% agreement was found by a meta analysis of 88 studies (Gershoff, 2002). Empirical studies which found an increased probability of 15 harmful side-effects of spanking are presented in Straus, Douglas, and Medeiros(In Press). For this article, the focus is on two of those effects: Assaulting a romantic partner and depression.

Spanking And Assaulting A Partner

Figure 7 shows that, for both the men and women students in this study, the more spanking they experienced as a child, the greater the percent who *severely* assaulted a dating partner in the previous 12 months. Figure 8 uses the 32 nations in the International Dating Violence Study as the units of study and shows that the higher the percent of students in a nation who were spanked or hit a lot, the higher the percent in their nation who severely assaulted a partner. The results using any assault, most of which are minor assaults, are parallel to those in Figures 7 and 8. The reason for focusing on severe assaults is to show that these results are not simply "lover's quarrel." They are evidence of link between spanking experienced as a child and major victimization of others as an young adult.

Spanking And Depression

A link between having been spanked as a child and an increased probability of depression has been found by at least 14 previous studies, for example, (Afifi, Brownridge, Cox & Sareen, 2006; Harper, Brown, Arias, & Brody, 2006; Straus, 2001, Chapter 5). To investigate whether that is true for the university students in the 32 nations of the International Dating Violence Study the measure of depressive symptoms described earlier was used. Figure 9 shows that, the more spanking experienced as a child, the higher the higher the score on the depressive symptoms scale, and that this applies to both men and women. Figure 10 shows that nations in which more students were spanked a lot as a child tend to be nations with more students who have depressive symptoms. Thus, as Greven (1990) argued on the basis of a historical study, national differences in CP of children are part of the explanation of national differences in depression.

CONCLUSIONS ABOUT VICTIMIZATION BY ROMANTIC PARTNERS

The results in this paper show that a large percent of university students are victims of physical assaults and psychological aggression by a dating partner in every major region of the world, in rich nations as well as poor nations. The percent assaulted by a dating partner is about three times greater than the percent victimized by a marital partner. Moreover, many of the victims of these physical and psychological attacks suffer physical and psychological injury.

A result that may come as a surprise to some readers is that about the same percent of men and women are attacked by a dating partner. This multi-nation result is consistent with what has been found in over 200 other studies mostly in the U.S. (Fiebert, 2010), but also in low economic development/male-dominant nations (Straus, 2011). However, although about the same percent of men and women are attacked, this study and many others shown that the adverse effect is greater for women victims. Women suffer more physical and psychological injury, especially when the attack is severe. Related to that is another result that some readers may find surprising: mutual violence (each attacking the other) is the predominant pattern and is associated with two to five times more injuries. That is a tragic finding because, when there is violence, the predominant pattern is mutual violence.

Is Most Partner Violence By Women Self Defense? One explanation for the approximately equal percent of women and men who assaulted a partner and the predominance of mutual violence is that it represents female victims respond in self-defense. The research on this issue, however, shows that only a small percentage of female assaults are in self-defense, such as 5% to 15% (Carrado, George, Loxam, Jones, & Templar, 1996; Cascardi & Vivian, 1995; Felson & Messner, 1998; Follingstad, Wright, Lloyd, & Sebastian, 1991; Pearson, 1997; Sarantakos, 1998; Sommer, 1996). One study did find higher rates of self-defense, but also found the percentage acting in self-defense was slightly greater *for men* (56%) than for women (42%) (Harned, 2001).

There is other evidence which casts doubt on the idea that that PV by women is primarily in self-defense. Eight studies providing data on who hit first have found that women initiate violent incidents in from 30 TO 73% of the cases (median = 45%); for example (DeKeseredy, Saunders, Schwartz, & Shahid, 1997; Saunders, 1986; Straus, 2005). Moffitt and colleagues (2001) found high rates of violence by women, even when male violence was statistically controlled.

CONCLUSIONS ABOUT BEING A VICTIM OF CORPORAL PUNISHMENT BY PARENTS

The most prevalent form of assault victimization experienced by the students in this study is in the form of CP by parents. High rates of spanking children are found almost everywhere. The data presented in this article understate the prevalence of parents hitting children because the question asked about whether the parents did this *a lot* and because many of the young adults studied do not remember what happened when they were between the ages of two and five, when spanking is most prevalent (Straus, 2010; Straus & Stewart, 1999). Despite that, the percentage of university students were "spanked or hit a lot" as a child ranged from 15% to 74% with a median of Moreover, spanking by loving parents is not a harmless method of correcting misbehavior as is widely believed. For the sample studied for this article, the more spanking experienced as a child, the higher the probability of physically assaulting a dating partner, and the higher the probability of being depressed as a young adult. Other studies have found many different harmful side-effects of spanking, as shown in a meta 88 studies (Gershoff, 2002).

Empirical evidence showing 15 harmful side-effects of spanking are presented in *The Primordial Violence: Spanking Children And Its Effects On Cognitive Development And Crime* (Straus, et al., In Press). *For children,* they found an increased probability of:

- Antisocial behavior *
- Delinquency
- Weakened bond between the child and the spanking parent
- Risky sex
- Lower IQ *
- Low educational achievement

For adults they found an increased probability of

- Depression
- Approval of violence against a partner under some circumstances
- Physically assaulting and injuring a marital
- Sexual coercion and physically forcing sex
- Assaulting a non-family person
- Physically abusing a child
- Drug use
- Property crime and violent crime (men only) *
- Arrested for a crime

The studies marked with an * used longitudinal data and found *change* in the variable subsequent to spanking. Except for the property crime and violent crime indexes, all the links listed apply to females as well males.

LIMITATIONS

Correlation Is Not Causation

All the results in this article are based on cross-sectional data. Consequently, caution is necessary concerning whether they indicate the correlations found reflect a cause-effect relationship. This is particularly important for the results on the correlations between spanking and PV and depression. The results presented do not take into account the fact that misbehavior causes spanking. That is correct, but it does not mean that when parents spank to correct misbehavior it does not have harmful side effects. There are at least 15 studies which used longitudinal data and therefore provide a basis for concluding that spanking does cause the problems studied, such as those listed in the previous section. These studies have found that when parents spank to correct misbehavior, although it corrects the misbehavior in that instance, the longer term effect is to *increase* the subsequent level of misbehavior (Straus, et al., In Press, chapter 19; Straus, Sugarman, & Giles-Sims, 1997).

Spurious Correlations. Another potential problem is that the relationships reported could be the result of confounding with underlying variables such as poverty and lack of parental warmth and support. That is also unlikely because this study and almost of the more than a hundred studies statistically controlled for those types of variables.

Risk-Factor Relationships. An important limitation of this study is one that it shares with almost all social science and medical research. It is that the relationships found are in the form of risk factor relationships, not one-to-one relationships. A risk factor is a condition which increases the *probability* of a disease or problem. Fortunately, or unfortunately (depending on the variables studied), a result in the form of a risk factor does not guarantee the outcome for those who have or experienced the risk factor. For example:

- **Smoking and death from smoking related disease:** A third of heavy smokers will die from a smoking related disease. However this statistic also means that two thirds of heavy smokers will not
- **Binge drinking and wife beating:** (19% of binge drinker assaulted their partner, which is three times the percent by non-drinkers (Kaufman Kantor & Straus, 1987). However, this statistic also means that 81% of the binge drinkers in that study did not beat their wives.
- **Pregnancy with HIV and child born with aids:** Less than half are born with HIV
- **Corporal punishment and assaulting a partner:** Three times as many men in this study and another study (Straus, 2001) who were spanked a lot as a child assaulted their partner. In the

study just cited, spanking was associated with an increase in the percent who assault a partner from 8% for those who did not experience CP to 24% for those who were spanked the most. This is three times greater probability of assaulting a partner, but it also indicates that 76% of those spanked the most do *not* assault.

IMPLICATIONS FOR THEORY, PREVENTION, AND TREATMENT

Victimization By Dating Partner

This study and many others have found that physically and psychologically victimizing dating partners of university students is a serious crime and health problem world-wide. These studies have also found that about the same number of male as female victims. These results call for a reconceptualization of maltreatment of marital and dating partners and new approaches to prevention and treatment based on that reconceptualization. In the following section only limited aspects of these theoretical policy and practice issues can be dealt with. They are presented more comprehensively in the publications to be cited below.

Theoretical Implications. The high percentage of university students victimized in all 32 nations in this study shows that violent victimization by partners applies to low and high violence nations, male-dominant nations as well as more gender equal nations, and to victimization of both men and women. The results in this article on violence by parents toward the students in this study suggest that one of the fundamental underlying explanations of PV is the near universality of violent socialization in the form of corporal punishment by parents.

Because half the perpetrators of PV are women, it is crucial to replace the conceptualization of PV as almost exclusively perpetrated by men. Instead, a family system conceptualization which recognizes that most PV is mutual is needed. Even when only one partner is violent, the nature of their relationship needs to considered, such as psychological aggression and coercive control by either partner, not just the male partner (Kim, Laurent, Capaldi, & Feingold, 2008; Straus, 2009a).

Prevention And Treatment Implications. A first implication for prevention and treatment of the types of victimization discussed in this article is that a substantial reduction in victimization of dating partners requires a substantial reduction in the victimization of children by parents. Efforts in that direction are taking place around the world, first in respect to corporal punishment in schools, and in some nations in respect to corporal punishment by parents (Durrant & Smith, 2011). Spanking children is more and more being seen as a violation of the rights of the child to be brought up without being the victim of violence (Durrant & Smith, 2011; Straus, et al., In Press; United Nations Committee on the Rights of the Child, 2006).

A second implication for prevention and treatment is that a substantial reduction in PV requires replacing prevention efforts directed exclusively to men and boys (the current situation) with programs *explicitly* addressed to both girls and women as well as boys and men (Straus, 2009a; Straus, In Press).

Third, treatment of offenders also needs fundamental change. The assumption that it is only violent *men* who need treatment must be replaced with Initial screening to determine whether the PV is unilateral or mutual and treatment needs to be based on that rather than *assuming* only the male partner is violent. Furthermore the nature of the treatment must similarly be based on an intake diagnosis rather than *assuming* that the "real" underlying cause is male-dominance and a patriarchal social system (Straus, 2009a; Straus, In Press).

Victim Services. None of these important changes should let us lose sight of the fact that despite equal rates of perpetration, the harmful effects of being a victim of PV are much more frequent and severe for women than for men. Consequently, although male victims also need help, the main effort needs to continue to be in services for women victims of PV.

At the same time, the greater need to help victimized women must not obscure the fact that men are victims of about a third of the injuries from PV (Archer, 2000), and depending the nation and time period, a fifth to a third of the homicide deaths (Catalano, 2006; Rennison & Welchans, 2000; Straus, 2005). Even though the effects are not as prevalent as from assaults by male partners, PV by women is a serious social and health problem that must be addressed (Straus, 2005). Moreover, as noted previously, the risk of injury and the probability of the violence continuing or escalating is greatest when both partners are violent (Straus & Gozjolko, In Press; Whitaker, Haileyesus, Swahn, & Saltzman, 2007), which is the situation that characterizes from half to two thirds of PV. Thus, violence by women is a threat to the safety and health of women. In addition, even when the male partner suffers no physical injury, the mere fact of attacking is legally a crime, is morally abhorrent, and has been shown by research to often be a traumatic experience for men as well as women, for example an experience which increases the probability of psychological problems such as depression. This study and a number of others have found these psychological effects for both male and female victims. The review by Hines and Douglas (2009) documents the adverse psychological effects for male victims, as did their study of a national sample of male victims (2010 A principle underlying the results presented in this article, and the conclusions and implications drawn from those results, is that violence in one sphere of life and in one sphere of society cannot be limited to those spheres. It tends to spill over into other spheres. In societies where parents are violent, children also tend to be violent. In societies were men are violent, women also tend to be violent. In societies where governments are violent, individual citizens also tend to be violent. Violence, usually for socially desirable purposes, is woven into the fabric of most societies. Thus, to reduce victimization, in addition to focusing on forms of criminal victimization, it is essential to attend to the use of violence for socially legitimate purposes because that provides the model for violence by individuals.

References

Afifi, T. O., Brownridge, D. A., Cox, B. J., & Sareen, J. (2006). Physical punishment, childhood abuse and psychiatric disorders. *Child Abuse & Neglect, 30*(10), 1093-1103.

Archer, J. (1999). Assessment of the reliability of the Conflict Tactics Scales: A meta-analytic review. *Journal of Interpersonal Violence, 14*(12), 1263-1289.

Archer, J. (2000). Sex differences in aggression between heterosexual partners: A meta-analytic review. *Psychological Bulletin, 126*(5), 651-680.

Archer, J. (2002). Sex differences in physically aggressive acts between heterosexual partners: A meta-analytic review. *Aggression and Violent Behavior, 7*(4), 313-351.

Carrado, M., George, M. J., Loxam, E., Jones, L., & Templar, D. (1996). Aggression in British heterosexual relationships: A descriptive analysis. *Aggressive Behavior, 22*, 401-415.

Cascardi, M., & Vivian, D. (1995). Context for specific episodes of marital violence: Gender and severity of violence differences. *Journal of Family Violence, 10*(3), 265-293.

Catalano, S. (2006). *Intimate partner violence in the United States*. Retrieved 1/9/2007. from www.ojp.usdoj.gov/bjs/intimate/ipv.htm.

DeKeseredy, W. S., Saunders, D. G., Schwartz, M. D., & Shahid, A. (1997). The meanings and motives for women's use of violence in Canadian college dating relationships: results from a National Survey. *Sociological Spectrum, 17*, 199-222.

Douglas, E. M., & Straus, M. A. (2006). Assault and injury of dating partners by university students in 19 countries and its relation to corporal punishment experienced as a child. *European Journal of Criminology, 3*(3), 293-318.

Durrant, J. E., & Smith, A. B. (Eds.). (2011). *Global pathways to abolishing physical punishment: Realizing children's rights*. New York: Routledge.

Felson, R. B., & Messner, S. F. (1998). Disentangling the effects of gender and intimacy on victim precipitation in homicide. *Criminology, 36*(2), 405-423.

Fiebert, M. S. (2004). References examining assaults by women on their spouses or male partners: an annotated bibliography. *Sexuality and Culture, 8*(3-4), 140-177.

Fiebert, M. S. (2010). References examining assaults by women on their spouses or male partners: An Annotated bibliography. *Sexuality & culture, 14*, 49-91.

Follingstad, D. R., Wright, S., Lloyd, S., & Sebastian, J. A. (1991). Sex differences in motivations and effects in dating violence. *Family Relations, 40*(1), 51-57.

Gershoff, E. T. (2002). Corporal punishment by parents and associated child behaviors and experiences: A meta-analytic and theoretical review. *Psychological Bulletin, 128*, 539-579.

Giles-Sims, J., Straus, M. A., & Sugarman, D. B. (1995). Child, maternal and family characteristics associated with spanking. *Family Relations, 44*(2), 170-176.

Grant, K., Marsh, P., Syniar, G., Williams, M., Addlesperger, E., Kinzler,

M. H., et al. (2002). Gender differences in rates of depression among undergraduates: measurement matters. *Journal of Adolescence, 25*(6), 613-617.

Greven, P. (1990). *Spare the child: The religious roots of punishment and the psychological impact of physical abuse*. New York: Alfred A. Knopf.

Harned, M. S. (2001). Abused women or abused men? An examination of the context and outcomes of dating violence. *Violence and Victims, 16*(3), 269-285.

Harper, F. W. K., Brown, A. M., Arias, I., & Brody, G. (2006). Corporal punishment and kids: How do parent support and gender influence child adjustment? *Journal of Family Violence, 21*(3), 197-207.

Hines, D. A. (2007). Predictors of Sexual coercion against women and men: A Multilevel, Multinational study of University students. *Archives of Sexual Behavior, 36*, 403-422.

Hines, D. A., & Douglas, E. M. (2009). Women's Use of Intimate Partner Violence against Men: Prevalence, Implications, and Consequences. *Journal of Aggression, Maltreatment & Trauma, 18*(6), 572 - 586.

Hines, D. A., & Douglas, E. M. (2010). A Closer Look at Men Who Sustain Intimate Terrorism by Women. *Partner Abuse, 1*(3), 286-313.

Kaufman Kantor, G., & Straus, M. A. (1987). The drunken bum theory of wife beating. *Social Problems. 34: 213-230. Also in Straus and Gelles 1990 Physical Violence in American Families: Risk Factors and Adaptations to Violence in 8,145 Families, edited by M. A. Straus and R. J. Gelles. New Brunswick, NJ: Transaction Publishers. A revised copy in (2003) J.D. Orcutt and D.R. Rudy (Eds.) Drugs, Alcohol, and social problems. New York: Rowman & Littlefield Pusblishers, Inc. (pp. 219-238).*

Kerley, K. R., Xu, X., Sirisunyaluck, B., & Alley, J. M. (2010). Exposure to Family Violence in Childhood and Intimate Partner Perpetration or Victimization in Adulthood: Exploring Intergenerational Transmission in Urban Thailand. [Article]. *Journal of Family Violence, 25*(3), 337-347.

Kessler, R. C., Molnar, B. E., Feurer, I. D., & Appelbaum, M. (2001). Patterns and mental health predictors of domestic violence in the United States: Results from the National Comorbidity Survey. *International Journal Of Law And Psychiatry, 24*(4-5), 487-508.

Kim, H. K., Laurent, H. K., Capaldi, D. M., & Feingold, A. (2008). Men's aggression toward women: A 10-Year Panel Study. *Journal of Marriage and Family, 70*(5), 1169-1187.

Kim, J.-Y., & Emery, C. (2003). Marital power, conflict, norm consensus, and marital violence in a nationally representative sample of Korean couples. *Journal of Interpersonal Violence, 18*(2), 197-219.

Moffitt, T. E., Caspi, A., Rutter, M., & Silva, P. A. (2001). *Sex differences in antisocial behavior: Conduct disorder. delinquency, and violence in the Dunedin longitudinal study*. Cambridge, UK: Cambridge University Press.

Pearson, P. (1997). *When She was Bad: Women and the Myth of Innocence* Toronto: Random House.

Rennison, C. M., & Welchans, S. (2000). *Intimate partner violence* (Special Report No. NCJ, 178247). Washington, DC: Bureau of Justice Statistics.

Sarantakos, S. (1998). *Husband abuse as self-defense*. Paper presented at the International Congress of Sociology.

Saunders, D. G. (1986). When battered women use violence: Husband-abuse or self-defense? *Violence and Victims, 1*(1), 47-60.

Sommer, R. (1996). Male and female perpetrated partner abuse: Testing a diathesis-stress model. Winnepeg, Manitoba: University of Manitoba, PhD Dissertation.

Stets, J. E., & Straus, M. A. (1989). The marriage license as a hitting license: A comparison of assaults in dating, cohabiting, and married couples. *Journal of Family Violence 4*(2), 161-180 (also reprtined in Straus and Gelles, 1990).

Straus, M. A. (1990). The Conflict Tactics Scales and its critics: An evaluation and new data on validity and reliability. In M. A. Straus & R. J. Gelles (Eds.), *Physical violence in American families: Risk factors and adaptations to violence in 8,145 families* (pp. 49-73). New Brunswick, NJ: Transaction Publications.

Straus, M. A. (1999). The Controversy over Domestic Violence by Women: A Methodological, Theoretical, and Sociology of Science Analysis. In X. Arriaga & S. Oskamp (Eds.), *Violence in Intimate Relationships* (pp. 17-44). Thousand Oaks, CA: Sage.

Straus, M. A. (2001). *Beating the Devil out of Them: Corporal Punishment in American Families And Its Effects on Children, 2nd Edition* (2nd ed.). New Brunswick, NJ: Transaction Publishers.

Straus, M. A. (2004). Cross-cultural reliability and validity of the Revised Conflict Tactics Scales: A study of university student dating couples in 17 nations. *Cross-Cultural Research, 38*, 407-432.

Straus, M. A. (2005). Women's violence toward men is a serious social problem. In D. R. Loseke, R. J. Gelles & M. M. Cavanaugh (Eds.), *Current controversies on family violence* (2nd ed., pp. 55-77). Newbury Park: Sage Publications.

Straus, M. A. (2008). Dominance and symmetry in partner violence by male and female university students in 32 nations. *Children and Youth Services Review, 30*, 252-275.

Straus, M. A. (2009a). Gender symmetry in partner violence: Evidence and implications for prevention and treatment. In D. J. Whitaker & J. R. Lutzker (Eds.), *Preventing partner violence: Research and evidence-based intervention strategies* (pp. 245-271). Washington D.C. : American Psychological Association.

Straus, M. A. (2009b). The National context effect: An Empirical test of the validity of Cross-National research using unrepresentative samples. *Cross-Cultural Research, 43*(3), 183-205.

Straus, M. A. (2010). Prevalence and societal causes of corporal punishment by parents in world perspective *Law And Contemporary Problems, 73*(2 Spring), 1-30.

Straus, M. A. (2011, November 17). *Assaults on partners by women in 27 male-dominant societies: What explains the high rate of assault?* Paper presented at the American Society Of Criminology, Washington, D.C.

Straus, M. A. (In Press). Gender symmetry and muruality in perpetration of clinical-level partner violence: Empirical evidence and implications for prevention and treatment. *Aggression and Violent Behavior.*

Straus, M. A., Douglas, E. M., & Medeiros, R. A. (In Press). *The primordial violence: Spanking children and its effect on cognitive development, and crime*. New York: Psychology Press.

Straus, M. A., Gelles, R. J., & Steinmetz, S. K. (1980 (2006)). *Behind closed doors: Violence in the American family* New York: Doubleday/Anchor Books (Re-issued Transaction Publications, 2006 with a new forward by Richard J. Gelles and Murray A. Straus).

Straus, M. A., & Gozjolko, K. L. (In Press). Intimate terrorism and injury of dating partners by male and female university students. *Journal of Family Violence*.

Straus, M. A., Hamby, S. L., Boney-McCoy, S., & Sugarman, D. (2010). Manual for the Personal and Relationships Profile (PRP). Durham, NH: University of New Hampshire, Family Research Laboratory. Available in: http://pubpages.unh.edu/~mas2/.

Straus, M. A., Hamby, S. L., Boney-McCoy, S., & Sugarman, D. B. (1996). The revised Conflict Tactics Scales (CTS2): Development and preliminary psychometric data. *Journal of Family Issues, 17*(3), 283-316.

Straus, M. A., & Mouradian, V. E. (1999, November 19). *Preliminary psychometric data for the Personal and Relationships Profile (PRP): A multi-scale tool for clinical screening and research on partner violence.* Paper presented at the American Society of Criminology, Toronto, Ontario.

Straus, M. A., & Ramirez, I. L. (2007). Gender symmetry in prevalence, severity, and chronicity of physical aggression against dating partners by University students in Mexico and USA. *Aggressive Behavior, 33*, 281-290.

Straus, M. A., & Stewart, J. H. (1999). Corporal punishment by American parents: National data on prevalence, chronicity, severity, and duration, in relation to child, and family characteristics. *Clinical Child and Family Psychology Review, 2*(2), 55-70. Also as "Prevalence, chronicity, and severity" , In Press, in *Murray A. Straus., Emily M. Douglas & Rose Anne Medeiros, The primordial violence: Corporal punishment by parents, cognitive development, and crime*. New York: Psychology Press.

Straus, M. A., Sugarman, D. B., & Giles-Sims, J. (1997). Spanking by parents and subsequent antisocial behavior of children. *Archives of Pediatric and Adolescent Medicine, 151*(August), 761-767. Also as "The Boomerang Effect" In Straus, Murray A., Emily M. Douglas and Rose Anne Medeiros. In Press. The primordial violence: Corporal punishment by parents, cognitive development, and crime. New York: Psychology Press.

Straus, M. A., & Sweet, S. (1992). Verbal Symbolic Aggression In Couples - Incidence Rates And Relationships To Personal Characteristics. *Journal Of Marriage And The Family, 54*(2), 346-357.

Sugarman, D. B., & Hotaling, G. T. (1989). Dating violence: Prevalence, context, and risk markers. In A. A. Pirog-Good & J. E. Stets (Eds.), *Violence in dating relationships: Emerging social issues* (pp. 3-31). New York: Praeger.

United Nations Committee on the Rights of the Child (2006). The right of the child to protection from corporal punishment and other cruel or degrading forms of punishment; General comment no. 8 Retrieved

June 28, 2006, from http://www.ohchr.org/english/bodies/crc/docs/co/CRC.C.GC.8.pdf

United Nations Development Programme (2005). Human Development Report 2005 (http://hdr.undp.org/).

United Nations Development Programme (2006). Human Development Report Retrieved Sept 20, 2007, from http://hdr.undp.org/hdr2006/statistics/indicators/230.html

Whitaker, D. J., Haileyesus, T., Swahn, M., & Saltzman, L. S. (2007). Differences in Frequency of Violence and Reported Injury Between Relationships With Reciprocal and Nonreciprocal Intimate Partner Violence *American Journal of Public Health, 97*(5), 941-947.

Papers on this and related topics can be downloaded from http://pubpages.unh.edu/~mas2. The work was supported by National Institute of Mental Health grant T32MH15161, and the University of New Hampshire.

Corporal Punishment, Depressive Symptoms and the Moderating Effect of Positive Parenting in a Multi-National Perspective

By

Alexandra V. Lysova

Abstract

There is still a strong debate on the pros and cons of Corporal Punishment (CP), and the practice remains common around the world. CP advocates declare that the love and care of a parent may eliminate the negative effects of CP. This paper explores the association between CP and depressive symptoms when moderated by positive parenting. The data are from the International Dating Violence Study (n=17,404 students in 32 Nations). Conclusions: CP has a negative effect on a child and is associated with a higher level of depressive symptoms among both male and female victims; positive parenting does reduce the negative effect of CP, but does not fully moderate it for children of either gender. Implications: The results serve as additional evidence of the necessity to stop using CP on children.

Discussion On Effects of Corporal Punishment

Corporal punishment (CP) is still one of the most difficult and controversial topics among both scholars and professionals discussing child-rearing issues. CP is being discussed all over the world (Lansford, 2010). The unabated attention to the issue of CP has been confirmed by the recent release of a volume of *Law and Contemporary Problems* (2010, Vol.73), dedicated to CP. This edition provides the most current empirical knowledge about the prominent views on the short- and long-term developmental effects of corporal punishment. Corporal punishment refers to "the use of physical force with the intention of causing a child to experience pain, but not injury, for the purpose of correction or control of the child's behavior" (Straus, 2001). Although "legitimate" CP (e.g., spank, slap) does not result in injury, it is possible that some of the same negative outcomes associated with abuse - violence that does result in injury - will be exhibited by children who are exposed to CP. Some believe that CP contributes to violence in later life; others believe spanking is a legitimate component of the overall process of discipline. Difficulties in discussing the issue of CP may also be exacerbated by the reliance of professionals and scholars on their own experiences of the appropriateness and effectiveness of CP without paying much attention to the relevant research literature (Friedman, Schonberg, & Sharkey, 1996). There is no consensus among professionals and scholars regarding the use of CP, especially spanking. The goal of this paper is to examine the effects of CP on children's wellbeing using a multinational dataset.

There have been hundreds of research studies in the fields of psychology, medicine, sociology, social work, family studies, and education, showing that CP is a risk factor for many social and psychological problems. A meta-analysis summarized the research linking CP to specific child outcomes by statistically combining existing data to discern the average effect of CP on children's well-being. It confirmed that there is "more harm than good" in applying CP to children (Gershoff, 2002, 2010). Meta-analysis cannot confirm whether CP definitively causes these consequences. Gershoff found a strong association between spanking and heightened child aggression (Gershoff, 2002). He further found a link between spanking and physical abuse of children on the part of parents. Previous research has confirmed such conclusions. Straus and Kaufman Kantor (1994) found persuasive empirical evidence showing CP to be a risk factor for later spousal abuse, child abuse, depression, suicide, and alcohol abuse. Other unintended effects of CP include disrupted child-parent relationships, reduced cognitive ability - e.g., lower levels of IQ (Straus & Paschal, 2009; Straus, 2009; Aucoin, Frick, & Bodin, 2006), increased adult aggression, and antisocial behavior.

Many studies have documented the various mental health problems (e.g., depression) associated with the use of CP on children. For example, Turner and Finkelhor (1996) found a positive association between the frequency of CP and both psychological distress and depression among youth, even after controlling for sociodemographic factors and physical abuse. In another study, children subjected to CP in combination with high level of parental anger showed symptoms of depression in young adulthood (Turner & Muller, 2004). In a sample of New Zealand children, Rodriguez (2003) found that children of parents who used harsher physical punishment and had higher abuse potential, and that the children demonstrated higher depressive or anxious symptoms. Based on these data, CP has been suggested to be considered a form of violence against children (e.g., Straus, 1994) or a potential predictor of physical abuse (e.g., Gershoff, 2010).

Despite this evidence, the topic of CP remains controversial and some scholars and professionals remain unconvinced of the harm of spanking children. The bulk of their criticism relates to the quality of the empirical research. In such instances, researchers criticize the correlational and point-in-time design of these studies (e.g.,

Baumrind, Larzelere, & Cowan, 2002; Colvard, 1996; Larzelere, 1996). They also contend that spanking must be considered in the broader context of the appropriate exercise of parental authority (Larzelere & Baumrind, 2010). According to such arguments, the focus should be less on the disciplinary tactic itself (e.g., spanking) and more on how and when the disciplinary tactic is used. Baumrind (1996) emphasized parents' decision to use CP, context, and parenting style in determining the negative or positive consequences of CP on children. Parents' overall parenting style is hypothesized to moderate the effects of CP by changing the nature of the parent– child relationship or the child's willingness to be socialized (Baumrind, 1996). CP used by a warm parent is considered as more likely to achieve positive outcomes and buffer the potential harmful effects of CP on children's behavior problems. According to Baumrind (1996, p. 831) "prudently used, spanking can effectively accomplish its limited goals with no more harm than alternative disciplinary tactics". Larzelere (1996) also found that reasoning bolstered by a form of discipline, such as CP, is highly effective at preventing future misbehavior.

In terms of the social policy, CP is currently legal in most of the nations in the world (Global Report, 2010). However, the worldwide trend away from CP is most clearly reflected in the twenty nine nations that have legally banned CP by 2010, including Sweden, Germany, Poland, Kenya and Tunisia (Global Report, 2010*)*. Despite the ongoing trend, between 70% and 90% of parents in the USA spank their children at least occasionally (Bender et al., 2007; Socolar et al., 2007; Straus & Paschall, 2009). Cultural variability in use and effects of spanking is generally assumed but not well confirmed (Lansford, 2010). There are also variations in attitudes on the use of spanking according to social class and racial and ethnic status (Giles-Sims, Straus, & Sugarman, 1995).

Research Questions

The current study adds to the existing research on CP by examining the impact of CP in childhood on later depression among young adults, and by considering moderating factors that may operate in this process. Specifically, this research (a) examines the impact of CP on depressive symptoms in young adults on a multi-national sample of students from 32 countries; (b) assesses the extent to which positive parenting and gender of a student moderate the impact of corporal punishment on depression.

A Stress-Process Framework

Given evidence concerning the potential negative effects of corporal punishment on the wellbeing of children, the stress-process model (e.g., Turner & Finkelhor, 1996) represents a particularly useful approach for studying these issues. This model has been widely and effectively used as a conceptual framework for examining the link between the social environment and individual consequences. Under this framework, CP would be considered as a stressful experience that evokes the negative impact on the physical and psychological health of individuals. Positive parenting or parental support will be tested as having potential moderating influence on effects of CP on children. On the one hand, parental support may increase the child's confidence, self-esteem and thus decrease distressing effects of CP (e.g., Baumrind, 1996). On the other hand, high parental support may exacerbate rather than reduce the negative effects of CP. In the situation of the high emotional attachment to their parents, children may construe CP as inconsistent, confusing and particularly distressing (Turner & Finkelhor, 1996). The current study will test these hypotheses.

Methods

The International Dating Violence Study

This research is part of the International Dating Violence Study (IDVS), which is being conducted by a consortium of researchers in all major world regions. Each researcher used a core questionnaire that was translated and then back-translated to maintain 'conceptual equivalence' (Straus, 1969) across the sites. A detailed description of the study, including the questionnaire and all other key documents, is available on the website of the International Dating Violence Study (2011) and in previous articles reporting results from this study (e.g., Douglas & Straus, 2006; Straus, 2010). The total sample of students in this study was 17,404 students at 68 universities in 32 nations.

Questionnaire Administration

The data were gathered using procedures reviewed by and approved by the boards for protection of human subjects at each of the universities in the study. The purpose of the study and the right to not participate were explained to all students. They were assured of anonymity and confidentiality, and given a debriefing form that explained the study in more detail and provided contact information for area social service agencies should the student participants need assistance.

Measures

There is a core questionnaire in English language that each member of the IDVS Research Consortium translated. This core questionnaire consists of demographic items, the *Revised Conflict Tactics Scales (CTS2*, Straus, Hamby, Boney-McCoy, & Sugarman, 1996), and the

Personal and Relationships Profile (PRP; Straus, Hamby, Boney-McCoy, & Sugarman, 1999).
For the current study, only the demographic information and PRP questions pertaining to corporal punishment, depressive symptoms, and positive parenting were used.

Corporal punishment. The question assessing experiences of CP was "I was spanked or hit a lot by my parents before age 12". The response categories were: (1) Strongly Disagree, (2) Disagree, (3) Agree, and (4) Strongly Agree.

Depressive symptoms. Depressive symptoms were measured by the Depressive Symptoms scale of the Personal and Relationships Profile (Straus, Hamby, Boney- McCoy, and Sugarman 1999). Respondents indicated their agreement or disagreement with the eight statements relating to disturbances in mood, dysphoric cognitions, and somatic disturbances experiences for the past year. Specifically, there were the following statements: "I usually wake up feeling pretty good", "I am so sad, sometimes I wonder why I bother to go on living", "I have thought about killing myself", "I am generally in a good mood", "I think good things will happen to me in the future", "I feel sad quite often", "My life is generally going well", and "I enjoy my day-to-day life". The reliability coefficient for this scale is .82.

Positive Parenting. A measure of positive parenting reflected the degree to which parents were loving, supportive and properly supervising their children. Respondents' quintile scores on six items were used to construct a measure of parental support. These items were: "Parents made sure I went to school", "Parents helped with my problems", "Parents helped me with homework", "Parents comforted when upset", "Parents helped me do my best", and "Parents cared if I got in trouble in school ". Each question was answered on a 4- point scale ranging from "strongly disagree" (1) to strongly agree (4) . The alpha coefficient for this scale is .68.

Limited Disclosure is measured by a subscale of the PRP (Straus et al. 2010). Since responses to questions in this study are influenced by the willingness to report (disclose) socially undesirable behaviors, The Limited Disclosure Subscale (LDS) can help to deal with this threat to validity.

Sociodemographics. Since both corporal punishment and depressive symptoms are likely to vary by child and family background characteristics, two sociodemographic factors and limited disclosure scale were considered.

Results

Prevalence of CP
The CP rate at each university was measured by the percentage of students who did not 'strongly disagree' to the question whether they were spanked or hit a lot - they were most likely to be exposed to CP. This decision was based on the assumption that students who did not experience CP would most likely strongly disagree with the statement that they were 'spanked or hit a lot'. It has been used in previous studies (e.g., Douglas & Straus, 2006). The median percent of students who experienced corporal punishment was 49.6%, and men reported of experiencing CP more often than women (57.2% of men, 46.3% of women, x^2 =174.5, p < .001). The ordering the university sites according to the student percentage who experienced "a lot" of CP, showed large differences between university sites. The ranking ranged from a low of 14.6% for a university in the Netherlands to a high of 74% of the students in Taiwan.

Association between Corporal Punishment and Depressive Symptoms

A bivariate correlation analysis between all variables of interest in this research revealed: As expected, level of corporal punishment is positively and significantly related to depressive symptoms (r = .19, p < .001) and negatively and significantly related to positive parenting (r= -.25, p<.001). It is worth noting that level of corporal punishment differs significantly by gender, limited disclosure, age and fathers' education. Men, younger children, respondents with less educated fathers and those who are likely to report socially undesirable behavior (with lower scores on the LS scale) indicate higher levels of corporal punishment.

An analysis of covariance (ANCOVA) further investigated the associations between corporal punishment and depressive symptoms. The result shows a statistically significant relationship between CP and Depressive Symptoms among students in 32 countries after controlling for the limited disclosure scale, respondent's age, father's education, and positive parenting scale (F(3)=5.37, p<.01). Students who were victims of CP had significantly higher scores on Depressive Symptoms than those who were not subjected to CP at home. For both men and women, being hit or spanked as children is associated with essentially the same increase in depressive symptoms, even though women, overall, have higher depressive symptoms (e.g., Turner & Finkelhor, 1996). Each of the independent variables (gender, CP, and positive parenting) has a statistically significant effect on the dependent variable Depressive Symptoms. All variables in the equation explain 28% of the variation in Depressive Symptoms.

Positive Parenting as a Moderator

Finally the effect of Positive Parenting on the association between CP and Depressive Symptoms is explained. Positive Parenting has five levels, where (1) corresponds to the lack of parental support and (5) to the highest scores of parental support. Students with lower scores on positive parenting have higher scores on depressive symptoms and those with high scores on positive parenting scale show less depressive symptoms. However, Positive Parenting does not thoroughly reduce the negative effect of CP. Regardless of whether the parents were caring and loving, being hit as a child by parents increases the probability of depression (e.g., 12.3% increase in Depressive Symptoms with lowest scores on Positive Parenting and 8.3% increase with the highest scores on Positive Parenting).

Discussion

This study provides further confirmation of the wide prevalence of the CP around the world. The number of students who experienced corporal punishment was almost 50 percent (range 15%–74%). All nations' median percentage of students who experience CP was 52% (54% of men and 52% of women). In almost all of the thirty-two nations, a larger percent of boys than girls experience CP. This result is consistent with many other studies (e.g., Giles-Sims, Straus, & Sugarman, 1995).

The current analyses showed that CP does have a negative effect on a child and is associated with a higher level of depressive symptoms among male as well as female victims. Data from the multi-national sample corroborates the results of many studies in the USA: Positive Parenting does reduce the negative effect of CP (e.g., Baumrind, 1996) but does not eliminate it for children of both genders (Turner & Finkelhor, 1996). Corporal Punishment is not beneficial to the well-being of children and young adults even in the context of supportive parent-child relationship. Thus, there is a need to stop using CP on children to prevent negative effects like the development of depressive symptoms. Moreover, both research in learning theory and the experiences of many parents have shown that discipline without corporal punishment can be authoritative, constructive, and successful (e.g., Cohen, 1996).

Limitations

Although this study is distinct in that it provides a test of the associations between CP and Depressive Symptoms moderated by the Positive Parenting for students at 32 countries, a few limitations need to be addressed in future studies. One limitation is that the data for this study come from a convenience sample. Thus, the results of this study cannot be taken as representative of these nations' citizens, of these nations' universities, nor of students in these countries in general. Second, the possible shortcomings may relate to the young adult participants' self-reported accuracy of the retrospective recall about childhood. Finally, the survey for this study was initially designed for Western students. It was translated from English into many other languages. But the lens through which students in other countries understand questions with sensitive material may be different from lens of Western students. The *CTS2* has demonstrated good cross-cultural reliability and validity (Straus, 2004). Nevertheless, caution should be taken when interpreting the results of this study, and replication is needed.

References

Aucoin, K.J., Frick, P.J., & Bodin S.D. (2006). Corporal Punishment and Child Adjustment, *Applied Developmental Psychology*, *27* (6), 527-541.

Baumrind, D. (1996). A blanket injunction against disciplinary use of spanking is not warranted by the data. *Pediatrics, 98*(4, Pt. 2), 828–831Baumrind, D., Larzelere, R. E., & Cowan, P. A. (2002). Ordinary physical punishment: Is it harmful? Comment on Gershoff (2002). *Psychological Bulletin, 128*(4), 580–590.

Bender, H.L., Allen, J.P., MceElhaney, K.B., Antonishak, J., Moore, C.M., O'Beirne K., Davis, S.M. (2007). Use of Harsh Physical Discipline and Developmental Outcomes in Adolescence, *Development and Psychopathology*, 19, 227-242.

Cohen, P. (1996). How can generative theories of the effects of punishment be tested? *Pediatrics, 98*(4, Pt. 2), 834-836.

Colvard, K. (1996). Spanking and triage: Response. *Pediatrics, 98*(4, Pt. 2), 807-808.

Douglas, E.M., & Straus, M.A. (2006). Assault and injury of dating partners by university students in 19 countries and its relation to corporal punishment experienced as a child. *European Journal of Criminology, 3* (3), 293-318.

Friedman, S.B., Schonberg, S.K., & Sharkey, M. (1996). Introduction. *Pediatrics, 98*(4, Pt. 2), vi.

Gershoff, E. T. (2002). Corporal punishment by parents and associated child behaviors and experiences: A meta-analytic and theoretical review. *Psychological Bulletin, 128,* 539-579

Gershoff, E. T. (2010). More harm than good: A summary of scientific research on the intended and unintended effects of corporal punishment on children. *Law and Contemporary Problems, 73,* 33-58 Giles-Sims J., Straus, M.A., & Sugarman D.B. (1995). Child, Maternal and Family Characteristics Associated with Spanking, *Family relations*, 44, 170-176.

Global Report (2010). *Ending legalized violence against children*. http://www.endcorporalpunishment.org/pages/pdfs/reports/GlobalReport2010.pdf. Accessed January 1, 2011.

International Dating Violence Study. http://pubpages.unh.edu/~mas2. Accessed August 12, 2011.

Lansford, J. (2010). The special problems of cultural differences in effects of corporal punishment. *Law and Contemporary Problems, 73,* 89-106.

Larzelere, R.E. (1996). A Review of the Outcomes of Parental Use of Nonabusive or Customary Physical Punishment. *Pediatrics, 98*(4, Pt. 2), 824-828.

Rodriguez, C.M. (2003). Parental Discipline and Abuse Potential Affects on Child Depression, Anxiety, and Attributions, *Journal of Marriage and Family, 65* (4), 809- 817.

Socolar, R., Savage, E., & Evans, H. (2007). A Longitudinal Study of Parental Discipline of Children, *Southern Medical Journal, 100* (5), 472- 477.

Straus, M. A. (1994). Should the use of corporal punishment by parents be considered child abuse? Yes. In M. A. Mason & E. Gambrill (Eds.), *Debating children's lives: Current controversies on children and adolescents* (pp. 197–203). Thousand Oaks, CA: Sage.

Straus, M. A. (2001). *Beating the devil out of them: Corporal punishment in*

American families and its effects on children (2nd ed.). New Brunswick, NJ: Transaction Publishers.

Straus, M. A. (2009). "Differences in Corporal Punishment by parents in 32 Nations and its Relation to National Differences in IQ." *Paper Presented at the 14th International Conference On Violence, Abuse And Trauma*, 25 September, San Diego, California. Retrieved December 20, 2010 from http://pubpages.unh.edu/~mas2/Cp98D%20CP%20%20IQ%20world-wide.pdf

Straus, M. A., & Kantor, G. K. (1994). Corporal punishment of adolescents by parents: A risk factor in the epidemiology of depression, suicide, alcohol abuse, and wife beating. *Adolescence, 29,* 543–561.

Straus, M.A. & Paschall M.J. (2009). Corporal Punishment by Mothers and Development of Children's Cognitive Ability: A Longitudinal Study of Two Nationally Representative Age Cohorts. *Journal of Aggression Maltreatment & Trauma*, 18, 459-483.

Straus, M.A. (1969). Phenomenal identity and conceptual equivalence of measurement in cross-national comparative research. *Journal of Marriage and the Family, 31,* 233-239.

Straus, M.A. (2004). Cross-cultural reliability and validity of the Revised Conflict Tactics Scales: A study of university student dating couples in 17 nations. *Cross-Cultural Research, 38,* 407-432.

Straus, M.A. (2010). Prevalence, societal causes, and trends in corporal punishment by parents in world perspective. *Law and contemporary problems, 73,* 1-30.

Straus, M.A., Hamby, S.L., Boney-McCoy, S., & Sugarman, D.B. (1996). The Revised Conflict Tactics Scales (CTS2): Development and preliminary psychometric data. *Journal of Family Issues, 17,* 283-316.

Straus, M.A., Hamby, S.L., Boney-McCoy, S., & Sugarman, D.B. (2010). *Manual for the personal and relationship profile (PRP).* Durham, NH: University of New Hampshire, Family Research Laboratory. Retrieved on August 17, 2011, from: http://pubpages.unh.edu/~mas2/PR10R14PRP%20Manual.pdf.

Straus, M.A., Hamby, S.L., Boney-McCoy, S., & Sugarman, D.B. (1999). *The personal and relationship profile (PRP).* Durham, NH: University of New Hampshire, Family Research Laboratory. Retrieved on May 28, 2009, from: http://pubpages.unh.edu/~mas2.

Turner, H.A. & Finkelhor, D. (1996). Corporal Punishment as a Stressor among Youth. *Journal of Marriage and the Family, 58* (1), 155-166.

Turner, H.A.& Muller, P.A. (2004). Long-Term Effects of Child Corporal Punishment on Depressive Symptoms in Young Adults: Potential Moderators and Mediators. *Journal of Family Issues, 25* (6), 761- 782.

Wife Abuse in Jordan

By

Diab M. Al-Badayneh

Introduction

Jordan is a developing country with a Human Development Index (0.76 (2006). Its area covers about 89 000 Km^2). It has a population of about 5 million people. Its illiteracy rate is 11.5, the fertility rate is 3.7 (children per woman). The biggest segment the population is younger than 15 years (48%). Jordanian citizens are Muslims (96%). 4% are Christians (The Jordanian Department of Statistics (DOS), 2007). Jordan society is a heterogeneous society. Families reside in urban or rural habitats. Some are nomads, others live in refugee camps.

In the general population, violence against women is widely regarded as a family matter. It is not perceived as a crime or as a serious social problem that affects large numbers of children and adults across their life span. It affects the generations to come due to its intergenerational transaction property.
Jordanian women are victimized psychologically, physically, and sexually by a wide range of behaviors that occur in a variety of cultural and social contexts (e.g. in family and in the workplace). There are no academic studies or accurate statistics that reveal the actual size of the problem in Jordan. However, it is fair to expect that its actual size would be larger than the official estimates. Such discrepancy might stem from misunderstandings of the different ways of social upbringing, of discipline, of beliefs in parents' rights (Araji and Carlson, 2001; Al-Badayneh, 2005; Chalk, and King, 1998; Djabari, 1998; Haj-Yahia, 2005, 1998b, 2002b, 2005; Patterson, 2004; Sheridan and Ghorayeb, 2004, and Zurayk, Sholkamy, Younis, and Khattab, 1997).

Al-Badayneh and Al-Shokour (2009) found: 90.2% of university students indicated that they witnessed, heard, or read something about child abuse. 75.3% of the sample experiences physical abuse during their childhood. Family members were reported to be abused by 87% of the sample. Aamiry (1994) studied a group of university students. 86% of the respondents experienced at least one type of family violence. Most prevailing abuse in their families were intimidation (75%), emotional abuse (40%), and physical abuse (33%). About half of the sample indicated that their mothers were victims of abuse. There was a clear order in the abuse: the father abused everyone, the mother abused children, and the male children abused the female children.

Historically, culture, laws, and social norms protected the right of the husband in most societies to use violence. This formerly uncontested "right" is now weakened by the women movement that increased awareness of women's rights. Research on violence against women is considered a complex multidimensional problem. Dimensions like family, local community, wife, husband, partner and macro social factors are related to victimization by family violence. (Araji and Carlson, 2001). Findings of Btoush and Haj-Yahia's study (2008) showed that in general, there was a high awareness of wife abuse and of the different types of abuse (mainly physical and psychological). The authors found a general tendency to oppose wife abuse, a tendency to blame the victim for abuse, and a lesser tendency to blame the abuse on the husband, marital problems, or on familial and societal conditions.

A major improvement in family issues in general and in the awareness of violence against women and children has been the establishment of the Jordan Family National Council. This council is headed by her Majesty Queen Rania. Its prime goal is the improvement of family affairs. A National framework for the protection of family violence was created in 2005 by Diab Al-Badayneh.

Research Problem

Wife abuse is a global phenomenon that occurs in family in all societies, and cultures. WHO describes violence against women as "the result of the complex interplay of individual, relationship, social, cultural and environmental factors" (WHO 2002). Wife abuse or intimate partner violence[1] (IPV) is a contemporary social problem that evolved from a husband's right to discipline his wife by physical means. While there is global concern regarding violence against women, very little is known about violence against women in Arab communities (Btoush and Haj-Yahia, 2008).

---

1 This term is not applicable to Jordanian society, dyadic relationship is socially accepted only within the framework of marriage.

According to the World Health Organization (1997), studies on domestic violence and its prevalence in 24 countries indicated a range of 20–50% of women being victims of physical abuse by their partners at some time in their lives. Approximately, 50–60% of these abused women are also raped by their abusive partners. According to the same report, violence against women in families is one of the precipitating factors of female suicide and homicides.

The United Nations (UN) Declaration on the Elimination of Violence Against Women defines wife abuse as "any act of gender-based violence that results in, or is likely to result in, physical, sexual or psychological harm or suffering to women, including threats of such acts, coercion or arbitrary deprivation of liberty, whether occurring in public or in private life" (United Nations General Assembly, 1993, p. 2). A review of 50 population-based studies performed in 35 countries prior to 1999 indicated that between 10% and 69% of women reported that they have been physically abused by an intimate partner at some point in their lives, and 10% to 30% of women reported that they have experienced sexual violence by an intimate partner (Garcia-Moreno, Jensen, Ellsberg, Heise, and Watts, 2005; Krug, Dahlberg, Mercy, Zwi, and Lozano, 2002). (Haarr, 2007).

Empirical data are available on the prevalence, types, and consequences of physical, sexual and psychological violence in many countries. There is an abundance of literature indicating that the most pervasive form of domestic violence is violence against women, committed by their intimate partners or ex-partners.

In Rakai, Uganda, 30% of women reported having ever been physically abused by their partners, and 20% were physically abused in the last year (Koenig, Lutalo, Wabwire-Mangen, Kiwanuka, Wagman, Zhao, (2003). A national survey of women in Brazil found that prevalence of physical abuse ranged from (13.2%) to (34.8%), and psychological aggression was (78.3%) (Calverton, Reichenheim, Moares, Szklo, Hasselmann, de Souza, Lozana, and Figueiredo, 2006). In Nicaragua, a study of married women reported lifetime IPV prevalence of (52%), and yearly prevalence of 27% (Ellsberget al. 1999). In Albania, 37% of married women reported this victimization (Burazeri, Roshi, Jewkes, , Bjegovic and Laaser, 2005).

42% of married Palestinian refugees in Jordan reported having ever been **beaten** by their husbands while the figure for the same group living in Lebanon was 22% (Khawaja and Barazi 2005; Khawaja and Twetel-Salem 2004).

High rates of acceptance of wife-beating are reported from Uganda (Koenig et al. 2003), Zimbabwe (Hindin 2003), India (Koenig, Stephenson, Ahmed, Jejeebhoy, and Campbell, 2006), Nigeria (Oyediran and Isiugo-Abanihe 2005). More than half of Palestinian men and women living in Jordan (Khawaja 2004) accept domestic violence. In a recent study from North India, Koenig et al. (2006) report that community-level norms concerning wife beating are significantly associated to the actual occurrence of physical violence. Yet only a few studies have looked at the risk factors for acceptance of wife beating.

In all studies, women were more likely than men to justify beating (Koenig et al. 2003). Researchers have reported rates of physical violence against Arab women ranging from 26% to 55% (Ammar, 2000; Diop-Sidibe, Campbell, and Becker, 2005; El-Zanaty, Hussein, Shawky, Way, and Kishor, 1996; Haj-Yahia, 1999, 2000c; Maziak and Asfar, 2003, Al-Badayneh, 2005c). Favorable attitudes toward violence against women and belief in the inferiority of women are socially accepted. Violence against women generally is perceived as a family matter, and not considered a crime or a social problem (Araji and Carlson, 2001; Patterson, 2004; Al-Badayneh, 2005; Djabari, 1998; Haj-Yahia, 2005, 1998b, 2002b, 2005; Zurayk, Sholkamy, Younis, and Khattab, 1997; Sheridan and Ghorayeb, 2004).

During 1989–1990, Jordan authorities reported 4,694 cases of physical abuse against women. In 1992 alone, they reported 4,856 cases of violence committed against women. Forty-two of these were murders and (34) were rapes. Between 1990 and 1993, there were 1,011 reported domestic violence cases in Jordan, of these. 97% of them were husband–wife abuse. From 1990–1995, Jordan authorities identified 503 cases of homicides; of these, 150 (=30.3%) were women killed by a family member due to "family honor" (Hadidi, 1996). In 1996, the hotline for abused women was established in Amman, the capital city of Jordan, with the financial support of the British government. During the first year of operation, about 4,000 cases of battered women reached this hotline. Some country officials recognize that domestic violence and crimes of "honor" in Jordan are a serious problem and are concerned about the human rights implications of such crimes (Husseini, 1996).

Family, Violence Against Women, and Culture in Jordan

Most literature on violence against women is concentrated on "Western" societies. This study contribute to the understanding the etiology of wife abuse in a developing country like Jordan. The aim of this research is to explore the problem of wife abuse in Jordan. And to identify personal, social, cultural factors associated with the problem.

The Jordanian social culture accepts violence against the child or the wife as a means of discipline. This acceptance is supported by cultural and social norms. The religion does not allow to harm someone physically, sexually or emotionally. Islam urges people to be good to animals e.g. when slaughtering them for food. According to Islamic texts, a woman went to hell because she let a cat starve. Another traditional story tells us that a man went to Paradise because he gave water to a thirsty dog (Al-Badayneh, 2005a, 2005b).

Jordanian society is a patriarchal society. Men have the power, privilege and control over women and children. This authority is based on material and social resources. Men are considered strong, independent, impassionate and aggressive. Women are held to be weak, submissive, passionate and peaceful. The distribution of power in Jordanian family is hierarchic, were male are superior and women and children are subordinate. It is still true: the husband is the ultimate ruler, controlling all property and all individuals residing in the household. Consequently, law and the social reality require the woman to obey her husband (Al-Badayneh, 2005; Araji and Carlson, 2001; Haj-Yahia, 2002b; Zurayk, Sholkamy, Younis, and Khattab, 1997, and Wallace, 1999).

According to this system, violence against women in the family can be seen as practicing the masculine power to achieve power and control over the wife (or any family members). It is a method of family (wife) discipline. Violence is culturally accepted in such a culture. From birth on, the son is taught masculine roles and role expectations (i.e., maintain family's honor, stability, and reputation). The first son is usually referred to his father as "father of the first son's first name ". When the father dies, the eldest son is expected to take the responsibility over the entire family (Abu-Hilal and Aal-Hussain, 1997; Elsaadawi, 1993; Najjar, 1994). Females are taught to be polite, passive, and docile. The husband assumes the role of financial provider, while the wife assumes the role of the caregiver, taking the responsibilities of child bearing and home making. The husband is considered "master of the family ". Men strictly regulate female behavior and sexuality. Men are responsible for imposing control to protect the family dignity and reputation (Bates and Rassam, 2001).

The patriarchal structure and lifestyle of the Jordanian family are also affected by major social values such as mutual support, mutual responsibility, family cohesion and solidarity, harmony among family members, and family privacy. Therefore, the family is expected to provide support and security at times of personal, spousal, family, and social distress. It is part of its collective identity, identification and responsibility. In this collective identity, pride is for all and shame is on all. Men are in the position of greater power, privilege, and control of women and children. Consequently they have the right to punish them for misbehavior (Al-Badayneh, 2005, Barakat, 1993;, Haj-Yahia, 2000, Haj-Yahia, 2002; Shalhoub-Kevorkian, 1997; Sheridan and Ghorayeb, 2004).

Family reputation is considered top priority. This priority is reflected in various spheres such as commitment, needs, aspirations, and social relationships (Barakat, 1993; Haj-Yahia, 1995, 2000; Nobles and Sciarra, 2000). The transformation of the extended family to the nuclear family has affected the patriarchal structure, the status of men and woman in the family, and the distribution of power within the family. The male position is weakened in the extended family, including his control over married males' family members and the family members living at home. But that is not so in the nuclear family: it maintained the patriarchal hierarchical structure. The husband is still at the top of the power pyramid (Haj-Yahia, 2002, Al-Badayneh, 2003). Man's control is not only on the personal life of woman and children but also on their social and financial resources. The man is responsible for providing financial support for his wife in exchange for her fidelity and her domestic services. The control of wife is not only a control of power and sex but also a control of finance. (Al-Badayneh, 2005). The honor of man is measured by the devotion of his wife. If the wife "deviates", restoring the honor is the responsibility of the husband - but not alone of the husband, but of family and tribe. Men have the authority to make all decisions. Because of the severe social stigma to this kind of crimes, the social reaction to them is very severe and ends up retaliation and sometimes by killing the female victim (Kulwicki, 2002). However, such deviations of wifes are very rare. It reaches an average of 25 cases per year in the period from 1990 to 2008). This is indeed rare compared to the figures reported in USA - 25% of all homicides in the U.S.A. are husband – wife killings (U.S. Department of Justice, 1995).

In Jordanian society, the behavior of men and women is strictly defined and formed on the basics of a patriarchal system, in which men are dominate (Al Krenaw and Graham, 2002). Success (pride) or failure (shame) of one family member is not a personal matter; it concerns the family as a whole. Thus, every family member assumes responsibility in most cases for the behavior, needs, and living conditions of the others (Haj-Yahia, 1995). Findings of Btoush and Haj-Yahia 's study (2008) showed a strong tendency to consider wife abuse a personal and familial issue rather than a social and legal problem.

The commitment to provide family members with assistance also derives from the belief that most family problems are an internal family matter and that outside parties should not be involved. This approach is all the more applicable when the family encounters problems that may harm its reputation or honor, or in situations that may cause shame, such as cases of wife abuse (Haj-Yahia, 2000, Haj-Yahia (2002), Al-Badayneh, 2008).

Family issues are viewed as belonging to private sphere. They occur behind closed doors. Society has not to interfere (Jaghab, 2005). For this reason wife abuse is not viewed as a social problem (Jaghab, 2005). If information about family violence and wife abuse reach the local community or relatives or friends, that stigmatizes the members of the family. It damages family reputation, unity, and dignity.

That results in strict role expectations for women. If the wife does not live up to these expectations, physical and cultural punishment results. When abused women request a divorce, they are usually socially ostracized, accused of being rebellious and of not caring about her family and children. To avoid such consequences, wives have to comply with social and cultural rules. Males are respected in the family. The behavior of women are the responsibility of her husband and her family. (Patai, 1969; Dobash and Dobash, 1992; Jaghab, 2005; Al-Badayneh, 2005, Al-Badayneh, 2007).

Method

The data were collected by questionnaires. The instrument covered these dimensions:

Sociodemographic Data.

Culture Aspects of Violence. Cultural aspects include questions for friends/relatives who believe in physical punishment as a method of discipline, exposure to family violence in young age, witnessing family violence. It asked for decision makers in family and financial issues in case the father was absent.

Beliefs Towards Violence. Questions explore the attitude towards (i.e., should all family members fear the husband? Should the wife obey the husband? Should all family members do so? Does the

husband have the right to punish his wife?)
Wife's Familial *Situation.* This section deals with respondent's satisfaction, family conflicts, wife commitment to marriage, wife propensity to leave, and attitude towards leavinge).

Prevalence of Family violence:
The Conflict Tactics Scale 2 (CTS2) was utilized to measure the conflict tactics used by the couple (Straus et al. 1996). The scale was modified and adopted to the Jordanian society.

Reliability:
Cronbach's Alpha was .93 for the bidirectional CTS2 scale, slightly less for women(.89), and for husband side (.87).

Validity and Reliability

Construct validity is used to estimate the validity of the scale. Theoretically, wife satisfaction with her marriage will be negatively correlated with violence against wife. A correlation of (-0.129, α=0.000) was found between wife satisfaction and the total CTS2 scale (husband). Also a correlation was measured between wife satisfaction and psychological aggression (0.152, α=0.000), physical assault, (0.131, α=0.000), sexual coercion, (0.116, α=0.000), and injury (0.079, α=0.001).

Participants

A final sample of 1,854 wives were selected randomly. The response rate was 96.5%. 98% of the respondents were married. 85 % of them were illiterate. 53% were unemployed.

Findings

Family Situation

43% of the participants indicated that they had a family disputes, 94% had family conflicts. Despite the presence of disputes and conflicts, 96% of women were committed to their families and satisfied (89%).
It seems to be a contradiction: wives reported conflicts, disputes and abuse - at the same time they are satisfied, committed to their families and had no intention to leave the relationship. But it is consisted with the social system, where wives accept abuse. They justify and internalize it. They try to avoid the negative stigmatization. They avoid being ostracized by other families. They fear stigma,

and they protect their personal and familial reputation. To avoid such consequences, wives have to comply with social and cultural rules. Males are respected in the family. Wife is the responsible of her husband and her family. This is consisted with the findings of previously conducted studies (Patai, 1969; Dobash and Dobash, 1992; Jaghab, 2005; Al-Badayneh, 2005).

Wife abuse is fostered by cultural and social expectations that support roles of men and women, which generally devalue woman. Findings showed more than half (57%) of the sample reported that they have friends who believe in using physical punishment as a way of discipline. On the micro level, violence against woman prevails in Jordanian family, as 98% of the sample reported some kind of wife abuse in the last 12 months. 63% witnessed or are aware of family violence (63%). 96% are aware of family violence in the local community.

In spite of gender inequality, and exclusion, and unequal distribution of power and control in the family, more than half of the sample (68%) reported that both husband and wife take joint decisions. About a third of the sample show the very traditional pattern: in 29%, the husband takes decisions alone. Only 3% of wives take decisions alone. Financial dependence of wife on her husband contributes to the situation of conjugal violence.

Family violence is accepted by wives: almost all participants (98%) totally agree to violence of the husband, a figure that is repeated in the community's acceptance of violence (96%) .

Distribution of Power and Control

Women share cultural beliefs that make them accept and internalize violence against them. The husband or a male member of the family members has the right to punish any family member or wife if proven guilty (if the member commits a misbehavior) (72%, 50% respectively). Obedience is owed to the husband (89%). Husbands are feared by all family members (22%). Control by the husband is accepted by all family members (28% respectively). Only (9%) of wives believed husband has the right to use violence during family dispute.

Wives internalize cultural beliefs that justified wife abuse and later on blaming themselves for being abused. This finding is consisted with Haarr's (2007) findings that most wives approved and accept wife beating and abuse by husband (Haarr, 2007).

Wife Definition of Violence

In this study, Jordanian women were asked for several dimensions of violence against them: physical, sexual, emotional, social, and economic abuse, sexual desertion (a husband's leaving the woman's bed and sleeping in a separate room), marrying another woman, (Gharaibeh and Al-Maaitah, (2002), and bequeath (Merath) neglect. All types of wife abuse were considered serious with an average around (2) on a scale of 4 (where 0= not serious)

About (50%) of the respondents believed that men have the right to physically hurt and sexually desert a rebellious wife. This definition is consistent with literature on other Arab societies (Al-Badayneh, 2005, 2006; Haj-Yahia, 2000a, 2000b; Hassan et al., 2004).

The traditional two forms of husband (partner) violence exist in Jordanian society. One form is **intimate terrorism** (IT), which embedded in general pattern of power and control (i.e., physical, and sexual violence). This type is rooted in patriarchal idea about gender and the social acceptance of violence against women. The second form is **situational couple violence** (SCV), which is a response to a situational violence (Leone, Johnson and Cohan, 2007; Johnson, 1995).

It is quite clear that the women see these behaviors as violence against them: 90% and more agree that that "shouting or insulting", "Pushing or grabbing" and "Kicking, or beating" is violence. Threatening, using weapons, forcible sex or threats to have oral or anal sex, beating with a sharp tool, throwing or slapping, financial neglect from family economics, food or shelter neglect, education neglect and health neglect are defined by more than 87% as violence. Measured on a scale from 0 (= not serious) to 4 (= very serious), the women ranked these violence acts against them with an average of seriousness rank of 2.3.

Post Wife abuse Feelings and Beliefs

In addition for the prevalence, this study looks for the emotional damage after the abuse. The women suffer many severe negative feelings after each violent incident. They feel insecure (80%), ashamed (81%), frightened (86%), controlled against their will (86%), feel caught up like in a prison (81%). These feelings are part of the social acceptance of violence, of inequality in gender roles and of social conformity omen believe they are helpless (87%), they can't escape their violent situation (88%), or depart the family (92%), they sacrify (92%).

Asked for their feeling after each violent incident, between agreed to these statements:

My investment to save my family is worth the attempt 92% (n=1697)
It is difficult to leave my husband 92%
Whatever I do I can't get away from the current situation 87%
I am afraid of him 86% (n=1594)
I feel I am programmed toward him 86%
I feel I am not controlling my own life 85%
I feel he owns me and I am controlled by him 84%
I cover up my injuries; I am afraid to reveal it to others 83%
I feel he can scare me without even touching me 83%
I feel he has frightening way of looking at me 82%
I feel shame from the things he did to me 81%
I feel as if I am in prison 81%
I feel insecure in my home 80% (n=1481)

Women are squeezed and trapped between their families of origin and their family of marriage. On the one side, the family of origin is the final provider in case the marriage fails (divorce). Then it provides support, protection and security. But on the other side, the family of origin pressures women to stay in the relationship, for reasons of maintaining the personal and familial reputation including their sense of dignity and their standing in the social network. The abuse by the husband threatens both, the family of origin and the marriage family. The wife tries to protect the survival of her marriage family by blaming herself. Crocker calls this "collective self-esteem" (Crocker and Luhtanen, 1990),

Abused women are usually very hesitant to seek help, so that they can preserve their family unity, reputation and their children's best interest as well as their self-image, esteem, and identity (Haj-Yahia, 1995, 2000b).

Wife reaction to husband violence against wife

Wifes has tried to call for help (81%) and most of this help came from her family of origin. Women fear to ask for help to avoid disclosure of her private life and to avoid social labels. When things get out of control, wife's family of origin usually sue the wife's husband (86%), but very small portion of the sample tried to call a police (2.5%) or a lawyer (2%). Women are considering family violence a personal issue. Only (32%), of women were willing to report family violence. Protection is offered by the family of origin, since the victim (wife) needs to continue to fulfill her roles as a wife, mother, sister, or daughter. Abused woman is characterized by: negative self image; "she deserved it"; taking the blame for an abuser's actions, guilt; anger, inability to protect herself, physical pain. (Walker, 1979).

The majority of abused wives continues to stay in their abusive relationship for fear of losing face, financial security, children, love, respect, (Choice and Lamke, 1997). Social embarrassment to her family and children, and social stigma are also significant factors for abused wife to stay in the abusive relationship.
Justifications for not reporting wife abuse can be attributed to insufficient information (63%), to insecurity what to do, (69%), fear from other people's reaction (64%), to the wish not to interfere in others business (69%). Women fear that reporting will not work (70%). They do not trust that government bodies will help (70%)
The reluctance of wives to report violence and to ask for help can be attributed to the following factors:

1. Lack of available services for abused wife.
2. Negative social stigma attached to the abused wife.
3. The expected harm to the reputation of wife and families.
4. The fear from generalized negative stigma to the other family members.
5. Wife's belief that nothing will be changed no matter what she will do.
6. Cultural acceptance of abuse.
7. Social belief that wife abuse is a private matter, not a public one.
8. Expected threats to the life of wife and children.

Wife Attribution of Causes of Violence Against Women

Women try to attribute causes of wife violence to external forces in order to avoid self-blame or husband blame. This kind of sympathy with the abuser can be attributed in light of **Stockholm Syndrome** or what is called (hostage syndrome), as the wife felt as if she is held in prison in her home There is a match between the abused wife and the hostage's case, because of the physical and psychological threatening by the husband. wife believes that that there is no way to be escaped, because the husband controls completely the whole situation, and that what the husband presents kindly sometimes is a result of isolating her from the external world, she develops a bond between her and her husband (Graham and Rawlins,1991, Kirchhoff 1999).

Conclusion and Discussion

The present study attempted to explore the current status of wife abuse in Jordanian society. To understand violence against wife in the Jordanian society, it is important to examine the status of women in Jordanian society, and to take into account several social and cultural dimensions, including the family structure and social values of the family.

Despite the economic, social, educational and cultural changes, reforms and transformation that have been taken place in Jordanian society over the past five decades, the family is still perceived the corner stone as a reference agent to individual behavior and actions. Jordanian society used to be dominated by extended family. This structure has started to change. Today, the Jordanian family is nuclear in its structure. At the same time, it is partially extended in its functions.

The control of wife is not only a control over power and sex but also a control of finance (Al-Badayneh, 2005a). The honor of man is measured by the devotion of his wife, so if the wife deviates, restoring the honor is not the responsibility of the husband only, but it is the responsibility of family and tribe. A man's honor is tied to the reputation (include sexual conduct of women in the family) particularly women, sisters, wife, daughters. Wife abuse is considered as a taboo issue and a private event that took place behind closed doors.

Jordanian society has undergone dramatic social and economic transformation. In a new era of cultural openness, and with the widespread equalization of education among the two genders and with women's entrance into the job market, new cultural challenges have emerged confronting traditional Jordanian social roles. One such basic challenge pertains to the position of women in Jordanian society, their rights, and the rights of their male counterparts, both in the public and the domestic arena (The Jordanian National Committee for Women, 1994).

Jordanian women are still bound by patriarchal patterns of lower social, economic, work, and educational status, cultural acceptance of violence, kinship, legalized and cultural discrimination, formal and informal social subordination and ingrained male dominance. Because women find themselves in a disadvantaged position in relation to decision-making within the family, supported by cultural acceptance of violence against women, their situation continuously exposes them to forms of family and institutionalized violence. Jordanians sustain both direct and indirect violence. In the first category, women suffer forms of physical assault, from beating to rape and murder. In the second, they are victims of cultural and social practices that cause material harm to women, such as child marriage.

Women were regarded as socially inferior to men and treated as minors. Women who rebelled against their subordinate positions were severely beaten. Women were told to preserve and to do the best to keep their marriage together. This is parallels of the feminist view that violence against women stems from the inequality and from the unjust distribution of power and control in the family.
Women and children are still considered the property of their husbands. Wife abuse becomes a result of **control and power** in the family. Attitudes and beliefs reinforced male status and power provide the rational for using physical violence to maintain men's superior position, thus any struggle on the part of the woman may be interpreted as a breach of loyalty, respect and role expectations that a wife is expected to give to her husband (Al-Badayneh, 2005a, 2005b; Btoush and Haj-Yahia, 2008; Kulwicki, 2002).

In traditional Jordanian society wife beating is common and is socially accepted. It is held justifiable if the wife was unfaithful or neglected her duties. Also wife abuse is justified if wives answered back or disobeyed, went outside the home without permission, or neglected the children, or refused to do as they were told, criticized her husband in front of her children.
Wife abuse occurs when the wife insults or disobeys her husband, does not follow traditional roles, disrespects family and friends, or has sexual relationships with someone than her husband. Exposure to family violence of origin has been identified as a risk factor for wife abuse and child abuse in the generation to come (Hadeed and El-Bassel, 2007).

Wife abuse is a result of a complex interaction of individual, social, cultural and environmental factors. It is a social problem that emerged from a cultural norm of husband's right to discipline his wife. Wife abuse is a violation of women basic rights and has severe negative consequences for health and safety of wife, her children and family.

References

Aamiry, A. (1994). Domestic violence against women in Jordan. AL-Raida, 11, 33-39, 65-66

Abu-Hilal, M. M., and Aal-hussain, A. A. (1997). Dimensionality and Hierarchy of the SDQ. In A non-Western Milieu: A Test of Self-Concept Invariance Across gender. Journal of Cross-Cultural Psychology, 28, 535-553

Ahmed, A. M., and Elmardi, A. E. (2005). A study of domestic violence among women attending a medical centre in Sudan. East Mediterranean Health Journal, 11, 164–174.

Ahmed, S. M. (2005). Intimate partner violence against women: Experiences from a woman-focused development programe in Matlab, Bangladesh. Journal of Health Population and Nutrition, 23, 95–101.

Al-Badayneh, Diab and Al-Shakur Manal, (2009). Relationship between personal and famial characteristics and Types of family violence among College students during their childhood. Arab Journal for Security Studies and Training, vol. 24, No. 48, pp 85-130

Al-Badayneh, Diab (1995). Suicide Victims in Jordan: A Sociological View. The Journal of Arts College. King Saoud University, , 7 (2), 567-605. Available athttp://digital.library.ksu.edu.sa/paper1973.html

Al-Badayneh, Diab (2005a). National Framework for Protection From Family Violence. NCFA, Amman.

Al-Badayneh, Diab (2005c) Violence in Jordan, from home to road. Violence in Universities Seminar, MU, Jordan.

Al-Badayneh, Diab, and Abuhejlah H., (2005) Relationship between Marital satisfaction and violence against wife in Al-Karak, Jordan. Mutah Journal For Studies and Research, Vol. 20, (6): 37-80.

Al-Badayneh, Diab (2006) Developing a General Crime Prevention Model (GCPM): family Violence Applications. Alfeker AlShorati Vo.. 57, (6): 37-80.

Al-Badayneh, Diab, Al-Tarawneh I., Al-Othman, H., and Abu Hasan R., (2009). Risk factors in Jordanian universities environment. YHC: Amman.

Al-Krenawi, A.,and Graham, J.R. (1998). Divorce among Arab Women in Israel. Journal of Divorce and Remarriage, 29, 103-119.

Ammar, N. H. (2000). In the shadow of the pyramids: Domestic violence in Egypt. International Review of Victimology, 7(1-3), 29-46.

Araji, S. K., and Carlson, J., (2001) Family violence including Crimes of honor in Jordan: Correlates and Perceptions of Seriousness. Violence Against Women 7;586-621 available at: http://vaw.sagepub.com/cgi/content/abstract/7/5/586

Arwa Oweis, Muntaha Gharaibeh, Ahlam Al-Natour and Erika Froelicher (2009).Violence Against Women: Unveiling the Suffering of Women with a Low Income in Jordan J Transcult Nurs 2009; 20; 69-76 Available at: http://tcn.sagepub.com/cgi/content/abstract/20/1/69

Bates, D., and Rassam, A. (2001). Peoples and cultures of the Middle East. Englewood Cliffs, NJ: Prentice Hall.

Belsky, J. and Stratton, P. (2002). An Ecological Analysis of the Etiology of Child Maltreatment. PP 95-110 in H. Hanks, P. Stratt and C. Hamilton (Eds). Early prediction and prevention of Child Abuse: A Handbook. Chichester, UK: Wiley.

Belsky, J. (1980). Child maltreatment: An ecological integration. American Psychologist, 35(4), 320-35
Belsky, J. (1993). Etiology of child maltreatment: A developmental-ecological analysis. Psychological Bulletin. 114(3):413-434.
Bersani CA, Chen H. (1988). Sociological perspectives on family violence. In V.B. Hasselt, RL Morrison, AS Bellack, M. Hersen, eds. Handbook of Family Violence (p. 57-86). New York: Plenum.
Bograd M. (1990). Feminist perspectives on wife abuse: An introduction. In K. Yllo, M. Bograd (Eds.). Feminist Perspectives on Wife Abuse (pp. 11-27). Newbury Park, California: Sage.
Btoush, R., and Haj-Yahia M., (2008). Attitudes of Jordanian Society Toward Wife Abuse. Journal of Interpersonal Violence Volume XX Number XX. Pdf file
Burazeri, G., Roshi, E., Jewkes, R., Jordan, S., Bjegovic, V., and Laaser, U. (2005). Factors associated with spousal physical violence in Albania: Cross-sectional study. British Medical Journal, 331 (7510), 197–201.
California Department of Justice. (1997). Domestic Violence Handbook: A Survivor's guide (Brochure). Sacramento, California: California Attorney General's Office.
Calverton, MD: ORC Macro. Reichenheim, M. E., Moares, C. L., Szklo, A., Hasselmann, M. H., de Souza, E. R., Lozana, J. A., and Figueiredo, V. (2006). The magnitude of intimate partner violence in Brazil: Portraits from 15 capital cities and the federal district. Cad Saude Publicia, 22, 425-437.
Care for Women International, *24*(4), 313-326.
Centre for Health and Gender Equity (CHANGE). (1999). Population reports: Ending violence against women. Baltimore: Johns Hopkins University School of Public Health and Centre for Health and Gender Equity. Available at http:/www.infoforhealth.org/pr/l11/ violence.pdf
Chalk, R. and King, P. A. (1998). Violence in Families: Assessing Prevention and Treatment programs. Washington, D.C.: National Academy Press.
Choice, P., and Lamke, L. K., (1997). A conceptual approach to understanding abused women's stay/leave decisions. Journal of Family issues, 18, 290-314
Chornesky, A. (2000). The Dynamics of Battering revisited. Affilia: Journal of Women and Social Work, 15, 480-501.
Coker, A. L., Davis, K. E., Arias, I., Desai, S., Sanderson, M., Brandt, H. M., and Smith, P. H. (2002). Physical and mental health effects of intimate partner violence for men and women. American Journal of Preventive Medicine, 23, 260–268.
Colman, A. (1996). Attitude Survey. Youth Studies, Autum 15 (1), 6.
Falchikov, N. (1996). Adolescent Attitudes to Abuse of Women. Violence,Sept/ Oct . Autumn 15 (1), 6
Crocker, J., and Luhtanen, R., (1990). Collective self-esteem and ingroup bias. Journal of Personality and Social Psychology, 58, 60-67
Deborah Capasso Richardson and Jennifer L. Campbell (1980) Alcohol and Wife Abuse: The Effect of Alcohol on Attributions of Blame for Wife Abuse Pers Soc Psychol Bull 1980; 6; 51-56
Department of Statistics (DOS), (2007). Jordan in Figures. General Indicators. Available at: http://www.dos.gov.jo/dos_home/jorfig/2007/jor_f_a.htm
Diop-Sidibe, N., Campbell, J. C., and Becker, S. (2005). Domestic violence

against women in Egyptwife beating and health outcomes. Social Science and Medicine, 62(2006), 1260-1277.
Djabari, L. (1998). The Syrian woman: reality and aspiration. In H. Afshar (Ed.), Women and empowerment (pp. 110-116). New York: St. Martin's Press.
Dobash RE, Dobash R. (1979). Violence Against Wives. New York: Free Press. Dodge KA.
Dobash, R.E., and Dobash, R.P. (1992). Women, Violence, and social change. London: Routledge.
Dobash, R.E., and Dobash, R.R. (1980). Violence Against Wives: A Case Against the Patriarchy. London: Open Books.
EL Saadawi, N.(1993). Women and Sex. In D.L. Bowen and E.E.A. Early (Eds.), Everyday Life in the Muslim Middle East (pp.81-83). Bloomington, ID: Indiana University Press.
Ellsberg, M. C., Pena, R., Herrera, A., Liljestrand, J., and Winkvist, A. (1999). Wife abuse among women of childbearing age in Nicaragua. American Journal of Public Health, 89(2), 241–244.
El-Zanaty, F., Hussein, E., Shawky, G.,Way, A., and Kishor, S. (1996). Egypt demographic and health survey 1995. Calverton, MD: Macro International.
Family Protection Administration (FPA) (2009). Annual Report (different years). Public Safety Department. Amman, Jordan.
Fawole, O. I., (2008) Economic violence to women and girls: Is it receiving the necessary attention?. Trauma Violence Abuse. OnlineFirst, published on May 21, 2008 as doi:10.1177/1524838008319255
Follingstad, D., and DeHart, D. D., (2000) Defining Psychological Abuse of Husbands Toward Wives: Contexts, Behaviors, and Typologies J Interpers Violence 2000; 15; 891-920
Galtung, J., (1990). Cultural violence. Journal of Peace Research, 27, 291-305
Garcia-Moreno, C., Jensen, H., Ellsberg, M., Heise, L., and Watts, C. (2005). WHO multi-country study on women's health and domestic violence against women. Geneva, Switzerland:World Health Organization.
Haarr, R. N., (2007). Wife Abuse in Tajikistan. Feminist Criminology 2007; 2; 245- 270, Available at: http://fcx.sagepub.com/cgi/content/abstract/2/3/245
Hadeed, L. F., and El-Bassel, N., (2007)Typologies of Abuse Among Afro-Trinidadian Women. J Interpers Violence 2007; 22; 479-497. Available at: http://jiv.sagepub.com/cgi/content/abstract/22/5/479
Hadidi, M. (1996). The National Institute of Medicine: The role of the forensic medicinein uncovering crimes committed against women. Unpublished manuscript.
Haj-Yahia, M. (2000b). Patterns of Violence against engaged Arab Women From Israel and Some Psychological Implications. Psychology of Women Quarterly, 24, 209-219.
Haj-Yahia, M. (2002a)Attitudes of Arab Women Toward Different Patterns of Coping With Wife Abuse. Journal of Interpersonal Violence, 17,721-745.
Haj-Yahia, M. M. (1995). Toward culturally sensitive intervention with Arab families in Israel. Contemporary Family Therapy, 17(4), 429-447.
Haj-Yahia, M. M. (1997). Predicting beliefs about wife beating among engaged Arab men in Israel. Journal of Interpersonal Violence, 12(4), 530-545.
Haj-Yahia, M. M. (1998a). Beliefs about wife beating among Palestinian women: The influence of their patriarchal ideology. Violence Against

Women, 4(5), 533-558.
Haj-Yahia, M. M. (1998b). A patriarchal perspective of beliefs about wife beating among Palestinian men from the West Bank and the Gaza Strip. Journal of Family Issues, 19(5), 595-621.
Haj-Yahia, M. M. (1999). Wife abuse and its psychological consequences as revealed by the first Palestinian National Survey on Violence Against Women. Journal of Family Psychology, 13(4), 642-662.
Haj-Yahia, M. M. (2000a). Patterns of violence against engaged Arab women from Israel and some psychological implications. Psychology of Women Quarterly, 24(3), 209-219.
Haj-Yahia, M. M. (2000b). Wife abuse and battering in the sociocultural context of Arab society. Family Process, 39(2), 237-255.
Haj-Yahia, M. M. (2000c). Wife abuse in the Palestinian Authority. Journal of International and Comparative Social Welfare, XVI, 59-73.
Haj-Yahia, M. M. (2002a). Attitudes of Arab women toward different patterns of coping with wife abuse. Journal of Interpersonal Violence, 17(7), 721-745.
Haj-Yahia, M. M. (2002b). Beliefs of Jordanian women about wife-beating. Psychology of Women Quarterly, 26(4), 282-291.
Haj-Yahia, M. M. (2002c). The impact of wife abuse on marital relations as revealed bythe Second Palestinian National Survey on Violence Against Women. Journal of Family Psychology, 16(3), 273-285.
Haj-Yahia, M. M. (2003). Beliefs about wife beating among Arab men from Israel: The influence of their patriarchal ideology. Journal of Family Violence, 18(4), 193-206.
Haj-Yahia, M. M. (2005). Can people's patriarchal ideology predict their beliefs about wife abuse? The case of Jordanian men. Journal of Community Psychology, 33(5), 545-567..
Haj-Yahia, M. M., (2002). Attitudes of Arab Women Toward Different Patterns of Coping With Wife Abuse. J Interpers Violence 2002; 17; 721-744 http://jiv.sagepub.com/cgi/content/abstract/17/7/721
Haj-Yahia, M.(2000b). Beliefs of Jordanian Women about Wife-beating. Psychology of Women Quarterly, 26,282-291.
Haj-Yahia, M.M.(1997). Predicting beliefs about Wife beating among engaged Arab men in Israel. Journal of interpersonal violence,12, 530-545.
Haj-Yahia, M.M., and Eldeson, J.L. (1994). Predicting the use of Conflict resolution Tactics Among Engaged Arab-Palestinian Men In Israel. Journal of Family Violence, 9, 47-62.
Haj-Yahia,M.M.(1998). Beliefs about wife-beating among Palestinian women ;The influence of their patriarchal ideology. Violence Against Women, 4,533-558.
Haj-Yahia,M.M.(2000a). Wife abuse and battering in the sociocultural context of Arab society. Family Process, 39,237-256
Hassan, F., Sadowski, L. S., Bangdiwala, S. I., Vizcarra, B., Ramiro, L., De Paula, C. S., Bordin, I. A. S., and Mitra, M. K. (2004). Physical intimate partner violence in Chile Egypt,India and the Philippines. Injury Control and Safety Promotion, 11(2), 111-116.
Hilton, N. Z. and Harris, G. T., (2005). Predicting Wife Assault: A Critical Review and Implications for Policy and Practice. Trauma Violence Abuse 2005; 6; 3-23 available: http://tva.sagepub.com/cgi/content/abstract/6/1/3

Hindin, M. J. (2003). Understanding women's attitudes towards wife beating in Zimbabwe. Bulletin of World Health Organization, 81, 501–508.

http://www.amanjordan.org/downloads/index.php?action=fileand id=67

Husseini, R. (1996, October). Domestic violence hotline. Jordan Times. p. 7. The Jordanian Penal Code Number 16, 1960. Amman: Jordan.

Hyde, S.H. (1996). Half the human experience: The Psychology of Women. New York, N.Y.D.C. Health and Company.

Jaghab, K.,(2005). Attitudes of Arab-American Women Towards Domestic Violence. The California School of Professional Psychology, San Francisco Bay Campus.

Jewkes, R., Levin, J., and Penn Kekana, L. (2002). Risk factors for domestic violence: Findings from a South African cross-sectional study. Social Science and Medicine, 55, 1603–1617.

Johnson, M. P. (1995). Patriarchal terrorism and common couple violence: Two forms of violence against women. Journal of Marriage and the Family, 57, 283–294.

Johnson, M.P. (1995). Patriarchal Terrorism and Common Couple Violence: Two Forms of Violence Against Women. Journal of Marriage and the Family, 57,283-294.

Johnson, M.P. (2001). Conflict and control: Symmetry and Asymmetry In Domestic Violence. In A. Crouter, A. Booth, and M. Clements (Eds.), Couples In Conflict (pp.95-104). Mahwah, NJ: Lawrence Erlbaum.

Johnson, M.P., and Ferraro, K. (2000). Research on Domestic Violence In the 1990s: Making Distinctions. Journal Of Marriage and the Family, 62,948-963.

Khawaja, M. (2004). Domestic violence in refugee camps in Jordan. International Journal of Gynecology and Obstetrics, 86(1), 67–69.

Khawaja, M., and Barazi, R. (2005). Prevalence of wife beating in Jordanian refugee camps: Reports by men and women. Journal of Epidemiology and Community Health, 59(10), 840–841.

Khawaja, M., and Tiltness, A. (2001). On the margins: Migration and living conditions of Palestinian camp refugees in Jordan. Oslo: Fafo Institute.

Khawaja, M., and Twetel-Salem, M. (2004). Agreement between husband and wife reports of domestic violence: Evidence from poor refugee communities in Lebanon. International Journal of Epidemiology, 33, 526–533

Khawaja, M., Linos, N., El-Roueiheb,Z., (2008). Attitudes of Men and Women Towards Wife Beating: Findings From Palestinian Refugee Camps in Jordan. J Fam Viol 23:211–218

Kishor, S., and Johnson, K. (2004). Profiling domestic violence: A multicounty study.

Kirchhoff, G.F. (1999). Why do they Stay? Why Don't They Run Away? In: van Dijk, J.M., van Kaam, R. and Wemmers, J. Caring for Crime Victims. Selected Proceedings of the 9th International Symposium on Victimology. Amsterdam, August 25-29, 1997. 221-238.

Koenig, M. A., Stephenson, R., Ahmed, S., Jejeebhoy, S. J., and Campbell, J. (2006). Individual and contextual determinants of domestic violence in North India. American Journal of Public Health, 96(1), 132–138.

Koenig, M., Lutalo, T., Wabwire-Mangen, F., Kiwanuka, N., Wagman, J., Zhao, F., (2003). Domestic violence in rural Uganda: Evidence from a community

based study. Bulletin of the World Health Organization, 81, 153–160.
Krug, E. G., Dahlberg, L., Mercy, J. A., Zwi, A. B., and Lozano, R. (2002). World report on violence andhealth. Geneva, Switzerland: World Health Organization.
Kulwicki, A. D., (2002). The practice of honor crimes: A glimpse of domestic violence in the Arab World. Issues in Mental Health Nursing, 23:77–87
Kulwicki, A., and Miller, J. (1999). Domestic violence in the Arab American population: Transforming environmental conditions through community education. Issues in Mental Health Nursing, 20(3), 199-215.
Leone, J. L., Johnson, M. P., and Cohan, C. L. (2007). Victim Help Seeking: Differences Between Intimate Terrorism and Situational Couple Violence. Family Relations, 56 , 427–439
Loseke, D. R.,(1991). Changing the Boundaries of Crime: The Battered Women's Social Movement and the Definition of Wife Abuse as Criminal Activity. Criminal Justice Review 16; 249-262. Available at: http://cjr.sagepub.com/cgi/content/abstract/16/2/249
Malcoe, L. H., Duran, B. M., and Montgomery, J. M. (2004). Socioeconomic disparities in intimate partner violence against Native American women: A cross-sectional study. BMC Medicine, 24, 2–20.
Maziak,W., and Asfar, T. (2003). Physical abuse in low-income women in Aleppo, Syria. *Health*
Mederer, H., and Gelles, R., (1989) Compassion or Control: Intervention in Cases of Wife Abuse J Interpers Violence 1989; 4; 25-43
Najjar, R. (1994). A Palestinian's struggle With Cultural Conflicts. In J.M. Bystydzienski and E.P.Resnik (Eds.), Women In Cross-Cultural Transitions (PP 39-44) Bloomington, In: Phi Delta Kappa Educational Foundation.
Oyediran, K. A., and Isiugo-Abanihe, U. (2005). Perceptions of Nigerian women on domestic violence: Evidence from 2003 Nigeria Demographic and Health Survey. African Journal of Reproductive Health, 9(2), 38–53.
Patai, R. (1969). Society, Culture, and Change. In the Middle East: Golden River to Golden Road. Philadelphia: University of Pennsylvania Press.
Patterson, M. D. (2004). Contextualizing human rights: A response to international family violence. In K. Malley-Morrison (Ed.), International perspectives on family violence and abuse: A cognitive ecological approach (pp. 473-500). Mahwah, NJ: Lawrence Erlbaum.
Rula Btoush and Muhammad M. Haj-Yahia (2008) Attitudes of Jordanian Society Toward Wife Abuse Journal of Interpersonal Violence Volume XX Number XX Month XXXX 1-24 http://jiv.sagepub.com
Schwertscharf, J. ,(2001). Male Attitudes Towards Violence Against Women California State University, Long Beach
Shalhoub-Kevorkian, N. (1997). Tolerating battering: Invisible methods of social control. International Review of Victimology, 5(1), 1-21.
Sheridan, L., and Ghorayeb, G. (2004). Lebanon. In K. Malley-Morrison (Ed.), International perspectives on family violence and abuse: A cognitive ecological approach (pp. 20 220). Mahwah, NJ: Lawrence Erlbaum.
Straus, M. A. and Sherry L. Hamby Sue Boney-McCoy, David B. Sugarman (1995). The revised Conflicts Tactics Scales (CTS2). Trauma Violence Abuse 2005; 6; 3 http://pubpages.unh.edu/~mas2/test%20form-CTS.htm
Straus, M. A. (1992). Sociological Research and Social Policy: The Case of Family Violence. Sociological Forum, Vol.7, No. 2, 211-237

Straus, M. A., (1999). The Controversy Over Domestic Violence by Women: A Methodological, Theoretical and Sociology of Science Analysis. Pp17-44 B. Arriaga and S. Oskamp, (eds.) Thosand Oaka, CA.: Sage
Straus, M. A., Hamby, S. L., Boney-McCoy, S., and Sugarman, D. B. (1996). The revised conflicts tactics scale (CTS2): Development and preliminary psychometric data. Journal of Family Issues, 17,283–316.
Straus, M.A., and R.J. Gelles (1986) Societal change in family violence from 1975 to 1985 as revealed by two national surveys. Journal of Marriage and the Family 48:465-479.
Straus, M.A., R.J. Gelles, and S.K. Steinmetz (1980) Behind Closed Doors: Violence in the American Family. New York: Doubleday/Anchor.
Thompson RS, Bonomi AE, Anderson M, Reid RJ, Dimer JA, Carrell D, Rivara FP (2006) Intimate partner violence: prevalence, types, and chronicity across adult women's lifetime. Am J Prev Med 30:447–457.
Tjaden, P., and Thoennes, N. (2000). The role of stalking in domestic violence crime reports generated by the Colorado Springs Police Department. Violence and Victims, 15(4), 427–441.
Todd I. Herrenkohl, Cynthia Sousa, Emiko A. Tajima, Roy C. Herrenkohl and Carrie A. Moylan (2008). Intersection of Child Abuse and Children's Exposure to Domestic Violence Trauma Violence Abuse 2008; 9; 84-99 http://tva.sagepub.com/cgi/content/abstract/9/2/84
U.S. Department of Justice. (1995). Criminal victimization in the U.S: National Crime Report. Washington, DC: Government Printing Office.
United Nations Fund for Women (UNIFEM). (1999). A world free of violence against women (U.N. global videoconference). New York: Author.
United Nations General Assembly. (1993). Declaration on the elimination of violence against women (Resolution Doc. A/REX/48/104). New York: Author.
Walker, L. (1979). The Battered Women. New York: Harper and Row.
Wallace . H. (1998). Victimology : Legal, Psychological, and social perspectives, Boston : Allyn and Bacaon.
World Health Organization (WHO) (1997). Violence against women. Geneva: Switzerland.
World Health Organization (WHO) (2002). World report on violence and health. Geneva: Krug, E. G., Dahlberg, L. L., Mercy, J. A., Zvi, A. B., Lozano, R. eds.
Zurayk, H., Sholkamy, H.,Younis, N., and Khattab, H. (1997). Women's health problems in the Arab world: A holistic policy perspective. International Journal of Gynaecology and Obstetrics, 58(1), 13-21

Institutional Victimization: Legislative Framework and Youth Maginalization in Post Apartheid South Africa

By

Robert Peacock

Abstract

Within a critical victimological framework this study focuses on the role of the state alongside the law in victimizing marginal and institutionalized youth in South Africa. For these disenfranchised and occupationally marginal youth who are unemployed or unemployable it could be said that a political struggle has been replaced by an economic struggle and their reactionary and victimizing mode of adaptation could be viewed as an outcome of the experiences of recurrent indignities and multiple deprivations associated with apartheid capitalism, class struggles and human rights abuses of the state. With a national average level of prison overcrowding of 45% (some prisons at more than 200%) this study assessed within a domestic and international human rights framework deprived prison conditions of a group of incarcerated youth in South Africa. Through purposive sampling 83 incarcerated adolescent male research participants were included in this study and an exploratory factor analysis (a two factor solution from a principle factor analysis) was conducted of prison conditions. A further correlation analysis between satisfaction with prison conditions and level of identity development of the incarcerated adolescents showed that although identity development was not influenced by physical prison conditions per se (primarily due to the compensatory nature of the prison gang) prison conditions - constructed as an outcome of abuse of power - impacted negatively on the physical well-being of the adolescent inmate and on his human rights.

Introduction

In an article called *Deviance as Strength* Nils Christie (2005) draws an analogy between elimination and confinement and the *garden state* (a term used by Christie to symbolize a state like Hitler's orderly Germany with the "ornamental plants" in the one category and annihilation of "weeds" or "deviance" in the other) to demonstrate how elimination and institutionalization have failed to improve the human condition. The failures of total institutions remind of course of the apartheid state. With a closer look at contemporary South Africa, and with reference to Christie's terminology, it would be more appropriate to refer to penal law as *pain law* when observing how the criminal justice system in South Africa continues to systematically deliver pain. Marginalized youth in South Africa continue to suffer in the aftermath of institutional and structural victimization (apartheid). What kind of society do we wish to create with the systematic imprisonment of different groups of society whose victimizing mode of adaptation can be viewed as an outcome of the experiences of recurrent indignities and multiple deprivations associated with apartheid capitalism and class struggles? It does not take much of a victimological imagination to recognize the grim consequences of mass imprisonment i.e. the transformation of family and community dynamics, exacerbated racial divisions or what Reiman (2004) refers to as "The rich get richer and the poor get prison." Christie (1981) mentions in *Limits to Pain* that although attempts are made to hide the basic character of punishment (punishment in the name of treatment and deterrence) the infliction of pain remains an undisputed reality. It poses fundamental questions about citizenship in a democratic and civilized society. Especially if this pain is inflicted on particularly vulnerable groups in society such as incarcerated children and youth or what Fattah (1997) describes in terms of cultural stereotypes as so-called "deserving victims", "disposable", "worthless" or structurally prone. Louk Hulsman (1997) reminds us to be aware how "penal language" is used to provide support to punishment, normalising and hiding in other words its very own victimogenesis (see the report on Hulsman in Kirchhoff 2005 p. 270 - 276). The following discussion will focus on a domestic and international legal framework seeking to protect children and adolescents who have been incarcerated in post apartheid South Africa – youth who have been caged, notwithstanding that in 1994, the first democratically elected State President of South Africa, Nelson Mandela, called for the removal of all children from prisons in South Africa in his first address to parliament (Lewis, 1997; Peacock, 2006).

However, it becomes firstly necessary to explain what is exactly meant with the concepts "child" and "adolescent". A definition of a "child" consistent with those contained in the African Charter on the Rights and Welfare of the Child ((1990) and in the UN Convention on the Rights of the Child (CRC) (1989) is a person below 18 years of age. Considering the dynamic nature of adolescence, researchers (Adamson, Hartman & Lyxell, 1999; Dreyer, 1980) agree that adolescence generally occurs during the period 12 to 22 years. This of course points to the arbitrariness of criminal law in relation to lifespan development in its attempts to determine when a person is an adult or child. The middle years of adolescence would usually refer to the period 15 – 18 years (Peacock, 2009).

Legal Framework

Louk Hulsman, penal abolitionist, expressed the profound thought "the efforts made are useless" in his book entitled *Peines Perdues* (co-authored with Jacqueline Bernat de Celis, in French) to signify the wastage associated with punishment (Hulsman, 2009). This wastage is demonstrated well by the expenditure of the Department of Correctional Services in South Africa (excluding the Departments of Safety and Security and Justice and Constitutional development) during the 2008/2009 financial year amounting to R12.3 billion – approximately one billion Euros a year - to accommodate a population of only about 165 000 inmates (Judicial Inspectorate of Prisons, 2009), but with very poor results indeed as the findings of this study will show.

Concerning useless efforts, it would be easy to argue that despite the spirit in which legal frameworks have been developed to ameliorate problematic situations (both nationally and internationally), and maybe at times with the best of intentions, the social and political environments in which legislation needs to be introduced can never be ignored. For instance, as with regard to only the political-punishment nexus, the Judicial Inspectorate of Prisons (2010) refers to the disregard and disposable nature of its recommendations on minimum prison standards contained in a substantial number of annual reports presented to the President of the Republic of South Africa.

The Child Justice Bill was recently passed by parliament seeking to create a child justice system (see Skelton (2009) to change the previous incoherent statuary provisions. These provisions were described as rendering in practice the exact opposite than the envisaged protection for marginalized youth (McLachlan, 1986; Peacock, 1989; South African Law Commission, 1997). South Africa has limited domestic resources. It is possible that therefore more pressures mounts to increasingly attend to the needs of so-called "pure" or "more deserving" victims (Christie, 1986) rather than to develop a comprehensive range of services for "disposable" or "worthless" victims, i.e the "child offenders." This lack of capacity may furthermore lead to the criminal justice system in South Africa adopting gradually a more punitive approach in its efforts to compensate for a lack of accountability in successfully addressing conflict in society. With this in mind the following discussion will provide a brief synopsis of international and domestic law seeking to govern the deprivation of liberty of children and adolescents.

Article 10(1)(b) of the International Covenant on Civil and Political Rights lays the foundation for the distinction between juvenile and adult prisoners. In this covenant it is stated that juveniles shall be separated from adult prisoners and be accorded with treatment appropriate to their age and legal status. The United Nations addressed the specific treatment of juveniles in detention in 1985 with the United Nations Standard Minimum Rules for the Administration of Juvenile Justice (The Beijing Rules), and together with the United Nations Rules for the Protection of Juveniles Deprived of their Liberty (1990), the aim is to establish minimum standards of treatment for incarcerated juveniles. In 1995 South Africa ratified the United Nations Convention on the Rights of the Child (1989). This convention is probably the most important internationally binding legal instrument dealing with children deprived of their liberty. Article 37 refers in specific to their rights.

South Africa is also a member of the African Union (formerly the OAU) and of the British Commonwealth. These bodies subscribe to the protection of the rights of children. Most notably is the African Charter on Human and Peoples Rights (ACHPR), which was adopted in 1986 and is relevant to countries on the African continent. The charter includes the recognition of human dignity inherent to any human being, while exploitation, cruel, inhuman or degrading punishment is prohibited.

Concerning the treatment and conditions of children deprived of their liberty the Correctional Services Act 111 of 1998 was passed. Its section 19 determines that child prisoners are subject to compulsory school education. The same section obliges Correctional Services to provide every child with "social work services, religious care, recreational programmes and psychological services" If practical, the Correctional Services have to ensure that child prisoners retain contact with their families through visits and other means.

The Bill of Rights (Chapter 2) of the Constitution of the Republic of South Africa (Act 108 of 1996), in particular section 28, which describes the rights of the child, and section 35, which describes the rights of arrested, detained and convicted persons, are of special relevance to children deprived of their liberty. Similarity exists between sections 10, 12, 14, 28 and 35 of the Constitution of the Republic of South Africa (Act 108 of 1996) and the contents of article 40 of the United Nations Convention on the Rights of the Child (1989). Article 40(1) of the United Nations Convention on the Rights of the Child (1989) prescribes to state parties to recognise the right of every child alleged as, accused of, or recognised as having infringed penal law to be treated in a manner consistent with the promotion of the child's sense of dignity and worth. This should serve to reinforce the child's respect for human rights and fundamental freedom of others. Treatment of the child should also take into account the child's age and the promotion of the child's integration in society in order for the child to assume a constructive role.

According to the Constitution of the Republic of South Africa (Act 108 of 1996, section 28):
Every child has the right not to be detained except as a measure of last resort, in which case, in addition to the rights a child enjoys under sections 12 and 35, the child may be detained only for the shortest appropriate period of time, and has the right to be treated in a manner, and kept in conditions, that take account of the child's age.

Section 28 states further:
"Every child has the right to be kept separately from detained persons over the age of 18 years" and "every child has the right to appropriate alternative care when removed from the family environment [and to] basic nutrition, shelter, basic health care and social services".

Section 33 states:
"Every child has the right to be protected from maltreatment, neglect, abuse or degradation." And: "Everyone who is detained, including every sentenced prisoner, has the right to have a legal practitioner assigned to the detained person by the state and at state expense if substantial injustice would otherwise result, and to be informed of this right promptly".

Section 35 stipulates:
"Everyone who is detained, including every sentenced prisoner has the right to conditions of detention that are consistent with human dignity, including at least the provision, at state expense, of adequate accommodation at least exercise [and] at state expense of reading material".

There are numerous regulations that describe the rights of the child offenders. However, these norms must be measured against reality. The result of such a comparison is that child offenders are victimized due to the lack of implementation of these rules.

Prison overcrowding and the right to adequate accomodation

Post-apartheid South Africa remains the country with the highest incarceration rates (3.5 per 1000 incarcerated) in Africa and indeed in the world (Judicial Inspectorate of Prisons, 2010). The Department of Correctional Services inherited from apartheid a measure of prison capacity of 3.34 square meters per prisoner in a communal cell - below international standards of four square metres per prisoner in a communal cell and six square metres for a single cell (Steinberg, 2005). Even by this measure prisons are 45% overcrowded with a great number of prisons between 200% and 400% (Judicial Inspectorate of Prisons, 2008). It therefore does not surprise that 12% of all prisoners do not have access to beds. They have to sleep on the floor. 22 prisons do not have eating utensils. 94 prisons do not have facilities to separate prisoners with contagious diseases from the others. Due to poor ventilation and sanitation, prisons can act as incubators for tuberculosis, relapsing fever and trench fever or water-borne diseases such as cholera, typhus or diarrhea (Robinson, Leo, Provic & Barber, 2003). Ablution areas are usually a general cause of concern, especially when considering all pervasive smells from such areas to the cells. According to a Human Rights Watch Prison Project (2005) and the more recent research of Sarkin (2008), poor hygiene, inadequate sanitation and a lack of clear water contribute in Africa to high levels of deaths in custody. It is hardly surprising that as a result of prison numbers violence, disease and death ravage prison populations. Unnatural deaths in prison increased since 2006 by 21% in South Africa (Judicial Inspectorate of Prisons, 2008). Although disease has always plagued African penal systems, that was before the onslaught of HIV/AIDS (Human Immune Virus/Acquired Immune Deficiency Syndrome). Estimates are that of the 10 000 prisoners released every month, 6 000 are HIV positive. This should also be read in conjunction with prisons functioning as an incubator for tuberculosis, an often deadly infection in association with HIV/AIDS (Peacock, 2006) or the potential devastating effects of the H1N1 flu virus. South Africa has been listed as one of the NEPAD countries (New Partnership for Africa's Development) severely lacking in medical access and care for its prisoners (Cherubin-Doumbia, 2004). This falls short of the constitutional test that prisoners must receive health care which is "adequate" to their circumstances.

The inmate is obliged to undergo a health assessment which may include testing for contagious and communicable diseases, both for purposes of individualized treatment required and to prevent the spread of airborne disease. This assessment has to be made immediately on admission to a correctional center. However, the

Judicial Inspectorate of Prisons (2009) has found that in a large number of cases detainees are not assessed upon admission or, in many cases, at any time thereafter, unless they specifically complain of an illness. For the period 1 April 2008 to 31 March 2009, the Inspectorate received
18 758 health complaints. During the following year, health complaints remained a major issue with the annual number rising to a national level of 22 053 complaints (Judicial Inspectorate of Prisons, 2009, 2010).

Also, most of the NEPAD countries under review do not provide adequate meals to prisoners. In fact, across Africa, nutrition is frequently poor or even non-existent. It is for instance reported in Mozambique that children receive decayed or maggot infested food and in Rumbek, Southern Sudan, no food is supplied unless the prison officials provide it from their own pockets (Sarkin, 2008). These findings concur with the local research of Peacock (2006) and Sloth-Nielsen (1998) reporting that children in custody frequently complain about being hungry, about the taste of the food and of loosing weight. An inadequate diet and disease are variables that affect the normal physical and psychosocial development of the incarcerated adolescent. This results in physical underdevelopment and under-activity. Berk (2003) highlights the critical importance of growth spurts in the human cortex during adolescence when the brain requires appropriate stimulation (dietary and otherwise) for the optimal development of human intelligence. Arrest of development may in turn impact negatively on the adolescent's ability to rationally calculate a risk-reward outcome when problematic situations are encountered, albeit during incarceration or eventually, upon release. Moreover, when internalising their inferior status within the context of substandard prison conditions, adolescents often experience themselves as "deserving" victims of institutional violence (Peacock, 2009). Idleness, fear and the inability to maintain a personal identity could all add to the stress associated with a lack of defensible space culminating in severe disturbances of the self, social withdrawal and the re-enactment of traumatic childhood experiences together with self-mutilating or suicidal behaviour (Peacock, 2006) According to the Judicial Inspectorate of Prisons (2006) the national crisis of chronic prison overcrowding in South Africa constitutes indeed a gross infringement of the most basic human rights of prisoners. Prohibition against inhumane and degrading treatment is found in a range of international human rights instruments. The ACHPR (1986) refers expressly to this prohibition indicating some awareness of the special risks associated with younger inmates.

Placing children in cages

In South Africa, everyone has inherent dignity and the right to have this dignity respected and protected (Constitution of the Republic of South Africa, Act 108 of 1996, Section 10). In addition, Section 28 prescribes the right to be treated in a manner, and kept in conditions, that take account of the child's *age*. Article 10(1)(b) of the International Covenant on Civil and Political Rights states that juveniles to be accorded with treatment appropriate to their *age* (emphasis of this author) and legal status. Article 40(1) of the United Nations Convention on the Rights of the Child (1989) prescribes that signatories - and South Africa has signed the Convention - have to recognise the right of every child alleged as, accused of, or recognised as having infringed penal law to be treated in a manner consistent with the promotion of the child's sense of dignity, taking into account the child's *age* (emphasis of this author).

The developmental stage of adolescence is generally referred to in life-span studies as the most critical developmental stage in human development (Peacock, 2006; Thom, 1988). According to the psychosocial theory of Erik Erikson (1958; 1963; 1968), the developmental stage of adolescence is in particular a critical and vulnerable phase for the establishment of a personal identity. Identity development reaches its peak during adolescence. This is due to the necessity of the individual to deal with considerable physical and cognitive changes and the need to acquire productive skills. To develop a strong personal identity, the adolescent has to consolidate previous identity developments with prevailing changes in physique, and outlook on life. In addition to this integration, the adolescent needs to finally resolve any possible crises experienced with previous developmental phases (such as trust versus distrust, autonomy versus shame and doubt, initiative versus guilt and industry as opposed to inferiority) and furthermore, to extend earlier identity development. The adolescent will then develop what Erikson refers to as the virtue of fidelity, or what could be termed as a commitment towards his own value system

When incarcerated, the preservation of self becomes a major challenge and an antithesis to the plight of the adolescent who is in particular confronted with the need to maintain inner sameness, however, in a hostile and deprived environment that is conducive to identity destruction. Previous research (Peacock, 2006), established a lower mean identity score amongst incarcerated adolescents in comparison to adolescent populations in open society. This result shows a less significant extension of earlier identity development phases amongst incarcerated adolescents. It demonstrates as well an inability to consolidate in prison these phases with prevailing changes in physique and outlook on life. An "arrest" of identity is usually accompanied by becoming 'identity conscious,' a painful awareness reflected by discrepancies between one's self-ideal and social identity. Due to the muting of both - autonomy and initiative - the adolescent most likely looses the capacity in prison to gain a sense of competence in personhood and to initiate sound decisions for him/herself. This all happens while behind a "prison mask", internal chaos, stress, alienation and fear may occur (Peacock, 2009). The destruction in prison of being an acceptable, respectable and worthy individual during the vulnerable and critical developmental age of adolescence is certainly not in compliance with minimum legal standards to be treated appropriately in terms of developmental age.

Rehabilitate rehabilitation

Most of the countries in Africa have emerged from a colonial past. Together with a prison system that was often used to procure the labour force for growing industries, one of the aims of imprisonment of the colonial regimes was rehabilitation. The influence of the West continues in current legislation in Africa, often reflecting European legislation of the late nineteenth and early twentieth century (Dissel, 2008).

Prison labour has been abolished in South Africa. From the objectives of the South African correctional system, as embodied amongst others, in section 35(2)(e) of the Constitution of the Republic of South Africa (Act 108 of 1996), section 2 of the Correctional Services Act (Act No 111 of 1998) and chapter 4 of the White Paper on Corrections (2005), the responsibility of the Department of Correctional Services (DCS) is first and foremost to correct offending behaviour in a secure, safe and humane environment to facilitate rehabilitation and avoidance of recidivism.

With reference to the warning of Hulsman on the deceiving nature of penal language, one needs to be aware of contradictions that lay at the heart of criminal justice systems (Ceretti, 2003). First of all, it remains an anomaly to remove individuals *from* society in order to assist them to adjust and function more successfully *in* society. Furthermore, how does one rehabilitate a victim of institutional and structural violence of apartheid in prison? Or how does one provide therapy in prison to the prevailing subcultures of violence in South Africa? In the name of rehabilitation it seems to be more a matter of the weak state making itself more visible by governing the lower classes, and where individuals within these classes to a large extent are controlled through their minor infractions (Christie, 1998). And one might add, at the expense of effectively addressing government corruption and organized crime.

With further consideration of the rehabilitation ideal, Muntingh (2001) refers to research of the World Health Organisation on "carceral suffering" as the disorienting result of the lack of meaning of time spend in prison. Often prisoners are unable to concentrate. They can not control their memory adequately. Many experience sudden "mind voids" and dizziness. Feelings of emptiness are also linked to self-negation when prisoners make themselves "invisible" in an effort to avoid constant observation, albeit from the other inmates, or prison staff. Bodily functions and senses are atrophied, for instance, eyesight deteriorates as a result of the confined space, whilst hearing becomes over-developed resulting in a hypersensitivity to noise. It therefore does not surprise that the suicide rate in prisons is six to seven times higher than outside. Tonry and Petersilia (1999) refer to young prisoners as the most likely group to commit suicide due to their particular susceptibility to prison stress. For those who do not succumb to suicide ideation, estimates of recidivism are between 85% and 94% (Peacock, 2006). With a social worker/prisoner ratio of 1 to 595 and a psychologist/ prisoner ratio of 1 to 11 223 in South African prisons, interventions of any kind are in any event virtually impossible (Cilliers & Smit, 2007). According to a recent report of the Judicial Inspectorate of Prisons (2010), the majority of the South African inmate population is detained in often overcrowded cells for 23 hours per day with only approximately 10-15 percent of sentenced inmates engaged in any work or rehabilitation programs.

The following discussion focuses on research procedures and techniques that were followed to assess institutional victimization, level of identity development and satisfaction with physical prison conditions of a group of male incarcerated adolescents in South Africa.

Research design

A quantitative research methodology was used for the purposes of this study. This allowed for a process of deductive analysis, moving from the theory of Erikson (1958; 1963; 1968) to the testing of the relationship between the variables rather than inferring from a specific case study (inductive reasoning) to the sample as a whole (Hagan, 1997). This approach allowed furthermore for the standardised measurement of the level of identity development of the research participants. The individual administration of semi-structured or non-directive interviews often associated with a qualitative research design (Esterberg 2002), is a lengthy and time consuming process and not suitable for a large sample. Our sample consists of 82 prisoners, and for such a sample, interviews are not suitable. A lack of standardisation of the data collecting process could render internal validity low, which together with the said time frame, were also points of criticism (Thom 1988) levelled against the research of Marcia (1967; 1975) on his assessment of different identity statuses. For the purposes of this study, it was therefore decided to assign numerical values to concepts in a self-administered questionnaire which in turn were statistically analysed in tandem with a standardised scale (Erikson Scale). This scale is described in the next paragraph.

The Erikson Scale and questionnaire

Ochse (1983) developed a standardised scale based on Erikson's theory specifically for the South African context. The scale can be used for both male and female adolescents (15–19 years) and has tested to be reliable in terms of cross-cultural comparisons of Afrikaans, English and African language speaking groups (Ochse & Plug 1986; Thom, 1988; Thom & Coetzee 2004). The reliability of the scale refers to the degree of relatedness of the individual items in one factor or scale/ construct (Rosnow & Rosenthal 1996). To determine the relatedness of the items in the identity development scale, the Cronbach alpha was calculated. Groves, Fowler, Couper, Lepkowski, Singer and Tourangeau (2004) explain that when many different questions are used to assess the same construct, the Cronbach alpha is a widely used method of determining reliability. The Cronbach alpha has a range of 0 - 1, where 0 is no internal consistency and 1 is the maximum internal consistency. A general rule of thumb for determining what constitutes a good internal reliability is given at 0.75 (Terre Blanch & Durrheim 1999). The Cronbach alpha of the Erikson scale is 0.78. The scale therefore is reliable. This confirms that the Erikson scale could be well utilised in different environments (Ochse & Plug, 1986; Thom, 1988; Thom & Coetzee 2004), e.g. in a correctional context as it is used here.

To assess the nature of the relationship between the prison environment, satisfaction with prison conditions and level of identity development achieved, a questionnaire was developed. Under the general information section, questions were included to capture essential data to describe the sample. Amongst others, aspects of relevance here were chronological age, cultural group, and nature of offence and length of prison sentence. This section consisted of nine questions. A Likert–type scale was developed for purposes of focussing on prison conditions, exposure to victimisation and gangsterism. This section consists of 11 questions with its respective sub-questions.

Twelve research participants were included in a pilot study prior to the undertaking of the entire data collection process. According to Babbie (1990) a pilot study is useful to anticipate and eradicate any problems in the field prior to undertaking the research. Furthermore, it served as an indicator of the time-frame (30–45 minutes) required for purposes of the completion of the Erikson scale and questionnaire.

Data collection

Permission was obtained from the Department of Correctional Services to conduct research on 100 research participants. Selected for participation were only male incarcerated adolescents in the middle years of adolescence (15 – 18 years) who could read, write and speak English. The research participants were provided with instructions on how to complete the questionnaire and Erikson scale. It was administered to small groups of approximately 12 research participants during a single session to further clarify any possible ambiguity or uncertainty as to the exact meaning of the single items. Special care was taken to assure the research participants of the confidential nature of the study. The purpose and nature of the research were also related to the participants. In accordance with the ethical principle of freedom from harm, it was discussed (and in addition was stated in a written note that accompanied the questionnaire and Erikson scale) that the participants could withdraw at anytime from the study if and when experiencing any emotional discomfort. A social worker from the Department of Correctional Services assisted to monitor the process of data collection, also to provide any possible after-care services in the event of a need for debriefing. None of the research participants terminated their participation prematurely. Their voluntary participation was guided by the principle of informed consent.

Sampling procedure

Due to practical constraints it was not feasible to collect a random sample of all incarcerated adolescents in South African prisons. A random sample within a single correctional centre would only yield randomly obtained data applicable to a single centre and would also not be representative of the universe of incarcerated adolescents in South Africa. It was therefore decided to employ a purposive theoretical sampling technique. According to this technique the aim was to create an operational population, in other words, a population that is theoretically constructed in such a manner that it represents the ideal (Bless & Higson-Smith 1995; Gilbert 1993). With identity development reaching its peak during adolescence (Erikson, 1959; 1968) the aim was to include adolescent male participants from the middle years of adolescence whose identity establishment is no longer dominated by physiological changes but rather develops along personal, social and cultural dimensions of personality (Adamson, Hartman & Lyxell 1999; Dreyer 1980; Thom 1988). In addition, it was imperative that all of the select elements of the sample could read and write English for purposes of the self-administration of the data collection instruments. Once the above-mentioned criteria were exhausted the sample size totalled 88 incarcerated adolescents in a select correctional centre. Due to incomplete and or corrupt data received from five participants, their responses were excluded from the study, arriving thus at a sample size of 83 research participants.

Description of sample

The following discussion focuses on characteristics of the sample, namely chronological age distribution, cultural and ethnic characteristics, home language as well as frequency distributions of offences committed and length of prison sentence.

The sample is made up of juveniles between 15 and 18 years of age (N=82). The mean age of the sample is 17.54 years. Most of them are 17 and 18 years old (89%). 31% of the respondents had attained Grade 10 education as their highest level. 48% had attained a lower level of formal education, 21% a higher level. A reason for this low incidence of a lack of formal schooling in the sample may be that only those who could read and write English were included in the study.

Regarding the racial background of the research participants, the majority of the participants, namely 77% (n=64) were African, 21 % brown (previously so-called "Coloureds"). The sample is ethnically very diverse, the participants described themselves as belonging to as many as 13 different ethnics. The largest ethnic group were Zulus (29%), followed by participants from the Tswana group (12.%), and finally the Afrikaans participants (11%). Most research participants (33%) spoke Zulu as their first language, followed by 16 percent who speak Afrikaans and 12 percent who speak Tswana.

Of the research participants, 96 % (n=80) were first time offenders while three (4%) were recidivists. Sentencing youth to prison as first time offenders violates clearly minimum international and domestic standards concerning the principle of detention as a last resort. This violation (multiply by 80) concurs with the research of

Odongo and Gallinetti (2005) on the treatment of children as first offenders in the South African criminal justice system. Indications are that at present there is a decline in the number of incarcerated children (Skelton, 2009). However, these figures do not account for the number of adolescents who are incarcerated from the ages18 to 22 and who are in terms of lifespan development *and* lifestyle and routine perspectives a particularly vulnerable group relating to victimization risk factors (Davis & Snyman, 2005; Peacock, 2006). The new "progressive" Child Justice Act passed by parliament in 2009, also provides for the incarceration of children under the age of eighteen years. The maximum prescribed sentence for a child of 14 years or older at the time of sentencing is 25 years in prison (Skelton 2009).

In accordance with the classification system of the Department of Correctional Services (DCS), the types of behaviour for which the research participants had been incarcerated are officially grouped into four categories/labels, namely, aggressive, economic, sexual and "other". The category, "other", includes social fabric "crimes", such as drinking in public, or trespassing as well as "offences" such as kidnapping, malicious damage to property, possession of burglary tools and an possessing as unlicensed firearm. None of the research participants were incarcerated for "narcotic offences" - a fifth category used by the DCS. This concurs with the research of Dissel (1999), which shows that imprisonment is seldom used for adolescents convicted of such conduct.

About half (49.4%) of the 82 research participants were in prison for "aggressive offences" such as murder, attempted murder, robbery, aggravating robbery and assault to cause grievous bodily harm. About a quarter (n=25) have been incarcerated for committing "economic offences" such as housebreaking, theft and fraud. Another 13% (n=11) have been sentenced to prison for committing "sexual offences" such as rape and indecent assault. The six 7% (n=6) who fall into the category "other" have been sentenced for kidnapping, malicious damage to property, possession of burglary tools and possessing an unlicensed firearm.

Data was also obtained to record the length of prison sentences. Only 13.25 percent (11) research participants had short sentences ranging from 3 to 11 months, 66.27 percent (55) had been sentenced for periods ranging between 1 and 5 years and 20.48 (17) received sentences exceeding five years. Despite their relatively long prison sentences, most of the research participants had not been in prison for longer than a year.

Data analysis

It was postulated that the level of identity development of the incarcerated adolescent will show a significant relationship will the level of satisfaction with physical prison conditions. It was therefore deemed probable that the incarcerated adolescent who has achieved a lower level of identity development, will display a lack of coping with deprived and victimising physical prison conditions. To statistically test this relationship between satisfaction with physical prison conditions and level of identity achieved, an exploratory factor analysis was conducted. The exploratory factor analysis of the data revealed two main factors:

Factor 1 includes variables that measure the physical conditions in the prison (size of your cell, your bed (bed and mattress), your bedding (blankets. sheets and pillows), washing facilities, toilets and food). Factor 2 includes exercise opportunities, reading material and fresh air in cell. The first factor reflects more basic needs whilst the second factor is associated with recreation, and could therefore be viewed as more aspiring or pertaining to higher needs.

The correlation analysis between factors 1 and 2, level of identity development and satisfaction with prison conditions resulted in insignificant correlation coefficients. Satisfaction with these two factors, or with its independent aspects, was therefore not influenced by degree of identity development of the research participants. From this it is construed that identity development is not influenced by prison conditions *per se*. Prison conditions may, however, impact on the physical well-being of the inmate or on his human rights. A lack of correlation between the level of identity development in particular and the *physical* environment, could be ascribed on the one hand to the intermediary effect of gangs in terms of satisfying needs in prison and on the other, to Erikson's (1963, 1968) extension of Freud's (in Maddi, 1980) concept of the psychosexual beyond the physiological, or intrapsychic, to include a social dimension of identity development. In this regard an assessment between the level of identity achieved and the compensatory nature of prison gangs in a victimizing, closed and deprived environment proved statistically significant as well as between the level of identity and psychosocial context in which inter-personal prison victimization took place. Demonstrating the compensatory and intermediary nature of the prison gang in terms of need satisfaction, in a broader victimizing context, explorative data was firstly collected.

The acquisition of tobacco, sweets and food in the prison economy was cited as the most important reason by 67% of the research participants to belong to a gang. This was followed by 63% who indicated the need for clothing and shoes revealing the deprived and thus victimising nature of the conditions in the so-called "correctional" environment of the research participants. A correlation analysis shows that incarcerated adolescents with a lower level of identity development are significantly more members of a prison gang than incarcerated adolescents with a high level of identity development - thereby demonstrating their own victimisation vulnerability. Also, those with a low level of identity development had significantly more friends that belong to a prison gang than those with a high level of identity development. This supports the importance of the psychosocial dimension of identity formation in prison (details in Peacock, R. & Theron, A. (2007).

Conclusion

This discussion demonstrated that children and adolescents need cognitively and socially rich environments but incarceration together with its destruction of being an acceptable, respectable and worthy individual during the vulnerable and critical developmental stages of childhood and adolescence, is certainly not in concert with treatment appropriate to developmental age. Incarceration is however promoted by minimum legal standards that provide moral and political justifications in the guise of humanist values for penal systems to inflict even more pain to deal with pain. Louk Hulsman (1997) reminds us of penal language and how it is used to provide support to punishment, normalising its own victimization.

References

Adamson, L., Hartman, G., & Lyxell, B. (1999). Adolescent identity – a qualitative approach: Self-concept, existential questions and adult contacts. *Scandinavian Journal of Psychology, 40*(1), 21-31.

African Charter on the Rights and Welfare of the Child (1999). Retrieved on January 14, 2005 from http://www.umn.edu/humanarts/africa/afchild.htm

Babbie, E. (1990). *Survey research methods* (2nd ed.). Belmont, CA: Wadsworth.

Berk, L.E. (2003). *Child development*. Boston: Pearson Education.

Bless, C., & Higson-Smith, C. (1995). *Fundamentals of social research: An African perspective*. Cape Town: Juta.

Ceretti, A. (2003). *A homage to Louk Hulsman* (Available from http://www.defensesocial.org/revista2003/04.pdf). Accessed on 30 March 2008.

Cherubin-Doumbia, G. (2004, July). African commitments to human rights: A review of eight NEPAD countries. *African Human Security Initiative*, Paper 2. Retrieved on February 12, 2005 from http://www.africanreview.org

Cilliers, C. & Smit, J. (2007). Offender rehabilitation in the South African correctional system: Myth or reality? *Acta Criminologica*, 20(2):83-101.

Chistie, N. (1981). *Limits to pain*. Oxford: Martin Robertson and Company.

Christie, N. (1986). The ideal victim. In E.A Fattah (ed.). *From crime policy to victim policy*. London: Macmillan.

Christie, N. (1998). Penal law and the civil society (available from http://folk.uio.no/christie/dokumenter/penal_law_columbia.htm). Accessed on 30 March 2008.

Christie, N. (2005). Deviance as strength. *Scandinavian Journal of Public Health*, 33(5): 7-11.

Correctional Services Act 111 of 1998. Pretoria: Government Printer.

Constitution of the Republic of South Africa, Act 108 of 1996. Pretoria: Government Printer.

Davis, L., & Snyman, R. (2005). *Victimology in South Africa*. Pretoria: Van Schaik.

Dissel, A. (1999). Children serving gaol sentences: A profile on children sentenced to prison. Retrieved on December 18, 2003 from http://www.csvr .org.za /papers /papdis7.htm

Dissel, A. (2008). *Rehabilitation and reintegration in African prisons.* In J. Sarkin (ed.). Human rights in African prisons. Cape Town: HSRC Press

Dreyer, H.J. (1980). *Adolescence in a changing society*. Pretoria: Academica.

Erikson, E.H. (1956). The problem of ego identity. *Journal of the American Psychoanalytical Association*, *4*, 56-121.

Erikson, E.H. (1958). *Young man Luther: A study in psychoanalysis and history.* London: Faber & Faber.

Erikson, E.H. (1959). Identity and the life cycle: Selected papers. *Psychosocial Issues, 1*, 1-171.

Erikson, E.H. (1963). *Childhood and society.* New York: Norton.

Erikson, E.H. (1968). *Identity, youth and crisis*. London: Faber & Faber.

Esterberg, K.G. (2002). *Qualitative methods in social research*. Boston: McGraw-Hill.

Fattah, E.Z. (1997). *Criminology: Past, present and future. A critical overview.*

London: Macmillan.
Gilbert, N. (1993). *Researching social life*. London: Sage
Groves, R.M., Fowler, F.J., Couper, M.P., Lepkowski, J.M., Singer, E., & Tourangeau, R. (2004). *Survey methodology*. New York: Wiley.
Hagan, F.E. (1997). *Research methods in criminal justice and criminology*. Boston: Allyn & Bacon.
Hulsman, L. (1997). Themes and concepts in an abolitionist approach to criminal justice.
Available from http://www.loukhulsman.org/Publication/, Accessed on 30 May 2009.
Hulsman, J. (2009). Louk Hulsman: A father of penal abolitionism and gardener of the world. *Acta Criminologica*, 22(2): i-iv.
Human Rights Watch Prison Project. (2005). *Prisons in Africa*. Retrieved on January 19, 2005 from http://www.hrw.org/advocacyprisons/africa.htm
International Covenant on Civil and Political Rights. Available from untreaty.un.org/humanrightsconvs/Chapt_IV.../CovenantCivPo.pdf. Accessed on January 15, 2005.
Judicial Inspectorate of Prisons. (2006). *Annual Report 2005/2006: Prisoners and prisons*. Office of the Inspecting Judge, Cape Town.
Judicial Inspectorate of Prisons. Annual Report 2007/2008: *Prisoners and Prisons*. Office of the Inspecting Judge, Cape Town.
Judicial Inspectorate of Prisons. Annual Report 2008/2009: *Prisoners and Prisons*. Office of the Inspecting Judge, Cape Town.
Judicial Inspectorate of Prisons. Annual Report 2009/2010: *Prisoners and Prisons*. Office of the Inspecting Judge, Cape Town.
Kirchhoff, G.F. (2005): Mediation in Criminal Justice: Theoretical Considerations and Practical Consequences. In: Vetere. E. and Pedro, D. (ERds.) Victims of Crime and Abuse of Power. Festschrift in honour of Irene Melup. Bangkok (UN Congress on Crime Prevention and Criminal Justice.) 2005.:264-285.
Lewis, S. (1997). *Juvenile diversion: Keeping children out of prison*. Unpublished MA dissertation, Rhodes University, Grahamstown.
Maddi, S.R. (1980). *Personality theories: A comparative analysis*. Homewood, IL: Dorsey.
Marcia, J.E. (1967). Ego identity status: Relationship to change in self-esteem "general maladjustment" and authoritarianism. *Journal of Personality, 35*, 118-133.
Marcia, J.E. (1975). Identity six years after: A follow-up study. *Journal of Youth and Adolescence, 5*(2), 145-160.
McLachlan, F. (1986). *Children in prison*. A study commissioned by Defence International, Institute of Criminology, University of Cape Town.
Muntingh, L. (2001a). *The case of offender reintegration*. Retrieved on December 18, 2003 from http://www.iss.co.za/Pubs/Monographs/52/Chap4.html
Ochse, R.A., & Plug, C. (1986). Cross-cultural investigation of the validity of Erikson's theory of personality development. *Journal of Personality and Social Psychology, 50*(6), 1240-1252.
Odongo, G. & Gallinetti, J. (2005). *The treatment of children in South African prisons: A report on the applicable domestic and international minimum*

standards. Cape Town: Civil Society Initiative.

Peacock, R. (1989). *Die manlike swart straatkind: 'n Verkennende psigokriminologiese ondersoek*. Ongepubliseerde MA-verhandeling, Universiteit van Pretoria.

Peacock, R (2006). *Identity development of the incarcerated adolescent: A comparative analysis.* Unpublished doctoral thesis, University of Pretoria.

Peacock, R. & Theron, A. (2007). Identity development of the incarcerated adolescent with particular reference to prison gang membership. *Acta Criminologica*, 20(3):61-74.

Peacock, R. (2009). Victimisation of adolescents in South African prisons. In O. Hageman; P. Schafer & S. Schmidt (eds.). *Victimology, victim assistance and criminal justice: Perspectives shared by international experts at the Inter-University Centre of Dubrovnik.* Monchengladbach/Kiel: Niederrhein University of Applied Sciences & Kiel University.

Reiman, J. (2004). *The rich get richer and the poor get prison: Ideology, class and criminal justice.* Boston: Pearson.

Robinson, D., Leo, N., Provic, P., & Barber, S.C. (2003). *Potential role of head lice, Pediculus humanus capitis as vectors of Rickettsia prowazeki.* Retrieved on December 5, 2004 from http:www.brightminds.uq.edu.au/ teachers/ resources /downloads/RobinsonEEAIPaper.pdf

Rosnow R.L., & Rosenthal, R. (1996). *Beginning behavior research: A conceptual primer*. Englewood Cliffs, NJ: Prentice Hall.

Santrock, J.W. (1986). *Life-span development*. Dubuque: Wm.C. Brown.

Sarkin, J (ed.). (2008). *Human rights in African prisons*. Cape Town: HSRC Press.

Skelton, A. (2009). *Acta Criminologica: The Southern African journal of Criminology,* 22(1): i-iv.

Sloth-Nielsen, J. (1998). *Children in prison in South Africa: A situational analysis*. Community Law Centre, University of the Western Cape.

South African Law Commission. (1997). *Juvenile justice.* South African Law Commission Issue, Paper 9, Project 106.

Steinberg, J. (2005). *Prison overcrowding and the constitutional right to adequate accommodation in South Africa.* Johannesburg: Centre for the Study of Violence and Reconciliation.

Terre Blanche, M., & Durrheim, K. (1999). *Research in practice: Applied methods for the social sciences*. Cape Town: University of Cape Town Press.

Thom, D.P. (1988). *n Psigologiese ontleding en vergelyking van die blanke en swart adolessent ten opsigte van ouer-kindverhoudings, portuurverhoudings, identiteitsontwikkeling en die vorming van n beroepsidentiteit*. Ongepubliseerde doktorale proefskrif, Universiteit van Suid-Afrika, Pretoria

Thom, D.P., & Coetzee, C.H. (2004). Identity development of South African adolescents in a democratic society. *Society in Transition, 35*(1), 183-192.

Tonry, M., & Petersilia, J. (1999). *Prisons: A review of research*. Chicago: University of Chicago Press.

United Nations Convention on the Rights of the Child (1989). Retrieved on December 10, 2005 from http://www.unhr.ch/html/menu3/b/kzcr.htm

United Nations Minimum Rules for the Administration of Juvenile Justice

(Beijing Rules). (1985). Retrieved on November 28, 2004 from http://www.unhcr.ch/html/ menu3/b/h_comp48htm

United Nations Rules for the Protection of Juveniles deprived of their Liberty. (1990). Retrieved on November 24, 2004 from http://www.unhcr.ch/html/ menu3/b/h_comp37.htm

White Paper on Corrections in South Africa. (2005). Pretoria: Government Printer.

Sexual Victimization

Rape in America: A Fifteen Year Followup

By

Dean G. Kilpatrick*, Ph.D. and
Heidi S. Resnick[1], Ph.D.

Rape is a devastating crime, and having accurate information about it is important for several reasons. First, having accurate information about the magnitude of America's rape problem, the key characteristics of rape cases, the extent to which cases are reported to law enforcement, and the impact of rapes on victims' lives is needed for public policy and program planning purposes. Public policy and funding decisions are frequently made based on available information, so better information can improve decisions about legislation, policies, and funding for criminal justice system (CJS) and victim assistance programs and services. Second, having accurate information about what rape is really like and how rape victims actually behave has the potential to address inaccurate stereotypes that contribute to victim blame and poor outcomes in the CJS process. Third, having good information about the proportion of rape cases that go unreported is important because it is a reflection of how well a society and its CJS is doing in creating an environment that encourages rape victims to report.

In the United States, the National Crime Victimization Survey (NCVS) has been described as the nation's primary source of annual information about the frequency, characteristics, and consequences of criminal victimization (Rand, 2009). The primary goal of the NCVS is to provide population estimates of the number of major crimes that occur each year among persons age 12 and older in the U.S. The NCVS measures rape, but, as noted by the National Research Council (2008) in a recent report on the NCVS, there have been major criticisms of the methods used by the NCVS to measure rape. These criticisms have emerged primarily because rape prevalence and incidence estimates derived from independent research studies using different scientific methods are virtually always larger than those obtained by the NCVS (e.g., Cook et al, 2011; Kilpatrick et al, 1992; Kilpatrick et al, 2007; Tjaden & Thoennes, 2006). There are numerous variables that impact measurement of rape in victimization surveys

---

1 Department of Psychiatry & Behavioral Sciences, Medical University of South Carolina, Charleston, SC

(e.g., Cantor & Lynch, 2000; Kilpatrick, 2004; Kilpatrick & McCauley, 2009), but one of the key limitations of the NCVS is the method used to screen for rape cases. As described elsewhere (Kilpatrick, 2004), an important component in victimization surveys is the quality of screening questions that cue respondents' memory about potential crimes they may have experienced. Not only should these questions cue memory, but they should also capture the elements of the crime that is the focus of the survey.

A study by Fisher and colleagues (Fisher, Cullen & Turner, 2000; Fisher, 2009) clearly demonstrated that major problems exist with the screening approach used in the NCVS. The study design involved conducting victimization surveys with two large national probability samples of U.S. female college students who were interviewed about rape and other sexual assaults they had experienced since the beginning of the school year. One sample was interviewed using a screening procedure and questions similar to those used in the NCVS. The second sample used a screening procedure and questions similar to those used in the National Women's Study (NWS) (Kilpatrick, Edmunds, & Seymour, 1992; Resnick et al, 1993) and the National Violence Against Women Survey (NVAWS; Tjaden & Thoennes, 2006). The latter screening procedure and questions were considerably more detailed and behaviorally specific than those used in the NCVS. All other methodological aspects of the two surveys were identical, so any differences in rape prevalence were attributable to the difference in screening approach and questions. Fisher et al, (2000) initially reported that the screening approach and questions based on the NWS and NVAWS yielded a rape prevalence estimate that was 11 times higher than the estimate obtained using the NCVS approach (1.7% vs 0.16%). A recent paper (Fisher, 2009) reported the difference between the two methods to be lower when a two-stage process was used in which followup questions gathered information about case characteristics, and these data were used to remove cases detected by screening questions but that did not include all elements of the crime. Fisher (2009) reported that many of the rape cases detected by the stage 1 screening questions were reclassified as other types of sexual assault based on followup information collected in the second stage, but she still found that the NWS/NVAWS approach yielded a higher prevalence even after making these adjustments. A recent paper by Cook and colleagues (2011) criticized the specific two stage process used by Fisher and argued that many legitimate rape cases may have been excluded by this two stage process.

However, these and virtually all other experts agree that the screening approach and questions used in the NCVS are not sensitive and miss far too many rape cases to enable the NCVS to be capable of providing a valid measure of the annual incidence of rape in the

U.S. Accordingly, because the NCVS dramatically underestimates the number of rape cases that occur each year, it cannot provide accurate data about potential changes in rape prevalence, or rape characteristics that may be occurring over time. Likewise, it cannot provide accurate information about potential changes in the proportion of women who report rapes to police because if consistently fails to detect most rape cases. The NCVS is not designed to detect cases of rape that occur outside of a one year measurement period, so it cannot tell us how many women have ever been raped. Finally, the NCVS does not include measures of the mental health impact of crime, so it tells us nothing about the extent to which rape increases risk of posttraumatic stress disorder (PTSD) and related mental health problems. Therefore, if we are interested in information about the magnitude, nature, or consequences of America's rape problem over time, the NCVS cannot provide it, and we must rely on studies conducted by independent researchers.

Our research group conducted two research projects that have the capacity to address several important questions that the NCVS cannot answer. These two projects were conducted 15 years apart and used virtually identical methodology, so they have the ability to provide estimates of the extent to which there have been changes over that period in the magnitude, nature, and consequences of rape in America. The methodology of these projects will be described in detail subsequently, but both projects involved conducting victimization surveys with national probability samples of adult women (age 18 and older) from telephone households who were asked about rape experiences using the type of screening question methodology that was demonstrated by Fisher (2009) to be superior to that used in the NCVS. In addition to being asked about recent cases of rape, women were also asked about rapes they had experienced at any time during their lives. Descriptive information was obtained about the characteristics of rape cases including whether the case was reported to police, and information was gathered about major mental health problems including PTSD and major depression (MD).

The first project, the National Women's Study (NWS), was funded by the National Institute on Drug Abuse and included three assessment waves beginning in 1989 and concluding in 1991. The NWS used random digit dialing telephone survey methodology to locate and interview a national household probability sample of 4008 adult women. The initial assessment obtained information about whether respondents had ever been forcibly raped at any time during their life prior to the interview. At one and two year follow up assessments, women were asked about forcible rapes they experienced in the one year periods between *waves 1and 2 and waves 2 and 3*. The NWS generated numerous peer-reviewed scientific publications (e.g.

Cougle, Resnick, & Kilpatrick, 2009; Kilpatrick, et. al.,1997; Resnick et. al.,1993), but a special document, Rape in America: A Report to the Nation (Kilpatrick et. al.,1992), was prepared focusing specifically on the rape data from the NWS. As described in this report, the lifetime prevalence of forcible rape was .1265, indicating that more than one out of eight adult women in the U.S. disclosed having ever been raped. The past year prevalence of forcible rape was .0071, indicating that approximately 71 of every 1000 adult women in the U.S. were forcibly raped during a one year period. Of these forcible rape cases, only 14.6% were reported to police. In summary, the NWS found that the burden of rape for women in America was substantial, with approximately one woman in eight having been forcibly raped at some point in her life, approximately 683,000 of whom were forcibly raped during the past year, and only 14.6% of all forcible rape cases were reported to police.

Since the NWS was conducted, there has been increased appreciation that force or threat of force is not the only tactic used by rapists. Two additional rape tactics that have received increased attention involve what we refer to as drug or alcohol-facilitated rape (DAFR) and incapacitated rape (IR) (Kilpatrick et al, 2007; Zinzow et al, 2010). Briefly described, DAFR involves rape that occurs after a perpetrator knowingly renders the victims unconscious via administration of alcohol or drugs and then engages in a sex act with them. Under the U.S. Federal Criminal Code (U.S.C. Title 18, Part 1, Chapter 109-A – Sexual Abuse), the term "sex act" is defined as any type of sexual penetration of the anal or genital opening; contact between the mouth and the penis, vulva, or anus; or penetration of the anal or genital opening by a hand, finger, or any object. In contrast, IR is defined as a rape involving a perpetrator who engages in a sex act with a person who has voluntarily consumed a sufficient amount of alcohol or drugs to render them either unconscious, incapable of appraising the nature of the conduct, or physically incapable of declining participation in or communicating unwillingness to engage in a sex act as defined above. Under the U.S. Federal Criminal Code as well as the laws of virtually all 50 U.S. states, DAFR and IR are felony crimes that carry major penalties of 10 years incarceration or more upon conviction. Previous studies including the NWS, the NVAWS, and the NCVS have not measured DAFR and IR (Kilpatrick & McCauley, 2009), and it is impossible to determine the full burden of rape upon women in the U.S. without assessing these types of rape.

In this paper, we will first present data from the NWS-R documenting the lifetime and past year prevalence of FR, DAFR, and IR among adult women in the U.S. Second, we will provide descriptive information and comparisons of forcible rape cases within

the NWS and NWS-R studies. Third, we will compare information on FR prevalence and reporting of FR cases to police among participants in the NWS and NWS-R to determine if there has been a significant change in FR prevalence or reporting of FR cases to police in the 15 years between the two studies. Finally, we will provide information on the extent to which FR increases risk of PTSD and major depression within the NWS-R study.
Method

Participants and Procedure

National Women's Study (NWS): The NWS was a longitudinal telephone survey involving a national household probability sample of 4,008 women. Among these women, 2,008 were a national household probability sample of U.S. adults (age 18 and older), and 2,000 were an oversample of women aged 18 to 34 years, the age at which victimization risk appears greatest. Sample weights adjusting for age and race were used in order for the sample to reflect the demographics of the US female population. Mean age for the weighted sample was 44.9 years (SD = 18.4 years). Most participants were White, non-Hispanic (80.2%), followed by Black, non-Hispanic (11%), Hispanic (5.4%), Native American, non-Hispanic (1.7%), or Asian, non-Hispanic (1.1%). Initial interviews (Wave 1) were conducted in 1989, with two follow-up assessment interviews conducted one and two years later. Multistage geographic sampling was used. Stratified samples of counties within areas defined as central city, standard metropolitan statistical area (SMSA), and non-SMSA within the four major regions of the country were generated as primary sampling units followed by systematic selection of residential telephone exchanges within sampling units and use of random digit dialing to identify households within strata. The woman in the household with the most recent birthday was selected for interview. Verbal assent was given by participants. Consent and completion rate was 85.2%. Sampling, interviewing, and monitoring procedures were conducted by the survey research firm of Schulman, Ronca, and Bucuvalas, Inc. (SRBI). Women were interviewed using a computer-assisted telephone interviewing (CATI) system. Experienced female interviewers conducted study assessments. Interviews lasted 35 minutes on average and included questions about a range of crime victimization experiences including forcible rape as well as mental health and behavioral functioning.

National Women's Study-Replication (NWS-R): A total of 3,001 women were interviewed from two U.S. national probability household samples: a) a sample of 1,998 women aged 18 to 34 and b) a sample of 998 women aged 35 and older, and 5 women who refused to provide their age. The combined data from the two samples were weighted by age and race using U.S. Census estimates. The mean weighted age for the entire sample was 46.58 (SD = 17.87). Most of the participants were White (76%), followed by Black (15%), Hispanic (5%), and Asian or Native American (4%). Random-digit-dial (RDD) methodology was used to survey a geographically stratified sample, with sample allocation proportionate to population distribution. Verbal informed consent was obtained. The cooperation rate was 65.3%. All interviews were conducted between January 23 and June 26, 2006. As with the NWS, sampling and interviewing procedures were conducted by SRBI and interviews were conducted using CATI procedures. If more than one eligible woman was present in a household, the woman with most recent birthday was selected for participation. Completed interviews averaged 20 minutes.

Measures

Rape Experiences

NWS:
Rape was defined as nonconsensual assault using force or threat of force involving some type of sexual penetration of the victim's vagina, rectum, or mouth. Detailed behaviorally specific questions to assess rape are described elsewhere (Resnick et al., 1993; Kilpatrick et al., 1997) and content is included within questions 1 through 4 described below in reference to the NWS-R methodology. At Wave 1, information was gathered about up to three rape incidents: a first, most recent, and worst incident if a woman reported a third incident that was perceived as being more severe or worse than a first/only or most recent incident.

NWS-R: Information was gathered about up to two rape incidents: A most recent and, for women with multiple rapes, first incident of rape. Rape was defined as penetration of the victim's vagina, mouth or rectum without consent. Questions were closed-ended and behaviorally specific. Women were asked:

1. *Has a man or boy ever made you have sex by using force or threatening to harm you or someone close to you? Just so there is no mistake, by having sex, we mean putting a penis in your vagina.*
2. *Has anyone, male or female, ever made you have oral sex by force or threatening to harm you? So there is no mistake, by oral sex, we mean that a man or boy put his penis in your mouth or someone penetrated your vagina or anus with their mouth or tongue?*
3. *Has anyone ever made you have anal sex by force or threatening*

to harm you? By anal sex we mean putting their penis in your anus or rectum.

4. *Has anyone ever put fingers or objects in your vagina or anus against your will by using force or threatening to harm you?*
5. *Has anyone ever had sex with you when you didn't want to after you drank so much alcohol that you were very high, drunk, or passed out? By having sex, we mean that a man or boy put his penis in your vagina, anus, or your mouth?*
6. *Has anyone ever had sex with you when you didn't want to after they gave you, or you had taken enough drugs to make you very high, intoxicated, or passed out? By having sex we mean that a man or boy put his penis in your vagina, anus, or your mouth?*

Case Definitions:
Forcible rape: All cases identified within the NWS were forcible rape cases based on endorsement of one or more types of unwanted sexual penetration due to force or threat as defined in questions 1 through 4 above. In the NWS-R, following initial screening using the 6 questions described above, specific case characteristic information about most recent and/or first incidents were used to further determine classification. Cases that included types of unwanted sexual penetration as defined by questions 1 through 4 based on specific incident characteristics (e.g. vaginal, anal, or oral penetration, reported physical or verbal threat) were classified as forcible rape incidents.

Drug or alcohol facilitated or incapacitated rape (DAFR/IR) was only assessed in the NWS-R study. Cases were defined as DAFR/IR if the victim was intoxicated and incapacitated via voluntary or involuntary consumption of drugs and/or alcohol during an incident.
Rape Characteristics:

In both the NWS and NWS-R, rape incident characteristics were assessed for each of up to 3 (NWS) or up to 2 (NWS-R) incidents of rape that included age of occurrence, relationship to the assailant (defined as stranger if respondent said they had never seen the perpetrator before or if they said they did not know the perpetrator well), and reporting to police or other authorities.
Mental Health Functioning: Posttraumatic stress disorder (*PTSD*) was assessed with a modified version of the National Women's Study (NWS) PTSD Module (Kilpatrick, Resnick, Saunders, & Best, 1989), which assessed each *Diagnostic and Statistical Manual of Mental Disorders*, 4th edition (*DSM–IV*; American Psychiatric Association, 1994) criteria with and yielded *DSM–IV* diagnoses of PTSD lifetime and/or current within the previous 6 months (see Kilpatrick et al., 2000). The NWS-PTSD Module was validated in the *Diagnostic and Statistical Manual of Mental Disorders, Fourth Edition* (*DSM-IV*),

PTSD Field Trial against a well-established structured diagnostic interview administered by trained mental health professionals with an interrater κ coefficient of 0.85 for diagnosis of PTSD. Comparisons between the NWS-PTSD Module and Structured Clinical Interview for *DSM-IV* yielded κ coefficients of 0.71 and 0.77 for current and 0.77 for lifetime PTSD, respectively (Kilpatrick et al., 1988). Major depressive episode (*MDE)* was assessed using the NWS Depression Module, a structured interview that targets MDE criteria using a yes/no response format for each *DSM–IV* symptom for lifetime and current prevalence within the prior 6 months. This module has been used in previous studies of mental health correlates of interpersonal violence and terrorism (e.g., Galea et al., 2002; Saunders et al., 1999). Diagnoses of probably PTSD and MDE required report of functional impairment or significant distress related to symptoms. We have previously reported findings from the NWS-R related to overall prevalence of rape including forcible and/or DAFR/IR incidents as well as prevalence of PTSD, depression, and drug and alcohol use or abuse (Kilpatrick et al., 2007; Zinzow et al., 2010; McCauley et al., 2010). In addition, we have described patterns of reporting to police of a most recent or only rape incident of any type (e.g., forcible, DAFR/IR) across the NWS and NWS-R studies (Wolitzky-Taylor et al., 2011). However, we have not previously reported statistical comparisons of lifetime and past year prevalence of FR which is most pertinent in terms of evaluation of change in prevalence over the 15 year time period given the relatively recent recognition of drug or alcohol facilitation or incapacitation as types of rape. Related to this issue, only FR was assessed within the NWS restricting the most meaningful comparisons across studies to FR. Similarly, we have not previously reported comparisons of the percentages of all *FR* incidents that are reported to police across the two studies. These comparisons provide an evaluation of whether FR prevalence and/or reporting of FR have increased, decreased, or remained unchanged across the two studies conducted 15 years apart.

Data Analysis

Prevalence of multiple types of rape (forcible, DAFR/IR) are presented based on the NWS-R study. The remaining analyses include comparison of prevalence of FR only across the NWS Wave 1 (baseline assessment) and NWS-R studies, and presentation of descriptive characteristics of all FR cases across the two studies including age of occurrence, relationship to assailant, and reporting of incidents to police. Two-tailed comparisons of proportions were conducted based on the prevalence within the two independent samples for lifetime and past year FR and percentage of all FR cases reported to police, yielding z-ratios (Lowry, 2011) for the estimate of significant differences. Logistic regression analysis of risk of PTSD and MD as a function of FR history within the NWS-R sample is also described.

Results

Rape Prevalence

Lifetime prevalence of any type of rape within the NWS-R general population sample was 18.0%, corresponding to an estimated 20.2 million women having experienced at least one FR(16.1%) and/or DAFR or IR (5.0%) (Kilpatrick et al., 2007). As previously reported, IR in which voluntary use of drugs or alcohol leads to inability to consent, resist or stop an assault (2.8%) was more prevalent than DAFR (2.3%) and alcohol was the substance most commonly involved in these rapes. Estimated annual prevalence of rape of any type was .94% with an estimated population prevalence of 1.1 million (Kilpatrick et al., 2007). Estimated annual prevalence was .74% and .42% for FR and DAFR/IR type rapes, respectively.

Prevalence of lifetime and past year FR as well as corresponding population estimates within the NWS and NWS-R is presented in Table 1.

Table 1. Comparison of Forcible Rape Prevalence from the NWS and NWS-R Studies

Sample	Lifetime Prevalence	Lifetime Population Estimate	Estimated Annual Prevalence	Past Year Population Estimate	Population of U.S. Adult Women (Year)
NWS (4,008)	12.6%	12.1 million	.71%	683,000	96,056,000 (1989)
NWS-R (3,001)	16.1%	18.0 million	.74%	829,000	112,068,000 (2005)

Z ratio comparisons were conducted to examine differences in lifetime and past year prevalence of rape over time comparing the NWS and NWS-R samples. Lifetime prevalence of FR was significantly higher within the NWS-R sample compared to the NWS sample as indicated by a z-ratio related to differences in proportion of positive cases within the two samples of 4.098, $p < .0005$. Past year prevalence of forcible rape did not differ across the two samples, $z = .087$, $p > .05$.

Case Characteristics

There were a total of 714 FR cases reported by 507 women within the NWS sample at Wave 1 assessment. Within the NWS-R sample, there were a total of 708 FR cases reported by 483 women who had experienced at least one or more forcible rapes. Data regarding age at time of rape within the NWS indicated that 29.3% of FR cases occurred prior to age 11; 32.3% occurred between the ages of 11 to 17; 35.4% occurred at age 18 or older; and 3.0% did not have an age specified by participants. Within the NWS-R, 23.0% of FR cases occurred prior to age 11; 29.0% occurred between ages 11 to 17; 44.6% occurred at age 18 or older; and 3.2% did not have an age specified by participants. Proportion of cases occurring prior to age 11 was significantly greater within the NWS as compared to the NWS-R sample, $z = 2.68$, $p < .05$. Proportion of cases occurring at age 18 or older was significantly greater in the NWS-R as compared to the NWS sample, $z = 3.54$, $p < .0005$.

Results related to perpetrator relationship within the NWS indicated that 22.8% of FR cases were classified as strangers to the victim; 8.5% were husbands/ex-husbands; 10.2% were boyfriends/ex-boyfriends; 10.6% were fathers/step-fathers; 16.0% were other relatives; 26.9% were other non-relatives; and 2.5% were not specified. Within the NWS-R, 26.4% of FR cases were classified as strangers; 9.9% were husbands/ex-husbands; 13.3% were boyfriends/ex-boyfriends; 8.1% were fathers/step-fathers; 15.4% were other relatives; 23.7% were other non-relatives; 2.8% were specified as "other"; and 0.8% of cases were not specified. With regard to percentage of all FR cases reported, only 14.6% of cases within the NWS and 17.7% of all cases within the NWS-R were reported to police or other authorities. The test of differences in proportions of reported cases indicated no significant difference across the two samples in percentage of all cases reported to police, $z = 1.59$, $p > .05$.

Mental Health Correlates

Prevalence of lifetime and current PTSD within the NWS-R sample was 16.8% and 8.8%, respectively. History of FR compared to no FR history was associated with increased risk of both lifetime PTSD (39.5% vs.12.5%), odds ratio = 4.56, 95% CI = [3.67, 5.67] and current PTSD (24.0% vs. 5.9%), odds ratio = 4.99, 95% CI = [3.83, 6.52]. Prevalence of lifetime and current MD within the NWS-R sample was 12.8% and 9.1% respectively. History of FR compared to no FR history was associated with increased risk of both lifetime MD (33.5% vs.8.8%), odds ratio = 5.25, 95% CI = [4.16, 6.64] and current MD (24.0% vs. 6.3%), odds ratio = 4.72, 95% CI = [3.62, 6.14]

Discussion

The most striking finding from the study was that there has been no decrease in burden of rape upon U.S. women in the period between the NWS and NWS-R. There was actually a significant increase in the proportion of U.S. adult women who had ever been forcibly raped from 12.6% to 16.1%. The estimated number of women in the U.S. who were ever forcibly raped increased from 12.1 million to 18.0 million. There was no significant change in the past year prevalence of FR (.71% vs .74%), but the estimated number of adult women forcibly raped each year increased from 683,000 to 829,000. When estimates of DAFR and IR from the NWS-R are added to FR estimates, projections are that almost one adult woman in five in the U.S. has been victim of some type of rape and that almost one out of one hundred adult women in the U.S. were raped in the year prior to the NWS-R assessment. When these estimates are projected to the population of U.S. adult women, an estimated 20.2 million women have been victims of some type of rape during their lives, and 1.1 million women were raped during the year prior to the NWS-R assessment.

These findings are in striking contrast to reports based on NCVS data suggesting that the rate of rape and sexual assault victimization decreased 56.9% from 2000 – 2009 (Truman & Rand, 2010). There are several reasons why the NCVS estimates differ from our NWS and NWS-R estimates including the previously discussed problems with the NCVS screening methodology and questions. Another reason is that the NCVS is focused primarily on attempting to measure the number of rape cases that occur each year and not on the number of women who are raped each year. Another reason is that the trend data from the NCVS are based on victimization rates primarily as opposed to actual number of cases of women affected. This is certainly reasonable to do because it corrects for changes in the population. However, victimization rates provide an inadequate and sometimes misleading picture under certain circumstances. For example, if the population is increasing and the victimization rate is unchanged, there will still be more cases of rape and more rape victims notwithstanding the fact that there has been no change in the victimization rate. The impact of an increased population of U.S. adult women from 96 million in 1989 to 112 million in 2005 on estimates of the number of U.S. women who were forcibly raped is illustrative. Although annual prevalence estimates of .71 and .74 were not significantly different, the increase in population resulted in an estimate that almost 150,000 more women were raped in 2005 than in 1989. This is important because victimization rates per se tell us little about the number of women who have been raped and who are likely to need services, and our findings suggest there are many more rape victims in the U.S. now than there were before as well as more women who were forcibly raped each year.

FR rape characteristics appeared to be similar across the two samples with the exception of age of occurrence. Within the NWS, there was a relatively increased proportion of all rape cases occurring prior to age 11 (29.3% vs. 23%), and within the NWS-R, there was a relatively greater proportion of all rape cases occurring at age 18 or older (35.4% vs. 44.6%). Regardless, more than one in five rape cases within the NWS-R occurred prior to age 11, and similar percentages of cases (32.3% and 29%) within the NWS and NWS-R occurred between ages 11 to 17. These findings indicate that rape is still a tragedy of youth among a sample assessed 15 years after the original NWS. While screening questions used to assess FR were parallel across the two studies, it is possible that the additional screening questions asking about DAFR/IR types of incidents may have cued women to recognize additional FR types of incidents that also included use of drugs or alcohol during the incidents. This may possibly relate to overall differences in prevalence of FR histories as well. It may be that women were more likely to report incidents that involved significant drug or alcohol use and that also met criteria as FR because of the additional screening items. It is also possible that there has been an actual but small increase in the age of greatest vulnerability over this 15 year period.

Data regarding perpetrator's relationship to the FR victim appeared to be similar across the two studies with the majority of incidents having been committed by someone known to the victim. Similarly, almost 19% of all FR cases in the NWS sample and approximately 23% of those in the NWS-R sample were perpetrated by an intimate partner (husband or boyfriend), or ex-partner. These data are inconsistent with stereotypic views of rape as being perpetrated by strangers and have important implications for prevention and appropriate responses to rape. Acknowledgement that rapes most often are perpetrated by someone known to the victim, occur at young ages as well as during adulthood, and may occur following incapacitation due to alcohol or drug use can be used to combat stereotypes and to develop prevention strategies. In addition, such information may positively change public attitudes, attitudes of those who may respond to women's disclosures of rape, service providers, and victims themselves.

Reporting of FR cases to police has not increased significantly across the 15 year period between the two studies (14.6 % vs. 17.7%). These NWS and NWS-R estimates of non-reporting differ substantially from NCVS estimates that over half of all rapes and sexual assaults are reported to police (Truman & Rand, 2010). As previously reported

(Kilpatrick et al., 2007; Wolitzky-Taylor et al., 2011), common reasons for not reporting an incident include fear of reprisal by assailants, not wanting others to know and not wanting family members to know about an incident, concern that there is not enough proof, fear of the criminal justice system, and lack of knowledge about how to report. Clearly, as previously noted, statistics based only on reported cases are not representative of all rape cases given that they represent a small minority of incidents. It is important to develop strategies to reduce barriers to reporting of rape. Reporting rape incidents may increase the likelihood that victims will receive needed services and the possibility that crimes may be investigated and perpetrators apprehended and dealt with in the criminal justice system in ways that might reduce crime and increase safety for individuals and society.

The mental health impact of rape is substantial, which is another indicator of the burden of rape on women in the U.S. Our findings indicated increased odds of lifetime and current PTSD and depression of greater than 4 in all analyses in association with FR history. Among those with FR history, approximately one third have met lifetime criteria for MD at some time in their lives and 39.5% have met criteria for PTSD. Based on our data, one in four women with history of FR met criteria for each disorder within the year prior to the study. Given the fact that most incidents are not reported, it is critical that those who have these serious mental health problems have access to efficacious treatment strategies. Empirically supported approaches are available that include cognitive behavioral strategies (Foa et al., 2009) that include prolonged exposure (Foa et al., 2005) and cognitive processing therapy (Resick et al, 2002). In an effort to increase dissemination of treatment, Dr. Connie Best and colleagues at the National Crime Victims Center along with Dr. Resick and colleagues developed an on line training program for clinicians in the use of cognitive processing therapy (CPTWEB 2011).

Finally, it is critically important for the NCVS to update and upgrade its methodology for measuring all types of rape (see Kilpatrick, 2004), There is a real need for better data on rape to be collected each year so we will be able to examine accurate trend data on a year-to-year basis. It is unfortunate that the best data we have on rape is from studies such as the NWS and NWS-R conducted by independent researchers. The encouraging news is that the Bureau of Justice Statistics is commissioning a pilot study designed to provide information that can be used to improve the NCVS's measurement of rape.

References

Cantor, D., & Lynch, J.P. (2000). Self-report surveys as measures of crime and criminal victimization. *Measurement and Analysis of Crime and Justice, 4,* 85-138.

Cook, S.L., Gidycz, C.A., Koss, M.P., & Murphy, M. (2011). Emerging issues in the measurement of rape victimization. *Violence Against Women, 17,* 201-218.

Cougle, J.R., Resnick, H. & Kilpatrick, D.G. (2009). A prospective examination of PTSD symptoms as risk factors for subsequent exposure to potentially traumatic events among women. *Journal of Abnormal Psychology, 118,* 405-411.

CPT-web (2011). National Crime Victims Research and Treatment Center. Retrieved from https://cpt.musc.edu/index.

Fisher, B.S., Cullen, F.T., & Turner, M.G. (2000). *The Sexual victimization of college women*. National Institute of Justice, U.S. Department of Justice.

Fisher, (2009). The effects of survey question wording on rape estimates: Evidence from a quasi-experimental design. *Violence Against Women, 15,* 133-147.

Foa, E.B., Hembree, E.A., Cahill, S.P., Rauch, S.A., Riggs, D.S., Feeny, N.C., et al. (2005). Randomized trial of prolonged exposure for PTSD with and without cognitive restructuring: Outcome at academic and community clinics. *Journal of Consulting and Clinical Psychology, 73,* 953-964.

Foa, E.B., Keane, T.M., & Friedman, M.J. (2009). *Effective treatments for PTSD: Practice guidelines from the International Society for Traumatic Stress Studies.* New York: Guilford Press.

Kilpatrick, D.G. (2004). What is violence against women? Defining and measuring the problem. *Journal of Interpersonal Violence, 19,* 1209-1234.

Kilpatrick DG, Acierno R, Resnick HS, Saunders BE, Best CL. (1997). A two-year longitudinal analysis of the relationship between violent assault and alcohol and drug use in women. *Journal of Consulting and Clinical Psychology, 65,* 834-847.

Kilpatrick, D.G., Edmunds, C.N., & Seymour, A.K. (1992). *Rape in America: A report to the nation.* Arlington, VA: National Victim Center & Medical University of South Carolina.

Kilpatrick & McCauley, (September, 2009). Understanding national rape statistics VAWnet: The National Online Resource Center on Violence Against Women www.vawnet.org

Kilpatrick D.G., Resnick, H.S., Ruggiero, K.J., Conoscenti, L.M. & McCauley, J. (2007). *Drug- facilitated, incapacitated, and forcible rape: A national study.* Final Report submitted June, 2007 to the National Institutes of Justice, Grant No. 2005-WG-BX-0006.

Kilpatrick D, Ruggiero KJ, Acierno R, Saunders BE, Resnick HS, Best CL. (2003). Violence and risk of PTSD, major depression, substance abuse/dependence, and comorbidity: results from the National Survey of Adolescents. *Journal of Consulting and Clinical Psychology, 71,* 692–700.

Lowry, R. (2011). Significance of the difference between two independent proportions, *VassarStats: Web Site for Statistical Computation.* Retrieved from http://faculty.vassar.edu/lowry/VassarStats.html.

McCauley, J.L., Ruggiero, K.J., Resnick, H.S., & Kilpatrick, D.G. (2010). Incapacitated, forcible, and drug/alcohol-facilitated rape in relation to binge drinking, marijuana use, and illicit drug use: A national survey. *Journal of Traumatic Stress*, 23, 132-140.

National Research Council (2008). *Surveying victims: Options for conducting the National Crime Victimization Survey.* Panel to Review the Programs of the Bureau of Justice Statistics. R. Groves, & D.L. Cork (Eds.), Committee on National Statistics and Committee on Law and Justice, Division of Behavioral and Social Sciences and Education. Washington, DC: The National Academies Press.

Rand, M.R. (2009). *Criminal victimization, 2008* (NCJ 227777). Washington, DC: U.S. Department of Justice, Bureau of Justice Statistics.

Resick, P.A., Nishith, P., Weaver, T.L., Astin, M.C., & Feuer, C.A. (2002). A comparison of cognitive-processing therapy with prolonged exposure and a waiting condition for the treatment of chronic posttraumatic stress disorder in female rape victims. *Journal of Consulting and Clinical Psychology, 70*, 867-879.

Resnick, H.S., Kilpatrick, D.G., Dansky, B.S., Saunders, B.E., & Best, C.L. (1993). Prevalence of civilian trauma and PTSD in a representative national sample of women. *Journal of Consulting & Clinical Psychology, 61*, 984-991.

Tjaden, P. & Thoennes, N. (2006). *Extent, nature, and consequences of rape victimization: Findings from the National Violence Against Women Survey.* US Dept of Justice, National Institute of Justice.

Truman, J. L., & Rand, M. R. (2010). *Criminal victimization, 2009.* Washington, D.C.: U.S. Department of Justice.

Wolitzky-Taylor, K.B., Resnick, H.S., McCauley, J.L., Amstadter, A.B., Kilpatrick, D.G., & Ruggiero, K.J. (2011). Is reporting of rape on the rise? A comparison of women with reported versus unreported rape experiences in the National Women's Study-replication. *Journal of Interpersonal Violence, 26*, 807-832.

Zinzow H, Resnick HS, Amstadter AB, McCauley JL, Ruggiero KJ & Kilpatrick DG. (2010). Drug- or alcohol-facilitated, incapacitated, and forcible rape in relation to mental health among a national sample of women. *Journal of Interpersonal Violence*, 25, 2217-2236.

Author Note

This research was supported by National Institute of Justice (NIJ) Grant #2005-WG-BX-0006 entitled Drug-Facilitated, Incapacitated, and Forcible Rape: A National Study (PI: Dean G. Kilpatrick, Ph.D.). Views expressed in this article do not necessarily represent those of NIJ.

We gratefully acknowledge the contributions of our co-investigator Dr. Kenneth Ruggiero and other co-authors of the final report (Kilpatrick, Resnick, Ruggiero, Conoscenti, and McCauley, 2007) for their contributions to the project.

Correspondence concerning this article should be addressed to: Dean Kilpatrick, National Crime Victims Research and Treatment Center, 67 President Street, MSC 861, Medical University of South Carolina, kilpatdg@musc.edu

Sexual Harassment in the University and in the Army in Israel

By

Sarah Ben-David, Inna Levy and Boaz M. Ben-David

1. Introduction

There are few characteristics that make a subject worth of academic discussion or academic research. The main characteristics include novelty, frequency, and severity of consequences. It is safe to say that sexual harassment embodies all of these characteristics, but one. The novelty isn't there. Sadly, sexually harassing behaviors are not new at all and can be found throughout history (Aaron, 1993), although, the term "sexual harassment" is relatively new, and the awareness to sexually harassing behaviors roused only in the late 70s of last century (Rosen and Martin, 1998).

1.1 Prevalence of sexual harassment

Despite of relatively high public awareness of sexual harassment, only 35%-45% of victims file official complaint (Adams-Roy and Barling, 1998; Gruber, 1990). Still, research shows that the majority of women (69% -90%) experience some form of sexual harassment at work (Baugh, 1997; Gruber, 1990; O'Hare and O'Donohue, 1998). Similarly, most of female students (60%-89%) (Mazer and Percival, 1989; Vaux, 1993) and female soldiers (63%-75%) (Bastin, Lancaster and Reyst, 1995; Firestone and Harris, 1994; Martin, 1990) experience some kind of sexual harassment. Unsurprisingly, minor cases of sexual harassment, like "sexual compliments and insinuation" and "unwanted sexual proposal", are more common than severe cases that include sexual assault (Gruber, 1990; O'Hare and O'Donohue, 1998).

1.2 Consequences of sexual harassment

Victims of sexual harassment suffer severe psychological, physiological and social negative consequences. Most of sexual harassing behaviors, and especially at the beginning stage, are vague and subtle. Therefore victims of sexual harassment, usually, are not sure that they understood and interpreted the situation correctly. Consequently victims feel confused, in doubt and blame themselves (Charney and Russel, 1994). They also suffer from wide range of psychological and physical consequences, including stress, anxiety, anger out-bursts, crying, insomnia, weight loss and digestion problems (Loy and Stewart, 1984). Negative consequences differ according to the severity of harassment. Some types of sexual harassment can induce post traumatic symptoms similar to those that combat trauma induces (Wolfe, Sharkansky, Read, Dawson, Martin, and Ouimette, 1998).

Sexual harassment invades one's personal and physical space (Wilson, 2000), and therefore creates hostile working environment (Charney and Russel, 1994). When the circle of people who are aware of the harassment becomes wider, when more and more people witness the harassment, victims begin to experience negative social reaction and blame attribution as well (Martin and Guadagno, 1999). Thus, sexual harassment can cause problems in victim's private life and effects victims' effectiveness at work (Pryor, 1995).

1.3 Sexual harassment types

As this review shows, different types of sexual harassment are characterized by different incidents rates and different consequences. Till (1980) distinguishes between five types of sexual harassment: gender harassment, seductive behavior, sexual bribery, sexual coercion and sexual imposition. Gender harassment refers to verbal and sexist harassing behaviors like inappropriate jokes and compliments. Seductive behaviors include sexual and romantic unwanted proposals. This category differs from sexual bribery and sexual coercion by the absence of promises to reward for sexual compliance and threats to revenge in case of refusal (accordingly). Sexual imposition includes behaviors that are considered as sexual abuse, sexual coercion and sexual assault.

1.4 Theories explaining sexual harassment

There are few theoretical arguments that try to explain sexual harassment (O'Hare, and O'Donohue, 1998). One of the arguments presents biological factor and states that men are more aggressive than women and have stronger sex drives. As a result men behave in sexually aggressive manner in different situations, including work settings. While some women find men's behavior unwanted and/ or offensive, men have no intention to harass the individuals they pursue. Thus according to this natural/ biological theory in most cases sexual harassment is a result of normal courtship (Tangri, Burt and Johnson, 1982).

Another explanation of sexual harassment states that sexual harassment can be explained only by the interaction between personality traits and organizational factors (Pryor, LaVite and Stoller, 1993). Pryor, LaVite and Stoller (1993) argue that there are people that have a tendency to become sexual harassers. These people usually are characterized by cognitive schemes that bind between sexuality and social superiority. Yet, these people may become sexual harassers only if situational factors allow it.

This situational approach is a subcategory of a wider organizational approach. According to the organizational approach sexual harassment is facilitated by organizational characteristics like: power differences, hierarchical structures and by the organizational climate (Tangri et al., 1982). The special position of authority creates the opportunity to abuse one's organizational power for purposes of sexual gratification. Though sexual gratification is not the only reason for sexual harassment in organization. Sexual harassment can be used as means of intimidation and control.

According to the organizational model not only power differences contribute to the occurrence of sexual harassment. Other contributing organizational characteristics include factors such as the ratio of males to females in the work place, occupational norms, definitions of duties attached to the job, career alternatives, and availability of grievance procedures. The organizational model emphasizes the contribution of elements such as work spaces privacy, dress codes, visibility of ranks and sings of seniority, job requirements like long working hours, business trips and etc. (O'Hare, and O'Donohue, 1998).

The socio-cultural model refers to the societal context in which sexual harassment occurs. This model addresses gender differentiation in the socialization process. While women are taught to be passive, to be obedient, to avoid conflict and to be sexually attractive, men are taught to be aggressive and assertive (Tangri et al. 1982). These differences in patterns of socialization preserve men's dominance over women. They also allow men to justify sexually aggressive behavior and cause women to blame themselves (Vaux, 1993). Thus, sexual harassment is both a manifestation of general male dominance (Farley, 1978; MacKinnon, 1979) and a mechanism for maintaining dominance over women, occupationally and economically, by limiting their growth or by intimidating them (Tangri et al. 1982).

The sex-role spillover model (Gutek and Morasch, 1982) focuses on the skewed sex ratio in favor of men. According to this model in this kind of environment sex roles become more predominant feature than work roles, thus facilitating sexual harassment. Women's singularity and distinctiveness makes their gender roles much more salient (O'Hare, and O'Donohue, 1998). Also, in organizations with sex ratios skewed in favor of men, like army, women tend to be employed in nontraditional jobs, which make women to stand out. Accordingly, Gutek and Morasch (1982) found that women, who were employed in nontraditional jobs, experienced more sexual harassment behavior and more negative consequences from sexual harassment than the average working woman.

Finally, the integrative model assumes that sexual harassment is too complex a phenomenon to be explained by one single factor, thus, it can be explained only by a combination of personal, organizational and sociocultural factors (O'Hare, and O'Donohue, 1998). The main idea is that sexual harassment happens when four main factors co-exists. These factors are: 1. Motivation on behalf of the harasser (e.g., sexual desire); 2. Lack of internal inhibitions against harassment (e.g., lack of viewing sexual harassment as illegal or immoral or/ and victim empathy); 3. Absence of external inhibitions against sexual harassment (e.g., lack of explicit grievance procedures and history of deficient actions in cases of sexual harassment); and 4. Overcoming victim resistance (e.g., the ability of the harasser to manipulate the victim so that she will not recognize and stop precipitating behavior to harassment) (O'Hare, and O'Donohue, 1998).

1.5 Goals and research questions

This article presents two studies on sexual harassment in Israel. The first study was conducted at the Tel-Aviv University and referred to female students. The second study was conducted at the Israeli Army and referred to female soldiers and female junior officers. The general goal of both studies was to examine the prevalence of different types of sexual harassment. In addition both studies examined situational characteristics and characteristics of victims and offenders.

2. Method

2.1 Participants

Tel-Aviv University sample:

The Tel-Aviv University sample included 625 female students. Most of them were in their twenties: 49% were at the 18-23 age range, 44% at 24-29 and just 6.5% were older than 30. 90.8% were single and 9.2% married. 90.5% were B.A. students, 8% were M.A.

students and 1.5% Ph.D. students. The majority of participants (89.3%) indentified themselves as secular. 7.9% defined themselves as traditional. Only 2.8% indicated that they were religious.

IDF (Israeli Defense Forces) sample (CSAWM, 2003):
The IDF sample included 1112 female soldiers that served mandatory service. The data regarding ages wasn't collected cause of IDF organizational interests. Though we know that the draft age is 18, that most of the soldiers are drafted in the first year after they finished high school. The mandatory service for women is two years. 22% of the participants were privates (0-8 month of army service). 46.4% were corporals (8-20 months), 27.1% were sergeants (20+ months) and 4.2% officers. Regarding participants' job definitions the distribution in the sample was as following: 13 % combat duties, 37% combat assistance duties and 50% home front duties (desk jobs). 1.4% finished less than 12 years of school. The majority (91%) had finished 12 years of school and got a matriculation certificate, and 0.8% had an academic education.

2.2 Measures

Tel-Aviv University research:
All participants were asked question regarding basic demographic data: age, academic degree and department, marital status and religiosity. Sexual harassment was measured through modified Sexual Harassment Questionnaire SEQ (Fitzgerald et al., 1988) in the Hebrew version (Avni 1990). The SEQ is a behaviorally based, 28-item survey. The respondents were asked to indicate whether each item on scale happened "never" (0), "once" (1) to "more than one" (2). The SEQ includes five sub-scales: gender sexual harassment, seductive behavior, sexual bribery, sexual coercion and sexual imposition. The study asked for sexual harassment by male faculty members' and for sexual harassment by male students. The data collected trough SEQ are considered to be indirect measure of sexual harassment prevalence (indirect SEQ measure of sexual harassment).
In addition every participant was asked directly if she was sexual harassed (direct measure of sexual harassment). If that was confirmed, participants were asked whether or not she reported the harassment; and what kind of treatment she thinks the complaint on sexual harassment will receive.

IDF (Israeli Defense Forces) research (CSAWM, 2003):
All participants were asked basic question regarding rank, army unit and the characteristics of work environment such as men to women

ratio and etc.. Sexual harassment was also measured through modified SEQ (Sexual Harassment Questionnaire) (Fitzgerald et al., 1988) in the Hebrew version (Avni 1990). The study asked for sexual harassment by commanding officer(s) and for sexual harassment by male soldier(s).
This research also made the distinction between indirect (SEQ) and direct measure of sexual harassment ("Have you ever been sexual harassed during your military service?"). Those respondents that gave positive answer on direct question were asked whether they reported the case, and if they didn't report they were asked "why?"

2.3 Procedures

Tel-Aviv University research:
The data was collected by Tel-Aviv University student association volunteers. They distributed questionnaires during first or last 20-30 minutes of lectures. Before the distribution the volunteers read the instructions and stated that the participation in this research is anonymous and voluntary.
IDF (Israeli Defense Forces) research:
The questionnaires were send by military mail system to all combat female soldiers and to a random sample of female combat assistances and home front clerks. The envelopes with the questionnaire included unmarked envelops with the research team returning address. This way, the participants were able to send back the questionnaire s after they answered under conditions of anonymity. The return rate was 41%.

3. Results and Discussion

3.1 Tel-Aviv University
The comparison between different faculties in prevalence of sexual harassment shows that female students from social science department reported the highest rates of sexual harassment (28% by students, 27% by academic staff). The lowest rates of sexual harassment cases were reported by students from medical sciences (10% by students, 9% by academic staff), with other departments in between.

The examination of differences between different types of sexual harassment shows that academic staff members and students are characterized by different pasterns of harassment. Rates of gender harassment (84% by academic staff, 67% by students) and seductive behaviors (67% by academic staff, 21% by students) lead. In clear distance are sexual assaults, sexual coercion and sexual bribery (ranking last, with 2% by students and 1% by academic staff). In each group, the students lead as perpetrators. Perhaps this finding indicates that low organizational status and young age may contribute to severity of sexual harassment.

3.2 IDF

The data based on indirect measure of sexual harassment in IDF sample shows that 81% of female soldiers experienced some kind of sexual harassment. Most of them (81%) reported gender harassment including sexual innuendos. 69% reported sexual suggestions, 52% reported incidents of touching and sexual body language. 26% reported bribery and 19% reported incidents of indecent exposure. Sexual coercion (8%) and sexual assault (and %) rank lowest. As expected, the less severe incidents of sexual harassment are more prevalent.

Referring to the organizational status of the perpetrator, sexual harassment by peer male soldiers is more frequent than sexual harassment by superiors. However, this finding is based on indirect questions, which do not take in to consideration participants' perceptions about behavior included in the questionnaire. Findings about female soldiers' perceptions of sexual behaviors show that organizational status of the perpetrator determines whether the incident will be defined as sexual harassment. Except for clear cases of sexual assault (rape), incidents involving peer soldiers were defined as sexual harassment much less than incidents involving commanding officer.

In addition to offender's status the research examined whether the organizational characteristics like nature of army base and nature of female soldier job contribute to harassment. There are no significant differences in rates of sexual harassment between open and closed military bases. There are no significant differences in harassment rates between the kind of jobs the soldiers performed - combat, combat assistance and home front jobs. The only difference was that combat female soldiers reported more peeping. This finding is understandable in light of the fact that combat female soldier frequently live in field/ combat conditions.

Another interesting finding shows that there is dependence between gender ratio and sexual harassment frequency. In units with skewed gender ratio in favor of men sexual harassment was more frequent than in units with even ratio or skewed ratio in favor of women. This finding supports the sex-role spillover theory (Gutek and Morasch, 1982).

3.3 Comparison between Tel-Aviv University and IDF

The comparison between female students and female soldiers reveals that female soldiers reported less gender harassment by superiors than female students (49% versus 67%). The difference in sexual bribery (female soldier 6%, students 1%) is significant while the other victimizations did not differentiate between soldiers and students. In case of sexual harassment by peers, there was no significant difference between female students and female soldiers in all categories except for sexual bribery.

In both groups, soldiers and students, gender harassment and seductive behavior was clearly leading, victimization by male students respectively peer soldiers leading.

Another view on the data regarding sexual harassment categories and organizational status of the harasser shows that peer harassment is much more prevalent in both organizations than superior harassment. This finding is consistent with findings of previous studies (Willness, Steel and Lee, 2007).

There is a striking difference between responses to direct and indirect questions. The responses to indirect question produce much higher rates of sexual harassment than responses to direct question, (indirect questions: soldiers 81% and students 68%, direct questions soldiers 21% and students 8%). The difference between direct and indirect questions is 60%, both in army and university sample. Assuming that direct question represents more truly sexual harassment rates, it seems that the actual rate of sexual harassment in the military is double than in the university. One in five 5 female soldiers reported sexual harassment. There are a few possible explanations for these findings: organizational difference between military and university, cultural differences and the fact that female soldiers are younger than female students and therefore more vulnerable to harassment. Last but not least, it is possible that due to the obligatory nature of military service, the same sexual behaviors can be perceived as more harassing by soldiers compared to university students.

Another difference emerges from data regarding victims' tendency to report sexual harassment. 80% of the students and 63% of the soldiers did not report sexual harassment to the authorities. These rates of unreported sexual harassment are much higher than those that were found in previous researches (Adams-Roy and Barling, 1998; Gruber, 1990)
According to the reason given by female students and soldiers it

seems that in both organization victims of sexual harassment do not trust official grievance procedures. The questions were asked slightly differently: while the students were asked about the expected treatment an official report would receive, the soldiers were asked in an open question why they did not report.

The majority of the students did not expect a fair treatment of such an report (60%). Seven percent even feared that the report would turn against them and hurt the reporter. In contrast to that, 28% expected a fair thorough treatment of their complaint. The remaining 5% expected that a complaint would be simply ignored.

Female soldiers gave these reasons: 48% answered to the open question that the incident was not severe enough to warrant reporting. 19% did not want to hurt the perpetrator. 14% feared negative social reactions. 7% expected a report to be inefficient. Another 7% did not know what to do. In these cases, clear reporting guidelines might be a remedy. 4% gave quite individual personal reasons: they expected never to see the perpetrator again. In this case, they saw no sufficient reason to report to the authorities. Only 1% stated that sexual harassment is an integral part of working with men.

These results show at the one hand that perceived severity of the harassment is important for reporting the event. Students indicated a considerable mistrust in the impartiality of the treatment of the report.

4. Summary and conclusion

The goal of this article was to introduce and compare finding on sexual harassment from Tel-Aviv University and IDF samples. The comparison shows that:

1. Indirect questions indicate that repeated sexual harassment is more frequent in university then in the army.
2. Direct question indicate that in general sexual harassment is more frequent in the army.
3. Gender harassment and seductive behaviors by academic staff are more frequent in the university then in the army committed by superiors.
4. There are no significant differences in frequency of peer harassment.
5. Female soldiers tend more to report the harassment than female students.

This comparison should be examined in reference to the main

difference between these two organizations. One major difference regards socio-economical status of possible victims and offenders. Military service is compulsory in Israel, thus almost all 18 years old men and women are recruited - there is no choice of the individual. IDF soldiers therefore come from all kinds of socio-economical groups. Academic studies at the university, however, are voluntary. They are a matter of choice, of good grades and financial ability. Students usually come from comparably higher social classes. *Educational and social background are quite different among soldiers.* important difference is in degrees of totality. IDF is a classic total institution that promotes obedience (Goffman, 1968). Academic studies promotes freedom of thought and teaches critical thinking. To the obvious power differential, there comes an age difference: University students are generally older - most of them are eighteen to twenty one years old. Soldiers are drafted at the age of eighteen. The army instructors are considerably younger than the academic staff. . That seemingly renders the female soldiers much more vulnerable.

In conclusion, sexual harassment exists even in those organizations that proclaim to treat men and women equally (university and army in general and combat units in particular). In spite of growing awareness to the issue of sexual harassment, women still feel afraid to complain. The findings presented in this article are a wake up call from the dream on gender equality. They show that a real equality does not yet exist.

References

Aaron, T. E. (1993). *Sexual harassment in the workplace: A guide to the law and a research overview for employees and employers.* Jefferson, NC: McFarland.

Adams-Roy, J., and Barling, J. (1998). Predicting the decision to confront or report sexual harassment. *Journal of Organizational Behavior, 19*, 329-336.

Avni, N. (1990). Psychological and demographical characteristics of sexual harassment against student. (Unpublished M. A. research). Tel-Aviv University, Tel-Aviv, Israel. (*in Hebrew*)

Baugh, S. G. (1997). On persistence of sexual harassment in the workplace. *Journal of Business Ethics, 16*, 899-908.

Charney, D. A., and Russell, R.C (1994). An overview of sexual harassment. *American Journal of Psychiatry, 151*, 10-17.

Chief of Staff Adviser on Women in Military (CSAWM) (2003). Sexual harassment in IDF - Results summery. Retrieved from the Web on January 10, 2009, http://www.aka.idf.il/yohalan/main/main.asp?catID=18283. (*in Hebrew*)

Firestone, J. M., and Harris, R. J. (1994). Sexual harassment in the U.S. military: Individualized and environmental context. *Armed Forces and Society, 21*, 25-43.

Fitzgerald, F. L., Shullman, S. L., Bally, N., Richards, M., Swecker, J, Gold, Y., Ormerod, M., and Weitzman, L. (1988). The incidence and dimensions of sexual harassment in academia and the work place. *Journal of Vocational Behavior, 32*, 152-175.

Goffman, E. (1968). *Asylums*. Harmondsworth: Penguin.

Gruber, J. E. (1990). Methodological problems and policy implications in sexual harassment research. *Population and Policy Review, 9*, 235-254.

Gutek, B. A., and Morash, B. (1982). Sex ratios, sex-role spillover, and sexual harassment of women at work. *Journal of Social Issues, 38*, 55-74.

Loy, P. H., and Stewart, L. P., (1984). The extent and effects of the sexual harassment of working women. *Sociological Focus, 17*, 31-43.

Martin, S. E. (1990). *On the move: the status of women in policing.* Washington DC: Police Foundation.

Mazer, D. B. and Percival, E. E. (1989). Student's experiences of sexual harassment at a small university. *Sex Roles, 20*, 1-22.

O'Hare, E. A., and O'Donohue, W. (1998). Sexual harassment: Identifying risk factors. *Archives of Sexual Behavior, 27*, 561-580.

Pryor, J. B. (1995). The psychological impact of sexual harassment on women in the U. S. military. *Basic and Applied Social Psychology, 17*, 581-603.

Pryor, J. B., LaVite, C. M., and Stoller, L. M. (1993). A social psychological analysis of sexual harassment: The person/situation interaction. *Journal of Vocational Behavior, 42*, 68-83.

Rosen, L N., and Martin L. (1998). Predictors of tolerance of sexual harassment among male U. S. army soldiers. *Violence against Women, 4*, 491-504.

Tangri, S. S., Burt, M. R.,and Johnson, L. B. (1982). Sexual harassment at work: Three explanatory models. *Journal of Social Issues, 38*, 33-54.

Till, F. J. (1980). *Sexual harassment: A report on sexual harassment of students*. Washington, DC: National Advisory Council on Women's Educational Program.

Vaux, A. (1993). Pragmatics assumptions in sexual harassment research: Being guided without being misled. *Journal of Vocational Behavior*, *42*, 116-135.

Willness, C. R., Steel, P., and Lee, K. (2007). A meta-analysis of the antecedents and consequences of workplace sexual harassment. Personnel Psychology, 60, 1, Article first published online: 22 FEB 2007.

Wilson, F. (2000). The subjective experience of sexual harassment: Cases of students. *Human Relations*, *8*, 1081-1098.

Wolfe, J., Sharkansky, E. J., Read, J. P., Dawson, R., Martin, J. A., and Ouimette, P. C. (1998). Sexual harassment and assault as predictors of PTSD Symptomatology among U.S. female Persian Gulf War military personal. *Journal of Interpersonal Violence*, *13*, 40-57.

Victims of Human Trafficking

Issues in Assisting Victims of Human Trafficking Worldwide

By

Jane Nady Sigmon

This article gives a brief overview of current global efforts to combat human trafficking is given. It discusses the role of the U.S. Department of State in eradicating modern slavery, and describes research of interest that the Office to Monitor and Combat Trafficking in Persons, chaired by the author, has supported.

The U.S. Department of State's annual *Trafficking in Persons Report* (*TIP Report*) is unique in its ability to focus global media attention on the issue of trafficking in persons as it discusses current trends, presents investigation and prosecution data, and assesses the efforts of nearly every country in the world to identify and protect victims, prosecute traffickers, and prevent the crime. The Report also serves as a key diplomatic tool for U.S. engagement with governments throughout the world and the individual country assessments guide the U.S. government's anti-trafficking foreign assistance priorities. The Office that this author represents, the U.S. State Department's Office to Monitor and Combat Trafficking in Persons (G/TIP), is responsible for producing the *TIP Report* as well as administering a grant program that is dedicated to addressing human trafficking globally. Though our funding is relatively small for a global program, approximately $21 million USD annually, we support projects in scores of countries

Slavery may be illegal in every country today, but it still exists in every country throughout the world. No country is immune. This heinous crime happens when one person completely controls another person, using violence and coercion to maintain that control. Traffickers usually target the most vulnerable members of society, exploiting their aspirations to create a better life and provide greater economic security for themselves and their families. Victims fall prey to deception and false promises of people who gain their trust, then exploit this trust for profit. Kevin Bales (1999) describes in his book, "Disposable People" the new slavery focusing on big profits and cheap lives. No longer about owning people like in the old slavery, today slavery is about controlling them completely. People, he writes, become completely disposable tools for making money.

Modern-day slavery is now recognized as a global challenge

that requires a global response and most governments have joined as parties to key international instruments designed to prevent, suppress, and punish perpetrators of trafficking in persons (TIP). However, the prevention, enforcement of laws, protection and assistance envisioned for victims are not a reality in many countries and, as a result, most traffickers are not apprehended or punished, and many victims of human trafficking are not identified and assisted.

The problem of human trafficking is a global issue. But, given the hidden nature of the crime and the lack of national estimates in most countries, there is little empirical data on which to base prevalence estimates. The most frequently cited numbers are those published by the International Labor Organization (ILO) in 2005, and are based on an extrapolation of 5,000 documented cases of forced labor throughout the world. The ILO's figures show more than 12 million people worldwide are trapped in some form of forced labor, including 2.4 million victims of sex trafficking, at any given time, and that more than half (56%) of all victims of forced labor are women and girls. Hundreds of thousands (600,000 to 800,000) are thought to be trafficked across international borders and millions are trafficked internally, within country borders. The annual profits from human trafficking are estimated at $32 billion USD, and it is described the fastest growing international criminal industry (ILO 2005, ILO 2009) .

In January 2009, at the launch of the ILO's 2009 global report entitled, *The Cost of Coercion*, Roger Plant, the head of the ILO Special Action Program to Combat Forced Labor, highlighted the increased vulnerability of migrants. He stated that in times of economic crisis, vulnerable workers – particularly migrants, including young women and even children – are more exposed to forced labor. Under conditions of hardship they would be taking more risks than before. *The Cost of Coercion* report notes that the highest numbers of forced labor victims (more than nine million) are found in Asia, in part because of the persistence of bonded labor systems and the widespread trafficking of women and children for both sex and labor. In their reports, both the ILO and the U.S. Department of State (DOS) describe how human trafficking manifests itself in many forms throughout the world in including: Commercial sexual exploitation, including the prostitution of children

- Forced or bonded labor
- Involuntary domestic servitude
- Debt bondage among migrant workers
- Child soldiers

Since adoption of the *United Nations (UN) Convention against Transnational Organized Crime* and the *UN Protocol to Prevent,*

Suppress and Punish Trafficking in Persons, Especially Women and Children (Palermo Protocol) by the UN General Assembly in 2000, we have made appreciable progress in our understanding of human trafficking. We have come to realize that more people are trafficked for the purpose of forced labor than commercial sex and that compelled service is found in nearly all sectors including:

- Forced prostitution
- Child prostitution
- Domestic work
- Agriculture
- Factories
- Mining
- Fishing industry

Several factors contribute to human trafficking and allow it to persist and thrive. These include: high profits and low risk as relatively few cases are prosecuted allowing traffickers at all levels to operate with impunity; the demand for cheap labor, which has enabled forced labor to penetrate the supply chains of majors goods; social and economic marginalization, which leaves many people with too few local choices for economic survival; political and economic instability, which disrupts jobs; official corruption, which undermines rule of law and good governance; and the globalization of trade, which has created labor routes far beyond borders and regions.

Human trafficking is recognized as a transnational crime that requires the cooperation of government officials and civil society in source, transit, and destination countries and it is often accompanied by other criminal activities. I mentioned two of the key tools in promoting international cooperation between UN Member States in the fight against human trafficking: the *UN Transnational Organized Crime Convention* and the *Palermo Protocol*. Together, they provide the legal framework for addressing human trafficking as well as a basic framework for victim and witness protection and assistance.

A key accomplishment of the *Palermo Protocol* was the first internationally agreed upon definition of trafficking in persons to guide the development of domestic laws to specifically address this crime. Article 3 (a) of the Protocol defines trafficking in persons in terms of three key elements:

- **The act(s):** the recruitment, transportation, transfer, harboring, or receipt of persons;
- **The means used:** threat or use of force or other forms of coercion, abduction, fraud, deception, abuse of power or of a position of vulnerability, or the giving or receiving of payments or benefits

to achieve the consent of a person having control over another person; and
- **The purpose of the act(s):** exploitation, including at a minimum, the exploitation of the prostitution of others or other forms of sexual exploitation, forced labor or services, slavery or practices similar to slavery, servitude or the removal of organs.

To meet the obligations of the *Transnational Organized Crime Convention* and the *Palermo Protocol,* UN Member States must adopt domestic criminal and civil laws necessary to make implementation a reality. The 2009 UN Office on Drugs and Crime (UNODC) *Global Report on Trafficking in Persons* provides evidence of remarkable global progress in combating TIP since the *Palermo Protocol* went into force in 2003. UNODC's *Global Report on TIP* attributes this progress to better legal frameworks and increased government attention and commitment of resources to combat TIP. The number of countries with TIP legislation more than doubled between 2003 and 2008 with 98 of the 155 (63%) reporting countries having enacted anti-trafficking laws that criminalize both sex and labor trafficking of children and adults. An additional 27 (17%) have less comprehensive TIP laws that cover sex trafficking only or children only. The majority of countries with no specific TIP offense are in Africa.

Despite these positive indications, according to the UNODC's *Global TIP Report*, nearly 40% of countries reported no human trafficking convictions. (UNODC 2009) In addition, much of the enforcement efforts have focused exclusively on sex trafficking. In 2008, only about 5% of reported prosecutions were for labor trafficking, evidence of the need to increase recognition of forced labor and improve practices in identifying victims of forced labor and investigating and prosecuting forced labor cases. The report also highlights challenges associated with the prosecution of trafficking crimes including issues that limit the interpretation of the data and thwart comparisons, such as the differences in national legislation, national criminal justice systems, capacities to collect criminal justice data, and capacities to detect TIP crimes UNODC 2009).

In 2000, the U.S. enacted comprehensive legislation to combat human trafficking, the Trafficking Victims Protection Act (TVPA), which adopts a victim-centered approach. Since its passage, it has been improved and amended three times. Key elements of the statute include the following:

- Affirmation that victims of human trafficking should be treated as victims, not criminals.
- Strengthening of U.S. criminal statutes and enhanced penalties for traffickers.

- Provisions for comprehensive services for identified victims who would otherwise not be eligible due to their immigration status.
- Provisions for immigration relief for foreign national victims to allow them to stay in the U.S. with a path to citizenship.
- Authorization of funding for public awareness, hotlines, training of law enforcement and others.

Reflecting the commitment of the U.S. Congress to combat human trafficking, the TVPA also authorized the establishment of the Office to Monitor and Combat Trafficking in Persons (G/TIP) within the U.S. Department of State, to provide global leadership on this issue. The responsibilities of this Office include:

- Production of the annual *Trafficking in Persons Report,* which is released in June;
- Face to face diplomacy with representatives of agencies working on TIP in order to encourage cooperation and improved responses on this issue;
- Funding and monitoring of anti-trafficking programs outside of the U.S.; and
- Engagement in public outreach and public awareness activities.

The U.S. Ambassador-at-Large to Combat Trafficking in Persons is the Director of G/TIP and also chairs the Senior Policy Operating Group (SPOG) on Trafficking in Persons, which regularly convenes more than ten different U.S. Government (USG) agencies that have some responsibility for trafficking in persons for discussions on the nation's response to human trafficking both domestically and abroad. In addition, the cabinet-level President's Interagency Task Force on Human Trafficking (PITF) is chaired by the Secretary of State and it meets annually to provide the highest level of attention to this issue. Together these high-ranking two bodies serve as the forum for inter-governmental dialogue and help to establish significant cooperation on policy and program issues that agencies share. Within the agencies of U.S. Government there is also excellent cooperation between G/TIP and the Department of Justice National Institute of Justice. Representatives of both agencies co-chair the Research Subcommittee of the Senior Policy Operating Group on human trafficking to ensure that our government's research agenda and projects are developed collaboratively.

The TVPA also mandated that the Secretary of State annually assess the efforts of foreign governments to combat human trafficking by applying certain "minimum standards" as outlined in the statute and issue the findings in the *Trafficking in Persons Report* (US Department of State 2009). The annual release of the *TIP Report* receives enormous media attention; its publication has prompted action by many countries and anti-trafficking advocates. In June 2011, the Secretary of State, Hillary Clinton, gathered hundreds of supporters for the release of the Report and described human trafficking as "an affront to our basic values and our fundamental belief that all people everywhere deserve to live and work in safety and dignity".

The *TIP Report* ranks countries in "tiers" based on the extent of their governments' efforts to implement the three "P" approach for the elimination of human trafficking: Prosecution of traffickers, Protection of victims, and Prevention of trafficking

The tires are defined in this way:

Tier 1: Countries whose governments fully comply with the TVPA's minimum standards for the elimination of trafficking.

Tier 2: Countries whose governments do not fully comply with the TVPA's minimum standards, but are making significant efforts to bring them into compliance

Tier 2 Watch List: Countries whose governments do not fully comply with the TVPA's minimum standards, but are making significant efforts to bring them into compliance AND: a) the absolute number of victims of severe forms of trafficking is very significant or is significantly increasing; b) there is a failure to provide evidence of increasing efforts to combat severe forms of trafficking in persons from the previous year, including increased investigations, prosecutions, and convictions of trafficking crimes, increased assistance to victims, and decreasing evidence of complicity in severe forms of trafficking by government officials; or c) the determination that a country is making significant efforts to bring itself into compliance with minimum standards was based on commitments by the country to take additional steps over the next year.

Tier 3: Countries whose governments do not fully comply with the minimum standards are not making significant efforts to do so.

It is the only State Department report that assigns countries a tier ranking. The 2009 *TIP Report* (US Department of State 2009) includes assessments of 175 foreign governments' efforts to combat trafficking along with recommendations for action. The *Report's* country narratives and country-specific recommendations provide diagnostic information for targeting anti-trafficking programming.

From 2001 to 2009, the USG invested approximately $620 million in programs to combat human trafficking globally. G/TIP's annual budget is around $21 million and our Office gives priority to funding projects in countries that are rated as Tier 3, Tier 2 Watch List, and some Tier 2 countries. To target limited funds effectively and provide potential applicants with information about funding priorities, G/

TIP names priority countries, based on several factors such as the *TIP Report* tier rankings; political will to improve the response to human trafficking; and a lack of economic resources within the country and from other donors to support anti-trafficking programs.

Each year in the fall, our Office publishes an annual solicitation requesting proposals and outlining priorities for funding. In response, we receive hundreds of applications; This year alone we received nearly 375 proposals requesting a total of nearly $290 million for projects in 57 countries. We provide funding to U.S.-based and foreign-based non-governmental organizations (NGOs), universities, public international organizations, and others. Generally, our Office supports capacity-building partnerships with foreign NGOs; the development of comprehensive services for victims of sex and labor trafficking; projects to improve the criminal justice and victim assistance response to labor trafficking; the implementation of victim-centered practices by criminal justice professionals (law enforcement officials, prosecutors, and judges); and action-oriented research and evaluation to enhance our understanding of this crime and the experience of victims and thus inform more effective programming.

Our Office recognizes that this is a very young field, and we must be fully committed to moving toward evidence-based programming, despite the limited body of research and evaluation in human trafficking. In 2005, G/TIP convened a group of trafficking in persons experts to identify gaps in human trafficking research. Among the most frequently cited research gaps were the prevalence of trafficking of men and boys and the experience of male trafficking victims. Early efforts to combat human trafficking in most countries focused on identification of women and girls who were victims of sexual exploitation, but anecdotal information about male victims was increasing along with our recognition that more attention must be given to this area. To address this data gap, in 2006, G/TIP solicited proposals for research on male trafficking victims

The research of Nikolic-Ristonovic (2009:99) shows that Serbian police and border officials have identified increasing numbers of male trafficking victims returning to Serbia after taking what they thought were well-paying construction jobs. However, the men had been threatened, had their passports taken away, had their movements restricted, and were not paid. Her research improved our understanding of how the horrific conditions of forced labor impact men and shed led on how little victim assistance exists for male victims of forced labor. She quoted a Serbian border official as follows:

> "They lived in poor conditions, they were housed in the barracks 20-40 people each; there was one bathroom for every 50-

> 60 of them, without the possibility to regularly take care of their hygiene and without an adequate diet. They were also threatened with "being sent to the war in Iraq," as well as that they would hurt their family members if they complain to someone or if they do not act according to what is demanded of them. The victims took the threats very seriously."

Our Office also supported researchers from the Harvard School of Public Health to study the health impact of human trafficking by reviewing health data on repatriated Nepalese girls and women who had been trafficked to India for sexual exploitation. These women and girls are considered particularly vulnerable to HIV infection because of their typically young age at trafficking, limited ability to negotiate condom-protected sex, and experiences of forced sex. Among the women and girls surveyed, 38 percent were HIV positive. The infection rate exceeded 60 percent among girls forced into prostitution prior to the age of 15. Girls trafficked at younger ages also reported a greater likelihood of servitude in multiple brothels and longer periods of brothel confinement associated with increased HIV infection risk of 2 to 4 percent for each additional month of captivity (Silverman et al. 2007). Additional data analysis conducted by Decker revealed that HIV+ sex trafficking victims were also more likely to have sexually transmitted infections (STIs), including Syphilis (2 to 1 ratio) and Hepatitis B (9 to 1 ratio) (Silverman et al. 2008).

Over the last few years, one of the most successful partnerships our Office has supported is a cooperative research initiative with the International Migration Organization (IOM). With more than 420 offices around the world, the IOM plays a critical role in the repatriation of many transnational victims of human trafficking. G/TIP works closely with the Counter-Trafficking Units (CTU) in Washington, DC and Geneva, Switzerland on programming and research and our funding supports projects in more than a dozen countries. IOM employs a comprehensive approach to trafficking in persons within the wider context of managing migration. The organization's approach to countering-TIP is governed by three main principles:

- Respect for human rights
- Physical, mental and social well-being of the individual and his or her community
- Sustainability through institutional capacity building of governments and civil society

G/TIP has been supporting the development of IOM's Global Counter-

Trafficking Database for approximately four years. This unique database provides a wealth of information for analysis and I am very pleased to describe it to this audience – as it may be of particular interest to researchers. Our funding supports the expansion of the database, analysis of trends, and the production of thematic reports. The database was developed to facilitate the internal management of information gathered from IOM's counter-trafficking and return and reintegration programs. It is a "closed system" that links IOM's Missions in both source and destination countries. By establishing case records in a manner that prevents duplicate entries, the database facilitates analysis of cross-border data. This standardized approach is used by nearly 50 IOM Missions in all regions of the world.

The initial pilot for the database was launched in South Eastern Europe nearly a decade ago for case management purposes. It has since expanded to include information from more than 13,650 victims that IOM missions have assisted in more than 85 source and 100 destination countries over a ten year period. Of these, 75% were international trafficking cases and 25 were internal trafficking cases. The individuals assisted range across all age groups, but the majority of the victims interviewed were between the ages of 18 and 24 years. Most are women Consistent with the patterns we have seen in the reports that I described earlier, 75% of the individuals were classified as victims of sex trafficking while only 20% were classified as victims of forced labor. However, a new trend is emerging in most places, and it can be seen here as well. The number of males identified as victims of trafficking and assisted by IOM has steadily increased, from the early years when males composed less than 5% of all victims in the database to about 24% in 2008. These trends are very similar to those found in UNODC's *Global Report on Trafficking in Persons (UNODC 2009).*

There are a number of strengths associated with IOM's primary victim data. These include consistency in collection methods; clear informed consent policies and procedures; and richness of information as data is collected over time, allowing for stories to unfold. However, there are also a number of limitations. First, the data is not representative of all trafficking victims. It is limited to cases identified and assisted by participating IOM Missions and thus nearly all of the cases are transnational – as would be expected given IOM's focus on migration. Second, the problems often occurring in the collection of information on human trafficking cases are also likely present, such as issues of trust and mistrust as well as reliability of self-reported data.

While recognizing its limitations, the analyses our Office has commissioned have contributed to our understanding of human trafficking and have expanded our thinking beyond previous assumptions. For example, the data reflects trends related to the increased recognition of the trafficking of males and older victim populations, and increased numbers of forced labor cases, including women in domestic work. Similarly, we have seen more male victims identified in the U.S. In 2006, only 6% of the trafficking victims certified by the U.S. Department of Health Human Services were male, versus 45% in 2008. In addition, in terms of U.S. trafficking prosecutions, the proportion of forced labor cases has increased slightly over recent years and the number of defendants charged with forced labor trafficking increased from 26 (in 2006) to 34 (in 2008).

IOM's analysis of the data also shows that traffickers are changing their methods of control: they are more coercive, using more female recruiters, and inflicting greater psychological abuse. Trends observed by the IOM are similar in many respects to the anecdotal reports that we have regarding TIP cases identified in the U.S. and from reports received from our grantees. This pattern recently prompted officials in the U.S. to amend the TVPA to more explicitly recognize coercion, not just physical violence, as a tool that traffickers use to enslave victims.

To further explore the situation of male trafficking victims, our Office also recently supported a thematic analysis of male victims served by the IOM. The final report entitled *Trafficking of Men – a Trend Less Considered: the Case of Belarus and Ukraine* was written by Rebecca Surtees of the NEXUS Institute in Vienna, Austria. The study examined the pre- and post-trafficking experiences of 685 Belarusian and Ukrainian men. The majority of males assisted were between the ages of 18-24. In contrast to the Ukraine where the majority of trafficked males were employed, in Belarus the majority were unemployed. Within this male population of victims seeking better circumstances most had children and some technical training. The men were trafficked for construction and labored seven days a week often 12 hours per day or more under exploitative conditions with no freedom of movement. Existing in cramped and unhygienic living conditions, they were often physically and psychologically abused or threatened with abuse.

In his interview, one of the male victims voiced the following:

> "When we came to get the money after the first month, the owner said he took the money for lodging, food and employment for our salaries and there was nothing left. We had an argument, he began to insult us and we went away with nothing. He also said that those who didn't want to work could

> leave, as there were other people to take our places. But where could we go? Our families were waiting for the money, and we had already borrowed some money to come there. So we worked for a month more. But again he said he had taken from the salaries money for medical assurance and to continue the visa. So there were only about 100USD left. I was happy to send even this money, as I left my wife and baby daughter at home... When the employer came to visit us, I asked him to pay me the salaries as I was going home [because I was sick]. But he only gave me money for the way home and said he would pay me the rest when I came back to work after being treated at home. During my five months of work there I earned about 300 USD".

In terms of the post-trafficking experience, most men exited the situation on their own (77.6% Belarusian men; 46.9% Ukrainian men). In Belarus, referrals were primarily from law enforcement where in the Ukraine trafficked men were more likely to seek out NGO support when their returned to their communities. Upon their return, many had faced economic and legal hardship stressing the importance of both short- and long-term accommodation and housing support. Furthermore, medical assistance was a primary need for victims of labor exploitation. Importantly, the men generally did not perceive themselves as victims; rather, they viewed their experiences as "failed migration". In conclusion, the study called for the development of more comprehensive assistance for these victims, including medical, psychological, and housing support tailored to their unique needs (Surtees 1999).

The IOM also produced a thematic report on re-trafficking (Kobe 2010). The analysis focused on the handful of TIP victims that had been assisted by the IOM on more than one occasion (n= 69). In 2003, the IOM introduced a question on re-trafficking into its standardized assistance form. A significant number of victims self-identified as having been trafficked more than once, some on three occasions. This is a relatively small number proportionately, given the tens of thousands of assisted victims. All of these victims were females and they all originated from South Eastern Europe. The average age at the first time of assistance was 20 with many under the age of 18. The average age at the second time of assistance was 21 with a significant decrease in cases of girls under the age of 18, suggesting that they had not stayed in their communities long after their return.

IOM's preliminary analysis of the re-trafficking data revealed information on exploitation patterns. At the first time of assistance, the majority of cases related to trafficking for sexual exploitation. Although sexual exploitation remained the most prevalent form of exploitation, there was an increase in the number of forced labor cases at the second time of assistance. The average time between the first and second time of assistance was 20 months, and the number of international trafficking cases increased among the re-trafficking cases. Furthermore, the majority of children were trafficked for sexual exploitation on both occasions. According to the IOM, the factors that contributed most significantly to re-trafficking were:

- Lack of family support upon return
- Stigmatization and inability to re-integrate into host society/ community/family, especially for victims of sex trafficking
- Deportation by law enforcement without necessary support
- Unwillingness to accept direct assistance
- Fear of or past negative experience with authorities
- Previous childhood trafficking experience
- Structural socio-economic push factors remain
- Desire to migrate remains upon return, but no safe or legal channels to do so
- Threats (personal and/or family) from traffickers upon return

G/TIP is continuing to support the IOM's work and the best practices for the collection, storage, and processing of standardized data on human trafficking and examination of the potential use of the core data elements by NGOs. While security concerns and protections limit database direct access to IOM counter-trafficking personnel, IOM is able to consider requests for sharing de-identified data following review of a data request. Researchers and others may inquire by emailing CTS-DB@iom.int and citing the purpose of the request and data fields of interest. Each data request is considered on an individual basis, and any data or information used from the database must be credited. Use of the data/information must adhere to the conditions prescribed by the IOM.

Human trafficking is a challenging field and millions of people are suffering today. We are committed to continuing to improve our efforts – with the knowledge that – what we do can make a difference.

Many members of this World Society of Victimology (WSV) are involved in the search for best practices. As researchers, academics, policy makers, and practitioners from all across the globe, they play unique and important roles in this effort. WSV is to be thanked for its work to advance knowledge in the field of human trafficking and for promoting communication and cooperation on this important topic.

References

ILO (2005) The International Labor Organization. (2005). *A global alliance against forced labour*, Global Report under the Follow-up to the ILO Declaration on Fundamental Principles and Rights at Work. Geneva, Switzerland: International Labour Office-Geneva.

ILO 2009 The International Labor Organization. (2009). *The cost of coercion*, Global Report under the follow-up to the ILO Declaration on Fundamental Principles and Rights at Work. Geneva, Switzerland: International Labour Office-Geneva

Kobe, A. (2010) The Causes and Consequences of Re-trafficking: Evidence from the IOM Human Trafficking Database. http://www.iom.int/jahia/webdav/site/myjahiasite/shared/shared/mainsite/published_docs/studies_and_reports/causes_of_retrafficking.pdf accessed on August 27, 2011.

Nikolic-Ristanovic, V. (ed.) (2009) The Victimology Society of Serbia. *Male trafficking in Serbia*. See http://www.vds.org.rs or http://www. prometej-beograd.rs/Viktimologija/MaleTrafficking.html accessed August 27, 2011

Silverman JG, Decker MR, Gupta J, Maheshwari A, Willis BM, et al. (2007) HIV prevalence and predictors of infection in sex-trafficked Nepalese girls and women. JAMA. 2007; 298: 536-42.

Silverman JG, Decker MR, Gupta J, Dharmadhikari A, Seage G.R. III, Raj A. Sexually transmitted co-infections among HIV-infected sex-trafficked women and girls, Nepal. Emerg Infect Dis [serial on the Internet]. 2008 Jun [*date cited*]. Available from http://www.cdc.gov/EID/content/14/6/932.htm

Surtees, R. The Nexus Institute, (2008) . *Trafficking of men – a trend less considered: the case of Belarus and Ukraine*. Geneva, Switzerland: IOM. Available on the internet http://publications.iom.int/bookstore/free/MRS_36.pdf, accessed August 27, 2011

UNODC (2009) UN Office on Drugs and Crime UNODC *Global Report on Trafficking in Persons*. Vienna. Austria. (UNODC). http://www.unodc.org/unodc/en/human-trafficking/global-report-on-trafficking-in-persons.html accessed August 27, 2011.

US Department of State (2009) Trafficking in Persons Report 2009. http://www.state.gov/g/tip/rls/tiprpt/2009/ accessed August 27, 2011.

Developing Need-based, Gender Specific and Empowering Approach to Supporting Victims of Trafficking

By

Vesna Nikolic-Ristanovic

What are the needs of victims of transnational trafficking, and how are the needs met by support services in destination/transit countries? The paper compares the situation in Serbia and Norway.

Introduction

Victims of transnational trafficking are often treated as illegal migrants rather then as crime victims. Victim services do not feel comfortable to support them. As a consequence, less assistance is available to foreigners as victims of trafficking. They seem to be stigmatized and excluded not only by ordinary people and institutions, but also by those who are supposed to give them assistance and support, including victim services.

This paper addresses challenges related to support of victims of cross-border crime, using example of victims of trafficking in people. The main aim of the paper is to explore victim support services available in **destination/transit countries**, with special emphasis on the needs of **foreign citizens** as victims of trafficking, how they are met and whether the services are comparable with services available to other crime victims.

Victim support of trafficked persons seems to be big challenge for both, for countries with well established victim support structures and for countries that do not yet have such structures. For countries with an existing support structure, the challenge is in the accommodation of existing services to the needs of foreign victims of trafficking. For the other countries, there is a need to create standards and to develop comprehensive and well organized victim support structures suitable to the needs of all victims.

Is there a difference between victims of trafficking and other crime victims? Do they really need special treatment? If yes, do they need to be excluded from support services available to other crime victims? Does victim support really meet the needs of trafficking victims? Is it victim or offender-centred? Is there a Proactive or reactive approach to victims?

The analysis is based on findings of research carried out in Serbia by Victimology Society of Serbia and FAFO Institute for Applied International Sciences from Norway, as well as on follow-up surveys in both Serbia and Norway. The article uses some preliminary findings of a survey conducted by the Victimology Society of Serbia's on male victims of trafficking as well.

The term "trafficking victim" encompasses victims of both sexes as well as children, regardless of the form of exploitation they suffer. Consequently, gender specific victim support is meant to take care of different (gender related) needs of male and female victims. The concept of victim support includes protection of victims and professional assistance, but also information and emotional support intended to help victim make own decisions and strengthen or regain the agency (empowering). It includes supporting vulnerable population/potential victims that may prevent victimisation by trafficking as well. Thus, victim support is defined as serving needs of victims because these needs exist and victims ask or agree to be assisted, regardless of what caused it (trafficking or other crime/ victimisation), what happened to offender and whether victim is identified as a such by others (see Recommendation Rec (2006)8 on Assistance to Crime Victims.[1]

Whether and how much victims of trafficking are different in comparison to other crime victims?

Victimisation that trafficking victims suffer is often long-term and multiple, including consequences of a number of specific crimes. Consequently, although its duration and combination of various crimes make it often unique and extremely traumatic experience for victims, they also can make it more or less similar with experiences of victims of other crimes. Since trafficking can have various forms, its consequences on victim can also be quite different and may range from long-term and very serious traumatic impact to short-term and less traumatic effect (Zimmerman, 2003; Nikolic-Ristanovic, 2005; Zimmerman, Hossain, Yun, Roche, Morison and Watts, 2006:2) . Exploring and understanding the complexity of consequences of trafficking on victim, as well as both similarities and differences between victims of trafficking and other crime victims is essential for assessment of victims' needs and for the creation of successful victim support and rehabilitation programs.

---

1 These definitions are very much in line with Recommendation Rec (2006)8 on Assistance to Crime Victims.

So far most information available relates to female victims of trafficking for sexual and some forms of labour exploitation. Findings of surveys conducted in Serbia (Nikolic-Ristanovic, 2005:89), as well as elsewhere (Farley et al., 2003; Zimmerman, 2003; Zimmerman, Hossain, Yun, Roche, Morison and , 2006) suggest that women victims of trafficking experience various forms of interconnected victimization, including physical, psychological and sexual violence, fraud, kidnapping and robbery, and are kept in isolation and under control in different ways. They are also forced to prostitution, to work as entertainers, to do domestic and/or other work, as well as to use alcohol and drugs. Women and children are sold and resold many times. Their documents are withdrawn from them. They are deceived about their validity. They are forced to work without payment. They are humiliated all the time. Victims' exclusion from relationships with people other than those from the "underworld", makes impossible or extremely difficult for them to ask for help from people outside. Victims who originally are involved in domestic prostitution without being trafficked also may suffer violence and control by their pimps and often do not have any other choice then to ask for the protection from even more abusive men who later became their traffickers (Nikolic-Ristanovic, 2005:91). Victimisation of children and male victims is much less explored. Available data suggest that they are also kept under more or less severe control, abused and exploited in various ways (Dowling et. al, 2007:13; IOM, 2007)

Asking for help may even more jeopardize trafficking victims. This is very much in connection to their status as illegal migrants, prostitutes and their otherwise involvement in illegal work. Thus, it is not unusual that they get arrested and experience severe victimization in relation to that. Moreover, survey findings suggest that asking for help may put them into risk of worse, including letal violence, from the trafficker (Nikolic-Ristanovic, 2002 and 2005). In this regard, trafficking bear ressemblance with other forms of long-term gender based violence. Similarly as in domestic violence, trafficking often includes many control tactics, which contribute significantly to the effectiveness of physical and sexual violence. Control tactics always imply the threats, keeping women continually 'on edge' and in fear, the lack of freedom of movement. But they include also economic and emotional abuse, isolation and other forms of control, increased debt, harm to their children and families and retrafficking (Nikolic-Ristanovic, 2005; Zimmerman, Hossain, Yun, Roche, Morison and Watts, 2006:2). The surveys conducted in Serbia, Moldova, Ukraine, Bulgaria, Check Republic, Italy and UK support the findings of Giobbe et al. (quoted by Farley et al., 1998:410), who described methods of coercive control exercised by pimps and customers over women in prostitution which are identical to the methods used by battering men to control women.

Trafficking has serious negative consequences on victims' health and on their relationships with close family and other people (Albert and Santos, 2004:60;Amnesty International Report on Kosovo, 2004:16; Nikolic-Ristanovic, 2005:94; Zimmerman, Hossain, Yun, Roche, Morison and Watts, 2006:11). In-depth interviews with victims and victim support personel, carried out in Serbia, revealed a clear link between trafficking and previous victimizations, including domestic and sexual violence, and other stressing events in the lives of victims, such as war, death of close relatives etc, resulting in continuity of victimization and continuation of traumas (Nikolic-Ristanovic, 2005:95). Similarly, findings of quantitave survey based on interviews with 207 women victims of trafficking showed that the prevalence of violence reported by women prior to being trafficked compares with some of the highest national prevalence levels of gender-based violence in the world (Zimmerman, Hossain, Yun, Roche, Morison and Watts, 2006:9).

Victims of trafficking suffer from wide range of traumatic symptoms, such as depression, anxiety, hostility, difficulty in sleeping, intrusive and re-experiencing symptoms, anger and irritability, dissociation, hyper-vigilance, double identity as well as intensive feelings of fear and insecurity, self-blaming, extremely low self-esteem and trust in other people (Amnesty International report on Kosovo, 2004:16; Albert and Santos, 2004:67, 69; Nikolic-Ristanovic, 2005:95; Zimmerman, Hossain, Yun, Roche, Morison and Watts, 2006:2). Important for victim support services, most of these consequences may meet criteria for Post Traumatic Stress Disorder. Many clients of shelters may be experiencing high level of distress and trauma symptoms. (Albert and Santos, 2004:67). However, there are many many victims who do not suffer from such serious consequences of trafficking (Zimmerman, 2003:6).

Victims of trafficking suffer from intensive self blaming and low self esteem. Low self-esteem and self-blaming are connected with both the loss of a control over the life and lack of confidence in other people. Additionally, psychological and social consequences of trafficking bear high resemblance with consequences of other forms of prolonged victimisation, such as domestic violence, child abuse, political terror, combat veterans experience (Herman, 1997), as well as torture and other traumatic events (Zimmerman, Hossain, Yun, Roche, Morison and Watts, 2006:2).

Finally, as a consequence of high level of both, the original trauma from trafficking and the additional risks of re-victimization and of retaliation from traffickers, victims of trafficking are among the most vulnerable witnesses, once they have decided to report and to testify against traffickers. Their vulnerability is related to stereotypes and prejudices towards gender based violence in general, and towards sexual violence and prostitution in particular. In this situation, victims of sex trafficking, similarly to victims of other forms of gender-based violence, are often left without proper protection. They are even victimized by those from whom this protection is supposed to come (i.e. police).

In addition, the effects of various crimes also contribute toward similarity of trafficking victims with other victims of gender-based violence, as well as victims of long-term abuse, frauds, robberies and marginalised groups in more general terms (e.g. migrants, women sex workers, those whose labour is exploited or who are forced to work, street children etc.) (Zimmerman, 2003:3 and Clawson, Small, Go and Myles, 2003:19).

Needs of trafficking victims – similarities and differences to other crime victims

Similarities in consequences lead to similarities in needs and coping of victims. Research on needs of trafficking victims, based on interviews with service providers and victims in USA, shows: trafficking victims problems are most similar to problems of domestic violence victims, immigrants/ refugees and sexually exploited persons (Clawson, Small, Go and Myles, 2003:19). Research carried out in Serbia, also based on interviews with service providers and victims (Nikolic-Ristanovic, 2005), reveals: similarly as victims of domestic violence and other victims of long-term abuse and stress, sex trafficking victims often cope in searching most of the time for the most appropriate response. They actually use acceptance of abuse as the most appropriate way of coping, taking into account their helpless situation and risks of worse violence if they resist. Like battered women (Walker, 1989:50), they don't attempt to leave the abusive situation, even when it may seem to outsiders that escape is possible (see Kirchhoff 1999). They neither can predict their own safety and do not feel they feel enough in control of their life after the escape.

However, much feminist work on violence (Kelly, 1987; Goudolf and Fisher, 1988), sought to demonstrate that even within the most constraining contexts, women acted – they used physical and psychological resistance strategies in the moments of violence, and developed coping and survival strategies both within ongoing abuse and with the aftermath. Learned Helplessness Theory suggested constant decreasing of and finally paralyzing of women's agency as the consequence of many unsuccessful attempts for action/escape (Walker, 1989:50). On the other side, Surviving Theory argues that the problem is not in women, since they do not actually stop seeking for help, but in the society which does not give them necessary support and assistance. (Goudolf and Fisher, 1988:13).

This apparent contradiction between victimization and agency is well pronounced by Lamb (1999:11) who suggests the notion „agentic victim" which implies agency as well as passivity, strength as well as harm, resistance as well as dissociation. Similarly, findings of the survey conducted in Serbia suggest a continuity of both victimization and coping. It shows as well the lack of appropriate support and protection. Victims constantly attempt escape or considers plans for the escape. Research in Serbia on more or less successful escapes, reveals (Nikolic-Ristanovic, 2005:117): most of the time women's coping primarily include their acceptance to work in prostitution in order to avoid violence. In the situations of extreme violence however, they sometime suddenly exercise agency through the escape. Similarly, battered women either suddenly leave or kill their abusers. Thus, as many other victims of violence, victims of trafficking may react out of fear for their lives, but also out of anger (Nikolic-Ristanovic, 2005:117). But, as Walker put it in relation to domestic violence victims, **this** anger is positive and empowering, and as Walker (1989:221) puts it, it feeds the "flames of esteem" for others and for self.

Similar as other victims, victims of trafficking need information, emotional support, outreach, referrals, legal, medical, financial etc. assistance, feeling of security from abusers/safe place to stay, compensation and witness support. The greatest needs of sex trafficking victims seem to be legal/paralegal services (99%), medical services (98%) and information/ referral services (97%).

However, trafficking victims also may have specific needs connected to their (illegal) migrant status, as well as to the complexity of consequences of lasting and multiple victimisations. As foreigners, trafficking victims are more isolated, know much less about the criminal justice system in destination country, do not have citizenship of destination country which makes it harder to serve their needs, their mental health needs are more extreme, they have higher safety concerns, have higher level of fear, etc. They need information in their own language, culturally sensitive support and assistance to leave abusive situation, based on understanding of continuity of both victimization and coping in the lives of trafficking victims (including acceptance of abuse as coping strategy); feeling in control of their decision to return home and testify against traffickers, and residence permits in the destination country (Clawson, Small, Go and Myles, 2003:19; Nikolic-Ristanovic, 2005: 117)

Services for victims: proactive or reactive approach?

Available information suggest that not only consequences but also barriers to access services for trafficking victims are similarity to those experienced by other victims of gender-based violence and other marginalised groups (Zimmerman, 2003:3). A recent survey carried out in Albania, Serbia and Moldova describes that a substantial number of women and girls were at least initially afraid of those who wanted to help them. They thought they were being transported to a new venue of exploitation (Brunovskis and Surtees, 2007:147).

Victims usually do not know where to turn for assistance (Surtees, 2007:239). But it is essential that they build up trust in support institutions (Brunovskis and Tyldum, 2004: 119; Zimmerman, 2003:5). Contact with support services is most likely to be established through "outreach programs" or mobility services directed at women in sex work or at those working in other sectors known to employ trafficked women (Zimmerman, 2003:5), children or men.

Victims in USA access their services most often through referral from other service providers and law enforcement (95%). They often hear about them through the word of mouth (54%) or through community outreach, including street outreach and outreach to other agencies/ organisations (51%). Service providers stress the importance of increased outreach in their areas as a means for locating victims who are "invisible and isolated". They also stressed improved collaboration among key partners (Clawson, Small, Go and Myles, 2003:24).

However, the crucial difference between supporting victims of trafficking in comparison to other crime victims lies in the fact that, that usually, victims of other crimes are legal residents. As such, they are automatically entitled to assistance. But victims of trafficking in destination countries can enjoy such entitlement not automatically. They need to be "officially certified". It is already a problem that victims of trafficking rarely self-identify themselves as victims and ask for support. Even bigger is the problem that other designated agencies have to recognise them officially. Consequently, it occurs that victims who want or even ask for help are rejected because they are not recognised as victims of trafficking. In other cases, the official procedure in not efficient and last too long. For example, research carried out in USA showed that certification of victim status is seen by service providers and victims as an external barrier to providing services to trafficking victims (Clawson, Small, Go and Myles, 2003:26). Access of foreign victims to services is dependent on certification of their status. „Differentiating between certified and not recognized victims, will leave women without the 'victim' label vulnerable for prosecution"(Skilbrei and Tveit, 2007:79).

Supporting victims of trafficking in Europe: meeting needs of victims or someone else?

Similarly as in USA (Clawson, Small, Go and Myles, 2003) and in Australia (Segrave et al.2009), in Europe the main challenge in supporting victims of trafficking seems to include the choice between victim-centred and offender centred approach, including especially the choice between giving priority to self-identification of victims and their identification by others. Consequently, it includes choosing between respecting victims' needs and wishes, while supporting them to make their own informed decisions, versus imposed victim status and assistance regardless of victim's needs and wishes.

The UN Convention against Transnational Organised Crime, together with its Trafficking Protocol (2000) called for an integrated and multi-agency approach that incorporates prevention of victimisation, victim protection and assistance, and prosecution of offenders. Recently the focus shifted from offenders to victims (e.g. "Brussels Declaration" and Council of Europe Convention on Action against Trafficking in Human Beings) (Goodey, 2004:31).

With this shift, a range of measures to victims of sex trafficking become available. These include safe accommodation, welfare payments, education, employment and health-care, as well as psychological counselling, information, witness support and protection, restitution and compensation from state, welfare payments, education, employment and health-care, short and long-term residence permit, and in some countries even possibility of permanent residence permit (e.g. the Netherlands and Belgium). Moreover, national referral mechanisms (Kroger, Malkoc and Uhl, 2004), as wider social frameworks for victim support and assistance, are designed and started to be implemented. National referral mechanism (NRM) is the process of identifying presumed trafficked persons by different stakeholders and co-operation among stakeholders to ensure the victims' referral to specialized services (so Kroger, Malkoc and Uhl, 2004:59).

However, in reality these measures have a lot of limitations and shortcomings. They are mostly applied to women and children victims of sex trafficking, although they are not adjusted to specific needs of children. In addition, as findings from recent research in South East Europe showed, they rarely serve victims of other forms of trafficking, and, in spite of increasing number of known cases of male victims of trafficking, both adults and minors, existing measures are mostly not adjusted to fit them (Surtees, 2006:16). These measures are mostly available under condition that victim cooperates with authorities regarding prosecution of offender. There is the possibility of granting permanent residence for trafficked persons on humanitarian ground in Belgium and Netherlands. But this option is extremely rarely used in practice (Anti-Slavery International, 2002:45; Smit, 2003).

The position of victims of trafficking is still determined by the fact that they are still treated as illegal migrants and criminals rather then as crime victims (Goodey, 2004: 32, Nikolic-Ristanovic, 2005:104).

Another big problem is the lack of respect for the agency of victims of trafficking. Reflection period and temporary resident permit, together with other assistance measures, are not only mainly available under condition of cooperation with state authorities. They also mean transition toward returning victim back to her country of origin. However, victims often have various reasons for not wishing to go back (Skilbrei and Tveit, 2007). This may be especially dramatic once they give testimony against traffickers (Nikolic-Ristanovic, 2005:109).

Support to victims of sex trafficking was largely developedparately from by feminist or more generalmen's groups as responses to violence against women. Thus, it seems that the special needs of victims of sex trafficking have been largely neglected by advocates and women's groups both in Western and Eastern European, i.e. Balkan countries.

The exclusion of trafficking victims from services for other victims contribute to their stigmatization, and, consequently to their refusal of assistance (Bjerkan and Dyrild, 2005:148; Brunovskis and Surtees, 2007:150;). In addition, those offering support exclusively to victims of trafficking often lack broader knowledge about victims' needs and/or violence against women, and this has negative consequences on standards of services trafficking victims obtain, but also on their number, choice, visibility and access to victims. On the Annual Conference of Victim Support Europe, held in May 2008 in Belgrade in a workshop on support for trafficking victims, all participants agreed that their organisations should support victims of trafficking. Some representatives maintained that their organization had first to expand their knowledge. Others said that they already support migrant victims.

There is a huge discrepancy between development of general victim services and development of services for victims of trafficking (Simeunovic-Patic, 2005:33). In reducing women to their traditional roles, some support organisations contribute to passivity of victims and control of their actions rather then empowering them to regain agency and control on their life (Andrijasevic, 2007:3).

Examples of Serbia and Norway

Serbia is the country which is emphasised by international organisations as the country with good practice regarding coordination of support and referral mechanism for trafficking victims (Kroger, Malkoc and Uhl, 2004:73). Norway recently developed its own model, which in some degree used experiences with national referral mechanism in OSCE participating countries in general, and in Serbia in particular. Support to trafficking victims was developed in Serbia in the context of very poorly developed social welfare system and general victim services, while the situation in Norway is quite opposite.

Both Norway and Serbia have nationally coordinated multi-agency frameworks for dealing with trafficking and national (governmental) referral mechanism that include cooperation between authorities and non-governmental organisations. In both countries most victims served are women victims of sex trafficking, in rare exceptions men or children. In Serbia there are not services specifically developed for them. Male victims usually are arrested, imprisoned and afterwards deported.

Children in Norway are responsibility of childcare unit, which means that they are not referred in the same way as adult victims. It is worth mentioning that children victims of trafficking are granted residence in Norway if they are unlikely to receive necessary care if they return to their country of origin (The Norwegian Government's Plan of Action to Combat Human Trafficking, 2006-2009:10). However, there is still no special referral subsystem for children in place in Serbia. Also, both foreign and Serbian minors (female and male) are sheltered alongside adult women, and offered practically the same protection, assistance, and integration programmes as adults. Even worse, minor victims are sometime referred to institutions for care of children with antisocial behaviour and treated as delinquents rather then victims.

Conclusion: toward a new approach

Apart from some specific needs, victims of trafficking have many similar needs as other crime victims, such as victims of violence against women, particularly victims of domestic violence. This may be strong argument for inclusion of, or coordination of support mechanism for trafficking victims within broader victim support service structure, including also services for women in prostitution. It is also the argument for gender sensible and victim-centred instead of offender-centred approach to victims of trafficking in destination countries. This shift in the approach should especially include abandoning the practice of discrimination of victims of trafficking as foreign citizens in comparison to indigenous people as crime victims.

Moreover, the shift toward victim-centred and gender specific approach is essential for empowerment of victims to regain agency and control on their lives (Nikolic-Ristanovic, 2005:86) and to make their own choices and decisions.

Victims should be able to make informed decisions as to what they consider to be in their best interest (Kroger, Malkoc and Uhl, 2004:69). This means that services need to take into account victim's wish whether to return to country of origin or not. They should inform police only when this is wished by the victim (WHO, 2003:26).

Policies must be abolished that keep women in their traditional passive roles by replacing one control (by criminal) by another (by criminal justice and victim support system). Victims of trafficking are to be trusted and treated accordingly both when they claim to be victims and when they refuse to be treated like that. Use of good practice in dealing with other victims, particularly victims of domestic and sexual violence, migrants and refugees (Zimmerman, 2003:7) may be helpful in assisting victims of trafficking.

References

Albert, I., Santos, I. (2004) '5 Day Workshop at the Shelter for Survivors of Human Trafficking' in G. Schinina (ed). *Psychosocial Support to Groups of Victims of Human Trafficking in Transit Situations,* Geneva: IOM.

Amnesty International Report (2004) 'So does it mean that we have rights?' Protecting the human rights of women and girls trafficked for forced prostitution in Kosovo.

Andrijasevic, R. (2007) 'Beautiful dead bodies: gender, migration and representation in anti-trafficking campaigns', *Feminist Review*, 86, p. 24-44.

Anti-Slavery International (2002) *Human Traffic, human rights: redefining victim protection*, Horsham:Anti-Slavery International.

Bjerkan, L. and Dyrild, L. (2005) A Sheltered Life in L. Bjerkan (ed) *The life on one's own: the rehabilitation of victims of trafficking for sexual exploitation*, Oslo:Fafo, p. 121-153

Brunovskis, A., Tyldum, G. (2004) *Crossing Borders. An Empirical Study of Transnational Prostitution and Trafficking in Human Beings,* Fafo-report 426. Oslo: Fafo.

Brunovskis, A. and Surtees, R. (2007) Leaving the past behind? When victims of trafficking decline assistance, Oslo:Fafo.

Clawson, H., Small, K., Go, E. and Myles, B. (2003) *Needs Assessment for Service Providers and Trafficking Victims,* National Institute of Justice.

Council of Europe Convention on Action against Trafficking in Human Beings, accessed at www.coe.int-trafficking, accessed at 20 January 2008

Dowling, S., Moreton, K., Wright, L (2007) Trafficking for the purposes of labour exploitation: a literature review. London: Home office.

Farley, M., Baral, I., Kiremire, M., Sezgin, U. (1998) 'Prostitution in five Countries: Violence and Post-Traumatic Stress Disorder', Feminism and Psychology, 8 (4), p. 405-426.

Farley, M., Cotton, A., Lynne, J., Zumbeck, S., Spiwak, F., Reyes, M., Alvarez, D. and Sezgin, U. (2003) 'Prostitution and Trafficking in Nine Countries: An Update on Violence and Posttraumatic Stress Disorder', in M. Farley (ed) Prostitution, Trafficking and Traumatic Stress, Binghamton:The Haworth Maltreatment & Trauma Press, p. 33-75

Goudolf, E., Fisher, E. (1988) Battered Women as Survivors, Toronto: Lexington Books.

Goddey, J. (2004) 'Sex trafficking in women from Central and East European countries: promoting a 'victim-centred' and 'woman-centred' approach to criminal justice intervention', Feminist Review, 76, p. 26-45

Goodey, J. (2005) Victims and Victimology:Research, Policy and Practice, Harlow:Pearson Education Limited.

Hedin, U. and Manssen, S. (2003) 'The Importance of Supportive Relationships Among Women leaving Prostitution" in M. Farley (ed) Prostitution, Trafficking and Traumatic Stress, Binghamton:The Haworth Maltreatment & Trauma Press, p.223-239

ICMPD (2006) Guidelines for the Development and Implementation of a Comprehensive National Anti-Trafficking Responses, Vienna:ICMPD.

ICMPD (2007) Transnational Referral Mechanism for victims of trafficking

– Draft.

IOM (2007) Trafficking of Men - A Trend Less Considered, GLOBAL EYE ON HUMAN TRAFFICKING, A Bulletin of News, Information and Analysis on Trafficking in Persons, No 1.

Kelly, L. (1987) Surviving Sexual Violence, Cambridge: Polity Press.

Kirchhoff, G.F.. (1999). Why do they stay? Why don/t they run away? In: van Dijk, J.J.M., van Kaam R.G.H. & J.Wemmers : Caring for Crime Victims: Selected Proceedings of the Ninth International Symposium on Victimology, Amsterdam, August 25-29, 1997. Monsey, New York, USA(Criminal Justice Press) p. 221-238.

Kroger, T, Malkoc, J. and Uhle, B. (2004) National Referral Mechanisms: Joining Efforts to Protect the Rights of Trafficked Persons – A Practical Handbook, Warsaw:OSCE/ODIHR

Lamb, S. (1999) 'Introduction' in S. Lamb (ed) New Versions of Victims: Feminist Struggles with the Concept, New York: New York University Press: 1-11.

Nikolic-Ristanovic, V . (2005) 'What victims went through and how they survived?' in Bjerkan, L. (ed) The life on one's own: the rehabilitation of victims of trafficking for sexual exploitation, Oslo:Fafo, p.71-118.

Nikolic-Ristanovic, V . (2002) Social Change, Gender and Violence: Post-Communist and War-Affected Societies, Kluwer Academic Publishers, Dordrecht, Boston, London: Kluwer.

Norwegian Government's Plan of Action to Combat Human Trafficking for 2006-2009, http:// www.jd.dep.no, accessed at 20 January 2008

Council of Europe. Committee of Ministers. Recommendation Rec(2006)8 of the Committee of Ministers to member states on assistance to crime victims. (Adopted by the Committee of Ministers on 14 June 2006 at the 967th meeting of the Ministers' Deputies) http://www.copii.ro/files2/29_RecomandareaCE_8_2006.doc, accessed August 31, 2011.

Rosa Project
http://www.rosa-help.no/pdf/rosa_english.pdf, accessed on 11 December 2007.

Smit, M. (2003) 'Trafficking in women: Dutch country report'. Contribution at the NEWR workshop on trafficking in women. Amsterdam April 25 and 26 2003, www.newr.bham.ac.uk/pdfs/Trafficking/Netherlands1.pdf, accessed at 22 January 2008

Segrave, M. , Milivojevic and S. Pickering: Sex Trafficking. International context and response. Cullompton and Portland (Willan) 2009.

Skilbrei, M. and Tveit, M. (2007) Facing Return: Perception of Repatriation among Nigerian Women in Prostitution in Norway, Oslo:FAFO.

Surtees, R. (2006) Evaluating Anti-Trafficking Victim Assistance in Southeastern Europe: a Strategic Planning Paper for the King Baudouin Foundation, Vienna: Nexus.

Surtees, R. (2007) Listening to victims: experiences of identification, return and assistance in South-Eastern Europe, Vienna: International Centre for Migration Policy Development

Zegarac, N. (2007) Deca govore (Children speak), Beograd: Save the children

World Health Organisation (WHO) (2003) Preporuke Svjetske zdravstvene organizacije za vodjenje razgovora sa zenama – zrtvama trgovine

ljudima (Guidelines of WHO for talking with women-victims of human trafficking), London: WHO
Walker, L. (1989) Terrifying Love, New York: Harper Perennial.
Zimmerman,C. (2003) The health risks and consequences of trafficking in women and adolescents:findings from a European study, London:London School of Hygien and Tropical Medicine, retrieved from www.lshtm.ac.uk on 7 July 2008.

Zimmerman, C., Hossain, M., Yun, K., Roche, B., Morison, L. and Watts, C. (2006) Stolen smiles: a summary report on the physical and psychological health consequences of women and adolescents trafficked in Europe, London:London School of Hygiene and Tropical Medicine, retrieved from www.lshtm.ac.ukgender violencee on 7 July 2008.

Disaster Studies

Victims of Global Environmental Change

By

Kieran G. Mundy

This essay introduces a human-centered scientific perspective of global environmental change victimhood and victimization. The typology of hidden victims of global environmental change (GEC) advanced is based on (1) identification of the type of environmental assault, (2) awareness of its victimizing potential and (3) the options available to reduce the victimizing force, and can also be applied to victimization at the community, regional, and global levels. While the type of the environmental assault is of secondary importance, the victimizing forces created have the potential to exacerbate existing global injustice and social inequity. This is explored in terms of the exponential growth of the human population and its' rapidly declining global resource base forcing within country and cross-border migrations into high-risk urban contexts. GEC injustice is also analyzed in terms of omissions by government and humanitarian agencies. GEC victimhood takes us beyond the orthodoxy of criminal law architecture and legal definitions of human rights, refugees, and displaced persons to a realistic consideration that perpetrators of environmental victimizing actions may be the victims of the victimizing forces they themselves have created. I propose that hidden GEC victims are a relatively small minority of a resilient majority who are not forced to, or who decide not to migrate, and who suffer long-term psychological, social and economic consequences of exposure to changing environmental conditions. The implications of GEC victimization inherent in an international aid response based on the Western discourse on the psychiatric implications of trauma are also discussed.

Introduction

Rather than enhancing earth systems sustainability, the triumph of neo-classical economic theory over environmental principle in the 20th century has created a global physical environment in the 21st century with the potential to victimize humanity on a scale never before experienced – or imagined. Unless global and national governance addresses this risk by putting people first, the decisions made on behalf of us all will fail to achieve justice for the victims of environmental change or shield vulnerable people from its potentially devastating impacts. The risk is not insubstantial as the global environmental crisis that has already begun could permanently and drastically constrain future global sustainability, or at worse, cause the extinction of intelligent life on the planet. The extreme severity of the risk of global environmental change to the human story deserves our utmost attention, even if some may argue, erroneously in my opinion, that its probability is relatively small.

Providing a victim's perspective on this threat is a challenge but has the sole and critical goal of alleviating and eliminating human suffering and pain. The aim is to understand the nature of individual vulnerability, a human-centered perspective on global environmental change in contrast to "top-down" socially constructed perspectives of climate justice advanced by interest groups who argue in the perceived humanitarian interests of those with whom they are charged to protect. How any environmental event plays out" as a victimizing force is the result of human decisions, a relativity reflected in the concept of weather itself as both a scientific construction based on meteorological statistics and one based on individual and group expectations of future climate that changes as societies, cultures, and knowledge evolve (Hulme, Dessai, Lorenzoni, & Nelson, 2009).

This essay aims to provide a theoretical framework for systematic analysis of global environmental change victimhood made from the point-of-view of the person – adult or child – who, for whatever reason, finds him or herself in a life context controlled by frequent, unpredictable, and threatening environmental events. Global environmental change does not have the temporal dimension of a natural disaster, such as a tsunami or earthquake, because it is an environmental catastrophe in slow motion – an imperceptible series of disasters that even those we assume most likely to be aware, cannot identify the threat or are aware of its potentially deadly impact. Focus is on the differential reaction of people to environmental assault and how they, as individuals and groups, cope psychologically and socially prior to the assault, and in the aftermath of the realization of that assault (see Dussich, 2008). Confronted with a potentially catastrophic environmental event, a tsunami for example, most people are able to identify the nature of the victimizing force, are aware of its victimizing potential, and respond by making a decision based on the options available to reduce the effect of the victimizing force – to get to higher ground, climb a tree, rush to a higher floor, or whatever. The majority, therefore, or those people able to identify the risk early enough, who are aware that tsunamis are deadly, and have the options available to avoid the ultimate victimization – death – are the survivors. From this majority are drawn a relatively small minority of high-risk people I describe as "hidden victims of global environmental change," or the higai-sha. These vulnerable people, perhaps children, women, or the elderly, but not necessarily so, are unable to identify the threat in time, are unaware of its victimizing potential, and do not have the personal and other resources (e.g., time to escape) to cope with the impending catastrophe and are subsequently victimized. Also, dependent on the nature of the event, a minority of people lose their lives. These people are the gisei-sha, or the sacrificed. Thus, the same victimizing force creates differential victimizing contexts and ways of coping ranging from behavioural modification to structural options available in countries to adapt to environmental change. The theoretical framework is simple—coping strategies or social adaptation determines either survival and/or victimization. Individuals and groups have a variety of options available, or limited or no options and, as a result, differential victimization outcomes range from death to survival to short and long-term physical, psychological, and social consequences.

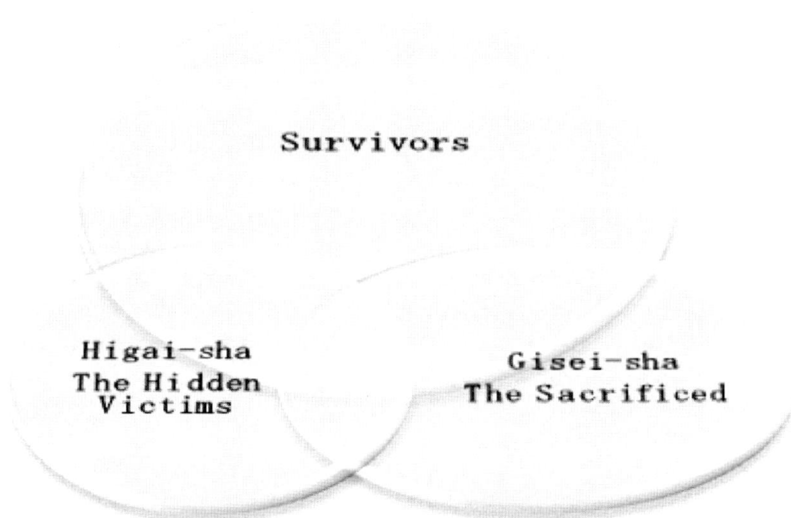

Figure 1. Categories of Global Environmental Change Victimhood

While my focus is not on the nature of the environmental assault, I critically accept the findings of biological, environmental and physical science alerting us to the dangers of abrupt or irreversible environmental changes due to human activities destabilizing Earth biophysical systems. Indeed, while the acrimonious debate over the anthropogenic origin of climate change proceeds, the window of opportunity to limit CO_2 concentrations in the Earth's atmosphere to less than 350 ppm, to halt the runaway loss of global biodiversity, and to reduce the human impact on the nitrogen cycle has closed, or is rapidly closing (Rockström et al., 2009). We have now entered an era of dangerous environmental change on Earth – the Anthropocene (Steffen, Crutzen, & McNeill, 2007) – with critical problems ahead for humanity in access to freshwater, ocean acidification, ozone layer depletion, atmospheric aerosol loading, land-use change, human-disrupted biogeochemical cycles, escalating biodiversity loss, chemical pollution, and climate change. But there is another dimension we rarely address, or choose to ignore because the ramifications are too overwhelming to confront. This is the ethical and moral issue that approximately 80% of the world's population, living mainly in the developing world, suffers the environmental impact of past carbon excesses as well as escalating volumes of greenhouse gas effluents released into the atmosphere by about 20% of Earth's population (International Energy Agency, 2009; UNFCCC, 2010). Paradoxically, rather than enhancing Earth systems sustainability, this injustice masquerading as an apparent triumph of neo-classical economic theory over environmental principle in the latter part of the 20th century has created a dangerous global physical environment in the 21st century with the potential to victimize humanity on a scale never before experienced – or imagined. The failure of our decision makers – political, industrial, and financial elites – to firstly, understand the magnitude and nature of this victimization by simply addressing the responsibility for and economic consequences of a singular dimension of global environmental change – climate change – and, secondly, to do little to ameliorate its impact should be viewed by future generations as a failure of governance for which we should be all held accountable.

The Victimizing Context

Focus on market manipulation to mitigate GHG emissions (Stern, 2007, 2009) and less focus on appeasement strategies of adaptation should be reframed to take account of the issues of climate justice and equity that are inextricably linked with victimization; that is, the search for justice for people vulnerable to the impact of global environmental change should not result in further victimization by creating additional injustice, inequity, vulnerability, and human insecurity. To define a global environmental change victim in this context is challenging because global environmental change, specifically climate change, is the consequence of the orders of complexity involving the explosion of the global human population (Bryant et al., 2009; Elverland, 2009; Myers, 2001; Warner, 2010; Tacoli, 2009), and is symbiotic with the rapid urbanization of the planet. This double-headed phenomenon is driven by declining child mortality in the developing world (WHO, 2010), natural increase, and massive numbers of people 'on the move' across the planet – a mobility disturbingly paralleled by a hidden migration of flora and fauna species towards the poles in response to global warming. The migration is within country primarily from rural to urban areas and/or cross-border from developing countries to mainly urban areas in the industrialized world. It is suggested that much of this human mobility as a result of unpredictable and declining rainfall is misrepresented and misinterpreted in the academic literature and mainstream media as ethnic or religious violence, as in the Guinea-Sudan-Sahel (GSS) region of Nigeria in West Africa (Fasona & Omojola, 2005).

The Earth's rapidly increasing population is forcing large numbers of people into what they perceive as secure urban environments (Burke, Miguelc, Satyanathd, Dykemae, & Lobell, 2009), but that in reality are milieu potentially exacerbating the risks of victimization. On a global scale, while most nation states guarantee human security for most of their citizens, at the same time limit personal options by erecting of borders –these may be virtual political borders as in the case of Timor Sea border separating Indonesia and Australia, or physically enforced "concrete walls," or wire-entangled "fences" that separate Bangladesh and India, Protestants and Catholics in 2010 Belfast, Israel and the West Bank, and Mexico and the United States border. Whatever the nature of these borders, they act to restrict the natural flow of people in response to changing climatic conditions, thereby enhancing vulnerability by creating a victimizing context defined not by the movement itself, but rather by the restriction on that movement. An example of this was observed during the Nigerian Civil War of May 30, 1967 to January 12, 1970, when the Biafran population was virtually encircled and isolated by Nigerian government forces causing starvation, mass death, and displacement of Igbos (Shelton, 2005). That is, state borders define, amongst a variety of mobile people of concern to the UNHCR and other humanitarian agencies, the concept of a refugee, asylum-seeker, and an internally displaced person (IDP) in the twentieth-first century.

The Century of the City

Rapid mass urbanization has creating a victimizing milieu of global proportions in the 21st Century. Explosive population growth and a declining global resource base directly related to global environmental change is forcing increasing numbers of people into high risk urban areas of the planet. In 2010 about one half of the world's population live in cities and urban areas that cover less than 1% of the Earth's surface, but use 75% of the world's energy and are responsible for 75% of its greenhouse gas emissions (The World Bank, 2008). To clarify this, by 2050 the proportion of the global population living in urban areas is predicted to rise to 70% (The World Bank, 2008), and developing and newly industrialized countries are projected to double their populations resulting in an eight-fold increase in the global demand for resources (Agenendt, 2010). Many of the world's mega-cities are located in the Low Elevation Coastal Zone (LECZ) of the Earth's surface comprising coastal and delta regions of major river systems only about 10 meters above mean sea level. While covering only 2% of the Earth's surface, the LECZ is home to 10% of the global population (:680 million people), the majority in Asia, and 60% of whom live in climate dependent megacities (:360 million people). Increases in global surface temperature, accelerated sea level rise accompanied by land subsidence and increasing saline freshwater supplies, and biodiversity loss pose particular environmental threats to urban areas with ballooning populations of immigrants supported by a declining resource base (Tacoli, 2009).

The enhancement of existing patterns of vulnerability within rapidly expanding urban areas in the developing world is driven by elites within these societies attempting to emulate the unsustainable consumption patterns of the West. With this caveat in mind, the global population will reach 7 billion next year (2011), a projected target to be achieved just 12 years after reaching six billion in 1999, and an increase from the previous level of five billion in 1987. By 2050 the world population will have grown by one third based on current population levels. Virtually all (97%) of the projected growth from 5.4 billion to 7.9 billion in 2050 will be in developing and newly industrialized countries (Population Reference Bureau, 2009), and will be highest in the 49 Least Developed countries (25% of all recognized countries) in which the population is projected to double from 828 million to 1.66 billion (Population Reference Bureau, 2009). Thirty-three LDCs are in Africa (16.8% of all recognized countries) and have the lowest relative incomes, highest economic vulnerability, and poorest human-development indicators. This is in stark contrast to projections of population decline by 2050 in countries in the developed world such as Germany, Italy, Japan, South Korea, Russia, and Spain. An additional layer of complexity is that nearly 90% of the planet's 1.2 billion youth (ages 15 to 24) live in developing countries with eight out of 10 in Africa and Asia. Globally, while the median age will rise over the next several decades in industrialized countries, in 2050 the population of countries such as Burundi, Afghanistan, Palestine, and Yemen will still have a median age of less than 24 (Agenendt, 2010). The differential victimizing milieu between rich and poor countries on Earth can be readily observed in fertility rates of Canada and Uganda, and are inconsistent with the Millennium Development Goals (UNFPA, 2009). Both countries have similar population today, but by 2050 Uganda is projected to have more than double Canada's population by 2050 due to enormous differences in lifetime births per woman – Ugandan women have 6.7 children on average, five more than the average for Canadian women (Agenendt, 2010), reflecting declining child mortality rates in the developing world (WHO, 2010).

As described above, victimization due to rapid global population growth in the next decades will be felt mainly in Asia. Currently more than four billion people, or nearly two-thirds of the global population live in Asia, a region with the longest coastline, the lowest above sea level land mass, more refugees, people in refugee-like situations or assisted by the UNHCR, returned refugees, returned IDPs and stateless persons than any other region on Earth (UNHCR, 2009), and with many of the world's megacities. While the size, form, structure, and function of these cities and their future growth trajectories pose major demographic, economic, environmental challenges and potential solutions to global sustainability, on this newly emergent life stage there is an increased risk of victimization due to global environmental change. This will be as further marginalization of vulnerable populations by exacerbating inequalities due to poverty (rich-poor), gender (male-female), age (the elderly), and culture, religion, race, and ethnicity. On an individual level, global environmental change forcing will result in an uneven distribution of victimizations. One way of examining this issue is to explore the links between population density (physical condition of with spatial and social dimensions), and the perception of crowding, a psychological condition involving a person's perception of constraints that result from limited space. Recent studies on neighborhood crime have used this approach to analyze neighborhood ethnic (or racial) heterogeneity due to factors such as residential concentration of ethnic and foreign-born minorities (Herzog, 2009).

Nevertheless, urbanization needs to be considered in context. Focus on IDPs and refugees as an underlying cause of urbanization fails to address the real issues facing the overwhelming majority of people who stay *in situ*—that is, the majority who do not migrate. For example, global estimates to the end of 2008 of the numbers of refuges, returned refugees, IDP protected/ assisted by UNHCR, including people in IDP-like situations, returned IDPs, and stateless persons was 0.49% (N = 34,415,751) of the total world population. In the Africa-Great Lakes, East and Horn of Africa, Western, and Southern Africa the estimate was 10,170,215 persons (UNHCR, June 10, 2009), or 1.02% of the total population (N = 1,000,010,000) of African states) (UNFPA, 2009). Finally, the total number of people directly or indirectly under the auspices of the UNHCR people is 0.49% of the world's population. In this context, it is important to focus on "the stayers" – perhaps about 60% of those who do not leave when threatened by environmental trauma.

Taking the above into consideration, the people most likely to migrate in an environmentally constrained future world will make the decision to do so well in advance, be well-informed of their options, and have the personal and economic resources to do so. For example, those living in some low-lying Pacific Island States will be the among the first people on Earth to be threatened by the sea-level rise, and are fully aware that they will eventually have to leave and have the potential option to do so, as regional powers will accommodate their resettlement. We do not view these people as victims in the sense that we are attempting to describe. Victims of global environmental change are a subset of people at risk of being victimized and drawn from the overwhelming majority of people who cannot use migration as part of the solution

Beyond the Bounds of Traditional Notions of Criminal Justice

The traditional notion of victimhood in the criminal justice system (von Hentig, 1948) describes that person who has been physically, financially or emotionally injured and/or had their property taken or damaged by someone committing a crime. In this sense, global environmental victims are clearly not victims of crime because there is no directly identifiable perpetrator of the crime, whatever that crime might be. The search for an environmental criminal to blame is a multi-layered procedure: we unwrap onion-layers of various causal agents until we find "the criminal" who may be prosecuted, possibly one such as 'Ali Jambi', a smuggler of illegal timber, on the run from the police in Indonesia, who has been tracked down to Singapore where he currently lives with impunity (EIA, 2008; Waters, 2010). But as we peel away the layers, we eventually arrive at a criminal source—the demand of people in the developed world for illegal rainforest timbers to build and furnish their homes and work places. In other words, we are the perpetrators of this specific global environmental crime. However, prosecuting environmental crime does nothing to eliminate suffering and pain due to that crime. In this sense, the concept of a global environmental change victim should be expanded to encompass the notions of either a "general victim," or one who has been physically, financially or emotionally injured and/or had their property taken or damaged by someone, an event, an organization or a natural phenomenon, as defined by Mendelsohn (1963), or a victim of the abuse of power (i.e., the use of organized powerful forces such that persons are injured physically, mentally, emotionally, economically, or in their rights, as a direct and intentional result of the misapplication of these forces) is that person whose human rights (based on national and international covenants) has been violated. As Kirchhoff (2008) argues, institutionalized top-down definitions or 'patterned reactions' are victimizing forces in themselves. We are aware that traditional and cherished concepts of punishment and state control seem threatened by participatory concepts such as victim participation in criminal proceedings/ restorative justice (mediation, victim-offender reconciliation, truth and reconciliation commissions), role of the victim in transitional justice, and UN instruments promoting human rights. The concept of a victim of global environmental change should also take us beyond these structural limitations to traditional ideas of justice, to encompass a vision of biosphere justice from the point-of-view of personal suffering and pain.

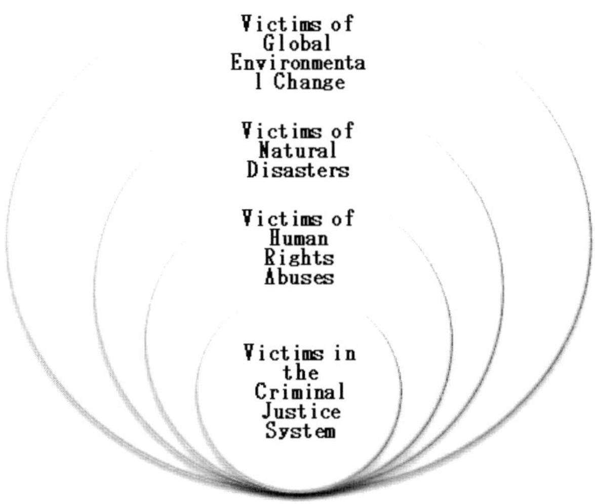

Figure 2. Global Environmental Change Victimhood as an Emergent Category of Crime Victimhood

Assaults on the Global Environmental Commons

While environmental assaults by elites on "the environmental commons" fall within the ambit of the traditional criminal justice system, at present there is little or no consideration of the construction of environmental victimhood in this process. Indeed, our focus should not be on the perpetrator of the biosphere crime, but rather the victim of the environmental assault. Are not some governments by acts of aggression (i.e., deliberate action) or omission (i.e., failing to act) victimizing the most vulnerable of their populations by locking down "the environmental commons," thereby denying equal access to sole sources of life-sustaining energy, air, food, and freshwater resources? Taken from the notion of "the Commons," I define it here as "the global commons of the Earth's biosphere" in all its dimensions – freshwater, the ozone layer, the natural geochemical (nitrogen and phosphorus) cycles of the Earth, the land and its vegetative cover, the oceans, and the biodiversity of the planet (IPCC, 2007a, 2007b, 2007c).

States do not have property rights over the global circulation of the atmosphere, just as they do not have property rights over the circulation of the planet's oceans, at least not beyond territorial borders (Fisher, 1993). Yet carbon-trading schemes privatizing the atmosphere normalizes the idea that States have "a 'property' right to pollute," and when a standardized share of that right has been under-utilized, that "right to pollute" the Earth's biosphere can be traded to someone else (see Stern, 2007, 2009). In the same sense, there can be no private property or "ownership" of national and international river-systems. Ethically and morally, but perhaps not legally, how can "an environmental common"—for example, the atmosphere and deep seas and with their life (human) sustaining resources be expropriated by a minority (viz., financial and political elites, and ordinary people subservient and economically dependent on those elites), as a valued resource – or a source of wealth –to the self-evident detriment of the majority of people on this planet.

To link mass human suffering, pain, and death with the decisions made by political, industrial and financial elites about the global environment is self-evident, but nevertheless difficult to establish under criminal law. At a macro-level, the failure of global governance at COP15 (UNFCCC, 2009) to agree to and urgently put-in-place strategies to reduce GHG emissions to safe limits should be considered as a major environmental assault with the potential to cause mass suffering and pain. Climate change, as everyone at COP15 was fully aware, is a temperature related – inter alia, water related – geophysical phenomenon of sea level rise, extreme drought and flooding, and major food shortages. Latest estimates of the risk of catastrophic sea level rise due to the rapid melt of the continental Greenland and West Antarctic ice sheets dramatically exceed IPCC (2007) projections (University of Toronto, 2009). COP15 delegates were also aware that if this (un)natural event was to happen it would have the potential for mass victimization of the planet's population. Rising sea level assault has already been responsible for creating the Earth's first homeless state as a direct result of failure of global governance – in Papua New Guinea, a remote community on the Carteret Islands in Bougainville is amongst the first recorded people on Earth to have lost their ancestral lands to rising sea levels.

The failure of national governments, particularly in the developing world, to rein-in the activities of multinational agrochemical companies, is the direct cause of food shortages and human suffering. The amount of nitrogenous chemicals in agricultural soil has long surpassed dangerous threshold levels described by Röckstrom et al. (2009), and directly threatens 75% of the world's poor who live in rural areas. As a result of unpredictable weather patterns and decreased crop yields, many of these people are poly-victimized by international agrochemical companies that aggressively promote reduced crop yields by forcing farmers already living on the margins of cultivation to buy patented genetically modified seed requiring expensive pesticides and herbicides, thereby making any existing environmental damage worse. These companies are also active in driving land system change, land-use, and land-cover change (LULCC) in developing countries at a rate, extent and intensity far greater than at any time in recorded history, resulting in irreversible changes in ecosystems and environmental processes at local, regional, and global scale (Rockström et al., 2009).

Over the past two decades the number of recorded natural disasters has doubled from some 200 to over 400 per year with nine out of every ten natural disasters in 2008 being climate-related (Holmes, 2008). While climate science is making progress in assessing whether or not these and other catastrophic events are natural or human-induced phenomena (Cai & Cowan, 2010), the cause of the victimizing force (whether earthquake, tsunami, wildfire, floods, hurricanes) is of little relevance for the victim whose sole interest is the scale and gravity of the victimization experienced, and the efforts made by others to alleviate suffering and pain. Victims and their victimizations are independent of cause – that is, no perpetrator needs be defined for a crime to have been committed.

The first step towards a legally defined idea of "a global environmental change victim" faces major obstacles, however. It requires, firstly, that rule-of-law architecture be reformulated to propel it into the twenty-first century and beyond traditional concepts of state control and punishment to consider that perpetrators of victimizing actions (in this case, to be even victims of their own unsustainable lifestyles) may be the victims of the victimizing forces they have themselves have created. "The criminal act" in this case, if indeed any has been committed, is indirect, and a poly-victimization ongoing over many years. That is, while a perpetrator is sought in the criminal justice system – the one who inflicts pain and suffering on someone else and can be held responsible for that action – the criminal act causing pain and suffering as a result of global environmental change, whilst encompassing personal violations, does not allow for blame to be apportioned to any other party (as with the blaming of human agents and agencies by victims of natural disasters), but still requires preventive measures, early warning measures, and appropriate responses to be taken by government agents to reduce the damage. While victims can blame governments and businesses for not acting with due care of the environment over decades, it is difficult, but not impossible, to establish "mens rea" - intentional criminal responsibility in judicial process. What makes people victims of catastrophic natural events are not acts of "mother nature," in themselves, but victimization by the accumulation over many years of ineffectual environmental policies and policy outcomes, negligence and the failure to act (e.g. the maintenance or restitution of bio-shields in coastal areas to alleviate the impact of tidal surges), lack of early warning of impending disasters (e.g. the 2004 Asian Tsunami), and early response to disasters (e.g. 'the U.S. response' to Hurricane Katrina in 2005 versus the Haiti earthquake in 2010). What also produces the victimizing force in all the above milieu is not only global environmental change and its concomitant (un)natural impacts, but a lack of preparedness of government and other agencies to respond to those victimizations. People living in the LECZ on the planet are not victimized by acts of "mother nature," but rather by poor governance, negligence, lack of early warning, and early response to disasters. The concept of victimization by environmental omissions has been recognized in the criminal justice system – the European Court of Human Rights that ruled failure to prevent or mitigate consequences of natural disasters amounts to a violation of the right to life and incurs state responsibility under international law (Popovski & Mundy, 2010).

Assaults on the Environmental Commons as a Violation of Human Rights

While the intent of a raft of international humanitarian treaties is to protect individual "rights," in reality the world continues to get it wrong and sideline the most vulnerable (Kayitesi-Blewitt, 2006). The failure of the West to act in 1994 Rwanda, for instance, resulted in the deaths of nearly 800,000 people in a mere 100 days, but this was not the greatest omission by those countries who had signed-off on the various international treaties that should have protected the most vulnerable of the Tutsi. Their greatest failure was that the survivors – the majority of those Tutsis who believed they would be protected by multi-layered and well-intentioned human rights that resulted in a false sense of human security – an extreme victimizing context in which those most vulnerable (the higai-sha), or those with no options were killed (the shigei-sha). Human rights are virtual rights that we can trace back to the ideals of liberty, fraternity, and equality in the French Revolution of 1789-99 and legalized by the

U.S. in the mid-twentieth century. Although we struggle to achieve this ideal protective rights context – the creation of a safe operating context for humanity – in reality, it does not exist, at least it did not for the survivors and victims of the Rwandan genocide, or of the small-scale murderous conflicts across most of sub-Saharan Africa in 2010. Members of the so-called Lord's Resistance Army (LRA) operating from bases in southern Sudan who kill, torture, maim, rape, and abduct large numbers of civilians, and virtually enslave numerous children do not really care about UN sanctioned human rights.

The human rights implications of global environmental change has not yet emerged as an issue of concern as clearly demonstrated in the Draft UN Convention on the Basic Principles of Justice for Victims of Crime and Abuse of Power debated at the Twelfth United Nations Congress on Crime Prevention and Criminal Justice (United Nations, 2010). The worthy aims to firmly establish the criminal justice system as "a central pillar in the rule-of-law architecture," to highlight "the pivotal role of the criminal justice system in development," and to emphasize "the need for a holistic approach to criminal justice system reform to strengthen the capacity of criminal justice systems in dealing with crime," raises profound issues of environmental (biosphere) justice and equity between generations, between the so-called developing and developed worlds, and between rich and poor within States. A human security perspective as outlined by Röckstrom et al. (2009) and normatively based on international human rights standards and practically directed to protecting and promoting the rights of victims has the potential to soften the impact of global environmental change victimization and to protect victims in terms of their ability to claim violations of rights. The challenge is to find an equitable distribution of responsibilities for global environmental change and the rights of GEC victims within this legislative context. GEC victimization from a human rights perspective is the abuse of power by organized powerful forces such that persons are injured physically, mentally, emotionally, economically, or their rights as perceived and defined by national and international covenants, have been violated as a direct and intentional result of the misapplication of these forces.

The fundamental purpose of the original human rights legislation was to legally immunize the world against the human pain and suffering caused by political extremisms in the first part of the twentieth century. While this legislation was not intended to address victimization due to environmental transgression, by implication it does offer a degree of legal protection for GEC victims. The basic treaty, the Universal Declaration for Human Rights (UDHR) ratified on December 10, 1948, proposes that "it is desirable for state parties to take all possible measures to reduce infant mortality and to increase life expectancy" (Article 3. The Right to Life), and that, "everyone has the right to a standard adequate for the health and well-being of himself and his family" (Article 25). The right to life, a right violated for many of the world's population threatened by the impending global environment crisis, is protected under Article 6 (1) International Covenant on Civil and Political Rights (ICCPR) adopted by the UN General Assembly on March 23, 1996 that states, "Every human being has the inherent right to life. This right shall be protected by law. No one shall be arbitrarily deprived of his life." Further, the right to life of children threatened by global environmental change is enshrined under Article 6 (1) of the Convention on the Rights of the Child (CRC) that entered into force on September 2, 1990 – "States Parties recognize that every child has the inherent right to life." Article (16) of the Convention Against Torture (CAT) of December 9, 1975 recognizes that "Each State Party shall undertake to prevent in any territory under its jurisdiction other acts of cruel, inhuman or degrading treatment or punishment which do not amount to torture as defined in article 1," but which could be interpreted to include acts of violence and murder as tools-of-trade of environmental criminals (EIA, 2008). In addition, Article 12 (a) of the International Covenant on Economic, Social and Cultural Rights (ICESCR) recognizes the right to the "highest standard of physical and mental health," and physical and mental health provisions are legally binding under Article 24 of the Convention on the Rights of the Child (CRC) and Article 12 (1, 2) of the Convention on the Elimination of All Forms of Discrimination against Women (CEDAW). The right to an adequate standard of well-being, inter alia, to not be victimized by global environmental change is only marginally protected under Article 2 (b) of the Draft UN Declaration on the Basic Principles of Justice for Victims of Crime and Abuse of Power, that recognizes "abuses of power; defined as acts or omissions that are not violations of national criminal laws but are violations of internationally recognized *jus cogens* norms."

Assaults on the Right to Food and Freshwater

It is now 14 years since the UN General Assembly legally recognized the right of every person to adequate food in Article 11 (1) of the International Covenant on Economic, Social and Cultural Rights (ICESCR) – "state parties recognize the right of everyone to an adequate standard of living for himself, his family, including <u>adequate food</u>, clothing and housing," and Article 11(2) – "the fundamental right of everyone to be free from hunger," yet today more than one billion people, or one sixth of Earth's population goes hungry, and five million children starve to death each year (Parker & Shapiro, 2008). To compound this milieu of suffering, and in blatant contravention of Article 12 (a) of the International Covenant on Economic, Social and Cultural Rights (ICESCR), Article 24 of the Convention on the Rights of the Child (CRC) and Article 12 (1, 2) of the Convention on the Elimination of All Forms of Discrimination against Women (CEDAW), severe nutritional deprivation and food insecurity, especially among children and other vulnerable groups, has the potential to create an unmanageable global mental health crisis (Parker & Shapiro, 2008). A future climate constrained world will see global environmental change impacting deleteriously on existing food shortages, specifically on the Indian subcontinent and in sub-Saharan Africa, regions already under stress from reduced food production and expected to become hotter and drier as a Greenhouse-world scenario unfolds (Fasona & Omjola, 2005; IPCC 2007a). For every 1.8 F° rise in temperature, grain production will drop 10% due to higher temperatures affecting grain-seed sterility, shifts in rainfall patterns and disruption of biogeochemical nitrogen and phosphorus cycles making previously arable land unsuitable for agriculture, accelerating erosion, desertification and reduced crop and livestock yields, rising sea levels making coastal land unusable and causing fish species to migrate, and the increased frequency of extreme weather disrupting agriculture (DuPont & Pearman, 2006).

The right to fresh water is fundamental to the right to health as articulated in the Universal Declaration for Human Rights, and in Article 12 of the International Covenant on Economic, Social and Cultural Rights (ICESCR). The right to freshwater and adequate food is an inherent right to life under Article 24 (c) of the Convention on the Rights of the Child (CRC), "To combat disease and malnutrition, including within the framework of primary health care, through, inter alia, the application of readily available technology and through the provision of adequate nutritious foods and clean drinking-water, taking into consideration the dangers and risks of environmental pollution," and the right, "To enjoy adequate living conditions, particularly in relation to housing, sanitation, electricity and water supply, transport and communications," as provided for under Article 14(2)(h) of the Convention on the Elimination of All Forms of Discrimination Against Women (CEDAW). By 2030, more than half the world's population (more than 3 billion people) will face freshwater shortages, or be dependent for their survival on too little freshwater at the wrong time of the year for growing crops, or on polluted water supplies. By 2020, regardless of what is done to mitigate greenhouse gases, from 75 to 220 million people in Africa will suffer the effects of drought (DuPont & Pearman, 2006).

Assaults on the Right to Physical and Mental Health

The negative impact on physical health of global warming is in contravention of Articles 3 (the Right to Life) and 25 (1) – "the right to a standard of living adequate for the health and well-being" - of the Universal Declaration for Human Rights, Article 6 (1) of the ICCPR, Article 12 (a) of the ICESCR, Articles 6 (1) and 24 of the CRC, and Article 12 of the CEDAW as outlined previously. Climate change is associated with abnormally high temperatures increasing health risks for infants, young children, the elderly, the poor, and those living in impoverished inner city areas who are less likely to have the financial resources to buy air-conditioners, or if they do have air conditioners, to afford the electricity to run them. If they live in poverty in developing countries, there may be no artificial escape from the heat. To further compound the inequity, children and the elderly are disproportionately represented amongst the poor. For example, 39% of all children in the USA live in low income families and 10% of people older than 65 live in poverty (Parker & Shapiro, 2008). People living in inner urban environments of mega-cities are also more likely to suffer the effects of higher temperatures (measured at up to 11°C hotter) than those living in rural areas (Huntington, Hemming, Gash, Gedney, & Nuttall, 2007). Some studies show that elderly men are more vulnerable to heat stress than elderly women, although the results are unequivocal. For example, in the 1995 Chicago heat wave, elderly men were two and a half times more likely to die than elderly women (Whitman et al., 1997). In the 1995 Chicago study, 2% of Hispanics died of heat related illness although making up 23% of the population at the time. In contrast, more than 50% of African Americans were more likely to die from heat stress than whites. These dramatic differences have been attributed to factors relating to poverty rather than to racial or ethic characteristics (Whitman et al., 1997). To compound these global environmental change victimizations, Cohen and Rotten (2003) demonstrated that an increase of 0.5°C showed evidence of significantly more criminal behavior.

Furthermore, the effects of bad air, especially due to depletion of the lung-damaging stratospheric pollutant, ozone, are magnified by age, poverty, geography, gender, race and ethnicity, and prior heart and lung disease. Higher predicted temperatures during summer as a result of climate change are predicted to lead to higher ozone concentrations, and the length of summer itself is predicted to increase in duration. A study of 50 cities in the eastern part of the US projected an increase of 60% more days with ozone levels higher than standard safe levels (Bell et al., 2007). The combination of high temperatures due to climate change, depletion of stratospheric O_3 and poor air quality is fatal (Parker & Shapiro 2008). In the 2003 heat wave in Western Europe, 45,000 people died, with peak fatalities occurring when temperatures and ozone concentrations were highest. The majority of these victims were elderly (English et al., 2009).

GEC Victim as an Emergent Category of Scientific Knowledge

While the natural, behavioral, and social sciences and the humanities have disparate methodologies defining who might present as GEC victims, as a behavioral science, victimology is not bound by the orthodoxy of criminal law architecture or by legal definitions of human rights, refugees and displaced persons. The voluminous research literature critically examining the common language used in describing "climate change refugees," "environmental migrants," (Brown, 2008), the range of social constructions of environmental "victimhood" legally defined by international instruments (UNHCR, 2009), or enshrined in national constitutions (The Council of Europe, 2008), are top-down subjective classifications and do not provide us with an objective understanding of GEC victimhood. The usage of the term "refugee" to define survivors of physical events linked with GEC is not only inconsistent with popular usage of the term as outlined in Article 1 of The 1951 Convention Relating to the Status of Refugees (see UNHCR, 2001), but dangerously misleading for well-intentioned relief effort.

Meta-analysis of the scientific datasets of the increased risks of the increased risks (viz. physical, psychological, social, financial) to people of global environmental change in terms of water and food stress, temperature-initiated physical and mental diseases, injury and fatalities due to catastrophic weather events such as unusually intense and frequent cyclones, hurricanes, floods, and so on, and to population displacement reveals that they do not adequately record suffering at individual level. On the contrary, the top-down perspectives described above often reflect the institutionalized and potential suppressive mechanisms of the State apparatus that depend on international legal formulations guaranteeing these apparent freedoms constituting "quality of life" as human rights—for example, the right to water, to food, to human security, and so on. That is, there is a difference between those people who feel that the denial of human rights and opportunities as legislated for by power elites defines them as GEC victims externally and those who are truly victimized by changing environmental circumstances perceive themselves. The concept of human security also struggles with the duality of how people perceive their own victimhood - their fears, what makes them insecure - from the tendency of external agencies to label particular groups as vulnerable, even if these assessments are based on scientific assessment. Many people probably do not fear war, genocide, a tsunami, or earthquake, as these are often abstract, non-imminent threats, but rather they do fear imminent threats such as not having enough food or freshwater to drink, losing their job, losing a loved partner, or child, disease, and so on.

Global environmental change victims can claim a personal identity –"I am a victim of changed environmental conditions," a bottom-up perspective that exists independently of any normative or institutional definition. Their victimhood derives from relative inter- and intra-individual fragility when confronted by some environmental trauma, and the relative individual lack of power to influence the behaviour of others perceived to be, or actually responsible for that victimization. Those people most vulnerable in any society, both physically and socially, are children, women, and the elderly, and it is to these vulnerable groups where the research effort stressing linkages, psychological factors, sociological factors should go to avoid secondary, or tertiary victimizations. That is, the true victims of global environmental change might not be those who are forced to, or who decide to leave in face of changing environmental circumstances. No case better illustrates this than the personal aftermath of Hurricane Katrina. The hidden victims of Katrina were drawn from that relatively smaller proportion (42%; N = 1,071,420) of non-evacuees living in Katrina-affected areas who choose to stay in New Orleans for whatever reason, or who simply could not afford to leave. Structural forces of social inequity clearly outweighed the threat and reality of the deadly forces of nature thereby ensuring the conditions for maximum victimization of vulnerable sub-groups but contrary to expectation of disproportionate numbers of blacks, women, children, and the elderly, the demographic composition of the non-evacuee and evacuee populations was similar (Fritz Institute, 2006).

Having in mind all caveats and uncertainties above, and realizing how premature and incomplete any definition of climate change victims could be, for the sake of opening a critical debate we tentatively propose a definition of global environmental change victims. A hidden GEC victim, or higai-sha is that living person who has been poly-victimized by repeated or an escalating series of environmental assaults to the extent that he or she can no longer function independently in either the short or long term due to physical and/or psychological damages, or indirectly due to significant deterioration of that person's physical, social, and economic milieu. To clarify the scientific terminology we seek to employ, a GEC victim is not that person who is a gisei-sha, or a sacrificed person to the impact of global environmental change.

Secondary GEC victims are "first responders," dependants, relatives, and other persons, including and especially, peers, in the violated behavioural space of the primary climate change victim who experience significant, but non-debilitating physical, social, economic, and/or psychological damages as a result of environmental assaults on the hidden GEC victim. Tertiary GEC victims are those persons whose secure behavioural space is influenced, but not violated by non-debilitating, short-term anxiety about the consequences of future climate change assaults. Tertiary climate change victims typically have no direct contact with either primary of secondary GEC victims and their victimization is the creation by states, interested parties, and individuals of a behavioural context, typically engendering fear and anxiety – but certainly a threat to an individual person's security – in which both primary and secondary GEC victimization is likely to occur.

Refugees, Survivors and Hidden GEC Victims

Who are those people standing unaware of the express train advance of the tsunami of global environmental change? Who are the most vulnerable? Why are they vulnerable? What is the nature of their vulnerability, and how do they express their vulnerability? Hidden victims of global environmental change may not necessarily be those who have left the victimizing milieu for, perhaps, another victimizing milieu; that is, environmental migrants/climate change refugees, or asylum seekers.

The Western Discourse on Victimization

The projected impact of global environmental change, and its most dangerous manifestation – climate change – raises the major ethical issue challenge of the 21st century in that those who contribute least to the problem bear the brunt of its consequences (Nobre & Hepburn, 2009 – the conference proceedings). However projections morph into the reality that presently the world's poorest people, most of whom live in developing countries, account for 95% of the deaths (gisei-sha) due to global physical disasters and have economic losses up to 20 times greater (as a percentage of GDP) than people living in developed countries (Angenendt, 2010). More than two-thirds of countries in sub-Saharan Africa have experienced armed conflict since 1960 resulting in millions of deaths and monumental human suffering (Burke, Miguelc, Satyanathd, Dykemae, & Lobell, 2009), and currently, a viral pandemic of opportunistic violent, and seemingly profit-oriented bloodshed committed against civilians by heavily armed bandits has broken out across the continent. If this scale of destruction and fighting was in Europe, it would be called "World War III" with the entire world rushing to report, provide aid, mediate and otherwise try to diffuse the situation (Shah, 2010). But, with impunity, the rebels predators of Africa steal other people's children, stick Kalashnikovs or axes in their hands, and make them commit stunning atrocities such as eastern Congo's rape epidemic, where armed groups in recent years have sexually assaulted hundreds of thousands of women, often so sadistically that the victims are left incontinent for life, or they have rammed assault rifles inside women and pulled the trigger (Gettleman, 2010). The linkages between drought and armed conflict in Sub-Saharan Africa have been demonstrated (Burke, Miguelc, Satyanathd, Dykemae, & Lobell, 2009). People in the developing world depend on rain-fed agriculture making them less ecologically, socially and individually resilient to transgressions of the planetary boundaries such as climatic variability, freshwater scarcity, disrupted biogeochemical cycles, and atmospheric aerosol loading (Rockström et al., 2009). Changes in rainfall patterns, a dimension of climate change, leads to increased vulnerability and, hence, food insecurity and poverty, which in turn, leads to increased political instability through horizontal inequalities that eventually culminates in violent conflict (Webersik, 2007).

Nevertheless, while we have no empirical data to support this claim as yet, the overwhelming majority of people, especially children, from the rebel-saturated Niger Delta to the human inferno in the Democratic Republic of the Congo, for example, should be able to theoretically maintain relatively healthy levels of psychological functioning during and after exposure to such intense stressors – at least a Western-defined type of resilience. Potentially traumatic events (PTEs) occur frequently and have affects on many levels including basic needs, functional impairment, physical and mental health (Resnick, Kilpatrick, Dansky, Saunders, & Best, 1993; Amstadter et al., 2009), as well as increasing the risk of a variety of psychiatric phenotypes. Fifty to 60% of the population in the U.S. (Ozer, Best, Lipsey, & Weiss, 2003), survive at least one violent or life-threatening situation during the course of their lives with acute distress from which they are able to recover, others react less intensely and for a shorter time, some apparently have no ill-effects but relapse with unexpected health problems, but most have no apparent disruption in their abilities to function at work or in close relationships (Bonanno, 2004, 2005). Further, as many as two to three adolescents report being exposed to psychological trauma which may include victimization (i.e. exposure to or witnessing community violence), severe physical injuries, unexpected or untimely loss, and life threatening disasters (see Ford, Elhai, Connor, & Frueh, 2010). Posttraumatic stress disorder (PTSD), major depression disorder (MDD), generalized anxiety disorder (GAD), substance use disorder (SUD) non-specific stress disorders (e.g. stress-related psychological and psychosomatic symptoms, sleep disorder), health problems (e.g. somatic complaints, medical conditions), daily living problems (e.g.

troubled interpersonal relationships) and psychosocial resources (e.g. social support, self-efficacy) (Kilpatrick et al., 2000; Norris, 2005), is only observed in 5% to 10% of survivors, although PTSD rates can reach as high as 17.8% for victims of physical assaults (Resnick, Kilpatrick, Dansky, Saunders, & Best, 1993). There are three well-documented and clinically significant psychiatric problems associated with victimization in adolescents – PTSD, MDD, and SUD as well as involvement in or being associated with juvenile delinquency (Ford, Elhai, Connor, & Frueh, 2010).

We are interested in defining the threshold between GEC resilience and GEC victimhood and, therefore, need to verify the 'life-boat approach to explaining vulnerability; that is, are PTSD rates in high-risk populations (e.g., refugees, IDPs, women, children, and the elderly) the same as predicted rates for poly-victimized GEC victims? Is there a dose-response relationship in terms of the severity and frequency of catastrophic events linked with GEC, and psychiatric outcomes. That is, is the victimization due to single stressor events that cause devastating physical harm, or that leave that person in a state of extreme confusion and insecurity (such as sexual abuse, violence, the threat of either, or the witnessing of either, particularly in childhood, the same as victimization caused by poly-victimization by catastrophic events linked with global environmental change? While resilience of high-risk populations, such as in the DRC, is a critical construct within the general traumatic stress response (Paton & Valanti, 2006), of the minority of those people we define as hidden victims – the higai-sha. The Western research literature on PTSD following natural disasters suggests that not all variance is explained by type of stressor experienced. Current consensus suggests the factors associated with victimization include (1) the more direct the exposure to the traumatic event, the higher the risk for emotional harm and prolonged effects (Sajid, 2007), (2) poly-victimization or the stepwise repeated victimization that increases the risk of psychiatric and behavioral problems, (3) gender, (4) prior experience of trauma, (5) personality (Acierno et al. 2009), and critically, (6) biological or genetic risk factors (Amstadter et al. 2009; Kolassa, Kolassa Ertl, Papassotiropoulos, & de Quervain, 2009; Ursano, Zhang, Li, Johnson, Carlton, Fullerton, & Benedek, 2009).

Children and adolescents are the hidden victims of the growing global environmental change in Africa. Rising food prices and inflation across the continent are exacerbating the vulnerability of especially children and adolescents with approximately 38 million children in Sub-Saharan Africa frequently witnessing violence in their homes (UN, 2006) and family poverty denying families the capacity to take care of their children, insulating their children from the hazards of child labor, child prostitution, child trafficking, and child slavery. Chronic and repeated exposure to GEC-linked environmental stressors and related adversities could be associated with severe psychiatric and psychosocial outcomes not only in childhood, but in adolescence and adulthood as well. These may include severe psychological distress (Finkelhor, Ormrod, & Turner, 2007), psychiatric disorders (Cuevas, Finkelhor, Ormrod, & Turner, 2009), delinquency (Cuevas, Finkelhor, Turner, & Ormrod, 2007), the increased risk of re-victimization, and of experiencing adversity other than victimization such as traumatic accidents and family breakup (Finkelhor, Ormrod, & Turner, 2007). However, in addition to clinical diagnoses of PTSD, MDD, and SUDs, poly-victimized adolescents were at risk of comorbid combinations of these disorders (Ford, Elhai, Connor, & Freuh, 2010). The risk and severity of internalizing and externalizing problems among poly-victimized children and adolescents suggests that healthcare providers and aid workers adopt sophisticated treatment, psychosocial and legal rehabilitation plans.

The Aid Response

The more direct and frequent the exposure to traumatic event, the higher the risk of more severe forms of victimization – that is, adolescent victims exhibiting psychiatric and behavioral problems were based on the sub-sets, 'no trauma', non-victimization trauma, community violence poly-victimization, and sexual and physical assault and abuse poly-victimization (Ford, Elhai, Connor, & Freuh, 2010). The increasing severity scale warrants much closer attention by health care providers and first aiders!

The framework issue is that the Western discourse on victimization and how to respond to that victimization only makes sense in the context of a particular cultural and moral framework and, therefore, becomes problematic in the context of other cultural and social settings (Keinzler, 2008). Thus, while the victim reacts by verbally and non-verbally communicating his or her victimization in a social and cultural context at the interpersonal (intra- and inter-familial), local community (neighbors, teachers, community leaders), and regional (e.g. sub-Saharan Africa), at the global level the response is largely structural or institutionalized. If this scale of destruction and fighting that is currently raging or has just ceased in nearly half of the countries in Africa was in Europe (the former Yugoslavia, for example), it would be called "World War III" with the entire world rushing to report, provide aid, mediate and otherwise try to diffuse the situation. Africa is largely ignored by the world today just as it was ignored in the 1990s - with such devastating and bloody consequence in Rwanda.

But how far should the West go to avoid secondary victimization of the higai-sha in the developing world – to relinquish institutionalized intervening (Western) therapies or legal positions in favor of protecting non-Western victims? Just as traditional and cherished concepts of punishment and state control in Japan, for example, seem threatened by participatory concepts such as victim participation in criminal proceedings, restorative justice, mediation, victim-offender reconciliation, truth and reconciliation commissions, the role of the victim in transitional justice, and UN international instruments, (see Kirchhoff & Morosawa, 2009), standardized psychiatric classifications of victimization (APA, 2000, 2010) are threatened by trans-cultural psychiatry. For example, the WHO Report on "Mental Health in Emergencies" (WHO, 2003) claims most acute mental health problems during acute emergency phases of any crisis are best managed by the principles of "psychological first-aid." During the reconsolidation phase it is recommended to educate humanitarian aid workers and community leaders in core psychological skills such as psychological first aid, emotional support, providing information, sympathetic reassurance, and recognition of core mental health problems. Similarly, the Inter-Agency Standing Committee (IASC, 2007) states that it is crucial to protect and improve people's mental health and psycho-social well-being in the midst of an emergency through (a) psychological first aid for people in acute trauma-induced distress by a variety of community workers and (b) care for people with severe mental disorders, including severe PTSD, by trained and supervised health staff only. These consensus criteria on approaches to trauma treatment largely ignore that no convincing evidence of the efficacy of advocated practices seems to exist (Pupavac, 2002; Summerfield, 1998).

Do the classifications of posttraumatic disorder (PTSD), major depressive disorder (MDD), and substance use disorder (SUD) exist as separate entities independent of the ways in which they are diagnosed, studied in 'atheoretical' frameworks, and treated as medical outcomes (Young, 1995, 2006), or do they only exist in their most severest manifestations? That is, is PTSD, MDD, and SUD as separate entities, or comorbid, a universal and cross-culturally valid psychopathological response to traumatic distress that may be applied to the hidden victims of the brutalities of the brainwashed boys and girls "child soldiers" of the Lord's Resistance Army (LRA) in northern Uganda in the 1980s (Gettleman, 2010). Can these victimizations be cured or ameliorated with (Western) clinical and psychosocial therapeutic measures? In contrast to the medicalisation of trauma survivors that reduces individual subjectivities to victims and, thereupon, patients (Kleinman & Kleinman, 1997), a relativist approach would suggest any psychological and/or physical trauma is embedded in the social and cultural frameworks of any society (Mollica, Caspi-Yavin, Bollini, Truong, & Lavelle, 1992; Kienzler, 2008).

Trans-cultural psychiatrists are making tentative steps to address "social suffering," a concept that combines Western with traditional healing strategies (Weine, 1998; Somasundaram, van de Put, Eisenbruch, & de Jong, 1999; de Jong, 2000; Lykes, 2002; Eisenbruch, de Jong, & van de Put, 2004; Lustig, Weine, Saxe, & Beardslee, 2004; Carr, 2006).

Humanitarian aid and development agencies, NGOs and international organizations that offer trauma counseling to GEC-affected populations should review the dominant grief work assumption upon which such aid is provided; that is, the critical importance of for "the victim" to "work through until 'closure'" the negative thoughts, memories, and emotions about loss and trauma (see Bonnano & Field, 2000). Indiscriminate "Crisis Intervention," or the provision of emergency psychological care to traumatized victims, or survivors with no trauma reaction at all so as to help them return to an adaptive level of functioning and to prevent or mitigate the negative impact of psychological and emotional trauma has proved to be ineffective and potentially harmful (Bonnano & Kaltman, 1999). Further, it lacks empirical support (Wortman & Silver, 1989), and may only be a plausible explanation for the most severe levels of grief and distress (Bonnano, Paps, & O'Neill, 2001). Mindful of these limitations, we propose that resilience, recovery, and victimhood be examined in terms of the blocking of the normal availability of potentials of the affected person to manage difficult situations (such as accessing water and food, coping with death of loved ones, loss of security, and so on). In this context, resilience concerns those people who, if exposed to traumatic stressors, can access their personal potentials to maintain relatively stable levels of psychological and physical functioning. The concept of recovery concerns the survivors of trauma who suffer less intensely than higai-sha and for shorter periods, or who recover quickly but experience unexpected problems later, and whose normal functioning is temporarily disrupted by threshold or sub-threshold psychopathology for a period of at least several months (Bonnano, 2004). The hidden victims - the higai-sha - are those people who experience severe victimization from which they are unable to recover. This differential and accelerating mechanism of blocked fulfillment of human needs at subsequently higher levels parallels Maslow's (1943) valuable, but neglected conceptualization of a hierarchy of human needs in pursuit of human self-actualization; that is, (1) physiological for survival—air, water, food, shelter, procreation, (2) safety—security, stability, law, order, (3) social—family and community, (4) esteem—status and recognition, and (5) self-fulfillment. Only when prior needs are satisfied does the individual person seek to address needs at a higher stage in the hierarchy. For long a fundamental tool in behavioral sciences and now increasingly accepted in the research literature on sustainable development management, Maslow's hierarchy of social needs is utilized in researches such as operational water resources management (Melloul & Collin, 2003), food management (Satter, 2007), transnational justice and victim recovery in terms of satisfying basic victim needs first and pursuing values such as reconciliation last (David & Choi Yuk-ping, 2005; Roberts, 2009), and in assessment of a global hierarchy of national development needs (Udo & Jansson, 2009).

Conclusions

This essay introduced to the research literature a theoretical framework for systematic analysis of global environmental change victimhood and victimization. The three-tiered typology of *shigei sha* (the sacrificed), survivors, and *higai sha*, or hidden victims of global environmental change advanced is a refinement of psycho-social coping theory (Dussich, 2008). Vulnerability in life contexts determined by frequent, unpredictable, and threatening environmental events were defined in terms of (1) identification of the type of environmental assault involved, (2) awareness of the victimizing potential of the assaults, and (3) the personal options available to reduce the victimizing force of the assaults. The theoretical framework proposed is relatively simple – coping strategies at the micro-level of analysis, and social adaptation at the macro-level determines either survival and/or victimization. It was established that individual or group identification of the risk of environmental assault and awareness of the inherent danger of such risk, and with different options available to reduce that victimizing force, may possibly result in differential victimization outcomes ranging from death to survival, and to short and long-term physical, psychological, and social consequences.

While critically accepting the overwhelming evidence of the science of global environmental change, the essay suggested that the nature of the environmental assault is of only minor consequence. Rather, it argued that focus should be on the victimizing forces created by global environmental change that have the potential to exacerbate existing gross injustice and social inequity. This phenomenon was explored in terms of the largely neglected relationship between the exponential growth of the global human population and its' rapidly declining global resource base forcing within country and cross-border migrations into high-risk urban contexts. In addition to concentration of the global human population in urban areas, the creation of victimizing milieu by the imposition of man-made virtual and physical borders preventing natural migrations of people due to changing environmental conditions was also raised. In addition, omissions or failures of governance and humanitarian agencies to reduce the impacts of victimizing forces were discussed.

The challenge of defining global environmental change victimhood and victimization took us beyond the orthodoxy of criminal law architecture and legal definitions of human rights, refugees, and displaced persons to a realistic consideration that perpetrators of environmental victimizing actions may be the victims of the victimizing forces they have themselves have created. The definition I proposed of a global environmental change victim is a bottom-up perspective existing independently of any relevant normative or institutional definition. In essence, the true or hidden victims of global environmental change are most probably not be those who are forced to leave their homes, or who simply decide to leave in face of changing environmental circumstances, but are a relatively small minority of the overwhelming majority of people who remain *in situ* and who demonstrate varying degrees of psychological, social and economic resilience during and after exposure to trauma.

Finally, it was proposed that the international aid response to natural disasters in general carries with it the potential risk of further victimization of affected populations. The framework issue is that the Western discourse on pre- and post-traumatic event psychiatric disorder and how that discourse is applied 'on the ground' victimization only makes sense in the context of a particular cultural and moral framework and, therefore, becomes problematic in the context of other cultural and social settings.

References

Acierno, R., Amstadter, A. B., Gros, D.F., Richardson L., Kilpatrick D. G., Trung, L.T., et al. (2009) A Pre-/Post-Disaster Epidemiological Study of Mental Health Functioning in Vietnam's Da Nang Province Following Typhoon Xangsane. *International Perspectives in Victimology,* 4 (1), 1-8.

Angenendt, S. (2010). The Perils of Population Boom. Why demographic ignorance can lead to conflict. German Institute for International Security Affairs, Berlin. DOI: 04.01.2010. Retrieved March 2, 2010, from www.ip-global.org.

Allden, K., Poole, C., Chantavanich, S., Ohmar, K., and Aung, N. N., et al. (1996). Burmese political dissidents in Thailand: trauma and survival among young adults in exile. *American Journal of Public Health*, 86 (11), 1561–1569.

American Psychiatric Association. (2000). *Diagnostic and Statistical Manual of Mental Disorders, Fourth Edition. Text Revision (DSMIV-TR).* American Psychiatric Association (Publ.)

American Psychiatric Association (2010). DSM-5: *Future of Psychiatric Diagnosis.* Retrieved June 4, 2010, from http://www.dsm5.org/Pages/Default.aspx.

Amstadter, A. B., Koenen, K. C., Ruggiero, K. J., Acierno, R., Galea S., Kilpatrick, D.G., and Gelernter, J. (2009). Variant in *RGS2* moderates posttraumatic stress symptoms following potentially traumatic event exposure. *Journal of Anxiety Disorders*, 23, 369-373.

Bell, M. L., Goldberg, C., Hogrefe, P. L., Kinney, K., Knowlton, B., Lynn, J., et al. (2007). Climate change, ambient ozone, and health in 50 US cities. *Climatic Change*, 82, 61-76, DOI:10.1007/s10584-006-9166-7.

Bonanno, G. A. (2004). Loss, Trauma, and Human Resilience: Have We Underestimated the Human Capacity to Thrive After Extremely Aversive Events? *American Psychologist*, 59 (1), 20 -28. DOI: 10.1037/0003-066X.59.1.20

Bonnano, G. A. (2005). Resilience in the Face of Potential Trauma. *Current Directions in Psychological Science*, 14 (3), 135- 138.

Bonnano, G. A., and Field, N. P. (2000). Examining the delayed grief hypothesis across five years of bereavement. *American Behavioral Scientist*, 44, 798-806.

Bonnano, G. A., and Kaltman, S. (1999). Towards an integrative perspective on bereavement. *Psychological Bulletin*, 125, 760-766.

Bonnano, G. A., Paps, A., and O'Neill, K, (2001). Loss and human resilience. *Applied and Preventive Psychology*, 10, 193-206.

Brown, O. (2008) Migration and Climate Change. *IOM Migration Research Series 31.*

Bryant, L., Carver, L., Butler, C. D., and Anage, A. (2009). Climate change and family planning: least-developed countries define the agenda. *Bulletin of the World Health Organization* 87 (11). DOI: 10.1590/S0042-96862009001100014

Burke, M. B., Miguelc, E., Satyanathd, S., Dykemae, J. A., and Lobell, D. B. (2009). Warming increases the risk of civil war in Africa. *PNAS*, 106 (49). DOI: 10.1073/pnas.0907998106

Cai, W., and Cowan, T. (2010), Evidence of impacts from rising temperature on inflows to the Murray-Darling Basin. *Geophysical Research Letters*, 35, L07701, 5 PP., 2008 . DOI:10.1029/2008GL033390

Carr, K. (2006). The Mobile Member Care Team as a means of responding to crisis. West Africa. In L. Barbanel, & R. Sternberg (Eds.), *Psychological interventions in times of crisis*. NY: Springer.

Coghlan, B., Ngoy, P., Mulumba, F., Hardy, C., Nkamgang Bemo, V, Stewart T., et al. (2007). *Mortality in the Democratic Republic of Congo*: An Ongoing Crisis. International Rescue Committee (IRC); NY, U.S.A.

Cuevas, C.A., Finkelhor, D., Turner, H.A., and Ormrod, R.K. (2007). Juvenile delinquency and victimization: A theoretical typology. *Journal of Interpersonal Violence*, 22, 1581-1602.

Cuevas, C.A., Finkelhor, D., Ormrod, R.K., and Turner, H.A. (2009). Psychiatric diagnosis as a risk marker for victimization in a national sample of children. *Journal of Interpersonal Violence,* 24, 636-652.

de Jong, J. (2000). Traumatic stress among ex-combatants. In N. Pauwels (Ed.), *War force to work force. Global perspectives on demobilization and reintegration*. Baden-Baden: Nomos Verlag.

DuPont, A,, and Pearman, G. (2006). *Heating up the planet: climate change and security*. Lowy Institute Paper 12. Lowy Institute for Public Policy: Double Bay, N.S.W.

Dussich, P. J. (2008). Psychosocial Coping: A Theoretical Model For Understanding General Victimization and Facilitating Recovery [Computer Software]. California State University, Fresno, U.S.A., and Tokiwa International Victimology Institute, Mito, Japan.

Environmental Investigation Agency (EIA). (2008). *Environmental Crime: A threat to our future*. EIA: London, UK.

Eisenbruch, M., de Jong, J. T., and van de Put, W. (2004). Bringing order out of chaos: a culturally competent approach to managing the problems of refugees and victims of organized violence. *Journal of Traumatic Stress*, 17 (2), 123–131.

Elverland, S. (2010).*"20 million Climate Displaced in 2008,"* Norwegian Refugee Council, 8 June 2009. Retrieved June 4, 2010, from http://www.nrc.no/?did=9407544).

English, P. B., Sinclair, A. H., Zev Ross, Z., Anderson, H., Boothe, V., Davis, C., et al. (2009). Environmental Health Indicators of Climate Change for the United States: Findings from the State Environmental Health Indicator Collaborative. *Environmental Health Perspectives*, 117 (11), 1673–1681.

Fasona, M. J., and Omojola, A.S. (21-23 June, 2005). *Climate Change, Human Security and Communal Clashes in Nigeria. Human Security and Climate Change*. An International Workshop Holmen Fjord Hotel, Asker, near Oslo. Centre for the Study of Civil War, International Peace Research Institute, Oslo (PRIO) & Centre for International Environmental and Climate Research at the University of Oslo (CICERO) for the Global Environmental Change and Human Security Program (GECHS).

Finkelhor, D., Ormrod, R. K., and Turner, H. A. (2007). Re-victimization patterns in a national longitudinal sample of children and youth. *Child Abuse and Neglect*, 31, 479-502.

Finkelhor, D., Ormrod, R. K., and Turner, H. A. (2009). Lifetime assessment of poly-victimization in a national longitudinal sample of children and youth. *Child Abuse and Neglect,* 33, 403-411.

Fisher, D. E. (1994). *Environmental Law*. The Law Book Company, North Ryde, Australia.

Ford, J.D., Elhai, J.D., Connor, D. F., and Freuh, B. C. (2010). *Journal of Adolescent Health*, (in press), 1-8.

Fritz Institute. (2006). Hurricane Katrina; Perceptions of the Affected. Retrieved 7 March, 2010, from www.fritzinstitute.com.

Gettleman, J. (2010). Africa's Forever Wars: Why the continent's conflicts never end. *Foreign Policy*, March/April 2010.

von Hentig, H. (1948). *The Criminal and His Victim*. New Haven: Yale University Press.

Herzog, S. (2009). Ethnic and immigrant residential concentration, and crime rates. *Journal of Criminal Justice*, 37 (5), 427-434.

Hulme, M., Dessai, S., Lorenzone, I., and Nelson, D. R. (2009). Unstable climates: Exploring the statistical and social constructions of 'normal' climate. *Geoform*, 40, 197-206.

Huntington C., Hemming D., Gash J. H. C., Gedney, N., and Nuttall, P. A. (2007). Impact of climate change on health: what is required of climate modellers? *Transactions of the Royal Society of Tropical Medicine and Hygiene*, 101 (2), 97-103.

Inter-agency Standing Committee (IASC). (2007). *IASC guidelines on mental health and psychological support in emergency settings*. Geneva: IASC.

International Energy Agency (IEA). (2009). CO_2 *Emissions from Fuel Combustion*. Retrieved June 3, 2010, from www.iea.org/co2highlights

IPCC (Intergovernmental Panel on Climate Change), (2007a) Climate Change 2007: *The Physical Science Basis. Contribution of Working Group I to the Fourth Assessment Report of the Intergovernmental Panel on Climate Change*. Solomon, S, Qin, D, Manning, M, Chen, Z, Marquis, M, Averyt, K, Tignor, M and Miller, H (eds). Cambridge University Press, UK. Retrieved, March 10, 2010, from http://www.ipcc.ch/ipccreports/ar4-wg1.htm

IPCC (Intergovernmental Panel on Climate Change), (2007b) *Climate Change 2007: Mitigation. Contribution of Working Group III to the Fourth Assessment Report of the Intergovernmental Panel on Climate Change*. Metz, B, Davidson, OR, Bosch, PR, Dave, R, Meyer, LA (eds), Cambridge University Press, UK. Retrieved January 6, 2010, from http://www.ipcc.ch/ipccreports/ar4-wg3.htm

IPCC, (2007c) Climate Change 2007: *Impacts, Adaptation and Vulnerability. Contribution of Working Group II to the Fourth Assessment Report of the Intergovernmental Panel on Climate Change*. Parry, ML, Canziani, OF, Palutikof, JP, van der Linden PJ, and Hanson, CE (eds.), Cambridge University Press, Cambridge, UK.

Kayitesi-Blewitt, M. (2006). Understanding development in Rwanda: the survivors' perspective. *Development in Practice* 16 (3 & 4), 316-321.

Kienzler, H. (2008). Debating war-trauma and post-traumatic stress disorder (PTSD) in an interdisciplinary arena. *Social Science and Medicine*, 67, 218-227. DOI:10.1016/j.socscimed.2008.03.030

Kilpatrick, D. G., Acierno, R., Saunders, B., Resnick, H. S., Best, C L., and Schnurr, P. P. (2000). Risk factors for adolescent substance abuse and dependence: Data from a national sample. *Journal of Consulting and Clinical Psychology*, 68 (1), 19-30. DOI: 10.1037/0022-006X.68.1.19

Kirchhoff, G. F., and Morosawa, H. (2009). The Study of Victimology. Basic considerationsfor the study of theoretical victimology. In F. W., Winkel, P. C., Friday, G. F. Kirchhoff., & R. Letschert (Eds.): *Victimization in a multi-disciplinary key: Recent advances in victimology*. Nimegen, NL (Wolf Legal Publishers), 271 – 312.

Kleinman, A., & Kleinman, J. (1997). The appeal of experience; The dismay of images; Cultural appropriations of suffering in our times. In A. Kleinman A., , Das, V. , and M., Lock (Eds.), *Social suffering*. Berkeley, CA: University of California Press, 1-24.

Kolassa, I-T., Kolassa, S., Ertl V., Papassotiropoulos, C., and de Quervain D. J-F. (2009). *The Risk of Posttraumatic Stress Disorder After Trauma Depends on Traumatic Load and the Catechol-O Methyltransferase Va[158] Met Polymorphism. Biological Psychiatry* (in press). DOI:10.1016/j.biopsych.2009.10.009.

Lustig, S. L., Weine, S. M., Saxe, G. N., and Beardslee, W. R. (2004). Testimonial psychotherapy for adolescent refugees: a case series. Transcultural Psychiatry, 41(1), 31–45. *Science and Medicine*, 43 (5), 889–900.

Lykes, B. (2002). A critical re-reading of post-traumatic stress disorder from a cross-cultural/community perspective. In D., Hook, & G., Eagle (Eds.), *Psychopathology and Social Prejudice*. Cape Town: University of Cape Town Press.

Maslow (1943). A Theory of Human Motivation. Originally published in *Psychological Review*, 1943, 50 (4), 370–396)

Mendelsohn, B. (1963) "The Origin of the Doctrine of Victimology" *Excerpta Criminologica,* 3, 30.

Myers, N. (2001), Environmental Refugees: Our Latest Understanding, *Philosophical Transactions of the Royal Society B: 356*, 16.1-16.5.

Mollica, R., Caspi-Yavin, Y., Bollini, P., Truong, T., and Lavelle, S. (1992). The Harvard Trauma Questionnaire: validating a cross-cultural instrument of measuring torture, trauma and posttraumatic stress disorder in Indochinese refugees. *Journal of Nervous and Mental Disease*, 180, 111–116.

Norris, F. M. (2005). *Range, magnitude, and duration of the effects of disaster on mental* health. Review update 2005. Retrieved on May 13, from http://www.redmh.org

Ozer E.J., Best, S.R., Lipsey, T.L., and Weiss, D.S. (2003) Predictors of posttraumatic stress disorder and symptoms in adults: A metanalysis. *Psychological Bulletin*, 129, 52-71.

Parker C. L., and Shapiro, S. M. (2008). *Climate Chaos: Your Health at Risk, What You Can Do to Protect Yourself and Your Family.* Praeger, NY. DOI: 10.1336/0275998584

Paton, D., & Volanti, J. (2006). Vulnerability to traumatic stress: personal, organisational and contextual influences. In J., Volanti, & D., Paton (Eds.), *Who gets PTSD? Issues of posttraumatic stress vulnerability*. Springfield, IL: Charles C. Thomas Publisher, Ltd.

Population Reference Bureau/ UN Population Division. *2009 World Population Data Sheet Aug. 12, 2009*. Washington, DC.

Popovski, V., and Mundy, K. G. (2010). Victims of Climate Change. *Sustainability Science* (In Press).

Pupavac, V. (2002). Pathologizing populations and colonizing minds: international psychosocial programs in Kosovo. *Alternatives*, 27, 489–511.

UNFPA (2010). State of the World's Population 2009. Retrieved on 1.5 May, 2010, from http://www.unfpa.org/swp/
Ursano R.J., Zhang L., Li, H., Johnson, L., Carlton, J., Fullerton, C.S, and Benedek, D. M. (2009). PTSD and traumatic stress: From gene to community and bench to bedside. *Brain Research*, 1293, 2-12.
Resnick, H. S., Kilpatrick, D. G., Dansky, B. S., Saunders, B. E., and Best, C. L. (1993). Prevalence of civilian trauma and postraumatic stress disorder in a representative sample of women. *Journal of Consulting and Clinical Psychology* 61, 984-991.
Rockström, J., Steffen, W., Noone, K., Persson, A., Chapin III, F. S., Lambin, E. F., et al. (23 September, 2009). Planetary Boundaries: Exploring the safe operating space for humanity. *Nature*, 461: 472-475. DOI:10.1038/461472a
Sajid. S. M. (2007). Unearthing the most vulnerable: Psychological impact of natural disasters. *European Journal of Psychiatry*, 21 (3), 320-231.
Satter E. (2007) Hierarchy of Food Needs. *Journal of Nutrition Education and Behavior* 39: S187-188. DOI 1016/j.jneb2007.01.003
Shah, A. *Conflicts in Africa. Global Issues*. Retrieved on May 15, 2010 from http://www.globalissues.org/issue/83/conflicts-in-africa
Shelton, D. L. (Ed.). (2005). "Biafra/Nigeria." Genocide and Crimes Against Humanity. Gale Cengage. eNotes.com. 2006. Retrieved February 2, 2010, from http://www.enotes.com/genocide-encyclopedia/ biafra-nigeria
Somasundaram, D. J., van de Put, Eisenbruch, C. M., and de Jong, J. (1999). Starting mental health services in Cambodia. *Social Science and Medicine*, 48, 1029–1046.
Steffen, W., Crutzen, P. J., and McNeill, J. R. (2007). The Anthropocene: are humans now overwhelming the great forces of Nature? *Ambio* 36, 614-621.
Stern, N. (2007). *The Economics of Climate Change: The Stern Review*. Cambridge University Press, Cambridge, UK.
Stern, N. (2009). *A Blueprint For a Safer Planet: How to Manage Climate Change and Create a New Era of Progress and Prosperity*. The Bodley Head, Random House, London.
Summerfield, D. (1998). The social experience of war and some issues for the humanitarian field. In P., Bracken, & C., Petty (Eds.), *Rethinking the Trauma of War*. NY: Free Association Books, 9-37.
Tacoli, C. (2009). Radical shift needed to end alarmism over climate-related migration. Institute for Environment and Development (IIED). Published online 19 August 2009, *Nature* 460, 943. DOI:10.1038/460943b
The Council of Europe. Parliamentary Assembly Doc. 11785, 23 December 2008 *Environmentally induced migration and displacement: a 21st century challenge Report. Committee on Migration, Refugees and Population*. Rapporteur: Mrs Tina ACKETOFT, Sweden, Alliance of Liberals and Democrats for Europe.
The World Bank/ The International Bank for Reconstruction and Development (2010). *Global Monitoring Report 2010. The MDGs after the Crisis.* Washington DC. Retrieved June 12, 2010, from http://siteresources.worldbank.org/INTGLOMONREP2010/Resources/6911301-1271698910928/GMR2010WEB.pdf
Udo V. E., Jansson, P. M. (2009) Bridging the gaps for sustainable development: A quantitative analysis. *Journal of Environmental Management*, 16 (1).

DOI: 10.1016/jenvman.2008/12.020

University of Toronto (2009, February 6). Collapse Of Antarctic Ice Sheet Would Likely Put Washington, D.C. Largely Underwater. *Science Daily*. Retrieved June 14, 2010, from http://www.sciencedaily.com / releases/2009/02/090205142132.htm

United Nations Framework Convention on Climate Change (UNFCCC), (December, 2009). Report of the Conference of the Parties on its fifteenth session, held in Copenhagen from 7 to 19 December 2009. Addendum. Part Two: Action taken by the Conference of the Parties at its fifteenth session. Retrieved June 14, 2010, from http://unfccc.int/meetings/cop_15/items/5257.php

United Nations Framework Convention on Climate Change (UNFCCC), (31 May, 2010). Bonn Climate Change Talks - June 2010. SBSTA 32, SBI 32, AWG-KP 12, AWG-LCA 10, Bonn. Retrieved 2 June, 2010, from http://unfccc.int/resource/docs/2010/sb/od01.pdf

UNHCR (United Nations High Commissioner for Refugees) (2006). *Convention and Protocol Relating to the Status of Refugees: Text of the 1951 Protocol Relating to the Status of Refugees, Text of the 1967 Protocol Relating to the Status of Refugees, and Resolution 2198 adopted by the United Nations General Assembly, UNHCR, Geneva*. Retrieved 7 June, 2010, from http://www.unhcr.org/protect/PROTECTION/3b66c2aa10.pdf (23.01.2010)

United Nations. (2010). Report of the Secretary-General on "Strengthening and coordinating United Nations rule of law activities", held in Salvador, 12-19 April 2010 2010, E/CN.15/2007/6, A/63/226, para. 44

United Nations Population Fund (UNFPA). (2009). State of the World Population Report 2009, Facing a Changing World: Women, Population and Climate. USA: UNFPA. Retrieved on 15 May, 2010, from http://www.unfpa.org/swp/

United Nations (29 August 2006). Rights of the Child: Promotion and protection of the rights of children. General Assembly Nations A/61/299

Warner, K. (2010): Global Environmental Change and Migration: Governance Challenges. In: Special issue on Governance and Complexity, Global Environmental Change.

Waters, J. (March, 2010). Following the proceeds of illegal logging in Indonesia: *Trends & issues in crime and criminal justice*, (391). Australian Institute of Criminology, Canberra, A. C. T.

Webersik, C. "Drought and armed conflict in Sub-Saharan Africa" Paper presented at the Annual Meeting of the American Political Science Association, Hyatt Regency Chicago and the Sheraton Chicago Hotel and Towers, Chicago, IL, Aug 30, 2007 <Not Available>. 2010-05-14 http://www.allacademic.com/meta/p210696_index.html

Weine, S. (1998). A prevention and access intervention for survivor families. National Institute of Mental Health. (RO1 MH59573–01).

Whitman, S., Good, G., E R Donoghue, E. R., Benbow, N., Shou, W., and Mou, S. (1997). Mortality in Chicago attributed to the July 1995 heat wave. American Journal of Public Health, 87, (9), 1515-1518.

World Health Organization (WHO). (2003). Mental health in emergencies. Mental health and social aspects of health of populations exposed to extreme stressors. Geneva: Department of Mental Health and Substance Dependence, World Health Organization, Geneva.

World Health Organization (WHO). Sixty-third World Health Assembly. World Health Assembly Journal, 5 (21) May 2010
Young, A. (1995). The harmony of illusions. Inventing post-traumatic stress disorder. Princeton, NJ: Princeton University Press.
Young, A. (2006). *'Inventing' posttraumatic stress disorder*. Retrieved 1 April, 2010, from: www.healingthewar.org

Victimological Perspective on the Rights and Presen Status of Disaster Victims: Indonesian Situation

By

Heru Susetyo

1. Introduction

Victims of disaster are among the most serious victims in contemporary world. Disasters take place all over the world at all times and have taken many lives. Kofi Annan, former UN General Secretary mentioned that number of deaths due to disaster were 669.000 people from 1994 – 2003 compared to 13.000.000 of death in conflicts. Number of refugees and internally displaced persons in 2003 were 35.000.000 (Malanczuk, 2005).

However, the current status of international law regarding disaster relief is considered to be highly unsatisfactory (Malanczuk, 2005). There is no definite, broadly accepted source of international law which spells out legal standards, procedures, rights, and duties pertaining to disaster response and assistance. No systematic attempt has been made to pull together the disparate threads to existing law to formalize customary law or to expand and develop the law in new ways. (IFRC in Malanczuk, 2005)

The principle of state sovereignty, still an ambiguous cornerstone of international law, has often been a major obstacle in the absence of bilateral or regional treaties. The experience with the Asian tsunami disaster in 2004 has underlined this major deficit. The prevailing principles on disaster victims (in this case is IDPs) are *soft law* which is a legally non binding principles and not a powerful one (Malanczuk, 2005).

If the current international law said so, victimology as a discipline has not confirmed whether disaster victims belong to study of victimology or not. Some scholars said that victimology deals only with crime victims. Others said that victimology should take into account all kind of victims and victimization regardless the causes of victimization.

This paper deals with the rights and present status of disaster victims from a victimological perspective, particularly from Indonesian situation, a disaster prone country which suffered from tsunami, earthquakes, volcanic eruption, landslides, and massive floods recently.

2. Disaster victimization

Disaster can be defined as a serious disruption of the functioning of a society causing widespread human, material, financial, and environmental losses which exceed the ability of the society to cope using its own resource (PNDCC, 1996)

Dejoras (1997) defines disaster and hazards. According to him, disaster is a sudden great misfortune, calamity, or a sudden calamitous event producing great material damage, loss, and distress. While the disaster includes the damage, hazard does not. Hazard is defined as a potentially damaging physical event, phenomenon or human activity that may cause the loss of life or injury, property damages, social and economic disruption, or environmental degradation. Hazards can include latent conditions that may represent future threats and can have different origins, natural (geological, hydro meteorological, and biological) or induced by human processes (environmental degradation and technological hazards).

Natural disasters roughly fall into three broad groupings: (1). Geological events, triggered by the internal workings of our planet; (2) Meteorological events, caused by variations in global weather patterns; (3) Biological disasters, resulting from the actions of living agents such as diseases or insect pest. They can occur separately or together, and are generally, although not always, unrelated. Natural disasters are also known as `acts of God` because they can strike with little or no warning and without any apparent direct human involvement (Coenraads, 2006).

Another form of disaster is technological disaster of technological accident. The Philippine Disaster Management System (1996) distinguishes natural disaster to technological accident and emergency which threaten human life, property and community as a whole. However, a technological accident is relatively preventable. It can be known and intervened by human knowledge and skills. Forms of technological disaster are as follows: transportation accident; industrial accident; construction accident; hazardous material accident; animal and plantation accident; epidemics and fires.

During and in the aftermath of the disaster, some countermeasures must be taken for the victims. Victims' needs generally are : Physical evacuation; relocation, shelter; food and water; clothes; medical needs; psychological needs; relief and construction issues; public health issues environmental and ecological issues disaster welfare information (Chockalingam, 2005).

The protection issues for victims are as follows (Malanczuk, 2005): access to humanitarian aid; discrimination; involuntary relocation to or exclusion from settlements and camps; camp security and military presence; protection of women and children; family reunification; access to education; loss of documentation; participation of internally displaced persons; voluntary return and resettlement and also property issues.

However, during and in the aftermath of disaster, the victimizer is not nature alone. In many cases, disaster victims have also been suffered from *secondary victimization* caused by people living around affected areas, by victim assistance efforts or by volunteers, by caregiver agencies, by law enforcement officials, by local or central or even foreign government and also by the media/ press.

3. Discourse of victims and scope of victimology

The United Nation Declaration of Basic Principles of Justice for Victims of Crime and Abuse of Power 1985 mentioned that "Victims" means persons who, individually or collectively, have suffered harm, including physical or mental injury, emotional suffering, economic loss or substantial impairment of their fundamental rights, through acts or omissions that are in violation of criminal laws operative within Member States, including those laws proscribing criminal abuse of power (http://www2.ohchr.org/english/law/victims.htm)

There are three definitions of victims: The crime victim, the universal concept of victims (Mendelsohn), and The victim of violations of human rights including crime (Kirchhoff & Morosawa, 2009).

Victims are socially constructed. It is not sufficient that persons claim the status of victims without **sufficient social acknowledgement** (social construction of reality) (Barkhuizen 2007, in Kirchhoff and Morosawa, 2009)

Hence, since its early beginnings, victimology has struggle with delineating its boundaries. An overview of the field reveals three main approaches in victimology. The first is *penal victimology*, which considers victimology as a branch of criminology and is focused on victims of crimes. The second approach is *general victimology*. It includes victims of all types, such as victims of accidents and natural disasters. The third approach is a human rights approach, which focuses on man-made victimizations of all kinds including genocide, torture, and slavery (Kirchhoff&Morosawa 2009, Wemmers 2009: 39).

If the notion of 'crime victim' is a relatively new phenomenon, victimology is an even newer concept. One of the first studies to examine crime victims was Hans von Hentig's book, *The Criminal and His Victim*. Published in 1948, this book examines the relationship between the criminal and the victim (Wemmers 2009: 33).
Ezzat Fattah (2002) defines victimology as the study of crime victims, their characteristics, their relationship to, and their interactions with, their victimizers, their role and their actual contribution to the genesis of crime, offers a great promise for transforming etiological criminology from a static, one-sided study of the traits and attributes of the offender into a dynamic, situational approach that views criminal behavior not as a unilateral action but as the outcome of dynamic processes of interaction. For Fattah, the study of the victims is and will always remain an integral part of criminology. Any attempt to separate victimology from criminology, or to treat it as an independent or autonomous discipline is bound to fail.

Shichor and Tibbets (2002) mention that Victimology is in the process of delineating its focus of study, defining its key concepts, theoretical approaches, refining its data-collection methods, and generally trying to establish itself as a legitimate and independent discipline. *Victimology focused on individual victims of violent crimes committed by individual perpetrators. Gradually, victimological studies expanded to organizations and corporations as victim and victimizers*

Kirchhoff (2005) defines Victimology as the scientific study of the victim of human rights violation (including crime), of victimizations and of reactions to both of those. It deals with victims of human rights violations (including crime). Victimology deals with empirically accessible social realities.

Victimology is interested in the process of becoming a victim (which social, group, institutional and individual conditions lead to the processes of victimization. Victimology looks at reactions, reactions to victims and reactions to victimization (Kirchhoff, 2005).

4. Abandonment of natural disaster victims

The United Nation General Assembly, in Resolution 45/ 100 declared the abandonment of victims of natural disasters without humanitarian assistance to constitute a threat to human life and an offence to human dignity.
The resolution invites all states whose populations are in need of humanitarian assistance to facilitate the work of organizations in implementing humanitarian assistance, in particular the supply of food, medicines, and health care, for which access to victims is essential (Raj Kumar, 2005).

There is a lack of attention to human rights protection and that measures need to be taken to address issues such as discrimination (this was echoed in the tsunami aftermath reports of India and Indonesia by Human Rights Watch and Amnesty International. Another problem is corruption and the need for transparency in the distribution of aid (Raj Kumar, 2005)

Current status of international law regarding disaster relief is considered to be highly unsatisfactory (Malanczuk, 2005). There is no definite, broadly accepted source of international law which spells out legal standards, procedures, rights, and duties pertaining to disaster response and assistance...no systematic attempt has been made to pull together the disparate threads to existing law to formalize customary law or to expand and develop the law in new ways....(IFRC in Malanczuk, 2005)

Fortunately, in 1997 The Red Cross and Red Crescent Societies initiated an international disaster response law called the Sphere Project. This contains guiding principles and practice on international disaster response. Therefore, up to now, the sphere project could be regarded as a humanitarian charter and as minimum standards common to all sectors in disaster response.

5. Victimological perspective on disaster victims

Disaster victims, no doubt, are among vulnerable persons seriously affected by victimization. The next question is whether victimology also encompasses disaster victims or not. When we talk about this matter, we certainly must bear in mind Mendelsohn and his 'general victimology' in mind.

Beniamin Mendelshon was the first person to use the word *victimology*. Mendelsohn lays the ground work for a new science, which he calls victimology and sees as a separate discipline from criminology. Mendelsohn's vision for the future of victimology is remarkable. In setting the parameter of this new science, Mendelsohn asks if victimology should include mass victimization, political victims as well as international victim. His response was that time will tell (Wemmers 2009 : 34).

Beniamin Mendelsohn continued to develop his ideas about victims for crime until he arrived at the theory of general victimology. *Its purpose was to help `victims of all kinds` -including victims of factors beyond human control* (Hoffman, 1992 : 90).

Mendelsohn developed the concept of victimity: *"whole of the socio-bio-psychological characteristics, common to all victims in general, which society wishes to prevent and fight, no matter what their determinants are* (criminal or others).

General victimology is inclusive and does not exclude any victims. This approach recognizes that the word "victimization" is used in many different contexts besides criminal victimization. As a result, it covers much more than criminology and is justified as a separate science. This broad approach recognizes that victimization is a subjective appraisal rather than the result of some objective, external criteria. Also, general victimology emphasizes the similarities in people's reactions to different types of victimization such as natural disasters (Wemmers 2009 : 40).

However, in general victimology, everyone is a victim and thus the limits of the science are blurred. Moreover, people's reactions to intentional victimization are structurally different than their reactions to unintentional victimizations (such as earthquakes). When intentionally harmed by another human being, common reactions include anger and loss of faith in others. These reactions are unique to man-made victimizations and do not occur when the victimization was the result of a natural disaster. Moreover, the causes of man-made victimization versus natural disasters are different. Understanding the causes of tsunami requires very different knowledge than understanding the causes of criminal victimization (Wemmers 2009 : 40).

Since the principal victims of disaster are the persons who are affected by the disaster, there is a need for them to receive the most immediate attentions. Victims of disasters include not only persons directly affected by the disaster, but also those indirectly harmed by the disaster such as a family, one of whose members has died or is otherwise adversely affected. (Chockalingam, 2005).

The victimological perspective on disaster centrally locates the victims in the discourse relating to disaster management. The victimological perspective regarding disaster management attempts to emphasize developing a framework whereby the rights of disaster victims are duly-protected, and victims receive the required assistance in the aftermath of disasters (Chockalingam, 2005)

Disaster victimization requires a response which places victims at the center of attention. The response mechanism needs to be based upon the needs of victims. There is a need to recognize the unique vulnerabilities of children and women during disasters. Recognizing the rights of disaster victims expand the scope of victimology. This expansion requires developing inter-disciplinary approaches to disaster management (Chockalingam, 2005)

A victimological account of disasters needs to be emphasizing the importance of developing a viable system of disaster preparedness that ensures that countries are better prepared for disaster and is able to respond to them. Such measures involve planning, recognizing the plight of disaster victims, and developing strategies for addressing their needs (Chockalingam, 2005).

Disaster victims have no equivalent perpetrator. Serious challenges to victims in coming to terms with their victimization. Disaster victims need more on relief and rehabilitation rather than assistance in court trial or legal aid (Chockalingam, 2005).

Last but not least, theoretical victimology should take serious note of disaster victims. It has (1) to formulate response strategies, and suggesting policies and mechanisms for providing the necessary assistance and other forms of relief to victims of disasters; (2) to identify key actors to participate in a network for disaster management; (3) to establish victim-focused approach in disaster management (Chockalingam, 2005).

6. Disaster victims in indonesian situation

Indonesia is really a disaster-prone country. Indonesia has replaced Bangladesh and India as the most disaster-prone nation on earth (Vitchek 2007). Whenever the word `Indonesia` appears on the list of headlines on internet site of *Yahoo News*, chances are that another enormous -- and often unnecessary -- tragedy has occurred on one of the islands of this sprawling archipelago. Airplanes are disappearing or sliding off the runways. Ferries are sinking or simply decomposing on the high seas. Trains crash or get derailed. Landslides are taking carton-like houses into ravines. Earthquakes and tidal waves are swallowing up coastal cities and villages. Forest fires from Sumatra are choking huge areas of Southeast Asia.

The scope of disasters is on a scale so vast that they cannot be discounted simply as the nation's bad luck or as the wrath of Gods or nature. Some of the disasters that have struck Indonesia are man-made; many are preventable; in all cases the possibility exists of reducing the human toll. Earthquakes alone do not kill people. Poor construction of houses and buildings are the culprits, together with the lack of preventive measures and preventive education (Vitchek 2007).

The number of victims and other losses resulted from the disaster in Indonesia, either man-made or natural disaster are tremendous. Since December 2004, Indonesia has lost some 200,000 people in various disasters, excluding automobile accidents, ethnic-religious conflicts and vertical conflicts. Indeed, many Indonesians experience their lives as equally dangerous and hazardous as those in war-torn parts of the world. Some of the disasters that have struck Indonesia are man-made; many are preventable; in all cases the possibility exists of reducing the human toll. On close scrutiny it becomes obvious that people die due to almost non-existent efforts to prevent the loss of life and the lack of basic education.

Indonesian parliament has enacted the *Disaster Management Act* (Undang-Undang Penanggulangan Bencana No. 24/ 2007) on 29 March 2007. Prior to this newly enacted bill, the existing regulations for disaster management were the Presidential Decree No. 3 year 2001 on *National Coordinating Board on Disaster Management and Refugees Handling* (Badan Koordinasi Nasional Penanggulangan Bencana dan Penanganan Pengungsi), Presidential Decree No. 111 year 2001 on the amendment of Presidential Decree year 2001 and National Coordinating Board Secretary Decree on Common Guidance in Disaster Management and Refugees Handling.

In accordance with the guidance issued by National Coordinating Board (through National Coordinating Board Secretary Decree No. 2 year 2001), Indonesian grand strategy in coping with disaster and refuges problem are as follows: (1) emergency response phase (2) empowerment phase (3) reconciliation phase; and (4) relocation phase. On the other hand, the measures to handle the refugees or Internally Displaced Persons (IDPs) are as follows: (1) emergency/

search and rescue; (2) data collecting; (3) emergency assistance; and (4) people's involvement.

Furthermore, based on own observation of this author while joining volunteering activities to assist the Aceh tsunami victims December 2004 – January 2005 and Yogyakarta earthquake victims in June 2006, the victim services program in Indonesia are roughly unorganized, unintegrated, and not really well-planned. Besides the fact that before 2007 Indonesia did not have any Disaster Management Act, the prevailing disaster management policies before 2007 were not adequate to cope with disaster response activities. There is a National Coordinating Board for Disaster Management and for the Handling of Refugees. It coordinates the disaster management and has branches all over provinces and regencies in Indonesia. But it could not integrate and coordinate the disaster countermeasures. The reasons are: the board has only limited jurisdiction. It has poor facilities. It is understaffed. It has a low budget. Its policies are not clear. There is a lack of coordination: when a disaster occurred, the victim service providers and caregivers, either coming from common people, NGOs, as well as from government bodies, ran their activities on their own without coordination among one and another
Other problems arise in the rehabilitation and reconstruction phase after a disaster hit: unequal and discriminative disbursement of financial assistance; misallocation in providing reconstruction funds; poorly managed data and also corruption.

When we come to the law, Indonesian laws concerning victims' issues are really insufficient to cope with disaster victims. 'Victims' in Indonesian "Law No. 13 of 2006 on Protection of Victims and Witnesses" are defined as persons who physically, mentally or economically suffered from any criminal actions. Therefore, disaster victims are outside of the scope of this law.

On the other hand, Indonesian "Law No. 24 year 2007 on Disaster Management" defines disaster victims as those who suffered from or lost their lives by disasters. This definition does not explain the indirect victims and the future victims who might be victims of secondary victimization in the aftermath of disaster.

Generally speaking, Indonesia does have disaster management policies. It has enacted a Disaster Management Act on March, 29th 2007. However, the policies as well as measures taken so far, are relatively far from perfect. Indonesia still need integrative policies and measures to handle the various problem of disasters. The newly enacted bill is really a blessing, but does not reach far enough.

Indonesia is poor, but it certainly has the capacity to protect some of its most vulnerable citizens (Vitchek 2007). The main problem is a lack of political will and a system whose priorities lie elsewhere. There is plenty of concrete and bricks to build dams and walls against tsunamis, to reinforce the hills around those towns, which are in danger of being buried by the landslides. One has simply to look around Jakarta where dozens of new shopping malls are springing up and at the palaces being built for corrupt officials.

Failure to deal with the problems of natural and man-made disaster is rooted in the combination of the dominance of profit achievement and the system's corruption. Local companies and officials have developed an uncanny ability to profit from everything, even from disasters and the suffering of fellow citizens. When the toll has to be calculated in hundreds of thousands of lost human lives, corruption becomes mass murder.
In the absence of an integrative provision of disaster management and disaster preparedness, the Indonesian people are really in danger. The government did react to the disaster by providing reliefs, emergency responses and enacting policies. However, those measures seemed to be a bureaucrative survival not a real product of radical and systematic learning. The coping capacity of the people remained low.

7. Conclusion

Current status of international law regarding disaster relief is considered to be highly unsatisfactory. There is no definite, broadly accepted source of international law which spells out legal standards, procedures, rights, and duties pertaining to disaster response.

There are ongoing debates whether victimology should covers only crime victims/ human rights violations victims or also general victims (incl. disaster victims). Theoretical victimology should take serious note of disaster victims. The victimological perspective regarding disaster management attempts to emphasize developing a framework whereby the rights of disaster victims are duly-protected, and victims receive the required assistance in the aftermath of disasters.

While the country's law on victim protection does not include disaster victims. Indonesian law on disaster management provides a poor and narrow definition on disaster victims. It seems that natural disaster victims are abandoned by both international and national law.

Lesson learned from Indonesia as disaster prone country,

International Law as well as Victimology should pay attention to disaster victims. Natural disaster may lead to man-made disaster since secondary victimization in the aftermath of disaster is very common. In this matter, disaster victims and crime victims are interrelated and interconnected.

Should scholars put the victims in general terms which also encompassing disaster victims, the problem of disaster victims will certainly not to be left alone. Victims are victims. They must get proper attention, regardless the causes of victimization.

References

Carter, N. (1991). *Disaster management: A disaster manager's handbook*, Manila, ADB.

Coenraads, R. (2006). *Natural disaster*, New South Wales, Millennium Publishing House.

Dejoras, Fortunato M. (1997). *Disaster preparedness A primer*, Manila, Lagat Ambakan Publishing, 1997.

Disasters, the Journal of Disaster Studies, Policy and Management Volume 30 Number 1 March 2006, Overseas Development Institute Blackwell Publishing, London.

Dussich, J.P.J. & Mundy, K. G. (ed). (2008). disaster victimization : understanding and responding to the impact and needs of disaster victims. Proceedings of the 3rd Symposium of the Tokiwa International Victimology Institute. Mito, Tokiwa International Victimology Institute.

Hagemann, O., Schaefer, P. & Schmidt, S. (eds.) 2009. *Victimology, victim assistance and criminal justice.* Perspectives shared by international experts at the Inter-University Centre of Dubrovnik. Monchengladbach.

International Perspectives in Victimology, Tokiwa International Victimology Institute Journal Vol. 1 No. 2 December 2004.

International Perspectives in Victimology, Tokiwa International Victimology Institute Journal Vol. 3 No. 2 December 2007

Kirchhoff, G. F. (2005). *What is victimology*. Monograph Series No. 1. Mito, Tokiwa International Victimology Institute, 2005.

Kirchhoff, G.F. and Morosawa, H. (2010): The study of victimology. Basic considerations for the study of theoretical victimology. In:Winkel, F.W., Friday P.C., Kirchhoff, G.F. and R. M.Letschert (eds.). Victimization in a Multidisciplinary Key: Recent Advances in Victimology. Selection of Papers presented at the 12th International Symposium on Victimology, 2006, Orlando, USA. Nijmegen (Wolf Legal Publishers WLP) 2009. Pp. 271 - 298.

Vitchek, A. (2007) "Indonesia: Natural disaster or mass murder?" The International Herald Tribune and The Financial Times. 12 February 2007.

Walsh, D. et. al. (2005) National incident management system, principles and practice, Boston, Jones and Bartlett Publishers.

Victims and Restorative Justice

Restorative Justice and Victims of Crime: Evidence and Possibilities

By

Heather Strang[1] PhD

Introduction

There is not very much we know in the social sciences with any degree of certainty. The variability in human behaviour often defeats us in predicting how people will react to what they experience. This is certainly the case in criminology, and it applies to crime victims as much as anyone else caught up in the criminal justice system. Victimology is a relatively new field of research because it is so recently that victims have been given the attention they deserve, so perhaps even less is known here than in other arms of criminological research. As well, their status as the 'forgotten third parties' (Sebba 19--) in the justice system has often militated against the assembly of high quality research findings about their common experience and needs.

When restorative justice (RJ) began to excite interest around the world in the early 1990s, it was not because potential benefits to victims were self-evident. Even if they had been, it is unlikely that governments and criminal justice agencies would have felt they were sufficient reason to pursue research in this area. But restorative justice is usually defined in terms that embrace the victims of crime. For example, Tony Marshall, a British advocate for RJ, has defined it as 'a process whereby all the parties with a stake in a particular offence come together to resolve collectively how to deal with the aftermath of the offence and its implications for the future' (McCold 1997). He perceives it as a transactional device for resolving disputes and conflict, just as Maori and others have for millennia (Braithwaite 2002) where both the person responsible for the harm and the person who experienced the harm are essential actors in the transaction. But the reality is that RJ would not have sustained attention if it did not have crime reduction potential. Rhetoric is rich around concern for crime victims but it seldom motivates governments to operate in their true best interests.

---

[1] University of Cambridge and the Australian National University

So it is ironic that fifteen years of research in restorative justice has yielded mixed results regarding its impact on offenders, with much depending on the demographics of the offender, the type and seriousness of the crime and especially whether or not the crime involved a personal victim. While there is no question that RJ can reduce future crime, there are nuances around whether and when it will reduce crime that require careful unravelling of the research findings (see for example Sherman & Strang 2007, Shapland *et al* 2007, 2008, 2009).

But when we look at the effect of RJ on crime victims, the evidence is now overwhelming. We can say with considerable certainty that victims of crime who agree to meet their offenders who admit responsibility for the harm experienced in face-to-face meetings, and who are accompanied by their families and friends, will most often find the experience a satisfying one, will say that they benefited from it in terms of their emotional restoration and would recommend it to other crime victims.

The benefits of RJ to the great majority of crime victims who agree to participate are so overwhelming that further research is not only unnecessary but probably also unethical. So why is it available to so few victims around the world? Why, when it is used, is it most often limited to victims of relatively trivial offences committed by youthful offenders? Why is RJ usually seen as a 'soft option' for offenders when the emotional cost for them is almost always so much higher here than in the formal justice system and the emotional restoration experienced by victims is so much greater?

In this paper I will first briefly discuss the processes and values that underpin RJ and that make it distinctively different from other ways of 'doing justice'. I will then lay out the evidence we now have about the effects and effectiveness of RJ for victims of crime, with special attention to its psychotherapeutic benefits. Following this I will discuss attitudes to RJ that may explain some of the reluctance to use it more widely in criminal justice, with special reference to a comparative attitudinal survey of Japanese and Australian citizens as a case study. The paper will conclude with a discussion of the wider potential for RJ to help victims in post-conflict societies transitioning from war and conflict.

RJ and Crime Victims: Processes and Values

RJ is haunted by confusion and ambiguity about its essential features, its *sine qua non* qualities. These problems have been canvassed by Chanova and Kirchhoff (2010), who describe the ways in which RJ practices are sometimes converted, or even subverted, into instruments of social control through traditional formal systems that employ punishment and repression as their primary tools. The Marshall definition mentioned earlier describes a widely accepted view of the *process* of RJ. It disposes of some the wilder flights of fancy of the popular media and even some politicians and policymakers where court-assigned tasks like picking up litter are sometimes called restorative. It encompasses what Braithwaite (2002) refers to as the 'bringing together [of] all stakeholders in an undominated dialogue about the consequences of an injustice and what is to be done to put them right' (p12). But the necessity for restorative core values in the encounter remains: parties that meet these process conditions could very well agree an excessively punitive outcome unless these values underpin the agreement.

So what are these values? Starting from the UN Universal Declaration of Human Rights, Braithwaite (2002) sets out a list of RJ values that include those to be found in all relevant international human rights agreements. He acknowledges that these may appear vague and inadequate for guiding how good restorative practices should be done but proposes they are essential for arriving at deliberative regulation of RJ achieved through conversations based on these broad principles.

These conversations have been lively over the past decade as advocates for the wider use of RJ have strived to articulate workable principles and, through them, to arrive at standards for practice that meet those principles. The United Kingdom Restorative Justice Council, for example, has set out 28 principles that constitute a fundamental ethical framework for RJ practice (Restorative Justice Council, 2004). They underpin the National Occupational Standards for restorative practice in the UK, and the Diploma in Restorative Practice now available in this country (Restorative Justice Council, 2010). They were also essential in the developing of the UK Best Practice Guidance which is endorsed by the Ministry of Justice (Restorative Justice Council 2011).

RJ and Crime Victims: What is the Evidence?

While it is highly desirable to have innovation in criminal justice based on good theory and strong values, it is essential to know whether the innovation is effective in the ways that are intended. At a minimum we need to be assured that any new practice will not increase crime, that the people caught up in criminal justice – victims, offenders, and anyone else affected by the crime – believe they are treated fairly and with respect and that they are satisfied with their experience. Furthermore, we need to be sure that the practice will be cost effective.

The programme of research in RJ with which the author has been involved over the past fifteen years, consisting of 11 experiments conducted in Australia (four) and the UK (seven) has tested a model of RJ that conforms to the processes and values outlined earlier. In the case of the Australian studies, known as the Re-integrative Shaming Experiments, the research team was responsible for the evaluation (Strang 2002), while the UK experiments were independently evaluated by a team from the University of Sheffield led by Professor Joanna Shapland, the author of a series of evaluation reports on this study between 2004 and 2008.

Each RJ case in these experiments involved a face-to-face meeting between all parties affected by the crime, usually lasting around 90 minutes but sometimes continuing for as long as three hours. In every case the offender had acknowledged responsibility for the harm at some point prior to the meeting. Friends and family of the victim and offender were invited to attend both to support and to express opprobrium (Braithwaite 1989). All parties talk directly to each other, often in highly emotional terms. A trained facilitator, who was expected to say very little, ensured that the meeting remained civil, remained on-topic and moved towards resolution. Discussion focused on three issues: what did everyone feel when the crime happened, who was affected by the crime and how, and what should happen next to repair the harm and make sure it did not happen again. The emphasis was always on how people felt rather than what actually happened so that the outcome focused on repair of emotional harm as well as any material claim (Strang 2002). All of the research upon which the conclusions are drawn about effectiveness is based on this model of RJ, which we call face-to-face conferencing.

The distinguishing feature of this body of research is that it employed the 'gold standard' of evaluation research, the randomised design (Sherman *et al* 2005; Strang 2002; Shapland *et al* 2007). Randomised controlled trials have a long history in medical research and are the standard required by organisations such as the US Food and Drug Administration for approval of drugs and medical devices (Pocock 1983). The great advantage of this method is that it can minimise the possibility of selection bias in comparing a 'new' way of doing business with an 'old' way. All cases coming into such a study, based on agreed eligibility criteria, are randomly assigned either to the experimental condition or the control condition on an equal probability basis. This makes very likely equivalence between the two groups not only on known variables, but also on variables which are unknown and perhaps not even imagined (Gartin 1995). It then follows that any post-treatment difference between the groups can be confidently attributed to the effects of the treatment rather than to the characteristics of the individuals making up each group.

In the Australian research, RJ was used *instead of* formal justice processing, that is, eligible cases were randomly assigned either to 'justice as usual' through the courts or diverted to RJ. Two of these four experiments involved personal crime victims, one of property crime and one of violent crime, while the other two had no direct victims (Strang 2002). In the UK experiments, serious adult crime was involved in nine of the eleven: they included robbery, burglary including aggravated burglary, and serious violence. The two remaining experiments involved juvenile property and violent offenders eligible for a pre-court disposal. Cases that complied with agreed eligibility criteria were randomly assigned either an RJ meeting *in addition* to 'justice as usual' through police action or the courts, probation and custody, or to 'justice as usual' without such a meeting (Shapland *et al* 2004). In both sites, eligibility criteria involved not only offence characteristics but also voluntary agreement to participate in RJ by all parties.

It is the consistency of the results for crime victims from all these eleven experiments that provides the strongest support for the view that enormous benefits can accrue to those who wish to participate in RJ. Despite substantial variations in offence types, social contexts, nationality, age, gender and race, victims have been consistent in their reactions to this way of doing justice. Before-after changes revealed by qualitative and quantitative data are all in the same beneficial direction (Strang *et al* 2006, Shapland *et al* 2007).

A telling measure of the value of RJ to these victims is found in their response to an interview question about why they decided to take part in the RJ meeting with their offender. Across all the study sites in both Australia and the UK, around two-thirds of them said that it was important to them to have the chance to express their feelings directly to their offender and to have a say in the way their case was dealt with by the justice system. In addition, almost 80 percent of victims in the UK studies said that it was important to them to have their questions to their offenders answered concerning the offence; this usually went to the question of 'why me?' and most often victims were greatly assured to find that their victimisation was opportunistic and that they had not been targeted intentionally. (Strang 2002, Shapland *et al* 2007).

Another critical dimension to the question of the value of RJ is that of procedural justice and perceptions of fairness. Tyler (1990) argues these consist of a number of elements around confidence: the impartiality of the process, its ethicality, its lack of bias, the likelihood of being able to correct any errors in the process and the individual's sense of control over the process. Victims in the Australian studies who had experienced RJ were asked detailed questions about all these dimensions: on almost all measures more than 85 percent of respondents said that they agreed they had experienced all of them and were very satisfied about the fair and respectful treatment they had received (Strang 2002). Victims who had experienced RJ in the UK studies were asked a more global question: 'Overall, how fair did you feel the criminal justice process was?' and almost three-quarters of them responded that they had found it fair. We should note though that these victims experienced both RJ and formal justice, because the experimental treatment consisted of RJ *in addition to* usual justice procedures, so their mental frame for answering this question differed from that of Australian respondents who had experienced RJ *instead of* court.

The most important indicators of the value of RJ to crime victims, however, were those where we are able to compare the views and attitudes of those whose cases were randomly assigned to RJ compared with those who did not experience RJ. The principle measure here in all these experiments was the extent to which victims were satisfied with their justice experience.

In Australia there was a statistically significant difference between those whose cases were assigned to RJ compared with those that were not: 46 percent of the court-assigned victims compared with 60 percent of the conference-assigned said they were satisfied. For various reasons, usually administrative, not all victims whose cases were *assigned* to RJ actually *experienced* RJ: significantly more victims who experienced RJ were satisfied, compared with those whose cases were dealt with in court (70 percent vs 42 percent) (Strang 2002). Unfortunately it was not possible to ask court-assigned victims to respond meaningfully to questions about their experience of fairness and respect: they had been effectively excluded from any part of the processing of their cases and had been largely unaware of any actions either by the police, the prosecution authorities or the courts. Many of them spontaneously commented that they felt their exclusion was unfair and unjust (Strang 2002).

Similar levels of satisfaction was expressed by victims in the UK studies (Shapland *et al*, 2007). Of the victims whose cases had been assigned to RJ (in addition to 'usual' justice procedures), 72 percent reported that they were satisfied with what the criminal justice system did about the offence compared with 60 percent of those whose cases were not assigned to RJ. Only 12 percent expressed any doubt about the outcome agreement reached at the end of the RJ meeting and almost all thought it was fair. Interestingly, given the highly variable length of time that had elapsed between the incident and the RJ meeting (from a few weeks to several years) more than three-quarters said that the RJ had been held about the right length of time after the incident. Furthermore, 78 percent of the RJ-assigned victims said they would recommend RJ to other crime victims and only five percent said they definitely would not. Shapland *et al* (2007) as the principal evaluators of the UK studies describe these findings as 'overall, a ringing endorsement of restorative justice.' (p43).

Although it is the results from randomised trials in RJ that have been emphasised, it is important to recognise that very similar findings have emerged from other evaluations as well. These have consistently shown that RJ benefits victims along several dimensions, principally in reducing emotional harm and increasing a sense of fairness.
For example, a number of studies have been conducted on victim-offender mediation in North America (see for example, Umbreit and Coates, 1992, 1993; Umbreit, 1994, 2001; Umbreit, Coates and Kalanj, 1994, Nugent *et al*, 2003). These report high levels of victim satisfaction arising from the chance to tell their offenders directly about the consequences of the crime and to obtain material and emotional reparation from the meeting.

Psycho-Therapeutic Benefits of RJ

Beyond those findings from all the RJ experiments that relate to macro-level victim views about both process and outcome, the London burglary and robbery experiments have also shed important light on the mental health benefits that RJ can provide. These had been hinted at in the earlier Australian research where RJ had been reported by victims to be very helpful in their recovery on a range of emotional dimensions. These included significant reductions after RJ compared with before in fear of and anger towards the offender and in anxiety levels about the crime, together with a range of other psychological improvements and, surprisingly but importantly, a reduction in desire to harm the offender (Strang 2002).

These findings led us to pursue some important questions around the psychological aspects of the RJ experience via a special 'experiment within the experiments' conducted by a member of the London research team, Caroline Angel, a qualified psychiatric nurse. Angel comments (forthcoming) that crime victims often have difficulty in accessing psychological care: indeed the mental trauma they have experienced is rarely recognised except in the case of special crimes such as rape (Foa & Kozak, 1986). And yet even low to moderate levels of post-traumatic stress symptoms (PTSS) are associated with higher rates of coronary heart disease, more physical symptoms of illness and more use of medical services compared with those without PTSS (Gillock *et al* 2005). It can also lead to economic burdens as well with lost working days and greater reliance on welfare benefits (Layard *et al* 2007).

Cognitive behavioural therapy (CBT), which can involve both cognitive restructuring of the memory of the trauma and desensitising individuals of things that remind them of the event, has been used with considerable success in post-traumatic stress disorder, especially for women (Schurr *et al* 2007), but the availability of trained therapists severely limits its application. Psychotherapeutic 'talking' treatment has also been applied but it tends to be expensive and its success not strongly evaluated

The working hypothesis was that a RJ meeting was a type of non-medical treatment that has theoretical connections with CBT (Sherman *et al* 2005). It provides many of the conditions required in CBT, including a re-living of the traumatic event in a safe setting (Foa & Kozack, 1986). Levels of PTSS were assessed via a standardised test, the Impact of Event Scale-Revised (IES-R) (Weiss *et al* 1997). This is an instrument designed to measure intrusion, avoidance and hyperarousal symptoms in those who have experienced a stressful life event (Angel, forthcoming).

The cases eligible for this special study were from the London experiments and concerned robbery and serious burglary committed by adult offenders (in the burglary study almost half of the victims reported having encountered the offender in the course of the crime). Nearly all of these RJ meetings were held in the prison where the offender had been remanded in custody, owing to the seriousness of the offence.

All eligible crime victims whose cases had been randomly assigned, whether to RJ or not, and who agreed to participate in the research, were telephoned following the finalisation of their cases in court (Angel 2005, Angel forthcoming).

The results of this study reveal that six months after the case had been finalised in the courts there was a substantial reduction in PTSS among those who had participated in RJ, compared with those who had not had the opportunity to do so. Whereas only 20 percent of victims with RJ remained with PTSS above sub-clinical levels after six months, 46 percent of the control group remained at this level. The difference was particularly clear for women, where 20 percent of the RJ group remained with PTSS compared with 56 percent of the control group. Angel (forthcoming) concludes that these results, especially for women, show that RJ can be both psychologically effective and cost-justified by victim health effects.

This analysis of the mental health benefits of RJ for crime victims concerns only one dimension of emotional restoration that victims want and secure from RJ. While lawyers may claim that financial restitution is their primary aspiration and the popular media, and even victim advocates, may clamour for punishment above all, when crime victims are asked what they want, their primary focus is almost invariably on the emotional aspects of the crime they have experienced and of their desire to participate in the way their case is dealt with by the justice system (Strang 2002). Indeed, their greatest wish is almost always for a sincere expression of remorse from their offender: in the Australian research the vast majority believed they should have received an apology. Of course the courtroom is a difficult setting in which to transact emotion and lawyers expressing remorse on behalf of offenders cut no ice with their victims, even when it might be completely sincere. RJ by contrast, presents a personal, even intimate, forum for apologies to be offered, and usually accepted, and thus provides the emotional restoration that victims need.

Possibilities for RJ

The evidence from fifteen years research clearly shows the benefits available from RJ for all crime victims who participate in the process. Of course this does not include all victims. Most victims never know who committed the crime against them; even if the offender is identified some of them will refuse to accept responsibility; even when offenders are willing to engage, some victims will prefer not to. It is likely that anger, fear and other emotions may make some victims (or their families) reluctant to take part in RJ. The level of reluctance may be influenced by the setting and by the seriousness of the offence. The way in which victims are invited to participate, however, seems to have more bearing on participation rates than any other factor: whereas the London experiments, which involved the serious crimes of burglary and robbery, had a take-up rate of over 50 percent, UK Youth Referral Panels dealing mostly with far less serious offences struggle to get victims to agree to take part at all. But RJ is clearly not for everyone and it is essential that no party be coerced into participation: we do not know whether victims who choose to take part have the capacity to self-select in such a way that they are more likely to benefit than those who decline (Sherman & Strang 2007)

But the future of RJ may lie partly in its past, especially in our biology and culture. It may be that the engine driving RJ encounters is the concept of empathy, defined not as an emotion but as a capacity for insight and understanding of the emotions of others (Sherman & Strang 2011). This capacity appears to be an essential element of our social selves, ubiquitous across human societies and even in other primates: de Waal (2009) writes of the empathetic behaviour of monkeys that seems essential to the success of small social groups. Certainly it is not surprising to find that Braithwaite (2002) suggests RJ 'has been the dominant model of criminal justice throughout most of human history for perhaps all the world's peoples.' (p 5).

With this history, combined with the clear research evidence on its effectiveness in reducing the harm experienced by crime victims it becomes the more puzzling why this more recent resurgence of interest in RJ for dispute and conflict resolution has not developed a greater head of steam. But traditional or conservative attitudes to crime and criminal justice are sometimes obstacles to RJ, regardless of the evidence base supporting its value. Indeed support for victims is often seen as a conservative political position and RJ advocates, especially in the United States, have worked with victim advocates to bypass conservative opposition (Roach 1997).

Some light is thrown on the bewildering ups and downs of RJ around the world over the past twenty years – sometimes making startling inroads on formal justice procedures, sometimes apparently stopped in its tracks by forces of inertia - by a paper that draws on the results of an attitudinal survey conducted in Australia and Japan (Huang *et al* 2011). The survey compares attitudes to punishment, rehabilitation and restorative justice in these two countries and investigates the influence of community participation, fear of crime and other independent variables on these attitudes including 'social capital', defined as the connections between individuals and the 'social networks, norms of reciprocity and trustworthiness that arise from them' (Putnam 2000: 19).

Claims have been made about the character of Japanese society and its propensity to favour shaming as a mechanism of social control (Braithwaite 1989). Because the role of shame in front of those one cares about is such an important explanatory mechanism in RJ (Braithwaite 2002), it is easy to assume that RJ would be an attractive and obvious tool for Japanese criminal justice. However, the research that Huang *et al* report reveals a much more complex and nuanced set of attitudes prevailing in Japan, attitudes quite unlike those most often held in Australia.

The survey shows that Japanese respondents perceived more benefits in RJ and were more open to taking part than Australians were; simultaneously the Japanese were more favourably disposed towards punishment as the appropriate response to crime both in terms of retribution and of prevention. Huang *et al* (2011) suggest that Australians are more cynical about justice generally than their Japanese counterparts. In both countries, respondents who feared that traditional values were decaying and who had high levels of fear of crime were more punitive and less restorative in their views. And in both countries, those respondents who attached more value to the rehabilitation of offenders were both more supportive of RJ and more opposed to punitive justice.

Perhaps unsurprisingly, the survey found that social capital was an important predictor of attitudes to RJ in both countries. Those respondents high in social capital supported RJ while more the more socially conservative supported more punitive measures. The survey shows these Australian respondents were significantly higher in social capital while the Japanese respondents tended to be more socially conservative. Huang *et al* conclude from these findings that the future of RJ may be closely linked to the extent of social capital in any society.

These findings coincide to a remarkable degree with those of Chankova and Kirchhoff (2009) who surveyed a number of professionals in Japan, all of whom had considerable knowledge of RJ in the criminal justice context. They find that, despite the perception of some outsiders that Japanese criminal justice is lenient and re-integrative, RJ is not yet widely practised in Japan, and that it makes up only a small part of formal social control. Furthermore, they suggest that although traditional restorative practices such as the emphasis on apology for wrongdoing remain important in Japan, they occupy a space in which changing values may in future see them altered according to Western conceptions and new interpretations of traditional understandings.

These findings may have important implications not only in relatively tranquil societies such as Australia and Japan but in much more troubled places too. The very idea of 'justice' is problematic in post-conflict societies recovering from war and violent civil strife; indeed it is the stark absence of social capital in their immediate aftermath that may be one of their defining features. Nevertheless, the former Deputy Chair of the South African Truth and Reconciliation Commission, Alex Boraine (2006) has suggested that in communities seeking transition from conflict five dimensions of justice are necessary: truth recovery, prosecution and accountability, institutional reform, reparations and reconciliation. No matter how desperate the post-conflict situation, he maintains, all of these dimensions are essential for recovery and all must be addressed in a holistic way, not as either/or propositions. It seems likely that RJ may be able to make important contributions to recovery along each of these five dimensions.

Boraine's concept of 'truth recovery' can be a troubled one. Braithwaite (2005:291) has observed that 'truth' in these circumstances may be a 'misleading shorthand...[because]...what matters is not so much revealing an objective truth as a process that all stakeholders in an injustice see as a high-integrity process for revealing what may end up as multiple truths...'. He adds that 'this kind of truth-seeking must be deliberative, attentive to multiple sources of evidence, open to public scrutiny and critiques.' In RJ meetings a discussion of the 'facts' of a case almost always leads to disputation, but skilled RJ facilitators can swiftly turn the discussion to the incontrovertible harm that the victims have suffered. This emphasis on harm has repeatedly been shown to be more productive in getting to questions about what should be done to repair it.

Beyond truth *per se*, research has confirmed the need that victims have for acknowledgement of what harm they have experienced. It is here that truth-telling intersects with accountability. If there is no knowledge there can be no accountability, but at the same time, knowledge is of little value without a process of accountability.

Boraine's dimension of prosecution and accountability, in the context of post-conflict societies, are often seen as synonymous with each other. As Aerten has observed (2008), it is generally assumed that prosecution brings relief to victims of human rights violations by acknowledging the facts and recognising the harm and injustice done to them. But there is little evidence for this view and actually these victims are rarely consulted on such issues. The reality is that no formal justice process is able to deal with all the crimes perpetrated during an armed conflict. Furthermore, it is not designed to address issues like the rebuilding of trust and respect in these communities – the building blocks of social capital. But RJ offers the possibility of community rebuilding from the bottom up, as the experience of places as diverse as Bougainville and Kosovo have shown (see, for example, Tschudi, 2008, Valinas & Arsovska, 2008).

Boraine's concept of institutional reform embraces much more than considerations of justice alone. But if institutions, like individuals, are prepared to take part in a restorative process about responsibility for abuses of power and other crimes, the outcome might be the basis for reform as well as for a more inclusive remaking of civil society. That remaking could give voice to grass-root entities that may make use of traditional conflict resolution processes that may previously have been ignored. These civil society groups may possess legitimacy of a kind absent in more formal judicial entities often implicated in state-based abuse of power. In the Democratic Republic of Congo, for example, such groups are said to play a crucial role both in promoting peace, in reporting human rights violations and in encouraging reconciliation (Franciscans International, 2006).

There is a clear right to reparations of the kind Boraine refers to in international law. The United Nations' Van Boven/Bassiouni Principles (United Nations General Assembly, 2005), developed in the context of gross human rights violations, encompass both material and emotional dimensions of harm. These are usually seen as the responsibility of the state to accomplish and they are clearly essential to the business of post-conflict recovery. But the state can be unreliable or even derelict in providing reparations, especially after civil strife. Research demonstrates that RJ with its individual focus and its emphasis on the obligations and networks of interdependency between those caught up in the crime can often render both material and emotional restoration more effectively than formal state justice (Strang, 2002, Shapland *et al*, 2007).

The concept of reconciliation, as Boraine describes it (2006) lies at the heart of RJ. It implies a future-oriented coming together of parties formerly in conflict. It may imply forgiveness, but that is not by any means essential. It certainly implies the need for an expression of sincere remorse or at least a common acceptance of past wrongs perhaps by more than one of the parties, and research has shown how critically important is apology in the resolution of disputes (Tavuchis, 1990). There is as well a real possibility for RJ to reduce the desire for revenge by either party (Strang, 2002). These findings reveal the importance in the practice of RJ of the concept of empathy, defined as the 'ability to identify what someone else is thinking or feeling, and to respond to their thoughts and feelings with an appropriate emotion' (Baron-Cohen 2011).

So RJ may be one of the most effective ways of addressing all the dimensions of justice in post-conflict societies outlined here. In the transitional time after armed conflict is ended when victims and perpetrators are emotionally and physically exhausted, RJ may come into its own as a process that does not require absolute clarity of right and wrong but rather allows for the complex and multi-layered nature of truth to emerge and provides a chance for devastated, divided communities to begin the process of renewal.

Conclusion

This paper has discussed the essential features of RJ that research has shown make it such a powerful tool for the restoration of victims. Its attention to the emotional dimension of victimisation is perhaps its most important feature, for it addresses precisely what is lacking for victims as they participate as best they can in formal justice procedures. The research lends strong support to the view that RJ deserves to be taken up more broadly around the world and applied in a wide range of circumstances where victims have suffered harm. This strong evidence base should be given the attention it deserves as governments consider the rights of victims in 21st Century criminal justice.

References

Aertsen, I. 2008. Racak, Mahane Yehuda and Nyabyondo: restoriative justice between the formal and the informal. In *Restorative justice and large-scale violent conflicts*, ed. I Aertsen, J. Arsovska, H.-C. Rohne, M. Valinas & K. Vanspauwen. Collompton, UK: Willan.

Angel, C. 2005. 'Victims meet their offenders: Testing the impact of restorative justice conferences on victims' post-traumatic stress symptoms'. PhD dissertation, University of Pennsylvania.

Angel, C., L. Sherman, H. Strang *et al.* Forthcoming. Longitudinal effects of restorative justice conferences on post-traumatic stress symptoms among robbery and burglary victims: a randomised trial. *Journal of Experimental Criminology.*

Baron-Cohen, S. 2011. *Zero Degrees of Empathy: A New Theory of Human Cruelty*, London, Allen Lane.

Boraine, A. 2006. 'Transitional Justice: A Holistic Interpretation', *Journal of International Affairs*, vol 60, 1, pp17-27.

Braithwaite, J. 1989. *Crime, Shame and Reintegration*. Cambridge: Cambridge University Press.

Braithwaite, J (2002), *Restorative Justice and Responsive Regulation*, Oxford: Oxford University Press.

Braithwaite, J. 2005. Between proportionality and impunity: Confrontation, truth, prevention. *Criminology* 43(2):283-306.

Chankova, D. & G Kirchhoff. 2009. Restorative approaches in Japan: state of affairs. *Scientific Research Journal of South-West University*, 2(2):21-30.

Chankova, D. & G. Kirchhoff. 2010. Restorative justice developments in Europe: sustainable success. *Tokiwa Journal of Human Science* 18:13-26.

De Waal, F. 2009. *The age of empathy: Nature's lessons for a kinder society.* New York: Harmony Books.

Foa, E. & M. Kozak. 1986. Emotional processing of fear: Exposure to corrective information. *Psychological Bulletin*, 99:20-35.

Franciscans International. 2006. Position paper. Paper presented at the fourth ordinary session of the African Commission on human rights, Banjul. http://www.franciscansinternational.org/docs/statement.php?id=475 (accessed January 3, 2009).

Gartin, P. 1995. Dealing with design failures in randomized field experiments: Analytic issues regarding the evaluation of treatment effects. *Journal of Research in Crime and Delinquency*, 32(4):425-445.

Gillock, K L, Zayfert, C, Hegel, M T & Ferguson, RJ (2005) 'Posttraumatic stress disorder in primary care: prevalence and relationships with physical symptoms and medical utilization'. *General Hospital Psychiatry*, vol 27, 1, pp 392-399.

Huang, H., V. Braithwaite, H. Tsutomi *et al.* 2011. Social capital, rehabilitation, tradition: Support for restorative justice in Japan and Australia. *Asian Criminology*. Published online 15 July 2011.

Layard, R, Clark, D, Knapp, M & Mayraz, G (2007). 'Cost-benefit of psychological therapy'. *National Institute Economic Review*, vol 202, 1, pp 90-98.

Nugent, W., M. Williams & M. Umbreit. 2003. Participation in victim-offender mediation and the prevalence and severity of subsequent delinquent behaviour: A meta-analysis. *Utah Law Review.* 2003(1):137-166.

Pocock, S. 1983. *Clinical trials: A practical approach.* London: John Wiley.

Putnam, R D (2000), *Bowling Alone: The Collapse and Revival of American Community*, New York, Simon & Schuster.

Restorative Justice Council. 2004. www.restorativejustice.org.uk/resource/rjc_principles_of_restorative_processes/, accessed 12 August 2011.

Restorative Justice Council. 2010. www.restorativejustice.org.uk/resource/2010_national_occupational_standards_for_restorative_practice_skills_for_justice/ accessed 12 August 2011.

Restorative Justice Council (2011) www.restorativejustice.org.uk/resource/best_practice_guidance_for_restorative_practice_2011 accessed 12 August 2011.

Roach, K. 1999. *Due process and victims' rights: The new law and politics of criminal justice.* Toronto: University of Toronto Press.

Schurr, P., Friedman, M. *et al.* 2007. 'Cognitive Behavioral Therapy for Posttraumatic Stress Disorder in Women: A Randomized Controlled Trial'. *Journal of the American Medical Association*, vol 297, 8, pp 820-830.

Sebba, L. 1996. *Third parties: Victims and the criminal justice system.* Columbus: Ohio State University Press.

Shapland, J., A Atkinson, E. Dignan *et al.* 2004. *Implementing restorative justice schemes (Crime Reduction Programme): A report on the first year.* Home Office Online Report 32/04. Home Office: London.

Shapland, J., A. Atkinson, *et al.* 2007. *Restorative justice: The views of victims and offenders. The third report from the evaluation of three schemes.* Ministry of Justice Research Series 3/07. London: Ministry of Justice.

Sherman, L., H. Strang, C. Angel *et al.* 2005. Effects of face-to-face restorative justice on victims of crime in four randomized controlled trials. *Journal of Experimental Criminology*, 1(3):367-395.

Sherman, L. & H. Strang. 2007. *Restorative justice: The evidence.* London: The Smith Institute.

Sherman, L. & H. Strang. 2011. Empathy for the Devil: Nature and Nurture in Restorative Justice in Karstedt, Susanne, Loader, Ian & Strang, Heather (eds) *Emotions, Crime and Justice*, Oxford, Hart.

Strang, H, L. Sherman, C. Angel *et al.* 2006. Victim evaluations of face-to-face restorative justice conferences: A quasi-experimental analysis. *Journal of Social Issues* 62(2):281-306.

Strang, H. 2002. *Repair or revenge: Victims and restorative justice.* Oxford: Clarendon Press.

Tavuchis, N. 1991. *Mea culpa: A sociology of apology and reconciliation.* Stanford, Cal: Stanford University Press.

Tschudi, F. 2008. Dealing with violent conflicts and mass victimisation: a human dignity approach. In *Restorative justice and large-scale violent conflicts*, ed. I Aertsen, J. Arsovska, H.-C. Rohne, M. Valinas & K. Vanspauwen. Collompton, UK: Willan.

Tyler, T. 1990. *Why do people obey the law?* New Haven: Yale University Press.

Umbreit, M. 1994. Crime victims confront their offenders: The impact of a

Minneapolis mediation programme. *Research on Social Work Practice* 4(4):436-47.

Umbreit, M. 2001. *The handbook of victim-offender mediation*. San Francisco: Jossey-Bass.

Umbreit, M. & R. Coates. 1992. The impact of mediating victim-offender conflict: An analysis of programs in three states. *Juvenile and Family Court Journal*:21-28.

Umbreit, M. & R. Coates. 1993. Cross-site analysis of victim-offender mediation in four states. *Crime and Delinquency* 39:565-85.

Umbreit, M., R. Coates & B. Kalanj. 1994. *Victim meets offender: The impact of restorative justice and mediation.* Monsey, NY: Criminal Justice Press.

United Nations General Assembly. 2005. *Basic principles and guidelines on the right to a remedy and reparations for victims of gross violations of international human rights law and serious violations of international humanitarian law,* UN Doc. A/RES/60/147 (also known as the Bassiouni Principles).

Valinas, M. & Arsovska, J. 2008. A restorative approach for dealing with the aftermath of the Kosovo conflict: Opportunities and limits. In *Restorative justice and large-scale violent conflicts*, ed. I Aertsen, J. Arsovska, H.-C. Rohne, M. Valinas & K. Vanspauwen. Collompton, UK: Willan.

Weiss, D. 2007. The impact of event scale:revised. In J. Wilson & C Tang (eds) *Cross-Cultural Assessment of Psychological Trauma and PTSD*. International and Cultural Psychology Series. New York: Springer.

Central Issues in Restorative Justice

By

Paul C. Friday[1], Ph.D.

One of the most significant developments in the field of criminal justice in recent years has been the emergence of a wide range of restorative justice/community justice programs. The focus on restorative justice has come about because the current policies and practices in criminal justice have been proving ineffective in reducing crime and in offering citizens confidence in and support from their legal authorities. The political "get-tough" rhetoric make politicians feel as though they are being effective but in reality recidivism rates have not been reduced and the victims of crime are no better off as a result of the legal interventions.

The primary reason that the criminal justice system per se cannot solve the problem of crime is that it does not focus on the true etiology of it – crime is a product of the development of a crime prone population within a family and community structure that enables individuals to be self-centered, self-involved, narcissistic and materialistic to the extent that their own interests supercede any interest in the well-being of others or the community itself. By focusing primarily on punishment, the criminal justice system reaffirms the importance of the individual as a separate identity and while affirming the outrage of the public and the victim the offender is basically shielded from intimate awareness of the harm that has been caused.

Restorative justice approaches are often view as "soft justice" or "no justice" by traditionalists who see the function of the criminal law to be that of punishment or retribution. But, as stated in the "*Handbook on Justice for Victims* on the use and application of the United Nations Declaration of Basic Principles of Justice for Victims of Crime and Abuse of Power (E/CN.15/1998/CRP.4/add.1 17 April 1998)", "Restorative justice is actually only a new term for an old concept. Throughout the history of humankind restorative justice approaches have been used in order to solve conflicts between

---

1 University of North Carolina- Charlotte, NC USA

parties and to restore peace to communities." (p.52). The terms restitution, reparation, compensation, reconciliation, atonement, redress, community service, mediation and indemnification are used within the literature. This indicates that the term "Restorative Justice" embraces concepts which do not necessarily have a common meaning, nor do existing programs and procedures in "Restorative Justice" necessarily give the same weight to all aspects involved._

The phrase "restorative justice" implies both process and outcome. It does not indicate a particular program, although programs and practices may be classified by the extent to which they advance restorative justice concepts. The term Restorative Justice is an effort to create an over-arching concept employing assumptions and processes different than those in a retributive or rehabilitative criminal justice process. The retributive process is a process that focuses primarily on the offender and the State. The retributive criminal justice system focuses on *process* rather than *outcome*. It appears that the "overriding issue is whether fair procedures are followed, not whether they produce a just result, a fair outcome for the accused, satisfaction for the victim or harmony in the community to which both the offender and victim belong." (McElrea, 1995:5). The rehabilitative criminal justice process concentrates on the needs of offenders to be rehabilitated.

The restorative process focuses on the victim and in some instances, the community. Restorative justice focuses mainly on restoring the health of the community, repairing the harm done, meeting victims' needs, and emphasizing that the offender must and can actively contribute to those repairs (Bazemore, 1996).
Restorative justice condemns the criminal act, holds offenders accountable, involves the participants, and encourages repentant offenders to work actively for their return into the good graces of society.

Restorative justice considers crime an act against the individual and the community rather than against the State (Barry, 1995). While restorative justice programs all seem to concentrate on the concrete conflict between victims and offenders, the degree to which they directly address community needs, varies. In essence, by focusing on "conflict" restorative justice addresses the same social phenomenon for which the law uses the term crime.

Restorative Justice seeks to balance the concerns of the victim and the community with the need to reintegrate the offender into society. It seeks to assist the recovery of the victim and enable all parties with a stake in the justice process to participate fruitfully in it.

In short, restorative justice

- Involves the victim, the offender, and the community in a search for solutions which promote repair, reconciliation, and reassurance. Goals are restitution and healing for victims, healing the relationship between victim and offender, accountability and healing for offenders, and healing for community (Zehr, 1990).
- Is all judicial or at least officially supervised initiatives which involve the offender *actively in* the restoration and in restitution of psychological , material, and/or social harm caused by the offense (Walgrave, 1995). If the social harm is to be restored and not the personal harm of victims, then the proponents of restorative justice speak of "symbolic restitution"," which means that the community receive services or payments from the offender.

Regardless of how it is practiced, restorative justice reflects a belief that justice should, to the greatest degree possible, do five things:

1) invite full participation and consensus;
2) Heal what has been broken;
3) Seek full and direct accountability;
4) Reunite what has been divided; and
5) Strengthen the community, to prevent further harms." (Sharpe, 1998, p.7.)

Restorative justice represents a paradigm shift from the retributive and/or rehabilitative approaches to crime (Friday, 1999) which have generally stressed that:

- Offenders must be punished
- Victims and offenders must be treated as adversaries
- Victims want offenders to be punished
- Victims benefit from the punishment of offenders
- Satisfying the needs of victims is not central to the judicial process
- Judges decide what is best for the victim and offender

Restorative Justice is sometimes referred to as the Balanced and Restorative Justice Model which seeks to address the need for sanctioning based on accountability measures that attempt to restore victims and also clearly denounce and provide meaningful consequences for offensive behavior, offer rehabilitation and reintegration of offenders, and enhance community safety and security (Bazemore and Umbreit, 1995).

The framework of restorative justice is, therefore, a combined emphasis on three priorities:

1. Restoration: Concern for providing services and support to victims whether or not there is an arrest. Restoration of community and social bonds is key to victim support as well as the prevention of future victimization. Restoration includes restoration or reparation of harm to the victim *and* restoration of offenders to community life through the acknowledgment of the harm done and the willingness to take accountability for their actions and their victims.
2. Accountability: Restitution, community service, and victim-offender mediation create an awareness in offenders of the harmful consequences of their actions for victims, require offenders to take action to make amends to victims, and, in the case of symbolic restitution, to the community. Whenever possible, victims should be directly involved.
3. Community protection: Intermediate, community-based surveillance and sanctioning systems channel the offender's time and energy into productive activities. A positive objective of this process is to provide supervision and provide incentives for offenders to make self-improvements by becoming competent - gain work experience, develop skills, interact positively in society and publicly demonstrate productive, competent behavior.

The primary assumptions associated with the Restorative Justice Paradigm are:

- Offenders accept responsibility for their criminal behavior
- Offenders and Community unite in recognition of harm done to the victim
- Opportunity for reconciliation through direct interaction between victims and offenders
- Reparation for the offense is given to the victims by offenders
- Offenders are not punished, but supported to repair the harm done and to seek help for their problems

Six principles shape the framework of restorative justice: the nature of crime, the goal of justice, the role of victims, the role of offenders, the role of the local community, and the role of the formal criminal/ juvenile justice system (OVC, 2000:3).

1. The nature of crime. Crime is a human process whereby humans violate both personal relationships and social relationships implied as a consequence of being part of a community. Crime is not merely an act of breaking laws of the State; it is a tearing of the social or community fabric. Crime is the violation of one human being by another.

2. The goal of justice. The proper goal of justice is to repair the damage done and restore relationships, both personal and communal, to their original state to the extent possible.
Criminal justice must be conceived not only as the imposition of justice on the criminal but also as the doing of justice for the victims. This means that a violation of the social order must be seen as an offense against society generally (the traditional criminal justice view) but also as an action that harms individuals.

3. The role of victims. Restoration for victims of crime can happen only if they have the opportunity to choose involvement in a justice process that meets their need for validation as individuals who have been hurt. Victim involvement may include receipt of information, dialogue with the offender, resolution of conflict with the offender, restitution, reduction of fear, heightened sense of safety, partial ownership of the process, resolving the experience, and renewal of hope.

4. The role of offenders. Restoration for offenders who commit criminal or delinquent acts can happen if they have the opportunity to accept their responsibilities and obligations toward individual victims and the community as a whole. Such opportunity may include defining their obligations, participating in safe, mediated face-to-face encounters with victims, understanding the impact of their own actions, providing restitution in creative ways, identifying their needs, having partial ownership of the process, resolving the conflict, and renewing hope.

Offenders must and should be held accountable for their actions. One element of accountability is retribution or 'just deserts.' Such sanctions should be just and equitable. Care should be taken to fashion culturally-appropriate punishments and to ensure that punishments are proportionate to the criminal act. Very serious crimes and serious recidivating offenders generally need and deserve incarceration both as a punishment and as a means of protecting society. This is not incongruent with restorative justice principles.

But so much of what is actually criminal, when one looks at the patterns of crime and arrests, is, while serious, relatively minor and may more effectively be dealt with by fines, restrictions of privileges, home confinement, and other measures that facilitate the offender's accountability not only to the state but also to the victim.

While accountability should include measured punishment for its own sake, it should go beyond punishment. It should include restitution to victims. Such restitution should be mandated by law. Accountability should also involve restitution to the community as a whole. A violation of the social order through crime also harms the community where it occurred, increasing fear on the part of citizens and engendering the use of otherwise more socially beneficial resources.

5. The role of the local community. Restoration for the local community can happen if its resources are brought to bear on the needs of victims and offenders as well as in prevention of delinquent and criminal acts. The affected communities also bear responsibilities. According to Young (1999), these responsibilities are of two kinds -those of the state, and those of the local community or neighborhood.

The responsibilities of the state include ensuring that appropriate laws and policies are in place in order to effect Restorative Justice *and to pay for its implementation*. Those legal policies should include the establishment of parallel rights for victims to those available to accused and convicted offenders, notably rights according victims participatory status in the justice system.

The responsibilities of the local community should include establishing and maintaining a practical system of programs and procedures that support Restorative Justice. Such a system would include: community policing, and committees like CONSEGU in Mexico that offer a comprehensive approach to the problem including efforts:

- To generate an Alliance between the society and government to fight the fear of crime and delinquency and to reestablish trust in Public Security Organizations,
- To promote citizen participation through the creation of state and Municipal Committees,
- To professionalize citizen participation in public security matters,
- To study and propose programs and actions of reform to the activities that the legal institutions develop for improvements in the Justice System (prevention, human rights and social

reintegration) and

- To support the authorities in their activities of prevention by providing them with information derived from citizen participation for the effective identification of problem areas to assist in fighting the incidence of high delinquency.

6. The role of the formal criminal/juvenile justice system. Restoration for the formal criminal/juvenile justice system can happen if it continues to work to ensure victim and offender involvement that genuinely engages all participants without coercion. As it seeks to promote justice in the community, this system must continue to monitor accountability, exhausting the least restrictive interventions for offenders before moving toward incarceration alternatives.

The Criminal Justice system *should aspire to achieve the restoration of both individual dignity and community bonds.* Restoration for offenders requires effort on their part as well as support from society. The criminal justice system needs to integrate into its sanctioning process mechanisms that enable offenders to acknowledge their violation of the social order and harm to the victim, accept their legal sanctions, and to make acts of contrition through remorse and shame, and through reparations to victims and the community.

The support from society should involve providing offenders with opportunity to return to their community with appropriate benefits such as medical or substance abuse treatment, or social or employment skills. It does not mean that society or victims have to forgive their past behavior or exonerate them, only that they should support opportunities for offenders to construct a new life as law-abiding (Young, 1999)

Use of Restorative Justice Programs

Some general themes are evident in the restorative justice literature. There appears to be some consensus that:

- Restorative justice programs should be generally available **at all stages** of the criminal justice process.
- Restorative processes should be employed only with the free and voluntary consent of all parties. The parties should be free to withdraw from the process at any point in time and the decision not to participate should never be interpreted as being uncooperative.
- Where restorative processes and/or outcomes are not possible,

criminal justice officials should do all they can to encourage responsibility of the offender toward the victim.

- The process should adhere to the core values of restorative justice and be directed at violations of legal standards, not moral, ethical standards *per se*.
- The restorative process must maintain a **balanced perspective** between victim, offender and community needs.
- Restorative justice is appropriate for both serious and less serious offenses and for juveniles as well as adults.
- The restorative process should preserve the independence and integrity of the judicial process and assure that only programs adhering to the core values of restorative justice be identified and acknowledged as restorative processes.

References

Barry, S. (1995). "Circle sentencing -- mediation and consensus: turning swords into ploughshares," Accord 14(1)

Bazemore, G. (1996). "Three paradigms for juvenile justice", Pp. 37-67, in B. Galaway and J. Hudson (Eds) Restorative Justice: International Perspectives. Monsey, NJ: Criminal Justice Press

Bazemore, G. and M. Umbreit. (1995). "Rethinking the sentencing function in juvenile court: Retributive or restorative responses to youth crime." Crime and Delinquency 41:296-316.

Friday, Paul C. 1999. "An overview of restorative justice programmes and issues" Report to the International Scientific and Professional Council of the United Nations. Milan

McElrea, F. W. M. (1995). "Accountability in the community: Taking responsibility for offending." Paper presented at the Legal Research Foundation Conference, Auckland, New Zealand, May.

OVC (Office of Victims of Crime) 2000. "Multicultural iplications of restorative justice: Potential Pitfalls." NCJ176348, April.

Sharpe, S. 1998. Restorative justice: A vision for healing and change. Edmonton Alberta: The Edmonton Victim Offender Mediation.

Walgrave, L. (1995). "Restorative justice for juveniles: Just a Technique or a Fully Fledged Alternative?" Howard Journal of Criminal Justice 34:228-249

Young, M. 1999. "Restorative community justice in the United States: A new paradigm." International Review of Victimology 6:265-277.

Zehr, H. (1990). Changing lenses: A new focus for crime and justice. Scottsdale, PA: Herald Press.

Restorative Justice for Victims of Bullying in Colleges in India

By

K. Chockalingam

Bullying freshmen by the seniors in colleges and universities in India have aggravated to serious proportions of physical and emotional abuse in the recent years. The matter has been dealt by the Supreme Court of India, which appointed a high level committee to suggest methods to prevent bullying and assure safety to the new students who join educational institutions. Several states in India also have formulated legislations, treating "bullying" as a criminal offence and providing punishment to deter the offenders who are also students. Despite these measures, the instances of bullying have not stopped or reduced. Instead of handling bullying from the traditional criminal justice perspective which has not given the desired results, the present paper suggests that India could apply the principles and method of restorative justice involving the victim (freshman student), his/her parents, the offenders (the senior students), his/her parents in a dialogue, which would facilitate the introspection by the offenders of the consequences of their acts and inducing them to come forward to offer restitution and also attain the feelings of repentance. This will also aim the reformation of the delinquent from indulging in the acts of bullying in future. From the perspective of the author, this is a fertile field completely unexplored, which in his opinion would bring in the desired results of the restorative justice to the victim, the offender and the community.

Introduction

Olweus, a leading authority on the subject of bullying and bully related issues, defines bullying, as "a student is being bullied or victimized when he or she is exposed, repeatedly and over time, to negative actions on the part of one or more students". He explains the phrase 'negative actions' as the behavior of someone who intentionally inflicts, or attempts to inflict, injury or discomfort on another (Olweus, 1993). Negative actions can be verbal behaviors such as threatening, taunting, teasing and calling names or by using physical contact such as pushing, hitting, kicking, punching or restraining another. It can be even without using words or physical contact, behaviors such as making faces or dirty gestures, intentionally excluding someone from a group, or refusing to respect another person's wishes. Bullying can be indulged in by a single person or a group and can be targeted against a single person or a group (Olweus, 1991; 1993).

Bullying is viewed as "repeated oppression, physical or mental, of a less powerful person by a more powerful person or group of persons". Bullying happens in the situations of power imbalance between people, and it is repeated behavior (Olweus, 1993; Rigby, 1996; Smith and Sharp, 1994 as cited in Wong, 2010). 'Bullying' among students in Indian Universities and colleges is locally known as 'Ragging', which is described as an extreme physical and mental torture of the freshmen by their seniors. In this whole paper, the act of bullying will be referred interchangeably as 'ragging' also because the laws passed by the different states in India use the terminology of 'ragging' to refer to the act of bullying. The act of bullying includes verbal, physical or sexual aggression on the victim.

In a brutal incident of bullying (which will also be referred as 'ragging'), a 23-year-old postgraduate student in computer applications Dande Devender Kumar from Andhra Pradesh state jumped into the railway tracks and killed himself when the pain of bullying was unbearable. Akhil Dev, a first year student of a college at Coimbatore, in Southern India was almost about to lose his eyesight as a consequence of bullying. The 20 year old student was thrashed by his seniors late in the night on March 7, 2009, the same day when another 19 year old medical student Aman Kachroo died as a consequence of bullying in the state of Himachal Pradesh in Northern India. There are several such cases of bullying reported in the media by when the cases are serious involving physical violence.

The Supreme Court of India had given an ultimatum saying students indulging in bullying must be punished and any delay in taking action by the institution should lead to stoppage of financial aid by the government and by the University Grants Commission, which is the highest regulatory and funding body in the field of higher education in India. The Supreme Court has also given elaborate guidelines to deal with the bullying menace in the educational institutions. There are many states in India who have passed separate legislations treating bullying as a criminal offence with stringent punishment of imprisonment. For example, the Tamil Nadu Prohibition of Ragging Act of 1997 in the State of Tamil Nadu in India defines the offence of bullying as, "ragging means display of noisy, disorderly conduct, doing any act which causes or is likely to cause physical or psychological harm or raise apprehension or fear or shame or embarrassment to a student in any educational institution and includes:

- Teasing, abusing or playing practical jokes on, or causing hurt to such student or,
- Asking the students to do any act or perform something, which such student will not in the ordinary course willingly do.

Punishment for bullying

The above law views bullying as a serious offence and provides severe penalty which states, "whoever directly or indirectly commits, participates in, abets or propagates 'ragging' within or without any educational institution, shall be punished with imprisonment for a term which may extend to two years and shall also be liable to a fine which may extend to 10000 rupees." Any student convicted of an offence under the above section shall be dismissed from the educational institution and such student shall not be admitted in any other educational institution. In spite of such severe punishments, the incidents of bullying continue to occur in educational institutions in different states of India. Despite several measures taken by the government, the solution to the problem of bullying is still elusive.

Background of the problem

The act of bullying involves pain and victimization to the victims who are fellow students in institutions of higher education in the Indian context. It is a human rights violation of the victim which takes several forms and magnitude. The behavior of the seniors who indulge in bullying include asking the fresher's to do petty menial jobs for them, writing their academic assignments, making them to spend money on parties to seniors, cleaning their rooms and clothes, asking them to do all odd jobs which are usually done by paid servants at one's home in middle and upper class families of India. The extremes of bullying go to the extent of homosexual behaviour and asking the juniors to strip and demonstrate vulgar postures and when resisted, leading to violence against them by the seniors (stopragging.org).

The word 'ragging' which literally means 'teasing' dilutes the enormous impact on the consequences of the conduct involved and undermines the seriousness of the social problem of bullying according to some sections of the population. For the several behaviours comprised within the conduct of ragging, the term 'bullying' is commonly used in other countries. The uniqueness of ragging in India is that it is indulged in by grown up students of colleges as compared to the behavior of bullying committed by young adolescents mostly in schools in other countries. In Japan, bullying has been a serious problem in schools and not in colleges. Since 1998 the rate of suicides among school children of ages between 10 and 17 being teased in schools has increased. In 2006, Prime Minister Shinzo Abe called for standards for punishing students that bully others in school and to impose severe punishments for teachers who ignore bullying in school. Unfortunately, Japanese law does not address bullying and even prohibits middle school children from being expelled from school for misconduct for bullying. In the case of U.S. , U.K. and other European countries, the problem of bullying is prevalent more in schools than in colleges and Universities.

Seriousness of bullying

Ragging was originally imported into India after the introduction of western system of education. But in course of time many of the vulgar and barbaric practices of ragging occurring in our college campuses have far exceeded in intensity than the ones prevailing in foreign countries. In some college/university campuses, bullying has degenerated into vulgar, brutal, sadist and even sexual abuse and harassment. The college/university authorities have failed to exercise adequate supervision and control the menace because of powerful student unions supporting the practice and the presence of non student anti-social elements residing in dormitories joining hands with seniors to bully the freshmen. When the behavior of ragging took serious proportions even to the extent of homicide, the states woke up and tried to respond to the serious situations by making special laws to prevent and punish the offence of ragging. In the state of Tamil Nadu, the legislation of the Tamil Nadu Prohibition of Ragging Act of 1997 was promulgated as a consequence of the ragging leading to the brutal murder of a freshman student in the medical school of Annamalai University in November 1996, which sent shock waves throughout the country as the father of the victim Naavarasu was the President of a premier state University at that time. Due to the pressure of the civil society and the media highlight of the incident, the Government of Tamil Nadu passed an ordinance, which became a law subsequently to deal with the problem of ragging.

R.K. Raghavan Committee on prevention of bullying in India

When the acts of bullying led to certain violent victimizations of freshmen in some colleges and when these were highlighted by the media, the Supreme Court of India took up the matter in the year 2007 and asked the Government of India to constitute a committee of experts with R.K. Raghavan the former chief of the Central Bureau of Investigation (CBI) as the Chair person with a few Vice Chancellors and educationists as members of the committee to study the problem and make recommendations for prevention of bullying and suggest remedial measures. This committee held series of discussions among themselves besides interviewing the different stakeholders such as teachers, researchers, students, teacher associations, student associations etc. and sought their views on the problem and the possible remedies from their perspectives.

Recommendations of the Raghavan Committee on Ragging

The Raghavan Committee submitted an elaborate report to the Government of India. The salient features of the report are:

- Primary responsibility for curbing ragging rests with academic institutions themselves.
- Ragging adversely impacts the standards of higher education.
- Incentives should be available to institutions for curbing the menace and there should be disincentives for failure to do so.
- Enrolment in academic pursuits or a campus life should not immunize any adult citizen from penal provisions of the laws of the land.
- Ragging needs to be perceived as failure to inculcate human values from the schooling stage.
- Behavioral patterns among students, particularly potential 'raggers' need to be identified.
- Measures against ragging must deter its recurrence.
- Concerted action is required at the level of the school, higher educational institution, district administration, university, State and Central Governments to make any curb effective.
- Media and the Civil Society should be involved in this exercise.

The Committee has made several other recommendations also (Vij, 2009).

Orders of the Supreme Court of India based on the Raghavan Committee on Ragging

On the basis of the Report of the Raghavan Committee on Ragging, the Supreme Court of India issued important orders, some of which include:

- The punishment to be meted out has to be exemplary and justifiably harsh to act as a deterrent against ragging.
- Every incident of ragging where the victim or his parent/guardian or the Head of institution is not satisfied with the institutional arrangement for action, a First Information Report (FIR) must be filed with the local police authorities without exception by the concerned institution. Any failure or negligence or deliberate delay in lodging the FIR with the police shall be construed to be an act of

culpable negligence on the part of the institutional authority. If any victim or his parent / guardian intends to file FIR directly with the police, that will not absolve the responsibility of the institutional authority from the requirement of filing the FIR.

- Courts should take up the ragging cases on a priority basis to send the correct message that ragging will be dealt with sternness.
- In addition, the Supreme Court directed that the possibility of introducing in the educational curriculum a subject relating to ragging shall be explored by the National Council of Educational Research and Training (NCERT) and the respective State Council of Educational Research and Training (SCERT).
- In the prospectus to be issued for admission by educational institutions, it shall be stipulated that in case the applicant for admission is found to have indulged in ragging in the past or if it is noticed later that he has indulged in ragging, admission may be refused or he shall be expelled from the educational institution.
- The Central and the State Governments shall launch a programme giving wide publicity to the menace of ragging and the consequences, which follow if any student is detected to have been involved in ragging.
- It shall be the collective responsibility of the authorities and functionaries of the concerned institution, and their role shall also be open to scrutiny for examination whether they have taken effective steps to prevent ragging and in case of their failure, action such as denial of any grant-in-aid or assistance from the State Government can be taken.
- The institutions shall form anti-ragging committees and squads. It shall be the job of the committee or the squad, as the case may be, to see that the Committee's recommendations are strictly adhered to and if there is any deviation, the same shall be brought to the notice of the Supreme Court forthwith.
- The Committee constituted pursuant to the order of this Court shall continue to monitor the functioning of the anti-ragging committees and the squads and shall also monitor the implementation of the recommendations to which reference has been made above (stopragging.org 2007).

Continuance of the problem

The practice of bullying has not stopped, though most of the states in India have passed legislations banning bullying among colleges and universities and the Supreme Court of India condemning the practice of bullying, has asked the college authorities to deal with the student offenders very firmly, even awarding them exemplary punishment,

Though the number of reported cases published in the media are much smaller- only 198 reported cases in the last one decade throughout India, extracted from the Coalition to Uproot Ragging from Education (CURE), www.noragging.com, there might be several hundreds of victims in many educational institutions in different states of India who might have been victimized due to bullying by seniors in varying degrees and still not reported the matter due to various reasons such as: people don't take it seriously as the number of reported incidents are not alarming; the colleges/educational institutions hush up the matter to avoid their reputation being affected; the perception of the college authorities on the erring students as not serious offenders; many victims are under fear to report as they have to continue in the same campus and hence console themselves that the problem is only temporary; over a period of time a culture has been created institutionalizing ragging as a common norm among the youth in colleges.

Failure of the punitive method

The traditional Criminal Justice System in dealing with offence and offenders in a formal way by the police and courts, ultimately punishing the offenders has failed to achieve the goals of the system worldwide. Neither has it prevented crime from occurring nor created deterrence among the potential offenders nor reformed the offenders who have indulged in crimes, which is evident from the increase in prison population in many countries (Fattah, E.A.,2002,p.308-309). Fattah rightly argues that justice paradigms have to change with the social evolution by taking stock of advances and new discoveries in the fields of criminology, victimology and penology and try to achieve the social objectives such as reconciliation, restoration, reparation and reintegration instead of continuing with the philosophical goals of expiation, atonement and retribution (Fattah, 2002).

Many victims often feel dissatisfied with the traditional methods of justice delivery. A vital question, which many victims want to have the answer, which they are not able to get from the traditional method, is "why it happened to them?" The adversarial method of justice does not go deep into the reasons for the offender to commit the prohibited act but restricts its role only to the limited purpose of establishing the '*mens rea*' or criminal intention of the offender. This method also precludes a dialogue between the offender and the victim. The victims have no opportunity to hear the explanations from the accused for the commission of the act. Moreover, the adversarial system does not take the responsibility to change the behavior of the offender but transfers the task of correcting the deviant behavior of the offender to the correctional agencies. The outcome of the treatment is not visible immediately (Young, 2001, p.xv). On the contrary: all these lacunae are addressed in a positive way in the restorative justice method as the offender and the victim enters into a dialogue and the there is a voluntary participation of the offender to agree for a change which is revealed through his assertion and commitment during the dialogue. Further, there is community involvement in preventing crime, responding to criminal behavior, supporting and assisting the victims, encouraging the reformation of the offenders, while holding the offender accountable for his misconduct through restitution, reintegrative shame, and remorse. The practices of restorative method adopted by the indigenous populations of the Maori in New Zealand, by Indian nations in US and Canada and by the Aborigines in Australia demonstrate the advantages of this method of justice delivery system (Young, 2001, p.xvi).

Now coming to the specific behavior of bullying in colleges in India, laws have been passed banning bullying in many states to abate the occurrence of bullying in colleges. The Supreme Court has taken up the matter seriously and directed the educational institutions to deal with bullying severely. The media has highlighted the gravity of the problem by reporting the instances whenever it became serious. Still the problem persists. Perhaps it aggravated. Thus we can say that legislations and the punitive method of handling of bullying through criminal law have not been effective or rather failed to achieve the goals. All the legislations passed are more offenders oriented than victim centered. They all aim at punishing the offenders and to a certain extent preventing bullying but not rendering justice to victims. Under the above circumstances restorative justice appears to be the better alternative, which is uniquely suited to render justice to victims of bullying by involving the victims who are the peers of the young student offenders and the community in the process of restorative justice. The primary goal of restorative justice is redress to the victim by treating it as society's obligation through active participation of the victim. It is a method of justice delivery to victims by respecting their wishes, meeting their needs and fulfilling their expectations (Fattah, 2002)

Restorative Justice

Historically restorative justice was the accepted way of handling crime in earlier societies (Van Ness 1993:252-7; Zehr 1990 1990:ch.7 cited in Johnstone, 2002).

Only from 12th century, the functions of crime control and dealing with the offenders was taken up by the power of the State, as a centralized agency. When the state took over the function of dispensing criminal justice, the earlier practice of asking the offenders to make up for the wrong through restitution to victims was abandoned. By the 19th century, the western powers imposed their model of state punishment on their colonized countries throughout the world driving away the native restorative justice practices. The process of abandoning the restorative justice and implanting the state punitive justice was almost complete during the twentieth century. According to anthropologists, only the native and aboriginal communities in certain countries escaped from the intervention of the state to do away with the practice of restorative justice, and in those societies even now this is the routine way of response to crime and other conflicts (Christie, 1977; Roberts 1979 cited in Johnstone, 2002, p.36-37). In the 1960s, colonized native peoples in North America, Australia, New Zealand and a few other countries undertook struggles to maintain their native traditions of justice based on their native values and customs which got acceptance by the State. The Advocates of restorative justice argue that it is worth to follow the examples of New Zealand Maori and Native Americans and recreate our own older methods of dispute resolution.

One of the major complaints against the conventional punitive justice is that it ignores the needs of crime victims (Zehr,1990) as crime is still perceived as an onslaught against the state, whereas crime at its core is a violation of a particular individual who has suffered physically, mentally and financially, besides a wrong against the society. Though the victim's position has been improving in some societies in the last two decades particularly after the adoption of the UN Declaration of Basic Principles of Justice for Victims of Crime and Abuse of Power, 1985 from the position of a mere witness to playing more active role in the criminal justice system as a result of long struggles by victim activists and victimologists, victims rarely feel the satisfaction of having got justice because punishment of the offender is the primary goal of punitive justice model and not care or restitution or other kind of services and relief to the victims. This is the main thrust of argument of the proponents of restorative justice as they say that the existing victim reforms do not basically alter the structural position of the victims in the criminal justice system. They perceive, rightly so, that despite the reforms in favor of victims achieved, in a punitive justice system, the victims' interests always remain secondary to the wider public interest represented by the State. This flaw will be rectified in the restorative justice approach, as the concern for the victims will be the primary objective (Van Ness, 1993).

In pursuance of the discussions on restorative justice during the Tenth UN Congress on the Prevention of Crime and the Treatment of Offenders, held in Vienna from 10 to 17 April 2000, in relation to the agenda item 'Offenders and victims: accountability and fairness in the justice process', the United Nations has recognized the value of restorative justice as an alternative method of conflict resolution. Therefore, the United Nations (2000) adopted a Declaration of "Basic Principles on the Use of Restorative Justice Programs in Criminal Matters". This Declaration defines 'restorative' justice programme as any programme that uses restorative processes or aims to achieve restorative outcomes. Restorative outcome has been defined as "an agreement reached as the result of a restorative process". For example, restorative outcome could result in restitution, community service and any other programme or response designed to accomplish reparation of the victim and community, and reintegration of the victim and /or the offender. This Declaration recommends the increased use of restorative programmes and incorporation of restorative approaches into criminal justice practices.

Further, this Declaration exhorts the member states to promote research on and evaluation of restorative justice programmes to assess the extent to which they result in restorative outcomes and serve as an alternative to the criminal justice process and provide positive outcomes for all parties.

According to Van Ness (2002, p.2), the restorative justice works with three principles and four values. The three principles of restorative justice are: Society should work to restore victims, offenders and communities who have been injured by crime. Victims, offender and communities should have opportunities for active involvement in the restorative justice process. Promoting justice, the government is responsible for preserving order, and the community for establishing peace (Van Ness, 2002, p.2).

The four values of restorative justice are: *Encounter, Amends, Reintegration and Inclusion*. These values are logically related to the first two principles mentioned above as these address the purpose and the participants in the restorative justice process (Van Ness, 2002, p.2).

Encounter

The key elements of the first stage 'Encounter' are: meeting, narrative, emotion, understanding and agreement. During the process of encounter the parties concerned are brought together in a meeting for a dialogue. All the stake holders - the victim, the offender and the community either themselves or through their representatives - express freely about what exactly happened, how the offence affected the victim and his/her family and how to address the harm caused. This kind of interaction among the parties involved is totally different from what happens in a courtroom, which insists, on legal principles, evidences and punishment. But in encounters, emotion is viewed as leading to arrive at understanding rather than impeding it. The parties frankly discuss the event, how it happened, the kind of damages caused, physically, emotionally and financially to the victims and their family. The offender gets an opportunity, may be for the first time, to look inward as to what made him to behave and cause the victimization and perhaps repent for the harm done. Thus, the parties come to understand each other and the consequences of the crime and the method by which the damage could be set right. When the parties have explored the personal, material and moral/spiritual repercussions of the crime they can come to an agreement that is specific to their situation and that is practical.

Amends

While encounter deals with restorative process, 'amends' deals with the unique outcome. Here the offender is encouraged to make amends for his crime. Restitution is one of the major ways, the amends could be achieved. The agreements arrived at during encounters usually have four elements when the offenders make amends to their victims, they are: apology, changed behavior, restitution and generosity. A genuine apology by the offender to the victim is a significant way of making amends in many cases. It is an unconditional acknowledgement of his wrong and places the offender in the powerless position of waiting to know whether his apology will be accepted by the victim and victim's family. Changed behavior of the offender is another way to make amends. The offender can make a promise and an agreement not to repeat the behavior. Behavioral changes in the positive direction could be shown by many other ways, such as seeking counseling to understand and get rid of the problem or concentrating in other activities like sports, fine arts etc. Restitution is probably the most suitable way to make amends. It involves monetary payment to the victim to meet all the losses incurred by the victim and his family. Particularly in victimizations involving hospitalization and medical treatment, the offer of the offender to meet the medical expenses for the injury caused by the offender would be a sign of acknowledgement of guilt and responsibility for his act and voluntary acceptance to meet the expenses for which the offender was responsible. Generosity of the offender is a step beyond the formal restitution or monetary payment for the losses caused. For example, the offender can commit himself to do voluntary free work to a non-profit organization dealing with children, elders, and women as a sign of repentance. These kinds of behaviours of the offender can even touch the heart of the victim and prove his genuine change of heart.

Reintegration

The essential significance of restorative justice is that both victim and offender have the opportunity to get reintegrated into their communities, which would relieve both of them from possible stigmatization. The reintegration process has three key elements: respect, material assistance and moral/spiritual direction. The offender in the process of reintegration should attain a position of a respectable member of the community, completely shedding his stigmatization. The victim also should be relieved of the stigmatization and gain respect from the community. Crimes always cause injuries and losses. To relieve the material losses suffered by the victim, material assistance like repairing the gadgets of the victim damaged by the offender should help reintegration. The participation of the offender/victim in moral/spiritual programs can relieve them from their emotional and moral stress.

Inclusion

Inclusion involves the participation of the victim, offender and affected community meaningfully in the subsequent justice process. This has three key elements: invitation, acknowledgement of interest and acceptance of alternative approaches. The responsible person for the justice process could issue an invitation to the affected parties to participate.

Apart from the interest served by both the victim and the offender to fulfill the obligations of the criminal justice system, the real interest of both the victim and the offender should be the focus in the inclusion. New approaches such as mediation, conferencing, circles and other forms of encounter, restitution, apology and other forms of amends should be accepted and encouraged. This will make the invitation to participate genuine and deep. Inclusion is the most important of the four values in the context of Nils Christie's observation that the State has stolen their crime from the victim and the offender (Van Ness, 2002).

Ideal components of Restorative justice

Hence ideally in a Restorative justice process, the following components would all be present:

- meeting of the parties involved
- communication between the parties
- agreement by the parties
- apology by the offender to the victim
- restitution to the victim
- change in the offender's behaviour
- respect shown to all the parties
- assistance provided to any party that needs it; and
- inclusion of the parties (Van Ness, 2002, p.6)

The goal should be restoration and not retribution

Both retributive and restorative theories of justice admit that a balance has been thrown off by the causing of the offence. As a consequence the victim who suffered the pain, loss and other sufferings deserves something and the offender who has preyed upon the victim owes something to the victim. There must be a proportional relationship between the act and the response. Retributive theory argues that pain will restore a sense of reciprocity. But in reality, shame and trauma suffered by the victim explain why the retributive approach fail to achieve what is either wished for the victim or the offender. As a form of punishment retribution seeks to vindicate and reciprocate, but is often counter productive. On the contrary, restorative justice theory argues that what in reality vindicates is acknowledgement of victims' harms and needs combined with efforts to make the offenders realize their responsibility, right the wrongs and address the causes of their behavior. By such vindication in a positive way, restorative justice has the potential to affirm both victim and offender and help them transform their lives.

Why restorative justice is specially suited for victims of bullying

- Victims and offenders are students and youth.
- Victims and offenders have long term goals of successful completion of studies and career building.
- Offenders do not have 'mens rea' or strong motives to harm the victims as most of them take bullying as fun and exhibit it to show their supremacy and power.
- The offenders had no opportunity to gauge the amount of damage they have done by their act of bullying and ascertain the harm resulted to their victims which is possible in the restorative session.

- The parents of the offenders and other family members with whom the offender has respect and affection can be involved in the dialogue with victims and their parents and other family members as both the parties are strangers and do not have any previous enmity or hatred towards each other.
- The offenders get an opportunity for repentance and reform.
- The victims and their family might forgive the offender if the offender expresses a genuine apology, realizes his guilt and shows his willingness to change.
- Both the victim and the offender can continue their education in the same institution without any disruption by establishing harmony and collegiality

Application of Restorative Justice to treat Bullying:
Some success stories of restorative justice

Wong et al, 2007 (as cited in Wong, 2010) conducted a two year longitudinal empirical study in Hong Kong from 2004 to 2006 on the effectiveness of the restorative whole school approach in four Government aided schools using experimental and control groups with a sample of 1480 students. The results showed contrasting findings between the two groups, with significant decrease in bullying behavior in the fully experimental group when compared to the control group. Braithwait (1989) argues that there is overwhelming evidence from US that restorative justice functions well and families who adopt restorative ways are more likely to have fewer delinquents than families who resort to more punitive and stigmatizing methods. Further he says that schools, like families have turned more restorative and less retributive than the brutal institutions of nineteenth century with more restorative conferencing programmes in contemporary schools (Hyndman, Thorsborne and Wood, 1996) According to Doi, a media correspondent in Japan, the Japanese culture promotes harmony and discourages confrontation. Hence confrontation is not acceptable. So, to confront a bully is not part of the Japanese culture. In fact 'Save Our Bullied Friends' is a newly formed group that holds talks about bullying at middle and elementary schools. This group makes efforts to address the problem in a non-confrontational manner. A father of one of the suicide victims has been appointed to the Nagano Prefectural Board of Education to act as a confidential mediator between schools and bullied students. He has visited with over 600 students so far. So in the recent times, Japan has recognized bullying as a massive problem, which is being discussed. (Read more at Suite101: Bullying in Japan: Harassment is world-wide. (http://www.suite101.com/content/bullying-in-japan-a10226#ixzz14fvgZDGo).

According to Olweus and Limber (2010), more than two decades of research has revealed that bullying can be decreased to a significant extent through school-wide efforts designed to reduce opportunities and rewards for bullying and to build a feeling of community among students and adults.

The application of restorative justice with success has been reported even in cases of conventional serious crimes like burglary in US. The following case study is presented as a typical example as to how it works and to demonstrate that if it can work successfully in traditional crimes like burglary why we cannot try this innovative method of dispute resolution in the case of bullying among students in the educational institutions in India and elsewhere. Following case studies from US are good examples of successful use of restorative justice in US. In a case of residential burglary, a twenty year old offender pleaded guilty to the burglary charge. During the sentencing hearing in the court, the youth offender was referred to the local victim-offender mediation programme. Though there was reluctance on the part of the offender to meet the victim initially, due to the efforts of the mediator, the offender agreed to a meeting. Similarly there was much more reluctance on the part of the victim too to meet the offender but with great efforts, the victim was also persuaded for a meeting with the offender. The mediation session was held in a community center in the presence of two trained mediators. After a lot of emotional outburst in the beginning, the offender admitted the full impact of what he had done and was ready to discuss a plan to make things right and agreed to pay $50 a month over a ten month period as restitution. After two months the victim's family visited the offender at his home on the invitation of the offender for a brief meeting and to review the process of restoration (Umbreit, 2001, p.85).

In the next case a teenage boy who was trying to hot-wire a brand new truck belonging to the victim, with the intention to steal from her house after midnight. During the investigation the police could prove his involvement in three separate car thefts earlier and later the young offender admitted to have stolen 41 vehicles over a period of three years. The case was referred to mediation services. Though he was in detention center, he never had any chance to face any of his victims and to know how his behavior had hurt his victims. He himself expressed his desire to meet one of his victims. When the matter was informed to the victim, in the beginning they were quite unwilling to meet the offender and finally the victim agreed to have the meeting. In the mediation session the offender narrated how he was initiated into criminal life. The victim explained what exactly had happened on the day when her car was stolen and finally how she got back the car but in a very nasty condition. She had to spend $700 to repair the car. The victim was very angry with the offender and wanted this money back. When the dialogue proceeded, the offender hung his head in shame. The victim heard the story of the boy how he was initiated into the crime and showed her anxiety that he should not get back to the gang. The boy promised that he would like to turn a good leaf though he said it was going to be tough when he comes out of the detention center. The victim and his family showed their real concern for the offender and offered their telephone number and told that he can meet them anytime if he needed to talk, needed support or for any reason.

> The offender's eyes were filled with tears and he thanked the victims profusely and he said he could not believe that the victims whom he harmed could care so much for him.

The victim decided not to pursue monetary restitution. When the boy returned from the detention center, the victims offered him all kinds of help to the boy in the challenge of his reformed life. The boy and his mother were in tears of gratitude to the victims for their concern and support despite the boys' behavior to them. The outcomes of the case studies demonstrated that humanistic dialogue driven principles played out in distinct ways with satisfactory settlement. The mediations resulted in high levels of satisfaction for both the victims and the offenders who participated.

Conclusion

The traditional justice system to deal with crimes has not been able to achieve its goals. Neither the offender nor the victim gets any benefit for improving their conditions. The community is also not satisfied with the outcome, as it does not provide security and peace to the people despite the fact the offender is punished. The data on recidivism and fear of crime among people in many countries support the conclusion that the punitive justice model followed in many countries is not a better alternative. Under these circumstances, restorative justice model is the promising method of affording justice to all parties concerned in a criminal offence as in this model, the offender, the victim and the community representatives are involved for a dialogue and facilitating an acceptable decision to resolve the issue. Though it is not claimed that punitive model should be completely replaced by the restorative model, it is proposed that in many cases, there is a lot of potential for the restorative justice model to work successfully with all parties concerned as it will provide a win-win situation to all. It is the strong case of the author of this paper that one such area where the restorative justice approach would be a better method to accomplish the repentance on the part of the offender with an assurance to the victim for restitution and promise of turning a good leaf by the offender would be bullying behavior and the victimization among college students.

References

Braithwaite, John (1989). *Crime, Shame and Reintegration.* New York: Cambridge University Press.

Fattah, E.A. (2002). From Philosophical abstraction to restorative action, from senseless retribution to meaningful restitution: just deserts and restorative justice revisited. In Weitekamp, E.G.M and Kerner, H.J. (Eds.), *Restorative Justice: Theoretical foundations.* (pp.308-309). Oregon: Willan Publishing,

Hyndman, M.,Thorsborne, M. and Wood, S. (1996) Community accountability conferencing: Trial report, Department of Education, Queensland, as cited in Braithwait, J. in "*Restorative Justice and a Better Future*" in http://www.iirp.org/article_detail.php?article_id=NDk4 accessed on August 11, 2010

Johnstone, G. (2002). *Restorative justice: Ideas, values, debates.* Oregon, US: Willan Publishing.

Johnstone, G. (2003). *A Restorative justice reader: Texts, sources, context*, US: Willan Publishing.

Olweus (1991). Bully/victim problems among schoolchildren: Basic facts and effects of a school based intervention program. In D.J.Pepler and K. H. Rubin (Eds.), *The development and treatment of childhood aggression* (pp. 411-448). Hillsdale, N.J.: Erlbaum.

Olweus, D. (1993). *Bullying at school: What we know and what we can do.* Oxford, UK: Blackwell.

Olweus, D. & Limber, S.P. (2010). Bullying at school: Evaluation and dissemination of the Olweus Bullying Prevention Program. *American Journal of Orthopsychiatry*, 80 (1), 124-134.

Pytel, B. : Bullying in Japan: Harassment is world-wide.
http://www.suite101.com/content/bullying-in-japan-a10226#ixzz14fvgZDGo accessed
on December 10, 2010.

Rigby, K. (1996). *Bullying in schools: And what to do about it.* London: Jessica Kingsley Publishers.

Smith, P.K. and Sharp, S. (Eds.) (1994). School bullying: Insights and perspectives. London: Routledge.

Stopragging.org (2007) http://stopragging.org/2007/05/21/full-text-of-the-supreme-courts-order-on-ragging-based-on-the-raghvan-committees-report/ accessed December 17, 2010.

Umbreit, M.S. (2001). *The handbook of victim offender mediation (p. 85-109).* San Francisco: Jossey-Bass.

United Nations (2000). Basic principles on the use of restorative justice programmes in criminal matters. Retrieved on September 2, 2010 from http://www.un.org/en/ecosoc/docs/2002/resolution%202002-12.pdf

Van Ness, D. (1993). 'New wine and old wineskins: Four challenges of restorative justice', *Criminal Law Forum*, 4:2, pp.251-76

Van Ness, D. W. (2002). The shape of things to come: A framework for thinking about a restorative justice system. In *Restorative justice: Theoretical foundations*. Ed. Elmar G.M. Weitekamp and Hans-Jurgen Kerner. Oregon: Willan Publishing.

Wong, D.S.W., Ngan, M.H. Cheng, H.K., and b S.K. (2007) *The effectiveness of restorative whole-school approach in tackling bullying in secondary schools*. Hong Kong: City University of Hong Kong, cited in Wong, D. (2010, p.190-191).

Wong, D. (2010). Adolescent bullying: The whole-school approach. In *The Promise of Restorative Justice—New Approaches for Criminal Justice and Beyond*, Ed. Dussich, J.P.J. and Schellenberg, J. Lynne Rienner Publishers, Colorado. pp. 181-194.

Weitekamp, E.G.M., & Kerner, H. (2003) Ed. Restorative justice in context: International practice and directions. Oregon, US: Willan Publishing.

Weitekamp, E.G.M., & Kerner, H. (2002) Ed. Restorative justice: Theoretical foundations. Oregon, US: Willan Publishing.

Young, M., (2001) "Foreword" in Umbreit, M.S. (2001). *The handbook of victim offender mediation* (p.xv.). San Francisco: Jossey-Bass.

Vij, S. (2009, September). *Ragging*. Retrieved December 17, 2010, from http://www.stopragging.org:

The Global Perspective on the UN Level

History of the Proposed UN Convention on Justice and Support for Victims of Crime and Abuse of Power

By

John P. J. Dussich, Ph. D.

The intention with this article is to recall the sequence of events that resulted in the development of the current draft Convention. To arrive at this task, seven key documents are here referenced as relevant to this discussion: 1st was the historical starting point for the granting of rights, the Magna Carta of 1217 which limited the power of the monarch, provided legal protections to all subjects equally, and emphasized the importance of the rule of law; 2nd was the Charter of the United Nations which was ratified on October 24th 1945 with the main objective being to foster international cooperation and prevent future wars; 3rd was the landmark UN Universal Declaration of Human Rights of 1948 following the end of World War II and the revelations of the Nazi Holocaust which joined nations together with one resolve, to promulgate in the world the "inalienable rights of all members of the human family": 4th was the unique UN Declaration of Basic Principles of Justice for Victims of Crime and Abuse of Power of 1985 to recognize the special rights of persons who had been harmed in violation of their legal liberties; 5th the evolving Draft UN Convention on Justice and Support for Victims of Crime and Abuse of Power proposed mostly by the World Society of Victimology for the future – possibly in 2015 to strengthen the principles of the 1985 Declaration; 6th the Resolution which is needed to introduce this Convention for a future Commission meeting; and, 7th the Recommendations which were accepted by the UN Commission on Crime Prevention and Criminal Justice as an official UN document for distribution at the Twelfth UN Congress on Crime Prevention and Criminal Justice in Salvador, Brazil in April 2009 and which represents the same basic text of the Resolution, but in an introductory statement format.

Early Roots:

A little known Romanian defense attorney, Beniamin Mendelsohn, began studying the victim/offender relationship to better defend his clients. He began publishing his results in 1937. After ten years and significant research which increasingly focused on types of victims he coined the word *victimology* in a 1947 speech in Bucharest and promoted its concept as the science of "victimity," the science of all victims (Kirchhoff, 2005). He referred to his concept as "general victimology" to distinguish it from "crime victimology," which is only concerned with crime victims. He also proposed the establishment of a society of general victimology, victimological research institutes, victim departments in all national governments, a journal of general victimology, the creation of victim treatment clinics and national victimology societies in each country (Viano, 1975a). Most of these proposals have come into being with the writings and collaboration and initiatives of other early pioneers such as Hans von Hentig of Germany and the USA (von Hentig, 1948), Stephen Schafer of Hungary and the USA (Schafer, 1968), Willem Nagel of the Netherlands (Nagel, 1959), Henri Ellenberger of Switzerland, France and Canada (Ellenberger, 1950), Israel Drapkin of Argentina, Chile and Israel (Drapkin and Viano, 1974), Ezzat Fattah of Egypt and Canada (Fattah, 1966), Koichi Miyazawa of Japan (Miazawa, 1966), Elias Neuman of Argentina (Neuman, 1984), Lolita Aniyar de Castro of Venezuela (Aníyar de Castro, 1969), Luis Manzanera of Mexico (Manzanera, 1988), Paul Šeparović of Croatia (Šeparović, 1962), Emilio Viano of Italy and the US (Viano, 1975b) and Hans Schneider of Germany (Schneider, 1975). These "first generation victimologists" not only laid the ground work for the scientific study of victims and provided the stimulus for advocating for victims' rights, they also gave us a vision for a victimology that would form the basis of a much greater understanding about victims that continue to humanize the way victims are treated today. This would be a victimology that would facilitate returning the balance between offenders and victims, and lead to a greater rationality for approaches to effective prevention of conflicts, treatment for victims and restoration of damages and injuries in the future.

Victimologists unite

In 1973 many of these pioneer victimologists promoted the idea for the First International Symposium on Victimology in Jerusalem, Israel which was coordinated by Israel Drapkin. This weeklong event started the momentum of a movement for the scientific study of victims, for victims rights and for victim assistance world wide. The proceedings of this event, was a set of six volumes that even today serve as the primary source document for victimological discourse (Drapkin and Viano, 1975). This core of dedicated scholars formed a professional alliance that quickly multiplied and in the following decades led to the creation of a new discipline. One of the first manifestations of this new identity took place in 1975, when a special two week long workshop was held in Bellagio, Italy organized by Emilio Viano, where many of these same scholars and other younger international victimologists, lawyers, and activists, totaling about 50 persons, came together to discuss this new evolving field of victimology. The product of this event was embodied in a book of proceedings which was the result of 12 days of intense discussions about the key issues confronting this neophyte field (Viano, 1976). In 1976 the 2nd International Symposium on Victimology was held in Boston, Massachusetts organized by Stephen Schafer who just seven year earlier had written the first English language text on victimology titled *The Victim and His Offender*. Three years later in 1979 the 3rd International Symposium on Victimology was held in Münster, Germany hosted by Hans Schneider. It was at this event, that the World Society of Victimology was founded with Schneider as its first president, Koichi Miyazawa its first vice president, John Dussich its first secretary general and Sarah Ben David its first treasurer.

The birth of the UN Declaration for victims

When this new organization, The World Society of Victimology, stepped out on the international stage, some of its founders had some thirty one years earlier witnessed the dramatic impact of the United Nations Universal Declaration of Human Rights passed on December 10, 1948. Thus, recalling the stark realities of the Nazi holocaust from the 1940s and its slaughter of about 6 millions persons, mostly Jews, and remembering the noble human rights principles that followed, and recently immersed in the crime wave from most of the countries that were involved in the Second World War, that started in the 1960s, the WSV wanted to take action on behalf of these crime victims. Dominant was the realization that there was an absence of specific rights for victims in most countries across the globe, and so plans were formulated to bring victims' rights to the community of nations in the form of a new declaration using the United Nations as the main vehicle. The beginning of this process was officially launched at the Fifth WSV Symposium held in Zagreb, Croatia in the then Yugoslavia in 1985 hosted by Zvonimir Šeparović, where LeRoy Lamborn and Irvin Waller urged the WSV to coordinate and promote a UN Declaration for Crime Victims' Rights. Immediately following this symposium many WSV members went to Milan, Italy where the United Nations was hosting its 7th Crime Congress and began a vigorous campaign to get a resolution accepted that would introduce a Declaration that could be adopted by the UN General Assembly in New York. In the process of those intense negotiations, both a Resolution and a Declaration were crafted. These were then send to the UN's Economic and Social Council (also known as ECOSOC) where they were reformulated in preparation for introduction to the United Nations General Assembly in New York City as Assembly Resolution 40/34. On November 29, of that same year, 1985, at the 96th Plenary Meeting, the United Nations General Assembly unanimously passed the "Declaration of Basic Principles of Justice for Victims of Crime and Abuse of Power!"

Victimologists, victim rights' advocates and victim service providers greeted this event with great joy and satisfaction. In a relatively short period, the World Society of Victimology, in cooperation with a handful of allied organizations, and the support of the governments of Canada, the Netherlands and the United States of America, had successfully nurtured in a significant international instrument that expressed a wide range of noble principles and rights on behalf of victims of crime and abuse of power. In essence it recommended that the billions of victims of crime and abuse of power, who had heretofore been largely ignored, be recognized and treated with respect for their dignity and their human rights. Just prior to 1985 these rights had been only the subject of academic lectures, the utterings of practitioners and the aspirations of victim rights lawyers. Finally, the community of nations formally declared a major shift in perspective, sentiment and in policy.

The challenge of implementing the new policies

The immediate question emerged, how to implement these basic objectives as they appeared in this new Declaration. What vehicle should we use to spread the word about these innovative changes? It was assumed that the Declaration would be self-evident once these principles were known and that after it was published, the needed changes would automatically follow. Translated into all six of the UN languages, the Declaration was then printed and distributed across the globe. Within less than a year, it was also available on the UN website. It was the subject of discussion and debate by victimologists in many national and international fora. However, in spite of the hype it received across the globe, the reality was that the much awaited implementations came very slowly and in only a few countries. This situation was intensely discussed at each of the following WSV symposia: Israel in 1988, Brazil in 1991, Australia in 1994, and in the Netherlands in 1997. It was also further discussed at the UN Security Council and in resolutions, from 1991 to 1995. Finally, the UN Expert Group Meeting on "Victims of Crime and Abuse of Power in the International Setting," held at Vienna in December 1995 recommended that specific actions be taken to remedy the problem of poor implementation (ECOSOC, 1997).

The Governments of the Netherlands and the United States of America agreed to act as host for two expert group meetings on victims of crime and abuse of power. One was organized by the United States Department of Justice at Tulsa, Oklahoma, in August 1996; and, the other was organized by the Ministry of Justice of the Netherlands at The Hague in March 1997. The results of those two expert group meetings, suggested that many countries did not have the necessary information about how to proceed with the recommended implementations of the Declaration, so the creation of a manual as a strategic guide for policy makers and of a handbook as a resource tool for practitioners were proposed. The USA agreed to publish these two documents and in 1999 these publications came into being and were distributed world-wide. Their effect was soon realized in that they were used for a wide range of training sessions in many national and international venues. Many countries accepted the challenges to implement those changes and the desired effect of these two documents began to be realized.

The dilemma of non-implementation continues

In spite of these important improvements, as early as 1997, at the WSV Amsterdam symposium, Professor Sam Garkawe of Australia and a WSV member, voiced concern that perhaps it was time for a convention; an instrument that would *require* all countries to follow the recommendations of the Declaration. He again brought up the need for a convention in April of 2005 at the Bangkok Crime Congress in his speech there. From subsequent discussions within the WSV, two issues emerged: the first, was the realization that new victimological information was now available from 20 years of research and experience; and, it became clear that many countries would not invest in the needed changes unless they were required to do so. Later that year (2005), in December, a group of experts was assembled under the coordination of the International Victimology Institute Tilburg (INTERVICT) at Tilburg University in the Netherlands under the leadership of its director, Professor Marc Groenhuijsen. Those who were invited to come were: Hidemichi Morosawa of Japan, Sam Garkawe of Australia, Marlene Young of the USA, Karen McLaughlin of the USA, Raj Kumar of India, Rianne Leschert of the Netherlands, Irvin Waller of Canada, Adedokun of Nigeria and Marianne of Austria. It was at this meeting that the actual first text of the convention was created. That first draft was distributed mostly within the WSV, and it soon produced many suggestions. Consequently a second version was written and published on the

INTERVICT and WSV websites (2005).

The next year (2006) at the WSV symposium in Orlando, USA, Professor Marc Groenhuijsen of INTERVICT organized a special workgroup to further consider changes on this second draft convention. After that symposium further changes were made and it was also published on the WSV and INTERVICT websites. This third version was labeled the December 2006 Convention. In 2008, under the leadership of Professor John Dussich, Director of the Tokiwa International Victimology Institute (TIVI) in Japan, a two day seminar was organized and hosted by TIVI. This working seminar focused on analytic critiques and recommendations aimed at changing the *content* of the convention; and, for the first time, a full day was devoted to creating a series of *strategies* that would aim at bringing the Convention closer to fruition. The products of these two days were published in a proceedings book, titled *Raising the Global Standards for Victims*, and represented changes in substance of the most recent modifications. Finally a new version was crafted by Sam Garkawe, Marc Groenhuijsen and John Dussich in December of 2009. After reformatting and typing this version, it was placed on the WSV and INTERVICT websites and dated February 8, 2010, where it is still today available as a source document for those working in the field of victims' rights.

Recognizing that only nations may introduce an agenda item to consider a convention, this version, now titled, "Draft UN Convention on Justice and Support for Victims of Crime and Abuse of Power," was ready to be brought before the UN Crime Commission in Vienna. A one-page draft Resolution was written by John Dussich to be used as the introduction so that a country might accept it and initiate the process of formally bringing the Convention to the Crime Commission table for consideration. It was hoped that the WSV might be able to find a few interested states in April 2010 at the 12th Crime Congress in Salvador, Brazil in anticipation of the May Crime Commission in Vienna which was held from the 17th-20th of May.

New strategies with the Convention

While significant inroads were made at the Crime Congress in Brazil, and two states did show some interest in supporting the Convention (Belgium and Canada), this support did not last and so ultimately the Resolution and the Convention were not supported by any member nations. In the aftermath of the weeklong Crime Congress in Brazil, the WSV Liaison Committee concluded that new strategic changes must be made. It was apparent that the Convention, which is a close replica of the 1985 Declaration, was either too much of a threat to prospective states who would not be in compliance if it were immediately adopted, even among those who had been major supporters of the original Declaration, or it was not a high enough priority compared to other international issues being considered among the various states.

A list of four new strategies were proposed by various members of the WSV Liaison Committee and are here presented:

1. To open a new pathway to the General Assembly at the UN Geneva office by considering the objectives embodied in the Convention as Human Rights issues; and thus, to pursue a course of action by way of ECOSOC's United Nations Human Rights Council (UNHRC) instead of only using the Commission on Crime Prevention and Criminal Justice in Vienna. We believe this new pathway will give us access to a host of different staff persons at the Geneva office and different NGOs to partnership with. Plus, the representatives from the various states, will have a different mindset with regard to victims which we hope will be more positive in our attempts to influence policy changes across the globe.
2. To create a sub-committee of our Liaison Committee to support victim issues in other UN instruments that are already being successfully adopted by the Commission, the Congress and ultimately by the General Assembly; and, to attach WSV support to these instruments. Examples would include those currently most prominent: victims of human trafficking; women and children victims; and, victims of organized crime. In each of these instances, major UN resources have been brought to bear on these topics, they have received positive responses by the majority of states, and they have passed all the critical points on their way to the General Assembly. Although, each of these are not directly for all crime and abuse of power victims, they each have a significant component that addresses some victims. Our organization wants to support these victims as well. So, we will begin to formally provide documentation reflecting the WSV support of these new allied instruments.
3. To develop mini-conventions that could address smaller parts of our current draft convention that would be more acceptable to member states and have a stronger link to mainstream crime prevention and criminal justice initiatives. An example would be a smaller convention on the issue of reducing victimization by applying recent research findings on "repeat victimizations" and "vulnerable persons." These two areas have become victimology "hot-topics" not yet significantly incorporated into any of the new UN instruments. It is our conviction that significant results could occur in reducing victimization if the research results would

be converted into policy. We would like to take on this challenge.

4. To increase the visibility of all the WSV Liaison Committee's initiatives we would establish site representatives for each of the three UN Headquarters: Vienna, Geneva and New York City. Their primary functions would be to keep the WSV informed of victim-relevant special events important for us to attend; develop closer relationships with victim-friendly UN staff persons at each site, maintain a constant WSV presence and local expertise at these locations, be present to vote on behalf of the WSV, and to join with other NGOs as they obtain approval with their respective instruments that also impact various types of victims. Some of these NGO-sponsored instruments clearly have mentioned special categories of victims and the WSV of course would have been pleased to join with these initiatives, but did not because of the preoccupation with our own Convention. With this strategy, will want to lend our support to a broader range of UN initiatives that are related to more types of victimsThe role of the WSV is to continually search for ways to advance research about victims, encourage scholarship and teaching in this field, promote the cause for victim rights and to raise the Global Standards for Victims whenever and wherever possible. It believes these four strategies will move us in that direction.

Reference

Aníyar de Castro, L. (1969). *Victimología,* Caracas: Venezuela.

Drapkin, I., and Viano, E. (Eds.). (1974). *Victimology,* Lexington, MA: Lexington Books.

Drapkin, I., and Viano, E. (Eds.). (1975). *Victimology: A new focus,* Lexington, MA: Lexington Books.

Ellenberger, H. (1950). Relations psychologiques entre le criminal et la victimize, *Revue Internationale de Criminologie et de Police Technique,* 103-121.

Fattah, E. A. (1966). Quelques problèmes posés à la justice pénal par la victimologie, *Annales Internationales de Criminologie (Paris) 5,* 335-361.

Kirchhoff, G. F. (2005). *What is Victimology?* Monograph Series No.1, Tokiwa International Victimology Institute. Tokyo: Seibundo Publishing Co., Ltd.

Manzanera, L. R. (1988). *Victimología: Estudio de la víctima,* México, D.F.: México Editorial Porrúa, S. A.

Miyazawa, K. (1966). *Basic problems and concepts of victimology.* Tokyo: Sekaishoin.

Nagel, N. (1959). Victimologie. *Tijdschrift voor Strafrecht, 1,* 1-26.

Neuman, E. (1984). *Victimologia: El rol de la víctima en los delitos convencionales y no convencionales,* Buenos Aires, Argentina: Editorial Universidad.

Šeparović, Z. P. (1962). Zrtva krivicnog djela (The Victim of a Criminal Offense), *Zbornik Pravnog fakulteta Zagreb: Croatia, No. 2.*

Schafer, S. (1968). *Victimology: The victim and his criminal; A Study in Functional Responsibility.* New York: Random House.

Schneider, H. J. (1975). *Viktimologie, Wissenschaft vom Verbrechensopfer,* Tubingen, Germany: J. C. B. Mohr (Paul Siebeck).

Viano, E. C. (1975a). Conclusions and recommendations: International Study Institute on Victimology Bellagio, Italy, July 1-12, 1975, cited in E. C. Viano (Ed.). *Victims and society,* Washington, DC: Visage Press Inc.

Viano, E. C. (1975b). *Victimology: A New Focus: Exploiters and Exploited-The Dynamics of Victimization,* Lexingon, MA: Lexington Books.

Viano, E. C. (Ed.). (1976). *Victims and Society,* Washington, D.C.: Visage Press.

von Hentig, H. (1948). *The criminal and his victim: Studies in the sociobiology of crime.* New Haven, CN: Yale University Press.

Developing Victim's Rights within the European Union: Past, Present and Future

By

Antony Pemberton and Marc S. Groenhuijsen

Introduction

The position of victims of crime has shown vast improvements since the 1970's. Thirty years ago it was correct to assert that the victim was the forgotten party of the criminal justice process, while this would be at odds with the actual situation of victims today(e.g. Groenhuijsen & Letschert, 2008). International bodies like the United Nations and the Council of Europe have developed a number of legal instruments, of which the UN Declaration of Basic Principles for Victims of Crime and Abuse of Power and the Council of Europe Recommendations 85(11) and 2006(8) are the most noteworthy.

Policy at the level of the European Union is laid down in the Council Directive 2004/80/EC relating to compensation to crime victims and the Framework Decision on the standing of victims in criminal proceedings of the 15th of March 2001 (2001/220/JHA.). The directive solely concerns the transmission of cross-border applications for state compensation. The Framework Decision is wider in scope. The main theme of the Framework Decision follows the international consensus visible in other international legal instruments. At its core it includes the following basic rights for victims of crime: to receive respect and recognition at all stages of the criminal proceedings (article 2); to receive information and information about the progress of the case (article 4); to provide information to officials responsible for decisions relating to the offender (article 3); to protection, of victims' privacy and their physical safety (article 8); to compensation, from the offender and the State (article 9); to receive victim support (article 13); and to participate in mediation for offences which are appropriate for this sort of measure (article 10).

The Framework Decision may be viewed as a milestone in the development of victims' rights (Groenhuijsen and Pemberton, 2009). It is the first so-called 'hard law' instrument covering a wide range of victims' rights available at the international level (For a description of the general distinction between soft law and hard law, see

Abbott and Snidal, 2000). Earlier international instruments like the UN Declaration and the CofE Recommendations did not contain legally binding obligations, while the Council of Europe Convention on compensation for crime victims did so, but had a (much more) restricted scope). The Framework Decision codifies rules at the supranational level concerning the legal position of victims that are binding concerning the domestic legal order of the member states.

The development of victims' rights within the European Union may be further enhanced by the adoption of the Treaty of Lisbon and the five-year plan for justice and home affairs within the EU, the 2009 Stockholm Programme. The 2009 Stockholm Programme calls for an integrated and coordinated approach to victims of crime and calls upon Member States and the European Commission to take a variety of measures, from strengthening legislation and policy to increasing research. The Lisbon Treaty specifically mentions the rights of victims of crime under the title of the 'Area of Freedom, Security and Justice' in its Article 82(2). The coming period will see the redrafting of the Framework Decision into a Directive on victims of crime, which will offer the European Commission more opportunities to see to the implementation of measures designed to promote the well-being of victims in the criminal justice system. The draft version of this Directive was put forward by the European Commission in May 2011, with adoption foreseen in late 2012.

So far, so good. However, as we shall set out in the first section of this paper, the transposal of Framework decision articles in domestic legislation and the enforcement of victims' rights paints a considerably less encouraging picture. It might be an overstatement to call the implementation of the Framework Decision a failure, but at least one may conclude, as we have done previously, that the impact has not been qualitatively different from previous soft-law instruments (Groenhuijsen and Pemberton, 2009). We will discuss the key findings and patterns in the results of recent research by our colleagues at the International Victimology Institute Tilburg (INTERVICT) and ourselves.

Subsequently we will consider the potential impact of the Stockholm Programme and the Treaty of Lisbon. Will the redrafting of the Framework Decision into a Directive automatically lead to better protection or is this a more complicated matter? In what way will characteristics of the EU (post-Lisbon) and differences in its member states impact the implementation and enforcement of victims' rights? This will lead us to reflect on the nature of victims' rights, as well as policy making within the European Union.

Assessing the impact of the Framework Decision

Some background on the Framework Decision on the standing of victims in criminal proceedings

The position of cross-border victims, those victimized in another state than their country of residence, lies at the heart of the EU Framework Decision on the standing of victims in criminal proceedings of 15 march 2001 (Groenhuijsen and Pemberton, 2009). The additional difficulties that these victims experience – they do not always speak the language, do not understand the host country's legal system and have often returned to their country of origin long before the trial – were linked to the central European notion of freedom of movement: the freedom of persons to travel without restrictions within the European common space. This consideration has been the main driver for European competence in the protection of victims of crime. But it is not practically feasible to regulate the position of cross-border victims without doing so for nationals as well, which means that the Framework Decision aims to synchronize the position of *all* victims of crime across the European Union.

It does so by requiring Member States to transpose Framework Decision articles into national law. Correct implementation of the Framework Decision entails the Member States providing evidence of national legislation - law in a formal sense - which mirrors the provisions of the Framework Decision. At set dates the Commission evaluates the extent to which Member States have implemented the Framework Decision. This scope, coupled with the limited sanctioning power vested in the Commission –who has to rely on Member States own reports to assess their performance, while only being in the position to 'name and shame' non-compliers, rather than impose any real sanctions - restricts the extent to which the Framework Decision should be expected to improve the position of victims of crime.

This impact was further constrained by the fact that some of its norms are phrased in a vague, open fashion, making it difficult to ascertain whether member states have, in fact, complied with them. When the European Commission issued a highly negative report on the progress of implementation of the Framework Decision in 2004, it quickly became apparent that there was much disagreement between the Commission and the Member States about the interpretation of the norms. Moreover it is highly questionable whether transposal into law should be the most relevant criterion in the assessment of the position of victims of crime. For many of the norms it is not the legislative provision, but enforcement in practice that matters. It is often not much use to have a law asserting a right to support or to receive information, if the actual support or reception of information in practice is not secured.

It should be noted that on all these counts the Framework Decision on the standing of victims of crime in criminal proceedings was quite a different beast from other Framework Decisions in the field of Justice and Home Affairs. These mostly concerned narrow, well-defined topics for which harmonization can realistically be considered a matter of mere legislative alignment.(The differences with the broad subject of victims' rights appear to have been overlooked in the negotiation of the Framework Decision for victims). The foreseen timeframe is a case in point. Most provisions should have been transposed within a year after adoption. Given that correct implementation might impact the whole criminal justice procedure of various EU-member states this is a highly optimistic target, if not an outright impossible one.

Studying the Framework Decision: Victims in Europe and Realizing Rights

Project Victims in Europe concerned the implementation of the EU Framework decision of victims in the criminal proceedings in the Member States of the European Union(van der Aa et al. 2010). It was developed by the Portuguese victim support organization APAV and the International Victimology Institute Tilburg on behalf of Victim Support Europe and queried both the legal as well as the practical/ organizational consequences of the Framework Decision. 97 experts from all EU-member states filled out the questionnaire on the legal consequences, while 218 experts considered the organizational and practical effects. The project's report (hereafter referred to as 'the APAV/ Intervict study') shows that many member states did not implement Framework articles in their legislation and where this is the case actual implementation of facilities for victims of crime is often lacking. In addition Intervict-researchers conducted a survey of victims rights as a part of the EU-project *Realizing Rights* (hereafter referred to as the RR-study; At the time of writing this contribution, the Realizing Rights study is yet to be published). Experts from 22 member states were tasked to provide a country-level report on the position of victims of crime. The RR-study confirmed the results of the APAV/ Intervict-study.

We will review the main findings of the RR-study and the APAV/ Intervict study. Each of the victims' rights: receiving information; compensation; to be heard in the criminal process; to legal aid and assistance; to protection; to support is discussed in turn. Within the right to be heard we have distinguished the victim's participation in the criminal justice procedure from measures designed to reduce the burden of witnessing. The right to mediation is included under participation in the criminal justice procedure.

Receiving Information

Nearly all member states grant victims the right to receive information. The APAV/ Intervict study revealed that information concerning the early stages of the criminal procedure is most widely available. Victims should be informed of the (outcome of the) police investigation of the offence and the prosecution of the suspect. Information on later stages, in particular the release of the offender, is often not made available to victims. Most member states do not notify victims of the release of the offender, which may be particularly problematic in the case of victims who run a high risk of repeat victimization.

The implementation of information rights leaves much to be desired. The APAV/ Intervict study observed that 'the systems for information dissemination may be there on paper, but according to most respondents they do not provide victims sufficient access to information in practice.' Results from the International Crime Survey show that generally speaking victims are not satisfied with the information they receive, although there is large variation in the proportion of victims receiving information across the European Union (Van Dijk et al, 2007; Van Dijk and Groenhuijsen, 2007). Generally speaking the countries in North-Western Europe do a better job informing victims, than the Mediterranean and Eastern European countries.

Compensation

According to the experts in the RR-study victims of violence are eligible for compensation either from the state or the perpetrator in all 27 countries of the European Union. Most continental countries allow victims to adhere their civil claim for reparation (the adhesion procedure or *partie civile)* to the criminal case, while the UK and Ireland, where this mode of participation is not allowed, have implemented so-called compensation orders. In addition most, if not all, member states have implemented some form of state compensation or criminal injuries compensation scheme (See also Matrix Insight (2008). The possible exceptions are Spain, Greece, Italy and Estonia.

These parsimonious and positive results conceal a more troubling and disparate reality. In many member states only a minute proportion of eligible victims access state compensation and it is questionable whether the grants awarded in the countries with fully functional schemes are sufficient to acknowledge the harm done to victims (Miers, 2007). Even in the most generous states, like the UK, the coverage rate of the scheme does not exceed 20% of those eligible.

Compensation within the criminal justice procedure, invariably takes a back seat to the ongoing trial of the suspect (Strang, 2002). Indeed, even when the offender is sentenced to pay compensation, adequate enforcement is most often lacking, with the onus mostly falling on the victim to ensure payment of compensation. This means that many victims have to wait years before compensation is paid and often do not receive the court-ordered award in full.

Participation in the criminal procedure

Both the APAV/ Intervict study and the RR-study confirmed that victims may be party to the proceedings in all member states of the European Union, except for those with adversarial systems (The UK and Ireland). And although it may fall short of party-status, the UK and Ireland afford victims a role in the criminal procedure as well. Victims have the right to submit a victim impact statement in these countries. The APAV/ Intervict study revealed that this instrument, which originated in common law countries, is in use in an increasing number of continental systems as well.

The possibilities to obtain compensation through the criminal procedure have already been noted above. According to the APAV/ Intervict-study most member states allow victims to take action against negative prosecutorial decisions, i.e. the decision to refrain from prosecuting a case. The main modes are either a right to private prosecution or the right to a review of the prosecutorial decision (See Brienen and Hoegen, 2000). Private prosecution is defined as 'a prosecution brought by a private individual or organization as opposed to a prosecution brought by or on behalf of the state.' The purpose of the institution of private prosecution is to act 'as a personal safeguard for the victim against an arbitrary decision of the authorities to dismiss his case or to refuse to undertake any action).' The latter allows the victim to challenge the non-prosecution decision, while in the former the victim can pursue the case him or herself, under certain circumstances.(These circumstances or conditions can vary from country to country. Sometimes it is limited to certain types of crime; in other jurisdictions the victim has to provide financial security in order to prevent frivolous private prosecution.

Finally many member states are increasing the possibilities to refer cases to victim-offender mediation and other forms of restorative justice. According to the APAV/ Intervict study mediation is mostly used in less severe cases, quite often involving juvenile offenders, although there are also member states (for instance Austria and Finland) that also allow more severe cases - even violence within the family – to be referred to victim offender mediation (see also Willemsens and Walgrave, 2007; Vanfraechem et al, 2010).

Superficially, it may appear that victim participation in the criminal

justice procedure is advancing across the European Union. However, the observations concerning compensation are also applicable to other victims' participation modes. There is a large gap between the formal and actual reality of victims' rights. Private prosecution of cases is a cumbersome and risky affair, which means that in most member states victims rarely opt for its use. Victim impact statements vary widely in their goals and their implementation, which in turn determines their effectiveness (Erez, 2004; Pemberton & Reynaers, 2011). The APAV/ Intervict study concluded that unfortunately it is still safe to say that the victims 'right to be heard' is not sufficiently implemented across the European Union. There is variation in implementation of this right, but there is no consensus as to the 'best practice' in this respect. Whereas the proponents of the 'citation directe' often suggest that this method allows victims to exert the most influence and is therefore preferable from a procedural justice perspective, opponents state that it actually puts victims in a vulnerable position, both financially and in terms of the threat of retaliation by the offender (e.g., Brienen & Hoegen, 2000).
As to the rise of restorative justice across the European Union, the main caveat here is that this is not necessarily a victim-focused development, although most participating victims find mediation or conferencing a positive experience (Sherman & Strang, 2007; Pemberton, Winkel and Groenhujsen, 2007). Depending on its implementation victim-offender mediation may be more or less victim-friendly, but most restorative justice programs are developed with the interests of (young) offenders in mind. Indeed, as Ashworth (2002) noted, without sufficient precautions restorative justice may result in using 'victims in the service of offenders'.[1]

Witnessing

A respectful treatment which recognizes the specific circumstances of the victims' ordeal is a cornerstone of any body of victims' rights.[2] According to the experts in the RR-study 16 member states have enshrined the right to be treated with dignity in national legislation. This right to dignity is of specific relevance when victims participate in the trial as a witness. The main concern with participation as a witness in both the pre-trial and trial phases is the prevention of

---

1 See also Pemberton, 2009; and the proposals offered in the "Statement on the position of the victim within the process of mediation", by the European Forum for Victim Services, London 2005.

2 Article 2 of the Framework Decision reads: "Every Member State ... shall continue to make every effort to ensure that victims are treated with due respect for the dignity of the individual during proceedings...".

secondary victimisation. In fact the term secondary victimisation was coined to describe the negative and harmful experience of victims being questioned and cross-examined with little respect for the ordeal they had been through (e.g. Frazier & Haney, 1996; Temkin, 2002). Attempting to minimize the risk of this happening has implications for the extent, length and repetitiveness of questioning. From the point of view of victims questioning should be kept to a minimum, particularly if victims are particularly vulnerable, as is the case with young victims, and victims of domestic or sexual violence.

Although most member states do allow for special treatment of vulnerable victims, most often defined as child victims or (female) victims of sexual and domestic violence, and have taken some (legislative) steps reduce the risk of secondary victimization, the APAV/ Intervict study ascertained that most of the respondents 'were not satisfied with the manner in which questioning of victims is undertaken in their jurisdictions. A majority finds the questioning to be unnecessarily intrusive and extensive. This in turn hampers victims' participation in the criminal justice system. This also applies to vulnerable victims. It is apparent from the results that the awareness of rights of vulnerable victims of crime is connected to more general emancipation issues. Treating victims of sexual and domestic violence with respect keeps equal pace with the more general phenomenon of female emancipation, with country-level implementation of these rights being a function of the general level of gender equality.[3]Matters are not improved by the inadequate and spotty implementation of article 7 of the Framework Decision, which relates to reimbursement of expenses incurred as a result from having to attend trial. The APAV/ Intervict study showed that 'in practice reimbursement of expenses leaves much to be desired.' Victims are unaware of the possibilities for reimbursement, with the application procedures being cumbersome.

Taken together the findings show that where many member states may pay legislative lip service to treating victims with dignity, the actual treatment of victims as witnesses in the criminal justice system is still far from ideal. Many victims, even in countries that have included the right to be treated with dignity in law, find the level of

---

3 This leads to the observation that in low gender equality countries female victims of domestic and sexual violence are worse off on three counts: their victimization rates are higher (Archer, 2006), societal norms are more likely to support the view that their abuse is permissible (Felson, 2002), while criminal justice authorities are less likely to treat them with respect when they have plucked up the courage to report their victimization.

respect and recognition proffered to them to be wanting.

Legal aid and assistance

According to the experts in the RR-study, most member states of the European Union are obliged to provide legal aid to victims of crime. This is the case in 19 of the 27 member states. However this mostly relates to provisions that apply to a wider group of legal participants and is normally contingent on the victims income, i.e. means tested, like it would be in cases in different legal spheres. According to the APAV/ Intervict study only a minority of EU member states provides victims with legal assistance, due to their victimisation. Even then these provisions apply to certain types of victims only. The APAV/ Intervict study furthermore showed that eligible victims in many states will not have effective access to aid and assistance due to unnecessarily cumbersome application procedures.

The means test, used for granting legal assistance, may have perverse effects in the cases of violence against women and children, depending on the way it is calculated. If household income is the criterion for granting aid, victims of abuse by a family member may be disadvantaged if the perpetrator is the main breadwinner. In these cases the victims' own personal income will be substantially lower than the household income, while the abuser can prevent the victim from accessing the household's resources.

Protection

According to the experts in the RR-study, in nearly all member states victims have a right to protection. It is open to question what the right to protection entails. In the APAV/ Intervict study a distinction was made between protection from the media and of a victims' privacy on the one hand and protection from (threats from) the offender on the other. Overall, the member states are aware of the significance of protection of victims against publicity and the offender. This is evident from the fact that a large majority has possibilities to hold hearings in camera, to restrict press coverage of cases, to limit disclosure of victims' personal information and to protect the victim through various practical and legal measures. However member states regularly opt for weaker mechanisms (hearings in camera at the discretion of the judge, restrictions on press coverage through a media code of ethics) or they do not provide the optimal combination of measures (restrictions on disclosure of victim's information, protection orders). A comparison between states is hazardous due to the difference in packages of protection measures and the variety in implementation of different protection measures.

Indeed in most cases it appears that protection measures are not primarily focused on the interests of the victim, rather than the successful prosecution of the offender. A number of member states specifically restrict protection measures to victims of organized crime or terrorism, for instance. Of course adequate protection of victims is of paramount importance in these cases, due to the high risk of retaliation by the 'suspect' and/ or his associates. However similar measures are not available for cases in which the victim runs similar risks, but in which the victim's cooperation is of less importance in the so-called fight against crime and/ or terrorism.

Support

According to the experts in the RR-study support (be that emotional, financial and/or practical) is available in principle in nearly all member states of the European Union and this also applies specifically to the cases of violence against women and children.

However the APAV/ Intervict study reveals that in many member states the actual delivery of support is anything but secured. Eight member states lack a national victim support organization, while in an additional seven victim support has not achieved national coverage. In fact: in only eight member states victim support has national coverage and in principle may offer all victims support. Even then demand for victim services outstrips the supply on offer: according to the last ICVS-sweep only one in six victims that would have welcomed support actually received it (Van Dijk and Groenhuijsen, 2007)

Funding is a main problem. One expert in the RR-study reported that there is just one shelter for 12 victims of violence against women or children in her or his member state. In other member states the situation is not that dire, but budget restrictions constrict the possibilities for delivery of support in nearly all member states. A large majority of experts in both the RR-study and the APAV/ Intervict study find the level of funding to be seriously inadequate. This is true even in countries like the United Kingdom and the Netherlands, which are relatively generous in the budgets on offer.

Concluding observations concerning the impact of the Framework Decision on the rights of victims of crime in the European Union

Pemberton and Rasquette (2010) reviewed the results of the APAV/ Intervict study. They find that the position of victims of crime across Europe has improved since the adoption of the Framework Decision, although it cannot be assured with confidence to which extent these improvements are a direct consequence of the adoption of the Framework Decision. A worthy benchmark for assessing improvement is the Brienen and Hoegen survey of 22 European countries that was completed in the year preceding adoption of the Framework Decision. See also Groenhuijsen and Pemberton, 2009 In any case it has not met the high expectations. In 2009, seven years after the deadline for transposition of most Framework Decision articles, still no EU Member State had correctly done so (see also Groenhuijsen and Pemberton, 2009).

According to their analysis three factors should be taken into account in the development of victims' rights across the Union:

1. *Importance of a victim-friendly national climate, including a victims' rights 'champion'.* The Framework Decision, albeit a hard-law instrument in nature, has not had qualitatively different effects from previous soft-law instruments. In general soft law can have a considerable impact on domestic legislation, when activists are successful in exposing gaps between international standards and governmental practice and are capable of marshaling popular support to bring their governments to effectively implement the provisions included in the soft law instrument (e.g. Keck and Sikkink, 1998). For this to succeed the norms must appeal to the political and public policy agenda, while the advocates need sufficient resources to gain traction. In similar vein compliance with the Framework Decision depended on Member States' willingness to do so and the existence of national civil society organizations that can rally support for the changes necessary in the instrument. These two factors (member states willingness and the availability of national victims' rights 'champions') coincide: the more victim friendly Member States of North and North-West Europe are more likely to have large and well-funded victim-oriented organizations: indeed the governments of these countries are mostly the primary benefactor of these organizations. They are acknowledged as primary stake-holders in the development of governmental policy and have easy access to the public through well-established ties with the media.
   However in Member States where the position of victims of crime is still relatively poor (the Mediterranean member states and the countries in Central and Eastern Europe that joined the EU since 2004) a victims' rights champion of a similar stature is most often non-existent. This implies a double disadvantage for activists attempting to mimic the developments in the more victim friendly areas: governments are less receptive to their views, while they have fewer resources to overcome this resistance. Taken together this means that the Framework decision, although it was intended to approximate the victims' position across the European Union, has ended up widening the gap between member states with more advanced victims' rights and those in which they have still to meet the most basic requirements This is similar to the findings concerning the implementation of human rights treaties, see Hafner-Burton & Tsutsui, 2007.

2. *Costs*. Implementation of victims' rights is severely constrained by budgetary considerations. The more funding needed, the less likely that a given provision will be adequately implemented. There is a funding gap between legislative provisions transposed into national law and compliance in practice. Victim Support, shelters for victims of violence in the family, adequate dissemination of information, full and timely compensation, an adequate level of protection, more generous possibilities for legal aid and advice all require accompanying legislative initiatives with funding to see actual enforcement of these initiatives. However most member states have not made sufficient means available to transcend the divide between 'law on the books' and 'law in practice'.
3. *Criminal justice 'barriers'*. The advance of victims' rights has often led to skepticism and even hostility of the criminal justice establishment (see also Pemberton & Reynaers, 2011). This may have subsided to a certain extent over the past three decades, but in many cases victims' rights may still be viewed as alien to the criminal justice system or as conflicting with core criminal justice values. Even the *perception* of the *possibility* that victims' rights *may* interfere with principles of criminal justice, more specifically with the notion of a fair trial, will lead to resistance. Conversely, criminal justice agencies will much easier endorse victims' rights where they are seen to be necessary to reach criminal justice goals. It has therefore proven to be easier to implement victims' rights that are uncontroversial or contribute to the goals of criminal justice agencies. As noted above, for instance, the aim of many protection measures is to secure the victims' testimony at trial, rather than the victims' own security interests.

From a Framework Decision to a directive: advancing the position of victims of crime?

The Treaty of Lisbon and victims of crime

The rights of victims of crime feature heavily in the EU's policy documents on criminal justice for the next five years. Not only is it one of the designated objectives in the Treaty of Lisbon (the treaty that replaced the EU-Constitution), but, in addition, the European Councils' Stockholm Programme of 2009 specifically acknowledges the unsatisfactory implementation of the current EU-victims' rights instruments and emphasizes the need for an integrated and coordinated approach to victims. The Stockholm Programme calls upon Member States and the Commission to take a variety of measures, from strengthening legislation and policy to increasing research.

In line with the Treaty of Lisbon the Framework Decision will be transformed into a Directive - *The EU-Directive establishing minimum standards on the rights, support and protection of victims of crime* - probably by the end of 2012. By definition a Directive is a stronger instrument than a Framework Decision: the Commission has more possibilities to review the progress in implementation and to sanction non-compliers. Individual complainants can use the provisions of a Directive, but not a Framework Decision, to bring a case before the European Court of Justice in Luxembourg. In theory, it therefore should be expected that Member States' compliance with EU-Directives will be an improvement compared to that with Framework Decisions. The transposal rate of currently existing Directives, for instances, is on average 96% (see Mastenbroek, 2003).

There are other developments that may impact victims' rights in the European Union. First of all due to the Lisbon treaty the 'community method' will apply to the area of freedom, security and justice, to which victims' rights policies belong. Where previously one single State could obstruct the adoption of legal acts, they will now be taken by qualified majority voting (QMV). Second there is the increasing use of the Open Method of Cooperation (OMC) and peer evaluation/ monitoring. The OMC provides a framework for cooperation between the Member States, whose national policies can thus be directed towards certain common objectives. Under this intergovernmental method, the Member States are evaluated by one another (peer pressure); with the Commission's role being limited to surveillance (the Commission may also initiate an OMC). In addition, Article 70 TFEU provides for the possibility of peer monitoring to facilitate full application of the principle of mutual recognition. Member States, in collaboration with the Commission, may conduct objective and impartial evaluation of the implementation of the Union policies referred to in this Title by Member States' authorities.

All of this can be listed as grounds for optimism. However, it remains to be seen whether the EU-directive and the simultaneous EU-developments will live up to any increased expectations. All three considerations concerning the EU-framework decision still apply, while the experience with this instrument suggests a stance along the lines of 'once bitten, twice shy' is in order. If anything, due to the current economic crisis within the EU (see for insightful commentary Roubini, 2011 or Skidelsky, 2011), costs are likely to be a more rather than a less important impediment to improving victims' rights across the European Union. Wider traditional criminal justice interests will continue to be an important factor: developments in other areas of criminal justice may shape victims' rights to a more significant degree than explicitly victim-focused efforts (see already

Garland, 2001). Victims' rights issues, at least in budgetary terms, are a minor element of criminal justice, which implies that small changes in other areas of criminal justice can have far-reaching consequences (Pemberton, 2010). Finally, as we will discuss further below, there is good reason to assume that a victim friendly climate and a 'victims' rights champion' will still be an important or even pivotal element in the translation of the Directives' provisions into victim policy.

Developing EU-policy: the fit with Member States' legislation
The European Union is a two-level polity (Scharpf, 1988). It derives its legitimacy from its Member States, who do the same from their citizenry. In turn, the European Union relies on the willingness and ability of Member States in the transposition and enforcement of European legislation. Member States' positions concerning EU-legislation anticipate the fit with their own legal order (Scharpf, 2009). In general, the stronger the instrument adopted, the more likely it is that it will reflect the lowest common denominator and reserve Member States' large discretion in its implementation (Lavenex, 2007). In addition it is often more likely that not all relevant aspects of a policy field become subject to approximation, but only in those where all actors' interests converge.

The experience with the Framework Decision has many similarities to the general features of EU-policy and legislation. The fit between Member States' legal order and the Framework Decision was a prime consideration in its drafting; more important than the stated goal of harmonizing and improving the position of victims of crime across the EU (Groenhuijsen & Pemberton, 2009). Given the poor level of implementation of the Framework Decision, it is quite likely that Member States will opt for a smaller scope of legislation and even vaguer provisions, although it is hard to imagine in what way one could succeed in drafting an instrument that would be more vague and open-ended than the Framework Decision itself.

In addition, there is a good chance that subsets of victim policy, either concerning certain types of victims only – for instance terrorism, trafficking in human beings or violence against women and children- or particular policy initiatives (the development of restorative justice) will take precedence over a more full-fledged and balanced approach to general victims' rights (see also Pemberton,2009) (For instance, see the extensive attention that the EU pays to victims of terrorism, the proposal for a European Protection Order and the Feasibility Study on EU Legislation in the Field of Violence Against Women, Children and Sexual Identity Violence and the Belgian initiative for a system of ministerial contact points concerning restorative justice. We ourselves are not immune to this tendency. Both of us have were involved in an advisory capacity in the drafting process of the Directive. In our efforts we have also seen fit to address problems in the current situation of victims rights and offer solutions that may well surpass the average standard of protection of victims rights in the European Union.. Finally the organizations representing victims' interests are mostly based in countries with relatively advanced levels of protection of victims' rights. As these organizations will be interested in the development of the Directive to further the position of victims in their own respective countries, this implies that the lobby will focus on improving on best practice in the EU, rather than assuring minimal standards.

In May 2011 the European Commission published a draft version of the Directive to be further negotiated by the Member States (see http://ec.europa.eu/justice/policies/criminal/victims/docs/com_2011_275_en.pdf, accessed 13-07-2011) In apparent contradiction to the expectations raised above, the wording of provisions contained in the draft Directive is (far) more concrete than in the Framework Decision, while the document is considerably more expansive as well (the draft Directive contains 30 articles, compared with the 18 contained in the Framework Decision). Even in comparison to earlier soft-law instruments the draft Directive is more concrete as well as more ambitious. Instead of being a set of minimum standards, it represents a significant advance on even the highest level of victims' rights available.

However, as we will discuss further below, there are other significant barriers to actual implementation of victims' rights on a European scale. It remains to be seen whether the draft Directive will pass through the negotiations unscathed. As noted, resources are a pre-eminent concern, which is likely to place pressure on relatively costly provisions. Alternatively, other elements of the Directive may seem appropriate methods of cost *reduction*, which increases the chance that these provisions will remain in the final version of the Directive. An example is the recent adherence of the British government to restorative justice as an element of cost reduction in the criminal justice system (although the responsible Ministry of Justice does have more substantive reasons for this as well: see their consultation document *Breaking the Cycl*, accessed 04-07-2011 in keeping with the example of New Zealand, where large scale restorative justice practices emerged in a similar drive to reduce costs (see for instance Maxwell and Morris, 1996).

The transposition and enforcement gaps

Once EU-legislation has been adopted it remains to be seen whether it becomes effective in practice. Even when it has been *transposed* in national legal order, challenges remain, in the sense that enforcement of EU-inspired national provisions may be insufficient or lacking all together. As discussed above this was particularly evident in the case of the Framework Decision. Importantly: many victims' rights can only be said to improve the position of victims of crime when they are sufficiently implemented in practice: a right to advice, support or information is not as important as actually receiving that advice, support and information, not in the least because without it, victims would not be aware of their rights. Enforcement of provisions is therefore a key element of implementation.

A recent examination of EU-directives shows that Member States differ in the extent to which they comply with the transposition and the enforcement of EU-legislation. Falkner & Treib (2008; Falkner et al, 2005; see also Borzel et al, 2010) find that there are different 'worlds of compliance' in the European Union.

In the first world, *'the world of law observance'*, the goal of compliance overrides domestic concerns. Transposition of Directives is on time and correct. Application and enforcement is also successful, while non-compliance is only evident when there are fundamental discrepancies with domestic legislation. This first world is visible in Denmark, Sweden and Finland.

In the second world, *'the world of domestic politics'*, obeying EU-rules is one goal amongst many. Timely and correct transposition is contingent on the absence of domestic concerns. When there are conflicting domestic interests at stake, the public supports Member State disobedience with European Union regulation. Finally, where EU-legislation is transposed, application and enforcement is often effective, which means that the main obstacle to compliance is political resistance at the transposal stage. Austria, Belgium, Germany, the Netherlands, Spain and the United Kingdom belong to this category.

In the third world, *'the world of transposition neglect'*, transposition of EU law is not a goal in itself. There is evidence of a posture of national arrogance towards EU-legislation, aggravated by administrative inefficiency. Without strong incentives and monitoring from the European Commission the result is often inactivity. Transposition shortcomings in enforcement are more prevalent than in the first two worlds, but definitely not as a rule. The world of transposition neglect includes Greece, France, Portugal and Luxembourg.

Finally, there is the *'world of dead letters'*. Here transposal is often swift and literal, without clear consideration of possibly conflicting features of the Member States' own legislation (also referred to as literal transposition, see Schimmelfennig and Sedelmeier, 2007). This is possible because the fourth world displays non-compliance in enforcement of EU-legislation: what is written in the statute simply may not become effective in practice. The causes may be sought in deficiencies in the working of the court system and other mechanisms of the rule of law, the lack of broad consultation of affected groups during the preparation of the laws (Treib, 2008) and/ or the relative weakness of civil society (Sissenich, 2010), which will hamper the detection of non-compliance and advocacy to ensure compliance. This applies to Ireland, Italy and the Central-Eastern European countries that joined the EU in 2004 and 2007 (in similar vein Sissenich, 2010).

It is important to note that the countries with the lowest level of protection of victims' rights belong to the 'world of dead letters' (compare Van der Aa et al, 2010). This does not bode well for the extent to which the EU Directive will raise the minimum level of victims' rights, as this logically entails a focus on the countries that are in effect the most 'EU-policy resistant'. A relatively unencumbered negotiation phase could then mask the fact that the resulting legislation will not be felt in any material sense in these jurisdictions. This implies that the more ambitious the Directive is, the more likely it is that the gap between victim-friendly and less friendly Member States will *widen*, rather than decrease, as is the stated aim of EU-policy in this field. Implementing transnational policies that go beyond the requirements of the Directive, as could be the case in an additional Open Method of Cooperation, are more likely to strengthen than dampen this effect.

More generally it is open to question whether the model of victims' rights and assistance that lies at the heart of international instruments and European Union legislation is not too contingent on the situation as is in Northern and North-Western Europe (and the non-European Anglo-Saxon countries), to be successful in different contexts. Victim assistance relies heavily on good governance, popular trust in key governmental agencies and an active role of civil society organizations in advocacy and service provision. In many countries in the world of dead letters, however, both governmental force and civil society are relatively poorly developed (Sissenich, 2010). Moreover, measures of the rule of law, control over corruption and trust in police and prosecution are consistently and significantly lower than in the countries that have formed the model for victims' rights legislation. This also applies to the broader institutional setting in which victims needs are expressed. For instance in Northern and North-Western Europe to a large extent victims (mental) health and compensation needs will be covered by their easy access to (mental) health providers and their high levels of insurance coverage.

The application of the single market analogy to victims' rights

Finally it is unclear to what extent the European Union's relative success in integration in the economic sphere, the establishment of the single market, can be translated to the area of Justice and Home Affairs in general and to victims rights specifically (Lavenex, 2007, Ouwerkerk, 2011). As Lavenex notes 'the adoption of the principle of mutual recognition in European Union (EU) justice and home affairs (JHA) co-operation can be seen as a typical case of institutional isomorphism where a policy concept that has proved useful in promoting integration in one area, the single market, has been borrowed to realize another area of integration, the 'area of freedom, security and justice'. This notwithstanding the marked differences between these spheres.

Mutual recognition within the single market removes obstacles to the flow of goods, services and people across the European Union and thereby enhances the rights of individuals engaged in trade, while reducing the regulatory scope of Member States. Within criminal justice mutual recognition removes obstacles to the flow of governmental acts, increasing the transnational enforcement capabilities of governments.

The characteristics of criminal justice - an intricate reflection of some of the most deeply felt norms and values of a polity (e.g. Duff, 2003) - will constrict the extent to which modes of multi-level governance that are available in other fields apply to criminal justice (see Hooghe and Marks (2001, 2003) define two ideal types of multi-governance, with Type I governance conceiving of dispersion of authority to general-purpose, nonintersecting and durable jurisdictions and Type II relating to task-specific, intersecting, and flexible jurisdictions. While the latter is organized according to principles of efficiency and is task and problem-oriented, the former is membership-oriented and is designed around (human) community. As a general rule criminal justice - although it is making a lurch in that direction in many countries (Garland, 2001; Tonry, 2004) - cannot be primarily motivated by principles of efficiency: it is inherently bound by principles of legitimacy. This legitimacy is closely connected to the beliefs and values of a community about the wrongfulness of certain acts and the way that society should respond to them (Robinson and Darley, 2007). The diversity of legal and cultural traditions and body of law determining the peculiarities of the criminal justice field in the various Member States raises the question whether the principle of mutual recognition could or even should be applied in all instances. While well described and/ or technical issues can expected to be suitable subjects for close integration, policy issues of a larger scope, which are more intimately connected to the core of criminal justice, should reckon with additional obstacles, which in cases may even render closer integration, synchronization and harmonization not only a difficult but even an undesirable goal. Imposition of provisions that are fundamentally at odds with communities' intuitions about criminal justice matters, as is a possible outcome of the procedure of Qualified Majority Voting (QMV), is likely to decrease the legitimacy of EU-policy, rather than achieve the goals laid out in these provisions. In sum: a too simplistic application of the *single market* analogy to criminal justice will err on both counts: there are problems of applying market-principles to criminal justice, while criminal justice across Europe is not a singular phenomenon. An interesting parallel can be found in recent thinking about international criminal justice, where there is increasing emphasis on the *ecological appropriateness* of justice responses after atrocities rather than a one-size-fits-all approach (Drumbl. 2007, Fletcher and Weinstein, 2002, Groenhuijsen and Pemberton, 2011).

These considerations have considerable bearing on the issue of victims' rights in the European Union. Victims' rights, as a rule, decrease rather than increase the efficiency of the criminal justice process. Rather than a roll back of government, victims' rights entail governmental action, directed at empowering victims. In other terms, they are intent on increaseing positive, rather than negative liberty (Berlin, 1969, see in different terms Groenhuijsen, 1996). The scope of victims' rights potentially implicates the whole criminal justice process: they are clearly not the type of well-described, technical matters which are conducive to European-wide integration.

The nature of victims' rights requires assessment of substantive policy outcomes, rather than transposal of legislative provisions. It is not immediately apparent that the European Commission is sufficiently competent, in terms of victimological knowledge and manpower, to successfully monitor these developments. Measuring the success and quality of victim policy within one member state is a significant challenge (see Van Mierlo and Pemberton, 2009), let alone in 27 countries that differ in many relevant aspects. The difficulties are increased by the fact that administrative capacity to review policy outcomes is likely to be far larger in the Member States than at the level of the European Commission. Developing a Brussels victim policy *panopticon* therefore will necessitate a large reduction in information: only general indicators can be taken into account. This will render EU-assessments, beyond the level of signaling extreme shortcomings, all but meaningless. The task is not made any easier by the fact that best practices and superior solutions are often situation-specific. What works in one country, culture or institutional environment may not be an appropriate means to an end elsewhere.

Conclusion and final remarks

The European Union stumbled into victim policy at the end of the 1990's. Europeans should enjoy unencumbered freedom of movement across the European Union, to which differences in the way they are treated when they fall victim to crime, may pose a barrier. As synchronizing the position of these cross-border victims is not feasible without a simultaneous attempt to harmonize the position of victims of crime in their own country, the European Union accepted competence to develop policy concerning all victims of crime.
The Framework Decision of 2001, which was the first legislative result of this line of reasoning, appears to have improved the positions of victims of crime in Europe to a certain degree. In the period after its adoption various Member States of the European Union strengthened victims' rights to information, participation, legal aid, support, protection, compensation and mediation and have attempted to reduce the burden of criminal justice for victims, in both an emotional and financial sense. Nevertheless the Framework Decision has not lived up to expectations: improvements have been made on shoe-string budgets, with transposal and enforcement of provisions depending on the associated costs and victim-related concerns have repeatedly taken a back-seat to other criminal justice goals. Moreover, instead of approximating the position of victims of crime across Europe, the Framework Decision has in effect widened the gap between the – in victimological terms- more and less advanced members of the European Union. In effect the Framework Decision has functioned as a soft law, rather than a hard law, international instrument: a victim friendly climate and a domestic victims' rights 'champion' are crucial in the realization of its provisions in practice.
Improving upon this assessment is an important objective of the EU's five year 2009-2014 Stockholm Programme, while the Treaty of Lisbon also specifically mentions this objective. The first step in this process, the draft of a EU-Directive establishing minimum standards on the rights, support and protection of victims of crime has recently was published by the European Commission in May 2011. On the face of it the Directive is a clear improvement on the Framework Decision. Not only is a Directive a stronger instrument, but the phrasing of its provisions is considerably less vague and more forceful than contained in the Framework Decision, while the list of subjects covered has increased substantially. Nevertheless challenges remain: costs and contradicting criminal justice goals will remain important obstacles, for instance. The negotiations necessary for the draft Directive to be adopted by the European Union may considerably weaken the text of the Directive and/ or

increase the emphasis on certain groups of victims or provisions to the detriment of others.

Once the Directive is adopted there is good reason to assume that that its effects will be less pronounced in countries with relatively poor standards of protection of victims rights. Results of research into the implementation of EU-policy reveal that in the so-called *world of dead letters*, transposal of EU-legislation is often literal: while the provisions are transposed, they are not necessarily enforced in practice. The Member States belonging to this world of dead letters -mostly the countries in Central and Eastern Europe that joined the EU after 2004- are also the ones with the poorest track record in victims' rights issues. Moreover many of the (implicit) assumptions underlying victims' rights - concerning good governance, the role of civil society, the rule of law and trust in criminal justice agencies - rely on the situation as it is in North and North-Western Europe, with the countries in the world of dead letters showing marked differences on all counts. These differences between Member States greatly reduce the likelihood that the Directive will serve to close the gap between more and less victim-friendly countries and even raise the minimum standards of protection across Europe.

Finally, as policy fields, criminal justice in general and victims' rights in particular are a far cry from the economic sphere, which is the original and natural habitat of the EU. It is apparent that the differences between these fields were not sufficiently recognized when the principle of mutual recognition was transferred to Justice and Home Affairs in the 1990's. For many criminal justice subjects tackled by the European Union this has not proved to be much of a problem, as they mostly concern minor subjects of a technical nature, but the extensive scope and the nature of victims rights strains the extent to which the single market is a credible metaphor. It also constricts the extent to which the European Commission can (and maybe should) function as an arbiter or monitor of the development of victims' rights across Europe.

That does not mean that we oppose European Union involvement in the development of victims' rights. To the contrary: we have great confidence in the ability of both the EU and the Commission to be a force for the good from the victims' perspective. However, in our view, the key-word here is *moderation*. Moderation should not be equated with a lack of ambition. Quite the opposite is the case. In this area, moderation is an essential element of realism. Effective reform of the criminal justice system on behalf of victims can only be attained by setting standards which are intrinsically appealing to the member States of the European Union. This requires a step by step approach. When it comes to victims' rights, the playing field does not allow for a giant leap.

References

Abbott, K.W. & Snidal, D. (2000). Hard and soft law in International Governance. *International Organization,* 54(3), 421-456.

Archer, J. (2006). Cross-cultural differences in physical aggression between partners: a social role analysis. *Personality and Social Psychology Review,* 10(2), 133-153.

Ashworth, A. (2000). Victims' rights, defendants' rights and criminal procedure. In Crawford, A. & Goodey, J. (eds.). *Integrating a victim perspective within criminal justice.* Aldershot. Dartmouth Publishing.

Berlin, I. (1969). *Four essays on liberty.* Oxford: Oxford University Press.

Börzel, T.A., Hofmann, T., Panke, D. *and* Sprungk, C. *(2010)* Obstinate and Inefficient: Why Member States Do Not Comply with European Law. *Comparative Political Studies,* 44(3), 1363-1390.

Brienen, M.E.I., and Hoegen. E.H. (2000). *Victims of crime in 22 European criminal justice systems.* Nijmegen, Wolf Legal Publishers.

Daly, K. & Stubbs, J. (2007). Feminist theory, feminist and anti-racist politics and restorative justice. in: Johnstone, G. & Van Ness, D.W. (red.) *Handbook of Restorative Justice.* Cullumpton, Devon, UK: Willan Publishing.

Drumbl, M. A. (2007). *Atrocity, punishment and international law.* Cambridge: Cambridge University Press.

Duff, R.A.(2003). Restoration and retribution. In: A. von Hirsch, J.V. Roberts, A. Bottoms, K. Roach, & M. Schiff (ed.) *Restorative and criminal justice: competing or reconcilable paradigms.* Oxford, UK: Hart Publishing: 115-134.

Erez, E. (2004). Integrating restorative justice principles in adverserial proceedings through victim impact statements. In: Cape, E. (ed.) *Reconcilable rights? Analysing the tension between victims and defendants.* London: Legal Action Group.

European Forum for Victim Services (2005). *Statement on the position of the victim within mediation,* EFVS, Lisbon.

Falkner G. & Treib O. (2008) Three worlds of compliance or four? The EU-15 compared to new member states. *Journal of Common Market Studies* 46(2):293-303.

Falkner, G., Treib, O., Hartlapp, M. and Leiber, S. (2005) *Complying with Europe: EU Harmonization and Soft Law in the Member States.* Cambridge: Cambridge University Press.

Felson, R.B. (2002). *Violence and gender re-examined.* Washington DC. American Psychological Association.

Fletcher, L. & Weinstein, H.M. (2002). "Violence and Social Repair: Rethinking the Contribution of Justice to Reconciliation." *Human Rights Quarterly* 24(3): 573-639 .

Frazier, P. A., and Haney, B. (1996). Sexual assault cases in the legal system: Police, prosecutor, and victim perspectives. *Law and Human Behavior.* 20: 607–628.

Garland, D. (2001). *The culture of control.* Oxford: Oxford University Press.

Groenhuijsen, M.S. (1996). Mensenrechten van slachtoffers van delicten en verdachten in het strafproces. In Brants, C.H., Kelk, C. & Moerings, M. (eds.). *Er is meer: opstellen over mensenrechten in internationaal en nationaal perspectief.* Deventer, NL: Gouda Quint.

Groenhuijsen, M.S. & Letschert, R.M. (2008). Reflections on the development and Legal Status of Victims' rights instruments. in: Groenhuijsen, M.S. & Letschert, R.M. (eds.) *Compilation of International Victims' rights Instruments*, Nijmegen, Wolf Legal Publishers, 2nd edition.

Groenhuijsen, M.S. & Pemberton, A. (2009) The EU Framework Decision on Victims. Does hard law make a difference? *European Journal on Crime, Criminal Law and Criminal Justice*, 17, 43-59.

Groenhuijsen, M.S. and Pemberton, A. (2011). Genocide, war crimes and crimes against humanity: a victimological perspective. In: Letschert, R.M., De Brouwer, A., Haveman, R.H. & Pemberton, A. (eds.).*Victimological approached to international crimes: Africa.* Antwerp: Intersentia.

Hafner-Burton, E.M. & Tsutsui, K. (2007). Justice Lost! The failure of International Human Rights Law to Matter where Needed Most. *Journal of Peace research*, 44(4), 407-425.

Hooghe, L,& Marks, G. (2001). *Multi-Level Governance and European Integration.* Lanham, MD. Rowman & Littlefield.

Hooghe, L. & Marks, G. (2003). Unravelling the Central State, But How? *American Political Science Review*, 97 (2), 233–43.

Johnstone, G. (2002). *Restorative Justice. Ideas, Values, Debates.* Cullompton: Willan Publishing.

Keck, M.E. & Sikkink, K. (1998). *Activists beyond borders: advocacy networks in international politics*. Ithaca, NY: Cornell University Press.

Lavenex, S. (2007). Mutual recognition and the monopoly of force: limits of the single market analogy, *Journal of European Public Policy*, 14(5), 762-779.

Mastenbroek, E. (2003). Surviving the Deadline: TheTransposition of EU Directives in The Netherlands., *European Union Politics* 4(4): 371–395.

Matrix Insight (2008). *The application of Directive 2004/80/EC relating to compensation to crime victims.* London. Matrix Insight.

Maxwell, G. & Morris, A. (1996) "Research on family group conferences with young offenders in New Zealand", in Hudson et al (ed). *Family Group Conferences: Perspectives on Policy and Practice* . Monsey, NY: Criminal Justice Press.

Miers, D. & Willemsens, J. (ed.) (2004). *Mapping restorative justice.* Leuven, Belgium: European Forum for Victim Offender Mediation and Restorative Justice.

Miers, D. (2007). Looking beyond Great Britain: the development of criminal injuries compensation. In Walklate, S. (2007). Handbook of Victims and Victimology. Cullumpton, Devon, UK: Willan Publishing.

Ouwerkerk, J.W. (2011). *Quid Pro Quo? A comparative law perspective on the mutual recognition of judicial decisions in criminal matters.* Cambridge/ Antwerp/ Portland: Intersentia

Pemberton, A. (2009). Victim Movements: from diversified needs to varying criminal justice agenda's. *Acta Criminologica*, 23(1), 1-23.

Pemberton, A. (2010). *The cross-over: an interdisciplinary approach to the study of victims of crime.* Antwerp: Maklu.

Pemberton, A., Winkel, F.W. & Groenhuijsen, M.S. (2007). Taking victims seriously in restorative justice. *International Perspectives in Victimology*, 3, 1, 4 – 14.

Pemberton, A. Kuijpers, K.F., Baldry, A.C. & Winkel, F.W. (2009). A nuanced

position. Intimate partner violence and restorative justice. In: Winkel F.W, Friday, P.C., Kirchhoff, G. F. & Letschert, R.M. (eds.). *Victimisation in a multi-disciplinary key. Recent advances in Victimology*. Nijmegen, Wolf Legal Publishers.
Pemberton, A. & Rasquette, C. (2010). Victims in Europe – Assessment of the implementation on the Framework Decision on the standing of victims in criminal proceedings: Preliminary results. In: Hartmann, J. (eds.) *Perspektiven professioneller Opferhilfe*, Wiesbaden, Germany. VS Verlag.
Pemberton, A., & Reynaers, S. (2011). The controversial nature of victim participation: Therapeutic benefits in victim impact statements. In: Erez, E., Kilchling, M. & Wemmers, J (ed.). *Therapeutic Jurisprudence and victim participation in criminal justice: international perspectives.* Durham: NC Carolina Academic Press.
Robinson, P.H. & Darley, J.M. (2007). Intuitions of justice: implications for criminal law and justice policy, *South California Law Review,* 81(1), 1-68.
Roubini, N. (2011). *The Eurozone's Last Stand*. http://www.project-syndicate.org/commentary/roubini40/English retrieved 01-10-11.
Scharpf, F. W. (1988). The Joint Decision Trap: Lessons from German Federalism and European Integration., Public Administration 66(3), 239–278.
Scharpf, F.W. (2009). Legitimacy in the multi-level European polity. *European Political Science Review* 1(2): 173–204.
Schimmelfennig, F. & Sedelmeier, U. (2007). Candidate Countries and Conditionality'. In: Graziano, P. & Vink, M.P. (eds). *Europeanization: New Research Agendas*. Houndmills. Palgrave Macmillan.
Schmidt, S.K. (2007), Mutual Recognition as a new mode of governance, *Journal of European Public Policy*, 14:5, 667–68.
Sherman, L. & Strang, H. (2007). *Restorative justice: the evidence*. London: Smith Institute.
Skidelsky, R. (2011). *The consequences of Angela Merkel,* http://www.project-syndicate.org/commentary/skidelsky45/English retrieved 20-10-11.
Sissenich, B. (2010). Weak states, weak societies: Europe's east-west gap. *Acta Politica,* 45, 11-40.
Temkin, J. (2002). *Rape and the legal process (2nd edition).* Oxford. Oxford University Press.
Tonry, M. (2004). *Thinking about crime: sense and sensibility in American penal culture*. Oxford: Oxford University Press.
Treib, O. (2008) 'Implementing and Complying with EU Governance Outputs. Living Reviews in European Governance, Vol. 1, No. 1. Available at http://europeangovernance.livingreviews.org/Articles/lreg-2008-5/.
Van der Aa, S. Van Merrienboer, R. Pemberton, A. , Rasquette, C. et al (2010). Project Victims in Europe: Implementation of the EU Framework Decision on the standing of victims in the criminal proceedings in the Member States of the European Union. Lisbon. APAV.
Van Dijk, J.J.M. (2007). World of crime. Thousand Oaks, CA. Sage.
Van Dijk, J.J.M., Manchin, R., & van Kesteren, J. (2007). *The burden of crime in the European Union.* Brussels: Gallup Europe.
Van Dijk, J.J.M. & Groenhuijsen, M.S. (2007). Benchmarking victim policies in

the framework of European Union Law. in: Walklate, S. (ed.). *Handbook of Victims and Victimology*, Cullumpton, Devon, UK: Willan Puiblishing.

Van Mierlo, F. & Pemberton, A. (2009). *Van tevredenheid naar kwaliteit: een meetinstrument voor de slachtofferzorg*. Tilburg: Intervict. (In Dutch: with an English summary).

Vanfraechem, I., Aersten, I. & Willemsens, J. (2010). *Restorative justice realities: empirical research in an European context*. The Hague: Eleven International Publishing.

Wemmers, J.J.M (1996). *Victims in the criminal justice system.* The Hague: WODC/ Kugler.

Willemsens, J. & Walgrave, L. (2007). Regional reviews: C: Europe. in: Johnstone, G. & Van Ness, D.W. (ed.) *Handbook of restorative justice*. Cullumpton. Devon, UK: Willan Publishing.

The Authors

Al-Badayneh Diab, Jordan, is Professor of Applied Criminology and Social Statistics at Mutah University, Jordan. He is president of Ibn Khaldun Center for Research & Studies (IKCRS). Al-Badayneh has published more than 150 articles and 20 books. His most recent books deal with Human Development and Terrorism in the Arab World and National Security in the Globalization Era and Understanding Terrorism (NATO) (edited). His research interests are: terrorism, violence, and corrections. He has received several awards, the latest research award (2009) came from IUA for his research on "Tolerance Values in the University Curriculum". Another research award came from Ministry of Higher Education and Scientific Research, Jordan for his work "Attitude towards Elderly in Jordan"; and "Best Book Translation Award", Philadelphia University, Jordan. For his translation to the "American Psychological Association Publication Manual". As a graduate student he was awarded K-S Award, Western Michigan University, USA. His name appears in the first edition of Who's Who Among International Students in American Universities & Colleges, USA.
E-mail: dbadayneh@gmail.com

Bastidas Zambrano, Laura Maria, Venezuela, is lawyer and criminologist from the University de Los Andes in Venezuela. She holds a Master of Criminal Sciences and Criminology degree from the Universidad de Carabobo and works as Prosecutor of the Ministerio Publico in Maracay.
E-mail: lauracrim@hotmail.com

Ben-David, Sarah (PhD) , Israel, is Associate Professor and the chair of the department of Criminology, Ariel University Center of Samaria. She previously held a position at Bar- Illan University, Department of Criminology where she also served as the head of the Department and the head of the Applied Criminology master programs. She is a life member of the World Society of Victimology (where she served for several years as a vice president), life member of NOVA, a member Association for the Treatment of Sexual Aggression (ATSA), the Israeli Society of Criminology (board member) and the Israeli Council for Criminology (chair). She is a licensed senior clinical criminologist, and the founder and the chair of the Professional Board of the Center for the Treatment of Sexual Offenders in the Community. Prof. Ben-David research focus is on issues in Victimology and sexual offending, and the interrelation of both this fields. She has published many articles in refereed journals and books, and co-edited several books.
E-mail: bendas@gmail.com

Ben-David, Boaz M., PhD. Canada, Assistant Professor, Department of Speech-Language Pathology, University of Toronto and Adjunct Scientist, Toronto Rehabilitation Institute, Ontario, Canada. My current research is focused on the cognitive and sensory aspects of communication and emotion perception in special population, such as older adults, traumatic brain

injury survivors and individuals with anxiety-related disorders. In his work, he acknowledges the victimological aspects affecting these populations. His recent research describes difficulties in emotional processing as a risk factor for offending and re-offending.
E-mail: boaz.ben.david@utoronto.ca

Cels, Johan, PhD, Representative in Japan United Nations High Commissioner for Refugees (UNHCR) has been working with the Office of the United Nations High Commissioner for Refugees (UNHCR) in various functions and countries, e.g., in Hong Kong, Northern Iraq and Eastern Turkey, Bulgaria, Switzerland, and Ethiopia. He is currently working as a Representative in Japan, appointed as of September 2008. Prior to that, he was a Senior Policy Advisor (Peace and Security) in New York, focusing on Sudan, Chad and Somalia, as well as on post-conflict recovery and peace building strategies. He also worked as a Project Leader for the Independent Commission on Human Security, co-chaired by Mrs. Sadako Ogata (former UN High Commissioner for Refugees) and Prof. Amartya Sen. He holds a Ph.D. in International Relations from the University of Notre Dame.
E-mail: CELS@unhcr.org

Chockalingam, Kumaravelu, Ph.D., India, is currently a Visiting Scholar at the Department of Criminology and Criminal Justice, University of Missouri in St.Louis, from the middle of October 2011 for three months. Earlier Dr.Chockalingam held the positions of Professor of Victimology at the Tokiwa International Victimology Institute (TIVI) and the Graduate School of Victimology besides serving as, Deputy Director of TIVI and then as Director of International Centre for different periods at Tokiwa University, Japan from 2005 until September 2011. His research interests include victim vulnerability, perception of crime victimization and elder victims. Besides his recent publications on these areas in the International Review of Victimology and International Perspectives of Victimology, he has also published on other victim issues. He is currently working on Intimate Partner Violence victims on the TIVI project. For the last two decades, he serves in the EC of WSV. Before joining TIVI, he was the Founding Head of the Department of Criminology in 1983 in the University of Madras, for 23 years until he was selected as the Vice Chancellor of the Monomania Sundaranar University in Tamil Nadu, in 2001 for three years. Professor Chockalingam founded the Indian Society of Victimology in 1992 and was its President for 15 years until 2007 and advocated for victim rights in India. His efforts through ISV resulted in the Tamil Nadu Government establishing a Victims Assistance Fund since 1995.
E-mail: profkcchoindia@yahoo.com

Davies, Andrew, USA, is doctoral candidate at the School of Criminal Justice, State University of New York at Albany. His research focuses on responses to victimization. Current projects include an investigation of the impact of risk perceptions on altruistic behavior and an exploratory, qualitative study of the impact of death penalty court processes on family-members of homicide victims in collaboration with Drs. Jim Acker and Bill Bowers.

He also has a second line of research concerning public (or 'indigent') defense policy which he conducts in collaboration with Dr. Alissa Worden. Andrew obtained an MA in history and an MSc in criminology from Oxford University before he became the Michael Hindelang Fellow of Criminal Justice at the State University of New York at Albany. He also worked for a time gathering mitigation evidence in capital cases and has extensive experience in policy evaluation research in New York State.
E-mail: andrewlucasblaize@gmail.com

Dussich, John P.J., PhD. USA, has degrees in Clinical Psychology (BS), Corrections and Criminology (MS), and Criminology and Sociology (Ph. D.). For 37 years he has been working mostly in the victimology field, specializing in victim services. He is the creator and founder of the National Organization for Victim Assistance - NOVA, which he launched in Fresno, CA in 1976 at the Second National Conference on Victim Assistance. He served as its first Executive Director for four years. He has also been active in the World Society of Victimology serving as its founding Secretary General (1979-85) serving first for two terms and recently a 3-year term (2000-03); he is its immediate past President (2006-09). He is the director of the Tokiwa International Victimology Institute and the editor-in-chief of its journal: *International Perspectives in Victimology*. He now teaches at the California State University, Fresno teaching. He is a trained disaster crisis responder and has logged hundreds of hours as a volunteer working with victims in disasters around the world. He has published 16 books, written 101 articles and made 196 presentations. His recent work concerns victims' rights at the United Nations. In August 2011 he was awarded Emeritus Professor status.
E-mail: jdussich@csufresno.edu

Friday, Paul C. , PhD, USA, is Professor and former chair of Criminal Justice at the University of North Carolina-Charlotte. He is currently the Director of the International Center for China Studies and holds adjunct professorships at Southwest University of Political Science and Law in Chongqing, China and China University of Mining and Technology in XuZhou, China. He received his Ph.D. in Sociology and Law from the University of Wisconsin-Madison in 1970. He was Assistant Professor at The Ohio State University until 1972. He directed the Criminal Justice Program at Western Michigan University until 1992. He has published six books and over 100 peer reviewed academic publications in the areas of Victimology, comparative and international criminology, violence and delinquency prevention. His latest books are Delinquency and Juvenile Justice in the Non-Western World (2006) and Different Responses to Violence: America and Japan (2004). He is a co-Editor of Victimization in a multi-disciplinary key:Recent advances in Victimology; Victimology in Transition from the 20th to 21st Century and Global Perspectives in Victimology, Friday is elected member of the Executive Committee of the World Society of Victimology and has served as Treasurer since 1997.
E-mail: pfriday@unc.edu

Groenhuijsen, Marc S., PhD, Netherlands, is professor of criminal law, criminal procedure and victimology at Tilburg University in the Netherlands. In 2005, he became the founding director of INTERVICT, the International Victimology Institute Tilburg. He has published widely on various victims' issues. He is president of the World Society of Victimology, member of the Board of Directors of the International Organization for Victim Assistance, and member of the Board of Directors of the International Society for Criminology. He also serves as a part-time judge in the Court of Appeal in Arnhem. Dr. Groenhuijsen is a member of the Royal Netherlands Academy of Arts and Sciences. Internationally, he belongs to the top researchers in the intersection of Administration of Criminal Law and Victimology. He has published over 250 articles and has authored or edited 24 books. The four volume work on the Dutch Criminal Procedure, can be considered as a standard reference work in this area for several decades to come. Dr. Groenhuijsen received several prestigious prizes/awards including the Dr. Hendrik Muller Prize for Behavioural and Social Sciences, awarded by the Royal Netherlands Academy of Arts and Sciences.
E-mail: m.s.groenhuijsen@uvt.nl

Hong, Young-Oh, PhD, Korea, is Research Fellow and Director of the Crime Trends and Statistics Center in the Korean Institute of Criminology. He holds a PhD in Social Psychology from Yonsei University, Seoul, Korea. He is member of the Korean Association of Victimology, the Korean Criminological Association, the Korean Psychological Association and the Korean Social and Personality Psychological Association. His research interests include victimology, juvenile victimization, corruption, decision-making and social cognition. He is currently conducting a national crime victimization survey in Korea.
E-mail: hong729@yahoo.co.kr

Levy, Inna, PhD., Israel, is a lecture at the Department of Criminology, Ariel University Center of Samaria, Israel, and she is a part of the Department of Criminology at Zefat Academic College. She received her Ph.D. in Criminology from Bar-Ilan University at 2007. Her doctoral thesis examined factor that contribute to victim-blaming and bystander-blaming. During her studies she received a Presidential scholarship for excellent Ph. D. students at the Bar-Ilan University. She is a member of Applied Criminologists Society and a board member of ELAM (Society for Prevention Sexual Offences). She conducted studies on sexual harassment in university and in the army. Her research interest includes issues in victimology, juvenile delinquency, criminal profiling, punitivism and statistics.
E-mail: inna_levy@bezeqint.net

Kilpatrick, Dean, PhD, USA, is a Distinguished University Professor of Clinical Psychology and Director of the National Crime Victims Research and Treatment Center at the Medical University of South Carolina. His gl;obally recognized research achievements and his many publications have been fundamental in understanding the risks and resilience in PTSD after traumatic events like disaster, terrorism and violent crimes. He has made

numerous contributions to improve evidenmce based clinical practice and teaching. He served as a founding member of South Carolina's first rape crisis center in 1974. He was appointed by South Carolina's Governor in 1984 to the Crime Victims Advisory Board and reappointed by Governor Carroll Campbell to a second term in 1991. Dr. Kilpatrick and his colleagues have received several grants from the National Institute of Mental Health, National Institute of Justice, and the National Institute of Drug Abuse supporting their research on the scope of violent crime and its psychological impact on victims. In 1985 he was given the National Organization of Victim Assistance Stephen Schafer Award for Outstanding Contributions to Victims Research. Dr. Kilpatrick serves as the Chairperson of the National Victims Center's Research Advisory Committee. In 1990, the US president presented him with the US Justice Department Award for Outstanding Contributions on Behalf of Victims of Crime.
E-mail: kilpatdg@musc.edu

Kim Jae-Min, PhD, Korea, is Associate Professor and Director of Police Science at Kyungil University, in Gyeongsangbuk-do, Republic of Korea. He is a director of the Korean Association of Victimology and of the Korean Criminological Association. As Senior Superintendent of the Korean Police Agency and as former professor of the Korean Police University, he became a member of the World Society of Victimology. He has published several articles, among them "A comparative study on the crime victim policies of providing the protection and support in Korea and Japan" in The Journal of Police Science, Vol. 8, No. 2, 2008.". Together with Ha, Ok-hyun he wrote "A study on the effective investigative interviewing skills on sexually abused children", Journal of Police Law, Vol. 7, No. 2, 2009. "A study on the police investigation related to collecting the verbal evidence from the disabled victims", The Journal of Police Science, Vol. 10, No. 2, 2010. "A study on the eligibility requirements and the process of the Korean Victim Compensation", The Korean Association of Criminology, Vol. 23, No. 1, 2011.
E-mail: dogoodwill@hanmail.net

Kirchhoff, Gerd Ferdinand, Dr. jur., Japan, is Professor of Victimology at Tokiwa University in Mito, Japan, Graduate School of Human Sciences (Dr. Program), Graduate School of Victimology (Master Program) and Member of the Tokiwa International Victimology Institute TIVI since 2003. Professor (em.) of Criminal Law, Criminology and Victimology at Hochschule Niederrhein, School of Social Studies, Moenchengladbach, Germany. He has published six books and about 90 academic peer reviewed articles. He is a co-Editor of 'Victimization in a multi-disciplinary key: Recent advances in Victimology"; and of "Victimology in Transition from the 20th to 21st Century" He is Founder and Co-Director of the Inter University Center Dubrovnik (IUC) Postgraduate Course on Victimology and Victim Assistance (CVVA annually since 1984), and is co-director of the African Postgraduate Course in Victimology and Victim Assistance. He is among the eight Founding Members of the World Society of Victimology (1970), served as elected member on the Executive Committee of the World Society of Victimology for several election periods, served for 15 years as

Secretary General and for three years as President of the World Society of Victimology. He teaches in international training courses financed by the Japanese Government, the last specializing in Assistance for War Victims in Colombia and in Nepal. He is Honorary Member of victimology associations in Argentina, Mexico and Serbia. Before specializing in victimology, he received the licence to be a judge in Germany and holds a doctorate in law from University in Giessen (Germany). Visiting Professor of Western Michigan University 1976 USA.
E-mail: gerd@tokiwa.ac.jp

Letschert, Rianne, PhD, Netherlands, is professor in international law and victimology, and Deputy Director of INTERVICT. She works on issues such as victims' rights and human security issues, more particular on international lawmaking in the field of victims' rights and victims of international crimes, in particular reparations. As Deputy Director she is, amongst others, responsible for the execution and coordination of the research programme of the Institute. In 2010, she was visiting researcher at the Lauterpacht Centre for International Law of Cambridge University (UK). She recently published the book 'The New Faces of Victimhood' (with Jan Van Dijk, Springer Press).
E-mail: R.M.Letschert@uvt.nl

Lysova, Alexandra V. , PhD is Trudeau Scholar at Centre for Criminology and Sociolegal Studies at University of Toronto (Toronto, Canada). Her research focuses on women's involvement in intimate partner violence in Canada, intimate partner/ family violence in Russia, Germany, and USA, alcohol-related violence, and female aggression. She has worked collaboratively on three cross-cultural studies on dating violence, corporal punishment, and sexual victimization. She has been actively involved in international collaboration with leading sociologists and criminologists as a Kennan Institute Scholar in Washington D.C., a Fulbright scholar at New York University, a visiting scholar through the German Alexander von Humboldt Foundation at the Max Plank Institute in Germany, and a visiting scholar through the Carnegie Research Fellowship Program at the University of New Hampshire. She holds the Medal for the Excellence in Scholarship given by the Russian Academy of Sciences. Recent publications appeared in the *Handbook of European Homicide Research, Nordic Studies on Alcohol and Drugs, Journal of Interpersonal Violence, Aggressive Behavior,* and *Polizei & Wissenschaft*. She has presented at international conferences and published in peer-reviewed journals (Russian, English and German). She is also a Professor at the Department of Psychology at the Far Eastern Federal University in Vladivostok, Russia.
E-mail: lysova_sasha@yahoo.com

Morosawa, Hidemichi, Japan, Chairperson of the Incorporated Educational Institution Tokiwa University, Professor of Criminal Law and Victimology, Doctor Course of Graduate School of Human Science, Graduate School of Victimology, and member of Tokiwa International Victimology Institute, Tokiwa University in Mito. He completed the Doctor Course of Law, Graduate School, Keio University, Japan (1971). He currently teaches Victimology, Criminal Law and Criminology at Tokiwa University Graduate Schools of Human Science and Victimology, at the same time teaches Victimology and Criminology at Keio University. The International Scientific and Professional Advisory Council of the UN Crime Prevention and Criminal Justice Program (ISPAC) nominated him as a member of the team to compose a standards manual of victim support (1995-1998). He has served as an Executive Member of the World Society of Victimology (WSV) since 2006. He was President of the 13th International Sympoisum on Victimology in Mito 1989 hosted at Tokiwa University. Additionally, he was the first Asian to be awarded the Certificate of Appreciation by the WSV in 1997. He gave keynote speeches at the WSV Symposia in Adelaide (1994), Stellenbosch (2003) and Orlando (2006). He was General Rapporteur in Amsterdam (1997). He is Member of the International Scientific and Professional Advisory Council of the United Nations Crime Prevention and Criminal Justice Program (2003-06). Board of the Scientific Council of Asian Crime Prevention Foundation (1992-now). Expert Committee of the Violence against Women of Japanese Government Cabinet Office (2004-now). Expert Committee of the Inmate Treatment Projects based on Victim Perspective of the Japanese Department of Justice (2004-now). Executive Board Member of the Japanese Association of Victimology (1990-now). Advisor of the Japanese Association of Crime Victims and Surviving Families (00-now). Advisor of the National Network of Victim Support in Japan (1998-now). Advisor of the Ibaraki Victim Support Center (1995-now). He published 23 books and 202 articles on Criminal Law, Criminology, Victimology and Criminal Policy. He lectured 186 public lectures all over Japan. He appeared on 311 TV programmes and 62 radio programs. He made 279 comments in the newspapers and 32 comments in the magazines. E-mail: morosawa@tokiwa.ac.jp

Mundy, Kieran Graham. PhD. is Deputy Director of the Tokiwa International Victimology Institute, Japan, and researches in the newly emerging area of victims of natural disasters and climate change. His published articles in this field have appeared in a number of sites, including in January 2012, Springer's eJournal Collection. He has extensive experience in teaching and research in refugee studies and psycho-trauma, is the Managing Editor of the peer-reviewed online journal *International Perspectives in Victimology*, and is involved in overseas development aid training courses conducted by the Government of Japan, most recently on victims of war and armed conflict in Nepal and Colombia. His articles focus on challenging the theoretical boundaries of the traditional criminal justice system — but not at the expense of the traditional approaches to victimological thinking. E-mail: marcusanton1201@eco.ocn.ne.jp

Nikolic-Ristanovic, Vesna, PhD, Serbia, professor of criminology, victimology, juvenile delinquency and child abuse at Belgrade University, Faculty for Special Education and Rehabilitation. She is director of Victimology Society of Serbia, member of Executive Committee of World Society of Victimology and president-elect of European Criminology Society. She was also the

founder and first editor-in-chief of *Temida*, journal on victimisation, human rights and gender. Her fields of experience and research include violence against women, war victimization, women's crime, war and crime, victim support, trafficking in people and truth and reconciliation. She initiated and successfully advocated for many legal and policy changes relevant for victims in Serbia. Nikolic-Ristanovic is currently principal researcher in the research project Development of methodology for crime recording as the basis for efficient crime control and prevention, implemented by Faculty for special education and rehabilitation, Belgrade University, funded by Serbian Ministry of science. Her latest publications include: Domestic violence in Vojvodina (2010, editor), Supporting victims of trafficking: towards reconciling the security of victims and states, *Security and Human Rights*, 2010, Possible application of yoga in victimology, 2010, Victims' Rights and EU: the Challanges of Victim Support (2011, edited with Copic). She is President elect of the European Society of Criminologgy.
E-mail: vnikolic@EUnet.rs

Noto, Chiori, Japan, was born in Shiraoi, Hokkaido to an Ainu mother and a non-Ainu Japanese father. After graduating from the Department of *Intercultural* Studies, Faculty of *Intercultural* Studies of Tomakomai Komazawa University in 2006, she became employed as a curator in a department of Shiraoi Town Hall focused on promoting policy related to the Ainu. In her position, she has worked together with local Ainu and non-Ainu Japanese to restore the natural environment of the Ainu people and plan and implement programs that promote Ainu culture, in line with the "Project for the Restoration of the Traditional Ainu Habitat," which was established from the 1997 "Law on the Promotion of Ainu Culture." Through exchange with different indigenous minority groups around the world, she is working toward improving the policies toward indigenous peoples in Japan. She is a member of the Ainu Association of Hokkaido. In 2011, she moved to the Foundation for Research and Promotion of Ainu Culture, Sapporo, and is currently working as staff for the Operation Department of the foundation.
E-mail: noto@frpac.or.jp

O'Connell, Michael, BSocSc MPubPol, Australia, **is** the first Commissioner for Victims' Rights in South Australia, was also the inaugural Victims of Crime Co-ordinator and Victim Impact Statement Coordinator. He teaches victimology in Australia and overseas. He is a life-member and Vice President of the World Society of Victimology; as well as Secretary of the Australasian Society of Victimology. He has written articles and chapters on victims of crime, criminal justice and crime prevention, and edited several books including co-editing the proceedings of the 1994 international symposium on victimology. He is a consulting editor for *International Perspectives on Victimology*. In 1995 he was awarded the Australian Police Medal for his victimological work; in 2003 he was a finalist in Australian of the Year 2004 (South Australia); and, in 2010 Victim Support Australasia acknowledged his contributions to victimology, advancing victims' rights and victim assistance with its National Award. Email:voc@agd.sa.gov.au

Okamura, Isao, Japan, is an attorney at law in Tokyo, originally from the Koichi Prefecture in Shikoku, Japan. He has served in a number of important posts, including serving as the President of the Daichi Tokyo Bar Association, Vice President of the Japan Federation of Bar Associations, and as a Committee Member of the Legislative Council. He also participated as an expert member at the Conference to Implement the Basic Plan for Crime Victims and at the Conference to Promote Crime Victim related Policies. In January 2000, he established the National Association of Crime Victims and Surviving Families (Asu no kai) and assumed the position of the Chairperson. He has been energetically working for the realization of victims' rights and for the restoration of those who are victimized.
E-mail: Okamura@NAVS.jp

Parra Fernandez, Yasmely del Carmen, Venezuela, graduated from the Faculdad de Ciencias Juridicas, Politicas y Criminologicas in Merida, Venezuela. She holds a Master degree from the School of Criminology, Universidad de Los Andes, Edo, Merida (Title of Thesis: Study on Distribution of Space and Time of Burglary and Vehicle Theft in the City of Merida) The works in the Ministry of the Interior and Justice. She cooperated with the national Victimization Survey in Venezuala (Encuesta Nacional de Victimisacio 2006 and 2009). She worked for the Autonomous Service of Hazard Identification and Aliens (SAIME) on the control of migration and mobilization in Venezuela. She was coordinating researcher of the Venezuelan national survey on victimization.
E-mail: yasmelyparra@yahoo.com.

Peacock, Robert, PhD., South Africa, is head of the Department of Criminology, University of Kwazulu-Natal in Durban where he is lecturing and conducting research in Victimology. At present he is a member of the Executive Committee of the World Society of Victimology. Since the Apartheid years in South Africa, he has been working in the specialization field of institutional victimization with children and adolescents as special focus groups. He has published extensively on the street child phenomenon, incarceration and adolescent identity. Most recent work refers to analyses of Victimology in the context of Transitional Justice with specific reference to the South African Truth and Reconciliation Commission and challenges to Reconciliation in Post Apartheid South Africa.
E-mail: peacock@ukzn.ac.za

Pemberton, Anthony, PhD , Netherlands, is a social scientist and associate professor of Victimology at the International Victimology Institute Tilburg, Tilburg University. Amongst others he has co-authored a book on victims of terrorism *(Assisting victims of terrorism: towards an European standard of justice, Springer, 2010)*, published a series of articles connecting social and clinical psychology to victimology in theories of restorative justice, (included in *The cross-over: an interdisciplinary approach to the study of victims of crime, Maklu. 2010)* and co-edited a volume on *Victimological Approaches to International Crimes, Intersentia, 2011*). In addition he completed evaluations of the Dutch victim impact statement and the European Union

Framework Decision on the standing of victims in criminal proceedings and was a key advisor to the European Commission in the drafting of the proposed EU-directive on victims' rights. Email a.pemberton@uvt.nl

Resnick, Heidi, PhD, USA, is a Professor of Clinical Psychology at the Medical University of South Carolina and a senior investigator at the National Crime Victims Research and Treatment Center. Dr. Resnick has conducted epidemiological and treatment outcome research related to the behavioral and mental health impact of sexual assault and other traumatic events. Her research has included development and evaluation of secondary prevention approaches implemented within primary care settings targeting problems of drug use and symptoms of posttraumatic stress disorder or other distress following sexual assault.
E-mail: resnickh@musc.edu>

Sigmon, Jane Nady, PhD, USA, serves as Senior Advisor to the Director of the U.S. State Department's Office to Monitor and Combat Trafficking in Persons. From 2006 through 2011, Dr. Sigmon served as Senior Coordinator for International Programs and administered the office's global foreign assistance program. As the Department of State's first crime victim assistance specialist (2000-2006), she developed the consular assistance to crime victims program for American victims overseas. She was Director of Research for the American Prosecutors Research Institute (1997-2000) and Executive Director of VALOR, the Victims' Assistance Legal Organization (1992-1997), where she founded the National Victim Assistance Academy. Previously in government, she directed the U.S. Department of Justice's Office for Victims of Crime (1987-1991) and was Associate Commissioner of the U.S. Children's Bureau (1985-1987). Dr. Sigmon earned a doctorate at Duke University. and she authored and co-authored articles, including *Combating Modern Day Slavery: Issues in Identifying and Assisting Victims of Human Trafficking Worldwide; Successful Adjudication Partnerships; The Tennessee Prosecutors' Caseload Study; and the National Victim Assistance Academy Text.* The American Society of Victimology presented her with the Ed Stout Innovation in Victim Services Award in 2009. Albertus Magnus College conferred the Honorary Doctor of Humane Letters in 2010.
E-mail: SigmonJN@state.gov

Strang, Heather, PhD., Australia, is Director of the Centre for Restorative Justice at the Australian National University and Deputy Director of the Lee Centre of Experimental Criminology, Institute of Criminology, University of Cambridge. She has been involved in many experimental tests of the effects of restorative justice in Australia and the United Kingdom and is currently analysing a ten year follow-up of victims and offenders who participated in the Australian study. She has published extensively in this area, including her victim-focused book, Repair or Revenge: Victims and Restorative Justice (2002) and numerous articles including her contribution to Shoham and Knepper's International Handbook of Victimology entitled 'Exploring the Effects of Restorative Justice on Crime Victims for Victims of Conflict in Transitional Societies'. Email address: hs404@cam.ac.uk

Straus, Murray A. , PhD, USA, is Co - Director of the Family Research Laboratory, University of New Hampshire and Professor of Sociology at the University of New Hampshire. A pioneer in research of family violence, he is considered one of the leading experts in the field. His studies on the effect of family violence on victims led to a paradigm change in this field, and he has led the way to a new understanding of the long term consequences of victimization in the family, leading to a new evidence based perception of couple violence, away from ideological biases. His most recent research looks at dating violence. He became famous as one of the first scientists to look at the long term effects of corporal punishment by parents. His Conflict Tactic Scales are among the most used instruments in empirical family violence research, measuring empirically victimization and offending in partner violence. He has authored and co-authored 15 books and more than 200 articles on crime, family and research methods.
E-mail murray.straus@unh.edu

Susetyo, Heru, Indonesia, is a senior lecturer and researcher at Faculty of Law University of Indonesia, Jakarta-Indonesia. His majors are victimology, social work and human rights. He is also a co-opted member of World Society of Victimology's Executive Committee and a co-founder of Indonesian Society of Victimology and Co-Director of the Indonesian Post Graduate Course on Victimology and Victim Assistance 2011.
E-mail: hsusetyo@ui.ac.id

Wang, Shr-Jie Sharlenna, PhD, Danmarkl, is a senior researcher and epidemiologist at the Rehabilitation and Research Centre for Torture Victims, in Copenhagen, Denmark. She received her Master of Public Health from Yale University School of Public Health and PhD in Clinical and Intervention Epidemiology from Swiss Tropical and Public Health Institute, Basel University. She has been working with war-affected and marginalised populations in Africa, Middle East and Southeast Asia since 1998. Prior to her work at the RCT, she served with the World Health Organization (WHO) in Sudan as public health officer and with Médecins Sans Frontières and other NGOs as an epidemiologist. Currently she is developing and validating a protocol to study lifetime exposure to violence and human rights violation and its lasting public health impact (with a focus on pain, injury and disability) among a traumatized population. She is member of World Society of Victimology, American Public Health Association and European Public Health Association. She is also a peer *reviewer* for several academic journals.
E-mail: sjw@rct.dk

Yamamoto, Lilian, PhD., Japan, is a Programme Associate in the Sustainable Urban Futures Programme at United Nations University Institute of Advanced Studies in Tokyo, Japan. She holds a law degree from Londrina State University, Brazil. After she was granted a Japanese government scholarship (Monbukagakusho), she did her master's studies at Kanagawa University in Japan. Her master's thesis was on the "Political Asylum and Protection under the Refugee Treaty in Brazil". In 2011, Lilian received her

Doctoral degree in international human rights law after completing her thesis on the "Past Violations and the Principle of Non-Retroactivity- The Practice in International Human Rights Bodies and International Criminal Tribunals". Her research topics include climate change and the sovereignty of island states, refugee protection system and international criminal courts. She also worked as a consultant for JALANA (Japan Association of Lawyers against Nuclear Arms), writing reports on the extraterritorial application of the American Declaration of the Rights and Duties of Man and on the continuing violations of human rights.
E-mail: liuka1980@hotmail.com

Index